Sovereign Immunity Under Pressure

Régis Bismuth • Vera Rusinova •
Vladislav Starzhenetskiy • Geir Ulfstein
Editors

Sovereign Immunity Under Pressure

Norms, Values and Interests

Springer

Editors
Régis Bismuth
Sciences Po Law School
Sciences Po
Paris, France

Vera Rusinova
Faculty of Law
National Research University "Higher School of Economics"
Moscow, Russia

Vladislav Starzhenetskiy
Faculty of Law
National Research University "Higher School of Economics"
Moscow, Russia

Geir Ulfstein
Department of Public and International Law
University of Oslo
Oslo, Norway

ISBN 978-3-030-87705-7 ISBN 978-3-030-87706-4 (eBook)
https://doi.org/10.1007/978-3-030-87706-4

This Springer imprint is published by the registered company Springer Nature Switzerland AG.
The registered company address is: Gewerbestrasse 11, 6330 Cham, Switzerland

Contents

Editors and Contributors

About the Editors

Régis Bismuth is a Professor of Law at Sciences Po Law School (Paris), specializing in public international law, international economic law, and international adjudication. He is the author of several publications in these fields and, more particularly, on the law of international organizations, sovereign immunity, extraterritoriality, anti-corruption law, economic sanctions, WTO law, international investment law and arbitration, State capitalism, sovereign debt, international standards, financial regulation, Internet regulation, and the responsibility of multinational corporations. He is Co-Editor-in-Chief of *The Law and Practice of International Courts and Tribunals* (LPICT) and Director of Studies of the French Branch of the International Law Association (ILA). Régis is also a member of the International Monetary Law Committee of the ILA (MOCOMILA) and a Fellow at the International Academy of Financial Crime Litigators. He has advised public institutions and private entities on matters of international law.

Vera Rusinova is a Professor at the Faculty of Law of the National Research University Higher School of Economics, where she heads the School of International Law. The main fields of her research activities comprise international human rights law, international humanitarian law, use of force, the theory of international law, and the application of international law to cyber operations. She is Co-Chair of the International Law Association's Committee on Use of Force: Military Assistance on Request. Vera is also a member of the Editorial Groups/Boards of "International Justice," "Journal of International Humanitarian Legal Studies," and "International Cybersecurity Law Review." Her lecture on "Human Rights in Armed Conflicts" was placed in the UN Audiovisual Library of International Law.

Vladislav Starzhenetskiy is an Associate Professor at the Chair of International Law, Faculty of Law of the National Research University Higher School of Economics. He also serves as Academic Director of the Master Program "Law of

International Trade, Finance and Economic Integration" and a researcher at the HSE Laboratory on Sanctions in International Law. The main fields of his research interests include jurisdictional immunities of states, economic sanctions, international protection of intellectual property, international civil procedure, and international human rights law. He is a member of the Editorial Group of the Russian "International Justice" Journal. Vladislav graduated from the Moscow State Institute of International Relations (MGIMO) with a degree in International Law. He received his Ph.D. for the dissertation dedicated to comparative analysis of property rights under the ECHR and Russian law. From 1998 to 2014, he has been working at the Russian Federation's Supreme Commercial Court and was heading the Department of International Law and Cooperation from 2011 to 2014.

Geir Ulfstein is a Professor of international law at the Department of Public and International Law, University of Oslo and Co-director of PluriCourts—Centre for the Study of the Legitimate Roles of the Judiciary in the Global Order, University of Oslo. He has been Director of the Norwegian Centre for Human Rights, University of Oslo (2004–2008). He has published in different areas of international law, including the law of the sea, international environmental law, international human rights, and international institutional law. Geir is General Editor (with Andreas Føllesdal) of two book series *Studies on Human Rights Conventions (Cambridge University Press)* and *Studies in International Courts and Tribunals (Cambridge University Press)*. He is President of the Norwegian Branch of the International Law Association, Co-Chair of the International Law Association's Study Group on the "Content and Evolution of the Rules of Interpretation," and is Chair of the Scientific Advisory Board, Max Planck Institute for Procedural Law, Luxembourg. He has been a member of the Executive Board of the European Society of International Law (2010–2016). He will deliver one of the special courses during the Hague Academy of International Law's 2022 winter session. He is also a member of the Norwegian Academy of Science and Letters.

List of Contributors

Giovanni Ardito Sapienza University, Rome, Italy

Giulia Bernabei Max Planck Foundation for International Peace and the Rule of Law, Heidelberg, Germany

Régis Bismuth Sciences Po Law School, Sciences Po, Paris, France

Stefano Dominelli University of Genoa, Genova, Italy

Rana M. Essawy Faculty of Law, Alexandria University, Alexandria, Egypt

Chimène I. Keitner UC Hastings Law, San Francisco, CA, USA

Apollin Koagne Zouapet Berlin-Potsdam Research Group 'International Rule of Law – Rise or Decline?', Berlin, Germany

Magdalena Matusiak-Frącczak University of Łódź, Łódź, Poland

Stefan Oeter Universität Hamburg Fakultät für Rechtswissenschaft Institut für Internationale Angelegenheiten, Hamburg, Germany

Facundo Pérez-Aznar Center for International Dispute Settlement, Geneva, Switzerland
University of Buenos Aires Law School, Buenos Aires, Argentina

Elisa Ruozzi University of Turin, Turin, Italy

Vera Rusinova Faculty of Law of the National Research University Higher School of Economics, Moscow, Russia

Pierluigi Salvati Link Campus University, Rome, Italy

Vladislav Starzhenetskiy Faculty of Law, National Research University "Higher School of Economics", Moscow, Russia

Geir Ulfstein Department of Public and International Law, University of Oslo, Oslo, Norway

Johannes Ungerer University of Oxford, Oxford, UK

Peng Wang Xi'an Jiaotong University School of Law, Xi'an, PR China

Anna Wyrozumska University of Lodz, Faculty of Law and Administration, Lodz, Poland

Editors' Introduction: State Immunity and the Need for a Global Discussion

Régis Bismuth, Vera Rusinova, Vladislav Starzhenetskiy, and Geir Ulfstein

States have always enjoyed the privilege of sovereign immunity before foreign courts. The rule of absolute immunity, based on the classic formula *par in parem non habet jurisdictionem*, reflected a state-centered approach that dominated the international legal order until recently. Suing foreign governments in national courts was not an option and the only remedy private parties could have hoped for was the diplomatic protection of their own State.

But that era of absolute sovereign immunity has progressively vanished in the twentieth century. The 2004 United Nations Convention on Jurisdictional Immunities of States and Their Property ('the UN Convention') eventually consolidated the rejection of an already old paradigm and served as a catalyst for subsequent changes. The UN Convention, the Council of Europe Convention on the Immunity of States, the case-law of the European Court of Human Rights, and the legislation of a significant number of states, have crystalized the recognition of a restrictive immunity rule.

Nevertheless, a closer look at the ongoing process of formation of the international customary law of State immunity reveals many contradictions and genuine tensions with some overarching objectives, principles or values. Suits against sovereigns before foreign courts often generate considerable political strains between affected states, and may give rise to new disputes in, for example, the International Court of Justice, the European Court of Human Rights, the European Court of

R. Bismuth (✉)
Sciences Po Law School, Sciences Po, Paris, France
e-mail: regis.bismuth@sciencespo.fr

V. Rusinova · V. Starzhenetskiy
Faculty of Law, National Research University "Higher School of Economics", Moscow, Russia
e-mail: vstarzhenetskiy@hse.ru

G. Ulfstein
Department of Public and International Law, University of Oslo, Oslo, Norway
e-mail: geir.ulfstein@jus.uio.no

R. Bismuth et al. (eds.), *Sovereign Immunity Under Pressure*,
https://doi.org/10.1007/978-3-030-87706-4_1

Justice. It is also worth mentioning that some powerful, non-Western countries (for instance, China) still adhere to the absolute immunity rule.

Furthermore, the rules on sovereign immunity are subject to rapid changes under the influence of evolving national legislation and the practice of national courts. Although not yet a reflection of a general practice, we are witnessing the formation of new domestic rules restricting sovereign immunity, such as a terrorism exception in the United States and Canada allowing victims of terrorism to sue foreign States and collect relevant compensation, and an expropriation exception granting jurisdiction to US courts in cases of property taken in violation of international law. Recent proposed exceptions to State immunity ranging from causing the COVID-19 pandemic to gaining unauthorized access to a computer in the United States are quite illustrative in this regard of this general trend of restricting sovereign immunity.

On the other hand, there is an opposite trend towards an expansion of State immunity from execution, by limiting the scope of seizable State property and by adding new procedural obstacles such as the requirement of prior judicial authorization for any measure of constraint targeting foreign State's property. This is the case for instance in France and Belgium where two new statutes on immunity from execution have been enacted recently.

The existing rules can also differ noticeably among different jurisdictions and be subject to different conditions, exceptions and reservations. Authors often emphasize the lack of a uniform understanding of basic elements of the restrictive immunity rule (including such concepts as acts *jure imperii* and *jure gestionis*, commercial transaction, implied or express waiver of immunity), and they diagnose an evolution of immunity law in different and sometimes, opposite directions. Another trend is the growing role of reciprocity principle (such as in Russia, China, Argentina, Brazil, Chile, Colombia, etc.) that subjects the granting of State immunity to reciprocal obligations of the foreign state concerned. It highlights serious concerns as to whether present and proposed revolutionary changes of the State immunity regime truly reflect a quest for justice and aim to ensure redress for victims, or rather serve as an instrument of lawfare and geopolitical domination that only works against 'enemy states' but never vice versa.

The rules of sovereign immunity are thus under serious pressure from various sides. They are criticized by human rights advocates for denying access to justice for victims of the most serious fundamental rights violations. But, although the International Court of Justice, in its 2012 judgment in *Jurisdictional Immunities of States*, rejected the argument that violations of *jus cogens* norms committed by armed forces can trump sovereign immunity, the discussion did not stop there and the dispute has shifted from an international to a domestic level, where national legislators and judges have attempted to find new solutions and balances based on their own constitutional values. This is the case, for example, with respect to the Italian Constitutional Court which, despite the aforementioned ICJ ruling, held in its judgment of 10 October 2014 that a foreign state committing war crimes cannot shield itself behind the screen of immunity. A similar issue was raised in Poland where one of the political parties questioned the validity of the renunciation of reparations made by the Polish communist government in 1953 and encouraged individual claims against Germany before Polish courts.

Concurrently, others have complained that existing restrictions on State immunity are interpreted too broadly by national courts and in a way that is abusive for foreign sovereigns, or that current approaches do not reflect, or do not sufficiently rely on positions and interests of non-western states. International financial and investment law may serve as another example where interests of investors collide with core interests of states. This conflict has triggered problems concerning the legal standards applied to waivers of immunity from jurisdiction or execution (should it be express or implied; should arbitration provision in bilateral investment treaties (BITs) per se constitute waiver from all kinds of State immunity); immunity from execution in disputes relating to sovereign defaults or the payment of arbitral awards and leading to the potential attachment of assets belonging to foreign Central banks, sovereign wealth funds or state-owned enterprises. The case of Russia denying jurisdiction of arbitral tribunals and resisting to enforce investment arbitration awards under the Energy Charter Treaty (the *Yukos* award of 50 billion USD), and recent 'Crimean cases' under the Ukraine-Russia BIT, are particularly illustrative. Another controversial issue is the lawfulness of the freezing foreign states' assets on such grounds as fight against terrorism or unilateral economic sanctions.

In the context of ongoing geopolitical power shifts and deepening multi-polarity, there is an overriding need for a global discussion on the most pressing issues on State immunity such as the difficulties in establishing the current state of international customary law in light of the divergent practice of states, policy implications of recent State immunity developments and main risks associated with it for international law, driving forces behind these developments and reactions of non-Western jurisdictions to ongoing erosion of the State immunity regime, and the role of international courts in the consolidation and interpretation of the law of jurisdictional immunities of states.

This volume explores three dimensions of the evolution of the State immunity regime: Part I looks at State immunity from a comparative perspective; Part II discusses more specifically the major trends relating to the interplay between State immunity and the protection of human rights as well as counter-terrorism; and Part III examines the various interplays between State immunity and the financial obligations of States.

Part I 'Sovereign Immunity from a Comparative Perspective: Weak v. Strong Immunity Regimes', deals with the diversity of existing regimes of State immunity at the national level. This part aims to explore different approaches of particular states to sovereign immunity, their general attitude to international law and attempts to understand why some States favour a weaker State immunity regime by multiplying exceptions or interpreting them broadly, while others continuously support a stronger one and sometimes rely on the doctrine of absolute immunity. Special attention is also paid to the application of the reciprocity principle that may trigger further fragmentation and disintegration of the global State immunity approach. This part includes an analysis of the national State immunity regimes of such players as the USA (see chapter by Chimène Keitner), Germany (by Stephan

Oeter), Russia (by Vladislav Starzhenetskiy), China (by Peng Wang), and also regional perspectives including Latin America (by Facundo Pérez-Aznar) and Africa (by Appolin Koagne Zoupet). This part also focuses on the role of the International Court of Justice in shaping the international law of State immunity and, in this regard, Giulia Bernabei also assesses the interpretative trends of the World Court and envisages the role that international courts at large are called to perform in this field.

Part II 'International Customary Law of Sovereign Immunity, Human Rights and Counter-Terrorism' highlights how human rights and counter-terrorism have shaped the law and practice of sovereign immunity. We have indeed witnessed attempts to limit immunity in cases involving violations of international peremptory norms. Anna Wyrozumska explores the extent to which a human rights exception to State immunity is recognised by domestic courts of the United States, Canada, Greece and Italy, the latter adopting a stance opposite to the ICJ ruling in *Jurisdictional Immunities of the State*.

Another compelling issue addressed by Eliza Ruozzi is how to bridge the gap between jurisdictional immunity and victims' rights. In this light, she explores how the rise and development of victims' rights can contribute to a progressive shrinking of State immunities, especially with regard to of the consolidation of the right to individual compensation.

Giovanni Ardito engages in an in-depth study of the of the European Court of Human Rights case-law in embassy-employment disputes in light of Article 6 of the European Convention on Human Rights and shows the difficulties the Strasbourg Court has faced in finding the proper balance between State immunity and the protection of human rights while relying on international customary law.

Finally, Magdalena Matusiak-Frącczak and Rana M. Essawy both focus in their respective chapters on the efforts of some States (USA and Canada) to counter State-sponsored terrorism by introducing so called 'terrorism exceptions' into their legislation, which permits individuals to sue foreign States before national courts by creating a private right of action. The most vital question here is whether the new State immunity exception is compatible with current international law, and how introduction of this rule by the USA and Canada intends, or not, to influence or reshape the international law of State immunity.

Part III 'Sovereign Immunity of States and their Financial Obligations' contributes to on-going debates related to the mixed and complex nature of States' financial obligations, which most often cannot be qualified as purely private or public ones, highlighting the often blurred distinction between *jure imperii* and *jure gestionis* acts, a distinction which is nonetheless of critical importance for the law of State immunity. In the absence of forum selection clauses, jurisdictional immunities are granted only with respect to *acta jure gestionis* in such cases. Recent cases involving sovereign debt restructuring by Argentina and Greece, show a high level of legal uncertainty as illustrated by the different legal approaches used in the EU and continental law as well as in Anglo-Saxon jurisdictions. In this Part, authors elaborate on perceptions of the underlying public-private law divide, cross-influences in public and private international law, and their consequences for State immunity.

Stefano Dominelli tackles the relationship between sovereign debt and State immunity in the framework of EU international civil procedure regulations and stresses the need for coordination between international public law and EU private international law. Another contribution by Johannes Ungerer highlights the lack of international consensus as to whether immunity can be raised by the issuing state through a public act of State that unilaterally modifies or lifts the obligation of repayment and suggests that differing perceptions of the underlying public-private law divide can be seen as an explanation of the divergent views.

Another burning question concerning States' financial obligations relates to highly politically sensitive issue of immunity from execution. Pierluigi Salvati explores the issue of immunity of the assets of foreign central banks and highlights a trend toward strengthening the immunity granted to foreign central banks from post-judgment enforcement measures while underlining some divergent approaches. Finally, Régis Bismuth's study shows how diplomatic concerns as well as economic interests have been prevalent in the context of the adoption of the new French statute on immunity from execution which significantly reinforces the protection enjoyed by State property. His chapter also points out that while the original declared intent was to devise a new framework based on customary international law, it turns out that it significantly and purposefully deviates from it in many ways.

This book is the result of a joint research project on Sovereign Immunity in International Law conducted by the PluriCourts Centre (University of Oslo, Norway), the National Research University 'Higher Schools of Economics' Law School (Moscow, Russia) and Science Po Law School (Paris, France). The contributors participating in the project represent not only well-known Western academic centres (University of Oslo, PluriCourts, Science Po, University of Turin, University of California, University of Hamburg, University of Genoa, University of Oxford, etc.), but also include authors representing the leading universities in China, Egypt, Argentina, Russia and Poland. One of the main aims of this volume is thus to contribute to a global discussion on the above-mentioned topics, and to search for solutions reflecting the future of the international customary law of State immunity.

Régis Bismuth is a Professor of Law at Sciences Po Law School (Paris), specializing in public international law, international economic law, and international adjudication. He is the author of several publications in these fields and more particularly on the law of international organizations, sovereign immunity, extraterritoriality, anti-corruption law, economic sanctions, WTO law, international investment law and arbitration, State capitalism, sovereign debt, international standards, financial regulation, internet regulation, and the responsibility of multinational corporations. He is Co-Editor-in-Chief of *The Law and Practice of International Courts and Tribunals* (LPICT) and Director of Studies of the French Branch of the International Law Association (ILA). Régis is also a member of the International Monetary Law Committee of the ILA (MOCOMILA) and a Fellow at the International Academy of Financial Crime Litigators. He has advised public institutions and private entities on matters of international law.

Vera Rusinova is a Professor at the Faculty of Law of the National Research University Higher School of Economics, where she heads the School of International Law. The main fields of her research activities comprise international human rights law, international humanitarian law, use of force, the theory of international law, and the application of international law to cyber operations. She is a Co-Chair of the International Law Association's Committee on Use of Force: Military Assistance on Request. Vera is also a member of the Editorial Groups/Boards of 'International Justice', 'Journal of International Humanitarian Legal Studies', and 'International Cybersecurity Law Review'. Her lecture on 'Human Rights in Armed Conflicts' was placed in the UN Audiovisual Library of International Law.

Vladislav Starzhenetskiy is an Associate Professor at the Chair of International Law, Faculty of Law of the National Research University Higher School of Economics (HSE). He also serves as an Academic Director of the Master Program 'Law of International Trade, Finance and Economic Integration' and researcher at the HSE Laboratory on Sanctions in International Law. The main fields of his research interests include jurisdictional immunities of states, economic sanctions, international protection of intellectual property, international civil procedure and international human rights law. He is a member of the Editorial Group of the Russian 'International Justice' Journal. Vladislav graduated from the Moscow State Institute of International Relations (MGIMO) with a degree in International Law. He received his PhD for a dissertation dedicated to comparative analysis of property rights under the ECHR and Russian law. From 1998 to 2014, he has been working at the Russian Federation's Supreme Commercial Court and was heading the Department of International Law and Cooperation from 2011 to 2014.

Geir Ulfstein is Professor of international law at the Department of Public and International Law, University of Oslo and Co-director of PluriCourts—Centre for the Study of the Legitimate Roles of the Judiciary in the Global Order, University of Oslo. He has been Director of the Norwegian Centre for Human Rights, University of Oslo (2004–2008). He has published in different areas of international law, including the law of the sea, international environmental law, international human rights and international institutional law. Geir is General Editor (with Andreas Føllesdal) of two book series Studies on Human Rights Conventions (Cambridge University Press) and Studies in International Courts and Tribunals (Cambridge University Press). He is President of the Norwegian Branch of the International Law Association, Co-chair of the International Law Association's Study Group on the 'Content and Evolution of the Rules of Interpretation' and is Chair of the Scientific Advisory Board, Max Planck Institute for Procedural Law, Luxembourg. He has been member of the Executive Board of the European Society of International Law (2010–2016). He will deliver one of the special courses during the Hague Academy of International Law's 2022 winter session. He is also a member of the Norwegian Academy of Science and Letters.

Part I
Sovereign Immunity from a Comparative Perspective: Weak v. Strong Immunity Regimes

Sovereignty, Humanity, and Justice: Reflections on U.S. Law of Foreign Sovereign Immunity

Chimène I. Keitner

Abstract This chapter offers reflections on aspects of the U.S. law of foreign sovereign immunity under the headings of Sovereignty, Humanity, and Justice. The enactment of the Foreign Sovereign Immunities Act (FSIA) in 1976 was motivated by a desire to depoliticize immunity determinations. However, some in Congress view the ability to create additional legislative exceptions to state immunity as an attractive tool in the foreign policy 'toolkit'. This contribution encourages a holistic approach to sovereign immunity doctrines that takes into account the human costs of immunity, while remaining mindful of the potential for systemic disruption created by idiosyncratic exceptions.

1 Introduction

The U.S. law of foreign sovereign immunity traces its roots to the earliest years of the Republic. As a doctrinal matter, this body of law is largely consistent with the restrictive theory, which insulates foreign states from the burdens of litigation for their public acts (*jure imperii*) but not for their private or commercial acts (*jure gestionis*). Other aspects of U.S. practice with respect to immunities are a product of the United States' distinctive constitutional structure and legal culture.

There are several noteworthy features of the U.S. approach to questions of sovereign immunity. First, the Foreign Sovereign Immunities Act of 1976 (FSIA) governs the immunities of states, including their political subdivisions and organs, and entities that are majority-owned by foreign states.[1] It does not govern the immunities of current or former foreign officials, whose immunities form the subject of other specialized statutes, and of a still-evolving body of federal common law.[2]

[1] See generally Stewart (2018); American Law Institute (2018), Part IV Ch. 5.

[2] Samantar v. Yousuf, 560 U.S. 305 (2010).

C. I. Keitner (✉)
UC Hastings Law, San Francisco, CA, USA
e-mail: keitnerc@uchastings.edu

R. Bismuth et al. (eds.), *Sovereign Immunity Under Pressure*,
https://doi.org/10.1007/978-3-030-87706-4_2

The FSIA also does not govern immunity from criminal proceedings, although its failure to state this explicitly has caused some consternation.[3]

Second, the FSIA places immunity determinations squarely in the hands of courts. In the decades preceding the statute's enactment, courts had come to rely on 'suggestions' of foreign state immunity or non-immunity from the executive branch. When interpretive disputes arise, courts employ the normal tools of statutory interpretation, which focus on the text, context, and history of the statute.

Third, the U.S. Congress has come to view the ability to create additional exceptions to foreign state immunity under the FSIA as a tool of foreign policy. Although the executive branch has taken the position that civil disputes with significant foreign policy implications are often unsuitable for judicial resolution, Congress has used the FSIA to channel certain claims against foreign states to U.S. courts, with predictably mixed results.

This essay offers reflections on aspects of the U.S. law of foreign sovereign immunity under the thematic headings of Sovereignty, Humanity, and Justice.[4] The enactment of the FSIA means that Congress defines the contours of State immunity from jurisdiction in U.S. courts. The decision to codify State immunity in 1976 was motivated in large part by a desire to depoliticize immunity determinations. However, a perhaps unintended consequence has been to create a perception in Congress that denying sovereign immunity can be viewed instrumentally as a tool in the foreign policy 'toolkit'. This contribution encourages a holistic approach to sovereign immunity doctrines that takes into account the human costs of immunity, while remaining mindful of the potential for systemic disruption created by idiosyncratic exceptions.

2 Sovereignty

The theme of State sovereignty has long figured prominently in U.S. foreign policy discourse. A pernicious strand of sovereigntist thought has occasionally led the United States to repudiate multilateral engagements, which was a hallmark of the Trump Administration. A more benign version has animated the United States' self-conception ever since the 1776 Declaration of Independence asserted the right of the thirteen former British colonies 'as Free and Independent States' to 'levy War, conclude Peace, contract Alliances, establish Commerce, and to do all other Acts and Things which Independent States may of right do'.

---

[3] See Keitner (2020a).

[4] This chapter builds on remarks delivered as the Alfred and Hanna Fromm Chairholder Lecture at UC Hastings Law on 26 January 2021. Readers might also be interested in a conversation between the author and Professor Ingrid Wuerth on related topics. Available at https://www.lawfareblog.com/lawfare-podcast-past-present-and-future-sovereign-immunity/.

The 1789 Constitution—which continues to govern the relationship among the branches of the U.S. government, and between the federal government and the 50 states—authorized the creation of federal courts (Article III) alongside the federal legislative (Article I) and executive (Article II) branches. To a perhaps surprising extent, case law on foreign sovereign immunity in U.S. courts has focused more on the proper allocation of domestic constitutional authority among these three branches than it has on relevant international law and practice. In part, this might be because Congress has the constitutional authority to violate customary international law, although the executive branch might not have that authority.[5] Because foreign state immunity has been governed by the FSIA since 1976, courts' primary task has been to interpret and apply the statute. That said, the *Charming Betsy* canon of statutory interpretation requires courts to avoid interpreting statutes to violate customary international law 'if any other possible construction remains'[6] International law considerations thus inform the executive branch's views on questions of state immunity, as well as the views of Congress and the courts. They will not, however, invalidate a clear Congressional enactment.

2.1 Foundations of State Immunity

Beginning in the 1790s, U.S. state and federal courts encountered claims to foreign State immunity in the context of *in rem* proceedings against foreign ships in U.S. ports. The most well-known of these early cases involved the *Balaou No. 5*, a French ship of war that two Maryland residents claimed was actually their ship, the *Schooner Exchange*. A threshold question was whether a U.S. court had jurisdiction to attach the ship, which had docked in the port of Philadelphia.

In his opinion for the Supreme Court, Chief Justice John Marshall began by noting the absence of applicable 'written law' or binding judicial precedent.[7] He therefore based his decision on the authority of what he called 'general principles' and 'common usage'.[8] He began with the axiom that '[t]he jurisdiction of the nation within its own territory is necessarily exclusive and absolute'.[9] But this absolute territorial jurisdiction has certain limits, he reasoned, based on the forum state's consent and the 'common interest impelling [sovereign states] to mutual intercourse'.[10] Because 'the ports of a friendly nation are considered as open to the public ships of all powers with whom it is at peace,' Marshall found that the *Balaou No. 5* had entered the Philadelphia port with the implied consent of the United States,

[5] See Dodge (2018).

[6] Murray v. Schooner Charming Betsy, 6 U.S. (2 Cranch) 64, 118 (1804).

[7] 11 U.S. (7 Cranch) 116, 136 (1812).

[8] Ibid.

[9] Ibid.

[10] Ibid., 137.

and that this implied consent entitled the ship to an exemption from local jurisdiction.[11] Private individuals or merchant vessels entering for the purpose of trade could not, however, claim such an exemption.[12] Under this analytic framework, the executive branch could play a role in immunity determinations by furnishing 'suggestions' to the court indicating whether or not a given ship met the factual predicates for immunity, as it had done in this case.

Disputes involving foreign ships formed the bulk of the foreign sovereign immunity docket through the early twentieth century.[13] Over time, suits against foreign states expanded beyond the admiralty context to include suits against foreign governments and agencies, as well as state-owned corporations. The executive branch continued its practice of suggesting immunity or non-immunity in selected cases. As a general matter, the State Department maintained that public vessels of war were entitled to immunity, but that government-owned merchant vessels and other vessels engaged in commerce were properly subject to U.S. jurisdiction.[14] Outside the admiralty context, state immunity also turned largely on whether or not a particular activity carried on by a foreign state, or by the agency or instrumentality of a foreign state, was deemed commercial in nature.[15]

2.2 *Adjudicating Commercial Activities*

The line between commercial and non-commercial activity was not always self-evident. Beginning in the 1940s, the Supreme Court established a practice of deferring to executive branch suggestions of immunity or non-immunity—not because the executive branch had a special talent for identifying commercial activities, but because '[w]hen the Secretary [of State] elects . . . to settle claims against the vessel by diplomatic negotiations between the two countries rather than by continued litigation in the courts, it is of public importance that the action of the political arm of the Government taken within its appropriate sphere be promptly recognized'.[16] The rationale for this new posture of judicial deference was rooted in the executive branch's role in diplomatic negotiations and its authority to settle international claims.

In 1952, the Department of State issued the Tate Letter, which formally announced that the United States would follow the 'restrictive' theory of immunity for foreign states.[17] Jack Tate was the Department's Acting Legal Adviser. The letter

[11] Ibid., 141.

[12] Ibid., 142.

[13] See Keitner (2019).

[14] The Pesaro, 277 F. 473, 479 (S.D.N.Y. 1921).

[15] See, e.g., U.S. v. Deutsches Kalisyndicat Gesellschaft, 31 F.2d 199, 200 (S.D.N.Y. 1929).

[16] Ex parte Republic of Peru, 318 U.S. 578, 587 (1943).

[17] 26 Dep't State Bull. 984-85 (1952).

canvassed the practice of numerous other countries and assessed a trend towards the restrictive theory, under which foreign states are immune from each other's domestic jurisdiction for suits based on their governmental acts, but not their commercial acts. Tate explained that the United States had long refrained from claiming immunity for its own merchant vessels in foreign courts, and that 'the widespread and increasing practice on the part of governments of engaging in commercial activities makes necessary a practice which will enable persons doing business with them to have their rights determined in the courts'.[18] The Tate Letter sought to clarify the broad outlines of the State Department's approach, but it arguably had the effect of 'thr [owing] immunity determinations into some disarray'.[19] Foreign states continued to pressure the Department to issue case-specific suggestions of immunity, and decisions about how to apply the restrictive theory became bound up with political considerations. The situation ultimately became untenable. The State Department, along with the Department of Justice, asked Congress to step in.

In 1976, Congress enacted the Foreign Sovereign Immunities Act (FSIA) to restore courts' authority over sovereign immunity determinations and to codify the restrictive theory.[20] The FSIA serves as a long-arm statute for asserting personal jurisdiction over foreign states and their agencies and instrumentalities. It creates a baseline of immunity from civil suit, subject to enumerated exceptions over which the federal courts can exercise subject-matter jurisdiction. Litigation under the FSIA has thus focused largely on whether or not a particular claim falls within a statutory exception to immunity. Meanwhile, the focus of intense lobbying has shifted from foreign states seeking case-specific suggestions of immunity from the executive branch, to claimants petitioning Congress to codify additional exceptions.

2.3 Construing Exceptions Narrowly

The underlying facts in FSIA cases can be compelling, as claimants seek redress for a wide range of injurious conduct. For example, in 1994, the D.C. Circuit Court of Appeals considered whether the Federal Republic of Germany was immune from claims brought by Hugo Princz, a Holocaust survivor and American citizen.[21] Mr. Princz sought to recover damages from Germany for injuries he suffered and slave labor he performed while imprisoned in Nazi concentration camps. But the FSIA does not have an enumerated exception to immunity for human rights violations, even when they amount to international crimes.

In the Court of Appeals, a majority found that the absence of an enumerated exception to immunity meant that Mr. Princz's suit could not proceed. The majority

[18] Ibid., 985.

[19] Republic of Austria v. Altmann, 541 U.S. 677, 690 (2004).

[20] See 28 U.S.C. § 1602 (2018).

[21] Princz v. Federal Republic of Germany, 26 F.3d 1166 (D.C. Cir. 1994).

observed that no state had likely 'ever violated [peremptory] *jus cogens* norms on a scale rivaling that of the Third Reich'.[22] However, it reasoned that the suit could not proceed under the FSIA's exception for waiver, because even an implied waiver 'depends upon the foreign government's having at some point indicated its amenability to suit'.[23] Absent such an indication by Germany, the majority was unwilling to find jurisdiction under the FSIA.

Judge Patricia Wald dissented on the grounds that Germany's inhumane treatment of Mr. Princz violated *jus cogens* norms of international law. In her view, the court should have treated the egregiousness of Germany's conduct as an implied waiver of its sovereign immunity.[24] She reasoned that '[i]n the mid-1940s, Germany could not, even in its wildest dreams, have expected the executive branch of the United States, as a matter of grace and comity, to suggest immunity for its enslavement and confinement (in three concentration camps) of an American citizen during the Holocaust'.[25] Moreover, *jus cogens* norms 'are by definition non-derogable, and thus when a state thumbs its nose at such a norm, in effect overriding the collective will of the entire international community, the state cannot be performing a sovereign act entitled to immunity'.[26] In Judge Wald's opinion, denying state immunity for *jus cogens* violations would also be consistent with international law's recognition of universal jurisdiction to prosecute such violations, and States' creation of international tribunals to adjudicate these acts.[27] She reasoned that, just as a state cannot invoke immunity to shield its officials from prosecution for international crimes, a state also cannot claim jurisdictional immunity for itself in foreign courts for the same conduct. In Judge Wald's view, international law supported construing the waiver exception to encompass violations of *jus cogens* norms.[28]

Because waiver is an enumerated exception to immunity under the FSIA, treating *jus cogens* violations as an implied waiver would provide a statutory basis for asserting jurisdiction over a foreign State. U.S. courts have not, however, adopted Judge Wald's reasoning. The Seventh Circuit Court of Appeals was especially critical of the suggestion that evolving conceptions of international law ought to dictate the meaning of the waiver exception, cautioning that '[c]ustomary international law can evolve unpredictably without reference to the understandings of courts or Congress,'[29] and that 'Congress's general desire to follow standards recognized under international law [in the FSIA] does not provide the foundation needed to support th[e] proposed reading of an implied waiver'.[30] This was so, the

[22] Ibid., 1174 (D.C. Cir. 1994).
[23] Ibid.
[24] Ibid., 1178.
[25] Ibid., 1179.
[26] Ibid., 1182.
[27] Ibid., 1183.
[28] Ibid., 1184.
[29] Sampson v. Federal Republic of Germany, 250 F.3d 1145, 1154 (7th Cir. 2001).
[30] Ibid.

court held, even though the plaintiff's Holocaust-era claims against Germany in that case 'allege[d] horrors which are beyond belief'.[31]

Foreign sovereign immunity blocked Mr. Princz's effort to seek a judicial remedy against Germany. But he ultimately succeeded in suing the German companies that had benefited from his forced labor, because they were not covered by the FSIA. Meanwhile, some in Congress proposed legislation to amend the FSIA to allow victims of genocide to sue foreign governments. Although that measure did not pass the Senate, Congress has adopted other exceptions to sovereign immunity, most notably in the terrorism context.[32] Eventually, the United States and Germany negotiated a settlement to provide reparations for almost 250 Americans who had survived Nazi concentration camps, including Mr. Princz. Settlements of claims against foreign states that were initially filed in U.S. courts have led some members of Congress, and some private parties, to view the threat of creating an additional statutory exception to state immunity as an effective pressure-point in diplomatic negotiations. But the executive branch, which conducts such negotiations, has generally opposed the creation of additional exceptions to state immunity from civil suit.

Unlike most other state immunity acts, the FSIA contains an exception for certain acts of expropriation.[33] This exception has allowed a measure of recovery for Holocaust-era property claims, but only for non-nationals of the expropriating state. In a recent case, claimants asked the U.S. Supreme Court to interpret the FSIA's expropriation exception to encompass the coerced sale to Prussia of a collection of medieval relics owned by German Jewish art dealers.[34] Although such 'domestic takings' do not violate the international law prohibition on expropriation, the claimants argued—and the D.C. Court of Appeals found in a related case—that the FSIA's language could extend to any 'tak[ing] in violation of international law'.[35] Because the Nazi government coerced the sale in conjunction with the international crime of genocide, the claimants argued that their German nationality should not act as a barrier to applying the expropriation exception.

A unanimous Supreme Court declined to read the statutory exception literally, and instead relied on the provision's 'text, context, and history' to exclude domestic takings.[36] It recognized that the expropriation exception is unique among state immunity acts, and attributed its existence to '[h]istory and context,' including the United States' long-standing efforts 'to protect the property of its citizens abroad as part of a defense of America's free enterprise system'.[37] Although the wording of the exception refers to 'rights in property taken in violation of international law,' the

[31] Ibid., 1146.

[32] See Sect. 4.2.

[33] 28 U.S.C. § 1605(a)(3).

[34] Federal Republic of Germany v. Philipp, 141 S.Ct. 703 (2021).

[35] Simon v. Republic of Hungary, 812 F.3d 127 (D.C. Cir. 2016).

[36] Philipp, 141 S.Ct. 714.

[37] Ibid., 713.

Court held that this language 'is best read as referencing the international law of expropriation rather than of human rights'.[38] Moreover, although this would have been sufficient to resolve the case, the Court went on to state in *dicta* that international law, according to the International Court of Justice's decision in *Germany v. Italy*, 'preserv[es] sovereign immunity for human rights violations'.[39] The Court thus declined 'to subject all manner of sovereign public acts to judicial scrutiny under the FSIA by transforming the expropriation exception into an all-purpose jurisdictional hook for adjudicating human rights violations'.[40]

As a structural principle of international law, foreign sovereign immunity preserves the system of diplomatic protection and espousal of claims, rather than direct access to judicial remedies. From a claimant's perspective, sovereignty operates as a barrier to having one's day in court. Diplomatic negotiations on behalf of injured parties can feel cumbersome, slow, and opaque. Diplomats and government lawyers must weigh a range of considerations in settlement negotiations, whereas attorneys representing private parties can focus single-mindedly on the interests of their clients. But precisely because foreign states are sovereign, and also owe a fiduciary duty to their own populations, it is not clear that resolving private claims in foreign courts will always produce the best result, viewed holistically. Private litigation can also complicate efforts to pursue foreign policy goals that require the cooperation of defendant states.

The FSIA's codification of a baseline of immunity derived from principles of foreign State sovereignty explains why a U.S. court could not adjudicate Mr. Princz's claims against Germany. But the FSIA does not codify absolute immunity. Rather, it reflects a series of political choices to delineate the reach of U.S. adjudicatory authority in disputes involving foreign States that also responds to other systemic needs and values, particularly in the commercial sphere. As a descriptive matter, a purely sovereignty-based theory of immunity has trouble explaining the restrictive theory, which treats State actors differently depending on the nature of their conduct. As a normative matter, structural principles of international law, and their domestic manifestations, do not exist solely to create stability and to preserve sovereignty. They also exist to protect and to promote other human values.

Although the FSIA does not contain an exception to immunity for international crimes or human rights violations, Congress has created civil causes of action and criminal penalties for certain internationally unlawful acts.[41] Thus, while the U.S. legal system recognizes certain prerogatives that flow from State sovereignty,

[38] Ibid., 712.

[39] Ibid., 713.

[40] Ibid.

[41] These include: Torture Victim Protection Act, 28 U.S.C. § 1350 note (2018); Genocide Accountability Act of 2007, 18 U.S.C. § 1091(d) (2018); Torture Convention Implementation Act of 1994, 18 U.S.C. §§ 2340–2340A (2006); War Crimes Act of 1996, 18 U.S.C. § 2441 (2018); Child Soldiers Accountability Act of 2008, 18 U.S.C. § 2442 (2018).

it does not necessarily treat the accoutrements of sovereignty as absolute. Some statutory provisions and judicial interpretations also give effect to other needs and values, including principles of humanity.

3 Humanity

In April 1945, Supreme Court Justice Robert Jackson—who would be appointed weeks later as chief prosecutor for the United States at Nuremberg—delivered an address at the annual meeting of the American Society of International Law. In his remarks, he reflected on the role of international law and international lawyers, observing that '[w]e still leave the traveler, the business man or the owner of property in a foreign country who suffers a violation of international law or treaty rights pretty much in the unhappy position of having no sure or easy remedy, and the bar still thinks of them as the affair only of diplomats'.[42] Justice Jackson recognized the limitations of a system of diplomatic protection and espousal of claims, which treated individual deprivations of rights at the hands of foreign governments as 'the affair only of diplomats'. Three years later, the U.N. General Assembly would adopt the Universal Declaration of Human Rights, which made deprivations of rights at the hands of one's own government a matter of inclusive international concern. Yet remedies for violations were—and remain—elusive.

The Nuremberg trials, in which Justice Jackson played a central role, have come to symbolize the potential for criminal proceedings against individuals who abuse the authority of the State to vindicate principles of humanity. They also stand for the idea that individuals can bear personal responsibility for certain violations of international law. The personalization of responsibility for atrocity crimes committed by 'men, not abstract entities' made clear that officials could not invoke State sovereignty to absolve themselves of culpability. It may also tend to absolve the broader population from a sense of collective responsibility by focusing blame on individual leaders.[43] State and individual responsibility can, and do, coexist. Yet although there has been a trend toward using domestic courts to impose consequences on individuals for international law violations, determinations of State responsibility have been left, by and large, to international bodies.[44]

[42] Jackson (1945).

[43] See Franck (2007).

[44] See Keitner (2013), noting that Germany appears not to have challenged Italy's conviction in absentia of Max Josef Milde for his role in a 1944 massacre in the Tuscan town of Civitella, even though it protested Italy's exercise of jurisdiction over the German state.

3.1 Civil Suits Against Foreign Officials

The potential role of U.S. courts in providing a forum for victims of international law violations to seek redress from individual perpetrators came into focus in a New York courtroom in October 1979. Peter Weiss, a New York lawyer, argued to the Second Circuit Court of Appeals that a Paraguayan police inspector-general violated international law when he tortured and killed Joelito Filártiga, the 17-year-old son of a political dissident in Paraguay.[45] The Convention Against Torture, a multilateral treaty, did not yet exist. Nevertheless, Weiss—with the support of expert affidavits from four international law professors, and a supportive brief from the Carter Administration—persuaded the court that there was a legal basis for asserting jurisdiction to adjudicate the plaintiffs' claims.

The U.S. government's brief, which proved decisive, affirmed that 'because torture is universally condemned and incompatible with accepted concepts of human behavior, the protection against torture must be considered a fundamental human right'.[46] In other words, even if some states still engaged in torture, none of them asserted a legal right to do so. The prohibition on torture could thus be said to have achieved the status of a customary international law rule. The positivist trend in international law means that one could not, and cannot, simply assert that all moral imperatives are also legal rules. But the repugnancy of torture, combined with President Jimmy Carter's view that 'moral principles were the best foundation for the exertion of American power and influence' in foreign affairs, created the conditions for interagency agreement on this forward-leaning brief.[47] The U.S. government also concluded that, in its view, the international law prohibiting torture could be privately enforced against a defendant who came within the court's personal jurisdiction under a then little-known provision of the U.S. code, 28 U.S.C. § 1350.

The *Filártiga* opinion opened a pathway for human rights litigation against foreign defendants in U.S. courts. But it left many questions unanswered. The Filártigas could not have sued Paraguay itself, unless Paraguay waived its immunity under the FSIA. The individual defendant, who was removed from the United States for having overstayed his visa, defaulted in the litigation. He thus did not argue that he enjoyed immunity under the FSIA. He did not claim that the suit against him should be treated as if it had been filed against Paraguay, because he had been acting in his official capacity as a police inspector-general. Consequently, the U.S. government did not have occasion to provide views on the question whether jurisdictional immunity could shield a former foreign official from allegations of torture.

---

[45] See Koh (2007).

[46] Memorandum for the United States as Amicus Curiae, Filartiga v. Pena-Irala, No. 79-6090 (2d Cir., May 29, 1980) 15.

[47] Koh (2007), p. 53, quoting Jimmy Carter, *Keeping Faith: Memoirs of a President* 143 (1982).

The U.S. record on this legal question is mixed, and has not yet been resolved at the Supreme Court level. Individual foreign officials can attempt to assert immunity based on their current role (status-based immunity) or based on the official nature of the challenged act (conduct-based immunity).[48] Some foreign officials who are not protected by the status-based immunity accorded diplomats and heads of state have instead successfully invoked conduct-based immunity as a basis for dismissing claims against them.[49] Others have not.[50] One court of appeals has suggested that *jus cogens* violations can never qualify as 'official acts' for immunity purposes,[51] whereas other courts have conflated the question of whether an official's act is attributable to the state for purposes of state responsibility with the separate question of whether the official can claim conduct-based immunity for that act.[52]

The executive branch maintains that, in both criminal and civil cases, it has the constitutional authority to make immunity determinations for individual officials absent an applicable statute. The State Department certainly has the authority to certify whether an individual qualifies for status-based immunity. However, it remains an open question whether the 1940s cases according deference to State Department determinations of immunity for foreign ships compel judicial deference on questions of conduct-based foreign official immunity.

3.2 Other Types of Domestic Proceedings

In the criminal context, U.S. courts have treated a decision to prosecute an individual as a conclusive determination that the official is not entitled to immunity. For example, the United States prosecuted a former Liberian official for torture committed in Liberia.[53] He is now serving a 97-year sentence in federal prison. In 2020, the United States indicted an alleged former Gambian 'death squad' member on torture charges in a Colorado district court.[54] More often, U.S. authorities will deny human rights violators entry to the United States, or remove them to their countries of origin if they have established residence in the United States without disclosing their role in persecution or other international crimes.[55] The United States has also become more proactive in imposing financial and other sanctions on individuals who belong to, or

[48] See Keitner (2010) and Stephens (2011).

[49] See Dogan v. Barak, 932 F.3d 888 (9th Cir. 2019).

[50] See Lewis v. Mutond, 918 F.3d 142 (D.C. Cir. 2019).

[51] See Yousuf v. Samantar, 699 F.3d 763 (4th Cir. 2012).

[52] See Matar v. Dichter, 563 F.3d 9 (2d Cir. 2009).

[53] U.S. v. Belfast, 611 F.3d 783 (11th Cir. 2010).

[54] Department of Justice, Office of Public Affairs, *Gambian Man Indicted on Torture Charges* (11 Jun. 2020).

[55] See Keitner (2015).

are associated with, foreign governments whose policies the United States condemns.

There remains a large degree of substantive consensus in the international community about what types of conduct violate basic norms of human dignity, both in peacetime and during armed conflict. There is also a consensus that, wherever possible, States should prevent and punish international law violations by their own officials, and that they should provide a remedy for any harm caused. The problem arises when a State does not provide redress. Must other States cajole compliance through diplomacy, or can courts play a more constructive role?

The Nuremberg Tribunal's legacy and the emphasis on individual responsibility in international law center values of humanity rather than State sovereignty. Yet the FSIA does not contain corresponding exceptions to State immunity, even for atrocity crimes. It does, however, contain certain exceptions for non-commercial activity that have enabled victims to seek redress in U.S. courts. In creating these selective exceptions, Congress has emphasized a value more often associated with judicial proceedings than with the conduct of diplomacy: the pursuit of justice.

4 Justice

Justice can mean different things to different actors, and it can be pursued in different ways. Victims of violent acts have sought to invoke exceptions to the FSIA to obtain civil redress for injuries suffered at the hands of foreign governments. Occasionally, they have succeeded.

4.1 Seeking Redress Under the Territorial Tort Exception

In 1976, exiled Chilean diplomat and socialist politician Orlando Letelier was assassinated in a car bombing in Washington, DC, that also killed Institute for Policy Studies researcher Ronni Moffitt. Among other avenues of redress, the victims' family members filed a civil lawsuit. The D.C. district court found that the plaintiffs could sue Chile under the tort exception to the FSIA, notwithstanding Chile's contention that the exception 'does not cover political assassinations because of their public, governmental character'.[56] This exception allows a suit 'in which money damages are sought against a foreign state for personal injury or death, or damage to or loss of property, occurring in the United States and caused by the tortious act or omission of that foreign state or of any official or employee of that foreign state while acting within the scope of his office or employment'.[57]

---

[56] de Letelier v. Republic of Chile, 488 F. Supp. 665, 671 (D.D.C. 1980).

[57] 28 U.S.C. §1605(a)(5).

In deciding this case, the court also found that the enumerated exceptions to the tort exception (under which Chile *would* be entitled to immunity) did not apply.[58] When Congress codified the territorial tort exception to state immunity, it inexplicably borrowed language from domestic Federal Tort Claims Act to preserve immunity for claims based on the exercise of 'discretionary functions'.[59] The *Letelier* court held that 'there is no discretion to commit, or to have one's officers or agents commit, an illegal act'.[60] It explained: 'Whatever policy options may exist for a foreign country, it has no 'discretion' to perpetrate conduct designed to result in the assassination of an individual or individuals, action that is clearly contrary to the precepts of humanity as recognized in both national and international law'.[61]

The Letelier plaintiffs established their right to relief by evidence satisfactory to the court, and the court entered damages judgments against Chile and several individual defendants.[62] When the claimants sought to execute upon assets belonging to Chile's national airline to satisfy the judgment, however, the FSIA's provisions on immunity from execution proved an insurmountable obstacle. The Second Circuit Court of Appeals found that the airline's assets could not properly be treated as belonging to Chile itself or executed upon under the relevant statutory provisions.[63] In the end, the families were only able to obtain a measure of compensation after the fall of the Pinochet regime, showing the limitations of domestic adjudication in securing relief.[64]

The territorial tort exception was not designed with political assassinations in mind, but it provided a basis for the Letelier claim to proceed in U.S. court. The Supreme Court has described this exception as providing jurisdiction over injurious acts, potentially including human rights violations, 'explicitly and with precision'.[65] The same clear intent to provide an exception to immunity characterizes Congress's enactment of terrorism-related exceptions to State immunity, which it has done on several occasions.[66]

---

[58] 488 F. Supp. 673.

[59] 28 U.S.C. §1605(a)(5)(A).

[60] 488 F. Supp. 673.

[61] Ibid.

[62] de Letelier v. Republic of Chile, 502 F. Supp. 259 (D.D.C. 1980).

[63] de Letelier v. Republic of Chile and Linea Aerea Nacional-Chile, 748 F. 2d 790 (2d Cir. 1984).

[64] See Dispute concerning responsibility for the deaths of Letelier and Moffitt (United States, Chile), 25 Rep. Int'l Arb. Awards 1, 11 (11 Jan. 1992).

[65] Federal Republic of Germany v. Philipp, 141 S.Ct. 703, 714 (2021).

[66] Federal Republic of Germany v. Philipp, 141 S.Ct. 703, 714 (2021), citing §§1605A(a), (h).

4.2 *Terrorism-Related Exceptions to Foreign Sovereign Immunity*

After the 1988 bombing of Pan Am Flight 103 over Lockerbie, Scotland, victims' families sought redress in part by filing civil claims against Libya in U.S. courts. Like other victims of state-sponsored atrocities, the plaintiffs argued that Libya's conduct should be treated as an implied waiver of its immunity under the FSIA.[67] The Second Circuit Court of Appeals acknowledged that '[t]he contention that a foreign state *should* be deemed to have forfeited its sovereign immunity whenever it engages in conduct that violates fundamental humanitarian standards is an appealing one'.[68] However, the court found that Congress did not intend the waiver exception to be applied in this manner. It also found that the territorial tort exception did not apply, because the victims were not killed in the United States.[69]

Because existing exceptions to the FSIA did not allow claims against Libya, victims' families lobbied Congress to create an additional exception.[70] Congress responded in 1996 by enacting a provision in the Anti-Terrorism and Effective Death Penalty Act (AEDPA) that allows suits to proceed against countries designated by the State Department as state sponsors of terrorism for acts of torture, extrajudicial killing, aircraft sabotage, hostage taking, and related material support, even if the actions occurred abroad.[71] In the end, Libya ultimately settled civil claims brought against it under the new exception as part of a comprehensive agreement negotiated with the U.S. and U.K. governments that also involved other core aspects of Libyan policy.[72]

Congress subsequently amended the state sponsors of terrorism exception to create a federal cause of action for U.S. victims of terrorism, and to allow plaintiffs to seek punitive damages.[73] The Supreme Court held in a case against Sudan that the punitive damages provision was not impermissibly retroactive.[74] In addition, Congress overrode a Presidential veto to pass legislation in 2016 that creates an exception to the FSIA for injuries caused in the United States by (1) an act of international terrorism in the United States and (2) a tortious act of a foreign state or its officials that is not merely negligent.[75] This amalgamation of a territorial tort exception with a terrorism exception prompted concern among foreign States given the lack of any

[67] Smith v. Socialist People's Libyan Arab Jamahiriya, 101 F.3d 239, 242 (2d Cir. 1996).

[68] Ibid. (emphasis in original).

[69] Ibid., 246.

[70] See Schwartz (2007), p. 563.

[71] Antiterrorism and Effective Death Penalty Act of 1996 (AEDPA), Pub. L. 104-132, 110 Stat. 1214, § 221(a) (1996).

[72] See Schwartz (2007), pp. 568–70.

[73] National Defense Authorization Act for Fiscal Year 2008 (NDAA), Pub. L. 110-91, 122 Stat. 3, §1803 (2008).

[74] Opati v. Republic of Sudan, 140 S.Ct. 1601 (2020).

[75] Justice Against State Sponsors of Terrorism Act (JASTA), Pub. L. 114-222, 130 Stat. 852 (2016).

geographic or other restriction on the 'tortious act' requirement, other than the negligence threshold.[76] Despite these concerns, Professor William Dodge has argued that the Justice for Sponsors of Terrorism Act (JASTA) is consistent with international law, because 'there appears to be no general and consistent practice of states followed out of a sense of legal obligation establishing that foreign states are entitled to immunity for acts of terrorism or material support of such acts'.[77] The American Law Institute's Restatement (Fourth) of the Foreign Relations Law of the United States indicates that the United Nations Convention on Jurisdictional Immunities of States and Their Property 'neither endorses nor precludes the removal of immunity for acts of state-sponsored terrorism'[78] JASTA does not modify the FSIA's provisions regarding attachment and execution, although previous amendments relating to state sponsors of terrorism have sought to make it easier to enforce judgments against those defendants' assets.

Considerations of international law were mentioned in Congressional debates over JASTA, but they were not determinative. One member of Congress, Representative Maloney, referenced international law in her remarks in support of JASTA by noting that people who conspired with the 9/11 hijackers in the 'planning, preparation, execution, and financing' of these horrific attacks 'walk the streets freely in foreign capitals today [and are] protected by a peculiar interpretation of international law that shields them from justice in U.S. courts for terrorist acts on U.S. soil'.[79] Acknowledging the 'concerns some have about [the bill's] possible effect on sovereign immunity,' she emphasized that 'it is narrowly focused and applies only to attacks committed on U.S. soil that harm U.S. nationals'.[80] In overriding President Obama's veto of JASTA, Senator Blumenthal emphasized that the United States need not fear reciprocal immunity-stripping measures 'as long as we do not engage in supporting or sponsoring the kind of violence that occurred on 9/11 here'.[81] Senator Cornyn added that '[i]f we allowed lawsuits against foreign governments for bar fights, contract breaches, drunk driving, then we should allow the victims of a terrorist attack on our soil the opportunity for their day in court as well'.[82] Moreover, in his view, 'JASTA is not a sweeping legislative overhaul that dramatically alters international law. It is an extension of law that has been on the books since 1976'.[83]

[76]For an argument that, in certain circumstances, exceptions to state immunity might be viewed as countermeasures, see Franchini (2020).

[77]Dodge (2016).

[78]American Law Institute (2018) § 460, Reporters' Note 11.

[79]Maloney C B. (NY). 'Justice Against Sponsors of Terrorism Act'. Congressional Record 162 (9 Sep. 2016), p. H5242.

[80]Ibid., p. H5242.

[81]Blumenthal R(CT). 'Justice Against Sponsors of Terrorism Act—Veto'. Congressional Record 162 (28 Sep. 2016), p. S6166.

[82]Cornyn J (TX). 'Justice Against Sponsors of Terrorism Act—Veto'. Congressional Record 162 (28 Sep. 2016), p. S6168.

[83]Ibid., p. S6168.

Representative Goodlatte also spoke in favor of overriding the President's veto, framing the issue as 'whether we should allow those who harm our citizens to hide behind legal barriers that are required by neither the Constitution nor international law'.[84] In his view, '[c]onsistent with customary international law, JASTA, for terrorism cases, removes the current requirement that the entire tort occur within the United States and replaces it with a rule that only the physical injury or death must occur on U.S. soil'.[85] Representative Scott, by contrast, expressed the view that 'JASTA abrogates a core principle in international law—foreign sovereign immunity,' and that it 'goes much further than any present exception or recognized practice of any national law'.[86] Representative Conyers similarly invoked 'the long-term interests of our country,' as well as the views of 'the national security experts, the international law scholars, and the President of the United States,' in support of his vote to sustain the President's veto.[87]

Ultimately, Congress overrode the veto by the required two-thirds vote in each chamber. JASTA had its intended effect of allowing claims against Saudi Arabia for its alleged support of the 9/11 terrorist attacks to proceed in New York court, although the prospects of recovery remain uncertain.[88] Yet as Professor Ingrid Wuerth has noted, JASTA 'has put aspects of U.S. foreign policy under the overlapping control of Congress, courts, the executive branch, and private litigants'.[89] This might provide litigants with a greater sense of control over the pursuit of their claims, but it does not necessarily guarantee a better outcome.

4.3 Other Proposed Exceptions

As described above, the FSIA has transformed the task of defining state immunity from one of identifying and applying 'general principles' (as in the *Schooner Exchange*) to an exercise in statutory interpretation. Although the legal basis for state immunity has shifted, the Supreme Court has consistently characterized

---

[84] Goodlatte R (VA). 'Justice Against Sponsors of Terrorism Act'. Congressional Record 162 (28 Sep. 2016), p. H6024.

[85] Goodlatte R (VA). 'Justice Against Sponsors of Terrorism Act'. Congressional Record 162 (28 Sep. 2016), p. H6024. Rep. Goodlatte also stated that JASTA 'would apply only to governments, not to individuals,' and that 'many countries have already done what we are proposing to do here today': p. H6027.

[86] Scott R (VA). 'Justice Against Sponsors of Terrorism Act'. Congressional Record 162 (28 Sep. 2016), p. H6027.

[87] Conyers J (MI). 'Justice Against Sponsors of Terrorism Act'. Congressional Record 162 (28 Sep. 2016), p. H6029.

[88] See Hamer and Green (2018).

[89] Wuerth (2016).

immunity as based on principles of comity.[90] Whereas Chief Justice Marshall viewed foreign sovereign immunity as essential to preserving the ability of foreign states to conduct governmental activities, however, the Supreme Court has suggested more recently that:

> Foreign sovereign immunity ... is *not* meant to avoid chilling foreign states or their instrumentalities in the conduct of their business but [rather] to give foreign states and their instrumentalities some protection from the inconvenience of suit as a gesture of comity between the United States and other sovereigns.[91]

This understanding of sovereign immunity as a gesture of comity rather than the fulfilment of an international legal obligation has tended to reduce the perceived political costs associated with creating additional statutory exceptions to immunity, although it has not led courts to interpret exceptions broadly.[92]

To date, proposed exceptions to the FSIA for acts ranging from causing the COVID-19 pandemic in the United States[93] to gaining unauthorized access to a computer in the United States[94] have not become law. As a general matter, the legislative branch seems much more eager than the executive branch to involve the judiciary in attempts to impose costs on foreign states for actions that adversely affect U.S. interests. To the extent that members of Congress are understandably responsive to the immediate needs of injured constituents, this institutional pressure makes some sense—although the COVID-19 proposal, which was not bipartisan, seemed aimed primarily at diverting blame away from inadequate U.S. efforts to control the spread of the coronavirus after it reached the United States. A problem with this political dynamic is that it places the executive branch in the unenviable position of appearing to oppose facilitating redress for U.S. claimants. The executive branch's consistent opposition to additional FSIA exceptions also means that the legislature has come to expect this reaction, and is thus more inclined to discount it. That said, if it becomes apparent that excessively permissive immunity rules create other problems—such as a retreat from the dollar and the U.S. financial system on account of concerns about attachment and execution—then Congress might become more cautious.[95]

---

[90] William Dodge has observed: 'The Court's characterization of sovereign immunity as comity does not preclude the possibility that some measure of immunity is required by international law. . . . But it does suggest that sovereign immunity in the United States cannot be understood exclusively in international law terms'. Dodge (2015), p. 2117 n. 275.

[91] Dole Food Co. v. Patrickson, 538 U.S. 468, 469 (2003) (emphasis added).

[92] For example, Mathias Reimann observed in 1995 that, because international law allows but does not require a human rights exception to state immunity, 'the decision Congress has to make about the amendment of the FSIA is largely a political one'. Reimann (1995), p. 423. As a general matter, Joan Donoghue, who now sits on the ICJ, noted 'judicial pleas for clarification' of the FSIA, and opined that '[a] more coherent and detailed FSIA' would serve U.S. interests, as well as those of foreign states and private parties. Donoghue (1992), pp. 494–495.

[93] See Keitner (2020b).

[94] See Keitner and Peters (2020).

[95] On related concerns in the context of U.S. sanctions policy, see McDowell (2019).

5 Conclusion

In international law, immunity functions as a structural, rather than substantive, rule. It allocates authority among states to adjudicate the conduct of certain actors in the international system. Whether it is treated as a matter of comity or customary international law in a given domestic legal system, political actors within that system must be convinced that the benefits of self-restraint outweigh the costs of placing certain types of disputes beyond the reach of domestic courts.

States have a variety of tools at their disposal to incentivize lawful conduct by other States, and to deter and attach consequences to unlawful conduct. Our goal as international lawyers must be to work towards a world in which more States comply with more substantive rules of international law more of the time—especially those rules designed to protect and promote human dignity. Domestic courts are part of the answer. But we should encourage a holistic approach to State immunity that takes into account the role immunity doctrines play in enabling a range of cross-border activities that also contribute to human flourishing. This means adopting a calibrated approach to immunity doctrine that recognizes its important structural role in facilitating what Chief Justice Marshall called the 'common interest' in 'mutual intercourse,' while also creating sufficient alternative pathways for individual redress so that immunity does not become the practical equivalent of impunity for the most egregious conduct.

References

American Law Institute (2018) Restatement of the law fourth, the foreign relations law of the United States

Dodge WS (2015) International comity in American law. Columbia Law Rev 115:2071–2141

Dodge WS (2016) Does JASTA violate international law?. JustSecurity. https://www.justsecurity.org/33325/jasta-violate-international-law-2/. Accessed 15 Apr 2021

Dodge WS (2018) Customary international law, change and the constitution. Georgetown Law J 106:1559–1591

Donoghue JE (1992) Taking the 'sovereign' out of the Foreign Sovereign Immunities Act: a functional approach to the commercial activities exception. Yale J Int Law 17:489–538

Franchini D (2020) State immunity as a tool of foreign policy: the unanswered question of certain Iranian assets. Va J Int Law 60:433–483

Franck TM (2007) Individual criminal liability and collective civil responsibility: do they reinforce or contradict one another? Wash Univ Glob Stud Law Rev 6:567–573

Hamer D, Green L (2018) JASTA keeps Saudi Arabia on Trial for 9/11 Terror Attacks: the US and its Foreign Sovereign Immunity Issue. EJIL: Talk!. https://www.ejiltalk.org/jasta-keeps-saudi-arabia-on-trial-for-9-11-terror-attacks-the-us-and-its-foreign-sovereign-immunity-issue/. Accessed 15 Apr 2021

Jackson RH (1945) Address by Mr. Robert H. Jackson, April 13, 1945. https://www.roberthjackson.org/wp-content/uploads/2015/01/Rule_of_Law_Among_Nations.pdf. Accessed 15 Apr 2021

Keitner CI (2010) The common law of foreign official immunity. The Green Bag 2d 14:61–75

Keitner CI (2013) Germany v. Italy and the limits of horizontal enforcement: some reflections from a United States perspective. J Int Crim Just 11:167–183
Keitner CI (2015) Prosecute, Sue or Deport? Transnational accountability in international law. Univ Pa Law Rev 164:1–10
Keitner CI (2019) Between law and diplomacy: the conundrum of common law immunity. Georgia Law Rev 54:217–296
Keitner CI (2020a) Prosecuting foreign states. Va J Int Law 61:1–48
Keitner CI (2020b) To litigate a pandemic: cases in the United States against China and the Chinese communist party and foreign sovereign immunities. Chin J Int Law 19:229–236
Keitner C, Peters A (2020) Private lawsuits against nation-states are not the way to deal with America's Cyber Threats. Lawfare. https://www.lawfareblog.com/private-lawsuits-against-nation-states-are-not-way-deal-americas-cyber-threats. Accessed 15 Apr 2021
Koh HH (2007) Filártiga v. Peña-Irala: judicial internalization into domestic law of the customary international law norm against torture. In: Noyes J (ed) International law stories. Foundation Press, New York, pp 45–76
McDowell D (2019) How 'sanctions overreach' could undermine the U.S. dollar's dominance. World Politics Review. https://www.worldpoliticsreview.com/articles/28418/ofac-sanctions-and-the-new-dollar-diplomacy. Accessed 15 Apr 2021
Reimann M (1995) A human rights exception to sovereign immunity: some thoughts on Princz v. Federal Republic of Germany. Mich J Int Law 16:403–432
Schwartz JB (2007) Dealing with a 'Rogue' State: The Libya Precedent. Am J Int Law 101:553–580
Stephens B (2011) The modern common law of foreign official immunity. Fordham Law Rev 79: 2669–2719
Stewart DP (2018) The Foreign Sovereign Immunities Act: a guide for judges, 2nd edn. https://www.fjc.gov/content/337316/foreign-sovereign-immunities-act-guide-judges-2ed. Accessed 15 Apr 2021
Wuerth I (2016) Justice Against Sponsors of Terrorism Act: initial analysis. Lawfare. https://www.lawfareblog.com/justice-against-sponsors-terrorism-act-initial-analysis. Accessed 15 Apr 2021

Chimène I. Keitner is Alfred & Hanna Fromm Chair in International and Comparative Law at the University of California Hastings College of the Law in San Francisco. She served as the 27th Counselor on International Law in the U.S. Department of State, and is an adviser on foreign sovereign immunity for the American Law Institute's Restatement (Fourth) of the Foreign Relations Law of the United States.

Sovereign Immunity from a Comparative Perspective: The Case of Germany

Stefan Oeter

Abstract The German approach concerning sovereign immunity clearly follows the Continental European tradition, which anchors sovereign immunities in international law, in particular in the general principle of sovereign equality. As an emanation of such general principle, and a body of rules deeply anchored in customary international law, sovereign immunities fall under the generalized incorporation of general rules of international law provided for in Article 25 of the German constitution, the Basic Law. German court practice has always applied rules of sovereign immunity as directly applicable norms. The Constitution even provides for a specific procedure in Article 100 para.2 Basic Law. The second part of this chapter will revisit the practice of courts and tribunals concerning jurisdictional immunities of foreign states. There exists a significant body of case-law on this issue—a case-law that has often struggled with the question how far immunity for acta *iure imperii* extends and where the realm of acta *iure gestionis* starts. In a third part, the chapter will look into the controversial issue of jurisdictional immunities of state officials.

1 Introduction

State immunity and the corresponding immunities of state officials constitute a well-established institution of international law that is routinely applied in international legal practice. At the same time, however, the scope of these immunities has become a hotly debated and quite controversial topic in the practice of states and international bodies, at least in certain regards.[1] One might only mention the conflict-laden

[1] See Fox and Webb (2015), pp. 335–478.

S. Oeter (✉)
Universität Hamburg Fakultät für Rechtswissenschaft Institut für Internationale Angelegenheiten, Hamburg, Germany
e-mail: stefan.oeter@uni-hamburg.de

R. Bismuth et al. (eds.), *Sovereign Immunity Under Pressure*,
https://doi.org/10.1007/978-3-030-87706-4_3

project of the ILC on Immunity of State officials from foreign criminal jurisdiction.[2] The practice of German state authorities on issues of sovereign immunity[3]—and also the surrounding academic debates[4]—mirrors such a parallelism of a long-standing and well-established institution of international law, on the one hand, and quite heated doctrinal debates on the scope of sovereign immunities, on the other hand. State practice in this regard is mostly practice of national courts and tribunals—and there exists a rather dense case law on issues of sovereign immunities in the German context.[5]

Such existence of an extended case-law results from two different factors, first, the practical importance of sovereign immunities in the daily operations of law, and, second, the institutional construction of the role of sovereign immunities in the German legal system. This second factor will be the topic of the first main part of this chapter. On a global scale there exist deep divides as far as the theoretical understanding of sovereign immunities is concerned[6]—where do they come from, are they the result of international law, expressions of comity in international relations, or mere products of national legislation? The German approach here clearly follows the Continental European tradition, which anchors sovereign immunities in international law, in particular in the general principle of sovereign equality.[7] As an emanation of such general principle, and a body of rules deeply anchored in customary international law, sovereign immunities fall under the generalized incorporation of general rules of international law provided for in Article 25 of the German constitution, the Basic Law (BL). It is generally accepted that the rules of sovereign immunity are covered by this provision, transforming them into part of the law of the land with a normative rank above ordinary legislation.[8] Court practice has always applied rules of sovereign immunity as a component of the legal order directly applicable to cases where questions of immunity are raised. The Constitution even provides for a specific procedure in Article 100 para.2 BL which entrusts the Federal Constitutional Court with the task of clarifying whether a general rule in the sense of Article 25 BL exists and whether it creates directly rights and duties for individuals—a procedure which has given rise to a number of Constitutional court decisions on various questions of sovereign immunity.

The second major part of this chapter will revisit the practice of courts and tribunals concerning jurisdictional immunities of foreign states. It is the scope of

[2] See International Law Commission. Current status of the work of the Commission and forthcoming deadlines: https://legal.un.org/ilc/status.shtml. Accessed 15 April 2021. See also for the substance of the debates: van Alebeek (2019), pp. 496–524.

[3] See the survey given by Hildner (2018), pp. 137–146. See also Ney (2015), pp. 32–39.

[4] For a survey of doctrinal debate in Germany see Pieper (2013), pp. 839–860.

[5] See only Herdegen (2020), Art. 25 GG, paras. 52–56.

[6] See Fox and Webb (2015), pp. 25–48; Orakhelashvili (2015), pp. 151–184; Damrosch (2019), pp. 40–60.

[7] See only Pieper (2013), pp. 842–844; Epping (2018), p. 211.

[8] See Koenig and König (2018), pp. 526–535, 539.

such immunities which has been disputed and which has led to a certain body of case-law—a case-law that has often struggled with the question how far immunity for acta *iure imperii* extends and where the realm of acta *iure gestionis* starts, with its resulting exception from the immunity of states. This part will also deal with the heated debate on potential exemptions from state immunity in cases of mass atrocities and crimes against international law—a debate which has had also a practical side with the prominent dispute between Germany and Italy on jurisdictional immunities, resulting in the prominent ICJ decision from 2012.[9] An additional sub-section will deal with issues of immunity to execution.

In a third main part, the chapter will look into the controversial issue of jurisdictional immunities of state officials. There are two main issues regarding immunities of state officials—the personal immunities of heads of state and members of government, and the functional immunities of other state officials as far as those act in official capacity.[10] In particular the latter one has led to a number of controversies, linked mostly to the question whether such functional immunities should recede into the background in favour of prosecution of crimes under international law on the basis of universal jurisdiction (as provided for in the Rome Statute). The organs of the German state take markedly different positions in that regard, with German diplomacy taking a cautious stance perceived by activists of international criminal law as rather conservative, whereas German criminal courts have positioned themselves in a much more activist manner, with a progressive approach that brushes aside traditional jurisdictional immunities.

2 Conceptual Construction and Constitutional Incorporation of Sovereign Immunity

As mentioned in the introductory part, Germany takes a markedly Continental European position in the conceptual dispute on the roots and constructive foundations of sovereign immunity. In the prevailing German understanding, sovereign immunity derives from the principle of sovereign equality of states, as one of the foundational general principles of international law.[11] The overarching guiding principle of sovereign equality that is of relevance here may be summarized in the old Latin maxim *par in parem non habet iurisdictionem*, literally translated as the equal shall not have jurisdiction over the other equal.[12] Such an understanding anchors the rules of sovereign immunity in the body of public international law.

[9] See ICJ, Jurisdictional Immunities of the State (Germany v. Italy: Greece intervening), Judgment of 3 February 2012. ICJ Reports 2012, p. 99.

[10] See Fox and Webb (2015), pp. 537–569; Franey (2015), pp. 205–252.

[11] See Pieper (2013), pp. 842–844; Epping (2018), p. 211.

[12] See Epping (2018), p. 211 (with references to the case law of the Reichsgericht of the Weimar Republic in footnote 725). See also Stoll (2011), para. 4.

Accordingly, sovereign immunity and its various emanations are understood as binding prerequisites resulting from the system of international law, directly creating legal obligations for states that impose a duty to respect the sovereign immunity of other states. Such an ascribed character as an objective rule of international law leaves no room for arguments of reciprocity, which would make the granting of immunity conditional upon reciprocal recognition of sovereign immunity by the other state.

With such a grounding in the realm of fundamental principles of international law, and the parallel existence of a generalized practice and a universal opinio juris which makes the rules of sovereign immunity in its practical implications also a rule of customary international law,[13] sovereign immunity is an obvious candidate for the category general rules of international law ('allgemeine Regeln des Völkerrechts'). This category is used in Article 25 BL, the provision of the Constitution that—in a rather generalized manner—incorporates the general rules into the German legal order as a directly binding part of the law of the land.[14] The provision reads as follows: 'The general rules of international law shall be an integral part of federal law. They shall take precedence over the laws and directly create rights and duties for the inhabitants of the federal territory'. This means that the rules of sovereign immunity (assuming that they constitute such general rules) become automatically part of the German legal order and apply as rules of federal law, with a rank in normative hierarchy above federal statutes but below the constitution.[15] They retain their character as rules emanating from international law, but are incorporated by the Constitution into the body of binding German law.

For a court confronted with an issue of sovereign immunity in a case, this means that the court must look into the academic writings of international law (and the relevant practice of superior courts trying to ascertain the existence and the concrete scope of such a general rule of international law). This will not always be easy because the details of such rules will often be contested in detail.[16] The fact that a general rule of sovereign immunity exists creates no troublesome problems—this is firmly established in doctrine of international law as well as international legal practice. What creates the real problems is the scope and shape of the relevant rule with regard to the issues raised in the concrete case. In such details the opinions put forward in academic writings, and also the relevant state practice, might diverge considerably. The Parliamentary Council, i.e, the body that drafted the Basic Law in 1948–49, was well aware of the resulting problem of ascertaining in a more or less authoritative manner the existence and scope of such general rules. It provided thus for a specific procedure in the Constitution that entrusts the Federal Constitutional Court with the task to issue guidelines on these issues. Article 100 para. 2 BL provides: 'If, in the course of litigation, doubt exists whether a rule of international

[13] See Pieper (2013), p. 843; Kau (2016), p. 163 para. 89.

[14] See Koenig and König (2018), pp. 526–531.

[15] See Herdegen (2020), paras. 78–79, but also Koenig and König (2018), pp. 531–535.

[16] See Epping (2018), pp. 212–222.

law is an integral part of federal law and whether it directly creates rights and duties for the individual (Article 25), the court shall obtain a decision from the Federal Constitutional Court'.[17] The specific procedure created for such purpose in Article 100 para. 2 BL envisages a reference procedure (a bit like the reference procedure going to the ECJ). A court confronted with an unsettled question concerning the existence and the concrete scope of a general rule of international law shall suspend its procedure and refer the involved question to the Federal Constitutional Court—and will later, after the constitutional court has handed down its (interim) judgment, decide the case on the basis of the construction given to the general rule by the FCC. This might cost some time, but takes care that there is a more or less consistent judicial practice in dealing with such general rules of international law. The mechanism contributes to safeguarding the overriding concern of legal security.

There is no subsequent statutory legislation which sets out the details of sovereign immunity. Statutes like the Gerichtsverfassungsgesetz (GVG), the federal statute on court organisation, simply refer to the existing rules on sovereign immunity. §§ 18 and 19 GVG merely refer to the diplomatic and consular immunities as provided for in the Vienna Convention on Diplomatic Relations and the Vienna Convention on Consular Relations. § 20 para. 1 GVG exempts from the jurisdiction of German courts all representatives of foreign states that are present on German territory on the basis of an official invitation of the German state. § 20 para. 2 GVG supplements this by providing that all other persons that are exempted from German jurisdiction according to general rules of international law or according to international legal agreements do also not fall under the jurisdiction of German courts.[18] The ball is thus played back into the field of Article 25 BL—German courts and tribunals cannot avoid the task of ascertaining whether a legal entity (a foreign state or a subsidiary of such state) or a foreign state official falls under the scope of sovereign immunity and is exempted from German jurisdiction. The constitution is clear in that regard. Only if the courts are in doubt whether a pertinent general rule of international law exists and/or what such rule might mean in detail, they may lodge a reference procedure asking the Federal Constitutional Court to ascertain authoritatively the scope of such rule.

3 Jurisdictional Immunities of States

The constitutional construction that determines the role of sovereign immunity in German law has a long tradition in constitutional history. The Weimar Constitution of 1919 had already contained a rule more or less identical with Article 25 BL,

[17] For the meaning of Article 100 para. 2 BL see e.g. Sieckmann and Kessal-Wulf (2018), pp. 987–990.

[18] Concerning § 20 GVG see Kissel and Mayer (2021), pp. 475–486.

namely Article 4 Weimarer Reichsverfassung.[19] As a result, there existed already a body of case law on issues of sovereign immunity decided by the Reichsgericht, the Supreme Court of the German Empire.[20] These decisions had clarified the existence of sovereign immunity as a general rule of international law, a matter that needed no further clarification by the Federal Constitutional Court.

3.1 *Differentiation Between Acta iure imperii and Acta iure gestionis*

The case law of the FCC on sovereign immunity thus could focus more on the operational details of sovereign immunity. A question that came up rather early, already in the early 1960s, was the issue of acta *iure gestionis*, i.e. whether a state is exempted from the jurisdiction of German courts if it has acted outside the realm of sovereign prerogatives, in particular pursuing commercial objectives.[21] The Reichsgericht had still upheld the classical doctrine of absolute state immunity wherever state organs are acting on behalf of the state, with only very limited exceptions.[22] The Federal Constitutional Court now stated that a general rule of international law that still exempts foreign states from jurisdiction, in the sense of sovereign immunity, does not exist anymore concerning commercial activities; the boundary line between the exercise of sovereign authority and acta *iure gestionis* has to be drawn according to the nature of the act in question—and such qualification should follow the differentiations established in national law.[23] Already a year before, in 1962, the FCC had to decide on the question whether the rules of sovereign immunity under international law exclude completely the possibility of suing a foreign state for correcting the land register (Grundbuch) concerning a real estate on which diplomatic premises have been built. The Constitutional Court gave a negative answer to this question, denying such an outright rejection of any jurisdiction on real estate registered in the local Grundbuch in Germany.[24] An

[19] See Koenig and König (2018), p. 515.

[20] See Reichsgericht VII 521/20 (1 July 1921) RGZ 102, 304, p. 306; Reichsgericht I 177/21 (10 December 1921) RGZ 103, 274, p. 275; see also from the time before, the era of the monarchy, Reichsgericht II 193/05 (12 December 1905) RGZ 62, 165, p. 167.

[21] See in general on this issue Fox and Webb (2015), pp. 395–434; Orakhelashvili (2019), pp. 105–124; Epping (2018), pp. 212–215.

[22] See the three decisions of the Reichsgericht cited above in n. 20 which all three were dealing with cases of what we would call today acta *iure gestionis*; the third decision (RGZ 103, 274) is already discussing the upcoming trend towards an exclusion of commercial activities from sovereign immunity, but still upheld the traditional position of an absolute immunity.

[23] See German (Federal) Constitutional Court 2 BvM 1/62 (30 April 1963) BVerfGE 16, 27–64, pp. 33ff.

[24] See German (Federal) Constitutional Court 2 BvM 1/60 (30 October 1962) BVerfGE 15, 25–43, pp. 34ff.

immunity concerning claims for payment resulting from reparation works at an embassy building was rejected in the same decision.[25] The distinction drawn between acta *iure imperii* and acta *iure gestionis* was confirmed in later decisions.[26]

The case law of the ordinary courts adjudicating in matters of private law follows these lines drawn by the Federal Constitutional Court.[27] It is the task of the competent national courts to draw the boundary line between acta *iure imperii* and acta *iure gestionis*. The decisive factors in distinguishing the two categories are mainly the object and nature of the state activity in question, and not so much the purpose of the act.[28] The case law has elaborated that there is a core of sovereign acts where state organs always exercise public authority, such as foreign relations powers, exercise of military power, legislation and adjudication.[29] This concerns also activities of policing and the levying of taxes.[30] Illustrative is a case decided by the Federal Supreme Court (Bundesgerichtshof) in 2016.[31] Subject matter of the decision was a claim concerning Greek bonds that had been placed on the international capital markets. The court admitted that the placing of the bonds on international capital markets was a commercial activity in the sense of acta *iure gestionis*. The bonds, however, had to be rescheduled in the wake of the financial crisis of 2008. Since the terms of the bond did not provide for a collective action clause, the Greek legislator made the majority decision of the bond holders accepting the terms of the rescheduling binding for all creditors, thus creating a kind of legislative surrogate for the (missing) collective action clause. The German Supreme Court qualified this legislative act as a sovereign act, with the character of an act *iure imperii*, and thus granted sovereign immunity. The underlying distinction between the *jure gestionis* character of the issuing of bonds (and the disputes arising in the context of these bonds), on the one hand, and the jure imperii character of the legislative change of the conditions of such bonds, on the other hand, has been taken up in a number of court cases dealing with the Greek bonds and the Greek legislators changes in the conditions of the bonds.[32]

The Kammergericht Berlin had to deal in 2010 with the issue of protection of cultural goods sent by a foreign state to Germany and with the status of cultural

---

[25] See German (Federal) Constitutional Court 2 BvM 1/60 (30 October 1962) BVerfGE 15, 25–43, pp. 42–43.

[26] See German (Federal) Constitutional Court 2 BvM 1/76 (13 December 1977) BVerfGE 46, 342–404, p. 364.

[27] See also Lengelsen (2011), pp. 71–89.

[28] See German (Federal) Supreme Court VI ZR 516/14 (8 March 2016), reprinted in 37 (2016) ZIP Zeitschrift für Wirtschaftsrecht, pp. 789ff.

[29] See Herdegen (2020), Art. 25 GG, para. 52.

[30] See German (Federal) Constitutional Court 2 BvR 736/13, Chamber Decision (17 March 2014), reprinted in 67 (2014) NJW Neue Juristische Wochenschrift, pp. 1723–1725.

[31] See German (Federal) Supreme Court VI ZR 516/14 (8 March 2016), reprinted in 37 (2016) ZIP Zeitschrift für Wirtschaftsrecht, pp. 789ff.

[32] See Hartwig (2018), pp. 739–742; Hartwig (2019), pp. 345–347. See also Reimer (2020), pp. 120–186; Bröhmer (2015), pp. 182–208.

institutes. In a case concerning cultural property of a foreign state that was brought to Germany in the context of cultural policy, in order to represent the culture of the sending country, the court qualified such cultural property as serving public purposes, thus covered by sovereign immunity. In another case concerning the Russian Center for International, Scientific and Cultural Cooperation, a subsidiary of the Russian Foreign Ministry, the court also affirmed the jure imperii character of the activities, and thus confirmed the existence of state immunity in the case.[33]

Another arena where the qualification of acts as jure imperii or jure gestionis has been very much disputed in judicial practice are labour law cases where teachers of schools run by third states as schools for their expatriates are concerned. In most cases the labour courts have rejected the immunity claims since the teachers concerned were hired locally with a private employment contract.[34] Only in the (rather exceptional) cases where teachers from the sending country with a status of public official were sent to Germany as representatives of their state in the School system, sovereign immunity was recognized for the labour dispute.[35] On the contrary, in labour law disputes concerning employees of consulates labour courts often accept the claim of sovereign immunity. This is regularly the case when the employees are involved in administrative matters, issue and certify official documents or are processing visa and passport affairs. A jure imperii character of the activities is regularly taken for granted in these cases, with a resulting confirmation of jurisdictional immunity.[36]

This court practice conforms entirely to the rules of the 2004 United Nations Convention on Jurisdictional Immunities of States and Their Property (not yet in force).[37] Although Germany has not signed the Convention and has not indicated that it intends to sign and ratify in future, German state authorities and the relevant national courts seem to accept that the 2004 UN Convention largely codifies existing customary law.[38] The (draft) Convention is rarely referred to, but German practice seems to be more or less in compliance with most of the rules laid down in the Convention, in particular as far as Articles 10 and 11 of the 2004 Convention are concerned.

[33] For the details of both cases see Hartwig (2013), p. 746.

[34] See e.g. Amtsgericht Bielefeld, 6 Ca 256/11 (4 May 2011), para. 30; Landesarbeitsgericht Köln, 10 Sa 575/11 (13 January 2012), paras. 50ff; Landesarbeitsgericht Nürnberg, 7 Sa 225/12 (6 November 2012), paras. 42ff.; Landesarbeitsgericht Nürnberg, 6 Sa 210/12 (7 March 2014), paras. 100ff.; Bundesarbeitsgericht, 2 AZR 216/17 (14 December 2017), paras. 12ff.; see also Hartwig (2019), pp. 342–344.

[35] See Landesarbeitsgericht Baden-Württemberg, 7 Sa 87/08 (27 February 2009), paras. 20ff.

[36] See Hessisches Landesarbeitsgericht, 16 Sa 650/14 (4 August 2014), paras. 18ff.; Arbeitsgericht Dortmund, 4 Ca 4214/14 (10 March 2016), para. 21; Landesarbeitsgericht Hamm, 11 Sa 406/16 (29 September 2016), paras. 38ff.

[37] For details of the 2004 UN Convention see Stewart (2005), pp. 194–211; commentary on the 2004 UN Convention by O'Keefe and Tams (2013).

[38] For some examples in this regard see Hartwig (2019), pp. 342–344.

3.2 *Territorial Tort Exception for Personal Injuries and Damage to Property*

There is one major exception to the overall picture of convergence in substance—and this relates to the issue of a potential tort exception for personal injuries and damage to property caused by state agents on the territory of another state (the forum state).[39] The 2004 UN Convention provides for such an exception from sovereign immunity in its Article 12.[40] German authorities very resolutely defend the position that such a tort exception, at least in the broad scope that is often given to Article 12, does not exist in customary law—and would also not be accepted by Germany as a rule de lege ferenda.[41] This contentious issue[42] seems to be the main reason why Germany is not willing to accept the 2004 UN Convention, as was some years ago stressed by a high-ranking official of the German Foreign Office.[43] Article 12 of the 2004 Convention does not explicitly exclude military activities on foreign soil from the scope of application of the provision—an ambiguity Italy made use of in the ICJ proceedings on the Jurisdictional Immunities of the State (Germany v. Italy) case. In light of the potential misinterpretations of the article, the German government finds it not suitable to envisage a ratification of the convention.[44]

The reasons for such reservation are easy to discern if one looks more in detail. The German state still has a lot of trouble with the nasty legacies of the Nazi regime, in particular concerning a number of massacres committed by German troops from the Wehrmacht and the SS when fighting against the partisans in Greece and Italy. Victims (and the descendants of victims) of a massacre committed in Distomo (Greece) in 1944 by SS troops had lodged proceedings at Greek courts in the late 1990s.[45] The district court as well as the Areios Pagos, the Greek Supreme Court, had denied sovereign immunity and had condemned Germany to a compensation payment of 37,5 Mio. Euro.[46] An attempt at execution in property of the German state was blocked by the Greek government. A subsequent proceeding before German courts claiming compensation for unlawful acts committed by agents of the German state failed in all instances, with a final judgment of the Federal Supreme Court (Bundesgerichtshof) rejecting the claims. According to the Supreme Court, the classical rules of the law of war, in particular Art. 3 of the IV Hague Convention, do not provide for individual compensation claims of individuals, but concern only the

[39] For details see Fox and Webb (2015), pp. 463–478.

[40] For the (disputed) character of Article 12 see Foakes and O'Keefe (2013), pp. 209–224.

[41] For details see Epping (2018), p. 217.

[42] See also Stewart (2005), pp. 201–203; Steger (2013), pp. 61–64.

[43] See Hildner (2018), pp. 144–146.

[44] See Hildner (2018), pp. 144–146.

[45] See only Boysen (2006), p. 364.

[46] For the details see Gavouneli and Bantekas (2001), pp. 198–204.

international relations between states.[47] The Court also mentioned that the principles of state immunity do not allow to execute the Greek judgments because they ignored basic principles of sovereign immunity. The Federal Constitutional Court rejected the constitutional complaint lodged against the decision, confirming largely the argumentation of the Supreme Court.[48] An attempt of the claimants to achieve an execution title for their Greek judgments in Italy was more successful. The Corte di Cassazione, the Italian Supreme Court, granted the title in 2008, denying the applicability of state immunity for such claims.[49] At the same time, victims of similar massacres in Italy had gone to Italian courts, again with success.

The Italian and the German government agreed to bring the issue before the International Court of Justice and started a proceeding known as the case Jurisdictional Immunities of the State (Germany v. Italy).[50] The subject matter of the dispute was quite controversial in both societies. In Germany there existed (and still exists) a strong current in the general public, but also in legal academia, that finds the insistence on state immunity in such cases to be a scandal and fights for an exemption of such tort claims from sovereign immunity, at least in cases of mass atrocities and crimes against international law.[51] The federal government, however, but also the federal courts, defend a much more traditional position and insist on state immunity as far as acts in the exercise of public authority are concerned, even if such acts were committed on foreign soil and blatantly violated rules of international law.[52] Not that these acts are legal—just to the contrary, they constitute a wrong under the rules of state responsibility. It is not up to individuals, however, to demand for compensation before foreign courts, so goes the argument, but a matter of inter-state negotiations to sort out the issue, with state immunity protecting these international negotiations against spoiling attempts from civil society. In the end, Germany was successful in the proceedings before the ICJ and the International Court of Justice ruled in its 2012 Jurisdictional Immunities of the State (Germany v. Italy, Greece intervening) decision[53] that state immunity shall not be pierced and should apply to such cases. Neither the argument of a territorial tort exception nor the line of reasoning that concludes from the ius cogens character of the human rights and law of armed conflict rules violated by German troops that sovereign immunity should

[47] See German (Federal) Supreme Court III ZR 245/98 (26 June 2003) BGHZ 155, 279.

[48] See German (Federal) Constitutional Court 2 BvR 1476/03 (15 February 2006), reprinted in 59 (2006) NJW Neue Juristische Wochenschrift, pp. 2542ff.; for a critique of the position argued by the BGH and the Constitutional Court see Boysen (2006), pp. 366–376.

[49] For details see Frenzel and Wiedemann (2008), pp. 1088–1091.

[50] For the substantive issues at stake in the proceedings see Tomuschat (2011), pp. 1107–1132; Pieper (2013), pp. 856–858; Steger (2013), pp. 22–34, 49–97.

[51] See e.g. Cremer (2003), pp. 144–163; Paech (2009), pp. 51–91; Tomuschat (2011), pp. 1119–1132; Uerpmann-Wittzack (2015), pp. 236–243.

[52] See also Kreicker (2012), pp. 113–115; Pieper (2013), pp. 857–858.

[53] See ICJ, Jurisdictional Immunities of the State (Germany v. Italy: Greece intervening), Judgment of 3 February 2012. ICJ Reports 2012, p. 99. See also Kloth and Brunner (2012), pp. 218–244; Blanke (2014), pp. 5–38.

not be applicable in such cases[54] found any sympathy with the majority on the ICJ s bench. The Court thus has confirmed the continued application of immunity rules for military activities on foreign soil.[55] This judgment has not closed the debate, however, since a number of international law experts from academia, but also human rights lawyers have expressed their discontent with the judgment and continue to fight for exempting mass atrocities and crimes against international law from the coverage of sovereign immunity.[56]

The ICJ judgment has also not brought an end to the wave of compensation claims lodged at Italian courts. Main reason for this is the judgment no. 238/14 of the Italian Constitutional Court[57] in which the Corte Costituzionale had declared the effects of the ICJ decision not to be compatible with the Italian constitution and, as a consequence, had denied the binding force of the decision for Italian authorities and courts.[58] The result of the Constitutional Court's judgment was not only that the tribunals of the original proceedings brought before the Corte Costituzionale, the tribunals of Firenze and Piacenza, decided their cases on the basis of a restrictive interpretation of state immunity that denied any jurisdictional immunity for Germany in the cases at hand.[59] The probably more important, and to a certain degree foreseeable result was a series of new claims against Germany brought before Italian courts.[60] The German government decided not to take part in the proceedings, instead sending a note verbale in each case to the Italian Ministry of Foreign Affairs (with a copy sent to the relevant court) in which Germany stressed that it enjoys sovereign immunity according to international law and that the Italian judiciary is barred from exercising jurisdiction.[61]

Such a strategy does not always work, however. In a comparable claim lodged in Turkey in 2012 where the Turkish courts at the beginning also ignored the jurisdictional immunities of Germany, the German government at first reacted again with a note verbale to the Turkish foreign ministry. After consultations with the Turkish government, the German Foreign Office decided to participate in the proceedings and to defend its position in the court proceedings.[62] After going through all the relevant instances of the Turkish court system, the claim finally was rejected, mainly due to the argument of state immunity. In the meantime, the German authorities were

[54] For this line of argument see only d'Argent and Lesaffre (2019), pp. 614–633.

[55] See Epping (2018), pp. 220–221.

[56] See e.g. Bothe (2015), pp. 99–115; Payandeh (2012), pp. 949–958.

[57] Corte Costituzionale, Sentenza no. 238/2014 of 22 October 2014.

[58] For the details of the judgment see Boggero (2016), pp. 203–224; Raffeiner (2016), pp. 451–473.

[59] For the details of these decisions see Oellers-Frahm (2016), pp. 193–202.

[60] See Hildner (2018), p. 142. See also Hector (2016), pp. 123–149.

[61] The text of the note verbale is reprinted in Hildner (2018), pp. 142–144. See also Hartwig (2018), pp. 743–744.

[62] For details see Hildner (2018), p. 139.

even forced to deposit a high security in order to avoid the execution in the plot of land upon which the German grammar school (Alman Lisesi) in Istanbul is built.[63]

3.3 Immunity from Enforcement

The immunity from adjudication has a corresponding rule for the phase where a title against a foreign state shall be executed with the adoption of writs of execution.[64] The case law of German courts recognizes that also for the phase of execution there exists a specific immunity rule, the immunity from enforcement (Vollstreckungsimmunität).[65] The lead case in that regard is a decision from the Federal Constitutional Court passed in 1977.[66] The owner of an office premise rented to the embassy of the Republic of the Philippines had pursued his claims for outstanding rental payments and repair costs with a judicial proceeding and had got a title against the Republic of the Philippines. When he tried to enforce that title, he applied for a writ of execution in the bank accounts of the Philippine embassy. The embassy went to court against the writ of execution claiming that sovereign immunity prohibited measures of enforcement in the embassy accounts. In a reference procedure according to Article 100 para. 2 BL the Federal Constitutional Court decided that the writ of execution was unlawful. It referred to the well-established general rule of international law that enforcement measures in property that is serving public purposes falls under the rules of sovereign immunity. Even if a title concerning activities of an acta *iure gestionis* character has been lawfully granted against a foreign state, state immunity excludes any measure of enforcement in goods and accounts that do not serve commercial purposes, but are necessary for the sovereign activities (hoheitliches Handeln) of the foreign state. The functioning of the embassy as a diplomatic mission is such a sovereign activity, and as long as the embassy account serves the maintenance of diplomatic activities, it is part of the core of sovereign immunity protected by international law. There may be difficulties, the Court pointed out, in drawing a boundary line on how elementary the use of the financial means deposited on an account is for the functioning of the embassy, but this must be evaluated in view of the typical abstract threats for the functioning of diplomatic activities, and does not presuppose a concrete threat to the functioning of the embassy.[67]

[63] See Hildner (2018), p. 139.

[64] See also Thouvenin and Grandaubert (2019), pp. 245–265.

[65] For details see Höfelmeier (2018), pp. 83–128, 181–207, 231–308; Lorz (2017), pp. 278–300, 344–402; Lengelsen (2011), pp. 131–149.

[66] See German (Federal) Constitutional Court – 2 BvM 1/76 – (13 December 1977) BVerfGE 46, 342–404.

[67] See also Schreuer (1985), pp. 521–542.

In a later case the Federal Supreme Court applied that line of argument also for a piece of land serving diplomatic purposes, ruling that execution in such a kind of property is barred by the rules of immunity.[68] The Federal Republic of Germany also insisted vis-à-vis Greece and Italy that land property registered for the German state as owner which is used by public entities serving purposes of cultural and scientific policy, such as the German Archaeological Institute in Athens and the Cultural Center Villa Vigoni at Lago di Como, still remains state property in sovereign use, thus protected by immunity from enforcement.[69] The ICJ confirmed this, at least for the case of the Villa Vigoni, in its 2012 judgment.

In a decision of 2005, the Federal Supreme Court further clarified the issue of public law versus private law nature of financial claims made subject to measures of enforcement. In the case at hand, an investor in Russia that had lost his investment due to state measures had got a title as a result of an investment arbitration. He tried to enforce the title with a writ of execution freezing the claim for fees of overflight and transit that a German air carrier was due to pay to the Russian air transport authorities. The Supreme Court qualified the air transport administration fees as being of a public law nature, with the consequence that immunity is extending to such claims.[70] The Court also had to deal with the issue of a potential renunciation of immunity, but argued that the arbitration consent did not imply a renunciation of immunity with regard to enforcement. This point became even more important in a judgment of the Federal Constitutional Court from 2006 concerning Argentinian bonds.[71] The Republic of Argentine had issued bonds on the international capital market that were governed by German law, with a comprehensive clause of renunciation concerning any claim of sovereign immunity. According to the wording of the contract, this extended even to execution into property of the Argentinian state serving public purposes. The warrant of distress tried to seize the accounts of the Argentinian embassy. The Constitutional Court argued in its decision that such a clause of renunciation concerning sovereign immunity does not automatically cover also diplomatic property necessary for the functioning of the diplomatic mission. Even if enforcement with regard to public property of Argentine in principle covered by sovereign immunity might be possible under such a clause, this does not per se cover also diplomatic property that is specifically protected under the Vienna Convention on Diplomatic Relations. A forfeiture of diplomatic immunity would require a specific consent from Argentine, a consent which did not exist in the case.[72]

---

[68] See German (Federal) Supreme Court – IXa ZB 19/03 (28 May 2003) NJW–Rechtsprechungs–Report 2003, 1218–1220.

[69] See Epping (2018), p. 222.

[70] See German (Federal) Supreme Court VII ZB 9/05 (9 October 2005) NJW–Rechtsprechungs–Report 2006, 198–201.

[71] See German (Federal) Constitutional Court – 2 BvM 9/03, (6 December 2006) BVerfGE 117, 141, 143–144.

[72] See also Epping (2018), p. 223.

The Federal Supreme Court further clarified the relationship between renunciation of sovereign immunity concerning the adjudication phase, the role of immunity in proceedings of recognition of arbitral awards and immunity from enforcement strictu sensu in two decisions from 2013 and 2016, both in the same proceedings of Walter Bau AG v. Kingdom of Thailand.[73] Background was a de facto expropriation of a toll road concession in Thailand. Under the bilateral investment treaty between Germany and Thailand from 2002, both parties had agreed to the possibility that the investor might directly go to an investment arbitration tribunal. This was qualified by the Supreme Court as a waiver of the immunity from adjudication. With a view to the relevant clause in the BIT, the Supreme Court found that the waiver of immunity extended also to the proceedings of recognition of the arbitral award, transforming the arbitral award into an internal title of execution.[74] With accepting the BIT, Thailand had subjected itself to such procedure. The immunity from enforcement is not covered by this waiver. The title may only be enforced with a view to commercial property of the state, not with regard to sovereign property serving public law purposes. When the investor tried to enforce the award with a writ of execution freezing the airplane used by the crown prince of Thailand for his regular travels to his estate in Bavaria, this led to a legal battle at German courts, with the Foreign Office trying to avoid damage to bilateral relations with Thailand.[75] The same investor standing behind the Thailand proceedings, the SME entrepreneur Franz Sedelmayer, also enforced a parallel investment tribunal award against Russia with a writ of execution concerning an office building in Cologne that belonged to the Russian Federation. Since the property, a former trade representation of the Soviet Union, served now only commercial purposes, he managed to enforce his title in the case, with a compulsory selling of the property.

3.4 State Enterprises

Specific problems of immunity arise in regard of state enterprises.[76] Historically such enterprises, if constituted as a separate legal subject, were not seen as being covered by sovereign immunities.[77] Since most of these enterprises were involved in commercial activities anyway and usually were registered as corporations of a private law nature, there was no reason to question the conventional wisdom. The

[73] See German (Federal) Supreme Court III ZB 40/12 (30 January 2013) Walter Bau AG v. Kingdom of Thailand and Federal Supreme Court I ZB 13/15 (6 October 2016) Walter Bau Ag v. Kingdom of Thailand.

[74] See Supreme Court III ZB 40/12, para. 14; Supreme Court I ZB 13/15, para. 18.

[75] See Kerler 'Geld aus Pfändung bei Thailands König soll bald an Gläubiger fließen' Augsburger Allgemeine of 6 June 2019.

[76] For a detailed analysis see Pullen (2012), pp. 69–257. See also Wiater (2017), pp. 148–184.

[77] For details see Fischer (1984), pp. 22–25. Epping (2018), p. 223.

conclusion that state enterprises which fulfil a public function and are entrusted with public authority may be covered by rules of sovereign immunity was drawn only in the early 1980s.[78] The topic became subject of a decision of the Federal Constitutional Court with the National Iranian Oil Company Case of 1983.[79] In the wake of the revolution in Iran 1979 several US and British companies had applied for (and got) a writ of execution against accounts of the National Iranian Oil Company in Frankfurt. Seized with the matter by a constitutional complaint, the Court decided that there was a violation of the obligation to refer the question of the scope of immunity to the Constitutional Court according to Article 100 para. 2 BL; in substance, however, the Court saw no violation of the general rule of sovereign immunity, since the National Iranian Oil Company was a legal subject separate from the Iranian state. Although its revenues are destined for the Iranian state budget, the company itself is organized as a commercial firm. An account with revenues from commercial transactions attributed to a state enterprise, the Court stressed, does not fall under the coverage of state immunity. The fact that the company operates for the benefit of the Iranian state and that the profits go to the budget of the state does not make a difference in that regard.[80]

4 Jurisdictional Immunities of State Officials

The principles of state immunity protect, as a logical extension, also state officials acting on behalf of the state. If such an extended immunity covering state agents would not exist, it would be all too easy to exert pressure on states by bringing their officials before court in foreign states. These immunities relating to state officials exist in two different versions—first the personal immunity of top representatives, such as the head of state, the head of government and the foreign minister, and, second, as a functional immunity of all state officials for acts in the exercise of public authority. The first one is an all-encompassing immunity, shielding the official entirely from the jurisdiction of other states, whereas the second variant is a purely functional immunity covering only the actions in official capacity.[81]

[78] See the references given by Epping (2018), p. 223. See also von Hoffmann (1984), pp. 42–47.

[79] See German (Federal) Constitutional Court – 2 BvR 678, 679, 680, 681, 683/81 – (12 April 1983) BVerfGE 64, 1–46.

[80] See German (Federal) Constitutional Court – 2 BvR 678, 679, 680, 681, 683/81 – (12 April 1983) BVerfGE 64, at 23, 42–44.

[81] For details see Fox and Webb (2015), pp. 537–569; Epping (2018), pp. 224–229.

4.1 *Personal Immunity of Heads of States and Members of Government*

The existence of a personal immunity for top representatives of foreign states has never been questioned in German doctrine and has not created any problem in the case law of German courts. It is routinely observed in German practice, although there exist some grey zones. In the 1980s there were coming up debates concerning the immunity of the head of the Council of State of the GDR, Erich Honecker. In the end, immunity was granted, and attempts to come around the personal immunity in order to prosecute Erich Honecker were aborted. The Federal Supreme Court in its 1984 decision on the issue acknowledged the absolute immunity of heads of state from criminal jurisdiction of third states during their terms of office. Persons enjoying such immunity, the court stressed, shall not be subject of criminal proceedings—with the result that any police or prosecutorial criminal investigation would be incompatible with the principle of personal immunity.[82] Only after 1990, after the GDR had perished, German courts could start criminal proceedings against Mr. Honecker.[83]

Another grey zone recently has come up concerning the King of Thailand and his personal estate in Bavaria. The Thai king, which clearly constitutes the head of state of a foreign state, is owning a private estate at the shore of the lake of Starnberg since many years, and he regularly spends parts of the year at this estate. This has continued even after he had become king. His regular (private) stays, including parts of his court, have given rise to some political quarrels on taxation and protocollary treatment in German internal politics. Despite these quarrels, German authorities have insisted on treating him according to protocol and do not negate his personal immunity. In response to a parliamentary question on 7 October 2020, Federal Foreign Minister Heiko Maas declared, in an attempt to tone down the debate: 'We have made it clear that political activities related to Thailand are not to be carried out from German soil. [. . .] It is not in line with the position of the Federal Government that [. . .] guests in our country conduct their affairs of State from here; this is something we would always clearly want to counteract'.[84]

The only issue that has led to controversies in that regard is the question how far personal immunities extend beyond the classical trials of head of state, head of government and foreign minister. Are also other members of government covered by the traditional personal immunities? German academia gives diverging answers to

---

[82] Federal Supreme Court, 2 Ars 252/84 (14 December 1984), juris, para. 2. See also information submitted by Germany to the ILC at its 66th session 2014. https://legal.un.org/ilc/sessions/66/pdfs/english/iso_germany.pdf. Accessed 15 April 2021.

[83] See Herdegen (2020), Art. 25 GG, para. 56 (with further references in footnote 1).

[84] See the GPIL blog post on that matter by Talmon and Wimmer. Germany tells Thailand's King not to rule from its soil. 26 October 2020. https://gpil.jura.uni-bonn.de/2020/10/germany-tells-thailands-king-not-to-rule-from-its-soil/. Accessed 15 April 2021.

this question.[85] The practice of German authorities demonstrates some unease with the question. Ministers from foreign governments may at least enjoy the treatment of ad hoc diplomats, granting them comparable forms of personal immunity.[86] But what if they are in transit or on a private visit in Germany? The question seems to be unresolved.

4.2 *Functional Immunity of State Officials*

Much more controversial than personal immunity is the range of functional immunity—and in particular the limits of such functional immunity.[87] The subject matter first had come up in a case decided in 1978 by the Federal Supreme Court. Following a request from the German Federal Criminal Police Office (BKA), the head of Scotland Yard had transmitted a report on dishonourable conduct of the plaintiff. The plaintiff went to court and sought a cease and desist order with regard to the accusations contained in the report. In the decision, the Federal Supreme Court stated that the measures taken by the head of Scotland Yard were official acts and therefore German jurisdiction was excluded, with the main argument the execution of police functions is part of the sovereign power of the state.[88]

In 1988, the Federal Administrative Court had to decide whether it was possible to summon the Indian minister of defence as a witness in an asylum procedure. In its decision the court stated that the principle of functional immunity would oppose such an order of summons, since the topics of evidence, such as the nature and scope of military action of Indian troops in Sri Lanka, the political motives for the deployment and the conduct of the troops during military operations are clearly acts jure imperii and make summoning him impermissible.[89]

Heated debates on the topic came up in the aftermath of German unification, with the question how to deal with the sizeable espionage apparatus of the GDR s Ministerium für Staatssicherheit. Before 1990, the treatment of foreign spies created no difficulty—if caught in action, they could be prosecuted in the framework of the German criminal law system. It is beyond doubt that spies acting under coverage in

[85] See e.g. Herdegen (2020), Art. 25 GG para. 56, on the one hand; Epping (2018), pp. 225–26, on the other hand.

[86] See Epping (2018), p. 225.

[87] See also van Alebeek (2019), pp. 496–524.

[88] See Federal Supreme Court, VI ZR 267/76 (26 September 1978) juris, paras. 16–17. See also information submitted by Germany to the ILC at its 66th session 2014. https://legal.un.org/ilc/sessions/66/pdfs/english/iso_germany.pdf. Accessed 15 April 2021.

[89] See Federal Administrative Court, 9 CB 47/88 (30 September 1988) juris, para.8. See also information submitted by Germany to the ILC at its 66th session 2014. https://legal.un.org/ilc/sessions/66/pdfs/english/iso_germany.pdf. Accessed 15 April 2021.

foreign territory do not enjoy functional immunity for their activities.[90] But what about higher officials of the GDR s secret service that never had left Eastern Germany? They are definitely state officials, they were not directly caught in action in Western Germany, and the fact that they could be put on trial simply resulted from the demise of the GDR, which had perished as a state. Western Germany s criminal courts were not reluctant in exercising criminal jurisdiction in these cases, and the Federal Constitutional Court confirmed that line in its judgment on the criminal trials against the members of the National Defence Council of the GDR concerning the shoot to kill policy at the inner-German border, with the argument that the GDR as a state did not exist anymore and that accordingly there was no room for an extended state immunity any more.[91]

The issue of functional immunity vis-à-vis criminal prosecution by foreign states has become even more controversial with the rise of international criminal law, in particular after the ratification of the Rome Statute and the enactment of the German Code of Crimes against International Law (Völkerstrafgesetzbuch).[92] The Völkerstrafgesetzbuch (VStGB) provides for universal jurisdiction of German criminal courts as far as crimes against international law covered by the four core crimes of the Rome Statute are concerned.[93] A number of cases have been prosecuted in the last years by the Federal Attorney (Generalbundesanwalt) who has exclusive competence for crimes under the VStGB. They concerned mostly militia leaders and members of non-state armed groups. With the current Al Khatib trial at the Oberlandesgericht Koblenz this has changed.[94] Accused in this trial are two members of the General Intelligence Service of the Assad regime in Syria, intelligence officials who were involved in rounding up demonstrators and opposition figures on the streets, jailing them in the secret service prison of Al Khatib, where they were systematically tortured and often murdered, It is beyond doubt that these accused committed their crimes as officials of the Syrian state, acting in official capacity. The question of functional immunity was accordingly raised, but the Federal Supreme Court (Bundesgerichtshof) very recently rejected the immunity objection, in a case concerning crimes of an officer of the Afghan national army. The passage on immunity in the judgment is very brief, dealing with the immunity question only

[90] See only Herdegen (2020), Art. 25 GG, para. 54 and more in detail: German (Federal) Constitutional Court –.2 BvL 19/91, 2 BvR 1206, 1584/91 and 2601/93 (15 May 1995) BVerfGE 92, 277, at 321–323. See also information submitted by Germany to the ILC at its 67th session 2015. https://legal.un.org/ilc/sessions/67/pdfs/english/iso_germany.pdf. Accessed 15 April 2021.

[91] See German (Federal) Constitutional Court – 2 BvR 1851, 1853, 1875, 1852/94 – (24 October 1996) BVerfGE 95, 96, 129–130.

[92] For the arguments speaking in favor of an exemption from functional immunities in cases of serious human rights violations and crimes against international law see van Alebeek (2008), pp. 301–364; Appelbaum (2007), pp. 137–182, 183–212, 238–272; Bröhmer (1997), pp. 143–188.

[93] See Werle and Jessberger (2014), pp. 159–161.

[94] See the post of Elisabeth Baier on Völkerrechtsblog. A puzzle coming together: The henchmen of Assad s torture regime on trial in Germany. 23 April 2020. https://voelkerrechtsblog.org/a-puzzle-coming-together/. Accessed 15 April 2021.

at the margins.[95] The decision was largely welcomed in circles of human rights lawyers and specialists of international criminal law, since it opens the gates for a rather expansive scope of criminal jurisdiction of German courts in prosecuting even foreign state officials when involved in war crimes and crimes against humanity.

The German Foreign Office is much more reluctant in its statements on the subject matter. The Foreign Office submitted several times comments on the current work of the ILC on Immunity of State officials from foreign criminal jurisdiction.[96] Even more pertinent are the statements of the German delegates at the Sixth Committee in debates on the relevant reports of the ILC.[97]

5 Concluding Remarks

Germany has followed throughout the twentieth century a prudent path in matters of state immunity, largely sticking to a conservative approach. Like nearly all countries it started at the beginning of the century with a very statist conception of absolute immunity. It embraced the new separation of acta jure gestionis from sovereign immunity in the 1960s and subsequently tried to make sense of the distinction between sovereign acts in the exercise of public authority (acta jure imperii) and commercial acts (acta jure gestionis) excluded from immunity. The Federal Constitutional Court which plays a decisive role in that regard, due to the general incorporation of general rules of international law provided for in Article 25 BL and the special reference procedure created with Article 100 para. 2 BL, has given important guidelines on this distinction and the implications that follow from it. The practice of the ordinary courts in private law matters has developed a rich case law on these matters, in addition also the labour courts. The decisional practice of these courts mostly remains in very traditional bounds, although the inherited distinctions become more and more difficult to operate, in particular in monetary policy and the issue of state bonds, where courts have to cope with grey zones where it is less and less clear whether state organs act in a purely commercial context, or are involved in implementing policies belonging to the realm of public law.[98]

A particularly prudent actor in this regard is the German Foreign Office. In the drafting process of the 2004 UN Convention it has shown itself as a very reluctant

[95] Not yet published, but see the blog post by Lorenz Rubner on Völkerrechtsblog. Rubner, Viel Lärm um nichts: Die funktionelle Immunität von Kriegsverbrechern. 9 February 2021. https://voelkerrechtsblog.org/archive/?cat=5108&keywords=funktionelle%20Immunit%C3%A4t#results. Accessed 15 April 2021.

[96] See ILC, Analytical Guide to the Work of the International Law Commission. Immunity of State officials from foreign criminal jurisdiction. https://legal.un.org/ilc/guide/4_2.shtml. Accessed 15 April 2021.

[97] See e.g. UNGA Sixty-seventh session, Sixth Committee, Summary record of the 21st meeting, UN doc. A/C.6/67/SR.21, p. 2.

[98] See Oeter (2015), p. 357.

actor, which voiced criticism with regard to some progressive tendencies, such as the attempts to establish a broad territorial torts exception. Due to the continuing queries on the meaning of Article 12 of the Convention, the German government has declared not to sign and ratify the 2004 UN Convention. The prudence shown by the Foreign Office results from a difficult situation that Germany is facing internationally. As a result of the unhappy legacy of the misdeeds of the Nazi regime, Germany still has to cope—even after 75 years—with a myriad of potential claims for compensation for the crimes committed by German state authorities in the early 1940s. The Foreign Office finds itself in the uncomfortable position to fend off such claims, despite them being often morally justified—and state immunity is the best tool it has in that regard. Accordingly, the Foreign Office has insisted on unfettered state immunity regarding military activities on foreign soil and has rejected any exception with regard to gross human rights violations and international crimes. Such defensive posture is even visible in its posture towards the ILC project on Immunity of State officials from foreign criminal jurisdiction where the delegates of the Foreign Office have expressed quite some scepticism towards too progressive approaches.

At the same time, however, there exist contrasting developments: The German criminal law system has embraced a conception of universal jurisdiction for international crimes not hindered by any type of immunity. A remarkable shift regarding the idea of international criminal justice happened in the 1990s, with Germany becoming one of the major advocates and champions of the idea of institutionalization of international criminal law.[99] In the course of the adoption and implementation of the Rome Statute, Germany enacted its new Code of Crimes against International Law (Völkerstrafgesetzbuch) which provides for universal jurisdiction concerning all the Statute's core crimes. This was not only enthusiastically embraced by human rights lawyers and activists of international criminal law, but also by the Federal Attorney (Generalbundesanwalt). The office of the Federal Attorney has set into motion a whole series of criminal proceedings against perpetrators of crimes against international law which were captured on German territory, including officials of states such as Afghanistan and Syria. Concerns of functional immunity of state officials have been discarded in that prosecution practice, a position recently confirmed by the Federal Supreme Court.

The contrast between the different positions taken by German state organs, and the different orientations shown by them, is remarkable. One might call it a contradiction, but if analysed more closely, it simply reminds us that the State is not a unified actor, but needs to be disaggregated as a network of different actors in detail. The professional socialisation and the resulting epistemic framework of the actors differ considerably. In the law of state immunities this becomes visible in a particular way. As I wrote five years ago, in the concluding remarks of the joint volume of the German and French societies of international law on Immunities in the Age of Global Constitutionalism : The roots of the law of immunities 'are to be found in

[99] For a seminal study on this shift of position see Steinke (2012), pp. 68–112.

international law, but its practice is mainly an issue of national administrative practice and court decisions. It is one of the few institutions of international law that rests on daily exercise in national legal practice, with a settled body of jurisprudence in most national legal orders. States may have disputes on issues of immunities in their international relations, may even go to court on these issues—but the day-to-day application does not take place in a purely diplomatic context, it involves a plethora of national law enforcement agents, from policemen over administrators, prosecutors to judges'.[100] What such a plurality of actors means in practice can be revisited in the German practice dealing with state immunity that was explained in this chapter.

References

Appelbaum C (2007) Einschränkungen der Staatenimmunität in Fällen schwerer Menschenrechtsverletzungen: Klagen von Bürgern gegen einen fremden Staat oder ausländische staatliche Funktionsträger vor nationalen Gerichten. Duncker & Humblot, Berlin

Blanke H-J (2014) Besteht Staatenimmunität bei Kriegsverbrechen im Lande des Forumstaates? Zur Entscheidung des IGH vom 3. Februar 2012 im Fall Jurisdictional Immunities of the State (Germany v. Italy, Greece intervening). Zeitschrift für öffentliches Recht 69:5–38

Boggero G (2016) The legal implications of Sentenza No. 238/2014 by Italy's constitutional court for Italian municipal judges: Is overcoming the 'Triepelian approach' possible? ZaöRV Zeitschrift für ausländisches öffentliches Recht und Völkerrecht 76:203–224

Bothe M (2015) Remedies of victims of war crimes and crimes against humanities: some critical remarks on the ICJ Judgment on the jurisdictional immunity of states. In: Peters A, Lagrange E, Oeter S, Tomuschat C (eds) Immunities in the age of global constitutionalism. Brill Nijhoff, Leiden, pp 99–115

Boysen S (2006) Kriegsverbrechen im Diskurs nationaler Gerichte: Der Distomo-Beschluss des Bundesverfassungsgerichts vom 15. Februar 2006. Archiv des Völkerrechts 44:363–379

Bröhmer J (1997) State immunity and the violation of human rights. Nijhoff, The Hague

Bröhmer J (2015) State immunity and sovereign bonds. In: Peters A, Lagrange E, Oeter S, Tomuschat C (eds) Immunities in the age of global constitutionalism. Brill Nijhoff, Leiden, pp 182–208

Cremer W (2003) Entschädigungsklagen wegen schwerer Menschenrechtsverletzungen und Staatenimmunität vor nationaler Zivilgerichtsbarkeit. Archiv des Völkerrechts 41:137–168

D'Argent P, Lesaffre P (2019) Immunities and jus cogens violations. In: Ruys T, Angelet N (eds) The Cambridge handbook of immunities and international law. CUP, Cambridge, pp 614–633

Damrosch LF (2019) The sources of immunity law – between international and domestic law. In: Ruys T, Angelet N (eds) The Cambridge handbook of immunities and international law. CUP, Cambridge, pp 40–60

Epping V (2018) § 7: Der Staat als die 'Normalperson' des Völkerrechts. In: Epping V, Heintschel von Heinegg W (eds) Ipsen: Völkerrecht, 7th edn. C.H. Beck, München, pp 76–232

Fischer P (1984) Staatsunternehmen im Völkerrecht. In: Fischer P, von Hoffmann B (eds) Staatsunternehmen im Völkerrecht und im internationalen Privatrecht (Berichte der Deutschen Gesellschaft für Völkerrecht, H. 25). C.F. Müller, Heidelberg, pp 7–31

[100] See Oeter (2015), p. 356.

Foakes J, O'Keefe R (2013) Article 12. In: O'Keefe R, Tams C (eds) The United Nations Convention on jurisdictional immunities of states and their property: a commentary. OUP, Oxford, pp 209–224

Fox H, Webb P (2015) The law of state immunity, 3rd edn. OUP, Oxford

Franey EH (2015) Immunity from criminal jurisdiction of national courts. In: Orakhelashvili A (ed) Research handbook on jurisdiction and immunities in international law. Edward Elgar, Cheltenham, pp 205–252

Frenzel EM, Wiedemann R (2008) Das Vertrauen in die Staatenimmunität und seine Herausforderung: Die Bewältigung von NS-Unrecht im Mehrebenensystem. NVwZ Neue Zeitschrift für Verwaltungsrecht 27:1088–1091

Gavouneli M, Bantekas I (2001) Prefecture of Voiotia v. Federal Republic of Germany, Case No. 11/2000, Areios Pagos (Hellenic Supreme Court), May 4, 2000. AJIL 95:198–204

Hartwig M (2013) Völkerrechtliche Praxis der Bundesrepublik Deutschland 2010. ZaöRV Zeitschrift für ausländisches öffentliches Recht und Völkerrecht 73:735–782

Hartwig M (2018) Völkerrechtliche Praxis der Bundesrepublik Deutschland 2016. ZaöRV Zeitschrift für ausländisches öffentliches Recht und Völkerrecht 78:717–788

Hartwig M (2019) Völkerrechtliche Praxis der Bundesrepublik Deutschland 2017. ZaöRV Zeitschrift für ausländisches öffentliches Recht und Völkerrecht 79:325–398

Hector P (2016) Zur gerichtlichen Durchsetzung von Staatshaftungsansprüchen für Militäreinsätze nach Völkerrecht und deutschem Recht – zugleich ein Beitrag zu Fragen der Staatenimmunität und des Verhältnisses von Völkerrecht und innerstaatlichem Recht. In: Bröhmer J (ed) Europa und die Welt: Festkolloquium zum 80. Geburtstag von Professor Georg Ress. Nomos, Baden-Baden, pp 123–149

Herdegen M (2020) Art. 25 GG. In: Herdegen M, Klein HH (eds) Maunz-Dürig: Grundgesetz-Kommentar 92. EL. C.H. Beck, München

Hildner G (2018) Staatenimmunität in der Praxis: Aktuelle deutsche Erfahrungen. Zeitschrift für öffentliches Recht 73:137–146

Höfelmeier A (2018) Die Vollstreckungsimmunität der Staaten im Wandel des Völkerrechts. Springer, Heidelberg

Kau M (2016) Der Staat und der Einzelne als Völkerrechtssubjekte. In: Graf Vitzthum W, Proelss A (eds) Völkerrecht, 7th edn. De Gruyter, Berlin, pp 141–252

Kissel OR, Mayer H (2021) Gerichtsverfassungsgesetz: Kommentar, 10th edn. C.H. Beck, München

Kloth M, Brunner M (2012) Staatenimmunität im Zivilprozess bei gravierenden Menschenrechtsverletzungen: Eine Anmerkung zu dem Urteil des Internationalen Gerichtshofs 'Jurisdictional Immunities of the State (Germany v. Italy: Greece intervening)' vom 3. Februar 2012. Archiv des Völkerrechts 50:218–244

Koenig C, König D (2018) Artikel 25 GG. In: Huber PM, Vosskuhle A (eds) von Mangoldt/Klein/Starck: Grundgesetz-Kommentar, vol 2, 7th edn. C.H. Beck, München, pp 515–555

Kreicker H (2012) Die Entscheidung des Internationalen Gerichtshofs zur Staatenimmunität – Auswirkungen auf das (Völker-)Strafrecht? Anmerkungen zum Urteil des IGH vom 3.2.2012 aus strafrechtlicher Sicht. ZIS Zeitschrift für internationale Strafrechtsdogmatik 7:107–123

Lengelsen RF (2011) Aktuelle Probleme der Staatenimmunität im Verfahren vor den Zivil- und Verwaltungsgerichten – unter besonderer Berücksichtigung des 'UN-Übereinkommens über die Immunität der Staaten und ihres Vermögens von der Gerichtsbarkeit'. Lang, Frankfurt am Main

Lorz S (2017) Ausländische Staaten vor deutschen Zivilgerichten: zum Spannungsverhältnis von Staatenimmunität und Recht auf Zugang zu Gericht. Mohr Siebeck, Tübingen

Ney M (2015) Sovereign immunities of states: a German perspective. In: Peters A, Lagrange E, Oeter S, Tomuschat C (eds) Immunities in the age of global constitutionalism. Brill Nijhoff, Leiden, pp 32–39

O'Keefe R, Tams C (eds) (2013) The United Nations Convention on jurisdictional immunities of states and their property: a commentary. OUP, Oxford

Oellers-Frahm K (2016) A never-ending story: the International Court of Justice – the Italian Constitutional Court – Italian tribunals and the question of immunity. ZaöRV Zeitschrift für ausländisches öffentliches Recht und Völkerrecht 76:193–202

Oeter S (2015) The law of immunities as a focal point of the evolution of international law. In: Peters A, Lagrange E, Oeter S, Tomuschat C (eds) Immunities in the age of global constitutionalism. Brill Nijhoff, Leiden, pp 355–366

Orakhelashvili A (2015) State immunity from jurisdiction between law, comity and ideology. In: Orakhelashvili A (ed) Research handbook on jurisdiction and immunities in international law. Edward Elgar, Cheltenham, pp 151–184

Orakhelashvili A (2019) Jurisdictional immunity of states and general international law – explaining the jus gestionis v. jus imperii divide. In: Ruys T, Angelet N (eds) The Cambridge handbook of immunities and international law. CUP, Cambridge, pp 105–124

Paech N (2009) Staatenimmunität und Kriegsverbrechen. Archiv des Völkerrechts 47:36–92

Payandeh M (2012) Staatenimmunität und Menschenrechte: zugleich Besprechung von IGH, Urteil v. 3.2.2012 – Deutschland gegen Italien. Juristenzeitung 19:949–958

Pieper SU (2013) Staatenimmunität – eine Bestandsaufnahme. In: Breuer M, Epiney A, Haratsch A, Schmahl S, Weiß N (eds) Der Staat im Recht. Festschrift für Eckart Klein zum 70. Geburtstag. Duncker & Humblot, Berlin, pp 839–860

Pullen J (2012) Die Immunität von Staatsunternehmen im zivilrechtlichen Erkenntnis- und Vollstreckungsverfahren. Peter Lang, Frankfurt am Main

Raffeiner S (2016) Jenseits der Staatenimmunität im deutsch-italienischen Staatenimmunitäten–Fall: Wege und Hürden nach dem Urteil der Corte costituzionale. ZaöRV Zeitschrift für ausländisches öffentliches Recht und Völkerrecht 76:451–473

Reimer R (2020) Staatenimmunität und Staatsverschuldung: hoheitliche Zwangsstrukturierung ausländischer Staatsanleihen vor nationalen Gerichten. Nomos, Baden-Baden

Schreuer C (1985) Zur Zulässigkeit von Vollstreckungsmaßnahmen in Bankkonten ausländischer Staaten. In: Barfuß W (ed) Festschrift für Karl H. Neumayer zum 65. Geburtstag. Nomos, Baden-Baden, pp 521–542

Sieckmann J-R, Kessal-Wulf S (2018) Artikel 100 GG. In: Huber PM, Vosskuhle A (eds) von Mangoldt/Klein/Starck: Grundgesetz-Kommentar, vol 3, 7th edn. C.H. Beck, München, pp 959–995

Steger R (2013) Staatenimmunität und Kriegsverbrechen: das IGH-Urteil im Verfahren Deutschland gegen Italien vom 03.02.2012. PL Academic Research, Frankfurt am Main

Steinke R (2012) The politics of international criminal justice: German perspectives from Nuremberg to The Hague. Hart, Oxford

Stewart DP (2005) The UN Convention on jurisdictional immunities of states and their property. AJIL 99:194–211

Stoll P-T (2011) State immunity. In: Wolfrum R (ed) Max Planck encyclopedia of public international law. OUP, Oxford

Thouvenin J-M, Grandaubert V (2019) The material scope of state immunity from execution. In: Ruys T, Angelet N (eds) The Cambridge handbook of immunities and international law. CUP, Cambridge, pp 245–265

Tomuschat C (2011) The international law of state immunity and its development by national institutions. Vanderbilt J Transnatl Law 44:1105–1140

Uerpmann-Wittzack R (2015) Serious human rights violations as potential exceptions to immunity: conceptual challenges. In: Peters A, Lagrange E, Oeter S, Tomuschat C (eds) Immunities in the age of global constitutionalism. Brill Nijhoff, Leiden, pp 236–243

van Alebeek R (2008) The immunity of states and their officials in international criminal and international human rights law. OUP, Oxford

van Alebeek R (2019) Functional immunity of state officials from the criminal jurisdiction of foreign national courts. In: Ruys T, Angelet N (eds) The Cambridge handbook of immunities and international law. CUP, Cambridge, pp 496–524
von Hoffmann B (1984) Staatsunternehmen im internationalen Privatrecht. In: Fischer P, von Hoffmann B (eds) Staatsunternehmen im Völkerrecht und im internationalen Privatrecht (Berichte der Deutschen Gesellschaft für Völkerrecht, H. 25). C.F. Müller, Heidelberg, pp 35–72
Werle G, Jessberger F (2014) Principles of international criminal law, 3rd edn. OUP, Oxford
Wiater P (2017) Der Staat als Investor: Staatsfonds und die süße Frucht der Staatenimmunität. Archiv des Völkerrechts 55:149–184

Stefan Oeter is, since 1999, a Professor for German and Comparative Public Law and Public International Law, at the Faculty of Law, University of Hamburg. He is member of the Permanent Court of Arbitration and member of the Academy of Sciences in Hamburg.

Russian Approach to State Immunity: If You Want Peace, Prepare for War?

Vladislav Starzhenetskiy

Abstract Russia has been considered for rather a long time, as one of the few remaining powerful protagonists of absolute immunity. But in 2015, it also switched from the absolute to restrictive (functional) doctrine of State immunity with the adoption of the new Federal Law. Why did Russia decide to switch to restrictive immunity? It seems implausible to explain this decision only by traditional reasons, such as by a need to protect the commercial interests of private parties vis-à-vis foreign States, or the pursuit of the more effective protection of human rights. In this chapter, we explore the reasons and motives that made Russia change its position towards State immunity, analyse specific features of the new 2015 Law and existing case-law in relation to foreign States in the Russian jurisdiction.

1 Introduction

In their research, Erik Voeten and Pierre-Hugues Verdier demonstrate that the majority of states have switched from an absolute to a restrictive immunity doctrine over the last 50 years.[1] As Xiaodong Yang put it 'the history of the law of State immunity is the history of the triumph of the doctrine of State immunity over that of absolute immunity'.[2] This tectonic shift is usually explained by two essential features of contemporary international law. Firstly, this is a need to protect the commercial interests of the private parties in response to a 'phenomenal increase of State trading, commercial and other activities in foreign countries'.[3] Secondly,

[1] Verdier and Voeten (2015).

[2] Yang (2012), p. 6.

[3] Yang (2012), p. 19.

V. Starzhenetskiy (✉)
Faculty of Law, National Research University, Higher School of Economics, Moscow, Russia
e-mail: vstarzhenetskiy@hse.ru

R. Bismuth et al. (eds.), *Sovereign Immunity Under Pressure*,
https://doi.org/10.1007/978-3-030-87706-4_4

this is a need to strengthen the international rule of law and to provide more effective protection of the most fundamental rights of individuals.[4]

The doctrine of restrictive immunity originates from Western legal culture.[5] At the same time, more and more non-Western states switch from the absolute to restrictive doctrine of State immunity. The 2004 United Nations Convention on Jurisdictional Immunities of States and Their Property ('UNCSI') also rejected the old paradigm of absolute immunity, and served as a catalyst for subsequent changes. These changes reflect the modern trajectories of international law development and current heated debates over such basic values of international law as state sovereignty, protection of human rights and the role of national/international courts.

Interestingly, Russia (often considered as one of the few remaining powerful protagonists of absolute immunity) has also switched from absolute to restrictive (functional) doctrine of State immunity in November 2015 with the adoption of the new Federal Law N.297-FZ 'On Jurisdictional Immunities of Foreign State and its Property in the Russian Federation' (2015 Law), as well as corresponding amendments to the Civil Procedure Code and Commercial Procedure Code. The new 2015 Law is largely based on the provisions of the UNCSI and provides instances where foreign states may be sued in Russia and may not invoke State immunity.

Why did Russia decide to switch to restrictive immunity? What were the motives behind this strategic decision, explicitly demonstrating Russian recognition (*opinio juris*) of the international customary law rule of restrictive immunity, having direct implications for the Russian foreign policy and relations with foreign States? Can such reasons as a need to protect the commercial interests of private parties, vis-à-vis foreign states, or the pursuit of the more effective protection of human rights explain such a decision? Our claim is that such an explanation would not be appropriate because of its oversimplification.

It is worth mentioning that the Russian approach to international law is usually characterised as different from the Western one.[6] Russia, in this context, is considered by Western scholars as a State-centred country with a strained relationship with Western perceptions of human rights and constituting the 'vanguard of challenging the dominance of Western liberal democratic states, in crafting the structure and substance of international law'.[7] In light of the growing academic interest in ongoing geopolitical power shifts, greater multi-polarity and non-Western approaches to international law, the Russian transformation of its State immunity law deserves a closer look.

In this paper we will explore the reasons and motives that made Russia change its position towards State immunity, analyse specific features of the new 2015 Law, and existing case-law, in relation to foreign States in Russian jurisdiction. This will help us to shed light on the Russian approach to jurisdictional immunities of states.

---

[4]Peters (2015), p. 3.

[5]For historical development see Fox and Webb (2015), pp. 133–166.

[6]Malksoo (2016).

[7]Roberts (2016), p. 280.

2 Evolution of the Russian Approach to State Immunity

It is hard to specify one single factor that led the Russian authorities to shift from the absolute to restrictive doctrine of State immunity in 2015. Rather, there were several key factors that gradually influenced the evolution of the Russian approach. They include traditional state-centrism, obligations under international law, development of doctrinal views, legislative and case-law changes, as well as foreign adverse proceedings.

2.1 State-Centrism: Values and Interests

Historically, Russia has always belonged to the group of countries with the strongest regimes of State immunity. This reverential attitude to jurisdictional immunities was inherited by the Russia Federation from its Soviet past. In the Soviet legal doctrine, absolute immunity of a foreign state was justified by the basic principles of international law, such as the sovereignty, independence and equality of states (*par in parem non habet jurisdictionem*). Mark Boguslavsky, prominent Soviet and Russian legal scholar, explained the Soviet attitude to State immunity in the following way: 'It is suggested that the very assessment of a state act, on the part of the court of a foreign state, has to be considered as a violation of sovereignty. Therefore, this doctrine (of restrictive immunity) contradicts the obligation to respect the sovereignty of a foreign state, and the principle of non-interference in the internal affairs of that state. It is a sovereign right of every state to determine the principles of the organisation of its social and economic system, and these must be respected by other states'.[8]

Traditional state-centrism remains constant in modern Russia despite certain fluctuations in the 1990s and beginning of 2000s. It highlights the superior role of state sovereignty in international relations and law and is intrinsically linked to what is perceived as the dignity and respect of the nation. This feature also reflects preferred diplomatic means of dispute resolution in the international arena, as well as general scepticism and cautiousness towards international litigation/arbitration, not to say about proceedings in foreign domestic courts. Such considerations, as international comity, stability in international relations, diplomacy and non-interference into domestic affairs would better fit and describe the Russian approach to international law than other values based on individualisation (respect of human rights, protection of property, right to fair trial).

Soviet and Russian support of the strong State immunity regime also has its pragmatic explanation. Firstly, it serves as an efficient legal tool for protecting state property abroad. Secondly, taking into account the role of a state in the economy, it might also be problematic to make a clear distinction between the acts, jure imperii

[8]Boguslavsky (1979), p. 169.

and jure gestionis, if we apply a functional approach to State immunity. As was pointed out by Mark Boguslavsky, '[t]he socialist state, as a sovereign, is vested not only with political, but also with economic power, and because of this unity of political and economic leadership the socialist state itself fulfils economic activities. It is impossible to split up the socialist state into two subjects: a sovereign power and an entity subject to private law rules. As already underlined, the state is one, but the expressions of its activity are manifold'.[9]

Even in the present, after the dissolution of the USSR, abolition of state monopoly of foreign trade and massive privatisation of state assets in Russia, this argument is not completely obsolete. Since 2005, the share of the state sector in the Russian economy has been steadily growing (this includes state corporations, state-controlled banks and commercial entities) and reached approximately 70% in 2019.[10] Thus, despite revolutionary social changes of the 1990s, Russia has recollected significant economic possessions owned by the state and state-owned companies. And of course, it remains interested in the effective protection of these assets in other jurisdictions as well.

2.2 *Russian Obligations Under International Law*

There are several international instruments which Russia signed and/or ratified since 1992 and which supported a shift to a restrictive approach towards State immunity.

Firstly, the European Convention on human rights (ECHR), that Russia signed and ratified in 1998. Article 6 of this Convention provides for the right to fair trial, that is guaranteed vis-à-vis sovereign states as well.[11] The Russian national courts' reluctance to accept jurisdiction and resolve cases with foreign states has already been condemned by the European court of human rights (ECtHR), in the case, *Oleynikov v. Russia*[12] that was decided in 2013.[13]

---

[9] Boguslavsky (1979), pp. 169–170.

[10] According to the Official Report on the state of competition in Russia in 2019 prepared by the Federal Antimonopoly Service of Russia (available at: https://fas.gov.ru/documents/686911). Accessed 15 April 2021.

[11] Guide on Article 6 of the European Convention. http://www.echr.coe.int/Documents/Guide_Art_6_ENG.pdf. Accessed 15 April 2021.

[12] ECtHR. Oleynikov v. Russia. No. 36703/04. Judgment of 14 March 2013.

[13] This case was initiated by the Russian citizen, Vladimir Oleynikov, who in May 1997, lent USD 1500 to the Khabarovsk Office of the Trade Counsellor of the Democratic People's Republic of Korea (the DPRK Trade Counsellor). After the DPRK Trade Counsellor had failed to repay its debt, Mr. Oleynikov sued the DPRK in the Russian court of general jurisdiction. His claim was returned, without examination, on the grounds that the Russian Code of Civil Procedure provided for absolute immunity of a foreign state. The ECtHR found violation of the applicant's right of access to the court that was not consistent with Article 6 of the ECHR. According to the Court, restriction on the right of access to court of Mr. Oleynikov had not been justified by the circumstances of the case, had been disproportionate and had impaired the very essence of his right of access to a court.

Secondly, these are the provisions of international investment treaties with other states that Russia signed[14] or ratified.[15] These treaties commonly include a special mechanism of investor-state dispute resolution based on an open arbitration clause, allowing investors to sue Russia in international investment arbitration. Such an arbitration clause is typically considered as a waiver of State immunity and states may not invoke sovereign immunity-related arguments in such disputes to avoid arbitration with private parties. Foreign investors successfully already used this option in disputes with Russia several times.[16]

Thirdly, it is also important to note that, in 2006, Russia signed the main international instrument related to restrictive doctrine—the UNCSI.[17] Although Russia subsequently did not ratify this treaty, this fact also supported a departure from absolute immunity.

2.3 Development of the Russian Legislation and Case-Law on State Immunity Before 2015

There were several attempts to soften, or even change, the absolute immunity rule in Russian law before 2015. From a chronological point of view, the first attempt was made in 1995, when the Federal Law 'On concession agreements' of 30.12.1995 was introduced. It included article 23, that prescribed that agreements concluded between the state and foreign citizens and foreign legal entities could provide for a waiver of immunity from adjudication, immunity from provisional measures and immunity from enforcement of judicial and/or arbitral award.

Interestingly, during this period, Russian courts moved towards restrictive immunity even faster than the law prescribed them to, showing unusual judicial activism. The Russian Constitutional Court, in its Ruling of 2 November 2000, examined the claim of Ms. Kalashnikova, a former employee of the information service of the United States Embassy in Russia, who was dismissed by the employer. The Russian courts of general jurisdiction rejected her claims, since she failed to present any evidence of the United States' consent to submit to the jurisdiction of the court according to Article 435(1) of the 1964 Code of Civil Procedure. The Constitutional

---

[14] Convention on the settlement of investment disputes between states and nationals of other states (Washington, 18.III.1965), which Russia signed on Jun 16, 1992, but still did not ratify. Another example is the Energy Charter Treaty that Russia signed in 1994, but revoked its signature in 2009.

[15] The total number of bilateral investment treaties (BITs) with Russia is 82 of which 70 were ratified by Russia and 65 are in force as of January 2021. A full list of BITs with Russia: https://www.economy.gov.ru/material/departments/d11/investicionnye_soglasheniya/. Accessed 15 April 2021.

[16] The total number of investment disputes against Russia reached 26 in 2019. Full list of them is here https://investmentpolicy.unctad.org/investment-dispute-settlement/country/175/russian-federation. Accessed 15 April 2021.

[17] Russian Government decree of 27.10.2006 N 1487-p.

Court reached the conclusion that: 'the formalistic application of Article 435(1) of the 1964 Code of Civil Procedure, by the courts of general jurisdiction, which refused to accept the claim of [Ms] Kalashnikova on the basis of this article, led to an inadmissible limitation of the claimant's rights with regard to an individual labour dispute . . . and thus to a violation of the right to judicial defence provided for in Article 46(1) of the Constitution of the Russian Federation'. Although the Court finally refrained from assessment of the constitutionality of relevant provisions of the Code of Civil Procedure, this signalled the need for changes in the legislation concerning State immunity.

Another interesting example was offered in 2001, by the Supreme Commercial Court, that instructed the lower commercial courts to differentiate the acts, jure imperii and jure gestionis, in deciding commercial cases involving State immunity.[18] The provisions of the Arbitrazh (Commercial) Procedure Code of 24.07.2002 subsequently contributed to an ongoing erosion of the absolute immunity rule and introduced article 251, 'Judicial Immunity'. The article proclaimed jurisdictional immunity of foreign states but specified that such immunity could be enjoyed only with regard to actions in sovereign capacity (acts jure imperii). Despite a new legislative approach, Russian commercial courts mostly favoured a pro-immunity approach,[19] with a few rare cases, when such immunity was not recognised.[20]

Finally, in 2005, the Russian Government presented the draft Law 'On jurisdictional immunity of a foreign state and its property' to the Parliament. However, this draft law based on the UNCSI provisions, and introducing general rule of restricted State immunity into the Russian legal system, was not adopted by the State Duma for reasons that are not public.

2.4 *Development of the Doctrinal Views*

The vast majority of prominent legal scholars in Russia (like Mark Boguslavsky,[21] Irina Khlestova,[22] Tatiana Neshatayeva)[23] and almost all PhD dissertations defended

[18] Information Letter of the Presidium of the Supreme Commercial Court of 18 January 2001.

[19] For example, State immunity was recognised in cases: A72-13414/2009 concerning privatisation of Serbian assets, A43-4888/2012 concerning recovery of debt out of a lease contract with the embassy of Belarus, A40-53648/12-133-481 concerning the recovery of commercial debt from European Reconstruction and Development Bank (as international organisation), etc.

[20] For example, case A55-34769/2009, concerning corporate succession and the Czech republic, case A40-46787/09-13-328 concerning the recovery of accident damages from the Embassy of the Democratic People's Republic of Korea.

[21] Boguslavsky (2000).

[22] Khlestova (2005a); Khlestova (2005b), p. 13.

[23] Neshataeva (1999); Neshataeva (2001), pp. 87–107.

in the period between 1991 and 2018[24] rejected the concept of absolute immunity as outdated and suggested, in their works, to follow a restricted immunity rule as the most appropriate in current circumstances. Support of the restricted State immunity regime in Russian international law academic circles has quickly become quite popular.

2.5 *Foreign Adverse Proceedings*

Our research reveals that, in 1995–2014, Russia lost several important and rather sensitive cases in foreign jurisdictions, where Russian State immunity was not (fully) appreciated and where Russia had to take active measures to protect its property from being seized and subsequently sold at public auctions. Four of the most significant of these cases deserve special mention, since they played an important role in the re-evaluation of the Russian position re State immunity.

2.5.1 The NOGA Case

In 1992, Swiss company, NOGA, concluded several contracts with the Russian Government for the supply of food and consumer goods. These agreements contained an arbitration clause and designated the Arbitration Institute of the Stockholm Chamber of Commerce, as a competent forum, to resolve disputes between the parties. Such disputes started in 1993 and Swiss company party soon referred the dispute for arbitration. In 1997, the Arbitration Institute of the Stockholm Chamber of Commerce rendered a decision against Russia, in the amount of several millions of US dollars. Russia refused to enforce this arbitration award and the company began hunting for Russian property abroad.

In 2000, NOGA succeeded in arresting the accounts of the Russian Embassy, the Permanent Delegation of the Russian Federation at UNESCO, the Commercial Bureau of the Russian Federation, Central Bank of Russia and the Russian sailboat, 'Sedov', in France, and in 2001, almost arrested Russian military aircraft, at the air show in Le Bourget. Subsequently, bank accounts were released[25] and seizures of property were declared illegal by the French courts. In 2005, at the request of the company, NOGA, in Switzerland, a collection of paintings (whose insurance value was estimated $1 billion) from the Russian State Pushkin Museum was seized. The Swiss Federal Council cancelled all decisions concerning the seizure' in the

[24] Shaykhutdinova (1991); Khlestova (2003); Chernichenko (2003); Demidov (2005); Lebedeva (2006); Gaididey (2006); Silkina (2007); Tumanov (2011); Shebanova (2011); Churilova (2018).

[25] Embassy of the Russian Federation in France, Permanent Delegation of the Russian Federation at UNESCO, Commercial Bureau of the Russian Federation in France v.Compagnie NOGA d'Importation at d'Exportation (NOGA), Decision of Aug 10, 2000, CA Paris (Fr.), excerpts reprinted in XXVI Y.B.Com.Arb 237 (2001).

protection of national interests'. In 2005, the assets of the Russian Federation were also seized in the International Air Transport Association, which Russia tried, unsuccessfully, to challenge in the Swiss courts.[26] In 2008, assets of Russian state-owned companies were frozen in France, with a value of several millions of euros, but were later unblocked.

The dispute allegedly ended up when, according to media reports,[27] a third person bought the Russian debts from the company, NOGA. Details of the deal were never disclosed.

2.5.2 The Sedelmayer Case

Mr. Franz Sedelmayer, a German national, decided to do business in Russia and entered into a joint venture with the Leningrad police department in 1991. The parties intended to supply specialised, imported equipment both for the police, and for commercial enterprises and individuals. The City police department made a contribution to the joint venture, in the form of 20 thousand square met res of land and the right to a 25-year lease of the 1908-built mansion on Kamenny Island. The German entrepreneur, in turn, paid for the renovation of the building, spending approximately two million dollars on it. Subsequently, the state authorities revoked their permission to use the building and asked the joint venture to vacate the premises without any compensation for renovation expenses.

Following this de facto expropriation of his capital contribution in the joint venture, Sedelmayer initiated arbitration, under the Germany-Russia bilateral investment treaty. In 1998, the Arbitration Institute of the Stockholm Chamber of Commerce rendered a decision against Russia and awarded Sedelmayer 2.35 mln USD plus interest.[28]

Russia refused to comply with the award and Sedelmeyer also started chasing for Russian state assets. He unsuccessfully tried to seize Russian property at the International Aerospace Show in Berlin, to foreclose on the Russian House of Science and Culture in Berlin (the so-called Russian House),[29] to freeze the payments of the Lufthansa company in favour of Russia for trans-Siberian flights etc.[30]

---

[26] Swiss Supreme Court, Decision 7B.2/2007, 15 August 2007, Moscow Center for Automated Air Traffic Control v. Commission de surveillance des offices des poursuites et des faillites du canton de Geneve, ASA Bull. 1/2008, 141–151.

[27] Russia's Finance Ministry Buys Noga Debts. http://www.kommersant.com/p842554/r_528/Noga_vs._Russian_Federation. Accessed 15 April 2021.

[28] Mr.Franz Sedelmayer v. Russian Federation, SCC, Award, July 7, 1998.

[29] Decision of 14 June 2010, Court of Appeals, Berlin, 1 W 276/09 (Germ.) http://www.italaw.com/sites/default/files/case-documents/italaw1524.pdf. Accessed 15 April 2021.

[30] Decision of Oct. 4, 2005, Federal Supreme Court, VII ZB 9/05 (Germ.) http://juris.bundesgerichtshof.de/cgi- bin/rechtsprechung/document.py?Gericht=bgh&Art=en&sid=6517d7e9cfb605db8841cd158bbcb8c2&nr=34320&pos=0&anz=1. Accessed 15 April 2021.

He managed to foreclose on the building of the Russian trade mission in Cologne, which, according to the German authorities,[31] was used for commercial purposes. The building was bought by the Russian State Property Fund.

Sedelmayer was then able to seize and sell a house belonging to the Russian trade mission in Stockholm.[32] In September 2014, the auction was held (the third in a row), and the building was sold for 12 million Swedish krone.[33] The Russian side insisted that the building was protected by diplomatic immunity, and challenged the actions of the Swedish authorities in the courts of Sweden, although unsuccessfully.

2.5.3 The Schneerson Library Case

The 'Schneerson Library' is a large and long-standing collection of Hebrew religious books and manuscripts, the first part of which was taken by Joseph Schneerson from Lubavitch (a village in Smolensk region of Russia) to Moscow, during World War I and subsequently nationalised in 1918, by the Russian Bolshevik government, on the basis of the Decree of the Council of People's Commissars on the scientific archives; the second part of the collection was captured by Nazi German troops in Poland, during World War II, and then returned to Russia as a military trophy. At the time of the dispute, books and manuscripts were kept in the Russian State Library and the Russian State Military Archive.

In the early 1990s, representatives of the Agudas Chasidei Chabad of United States, a non-profit Jewish organisation, incorporated in New York, tried to use all available legal procedures in Russia to acquire the 'Schneerson Library' to their ownership, but after a series of controversial judgments in 1992, the Plenum of the Russian Supreme Commercial Court finally decided to leave the collection in state ownership. Russia claimed that the Library was part of Russia's national heritage.

After that, in 2004, Agudas Chasidei Chabad of United States filed a lawsuit against the Russian Federation, as well as its Ministry of Culture and Mass Communication, the Russian State Library, and the Russian State Military Archive (all collectively referred to as 'Russia') in the US District Court of Columbia, seeking to obtain possession of the Library. Russia moved to dismiss the claims on grounds of foreign sovereign immunity, forum non conveniens, and the act of state doctrine. In 2006, the US District Court rejected all claims against the Russian State Library on the basis of the US Immunity Act, but not to the Russian State Military Archive.[34] The parties filed an appeal, and on June 13, 2008, the US Court of Appeals for the District of Columbia ruled that Russia had no jurisdictional immunity in this dispute.

[31] Decision of 18 March 2008, Court of Appeals, Cologne, 22 U 98/07 (Germ.) available at http://www.italaw.com/sites/default/files/case-documents/ita0764.pdf. Accessed 15 April 2021.

[32] Russian Federation v. Franz J. Sedelmayer, Decision of July 1, 2011, Supreme Court, Ö 170-10 (Sweden)(English translation). See also Wrange (2012), pp. 347–353.

[33] http://www.top.rbc.ru/economics/12/09/2014/948746.shtml. Accessed 15 April 2021.

[34] Agudas Chasidei Chabad v. Russian Federation. 466 F. Supp. 2d 6, 10–14 (D.D.C. 2006).

After that, Russia decided to withdraw from the court proceeding on merits, insisting a lack of jurisdiction and authority of the US court to adjudicate rights in cultural property that always had been located in the Russian Federation. In 2010, the US District Court delivered a default judgment against Russia[35] and ordered Russia to 'surrender to the United States Embassy in Moscow, or to the duly appointed representatives of . . . Chabad . . . the complete collection'.

What were the legal arguments used by the US courts to deny Russian State Immunity in this dispute? Rendering their judgments against Russia, the US courts were relying on so called 'expropriation exception' contained in the Foreign State Immunities Act (FSIA) (28 U.S.C. § 1605(a)(3))[36] and came to the conclusion that (1) Agudas Chasidei Chabad had property interests in the Library as it accumulated, with a succession of Rebbes acting as custodians for the benefit of Chabad and its followers; (2) the Library owned by the worldwide Chabad organisation represented by the US Jewish organisation was taken by Russia in violation of international law in 1917–1925, 1945 and retaken in 1991–1992; and that the takings of the Library were not for a public purpose, were discriminatory, and occurred without just compensation; (3) the Library was in the possession of the Russian state agencies (State Archives and State Library); (4) the Russian State Archive and Russian State Library were engaged in commercial activities in the US, since they, several times, were paid royalties by US companies for the reproduction and sale of materials worldwide, including the US, for a value of less than USD 100,000. Russia predictably refused to comply with the final court judgment and declared it 'null and void'.[37]

On January 16, 2013, the US Court granted a motion for civil contempt sanctions, ordering Russia to pay monetary sanctions of $50,000 per day, payable to the plaintiff.[38] In 2015, the US District judge granted a motion for interim judgment of the accrued sanctions in the amount of $43,700,000.[39] Since 2015, Chabad has taken steps in the US jurisdiction, to enforce the Court's sanctions order and

[35] Agudas Chasidei Chabad of U.S. v. Russian Fed'n (Chabad II). 729 F. Supp. 2d 141 (D.D.C. 2010).

[36] It provides in relevant part that: A. A foreign state shall not be immune from the jurisdiction of courts of the United States or of the States in any case- (3) in which rights in property taken in violation of international law are in issue and that property or any property exchanged for such property is present in the United States in connection with a commercial activity carried on in the United States by the foreign state; or that property or any property exchanged for such property is owned or operated by an agency or instrumentality of the foreign state and that agency or instrumentality is engaged in a commercial activity in the United States.

[37] Comment of the Russian Ministry of Foreign Affairs of 11.08.2010: 'This verdict is null and void from a legal point of view, represents gross violation of generally accepted norms and principles of international law, in particular the principle of jurisdictional immunity of states, according to which courts of one state cannot consider claims against other states and their property without the express consent of the latter'.

[38] Agudas Chasidei Chabad of U.S. v. Russian Fed'n (Chabad IV),915 F.Supp.2d 148 (D.D.C.2013).

[39] Agudas Chasidei Chabad of U.S. v. Russian Fed'n (Chabad II). 128 F.Supp.3d 242 (2015).

judgment and is seeking discovery about Russian assets from certain U.S. financial institutions via subpoena.

On July 1, 2013, the Ministry of Culture of the Russian Federation and the Russian State Library, on their side, filed a lawsuit with the Moscow Commercial Court, against the Library of Congress and the United States of America, demanding the return of seven books from the Schneerson library collection, loaned to the US in 1994, in the course of inter-library exchange for 60 days. The USA declined to participate in the court proceedings. Considering the claim, the court did not recognise the State immunity of the USA and its organs, since the dispute, according to the court, did not affect the sovereign functions of the United States; the inter-library exchange was qualified as an act jure gestionis. On May 29, 2014, a default judgment[40] was delivered by the Russian court, that ordered the Library of Congress and the USA to return the books received, and to pay USD 50,000 in fines for every day the seven books are not handed over.

Subsequently, the Russian Government decided to transfer the Schneerson library, which is regarded by Russia as part of its national cultural heritage, to the Jewish Museum and Tolerance Centre in Moscow.[41] Russian President, Vladimir Putin, stated in this regard, 'I hope that moving the Schneerson library to the Jewish Museum and Tolerance Centre will put an end to this problem once and for all'.[42]

This case has seriously affected US-Russia relations. All art loans, exchanges of exhibitions, most of the joint cultural projects between libraries and museums of both countries have stopped. There are serious and mutual concerns of potential seizure and subsequent forced sale of cultural objects. It would be hard to disagree here with the opinion of Irina Tarsis and Elizabeth Varner, that 'this stalemate demonstrates the challenge of attempting to resolve historical international disputes through national court systems. Perhaps it is time to return to diplomatic channels for resolving the standstill or to consider an alternative dispute resolution mechanism such as arbitration'.[43]

2.5.4 The Yukos Case

In 2002, the company, Yukos, directed by one of the richest Russian Oligarchs, Mikhail Khodorkovskiy, became the subject of a series of tax audits and proceedings and was subsequently found guilty of repeated tax fraud, in particular, for using an illegal tax-evasion scheme, involving the creation of sham companies. Uncompromising and hasty execution of tax debts, unanimously recognised by the Russian courts, resulted in the company's demise and bankruptcy.

[40] Case № A40-82596/13.

[41] https://www.jewish-museum.ru/en/libraries/schneerson-library/. Accessed 15 April 2021.

[42] https://ria.ru/20130613/943178957.html. Accessed 15 April 2021.

[43] Tarsis and Varner (2014).

The management and shareholders of Yukos company sued Russia, domestically and internationally, trying to convince judges and investment arbitrators that the company's assets were de facto expropriated, for political reasons and contrary to international law.

European Court of Human Rights

The ECtHR, in its very close 4-3 chamber judgment of 20 September, 2011, in the case *OAO Neftyanaya Kompaniya Yukos v Russia*[44] came to the conclusion that tax proceedings against the company were not politically motivated and that Yukos was not treated differently from other companies; the Court also confirmed large-scale tax evasion schemes used by the Yukos company and its obligation to pay taxes to the Russian budget. At the same time, the ECtHR found several violations of Article 1 of Protocol No 1 of the ECHR, including the unlawful imposition and calculation of penalties in a certain tax period and failure to strike a fair balance in enforcement proceedings. The ECtHR, by judgment of 31 July 2014, awarded to the former shareholders of Yukos company a just compensation in an unprecedented amount of EUR 1,866,104,634.[45]

The Russian Constitutional Court, in its judgment of 19 January 2017, N 1-P, subsequently blocked the execution of the 2014 ECtHR judgment[46] as being contrary to the Russian Constitution and public order. The main argument advanced by the Russian Constitutional Court was that the ECtHR failed to take into account the specific social and historical context in Russia at that time, did not pay attention to the fact that the former majority shareholders were those who organised illegal tax-evasion schemes, and in no way, could be reimbursed for that in any form. The Constitutional Court concluded that payment of compensation, in such a context, is impossible because it contradicts the constitutional principles of equality and justice in tax relations. In other words, this would constitute a legalisation of tax crimes which is unacceptable.

Investment Arbitration

On 18 July 2014, the tribunal in the three parallel *Yukos* arbitrations against Russia, brought under the Energy Charter Treaty, has rendered the largest ever awards in the history of international arbitration (totalling US$50.2 billion in damages).[47]

[44] OAO Neftyanaya Kompaniya Yukos v Russia Appl No 14902/04 (ECtHR, 20 September 2011).

[45] OAO Neftyanaya Kompaniya Yukos v Russia (Just Satisfaction) Appl No 14902/04 (ECtHR, 31 July 2014).

[46] Russian Constitutional Court, Judgment N 1-P of 19 January 2017.

[47] See Yukos Universal Ltd. v Russian Federation, PCA Case No. AA 227, UNCITRAL ad hoc arbitration, Final Award, 18 July 2014; Veteran Petroleum Ltd. v Russian Federation, PCA Case

This case raised many sensitive legal issues. Russia challenged the jurisdiction of the investment tribunal on several grounds. Firstly, the Energy Charter Treaty was not ratified by Russia and such ratification was required under the Russian Constitution in order to constitute valid consent for arbitration. Secondly, it stressed that the dispute was essentially an internal one between Russian businessmen (shareholders of Yukos) and the Russian state; it did not involve any foreign investors or foreign investments. Thirdly, the dispute concerned massive tax evasion, and other illegal activities of Yukos Company and its shareholders. Fourthly, the tax measures constituted the core of the Russian sovereign powers and were not covered by the Energy Charter Treaty.

The Russian government challenged these awards in the Dutch courts. On 20 April 2016, the District Court in The Hague set them aside, holding that the Tribunal could not have established jurisdiction, based on the provisional application of the Energy Charter Treaty. The Hague Court of Appeal, in judgment of 18 February 2020, rejected Russia's claims and quashed the judgment of the District court of 20 April 2016. The case is now pending in the Supreme Court of the Netherlands.

In the meantime, former Yukos shareholders initiated enforcement proceedings against Russia in the EU, US and other countries, where they applied for discovery, arrests and seizure of property allegedly belonging to Russia.[48] Russia continues to resist enforcement of the *Yukos* awards and actively uses arguments based on State immunity as well.

2.6 Assessment: Reciprocity Principle

Our analysis shows that the transition to a restrictive State immunity regime in Russia was influenced by several conflicting factors at the same time, both internally and externally. There were indications of the ongoing erosion of the old traditional state-centred approach to State immunity in Russia but it retained its dominance for a long time. In 2015, the situation finally changed. The explanatory note to the draft 2015 Law leaves little room for discussion about what factor was decisive. It clearly suggests that the new law was needed for counterbalancing relations with foreign states that disregard Russian State immunity on the basis of the reciprocity principle.[49]

No. AA 228, UNCITRAL ad hoc arbitration, Final Award, 18 July 2014; Hulley Enterprises Ltd. v Russian Federation, PCA Case No. AA 226, UNCITRAL ad hoc arbitration, Final Award, 18 July 2014.

[48] More information about judgments in Yukos case: https://jusmundi.com/en/document/decision/en-yukos-universal-limited-isle-of-man-v-the-russian-federation-judgment-of-the-hague-court-of-appeal-tuesday-18th-february-2020#decision_6812. Accessed 15 April 2021.

[49] It says, in particular, that Russia '*is forced* to waive its immunity' (emphasis added) and mentions two examples (commercial transactions and bilateral investment treaties); stresses that 'the number

The cumulative effect of foreign litigations against Russia, multiplied by serious tensions in relations with the West, in the context of the Ukrainian crisis of 2014, reached the highest political level in 2015. And if the NOGA and Sedelmayer cases were finally settled, and Russia decided not resort to any reciprocal measures against relevant states (at the end, there were persuasive legal grounds to honour these commercial debts and explicit waiver of the State immunity in relevant arbitration agreements), the Schneerson library and Yukos cases were completely different in this regard, since Russia never waived its State immunity and the issues raised in both cases were of vital public importance. The n on-recognition of State immunity in the latter cases was perceived by the Russian political elites as a direct assault on Russian sovereignty, its exclusive powers to regulate tax policy and preserve cultural heritage within its own territory, and as illegitimate, humiliating, and offensive actions against Russia, as subject of international law in general. It would also be true to say the ongoing erosion of the State immunity regime, on a global level, represented a threat to the essential interests of the Russian state.

In such circumstances, the reciprocity principle plays a special role. According to the theory of international law, 'as long as the international legal order lacks the centralised enforcement machinery and thus has to live with auto-determination and self-help, reciprocity will remain the principle leitmotiv, a constructive, mitigating and stabilising force, the importance of which can hardly be overestimated'.[50] The reciprocity argument in international relations and international law is often used to identify the problem, to show displeasure with unfriendly actions, demonstrate their unacceptable character and to provide a clear message to other states concerned that retribution may follow. It can serve as an effective deterrence, a chilling effect measure and inducement for diplomatic negotiations in order to avoid the negative consequences of reciprocation. As was pointed out by Shahrad Nasrolahi Fard, 'the tit-for-tat policy view of reciprocity in international law, where a State can be retaliated against or be punished if and when it has deviated from co-operation is essential for the international community'.[51]

The reciprocity principle is one of the core features of the Russian politics of international law. Russia has often and consistently applied this principle in relations with other States. We may find numerous examples of it, starting from international

---

of claims against the Russian Federation and its bodies in foreign courts is steadily increasing, while the consent of the Russian Federation, to participate in such court proceedings is not being sought'; suggests to limit jurisdictional immunities of foreign states, based on international law, legislation and case law of foreign countries and relies on the reciprocity principle, that allows the limiting of jurisdictional immunities of a foreign state accordingly ('in order to ensure the balance of jurisdictional immunity, granted to a foreign state in accordance with the laws of the Russian Federation and the jurisdictional immunity accorded to the Russian Federation in that foreign country').

[50] Simma (2000), pp. 29–30.

[51] Fard (2014), p. 279.

security and disarmament to economic sanctions,[52] visa issues, diplomatic staff and property controversies etc.[53]

Thus, resort to reciprocity, in the context of State immunity, is not surprising. Being unable to prevent lawsuits against it, in foreign courts and to preclude future enforcement measures regarding its state property by diplomatic means, Russia reserved the right to act reciprocally. Reciprocity serves as a legal ground to deny the benefits of jurisdictional immunities to defendant states that breach Russia's sovereign rights and to impose sanctions on them by way of retaliation. Such a model has already been tested in the mirror litigation concerning the Schneerson library against the US, and this example gives a good insight on how Russia can apply direct reciprocity in the future.

The reciprocity provision was considered by the Russian commentators as one of 'fundamental importance' and as 'providing a legal opportunity to, in a certain way, protect Russian property abroad from recovery, since it becomes disadvantageous for foreign states to limit the State immunity of Russia'.[54]

To sum up, the new 2015 Law was primarily needed as a defensive mechanism, to deter ongoing and potential attacks on Russian sovereignty and Russian property abroad and to act reciprocally.

3 Russian 2015 Law on State Immunity: An Overview

The 2015 Law is largely based on the provisions of the UNCSI. It proclaims general principle according to which, a foreign state enjoys State immunity in Russia, with the exceptions laid down in the law (art.1). It contains the same list of proceedings (art.7–13) in which State immunity cannot be invoked (commercial activity, labour disputes, participation in legal entities and other collective bodies, possession and use of property, tort disputes, protection of intellectual property, and disputes arising out of operation of ships); recognises three distinct kinds of State immunity – from adjudication, from provisional measures and from execution (art.2). There are three instances when a state would be deemed to have expressly consented to the exercise of jurisdiction by a Russian court (by international agreement, in a written agreement and by declaration before the court, or by a written communication); moreover, consent for adjudication does not mean automatic waiver of the other two kinds of

[52] One of such recent examples in context of sanctions against Russia is the 2018 Federal Law N 127-FZ 'On Measures of Reaction (Counteraction) to Unfriendly Actions of the United States of America and Other Foreign States'.

[53] For example, in December 2016 US expelled 35 Russian diplomats and shut down two Russian diplomatic estates in the US. Russia replied by order to America to cut the number of diplomatic staff it had in the country and had seized a dacha compound and warehouse used by US officials. https://www.independent.co.uk/news/world/europe/russia-us-property-seize-moscow-diplomats-expel-new-sanctions-putin-trump-kremlin-nato-a7864346.html. Accessed 15 April 2021.

[54] Bessonova (2016), p. 41.

State immunity, related to measures of constraint (art.5). The 2015 Law provides the same list of property that is immune in the context of measures of constraint, as mentioned in article 21 of the UNCSI. The procedural issues of State immunity are regulated by Civil and Commercial Procedural Codes respectively and are in accordance with the provisions of part V of the UNCSI.

From an international law perspective, the provisions of the 2015 Law mean that Russia has accepted State immunity exceptions enshrined in the UNCSI, recognised them as reflecting current international customary law, and amore or less balanced solution for competing interests in international law. This list of exceptions is perceived as exhaustive and not subject to broad/extensive interpretation.

Apart from common rules, there are several specific provisions in the Russian legislation that differ from UNCSI. The most important of them are the following.

Firstly, it is incorporation of the reciprocity principle, in article 4 of the 2015 Law, article 256.9 of the Commercial Procedure Code and article 417.9 of the Civil Procedure Code. It declares that jurisdictional immunities of a foreign state and its property can be limited reciprocally, if it is established that Russian State immunity is restricted in that foreign state. If such an issue arises in the course of proceedings, the court will need to compare the scope of jurisdictional immunities granted to Russia in a foreign state and the scope of jurisdictional immunities granted to a foreign state in Russia. The court dealing with a case may invite parties to submit their evidence on this legal issue and can likewise rely on the opinion of the Russian Ministry of Foreign Affairs, that is empowered to advise the court on this matter.

If it is established that reciprocity does not exist, the defendant state accords a lower level of jurisdictional immunities to Russia and less than the minimum standard under international customary law (enshrined in the UNCSI) and Russian law, it will lead to a reciprocal and proportionate denial of immunity. In other words, Russia can limit the State immunity of the defendant state, but not extend it above what is provided by the 2015 Law. However, in international treaty, the contracting parties can agree otherwise.

Secondly, Russian legislation follows a complex approach in the classification of 'commercial' nature of transactions; part 4 of article 7 of the 105 Law prescribes the Russian courts to consider the nature and purpose of transactions on a cumulative basis; the nature and purpose of transaction have equal meaning, neither is prioritised. It differs from provisions of article 2 (2) of the UNCSI, where the 'nature' test would generally have precedence. The scope of State immunity in commercial matters under Russian law can be more extensive and can cover transactions that have a commercial nature but are made exclusively for sovereign purposes (such as, for example, vaccine production and sales of contracts for public health purposes, or construction contracts for military purposes). This approach is less predictable than the one offered by the UNCSI; it favours the State's interests more but does not explain how to reconcile the nature and purpose tests if they result in a different outcome, whether factors of fairness and justice should also be considered. The Russian courts would need to develop some additional criteria for differentiation between the acts jure imperii and jure gestionis.

Thirdly, the 2015 Law contains a rather broad tort exception (art.11) that covers not only personal injuries and damage to property but also defamation claims. State immunity can be lifted if defamation took place on the territory of Russia (in whole or in part) and the injurer was present in Russia when such action occurred. In the context of modern technologies and internet, the proposed solution may raise many controversies. It would be hard to conceive a foreign state (or its officials) being involved in the defamation of a Russian person on the territory of Russia. The only apparently suitable case might concern diplomatic and consular activities of a foreign state; however, lex specialis rules, in regard of diplomatic and consular immunities under international law should apply in this situation, not Russian domestic law. Therefore, the reasons for extending this State immunity exception to defamation are not entirely clear.

Fourthly, the new State immunity regulation provides for an active role of the Ministry of Foreign Affairs in court proceedings against foreign states. It is empowered to prepare official opinion on the scope of jurisdictional immunities granted to Russia in a foreign state (article 4 of the 2015 Law), upon request of the court or on its own initiative advise the court, in particular, on the status of an entity involved in the case as a foreign state, on application of State immunity in relation to the dispute in question, the immunity regime of specific property of a foreign state located on the territory of Russia, the immunity regime in the context of provisional measures and execution of judgment, (article 256.8 of the Commercial Procedural Code, article 417.8 of the Civil Procedure Code), to assist in the service of documents to a foreign state (article 256.6 of the Commercial Procedure Code, 417.6 of the Civil Procedure Code). These procedural safeguards are aimed at objective, balanced and impartial resolution of disputes, especially in cases when a foreign state declines to participate in court proceedings and fails to present its detailed counter-arguments against the claim.

4 Post 2015 Developments

The adoption of the 2015 Law has been an important and symbolic step towards recognition of the restrictive State immunity rule. In this section, we assess the extent to which Russia has actually changed its approach to State immunity in both dimensions, internally and externally. We will look at the application of the 2015 Law by the Russian courts and official position of Russia vis-à-vis other subjects of international law.

4.1 Case Law Based on 2015 Law

After 2015, the number of cases against foreign states has increased both in commercial and general jurisdiction courts. The spectrum of disputes ranged from claims of unlawfulness of military operations to labor and civil disputes.

Overall assessment of case law demonstrates that Russian courts continued to follow a rather cautious approach, granting State immunity in all cases when the issue was connected with sovereign activities of foreign state,[55] precluding attempts to recover compensation for damage caused by Germany during World War II,[56] favouring pro-state immunity interpretation in labour disputes,[57] defamation claims,[58] with rare exceptions related to property,[59] and tort[60] disputes.

The courts set up a high standard for the waiver of immunity concerning arbitration agreements. In one of the cases concerning interpretation of arbitration clause in international investment treaty, courts explained that international law requires that consent to arbitration must be explicit, clear, and unambiguous. In case of doubt narrow interpretation in favour of a state should prevail.[61]

[55] The court dismissed claims against Azerbaijan concerning its allegedly unlawful military attack on Armenia (case N 66-6579/2020). The claim against the US about challenging visa cancellation also was dismissed based on State immunity (case 33-30996/2017). Courts granted State immunity to Austria and Belgium in disputes concerning refusal to grant citizenship (cases 33-6594/2016, 66-3326/2020, 33-32,835/2019).

[56] Case 66-1161/2020.

[57] In cases when foreign Embassies claimed immunity and were supported by written expert opinions of the Russian Ministry of Foreign Affairs, courts presumed that labour disputes related to sovereign activities of the defendant states and terminated proceedings. For example, in case 88-23984/2020 against the Embassy of Switzerland the court concluded that the employee was responsible for official functions, including translation and interpretation, preparation of both notes and letters, acceptance of documents, and was a member of the administrative and technical staff of the Embassy. Similar conclusion was reached by courts in a number of cases against the Embassy of France concerning termination of labour relations with the Department of the Trade and Investment Representation of the French Embassy in the Russian Federation (case 33-37980/2018 and others), the dismissal of a telephone operator of the Japanese Embassy (case 33-2981/2018), the dismissal of the Head of German School and Nursery of the German Embassy (case N 4г\10-622\2018), passport and visa officers in the Consular and Legal Department of the German Embassy (cases 33-10576/2018, N 33-10575/2018).

[58] The court terminated proceedings against Lithuania in case A40-165646/2016 concerning defamation as all actions took place on the territory of a foreign State.

[59] Courts lifted State immunity in case against the Embassy of Kazakhstan related to use of common property in the apartment complex (case N 5-АПГ19-12); the compensation of damages under lease contract against the Embassy of Kazakhstan (cases 66-568/2021, 66-7225/2020).

[60] The Appeals Court instructed the lower courts that dispute relating to damages resulting from the gas explosion in the apartment rented by the US Embassy could fall under tort exception to State immunity under the 2015 Law (case 66-1692/2020).

[61] Case A40-64831/2014. In this case the Kyrgyz Republic successfully challenged investment arbitration award based on provisions of the Investor Protection Convention of 28 March 1997.

So far, one of the most controversial issues[62] were legal consequences of the investment arbitration clause contained in the bilateral investment treaty for subsequent recognition enforcement proceedings. In the case *Tatneft v. Ukraine*[63] that dealt with enforcement of investment arbitration award of 100 mln USD against Ukraine in favor of the Russian company,[64] the central question was whether by entering into arbitration agreement Ukraine has automatically given its consent to jurisdiction of foreign courts in recognition and enforcement proceedings at the same time (the concept of 'implied waiver'). Opinions of judges were not unanimous in this regard. Finally, the Cassation commercial court ruled in June 2019 that Ukraine cannot use State immunity defense against recognition and enforcement of arbitral award.[65] However, in another case about recognition and enforcement of arbitration award against the Kyrgyz Republic the Moscow city commercial court[66] reached a different conclusion, denying recognition and enforcement using public policy and State immunity arguments. The latter decision seems more coherent with the Russian conservative State immunity approach and standards applicable to the waiver of State immunity. Owing to the lack of uniform case law on this matter, it is for the Supreme Court of Russia to clarify it and say a final word.

4.2 *Russian Official Position*

On the international arena, Russia remains an active protagonist of the strong State immunity regime. Russia is consistently stressing the importance of this rule in international law and international relations, and condemning other states for disregarding these basic rules.[67]

For example, paragraph 8 of the Joint Declaration of the Russian Federation and the People's Republic of China on the Promotion of International Law (25.06.2016) states that: 'The Russian Federation and the People's Republic of China assert that international obligations regarding immunity of States, their property and officials must be honoured by States at all times. Violations of these obligations are not in

[62] Vyalkov (2017).

[63] Case A40-67511/2017, A63-15521/2018.

[64] More information about this dispute https://www.italaw.com/cases/4736. Accessed 15 April 2021.

[65] Interestingly, in parallel proceeding in Ukrainian courts Russian State immunity was also denied when enforcing arbitration award under the same Ukraine-Russia BIT. See, Everest Estate LLC and others et al. v. The Russian Federation as represented by Ministry of Justice Case No 796/165/2018 (25 January 2019).

[66] Case A40-230382/18-143-922.

[67] See, for example, the comment by the Russian MFA Information and Press Department on the US passing the Justice Against Sponsors of Terrorism Act with extraterritorial jurisdiction. https://www.mid.ru/en/web/guest/kommentarii_predstavitelya/-/asset_publisher/MCZ7HQuMdqBY/content/id/247912. Accessed 15 April 2021.

conformity with the principle of sovereign equality of States and may contribute to the escalation of tensions'.

Recently, Russia has supported the UN Basic Principles on Sovereign Debt Restructuring Processes that, inter alia, also favours rather conservative and protective approach to sovereign immunity. Paragraph 6 of the Resolution adopted by the General Assembly on September 10, 2015 N.69/319 states that 'Sovereign immunity from jurisdiction and execution regarding sovereign debt restructurings is a right of States before foreign domestic courts and exceptions should be restrictively interpreted'.

In June 2016, the Russian Ministry of Foreign Affairs issued the Declaration on Jurisdictional Immunities of State Owned Cultural Property[68] in support of the Council of Europe initiative[69] that mentions, inter alia, that 'property of a State forming part of its cultural heritage or its archives or forming part of an exhibition of objects of scientific, cultural or historical interest, and not placed or intended to be placed on sale cannot be subject to any measure of constraint, such as attachment, arrest or execution, in another State'.

Thus, the existing case law under the 2015 Law and Russian official statements convincingly demonstrate that there was no radical departure from the previous position supporting a strong State immunity regime. At the same time, the increase of the number of cases against foreign states in the Russian courts and instances where sovereign immunity was lifted show that restrictive rule of State immunity is steadily taking root in Russia.

5 Immunity of Foreign State Officials

Just like in case of jurisdictional immunities of states and their property, Russia adheres to a strong regime of immunity of foreign state officials.[70] Perhaps, the best way to describe it would be to cite Roman Kolodkin, Special Rapporteur of the International Law Commission: 'it is difficult to talk of exceptions to immunity as having developed into a norm of customary international law, just as, however, it is impossible to assert definitively that there is a trend toward the establishment of such a norm'.[71]

Russian law subjects criminal liability of foreign officials to consent of the relevant state and provisions of international law.

---

[68] https://www.mid.ru/en/foreign_policy/legal_problems_of-international_cooperation/-/asset_publisher/HCN0yFLs7lFy/content/id/2302033. Accessed 15 April 2021.

[69] https://www.coe.int/en/web/cahdi/news-cahdi/-/asset_publisher/FL6bNvghtkKV/content/declaration-on-jurisdictional-immunities-of-state-owned-cultural-property?inheritRedirect=false. Accessed 15 April 2021.

[70] More about Russian position on immunity of state officials see Abashidze and Shatalova (2017).

[71] Kolodkin, Special Rapporteur, Second report on immunity of State officials from foreign criminal jurisdiction, UN Doc. A/CN.4/631, 10 June 2010, p. 56, para. 90.

According to article 11 of the Russian Criminal Code criminal liability of diplomatic representatives of foreign states and other citizens who enjoy immunity must be resolved in accordance with the norms of international law (in particular, 1961 Vienna Convention on Diplomatic Relations, 1963 Vienna Convention on Consular Relations), in case they commit a crime on the territory of Russia. In case a crime is committed abroad criminal liability is also determined by applicable international law rules (article 12 of the Russian Criminal Code).

The Plenum of the Supreme Court of Russia 'On Application of the Generally Recognized Principles and Norms of International Law and International Treaties of the Russian Federation' of 10.10.2003 N.5 explained in par. 7 that the range of persons who enjoy immunity includes, for example, heads of diplomatic missions, members of missions holding diplomatic rank, and members of their families, if the latter are not citizens of the host state. Other persons enjoying immunity include, in particular, heads of state, government, heads of foreign affairs of states, members of the staff of a diplomatic mission who carry out administrative and technical services to the mission, members of their families living with these persons, as well as other persons who enjoy immunity in accordance with the generally recognized principles and norms of international law and international treaties of the Russian Federation.

Another important provision is article 3 (2) of the Russian Code of Criminal Procedure according to which procedural actions against persons who enjoy immunity under universally recognized principles and norms of international law and Russian Federation treaties can be carried out only with the consent of a foreign State. Russian Ministry of Foreign Affairs advises the law enforcement agencies with regard to presence and scope of immunity of such person.

6 Conclusion

Our study confirms that Russia remains an active advocate of the strong state immunity regime. This approach reveals essential interests of the Russian politics of international law and secures underlying values such as the superior role of state sovereignty, diplomacy, international comity, and stability in international relations. However, the picture is not black and white, and values other than state-centrism, including respect of human rights and right to fair trial, also matter, however to a lesser degree.

Russia's example highlights the importance of reciprocity in formation and application of international customary law. This factor has been the main driving force of Russian transition to restrictive rule of State immunity. The need to balance relations with other states applying the restrictive immunity against Russia as well as to provide certain deterrence against the decline of the State immunity regime on the global level elucidate the introduction of the 2015 Law. In this context change of the Russian position is, perhaps is best to describe not in terms of voluntary acceptance of liberal rules on State immunity but by necessity and precaution.

The Russian trajectory of a weakening State immunity regime and reasons behind the recognition of restrictive doctrine allow us to make several observations for the future.

Firstly, the Russian jurisdiction is unlikely to become a major battlefield for disputes against foreign states, excluding reciprocal responses to lawsuits against Russia in foreign jurisdictions. Russian legislature contains many different safeguards securing a solid State immunity regime and the existing case law is receptive to arguments based on sovereignty (par in parem non habet jurisdictionem) and international comity. At the same time, a certain minimum level of protection against violations committed by foreign states on the territory of Russia will be granted, especially in the light of the Russian international obligations under the ECHR.

Secondly, diplomacy will continue to play an important role in the resolution of disputes with foreign sovereigns. Russian law envisages a special and active role of the Ministry of Foreign Affairs that should work closely with parties to a dispute and judicial authorities, mitigating potential negative effects of adversarial proceedings and supporting search for mutually acceptable solutions.

Thirdly, Russia's position with emphasis on reciprocity may further trigger the disintegration of international customary law on State immunity. Hypothetically, it may lead to the formation of a spectrum of different State immunity regimes, ranging from strong to weak ones. Applicable State immunity rules will not be uniform but will depend on reciprocal obligations of foreign states vis-a-vis Russia. In such a case it would be much harder to find a common denominator for a consistent state practice in the context of international customary law.

References

Abashidze A, Shatalova S (2017) International crimes exception to the immunity of state officials from foreign criminal jurisdiction: the Russian perspective on the work of the international law commission. Neth Int Law Rev 64(2):213–236

Bessonova AI (2016) Procedure for considering disputes with a foreign state in the Russian Federation. Arbitration and civil procedure 11:36–41 [Бессонова А И (2016) Порядок рассмотрения споров с участием иностранного государства в Российской Федерации // Арбитражный и гражданский процесс. N 11. С. 36–41]

Boguslavsky M (1979) Foreign State immunity: Soviet doctrine and practice. Netherlands Yearbook of International Law (Alphen aan den Rijn), vol X

Boguslavsky M (2000) Application of state immunity principle and problem of legislation regulation. In: Bogulavsky M, Svetlanov A (eds) International private law, TON-Ostozhie, Moscow [Практика применения принципа иммунитета государства и проблема законодательного регулирования in Международное частное право: современная практика. Сборник статей под ред. М М Богуславского и А Г Светланова (2000) М.: ТОН, Остожье]

Chernichenko O (2003) Thesis (Ph.D.), International law aspects of jurisdiction. Diplomatic Academy on the Russian MoFA, Moscow

Churilova N (2018) Thesis (Ph.D.), international legal grounds of jurisdictional immunity of the state. MGIMO University, Moscow

Demidov I (2005) Thesis (Ph.D.), state as subject of international law. Saratov State Academy of Law, Saratov

Fard SN (2014) Is reciprocity a foundation of international law or whether international law creates reciprocity?. Thesis (Ph.D.), Aberystwyth University. https://ethos.bl.uk/OrderDetails.do?uin=uk.bl.ethos.606508 Accessed 29 Mar 2021

Fox H, Webb P (2015) The law of state immunity, 3rd edn. OUP, Oxford

Gaididey J (2006) Thesis (Ph.D.), constitutional foundations of state immunity. Volgograd Academy of the Ministry of Interior, Volgograd

Khlestova I (2003) Thesis (Ph.D.), problems of the jurisdictional immunity of a foreign state. Institute of Legislation and Comparative Law under the Government of Russia, Moscow

Khlestova I (2005a) On Accession of Russia to the European Convention on State Immunity of 1972. J Russian Law (5) [Хлестова И О (2005) О присоединении России к Европейской конвенции об иммунитете государства 1972 г. Журнал российского права, № 4]

Khlestova I (2005b) UN Convention on jurisdictional immunities of states and their property. Int Commer Arbitr 4):13 [Хлестова И О (2005) Конвенция ООН о юрисдикционных иммунитетах государств и их собственности. Международный коммерческий арбитраж. № 4. С. 13]

Lebedeva M (2006) Thesis (Ph.D.), immunity of foreign state from provisional measures in private international law. Institute of Legislation and Comparative Law under the Government of Russia, Moscow

Malksoo L (2016) Russian approaches to international law. OUP, Oxford

Neshataeva T (1999) On jurisdictional immunities. Vestnik of the Supreme Commercial Court (9) [Нешатаева Т Н (1999) О судебных иммунитетах, Вестник ВАС РФ. № 9]

Neshataeva T (2001) International Civil Procedure. DELO, Moscow [Нешатаева Т Н Международный гражданский процесс. Дело, 2001]

Peters A (2015) Immune against constitutionalisation? In: Peters A et al (eds) Immunities in the age of global constitutionalism. Martinus Nijhoff, Leiden, pp 1–22

Roberts A (2016) Is international law international? Cambridge University Press, Cambridge

Shaykhutdinova G (1991) Thesis (Ph.D.), Jurisdictional immunity of state. Kazan University, Kazan

Shebanova N (2011) Thesis (Ph.D.), Russian property abroad: regulation and protection. Saint-Petersburg State University, Saint Petersburg

Silkina I (2007) Thesis (Ph.D.), contemporary issues of jurisdictional immunity of foreign state and its property. MGIMO University, Moscow

Simma B (2000) Reciprocity. In: Encyclopedia of public international law, vol 4. North-Holland, Amsterdam, pp 29–30

Tarsis I, Varner E (2014) Reviewing the Agudas Chasidei Chabad v. Russian Federation, et al. Dispute. ASIL Insights 18(8)

Tumanov E (2011) Thesis (Ph.D.), Recent Trends in development of State Immunity in private transborder relations. Russian State Humanitarian Institute, Moscow

Verdier P-H, Voeten E (2015) How does customary international law change? The case of state immunity. Int Stud Q 59(2):209–222

Vyalkov A (2017) Jurisdictional immunities of foreign states at the stage of recognition and enforcement of arbitral awards in Russia. Mezhdunarodnoe pravosudie 4:89–121

Wrange P (2012) Sedelmayer v Russian Federation. Am J Int Law 106(2):347–353

Yang X (2012) State immunity in international law. CUP, Cambridge

Vladislav Starzhenetskiy is an Associate Professor at the Chair of International Law, Faculty of Law of the National Research University Higher School of Economics. He also serves as an Academic Director of the Master Program 'Law of International Trade, Finance and Economic Integration' and researcher at the HSE Laboratory on Sanctions in International Law. The main fields of his research interests include jurisdictional immunities of states, economic sanctions, international protection of intellectual property, international civil procedure and international human rights law. He is a member of the Editorial Group of the Russian 'International Justice' Journal. Vladislav graduated from the Moscow State Institute of International Relations (MGIMO) with a degree in International Law. He received his PhD for the dissertation dedicated to comparative analysis of property rights under the ECHR and Russian law. From 1998 to 2014, he has been working at the Russian Federation's Supreme Commercial Court and was heading the Department of International Law and Cooperation from 2011 to 2014.

Too Hard-Won to be Wasted … Sovereignty, Immunities and Values: A (Sub-Saharan) African Perspective

Apollin Koagne Zouapet

Abstract The analysis of African practice on sovereign immunities is both absent in the work of international lawyers and made up of generalisations in the few works that do address it. On the one hand, probably because of the difficulty of accessing documentation on the practice of African states, few, if any, chapters are devoted to the African perspective in the numerous books on the subject. On the other hand, due to the high media coverage, African practice has sometimes been summarized in terms of the crisis between the African Union and the International Criminal Court. This chapter attempts to highlight the African perspective on sovereign immunities, highlighting the values, tensions and divergences that inform it. It reveals a much more mixed picture that is indicative of the dynamics running through the continent that impact efforts to define an African vision of international law.

1 Introduction

Quick bibliographical research on the issue of immunities and Africa leads to two observations. The first relates to the very little, if any, general studies on African immunity practice. The very many monographs and treatises devoted to the issue rarely have chapters focusing on African practice. While there are almost always chapters devoted to many Western countries (France, the United States, Great Britain Germany…) and sometimes now China, African States are relegated to a 'cosmetic' role, their practice and position being convened to confirm conclusions already drawn.[1] Here we are very often in the field par excellence of the 'Them too' approach, a practice that consists of international lawyers in using the principles and rules identified in the national legal orders of the West to seek their confirmation in the legal orders of the countries of the South. The approach is thus within a logic that

[1] See amongst others, Fox and Webb (2013); Orekhelashvili (2015); Peters et al. (2014); Reinisch (2010); Ruys and Angelet (2019); Verhoeven (2004).

A. Koagne Zouapet (✉)
Berlin-Potsdam Research Group 'International Rule of Law – Rise or Decline?', Berlin, Germany

R. Bismuth et al. (eds.), *Sovereign Immunity Under Pressure*,
https://doi.org/10.1007/978-3-030-87706-4_5

induces a selectivity of the materials that will be retained, only those confirming or reinforcing Western principles being highlighted, to the exclusion of those that contradict them.[2]

If the difficult access and low dissemination of the practice of African states partly explain this lack of consideration of African practice in the debate on immunities, they do not justify it. This 'ignorance' of Africa reveals the sign of a more serious pathology of international law, a 'legal ethnocentrism'[3] that continues to consider and maintain the West as the centre of proposal and formulation of universal norms, while other regions of the world are reduced to a role of validating or contesting proposals, without being able to formulate proposals themselves. This legal ethnocentrism is co-written by African authors who even when they have access to African materials conduct the analysis through the prism of Western practice. Thus, the rare court decisions and acts that are commented on are so under a Western-centric approach, the relevance and 'correctness' of the African judge's reasoning being assessed in relation to its conformity with the conclusions of his/her Western counterparts. No attempt is made to understand the position of African countries, but rather to show them the way to follow to be on the right side of history.[4]

This is particularly true, and this is the second observation, in the area where reference to Africa is abundant in studies on immunities in international law: the immunities of sitting leaders, especially before international criminal courts. Indeed, the crisis between African states and the African Union on the one hand, and the International Criminal Court and the United Nations Security Council on the other hand has defined the perception of the 'African perspective' on immunities. In the 'hero-villain trend' characteristic of the international criminal justice debate',[5] the African position was quickly judged 'scandalous',[6] without always taking the time to understand it. Here, the argument of values deemed essential and universal leads to the discrediting of any contestation or proposal that does not go along with what is considered to be the progress of international law. The feeling of cultural superiority and values that dominated the colonial period still seems to persist in the norm-making process of international law, despite the significant changes in international relations over the last 60 years.

In so doing, international law, or at least part of the discourse within it, perpetuates what African states and other states of the South were reproaching it for in the aftermath of their independence. Challenging a European-centred international law, Africans claimed both the existence of international law in pre-colonial Africa and the imperative for international law to take into account their aspirations and needs

---

[2] See Koagne Zouapet (2021), p. 22.

[3] According to Jouannet, liberal Western democracies have instilled in international law a 'certain legal ethnocentrism'. Jouannet (2008), p. 62.

[4] See for example Schlemmer (2011); Gericke (2014), pp. 2620–2622; Jenson (2013).

[5] Tladi (2015), p. 3.

[6] See Pellet (2019), p. 8.

from now on. Beyond the contestation of specific rules, African states did not question the existence of an international law that should govern their relations with other states, nor their submission to these rules. What they were contesting was the idea of a Eurocentric international law that did not take into account their specific requirements and needs, and reflected their specific interests.[7] Behind the discourse of these States, there was the underlying idea of a third world vision, if not specifically African, of what the international legal order should be.

It is in this latest perspective that the present contribution seeks to fit in. It will be a question of exposing and analysing the practice of Africa and African States not in relation to other regions of the world, but by trying to understand the legal reasoning followed, and above all the socio-political context that irrigates and conditions it. As I have written elsewhere, while it bodes well that international politics and international law should not be confused, the fact remains that one cannot deny the influence that social reality has on the orientation of the international system and in particular on the regime of immunities in international law.[8]

This study thus highlights the fact that immunity law in Africa remains deeply marked by an attachment to sovereignty and the representation that African countries make of it. Indeed, outside of states and the framework of Western academics, sovereignty, and the institutions that are perceived as attached to it, such as immunities, are still seen as necessary to preserve a freshly and hard-won independence. Independence and sovereignty, considered the supreme objective during the hard years of liberation and conquered sometimes at a heavy cost of blood and human life, are precious goods that must be kept intact and whole, and which cannot be renounced without betraying the memory of the martyrs sacrificed.[9] To this must be added the past instrumentalization of international law and the fear of alienation of decision-making power. Africans are aware of the vulnerability of their young states, and of the fact that their political independence is not sufficient to ensure their real independence from former colonial and other hegemonic powers of international society.[10] In Africa more than elsewhere, the tension highlighted in the title of this book is perfectly illustrated: immunities are at the centre of a process of searching for a delicate balance between various sometimes antagonistic interests, values that are sometimes difficult to reconcile, and the desire to be part of the project of building a truly international community.

The greatness and prestige of the State are then closely linked to the immunities of the State, other public entities and governments. Section 2 of this article will thus demonstrate that although African States have gradually adopted a functional conception of immunities in the economic field, they are more reluctant to adopt a restrictive approach to immunities when this relative immunity means subjecting sovereign entities to the rigours of forced execution. This reservation turns into

---

[7] See Okoye (1972), p. 178.

[8] Koagne Zouapet (2020), p. 43.

[9] Yakemtchouk (1972), p. 19.

[10] Yakemtchouk (1972), p. 19.

genuine resistance, even hostility when the waiver of immunities is perceived as jeopardising the very essence of hard-won sovereignty, i.e. the return to a disguised colonial yoke. Indeed, the link that some authors make between sovereign and State officials' immunities is part of the African perspective on immunities.[11] Perhaps because of the nature of political systems and the high degree of personalisation of power in some countries, leaders, and in particular the head of State, embody the sovereignty of the state itself. Whatever one's opinion on the appropriateness of such an approach in a regional legal order that enshrines democracy as a fundamental principle is,[12] one cannot have even a cursory view of the African perspective on immunities without addressing this aspect. Section 3 will therefore be devoted to the immunity of sitting officials in criminal matters.

A final methodological clarification must be made. In addition to the above-mentioned difficulty in having access to the material needed for such a study (case law, repertoire of practice, etc.), there is the danger of simplifying and generalising a plural and sometimes heterogeneous reality. If the study has chosen to focus on sub-Saharan Africa, it is notably because of the existence of groupings such as the Organisation for the Harmonisation of Business Law in Africa (OHADA), which leads to a certain unification of practices, and the practice in Eastern and Southern Africa of enriching common case law through mutual citations.[13] Despite all this, it remains, that the issue of immunities in Africa and sub-Saharan Africa is still fraught with tensions that reflect both the convergence of interests on certain points and the divergence of views on the values to be protected.

2 Renouncing Immunities While Preserving the 'Prestige' of the State in Economic Field

Initiated by few states, the rule of relative immunity would have been progressively enshrined by effect of reciprocity in customary international law in certain matters. It is generally accepted that the transition from absolute immunity to immunity reduced to acts of public authority took place from the 1920s onwards when the Belgian and Italian courts gradually called into question the absolute nature of State immunity. In 1952, the U.S. Department of State also announced its decision to

[11] See Crawford (2012), p. 487; Dyani-Mhango (2020), p. 332.

[12] See articles 3(g), 4(m) of the Constitutive Act of the African Union; African Charter on Democracy, Elections and Governance adopted on 30 January 2007.

[13] See for example Mazila v The Government of the Islamic Republic of Iran (A13/2015) Namibia High Court Main Division [NAHCMA] 24 (13 February 2015), paras. 17–18; Minister of Foreign Affairs v Michael Jenrich, Standard Chartered Bank Zimbabwe, Sheriff of Zimbabwe, Supreme Court of Zimbabwe [ZSC], 19 March 2018 & 31 October 2018, pp. 16–17; The International Committee of the Red Cross v Phyllis Sibanda, MunyamaNgangura, ZSC, 30 September 2003 & 13 January 2004, p. 6; Dube and Rabasha v American Embassy/Botusa, First instance judgment, case n° IC 897/2006, 30 October 2008, Botswana Industrial Court, para. 8.

change its immunity policy, arguing in what is commonly referred to as the 'Tate Letter' that this decision was due to the increasing involvement of governments in commercial activities.[14] Gradually this practice has become more widespread and the principle now seems to be generally accepted: immunity is not absolute and depends on the act or behaviour in question. The few existing treaties regulating immunities enshrine the principle. Thus, both the European Convention on State Immunity, signed in Basel on 16 May 1972, and the United Nations Convention on Jurisdictional Immunities of States and Their Property of 16 December 2004 declare immunity in principle, but with very many exceptions. The development of the practice of qualified immunity would be partly due to the explosion in the growth of international trade and investment, which has led to the recognition that there would be an unfair imbalance if private litigants were denied judicial recourse in situations where States and governments engage in commercial activities outside what might ordinarily be called official governmental functions.[15] The principle is therefore in the field of economic law of the emergence of a customary rule of immunity limited to acts of public authority, based on the distinction *jus imperii-jus gestionis.*

However, the assertion of the emergence of such a customary rule does not in any way mean that the practice is universal and that there is no opposition to the principle which is in the process of being consolidated.[16] It, therefore, remains interesting to examine African practice to establish either that it participates in the consolidation of the emerging rule or that it contests it in whole or in part, contributing to define the contours of the rule. The birth of the rule having generally preceded the accession of African States to international sovereignty, the latter, faced with the requirement to participate in international trade to ensure their development, have gradually accepted an exclusion of immunity from jurisdiction for 'commercial transactions'. This adherence to functional conception was also guided by a logic of reciprocity. Reluctant African states had to adopt the regime of relative immunities also because of the numerous proceedings they faced before foreign courts, especially Western ones, and the refusal of the latter to recognise immunity based on the *jus imperii-jus gestionis* criterion. However, this admission of the functional conception of immunities in the economic field remains very cautious and is accompanied by a strong attachment to immunity from execution, any forced execution appearing to be too prejudicial to the figure of the sovereign state.

[14] Letter from the Secretary of State, Jack B. Tate to the Attorney General dated 19 May 1952. See for a historical overview, Fox (2019), pp. 21–30.

[15] Alderton (2009), p. 702.

[16] See Koagne Zouapet (2020), pp. 89–140.

2.1 Exclusion of Immunity from Jurisdiction for 'Non-Sovereign Acts'

The transition from the doctrine of absolute immunity to that of relative immunity consisted in a complete redefinition of the rationale and scope of the principles on the basis of which a State could expect another State to recognise its immunity from jurisdiction. The maxim *par in parem non habet imperium* now applies not only because the State is a sovereign entity, but also and only if, in addition to this, the act complained of before the foreign court is an act of sovereignty.[17] This reversal of the presumption would be due to a significant change in the concept of sovereignty, as a result of the diversification of international actors and advances in international law, which has led many States to adapt and relativise immunity, limiting it to acts of sovereignty as opposed to acts of a private and commercial nature.[18] As noted earlier, this movement, which began in the mid-twentieth century, preceded the accession to independence of many Africans states, who hardly contributed directly to the emergence of the rule. However, African states do not seem to contest the rule whose customary nature they recognise. This is mainly the work of judges who apply the rule by reaffirming its customary nature. In the words of the Supreme Court of Zimbabwe: 'The doctrine of restrictive sovereign immunity has become accepted worldwide as a principle of customary international law. [...] Where therefore any sovereign state is sued in our courts for public governmental acts, it can successfully plead immunity. However, where a sovereign state is sued for private commercial activities it cannot successfully plead or raise the defence of sovereign immunity to avoid the fulfilment of its obligations'.[19]

To arrive at this conclusion, African judges, particularly from the common law tradition, construct their arguments in two stages. First, they recall the customary nature of the rule of relative immunity, often relying heavily on British case law and authors. These excerpts from the case-law of the former colonial power and authoritatively cited authors, without one always knowing the criteria for choosing these authors rather than others and the value of their writings, are used to demonstrate both the existence of the rule and its *raison d'être*.[20] Next, the judges emphasise the place of international customary law in their national legal order: 'Customary

[17] Chukwuemeke Okeke (2018), pp. 97–101.

[18] Koagne Zouapet (2020), p. 90.

[19] Minister of Foreign Affairs v Michael Jenrich et al., 2018, ZSC, p. 15. See also Eastern African Development Bank v Blueline Enterprises Limited, 2011, Tanzania Court of Appeal [TZCA] 1; Concorp International Ltd v East and Southern Africa Trade and Development Bank, 2013, Uganda Supreme Court [UGSC] 18; Dube and Dube and Rabasha v American Embassy/Botusa, First instance judgment, case n° IC 897/2006, 30 October 2008, Botswana Industrial Court, para. 10.

[20] The International Committee of the Red Cross v Phyllis Sibanda, Munyama Ngandura, SC 48/03, 2004, ZSC, pp. 3–5; Angola v Springbok Investments (Pty) Ltd, Application for review, MISCA n° 4/2002, 12 October 2003, Botswana High Court, para. 8.

international law need not to be incorporated into our law by or under an Act of Parliament. It is part of our law by virtue of it being customary international law'.[21]

In South Africa, these jurisprudential developments were translated into law in 1981 by the Foreign States Immunities Act (FSIA). Under Section 4(1) of the Act, immunity from jurisdiction does not apply in proceedings relating to commercial transactions entered into by the foreign state, or a contractual obligation of a foreign state to be performed wholly or partly in the Republic. With this recognition by African states of a functional approach to immunity from jurisdiction limited to acts of public authority, the main difficulty for the African judge is to determine which act is 'non-sovereign' or relates to 'commercial transactions'.

Indeed, while the theory of relative immunity seems to have broad support among states, in Africa and the rest of the world, the main difficulty lies in defining what is a sovereign act (*jure imperii*) and what is not (*jure gestionis*). What is the criterion for the distinction: should it be limited to the nature of the act or, on the contrary, should the objective pursued by the state be taken into consideration? The criterion for this distinction has been the subject of much debate and continues to divide national courts, without it being possible to identify a consensual practice.[22] In Zimbabwe, 'the courts distinguish *acta jure imperii* from *acta jure gestionis* by referring to the nature of the state transaction or the resultant legal relationships, and not to the motive or purpose of the State activity'.[23] Beyond the purpose pursued, what is decisive in the eyes of the Zimbabwean judge is that the act must be 'an act of a private law character such as a private citizen might have entered into'.[24] Relying on Zimbabwean case law, it is this criterion that is also used by the Kenyan judge.[25] This is also the solution adopted in South Africa by the FSIA, which states in Section 4 (3) that the test for what will constitute a commercial transaction is objective and based upon the nature of the transaction.[26]

Thus for the South African judge, as for his Zimbabwean and Kenyan counterparts, the assessment of whether an act is sovereign or not is made by isolating the disputed act from all the activity carried out by the State. If it is an act that can be performed by a private person, then it is considered not to be covered by immunity from jurisdiction. States which opt for this criterion, therefore, favour a greater restriction of the principle of immunity, since this criterion makes it possible to

---

[21] Minister of Foreign Affairs v Michael Jenrich et al., Supreme Court of Zimbabwe, p. 20, after quoting Section 326 of the Constitution. In the same vein, Angola v Springbok Investments (Pty) Ltd, Application for review, MISCA n° 4/2002, 12 October 2003, Botswana High Court, para. 7; *Inter-Science Research and Development Services* (Pty) Ltd *v* Republica Popular De *Mocambique* 1980 (2) SA 111.

[22] See Koagne Zouapet (2020), pp. 90–103.

[23] Backer Mc Cormac (PVT) Ltd v Government of Kenya, Zimbabwe High Court, ZLR 185 (1).

[24] The International Committee of the Red Cross v Phyllis Sibanda, Munyama Ngandura, SC 48/03, 2004, ZSC, p. 5.

[25] Edna S. Ouma v The Government of the Arab Republic of Egypt, civil case 160 of 2004, High Court of Kenya, 2009.

[26] Strydom (2019), p. 670.

distinguish between the various activities of the State and allows immunity to be confined solely to activities that are strictly carried out in the exercise of public authority. Conversely, consideration of the purpose of the act tends to broaden the scope of immunity, since any activity carried out by the State has as its purpose the common good, the general interest. If the disputed act could be exercised by a private individual but is part of a sovereign activity of the foreign State, the latter will be able to invoke its immunity.[27]

It is this second criterion, that of the objective pursued, which is retained by some African judges. Thus, the judge of the High Court of Namibia dismisses an action on the ground that the plaintiffs could not prove that they were in a business relationship with the Iranian Embassy in Windhoek. According to the judge's reasoning, only proof of the existence of a commercial relationship between the plaintiffs and the foreign embassy, or that the mosque (the subject of the dispute) was used for commercial purposes, or that the beneficiary of immunity had waived it, is such as to rule out the immunity enjoyed by the foreign State and its embassy.[28]

One of the areas where there seems to be a consensus, irrespective of the criterion used, is that of employment contracts. The South African FSIA (Section 5) specifies the scope of contractual employment relationships that are not covered by immunity: where the employment contract has been concluded in the State of the forum or is to be performed in whole or in part in the territory of that State; where the contract has been concluded by a national or resident of the State of the forum; or where the worker is not a national of the State not party to the dispute at the time the case is brought before the court. However, the judge of the host State does not have jurisdiction, when the contract of employment provides for the jurisdiction of another judge (Section 5(2)(a)). In this hypothesis, moreover, it is more a question of the effect of the autonomy of will of the contracting parties than of immunity of the foreign State. On the other hand, it is indeed immunity that prevents the court of the forum from receiving an action relating 'to the employment of the head of a diplomatic mission or any member of the diplomatic, administrative, technical or service staff of the mission or to the employment of the head of a consular post or any member of the consular, labour, trade, administrative, technical or service staff of the post' (Section 5(2)(b)).

Thus, in South Africa and as in other African countries, judges rule out immunities in disputes between diplomatic missions and foreign states and their employees who have not been assigned to sovereign tasks. As the Supreme Court of Zimbabwe explains, an employment contract 'clearly, is an act of a private law character such as a private citizen might have entered into.[29] In the same vein, in the *Bah v Libyan Embassy* case, the Botswana Industrial Court held that an action of legal suit arising out of breach of an employment contract and or the national

---

[27] Koagne Zouapet (2020), p. 92.

[28] Mazila v The Government of the Islamic Republic of Iran [2015], NAHCMD 24, paras. 19–23.

[29] The International Committee of the Red Cross v Phyllis Sibanda, Munyama Ngandura, SC 48/03, 2004, ZSC, p. 6.

Employment Act involves a private law transaction and is justiciable. There is, according to the Court, no reason why the foreign State or its embassy should be immune from a legal suit of this nature, if the applicant is not challenging a governmental act, but is 'merely' seeking compliance with the Employment Act.[30] In the case of *Dube Rabasha v American Embassy*, the Botswanan judge goes even further and insists on the nature of the protected rights and the universality of labour law values to which both Botswana and the defendant State are attached to justify the exclusion of immunity and jurisdiction. For the judge, when a State such as the United States decides to become a member of the International Labour Organization (ILO), it accepts the fundamental principles enshrined in the ILO Constitution and other important texts such as the 1944 Declaration of Philadelphia and therefore has an obligation to give effect to these principles, including in its embassies and consulates.[31] It is clear from the reasoning followed by the judge that the nature of the rights protected fully justifies and explains the evolution of the customary rule of immunity in labour relations.

This desire to protect the worker, traditionally regarded as the weaker party, and to provide him/her with a legal remedy against a particularly powerful employer, pushes even the most conservative African judges on the subject of immunities to admit the exception, including against international organizations. Thus, despite his/her usual caution and reluctance to accept exceptions to international immunities, the Cameroonian judge seems more inclined to admit applications relating to employment contracts. Without going so far as to assert the existence of a customary exception enshrined in international law, his/her strategy is to seek to 'find' in the attitude of the immunity beneficiary a tacit waiver of immunities. This activism translates into assimilation to the renunciation of any equivocal attitude on the part of the defendant benefiting from immunity. Thus, for example, the judge considered that by agreeing to defend itself before the labour inspector during the conciliation attempt, the Bank of Central African States (BEAC) tacitly waived the 'privilege of jurisdiction' it invokes.[32] Similarly, the waiver of immunity was deducted from the terms of termination of the contract: according to the judge, the holder of immunity had waived immunity by referring to the provisions of the Cameroonian labour code for the termination of the employment contract.[33] This is a questionable confusion between applicable law and waiver of immunity which can only be explained by the judge's desire to bring the dispute to his courtroom and not leave the employee without legal recourse.

[30] *Bah v Libyan Embassy,* Application to Industrial Court, case n° IC 956/2005, 28 November 2005, Botswana Industrial Court.

[31] Dube and Dube and Rabasha v American Embassy/Botusa, First instance judgment, case n° IC 897/2006, 30 October 2008, Botswana Industrial Court, para. 22.

[32] Tribunal de Grande Instance du Mfoundi (Cameroun), Ngolle Matouke c. BEAC, jugement social n°117 du 19 mars 2001.

[33] Tribunal de Grande Instance du Mfoundi (Cameroun), Kuidjeu GassamFélicité c. CICR, jugement social n°153 du 2 septembre 2002.

While this desire to protect employees without recourse to employers enjoying immunity initially justified the extension of the exclusion of immunities in respect of employment contracts to the regime applicable to international organizations,[34] the Zimbabwean Supreme Court reversed its earlier jurisprudence, emphasizing that the established exception for States does not apply to international organizations. The Court justifies this decision by the difference in the basis of State immunities and those granted to international organisations: if international organisations were required to comply with the laws of all member states in which they have to operate, this would make it impossible for them to exercise their 'universal mandate'. This leads the judge to enshrine absolute immunity for international organizations, including in labour disputes: 'The restriction that has been put on sovereign immunity cannot be extended to the immunity of international organisations, because the purpose of the immunity they enjoy has always been defined in terms of the nature and scope of their functions as described in the instruments by which they are established. The functional immunity of international organisations thus remains absolute'.[35]

2.2 A Desire to Preserve Immunity from Execution

The absence of immunity from jurisdiction does not necessarily imply the absence of immunity from execution. The distinction between the two phases of immunity is indicated by the autonomy of the waiver in each phase of the judicial proceedings. The fact that the State waives immunity from jurisdiction i.e. agrees to submit to the jurisdiction of the courts of another State or to participate in a judicial proceeding, does not imply that the State submits to enforcement measures. The regime of coercion is certainly one of the most difficult problems to solve, as coercive measures against a foreign State are considered to be more important infringements of sovereignty than submission to jurisdiction. When applied to enforcement measures, the purpose of immunity is not to deprive the State of the material means necessary for the performance of its functions. This may explain the cautiousness of codification efforts in what has been called the 'last bastion of immunities'.[36] This led the United Nations International Law Commission (ILC) to adopt a conciliatory position, which is reflected in Articles 18 and 19 of the UN Convention on Jurisdictional Immunities of States and their Property.

While in other parts of the world, some courts have been hostile to the idea of maintaining a broad scope of immunity from execution, arguing that the right to a

[34] The International Committee of the Red Cross v Phyllis Sibanda, Munyama Ngandura, SC 48/03, 2004, ZSC, p. 7.

[35] Minister of Foreign Affairs v Michael Jenrich et al., Supreme Court of Zimbabwe, p. 16.

[36] Hafner and Lange (2004), p. 68.

fair trial implies the right to execution,[37] African judges have generally taken the view that the exclusion of immunity should be very restrictive in order to respect the 'dignity' of the foreign state.[38] Even the South African FSIA which, as we have seen, largely enshrines relative immunity from jurisdiction, is more conservative on immunity from execution. Indeed, under Section 14 FSIA, even if the claim against a foreign state falls within the exceptions to the general immunity from jurisdiction, the property of foreign state remains immune from processes of enforcement by the South African courts as long as it does not concern state property used for commercial purposes. The most significant example of this attachment of African states to the immunity from execution is that of the OHADA space where, despite the stated desire to establish a framework granting judicial certainty to attract investors, the 'unseizability' of the property of public entities has been maintained despite criticism. On the other hand, the Fick decision handed down by the South African Constitutional Court will also be of interest because, by also mobilising the 'dignity' argument, it seems to be laying the foundations for a challenge to the quasi-absolute conception of immunity from execution which has hitherto seemed to prevail on the continent.

2.2.1 The 'Unseizability' of the Property of Public Entities in the OHADA Region

The principle is clearly stated in Article 30 §1 of the Uniform Act on the organisation of the simplified procedures of recovery and enforcement of the OHADA:[39] forced execution and conservatory measures do not apply to persons who benefit from immunity of execution. The only exception to this principle is the compensation of certain, liquid and payable debts. §3 of Article 30 specifies that only debts resulting from an acknowledgement by public persons of these debts or from a title having an enforceable character on the territory of the State where the said persons and companies are located can be considered as certain. For Cameroonian judges, Article 30 means that in the absence of voluntary enforcement, conservatory measures and enforcement measures as such are prohibited against the beneficiaries of immunity from execution, whatever the nature of the activity they carry out and whatever the use of the property subject to the enforcement measure.[40]

[37] See for a presentation and discussion of the diverging national jurisprudence on this issue, Koagne Zouapet (2020), pp. 118–123.

[38] See Angola v Springbok Investments (Pty) Ltd, 2003, Botswana High Court, para. 16.

[39] Parties to the Port Louis Treaty of 17 October 1993 on the Harmonisation of Business Law in Africa (revised on 17 October 2008 in Quebec, Canada) are currently: Benin, Burkina Faso, Cameroon, Central African Republic, Chad, Congo, Comoros, Democratic Republic of Congo, Gabon, Guinea, Guinea-Bissau, Mali, Niger, Senegal and Togo.

[40] See Tribunal de Grande Instance du Wouri (Cameroun), ordonnance du président sur requête n°0339, 13 novembre 1998, SNIF c. ONPC; Tribunal de Grande Instance de la Menoua

Refusing to follow those who urged it to interpret the Uniform Acts in a manner consistent with the preamble of the Constitutive Treaty, which aims to guarantee the legal security of economic activities, to promote their development and encourage investment,[41] the OHADA supranational court, Cour Commune de Justice et d'Arbitrage (CCJA), considered that a public company cannot, even by virtue of a national law, be subject to the same regime as private companies and therefore deprived of its immunity from execution. Such a measure to deprive a public company of its immunity from execution is, according to the Court, contrary to Article 30 above and inapplicable following Article 10 of the OHADA Treaty.[42] For the Court, the absolute nature of immunity from execution is not subject to any derogation outside the case mentioned by the Uniform Act, even if the national law subjects public companies to the rules of private law.[43] The only strategy to reduce the scope of Article 30 is for States to make the targeted entity lose its public nature, this public nature alone being sufficient to grant the entity immunity from execution.

CCJA has nevertheless excluded the benefit of immunity from execution for mixed economy companies owned in equal parts by private persons and the state.[44] The Court has thus partly responded to the criticism of certain authors that it has an overly rigorous or even rigid approach to the question of immunity, which is not in line with the general objective of OHADA. For these authors, if the protection granted to the State and its branches is understandable because of their public service mission, the protection granted to public industrial and commercial companies is less understandable as soon as those companies behave like private ones without being subject to the same rules. The immunity from execution of Article 30 has the disadvantage of instituting a 'right not to pay' which legal persons under public law, in particular public companies, use against their commercial partners even if the claim is indisputable.[45] This is all the more true as the only exception allowed, compensation, is subject to strict conditions. Compensation does not cover all categories of creditors, but only those who are both creditors and debtors of the same public person. Moreover, Article 30 § 3 specifies that the debt is certain if it is the subject of an acknowledgement of debt issued by the public debtor or is attested by an enforceable title.[46] It is therefore sufficient for the public debtor to contest the

(Cameroun), ordonnance présidentielle de référé n°12, 11 septembre 2000, Tonye Dieudonné c. Université de Dschang.

[41] See for example Kenfack Douajni (2002), p. 5.

[42] CCJA, arrêt n°043/2005 du 7 juillet 2005, Aziablevi Yovo et a. c. Société Togo Télecom.

[43] CCJA, 3ème chambre, arrêt n°024/2014 du 13 mars 2014, Koutouati A. Akakpo Danwodina et dix-huit autres c. Société Togo-Port dite Port autonome de Lomé.

[44] CCJA, Troisième chambre, Mbulu Museso c. La Société des Grands Hôtels du Congo S.A. et autres, pourvoi n°112/2016/PC du 30/05/2016, arrêt du 26 avril 2018.

[45] De Saba (2016), p. 260.

[46] According to Article 33 of the Uniform Act on Enforcement, the following are enforceable titles: court decisions bearing the executory formula and those which are enforceable on the original; foreign acts and court decisions as well as arbitration awards declared enforceable by a court decision, not subject to an appeal suspending enforcement, of the State in which this title is invoked;

debt or refuse to recognise it for the compensation not to take place. But this criticism seems to confuse effect and cause. As Sawadogo points out, the Court is applying the stated legal rule correctly. What is open to criticism is the provision itself, which is written in an absolutist style, making no distinction between public persons.[47] The CCJA judge has very little room for manoeuvre to attempt a revolution like that initiated by the South African judge.

2.2.2 The *Fick* Case: A South African Revolution for the Dignity of the Continent?

On 27 June 2013, the Constitutional Court of South Africa issued a groundbreaking ruling in many respects.[48] Against the tense political backdrop of a crisis between the Southern African Development Community Tribunal (SADC Tribunal) and Zimbabwe and a backlash against the Tribunal,[49] the South African Constitutional Court's decision raises important questions regarding the enforcement of international court decisions in South Africa. The Constitutional Court held that South Africa was obliged by its treaty obligations as a member of SADC to enforce the decision of the SADC Tribunal against Zimbabwe in South Africa domestic courts. The Court did so by 'developing' the common-law doctrine of enforcement of foreign judgments to include those of the SADC Tribunal. Secondly, the Court held that in this case Zimbabwe was not protected by the immunity from civil jurisdiction and execution usually accorded to foreign states by both international law and South African domestic law.

On this second point, which is the only one of interest for this study,[50] the Court's reasoning is bold, to say the least. After acknowledging that Zimbabwe enjoys immunity in principle in South Africa under the FSIA, it nevertheless asserts that this State has waived its immunity following Section 3 (1) FSIA. It reaches this conclusion by noting that both South Africa and Zimbabwe are obliged under Article

conciliation reports signed by the judge and the parties; notarial deeds bearing the executory formula; decisions to which the national law of each State party attaches the effects of a court decision.

[47] Sawadogo (2008).

[48] Government of the Republic of Zimbabwe v Fick and others, CCT 101/12, [2013] ZACC 22.

[49] The SADC Tribunal is an international jurisdiction established within the SADC framework to ensure adherence to, and proper interpretation of the provisions of, the SADC Treaty and subsidiary instruments, and adjudicates upon disputes referred to it. The decision of the Constitutional Court concerned the possibility of enforcing a decision of the SADC Tribunal against the Government of Zimbabwe in South Africa. The SADC Tribunal decision in issue was Mike Campbell (PvT) Limited and others v The Republic of Zimbabwe, which examined the legality of the policy of government expropriation of farms in Zimbabwe. See for an overview of this crisis and the backlash against the SADC Tribunal Alter et al. (2016); Obonye (2013); Scholtz and Ferreira (2011); Nathan (2013).

[50] For comments on the whole decision, see Woolaver (2015); Frimpong Oppong and Niro (2014); de Wet (2014).

32 of the SADC Tribunal Protocol to implement the decisions of the Tribunal and to take all necessary measures to do so. By accepting this obligation to enforce, Zimbabwe and the other SADC States have, according to the Braamfontein Court, waived their immunity from enforcement in any proceedings in another Member State relating to the enforcement of a Tribunal decision against them. However, the Court's reasoning is not convincing.

First, the judges confuse acceptance of the jurisdiction of an international tribunal with the waiver of immunity. The SADC Tribunal is exercising jurisdiction over Zimbabwe not because Zimbabwe has waived its immunity, but because it has consented to its jurisdiction. If a State not party to the Tribunal's Protocol were to be brought before the Tribunal, the Tribunal would refuse to adjudicate not because the State in question enjoys immunities, but because it has not consented to the Tribunal's jurisdiction. Secondly, the Court's inference that immunity has been waived is problematic. Indeed, even leaving aside the confusion noted above, it is difficult to conclude that Article 32 of the Protocol of the Tribunal constitutes a waiver of immunity. Waiver of immunity from execution cannot be presumed: it must be clear, express, and explicit. This is a requirement of customary international law that is also found in South African law, the FSIA. This law on which the judge relies further specifies in section 14 (1) that the foreign state's discretionary decision to waive its immunity from execution must be specific. Yet, as has been pointed out, 'if waiver is fixed to a once-off event such as the ratification of a multilateral treaty, it constitutes a waiver for all future incidents, which is irreconcilable with a foreign state's sovereign power to decide in each specific case what course of action to take'.[51]

Nevertheless, the decision of the Constitutional Court is particularly interesting since it offers interesting prospects for the enforcement of international arbitral awards. Should it be considered, following the Court judgment, that the States Parties to the Convention on the Settlement of Investment Disputes between States and Nationals of Other States (the ICSID Convention) have also waived their immunity and that an ICSID arbitral award against a State Party can be enforced in any other State Party?

Indeed, Article 32 of the SADC Tribunal Protocol was drafted in different terms from those found in the statutes of other international courts: it does not limit the binding nature of the decision and the obligation to enforce it to the State party to the dispute but extends it to all States parties to the Protocol.[52] It was rightly pointed out

---

[51] Strydom (2019), p. 683.

[52] 'Article 32: Enforcement and execution. 1. The law and rules of procedure for the registration of enforcement of foreign judgments in force in the territory of the State in which the judgment is to be enforced shall govern enforcement. 2. States and institutions of the Community shall take forthwith all measures necessary to ensure execution of decisions of the Tribunal. 3. Decisions of the Tribunal shall be binding upon the parties to the dispute in respect of that particular case and enforceable within the territories of the States concerned. Any failure by a State to comply with a decision of the Tribunal may be referred to the Tribunal by any party concerned. 5. If the Tribunal establishes the existence of such failure, it shall report its finding to the Summit for the latter to take appropriate

that this article is closer to Article 54 of the ICSID Convention, which provides that arbitral awards made under the Convention are binding on all States parties to the Convention.[53] Similar formulations can be found in Article III of the New York Convention on the Recognition and Enforcement of Foreign Arbitral Awards and Article 35 (1) of the UNCITRAL Model Law on International Commercial Arbitration.[54] If one follows the reasoning of the *Fick* case, one should conclude that by subscribing to this article, States have waived their immunity and therefore their contractor with an arbitral award could have it enforced in any other State Party without being subject to any immunity from execution.[55]

With specific regard to arbitral awards, case law and practice seem to be divided as regards the effect of the arbitration clause on immunity from execution. A review of the decisions indicates that national judges do not agree on the limit of the scope of immunity from jurisdiction and immunity from execution concerning arbitral awards. In the absence of a conventional clarification, the submission of the exequatur procedure to the rules of immunity from jurisdiction or execution depends on the appreciation of each national legal order or judge.[56] It is on the basis of values that the South African judge chooses to consider any waiver of immunity from jurisdiction as a waiver of immunity from execution.

Indeed, the Constitutional Court emphasises both the importance of access to justice and the rights that were protected by the SADC Tribunal decision. The Court believes it is necessary to recall that 'this application concerns the enforcement of the costs order granted by the Tribunal against Zimbabwe. The origin of that costs order is a dispute that implicates human rights and the rule of law, which are central to the treaty and our constitution. A constitutional matter does, therefore, arise here in relation to access to courts which is an element of the rule of law'.[57] It is therefore with regard to the value of the rights that the decision sought to protect that immunity from execution cannot be granted. The Court makes no secret of the balancing of interests which it has undertaken and which justifies its decision: 'An observance of the right of access to the courts would therefore be hollow if the costs order were not be enforced. To give practical expression to the enjoyment of the right, even in

action'. The new wording resulting from the amendment of the Protocol on 18 August 2014 is slightly different. Article 44, which in the new Protocol is devoted to the enforcement and execution of the Tribunals decisions, is formulated in slightly more restrictive terms.

[53] Article 54(1): Each Contracting State shall recognize an award rendered pursuant to this Convention as binding and enforce the pecuniary obligations imposed by that award within its territories as if it were a final judgment of a court in that State. A Contracting State with a federal constitution may enforce such an award in or through its federal courts and may provide that such courts shall treat the award as if it were a final judgment of the courts of a constituent state.

[54] Woolaver (2015), pp. 226–227.

[55] In the case of ICSID arbitration, Article 55 of the ICSID Convention states that 'Nothing in Article 54 shall be construed as derogating from the law in force in any Contracting State relating to immunity of that State or of any foreign State from execution'.

[56] See Koagne Zouapet (2020), pp. 202–204.

[57] Government of the Republic of Zimbabwe v Fick and others, para. 21.

relation to judgments or orders of the Tribunal, articles 32(1) and (2) of the Tribunal Protocol and section 34 of the Constitution must be interpreted to grant successful litigants access to our courts for the enforcement of orders, particularly those stemming from human rights or rule of violations provided for in treaties that bind South Africa'.[58]

In an activism of which it is now accustomed,[59] the Court not only sets up the Bill of Rights of the South African Constitution as a supreme norm imposing itself on foreign states, but also constitutes itself as the guardian of the rule of law in the SADC legal order, and even as an agent for the restoration of the dignity of the African continent. Indeed, right at the beginning of the decision, in the very first sentence, the Court regrets that 'For the right or wrong reasons, or a combination of both, Africa has come to be known particularly by the western world as the dark continent [sic], a continent which has little regard for human rights, the rule of law and good governance'.[60] Contrary to his/her colleagues who see in the maintenance of immunity from execution the means of preserving the 'dignity' of African countries and the Continent, the South African judge is convinced that it is, the exclusion of immunity from the 'the need to respect, protect and promote human rights, democracy and the rule of law' that will ensure the restoration of this dignity. The legal regime of immunities thus appears to be an indicator of the tensions around the values and interests that should guide the African approach to international law.

3 The Immunities of the Sitting Officials or the African Disagreement About the Values to be Protected

One of the dynamics that run through international immunity law today, giving rise to tensions, is undoubtedly that of reconciling the immunity regime with the imperative of protecting the human person. The access of individuals and private operators to international courts as well as the repression of serious violations of human rights, qualified as international law crimes, are indeed one of the characteristic features of a more anthropomorphic international law. This international law places human person and humanity at its hearts, and affirms the superiority of norms derived from these values over all others. This 'law of the international community', which transcends the classical law of coexistence and cooperation, is above all a law that seeks to promote certain essential aspects and interests of the 'international community' as a whole.[61] To achieve this, this 'new international law' introduces

[58] Ibid., para. 62.

[59] See on this judicial activism of the South African Constitutional Court and international law, Koagne Zouapet and Plagis (2019).

[60] Government of the Republic of Zimbabwe v Fick and others, para. 1.

[61] Koagne Zouapet (2020), p. 247.

new institutions such as universal jurisdiction or the Criminal Court, while promoting the restriction of the scope of immunities.

By opposing these new institutions and mechanisms, it is the universality of the system that the African Union (AU) seems to want to challenge.[62] The pan-African organisation, supported by many states on the continent, decries a system that does not take sufficient account of values that are just as essential in their eyes and that immunities preserve. Faced with the challenge of reconciling what appear to be conflicting interests, the AU opts for immunities because of their social utility. But this choice is far from unanimous and some African states, pushed by national judges, are making the opposite choice in the name of the fundamental importance of human rights and the fight against impunity. The battle over the immunities of incumbent leaders in criminal matters is thus the 'soul of international law'[63] in Africa.

3.1 *The AU's Choice: Immunities in the Name of Equality and Peace*

The African objection to an evolution of the legal regime of immunities in international criminal law was mainly based on the reminder of the purposes that this regime serves. It would be a tool to protect sovereignty and resist neo-imperialism which, under the guise of universal values, would lead to the undermining of equality between States. The first of this section will return to the argument developed, which insists on the important purposes that immunities serve. Second paragraph will then outline the efforts of the AU and African states to challenge this universality within the regional framework through the creation of an African criminal court.

3.1.1 The Attachment to Immunities for Their Social Functions: A Bulwark Against Imperialism and Instrument of Peace

The context of the crisis between the ICC and African states may provide a better understanding of the reasons for the AU's 'objection' to the evolution of the sovereign immunities regime in international law. As mentioned above, many African states see the violation of the immunities of their leaders, and in particular the Head of State, as a direct attack on the dignity of the state and its sovereignty. In many regimes, the Head of State continues to 'embody' national unity and personifies the state.[64] The protection of the Head of State and other state leaders is

[62] See Tladi (2009), pp. 62–64.

[63] Tladi (2009), p. 57.

[64] See for example article 5 (2) Constitution of Cameroon; article 54 Constitution of Côte d'Ivoire.

therefore both symbolic (a sacredness of those who embody sovereignty) and pragmatic (protecting them from pressure and allowing them to defend the country's sovereignty without fear).

The tension between African states and the ICC arose following the first extra-African referrals to the court for crimes committed in Africa. If until then the ICC's action on the Continent had always been at the initiative of African states, the decisions of the United Nations Security Council to refer the situation in Darfur for crimes committed since 1 July 2002,[65] and the crisis triggered in the Libyan Arab Jamahiriya on 15 February 2011[66] quickly aroused the ire of many African leaders. Following these referrals, arrest warrants were issued, in particular against Sudanese President Oumar Al-Bashir on 4 March 2009 for war crimes and crimes against humanity, then on 12 July 2010 for genocide; an arrest warrant was issued against the Libyan 'Guide' Muammar Gaddafi on 27 June 2011. To justify its opposition to the judgement of these heads of state, the AU argues values defended.

The first argument put forward is that of peace. The desire to preserve Al-Bashir's immunity is the result of a delicate balancing act between two interests to which African states are committed. The Assembly of Heads of State and Government, in its first resolution on the issue in 2009,[67] underlined this fact. On the one hand, the resolution 'reiterated the AU's unflinching commitment to combating impunity and promoting democracy, the rule of law and good governance throughout the entire Continent, in conformity with its constitutive Act'.[68] On the other hand, the Assembly cautioned that 'in view of the delicate nature of the peace process underway in the Sudan, the indictment of Al-Bashir could undermine the efforts aimed at facilitating the early resolution of the conflict in Darfur'.[69] This need to weigh up interests will be repeated repeatedly by the AU in the fifteen or so resolutions that will follow on the arrest warrants for Al-Bashir, Gaddafi and Kenyan president Uhuru Kenyatta. For African states, although the fight against impunity is an essential value to be defended, they believe that it remains subordinate to the higher value of maintaining and restoring peace.

In Maluwa's words, the 'AU's decision not to cooperate with the ICC on the Al-Bashir indictment should not be seen as a rejection of the universality of the norm against impunity, still less of the values that underlie it. In advocating for the withholding of cooperation with the ICC on the indictment and arrest warrant, the AU and the African States that support that position are not contesting the existence of the norm against impunity, but arguing that the competing norm of securing and

[65] Resolution 1593 (2005) / adopted by the Security Council at its 5158th meeting, on 31 March 2005, UN Doc. S/Res/1593 (2005).

[66] Resolution 1970 (2011) adopted by the Security Council at its 6491st meeting, on 26 February 2011, UN Doc. S/Res/ 1970 (2011).

[67] Assembly/AU/Dec.221 (XII), Decision on the application by the International Criminal Court (ICC) Prosecutor or the indictment of the President of the Republic of Sudan (3 February 2009).

[68] Ibid., para. 6.

[69] Ibid., para 2.

preserving peace should be given priority in the particular circumstances of the Darfur conflict'.[70] This is the argument that has also been put forward by South Africa to justify its desire to withdraw from the Rome Statute. The Minister of Justice explained to the Assembly of States Parties to the Rome Treaty that South Africa's withdrawal was justified by the country's inability to deal with regional peace and security matters as a result of the Rome Statute's removal of immunities for sitting heads of state.[71] Thus, the purpose of the withdrawal from the Rome Statute 'is not to do away with the prosecution of the perpetrators of international crimes, but to make provisions for the confirmation of immunities for certain people'.[72] The immunity of the sitting officials is therefore not defended as such but as a means of preventing a third actor from challenging peacemaking efforts.

The argument, which can be criticised, raises the delicate question of the relationship between justice and peace.[73] For the AU and some African states, a choice has been made in favour of peace, even if it means sacrificing justice. In the cases of Darfur and Libya, the AU's reluctance to see sitting leaders on trial was justified by assumed political considerations. The pan-African organisation believes, in good faith or out of an ethic of responsibility, that the insistence on justice in these two cases is an obstacle to peace, and that the determination to see justice done is, in these contexts, an impediment to peace and reconciliation between the parties to the conflict.

The second argument in support of the objection of African states to the evolution of the regime of immunities for sitting leaders is closely related to the rationale of immunities in international law: to ensure and preserve the equality of states. By reaffirming the maintenance of the immunities of African heads of state, including before the ICC when they are not parties to the Rome Statute while denouncing this judicial institution as a tool of neo-colonialism of the Western powers, the African states recalled that immunities make it possible to avoid that the objective of the fight against impunity results in the institutionalisation of a difference of treatment between states according to their power.

It has been pointed out that this reaction can be justified by disillusionment with the real role of an International Criminal Court, which many Africans hoped would be the vehicle and symbol of the advent of a new era of accountability for the leaders of the great powers, accused of being responsible for past crimes on the African continent. The ICC would thus have helped stem the tide of impunity that is allegedly responsible for many of the conflicts and major violations of international criminal law that have occurred, and continue to occur, on the Continent. As such,

[70] Maluwa (2019), p. 329.

[71] ICC ASP General Debate, opening statement by Adv Tshililo Michael Masutha, MP, Minister of Justice and Correctional Services, Republic of South Africa, Sixteenth session of the Assembly of State Parties of the International Criminal Court, New York, 4 – 14 December 2017, p. 3. See Dyani-Mihango (2020), p. 320.

[72] Dyani-Mihango (2020), p. 324.

[73] See the critical analysis of this position by Tladi (2009), pp. 67–69.

the rapid and widespread ratification of the Rome Statute by African states was based on this hope and also on the expectation of a new era marked by 'rigorous' compliance with the new rules of engagement in international criminal justice. The ICC was the beacon of this hope for the continent.[74] Africans seem to be hallucinating that the best legal instruments can suffer from variable geometry in their application.[75] It can be seen that the ICC carries out its mandate more easily on the territory of African states that are more inclined to cooperate with it, unlike other countries that are more reluctant to the intervention of an external institution. Moreover, there are fewer opportunities to clash with the interests of a great power on this continent.[76]

African states, and scholars who decry imperialism disguised as repression of serious crimes,[77] see it as a new 'civilising mission' of the West against African barbarians. Behind the rhetoric of protection of the human person and universal repression of serious crimes, there is still sometimes the underlying vision of 'western thought and western law as essential liberating and beneficial, capable of bringing about 'development' and well-being while overcoming oppression, discrimination and prejudice'.[78] This new paradigm makes it possible to distinguish between the 'good' state which 'controls its demonic proclivities by cleansing itself with, and internalizing human rights', and the 'evil' state which 'express itself through an illiberal, anti-democratic, or other authoritarian culture'.[79]

Thus, preserving the immunities of sitting officials even before international criminal courts is the only way to preserve the principles of sovereign equality of states and non-interference enshrined in the UN Charter. Indeed, for many African states, denying immunities to sitting leaders before international criminal courts would have exactly the same effect, given the reality of international politics, as allowing national courts to try sitting leaders. The decision on whether to prosecute, who to prosecute and when to prosecute, is a highly political decision that takes into account considerations other than the mere fight against impunity:

> international justice is a hotly contested 'political space' where the considerations that inform important decisions such as whom to prosecute and how to prosecute them may have very little to do with the ideals of transitional justice (with its focus on 'the reclamation of language and the rediscovery of victim's voices in post-conflict contexts) and more to do with the interests/motivations of the 'big powers' which often determine international outcomes.[80]

---

[74] Ngwaba (2015), p. 96.

[75] Kamto (2013), p. 147.

[76] See for analysis of the alleged loss of credibility by the ICC, Ssenyonjo (2017), pp. 758–762.

[77] See Obo and Ekpe (2014). For a criticism of these positions, Tladi (2009), pp. 65–67; Ssenyonjo (2017), pp. 770–773.

[78] Glenn (2014), p. 272. On regional approaches to international law and imperialism of 'universal values', see Koagne Zouapet (2021), pp. 27–33.

[79] Mutua (2001), p. 203.

[80] Ngwaba (2015), p. 97.

This would, in effect, allow some of the more powerful states to exert pressure on the leaders and policies of the Continent's weaker countries. Drawing the consequences of this reality, African states will launch a counterattack against the emergence of a customary norm that would enshrine the absence of immunity of the incumbent leader before international jurisdictions.

3.1.2 The Contested Objection to the Exclusion of Immunity in International Criminal Justice

On 27 June 2014, the Heads of State of the member countries of the African Union, meeting at the twenty-third ordinary session of the Organisation in Malabo, added a new line to the already tumultuous history of the continental jurisdiction in Africa.[81] An amendment to the Maputo Protocol on the Statute of the African Court of Justice and Human Rights gave life to the African Court of Justice and Human and Peoples' Rights (ACJHPR), which thus replaced the African Court of Justice and Human Rights (ACJHR) still in gestation. This reform occurring against the backdrop of the above-mentioned crisis between the AU, some African countries and the ICC has led to the mistaken belief that the creation of an African criminal court was a simple response to this crisis. While it cannot be denied that the crisis may have exacerbated the desire of African states to establish a regional criminal court, it is wrong to see this crisis as the starting point for African thinking on the creation of such a court in Africa. Long before and during the drafting of the African Charter on Human and Peoples' Rights, the idea of a regional court with jurisdiction over international crimes had already been raised, but was rejected by the committee of experts responsible for drafting the future Charter. They had considered such an initiative premature, particularly because the Convention against Apartheid provided for an international criminal jurisdiction and the United Nations was already working on the establishment of a jurisdiction competent to judge all crimes under international law.[82]

In any case, by initiating the process of developing a regional criminal law subsequent to, and even concomitant with, the friction with the ICC, African countries and the AU have suggested that the creation of an African regional court is a defiance of the ICC and a desire to protect the leaders of African countries who might be prosecuted by the Hague court. The divergence has focused on the immunities of sitting leaders before the international criminal courts. As early as 2013, the Assembly of Heads of State and Government and the AU affirmed that under customary international law, 'Heads of State and other senior state officials are

---

[81] The pan-African organisation seems to be looking for a jurisdictional model that it is far from having found. See Koagne Zouapet (2017).

[82] See Abass (2017).

granted immunities during their tenure of office'.[83] This immunity, according to African leaders, is not only limited to foreign jurisdictions but also to international jurisdictions. Therefore, 'no charges shall be commenced or continued before any International Court or Tribunal against any serving Head of or Government'.[84] This position was enshrined in the Malabo Protocol. According to Article 46Abis of the Statute of the future ACJHPR, 'No charges shall be commenced or continued before the Court against any serving AU Head of State or Government, or anybody acting or entitled to act in such capacity, or other senior state officials based on their functions, during their tenure of office'.

One may wonder about the scope and validity of such a provision, which seems to contradict the Rome Statute, in particular Article 27 (2), and an emerging rule of customary law. This call for few quick remarks. First, it makes no sense to assess the validity of Article 46Abis against the Rome Statute.[85] 'The Rome Statute is not a *primus inter pares* among treaties and cannot fetter the competence of its States Parties to deploy their consent in international law'.[86] Secondly, it is not demonstrated that Article 27 (2) of the Rome Statute, which excludes immunities before the ICC, is a codification of customary law. Responding generally to the question, the Trial Chamber of the International Criminal Tribunal for the former Yugoslavia (ICTY) considered that the Rome Statute could 'in many areas' be considered to reflect the *opinio juris* of a large number of States.[87] The Rome Statute itself emphasises that it is not a codification, at least in some of its provisions, of customary law. Articles 6, 7(1), and 8(2), for example, state that the definitions of the crime of genocide, crimes against humanity, and war crimes apply only 'for the purposes of the Statute'. Similarly, Article 10 provides that 'Nothing in this Part shall be interpreted as limiting or prejudicing in any way existing or developing rules of international law for purposes other than this Statute'. Of course, this does not alter the fact that the definitions in the Statute have a great influence on the development of customary international law. But it would still have to be shown that a specific provision reflects customary practice. Thirdly, even assuming that Article 27(2) of the Rome Statute is a codification of a customary rule, *quod non*, it is doubtful that it sets out a rule of *jus cogens* from which no derogation would be permitted within the meaning of Article 53 of the Vienna Convention on the Law of Treaties. States are always free to modify a possible international customary rule in relations between them, as long as it is not imperative.[88]

---

[83] Ext/Assembly/AU/Dec.1 (October 2013), Decision on the Africa's relationship with the ICC, para. 9.

[84] Ibid., para. 10(i).

[85] See for example Murungu asking whether extending jurisdiction of the African Court to cover criminal matters (along with article 46Abis) 'has a legal basis under the ICC Statute'. Murungu (2011), p. 1077.

[86] Abass (2017), p. 21.

[87] ICTY, Trial Chamber, Anto Furundzija, IT-95-17/1-T, 10 December 1998, para. 227.

[88] See on the possible customary value of Article 27 (2) of the ICC Statute, Koagne Zouapet (2020), pp. 334–341.

Finally, concerning the existence of an international customary norm excluding immunity before international criminal courts, one may have some doubts. The often-cited precedents (Statutes of the International Military Tribunals of Nuremberg and Tokyo, International Criminal Tribunals for the former Yugoslavia and for Rwanda amongst others) are not entirely convincing. The provisions referred to, in particular Articles 7 and 6 of the statutes of the Nuremberg and Tokyo IMTs respectively, which are often cited as normative precedents, did not relate to immunities but to individual criminal responsibility. They aimed at ruling out the imputation of the act of the organ to the State, which would have the effect of excluding individual responsibility of that organ, and expressed a refusal to take into account official functions as constituting a cause exonerating responsibility. However, the rules conferring immunities on a subject and those exempting it from responsibility are distinct. This is probably the reason why the two principles are set out in two separate paragraphs of Article 27 of the Rome Statute. In the case of the ICTR and ICTY, the exclusion of immunity stemmed less from the international nature of these courts than from the fact that they were created by the United Nations Security Council, which under the UN Charter had the power to waive immunities before these tribunals.[89]

It is true that there is no precedent, before the African one, for stipulating the immunity of incumbent leaders before an international criminal tribunal. Nevertheless, it would be incorrect to draw on that basis the conclusion of a customary norm of no immunity before an international criminal court.[90] Therefore, 'if customary international law neither requires nor precludes the immunity before international courts and tribunals, then as matter of law the AU is free to include or exclude immunities as a bar to prosecution as it deems fit. [. . .] the existence or not of immunities before international courts and tribunals is dependent not on rules of customary international law but rather on the constitutive instrument establishing the court or tribunal'.[91]

While one cannot ignore the general tendency of African states to be cautious about challenging the immunities of public entities,[92] one cannot ignore the fact that the position of the African Union remains contested within the Union itself by many states that have refused any mass denunciation of the ICC Statute. Amongst African Union member states, some, prompted by strong statements by national judges, remain committed to the Rome Statute and the current wording of its Article 27. The lack of real unanimity on this issue probably also explains the lack of enthusiasm observed so far for the ratification of the Malabo Protocol.

---

[89] Koagne Zouapet (2020), pp. 334–338.

[90] Tladi (2015), pp.1315.

[91] Tladi (2015), p. 15.

[92] See Sect. 2 above.

3.2 The Organisation of Resistance by National Jurisdictions: The Affirmation of the Pre-eminence of Human Rights and the Fight Against Impunity

The refusal of African States Parties to the Rome Statute to execute the arrest warrant issued by the ICC against Al-Bashir, based on the common position developed within the AU, has led to legal proceedings against them to assess the legality of their refusal. While the ICC's decisions reminding these states of their obligation to arrest and transfer a sitting president were foreseeable in light of the position the Court had previously defended,[93] it was the domestic proceedings against these states that highlighted the resistance of national judges to the AU's recommendations. National judges refused to subordinate the obligation of states to facilitate the repression of crimes under international law, in particular by arresting and transferring a sitting head of state to the ICC, to the obligation to respect the immunities that the head of state would enjoy under international law. Without denying this conflict of norms, national judges clearly indicate their preference for the repression of crimes under international law in the name of the imperative to protect the human person.

The approach of the South African Supreme Court of Appeal is illustrative of both the awareness of national judges of the shortcomings of international law on this issue and their willingness nevertheless to assert the superiority of the repression of crimes under international law over immunities. In reviewing the legality of the South African government's refusal to arrest Al Bashir and transfer him to the ICC, the Supreme Court of Appeal did not challenge the fact that Al Bashir enjoys immunities as a sitting head of state.[94] The Supreme Court of Appeal analyzed the Rome Statute and found that there is tension between articles 27 and 98.[95] Compelled to limit itself 'to assess the state of customary international law as it stands at the present time and apply it,'[96] the Court notes 'with regret' that there are no rules in customary international law which exclude the immunity of the head of state in office in the case of a violation of a norm of *jus cogens*, nor which enshrine such an

[93] See The Prosecutor v Omar Hassan Ahmad Al Bashir, ICC-02/05-01/09-139-Corr-Anx, Annex: Corrigendum to the Decision Pursuant to Article 87(7) of the Rome Statute on the Failure by the Republic of Malawi to Comply with the Cooperation Requests Issued by the Court with Respect to the Arrest and Surrender of Omar Hassan Ahmad Al Bashir, ICC, Pre-Trial Chamber I, 15 December 2011; The Prosecutor v Omar Hassan Ahmad Al Bashir, ICC-02/05-01/09-140, Decision pursuant to article 87(7) of the Rome Statute on the refusal of the Republic of Chad to comply with the cooperation requests issued by the Court with respect to the arrest and surrender of Omar Hassan Ahmad Al Bashir, ICC, Pre-Trial Chamber I, 15 December 2011; The Prosecutor v Omar Hassan Ahmad Al Bashir, ICC-02/05-01/09-302, Decision under article 87(7) of the Rome Statute on the non-compliance by South Africa with the request by the Court for the arrest and surrender of Omar Al-Bashir, ICC, Pre-Trial Chamber II, 6 July 2017.

[94] The Minister of Justice and Constitutional Development and Others v The Southern Africa Litigation Centre, case 867/15, Supreme Court of Appeal [SCA], 15 March 2016.

[95] Ibid., para. 40.

[96] Ibid., para. 73.

exclusion before foreign courts in the case of crimes under international law.[97] The Court also concludes that Article 27 (2) which excludes immunity before the ICC is only binding on States Parties to that Convention and cannot be applied to non-States Parties who have not consented to this rule. This leads the Court to concede that this 'provides justification for African states to refuse to arrest and surrender President Al Bashir, because he is entitled as the head of state of Sudan to immunity *ratione personae*'.[98]

However, refusing to accept what seems to it to be a failure, the Supreme Court of Appeal will seek ways to promote the law that would allow a now democratic state, which has long been an 'international pariah', 'to play a full role as an accepted member of the international community'. South Africa became 'an integral and accepted member of the community of Nations' by enacting the Implementation of the Rome Statute of the International Criminal Court Act 27 of 2002 (Implementation Act).[99] It is with this agenda of ensuring that South Africa remains an accepted member of the international community that the Court will conclude that by adopting the Implementation Act the country was admitting that no immunity, including that of a sitting foreign head of state, would constitute an obstacle to its cooperation with the ICC.[100] In the end, it does not matter that the paradoxical situation arises that the immunities of a foreign head of state are invocable and enforceable under the Rome Statute, but not under the South African national law that implements that treaty.[101] Assuming its activism for the noble purpose it serves, the Court recognizes 'that in doing so South Africa was taking a step that any nations have not yet taken. If that puts this country in the vanguard of attempts to prevent international crimes and, when they occur, cause the perpetrators to be prosecuted, that seems to me a matter for national pride rather than concern. It is wholly consistent with our commitment to human rights both at a national and an international level. And it does not undermine customary international law, which as a country we are entitled to depart from by statute as stated in s 232 of the Constitution. What is commendable is that it is a departure in a progressive direction'.[102]

The same logic was followed by the Court of Appeal of Nairobi which decides on the failure of the Kenyan Government to execute ICC warrants for the arrest of President Al Bashir.[103] In an even more problematic move in terms of international

[97] Ibid., para. 84.

[98] Ibid., paras. 59–60.

[99] Ibid., para. 63.

[100] Ibid., para. 103.

[101] Judge Ponnan in his separate opinion underlines this paradox. Minister of Justice and Constitutional Development and Others v The Southern Africa Litigation Centre, case 867/15, Supreme Court of Appeal [SCA], 15 March 2016, para. 122.

[102] Minister of Justice and Constitutional Development and Others v The Southern Africa Litigation Centre, case 867/15, Supreme Court of Appeal [SCA], 15 March 2016, para. 122.

[103] The Attorney General and others v The Kenya Section of International Commission of Jurists, civil appeal n° 105 of 2012 consolidated with criminal appeal n° 274 of 2011, Court of Appeal (Kenya), 16 February 2018.

law, the Kenyan court endorsed the position of the High Court, which had stated that 'the doctrine of universal motivation was a *jus cogens* obligation under international law and States were authorized to arrest and prosecute persons implicated in international crimes regardless of their nationality.[104] The Court of Appeal will then, without any demonstration other than the number of States parties to the Rome Statute that it has identified (98), assert that article 27(2) of the Rome Statute is a codification of customary law and is binding even on States not party to the Statute. Moreover, it points out, 'when a State engages in acts which are contrary to *jus cogens* norms, then by implication it waives any rights to immunity for stepping out the sphere of sovereignty'. The Court can, therefore, reject the position of the African Union that Kenya has put forward to justify its failure. All the more so since, like the South African judge, the Court of Appeal came to the view that, under the legal system of Kenya, there was no exception to the obligation of the State to cooperate with a request for assistance of the ICC and that the immunities otherwise enjoyed by President Al Bashir provided no exception to that rule.[105]

Whether it is the decision of the Supreme Court of Appeal of South Africa or the Nairobi Court of Appeal, the reasoning and conclusions followed by the judges are unquestionably flawed in their engagement with and application of international law. What makes them admirable, however, is the manifest will of the judges to act as a counterweight to political power and not to leave it to national executives and the AU alone to define the values that should guide the foreign legal policy of African states and the continent. For these national judges, it is a question of subjecting sovereignty to a value that seems greater to them: the dignity of the human being.

4 Conclusion

In an article published in 2011, Christian Tomuschat wrote that'colonialism is a word of the past. It does not afflict the contemporary world'.[106] This view that many Westerners have of colonisation as a relic of the past is not always shared by people in the South. For many populations and human groups around the world, the memory of colonisation and the role of international law in legitimising it is too vivid for them to believe without reservation the former colonial powers when they claim that they have changed and proclaim a new, more intrusive conception of law based on values presented as universal. The former colonised cannot reasonably be blamed for being distrustful and cautious with an international law that has sometimes been the tool of their enslavement and subjugation.[107]

[104]Ibid.

[105]Ibid.

[106]Tomuschat (2011), p. 221.

[107]Koagne Zouapet (2021), pp. 33–34.

The reluctance of African states to see the immunity regime evolve is explained on the one hand by the fear that the evolution of the immunity regime will result in a challenge to their sovereignty and serve as a Trojan horse for certain states to establish their domination. The battle over the immunity regime is also a fight to ensure that their voice counts on the international scene. As a tool to protect sovereignty, immunities are also the field of expression of sovereignty. The hard-won sovereignty enables African states and other 'weak' states, to have a real say in the process of developing international law, which they would lose if the law were 'deformalised' in the name of the universality of values. While committed to these values, African states and the African Union stress the difficulty of implementing them in an inherently unequal society. They are aware of the different power relations that make it difficult to implement idealistic principles: this is still a world in which 'one's chance of getting nabbed for committing a 'universal crime' varies with the inverse square of the distance from London to Brussels'.[108] In the absence of reciprocity in challenging sovereign immunities, at least in some areas, African states support the regime that preserves even illusory legal equality.

Less than an attachment to the immunities themselves, it is an attachment to what they represent that African states seem to defend. The challenge is to persuade them not only of the need for the desired change but above all that it meets the aspirations of all peoples, including the peoples of Africa. It is in this delicate and complex area that national judges in Africa are gradually investing themselves, sometimes awkwardly, often with cautious boldness, but always with great conviction.

References

Abass A (2017) Historical and political background to the Malabo protocol. In: Werle W, Vormbaum M (eds) The African criminal court. Asser Press, The Hague, pp 11–27

Alderton M (2009) Immunity for heads of state acting in their private capacity-Thor shipping A/S v. The 'AL DUHAIL'. Int Comp Law Q 58:702–711

Alter KJ, Gathii JT, Helfer LR (2016) Backlash against international courts in West, East and Southern Africa: causes and consequences. Eur J Int Law 27:293–328

Chukwuemeke Okeke E (2018) Jurisdictional immunities of states and international organizations. OUP, New York

Crawford J (2012) Brownlie's principles of public international law, 8th edn. OUP, Oxford

De Saba A (2016) La protection du créancier dans le droit uniforme de recouvrement des créances de l'OHADA. Thèse de doctorat en droit. Université de Paris I pantheon-Sorbonne

De Wet E (2014) The case of Government of the Republic of Zimbabwe v Louis Karel Fick: a first step towards developing a Doctrine on the status of international judgments within the domestic legal order. Potchefstroom Electr Law J 17:554–612

Dyani-Mihango N (2020) Reflecting on South Africa's attempt to withdraw from the Rome Statute in favour of immunities for sitting heads of state: an analysis of the international crimes Bill 2017. Afr J Int Comp Law 28:319–351

[108] Kennedy (2007), p. 642.

Fox H (2019) The restrictive rule of State immunity – the 1970s enactment and its contemporary status. In: Ruys T, Angelet N (eds) The Cambridge handbook of immunities and international law. CUP, Cambridge, pp 21–39
Fox H, Webb P (2013) The law of state immunity. OUP, Oxford
Frimpong Oppong R, Niro LC (2014) Enforcing judgments of international courts in national courts. J Int Disp Settlement 5:344–371
Gericke SB (2014) The interplay between international law and labour law in South Africa: piercing the diplomatic immunity veil. Potchefstroom Electr Law J 17:2601–2634
Glenn HP (2014) Legal traditions of the world, 5th edn. OUP, Oxford
Hafner G, Lange L (2004) La convention des Nations Unies sur les immunités juridictionnelles des États et de leurs biens. AFDI 50:45–76
Jenson LC (2013) The restrictive theory of sovereign immunity and the Chinese–African relationship. Transnatl Law Contemp Probs 22:563–598
Jouannet E (2008) What is the use of international law? International law as a twenty–first–century guardian of welfare. In: Ruiz Fabri H, Jouannet E, Tomkiewicz (eds) Select proceedings of the European Society of International Law volume I 2006. Hart, Oxford, pp 51–96
Kamto M (2013) L'affaire Al–Bashir' et les relations de l'Afrique avec la Cour pénale internationale. In: Kamga M, Mbengue MM (eds) Liber amicorum Raymond Ranjeva. L'Afrique et le droit international: variations sur l'organisation internationale. Pedone, Paris, pp 147–170
Kenfack Douajni G (2002) L'exécution forcée contre les personnes morales de droit public dans l'espace OHADA. RCArb 18:3–12
Kennedy D (2007) One, two, three, many legal orders: legal pluralism and the cosmopolitan dream. N Y Univ Rev Law Soc Change 31:641–659
Koagne Zouapet A (2017) L'Union Africaine à la recherche de son introuvable juridiction. In: Mvele G, Zang L (eds) L'Union Africaine quinze ans après, vol 1. L'Harmattan, Paris, pp 279–298
Koagne Zouapet A (2020) Les immunités dans l'ordre juridique international. Le prisme de la constance. Pedone, Paris
Koagne Zouapet A (2021) Regional approaches to international law (RAIL) rise or decline of international law? KFG working paper series n°46
Koagne Zouapet A, Plagis MA (2019) Braamfontein encroaching? An internationalist reading of the South African Constitutional Court judgment on the SADC Tribunal. South Afr J Human Rights 35:378–403
Maluwa T (2019) The contestation of value–based norms: confirmation or erosion of international law? In: Krieger H, Nolte G, Zimmermann A (eds) The international rule of law: rise or decline? OUP, Oxford, pp 311–334
Murungu CB (2011) Towards a criminal chamber in the African Court of justice and human rights. J Int Crim Just 9:1067–1088
Mutua M (2001) Savages, victims and saviors: the metaphor of human rights. Harv Int Law J 42:201–246
Nathan L (2013) The disbanding of the SADC tribunal: a cautionary tale. Human Rights Q 35:870–892
Ngwaba U (2015) The ICC, Africa and the travesty of international criminal justice. In: L'Afrique et le droit international penal. Pedone, Paris, pp 89–104
Obo UB, Ekpe D (2014) Africa and the international criminal court: a case of imperialism by another name. Int J Dev Sustain 3:2025–2036
Obonye J (2013) Neutering the SADC tribunal by blocking individuals' access to the tribunal. Int Human Rights Law Rev 2:294–321
Okoye FC (1972) International law and the New African States. Sweet & Maxwell, London
Orekhelashvili A (ed) (2015) Research handbook on Jurisdiction and immunities international law. Edward Elgar Publishing, Cheltenham/Northampton

Pellet A (2019) Values and power relations - the 'disillusionment' of international law? KFG working paper series n°34
Peters A, Lagrange E, Oeter S, Tomuschat C (eds) (2014) Immunities in the age of globalism. Brill Nijhoff, Leiden
Reinisch A (ed) (2010) Challenging acts of international organizations before national courts. OUP, Oxford
Ruys T, Angelet N (eds) (2019) and Ferro L (ass ed) The Cambridge handbook of immunities and international law. CUP, Cambridge
Sawadogo FM (2008) L'acte uniforme portant procédures simplifiées de recouvrement et voies d'exécution. In: Formation des juristesbéninois au droit OHADA, online
Schlemmer EE (2011) Tanzanian court of appeal, functional immunity and the east African development bank. South Afr Yearb Int Law 36:261–282
Scholtz W, Ferreira G (2011) Much Ado about nothing? The SADC tribunal's quest for the rule of law pursuant to regional integration. ZaöRV, 331–358
Ssenyonjo M (2017) African States failed withdrawal from the Rome Statute of the international criminal Court: from withdrawal notifications to constructive engagement. Int Crim Law Rev 17:749–802
Strydom H (2019) South African law on immunities. In: Bradley CA (ed) The Oxford handbook of comparative foreign relations law. OUP, Oxford, pp 666–684
Tladi D (2009) The African Union and the international criminal Court: the battle for the soul of international law. South Afr Yearb Int Law 31:57–69
Tladi D (2015) The immunity provision in the AU amendment protocol separating the (doctrinal) wheat from the (normative) Chaff. J Int Crim Just 13:3–17
Tomuschat C (2011) Asia and international law: common ground and regional diversity. Asian J Int Law 1:217–231
Verhoeven J (ed) (2004) Le droit international des immunités: contestation ouconsolidation ? Larcier, Bruxelles
Woolaver H (2015) Domestic enforcement of international Judicial decisions against foreign states in South Africa: government of the Republic of Zimbabwe Fick. CCR pp 217–244
Yakemtchouk R (1972) L'Afrique en droit international. LGDJ, Paris

Apollin Koagne Zouapet is a Postdoctoral Fellow at the Berlin-Potsdam Research Group 'International Rule of Law – Rise or Decline?' He holds a PhD in law (University of Geneva) and the Diploma of The Hague Academy of International Law. Before joining the Berlin Potsdam Research Group, he was a Judicial Fellow at the International Court of Justice, Visiting Fellow at the Max Planck Institute Luxembourg and Associate Researcher at the International Relations Institute of Cameroon (IRIC).

State Immunity Regimes in Latin America: A First Approximation to a Global Analysis

Facundo Pérez-Aznar

Abstract Latin American states have a long and rich tradition concerning jurisdictional immunities of states and their property. This chapter analyses how Latin American countries approach state immunity in their regional treaty law, legislation, practice and case-law. The analysis pays special attention to the attitude of these states to the provisions of the 2004 UN Convention on Jurisdictional Immunities of States and Their Property, the exceptions to state immunity that may exist, the evolution of relevant case-law, the different approaches concerning immunity from execution and also the role of the reciprocity principle. The article analyses how these traditions may have an impact on the emergence of new international customary law rules in this area.

1 Introduction

The issue of state immunity involving Latin American countries is often analysed when claims are initiated against countries from the region before the national courts of capital exporting countries. The causes of these claims can be varied. A cause that has important relevance nowadays is the issuance of sovereign bonds in order to obtain financial resources. Some of the contracts entered into for this purpose are subject to foreign legislation and jurisdiction and can contain a waiver of immunity from jurisdiction or execution.[1] On occasions, states have incurred default of payments and have proceeded to restructure their debt, deferring the payment of the bonds or proceeding to carry out an exchange. These situations have generated numerous claims involving state immunity before the local tribunals of capital exporting countries.

[1] On this issue, see González Napolitano and Lozza (2015), pp. 725–760.

F. Pérez-Aznar (✉)
Center for International Dispute Settlement, Geneva, Switzerland

University of Buenos Aires Law School, Buenos Aires, Argentina
e-mail: facundo.perez@graduateinstitute.ch

R. Bismuth et al. (eds.), *Sovereign Immunity Under Pressure*,
https://doi.org/10.1007/978-3-030-87706-4_6

One of the effects of the relevance of state immunity in capital exporting countries is that state immunity in Latin American countries and how they deal with it in their international practice, treaty law, local legislation, and before their national courts, is quite often forgotten. This chapter attempts to make a first global approximation of that issue and convers more than ten countries from the region.

Latin American states have a long and rich tradition concerning jurisdictional immunities of states and their property. The region was a pioneer in the regulation of state immunity through a plurilateral international agreement, and there are different treaties at the regional level that regulate, directly or indirectly, different aspects of state immunity. At the same time, there have been interesting attempts to codify rules on state immunity at the regional level. State practice, in the form of interventions before international conferences, international organizations or in the enactment of circular notes addressed to foreign states representatives, is also ample. In addition, some countries have enacted local legislation regulating certain aspects of state immunity.

The experience of Latin American countries with state immunity includes considerable case-law that goes back to the nineteenth century. Nowadays, the disputes that are aired before local courts in the region relating to state immunity are mainly labour claims between local nationals or residents that have a labour relationship with foreign countries or their diplomatic or consular representations (rather than states engaged in economic activities and transactions with private partners, as it happens in capital exporting countries). However, interesting disputes dealing with different aspects of state immunity can be identified.

The regulation and application of rules on state immunity in Latin America bring different issues. These issues include: the interaction between consular, diplomatic law and state immunity; the source and extension of exceptions to state immunity applied by national courts; the different approaches concerning immunity from execution; the role of the reciprocity principle and the interaction between state immunity and human rights; the attitude of countries with respect to the 2004 UN Convention and the impact of state practice and case law in the emergence of new international customary law rules in this area.

In order to adequately delimit this topic in this first evaluation, we will approach state immunity in the following manner: (i) in most cases, we will focus on publicly available judicial decisions, legislation and state practice, knowing that some countries from the region do not have all these resources online; (ii) in our analysis of case-law, we will only include cases related to state immunity brought before Latin American national courts, excluding, consequently, cases in which Latin American countries, or their diplomatic or consular representatives have been involved before foreign courts; (iii) we will focus on those decisions issued by the highest courts of justice of countries from the region, but not their lower courts, which in some cases can be very interesting for the topic under analysis; (iv) in general, the analysis in each country will begin with those judgments where a change towards relative immunity can be identified, without analysing the cases prior to these decisions.

The present work is divided as follows. First, it analyses the relevant treaties on state immunity for the region, focusing on those treaties concluded at the regional level and the work on state immunity carried out at the Organization of American States (OAS). Second, it explores the national legislation at the regional level dealing with state immunity and the practice of some countries of issuing of circular notes. Third, it deals with the development of case-law in the region and the move from absolute to relative immunity from jurisdiction. Fourth, it inquires how national courts deal with immunity from execution. Fifth, it scrutinises the position taken by national courts as regards the UN Convention, the principle of reciprocity and the interaction between immunity and human rights. Finally, it ends with some concluding remarks.

2 Relevant Treaties on State Immunity for Latin America

The first relevant treaty on state immunity for the region is the 2004 United Nations Convention on Jurisdictional Immunities of States and Their Property (UN Convention) and the works before the International Law Commission (ILC) of the United Nations, which derived in that treaty. Latin American countries have actively participated in the work of the ILC on state immunity from a very early period.[2] During the adoption of the Convention by the General Assembly in 2004, the representative of Brazil, speaking on behalf of the state members of the Rio Group,[3] expressed satisfaction about the completion of the work, welcomed the preamble of the Convention's statement that the jurisdictional immunities of states and their property were generally accepted as a principle of customary international law and expressed their conviction that such an instrument would enhance the rule of law, legal certainty and the harmonization of practice in that area.[4] However, only Mexico and Paraguay from the region signed the Convention during the period opened for signature (from 17 January 2005 until 17 January 2007) and only Mexico

[2] See, for example, the information and comments received in 1981, included in the document A/CN.4/343 of 14 April 1981 (including Brazil replies to the questionnaire sent by the ILC). https://legal.un.org/ilc/documentation/english/a_cn4_343.pdf. Accessed 15 April 2021. See also document A/CN.4/343/Add.2 of 16 April 1981 (including materials submitted by Argentina, Chile and Colombia). https://legal.un.org/ilc/documentation/english/a_cn4_343_add2.pdf. Accessed 15 April 2021. The comments and observations on the draft articles received in 1988 were reproduced in YILC, 1988–II–1 (including those of Brazil, Chile, Mexico and Venezuela from Latin America). https://legal.un.org/ilc/documentation/english/a_cn4_410.pdf. Accessed 15 April 2021. From these comments of Latin American countries, it can be seen a strict position concerning absolute immunity from jurisdiction.

[3] The Rio Group included Argentina, Brazil, Bolivia, Chile, Colombia, Costa Rica, Dominican Republic, Ecuador, El Salvador, Guatemala, Guyana, Honduras, Mexico, Nicaragua, Panama, Paraguay, Peru, Uruguay and Venezuela.

[4] See Summary record of the 13th meeting: 6th Committee, held at Headquarters, New York, on Monday, 25 October 2004, General Assembly, 59th session, document A/C.6/59/SR.13, p 7. https://digitallibrary.un.org/record/544568. Accessed 15 April 2021.

has ratified it, in 2015.[5] As we will see later on, besides the lack of ratification, national courts from different countries in the region have quite often referred to the UN Convention.

Apart from the UN Convention, there are different treaties at the regional level that regulate, directly or indirectly, diverse aspects of state immunity.

The Bustamante Code, adopted at the Sixth Inter-American Conference at Havana in 1928 includes some provisions on state immunity (Articles 333 to 339) applicable to those countries that have ratified it (Bahamas, Bolivia, Brazil, Chile, Costa Rica, Cuba, Dominican Republic, Ecuador, El Salvador, Guatemala, Haiti, Honduras, Nicaragua, Panama, Peru and Venezuela).[6] The Code provides that national courts of a contracting state shall be incompetent in cases against another contracting state, with the following exceptions: in cases of express submissions or counterclaims,[7] in real or mixed actions where the foreign contracting state has acted as an individual or private person[8] and in universal proceedings (*juicios universales*, e.g. distribution of a bankrupt's or decedent's effects).[9] The Code further provides that national courts shall not adopt coercive or other measures which have to be executed within the diplomatic or consular premises or their archives or correspondence, without the consent of the state.[10] Xiadong Yang notes that, given the adherence to it by the American countries, the Code can be regarded as reflective of generally accepted exceptions to immunity at that time.[11] The Bustamante Code adheres to the absolute immunity from jurisdiction with limited exceptions and

---

[5]See United Nations Treaty Collection, Privileges and Immunities, Diplomatic and Consular Relations, etc. Chapter III (2004). https://treaties.un.org/Pages/ViewDetails.aspx?src=IND&mtdsg_no=III-13&chapter=3&clang=_en. Accessed 15 April 2021.

[6]Bustamante Code: Convention on Private International Law (Habana, 20 February 1928) 86 LNTS 111 (English text on p. 246). The Convention entered into force on 25 November 1928. Information on the treaty and ratifications: http://www.oas.org/es/sla/ddi/tratados_multilaterales_interamericanos_A-31_Codigo_Bustamente_firmas.asp. Accessed 15 April 2021.

[7]Article 333 of the Bustamante Code provides: 'The judges and courts of each contracting State shall be incompetent to take cognizance of civil or commercial cases to which the other contracting States or their heads are defendant parties, if the action is a personal one, except in case of express submission or of counterclaims'. Article 334 provides: 'In the same case and with the same exception, they shall be incompetent when real actions are exercised, if the contracting State or its head has acted on the case as such and in its public character, when the provisions of the last paragraph of Article 318 shall be applied'. Article 318, last paragraph, provides, '[t]he submission in real or mixed actions involving real property shall not be possible if the law where the property is situated forbids it'. (The Bustamante Code, 1928).

[8]Article 335 of the Bustamante Code provides: 'If the foreign contracting State or its head has acted as an individual or private person, the judges or courts shall be competent to take cognizance of the cases where real or mixed actions are brought, if such competence belongs to them in respect to foreign individuals in conformity with this Code'.

[9]Article 336 of the Bustamante Code provides: '[t]he rule of the preceding article shall be applicable to universal causes (juicios universales, e.g., distribution of a bankrupt's or decedent's effects), whatever the character in which the contracting foreign State or its head intervenes in them'.

[10]Bustamante Code, Article 339.

[11]Yang (2012), p. 445.

absolute immunity of execution. The main criteria for exceptions to immunity from jurisdiction is when the contracting state acts as an individual or private person.[12] It has been quite common for local courts of the contracting states to refer to the Bustamante Code, however, references to the Code by the highest courts of Latin American countries in the last 30 years are rather limited.

Another relevant treaty on state immunity for the region is the international commercial navigation treaty signed by Argentina, Bolivia, Brazil, Chile, Colombia, Paraguay, Peru and Uruguay at Montevideo on 19 March 1940.[13] The treaty recognises, in Article 35, the immunity of 'men-of-war, yachts, airplanes, hospital, coast guard, police, sanitation, supply, public-works vessels, and other vessels which are the property of the state, or operated by it, and which are employed, at the time when the claim arises, in some public service outside the field of commerce'.

Finally, the 1984 Inter-American Convention on Personality and Capacity of Juridical Persons in Private International Law provides in Article 7 that each state party and the other juridical persons organized under the public law of such state shall enjoy the status of a private juridical person 'without prejudice to their invoking immunity from jurisdiction, where appropriate'.[14]

As can be seen, these treaties signed at the regional level regulate, directly or indirectly, different aspects of state immunity. However, they are applicable only to those countries that are bound by them. This produced the issue that state immunity in the region remains largely ruled by general international law. Notwithstanding this, these treaties have had an impact in the regional development of state immunity.

3 The Attempts of Codification at the Organization of American States

During the last 50 years the issue of state immunity has been dealt by the OAS, in particular the Inter-American Juridical Committee (IAJC) in different periods.

The IAJC in its regular session of 1971 undertook a study of the immunity of states from jurisdiction. In subsequent years the IAJC produced different studies and

[12] Romero (2010), p. 240.

[13] Treaty on International Commercial Navigation Law, signed at Montevideo, 19 March 1940, 37 AJIL (1943), Supp., p. 109 (emphasis added). This treaty was ratified only by Argentina and Paraguay. Information on the treaty: http://www.oas.org/juridico/spanish/firmas/f–13.html. Accessed 15 April 2021.

[14] Inter–American Convention on Personality and Capacity of Juridical Persons in Private International Law, adopted at La Paz, Bolivia on 25 May 1984 and entered into for on 9 August 1992 (emphasis added). The convention was ratified by Brazil, Guatemala, Mexico and Nicaragua. See http://www.oas.org/juridico/english/treaties/b–49.html. Accessed 15 April 2021.

reports on the topic. In the regular session of 1983, the IAJC approved the Draft Inter-American Convention on Immunity from the Jurisdiction of States.[15]

The 1983 Draft Convention adheres to the theory of restrictive immunity from jurisdiction and absolute immunity of execution. Chapter I includes the general provisions. Article 1 provides that a state enjoys immunity from the jurisdiction of any other state. Article 2 defines what is understood as state for the purposes of the Convention. Article 3 provides that the state will enjoy immunity from jurisdiction by the acts that it enhances in the exercise of its state power. Notwithstanding that general rule, Article 4 provides that the states may be brought before the jurisdictional bodies of another state in the cases contemplated in the Convention. Chapter II deals with the exceptions to the immunity from jurisdiction. The states will not invoke immunity from jurisdiction with respect to claims that refer to trade or commercial activities that have been carried out in the territory of the state of the forum, understood as the performance of a particular transaction or commercial or trading act pursuant to the ordinary trade operations (Article 5). In addition, states shall not invoke jurisdictional immunity either in labour matters, in universal proceedings, in actions involving real property located in the state of the forum, in tax matters related to commercial activities, in cases of tort liabilities related to commercial activities, and in issues related to court costs (Article 6). On the other hand, the jurisdictional bodies of a state shall exercise jurisdiction over another, when the latter state: (a) initiates proceedings before them, (b) responds to a claim or intervenes in the process or (c) submits a counterclaim (Article 7).

Chapter III of the 1983 Draft Convention includes different, procedural rules. Among them, it provides that in order to notify a foreign state of a claim, the competent jurisdictional body of the forum state shall send letters rogatory to the respective jurisdictional body of the foreign state, through the Ministry of Foreign Affairs of the forum state (Article 9). As regards immunity from execution, it is provided that the final judgments rendered within the framework of the Convention will be executed in the foreign state that has intervened in the proceedings (Article 14) and that the foreign state shall always enjoy immunity with respect to acts of execution or preventive measures, unless it expressly waives immunity (Article 15). In the end, the 1983 Draft Convention did not become a treaty and the works on state immunity at the IAJC were interrupted for almost two decades.

In its session of 2012, the member of the IAJC from the US, Mr. David P. Stewart, proposed to the plenary of that body to work on an instrument on the immunity of states in transnational litigation. The plenary accepted the proposal and appointed Mr. Carlos Mata Prates as rapporteur to work on that particular topic. A questionnaire on the situation of state immunity was sent to the member states of

[15] OAS Draft (1983) The Inter–American Judicial Committee of the Organization of American States, Inter–American Draft Convention on Jurisdictional Immunity of States, approved on 21 January 1983, 22 ILM 292.

OAS and the issue was discussed in subsequent sessions, based on three reports submitted by the rapporteur.[16]

The report prepared by the special rapporteur in 2017 includes a brief analysis of the responses to the questionnaire submitted by states.[17] It is noted that only 12 states sent responses to the questionnaire.[18] Regarding the existence of national legislation on state immunity, it is stated that eight states answered that they do not have legislation of this nature, while three stated that they do have national regulations on the subject and in some cases a detailed law on the matter.[19] As for the body in charge of deciding on immunity from jurisdiction in a case brought to a resolution, it is stated that this is mostly done through the judicial system. Regarding the scope of immunity from jurisdiction of the states, it is stated that all the answers coincide in its restricted scope in accordance with the type of activities carried out.

During the discussions in the ordinary session of the IAJC of 2017, the special rapporteur expressed doubts about continuing the report, considering that it did not have sufficient answers to have a global vision of the practice of the countries in the Americas and that no new rules were required in the current state of affairs, in the light of the existing conventions and customary norms.[20] The IAJC however continued its work on the topic of immunities of international organizations and, in 2018, it adopted a 'Practical Application Guide on the Jurisdictional Immunities of International Organizations'.[21]

The work of OAS on state immunity shows the importance of the topic for Latin America. Although the 1983 Draft Convention did not become a treaty, it had an important impact on the development of state immunity in the region. The 1983 Draft Convention adheres to the theory of restrictive immunity from jurisdiction and absolute immunity from execution. The state would enjoy immunity from jurisdiction by the acts that enhance the exercise of its state power, but would not be able to invoke immunity from jurisdiction with respect to claims that refer to trade or commercial activities.

[16] The rapporteur submitted the following three documents: CJI/doc.480/15, CJI/480/15 rev.1, CJI/doc.530/17.

[17] See 'Immunity of Jurisdiction of States. Scope and Validity (presented by Dr. Carlos Mata Prates)' CJI/doc.530/17. The document is included in the Annual Report of the Inter–American Juridical Committee to the General Assembly 2017 OEA/Ser. Q, CJI/doc. 551/17, pp. 124–132.

[18] These states are Bolivia, Brazil, Colombia, Costa Rica, Dominican Republic, El Salvador, Jamaica, Mexico, Panama, Paraguay, United States, and Uruguay. The responses by these states are not publicly available.

[19] For the case of Mexico compare with Reyes Moncayo (2017), pp. 77–97.

[20] See discussion on 'Immunity of States' in Annual Report of the Inter–American Juridical Committee to the General Assembly 2017 OEA/Ser. Q, CJI/doc. 551/17, pp. 119–124.

[21] See Organization of American States, Immunities of International Organizations (2003–2020). http://www.oas.org/en/sla/iajc/themes_recently_concluded_Immunities_International_Organizations.asp. Accessed 15 April 2021.

4 National Legislation in the Region Related to State Immunity

In general, Latin American countries have not enacted local legislation related to state immunity. That means, in practical terms, that national courts apply international rules on state immunity, embodied in treaties and in customary international law.

One exception to this situation is the case of Argentina.[22] There are three important pieces of legislation on the subject in that country. First, Decree-Law No. 1285/58, which organizes the national justice system, includes some provisions dealing specifically with cases involving foreign states. The law provides that no claim against a foreign state will be initiated 'without requiring previously from its diplomatic representative, through the Ministry of Foreign Relations and Worship, the agreement of that country to be put to trial'.[23] Therefore, when an Argentine judge receives a claim with a foreign state, he or she must previously request its approval through the Argentine Ministry of Foreign Affairs. The law also provides that the executive branch can declare by decree the lack of reciprocity in relation to a particular foreign state.[24] Thus, in such a case of a declaration of lack of reciprocity, the immunity from jurisdiction of the foreign state would not be recognized, and the claim would be submitted before Argentine courts. Argentine government included this reference to reciprocity as a reaction to a lawsuit initiated in 1959 before Italian courts against Argentina, without its consent.[25]

Second, Law No. 24,488 passed by the Argentine National Congress in 1995, specifically regulates the immunity from jurisdiction of foreign states before Argentine courts.[26] This law adopts the theory of restricted immunity. Law No. 24,488 provides as a general rule in Article 1 that foreign states are immune to the jurisdiction of Argentine courts, with the terms and conditions established in the law. Article 2 deals with the exceptions to the general rule. Under this Article,

---

[22] On the issue of state immunity in Argentina, see González Napolitano and Lozza (2015), pp. 725–760.

[23] Decree–Law 1285/58, dated 4 February 1958 (B.O. 7 February 1958), ratified by Law 14,467 (B.O. 29 September 1958), Article 24, para. 1.

[24] Decree–Law 1285/58, dated 4 February 1958 (B.O. 7 February 1958), ratified by Law 14,467 (B.O. 29 September 1958), Article 24, para. 1.

[25] Goldschmidt (1974), pp. 403, 500.

[26] Law No. 24,488, enacted on 31 May 1995 and partially promulgated on 22 June 1995 (B.O. 28 June 1995). This law was invoked by Italy and discussed in Jurisdictional Immunities of the State (Germany v. Italy: Greece intervening), Judgment of 3 February 2012. The ICJ noted that nine of the ten States referred to by the Parties which have legislated specifically for the subject of State immunity had adopted provisions to the effect that a State is not entitled to immunity in respect of torts occasioning death, personal injury or damage to property occurring on the territory of the forum State (among them, Argentina Law No. 24,488 (Statute on the Immunity of Foreign States before Argentine Tribunals) 1995, Art. 2 (e)). See Jurisdictional Immunities of the State (Germany v. Italy: Greece intervening), Judgment. ICJ Reports 2012, 99, p. 130, para. 70.

foreign states may not invoke immunity from jurisdiction in the following cases: (a) when they expressly consented that Argentine courts have jurisdiction over them, through a treaty, a written contract or a declaration in a specific case; (b) when they are the subject of a counterclaim directly linked to the main claim initiated by them; (c) when the claim is of a commercial or industrial activity carried out by the foreign state and the jurisdiction of the Argentine courts arises from a contract or from international law; (d) when they are sued for labour claims by Argentine nationals or residents in the country; (e) when they are sued for damages and losses arising from crimes or acts of negligence committed in the territory; (f) when dealing with actions on immovable assets that are located in Argentina; (g) when dealing with actions related to the foreign state acting as an inheritor or legatee of property in the national territory; (h) when they agreed in writing to submit to arbitration any claim related to a commercial transaction and the claim relates to such agreement.[27]

The law includes some procedural provisions. Among them, Article 7 provides that in the case of a lawsuit against a foreign state, the Ministry of Foreign Affairs may express its opinion on some aspects of the outcome before the intervening court, in its *amicus curiae* character. Law No. 24,488 deals only with immunity from jurisdiction, but not with immunity from execution, a matter that is not expressly regulated at present (with the exception of the assets of foreign central banks and foreign monetary authorities, regulated by Law No. 26,961) and is decided, in a case-by-case basis by the Argentine courts. If this law can be taken at its face value, then Argentina seems to adhere to relative immunity from jurisdiction and absolute immunity from execution.[28] Some authors consider that Law No. 24,488 contributed to the regulation of immunity from jurisdiction in Argentina, although it left several loopholes.[29]

Third, in 2014, the Argentine National Congress passed Law No. 26,961 in order to specifically regulate the immunity from jurisdiction of central banks and other monetary authorities before Argentine courts, as well as the immunity from execution of their assets.[30] Law No. 26,961 establishes that foreign central banks and other foreign monetary authorities are immune from the jurisdiction of the Argentine courts, with the following exceptions: (a) express consent in writing through a treaty, contract, arbitration agreement or through a declaration after the initiation of a claim; (b) counterclaim based on the same legal relationship or on the same facts as the main claim; and (c) when the claim relates to an activity outside its own functions

[27] Article 3 of Law No. 24,488 provides that if claims are brought before the Argentine courts against a foreign State involving alleged violations of the International Law of Human Rights, the intervening court will limit itself to indicate the plantiff to the international protection organ where the claim can be submitted if it corresponds. However, this article was vetoed by the Executive Power of the Nation. Article 1 of Regulatory Decree No. 849/95 B.O. 28 June 1995.

[28] Yang (2012), p. 651.

[29] Zuppi, La inmunidad jurisdiccional de los Estados extranjeros ante los tribunales argentinos conforme a la ley 24.488, El Derecho, t 166, pp. 866–877.

[30] Law No. 26,961, enacted on 6 August 2014 and promulgated on 7 August 2014 (B.O. 8 August 2014).

and the jurisdiction of the Argentine courts arises from the invoked contract or international law (Article 1). Likewise, the assets of a foreign central bank or a foreign monetary authority enjoy immunity from execution and seizure before Argentine courts with respect to any coercive measure that could affect them (Article 2). The law establishes reciprocity as a condition for immunity from execution and seizure, by providing that said immunity shall be applicable to the same extent as the assets of the Central Bank of Argentina enjoy immunity, in accordance with the legislation of the country to which the foreign central bank or the foreign monetary authority in question belongs (Article 3). The cases of exception to immunity from jurisdiction in Law No. 26,691 are stricter than those included in Law No. 24,488.

Moving to Chile, a relevant piece of legislation on that country is Decree-Law No. 2,349 of 1978 which, provides a rule of reciprocity for state immunity, by indicating that 'any foreign State and its organs, institutions and companies may invoke in Chile immunity from jurisdiction or execution, as the case may be, on the same terms, to the same extent and with the same exceptions as its own legislation grants to the State of Chile or to its organs, institutions and enterprises'.[31]

In the case of Costa Rica, Executive Decree No. 15877-RE of 1984 regulates the immunities and diplomatic and consular privileges of states and international organizations. That regulation in Article 39 provides that the premises of diplomatic missions, consular offices and international organizations, as well as their archives and belongings, are inviolable and enjoy immunity against search, requisition, confiscation, expropriation and all kinds of intervention.[32]

In the case of the Dominican Republic, the Law on Private International Law provides in Article 26 that the general scope of the jurisdiction of the Dominican courts will be determined 'without prejudice to the cases of immunity from jurisdiction and execution of the State and its bodies established by the rules of Public International Law' and that the Dominican courts 'will restrictively apply the scope of the immunity established in this article, limiting it to acts that imply the exercise of public power (*acts iure imperii*)'.[33]

Finally, it is important to note that in 2005 there was in Mexico an initiative proposing the enactment of a law on state immunity, with the objectives of determining the cases in which the Mexican State grants immunity to foreign states and to specify the procedure for officials, agencies and entities of the Mexican government to waive the immunity that corresponds to Mexico.[34] The draft followed a restrictive approach as regards state immunity since it establishes exceptions to the general rule of immunity, but at the same time requires, in order to recognize such immunity, that the Mexican state has been given reciprocal treatment.

---

[31] Chile, Decree Law No. 2,349 of 13 October 1978, Article 9. Diario Oficial (28 Oct 1978).

[32] Costa Rica, Executive Decree No. 15877–RE (29 Nov 1984).

[33] Dominican Republic, Law No. 544–14 on Private International Law G. O. 10787 (18 Dec 2014).

[34] Mexico (15 Dec 2005) Gaceta del Senado, LIX/3PPO–145/7564. https://www.senado.gob.mx/64/gaceta_del_senado/documento/7564. Accessed 15 April 2021.

As can be seen, the regulations providing for state immunity are rather the exception in the region, and in most countries the issue of state immunity is governed by international law, being customary international law or treaty law (mainly for those countries that have ratified the Bustamante Code and the UN Convention in the case of Mexico). Argentina, one of the few exceptions in the region with this type of regulation, applies the principle of relative immunity from jurisdiction and absolute immunity from execution. In the case of Dominican Republic, if one takes the text of applicable legislation at its face value, it could give the impression that it grants relative immunity both to jurisdiction and execution. In the case of Argentina (as established in Decree-Law No. 1285/58 and Law No. 26,961) and Chile (as established in Decree Law No. 2,349 of 1978) reciprocity plays an important role.

5 The Practice of Issuing Circular Notes

It has been quite common for countries in the region, by their ministries of foreign affairs or labour, to issue circular notes addressed to foreign representations in these countries, where they describe the rules applicable to state immunity, mainly with respect to labour claims.

In the case of Brazil, the number of labour claims against foreign states and the consolidation of the position of relative immunity to jurisdiction followed by the Brazilian courts led the Ministry of Foreign Affairs to issue a circular note to foreign delegations explaining the limitations on immunity in labour matters. The statement addressed to diplomatic missions accredited in Brazil emphasizes the inapplicability of immunity from jurisdiction, when dealing with acts *iure gestionis*, such as those derived from labour contracts.[35] The reasons for the enactment of the statement were: (i) the Vienna Convention on Diplomatic Relations (VCDR) of 1961, as well as the Vienna Convention on Consular Relations (VCCR) of 1963, do not regulate immunity with respect to claims derived from labour relations between the accrediting state and persons hired in the territory of the accredited state; (ii) in light of this, the Brazilian courts, 'in line with current legal thinking', established case-law in the sense that 'foreign legal entities of public law do not enjoy immunities in the field of acts *iure gestionis*, such as working relationships established locally'; and that (iii) the Brazilian Constitution, in force since 1988, determines, in its Article 114, that the labour justice is competent to know and judge in such disputes.[36]

Other countries in the region have followed a similar approach. In the case of Mexico, adherence to the doctrine of restricted immunity since 1995 has been

[35] Brazil, Ministry of Foreign Affairs, Circular Note No. 560/DJ/DPI/CJ (14 Feb 1991), reproduced, for example, in the judgment RE 222368 AgR of the SFT of Brazil (30 Apr 2002).

[36] Ibid.

established by various circular notes that the state sends to the representatives of foreign states accredited in Mexico, in order to inform them of the procedure to follow when they are the subject of labour lawsuits before Mexican courts.[37] Likewise, in Chile, by means of different circular notes, the Ministry of Foreign Affairs has asked the different embassies and international organizations to adopt the necessary measures for compliance with labour and social security regulations, bearing in mind that with respect to cases related to non-compliance with said regulations, it is not appropriate to apply immunity from jurisdiction, since the first obligation of a state is to respect the legislation of the country where they are located, especially labour laws, although immunity from execution applies.[38] In the case of Costa Rica, a circular note of 2008, states that diplomatic agents enjoy the immunity of civil and administrative jurisdiction, with some exceptions, notwithstanding that the accrediting state may waive the immunity from the jurisdiction of its diplomatic agents and the persons enjoying immunity.[39]

6 The Move from Absolute to Relative Immunity by National Courts in the Region

During most of the twentieth century, the highest local tribunals of Latin American countries followed the doctrine of absolute immunity from jurisdiction. The situation started to change by the end of the 1980s in Brazil, with the *Genny* case, and by mid 1990 in the rest of Latin American countries, influenced in part by the *Manauta* case in Argentina. Nowadays, most countries follow the theory of relative immunity from jurisdiction. In the following paragraphs, we will analyse the main cases before the highest courts in each country dealing with immunity from jurisdiction.

6.1 Brazil

Brazilian alignment with a progressive trend on state immunity started with the famous judgment *Genny de Oliveira v Embassy of the German Democratic Republic* in 1989, related to a labour claim.[40] In its judgment, the Supreme Federal Tribunal

[37] See Reyes Moncayo (2017), pp. 77–97; Secretariat of Foreign Relations of Mexico (19 Jun 2006) General Directorate of Protocol Circular PRO07130. https://sre.gob.mx/images/stories/docnormateca/dgp/circulares/pro07130.pdf. Accessed 15 April 2021.

[38] Circular notes No 371 (16 Oct 1997), No. 172 (17 May 1999) and No 108 (10 Apr 2000), enacted by the Ministry of Foreign Affairs. See SCJ of Chile, judgment 1,224–2013 (30 Jan 2013).

[39] Circular No 0009–08 UAL dated 22 April 2008, by the Legal Department of Labour Inspection. See Briones (2012), pp. 57–59.

[40] SFT of Brazil, Civil Appeal No 9.696–3/SP, Genny de Oliveira v Embassy of the German Democratic Republic, judgment of 31 May 1989.

(SFT), breaking with a long tradition, changed its understanding in order to allow, in certain cases, limitations on state immunity. In that case, the SFT considered that there is no immunity from jurisdiction for the foreign state, due to a labour nature of the claim. The main reason that the SFT reached that conclusion was that Article 114 of the Federal Constitution of 1988, expressly included in the competence of the labour justice of Brazil claims between workers and employers 'including the entities of foreign public law', thus eliminating the immunity of foreign states in claims of a labour nature. In the decision, Judge Francisco Rezek, who would later be appointed as a judge at the International Court of Justice (ICJ), considered that 'we can no longer say, in this Plenary, that there is a solid rule of customary international law [of absolute immunity], as soon as the United States of America, Great Britain and as many countries in the northern hemisphere disagree with that rule'.[41] This line of reasoning has been followed in subsequent years by the STF and the Supreme Tribunal of Justice (STJ) of Brazil.

There are important decisions in Brazil dealing with relative immunity and the distinction between acts *iure imperii* and acts *iure gestionis*. The STJ considered that acts of commerce, such as a credit related to the supply of materials for the construction of an embassy, were not covered by immunity, as they were within the scope of acts *iure gestionis*.[42] In another judgment, the STJ considered that in cases where the object at issue is based on relations of a purely labour, commercial or civil nature, such as a claim to obtain reparation for the alleged breach of a verbal contract entered into with the defendant for the preparation of a project for an international exhibition, felt in the category of acts *iure gestionis*.[43]

An important recent decision of the STF, which summarises the position of that tribunal regarding state immunity, is the case of 2017 related to the sinking of a fishing vessel in the Brazilian coast by a German submarine during WWII.[44] In its decision, the STF recalled the applicability of relative immunity from jurisdiction when it involves civil, commercial or labour relations, noting that immunity remains prevalent in the case of an act *iure imperii* as in that case, which related to an act of war. The STF considered that its jurisprudential understanding was consolidated in the sense that immunity from jurisdiction related to acts *iure gestioinis* is inapplicable, while immunity from execution remains absolute in all acts of the sovereign state in foreign territory, in the light of the VCDR.

[41] Ibid.

[42] STJ of Brazil, judgment of 21 October 1990, Ag 757/DF.

[43] STJ of Brazil, judgment of 20 May 2010, RO 26/RJ.

[44] SFT of Brazil, judgment of 5 November 2017, ARE 954858 RG.

6.2 Argentina

Already in 1921, the Supreme Court of Justice (SCJ) of Argentina referred to the distinction between acts *iure imperii* and acts *iure gestionis* in relation to the immunity of a state from jurisdiction.[45] However, the SCJ has started to follow a consistent position of restrictive immunity from jurisdiction since the case of *Manauta v Embassy of the Russian Federation*, rendered in 1994.[46] The claimant in that case, who had been employed by the Embassy of the Soviet Union in Argentina, claimed damages from the Russian Federation as the successor, for non-payment of social security contributions, union contributions and family allowances. The Court held that what was at issue was not a governmental act since the dispute related to the performance of obligations concerning employment and welfare contributions, so that the normal activity of a diplomatic representation was in no way involved. The Court considered that it is 'no longer possible to maintain that absolute immunity from jurisdiction constitutes a rule of general international law, because it is not followed in a uniform way and there is no legal conviction that it is binding'.[47] According to the Court, proof of this was provided by the modern legislative texts that followed the restrictive theory, such as the European Convention on Immunity of States of 1972, the Foreign Sovereign Immunities Act of the United States of 1976, the State Immunity Act of the United Kingdom of 1978, and the project on immunity from jurisdiction prepared by the ILC.[48] The SCJ also ruled that the requirement to request the agreement of the foreign state to be put to trial provided for in Decree-Law No. 1285/58 was not applicable because a governmental act was not in question, since the dispute brought referred to the fulfilment of labour and social security obligations.[49] The *Manauta* decision produced a breaking with the long tradition of the SCJ of applying the thesis of absolute immunity where a foreign government could not be brought to court before the national courts without its own consent, which had been applied previously in several decisions of the SCJ.[50]

---

[45] SCJ of Argentina, Judgment of 14 November 1921, Romay, Antonio v Royal Commission on Wheat Supplies. Corte Suprema de Justicia de la Nación (CSJN) Fallos, vol 135, p. 259.

[46] SCJ of Argentina, judgments of 22 December 1994, Manauta, Juan José and others v Embassy of the Russian Federation. CSJN, Fallos, vol 317, p. 1880.

[47] Ibid.

[48] Ibid.

[49] Ibid.

[50] SCJ of Argentina, judgment of 20 February 1892, Plenipotentiary Minister of the Republic of Chile v Porta, Carlos, CSJN, Fallos vol 47, p. 248; judgment of 26 February 1916, Baima and Bessolino v Government of Paraguay, CSJN, Fallos, vol 123, p. 58; judgment of 28 December 1916, National Treasury v Mones Cazón, Rodolfo, CSJN, Fallos, vol 125, p 40; judgment of 16 July 1937, Ibarra and Cía. v Capitán vapor "Ibaí", CSJN Fallos, vol 178, p 173; judgment of 21 November 1949, Townshend de Briochetto, Muriel Olga v Canada Commercial Department Office, CSJN, Fallos, vol 215, p 252; Judgment of 12 November 1951, Oppenlander de Soska, Nelly E. v Embassy of Ecuador or Arturo Borrero or Borrero Bustamante, CSJN, Fallos, vol

In addition, from the enactment of Law No. 24,488 in 1995, the SCJ of Argentina has had the opportunity to interpret several of the exceptions to state immunity from jurisdiction contemplated in Article 2 of that law,[51] including the term 'commercial activity'.[52] Nevertheless, the Court has refused to apply Law No. 24,488 by analogy to the cases of immunity from jurisdiction of international organizations, or to immunity from execution of foreign states.

In recent decisions, the SCJ of Argentina has had an opportunity to address whether different activities carried by the state were considered acts *iure imperii* or *iure gestionis*. The Court, following the approach of the general attorney, rejected claims by virtue of the principle of immunity from jurisdiction contained in Article 1 of Law 24,488 because the act that generated the claim was in the event of an armed conflict, being an act *iure imperii*.[53] In a claim for damages caused by intelligence agents of a foreign state in the territory of that state the SCJ recalled that acts *iure imperii* were covered by the immunity enshrined in Article 1 of the aforementioned law.[54] The Court considered that the fulfilment of the obligation contained in a legacy in favour of a foreign government did not affect the normal development of the embassy, thus immunity from jurisdiction was not present.[55] In another case, the SCJ followed the approach of the general attorney in the sense that the issuance of phytosanitary certificates by the authorities of a foreign government, within the framework of an international sale, cannot be considered an act *iure gestionis*, being an activity that reflects the exercise of *imperium* by the state and,

221, p. 171; judgment of 24 June 1976, Gómez, Samuel v British Embassy, CSJN, Fallos, vol 295, p 176; judgment of 24 June 1976, Lopez Elsa and other v France Embassy, CSJN Fallos, vol 295, p. 187; judgment of 1 September 1992, Compañía Arenera del Río Luján SA. v De Castro, Francisco and others regarding compensation, CSJN, Fallos vol 315, p. 1779; judgment of 16 December 1993, Amarfil Albornoz, Mirta Susana and other v Consulate of Chile and others regarding payment in pesos – Labor Court, CSJN Fallos, vol 316, p. 3111.

[51] SCJ of Argentina, judgment of 1 September 1998, Saravia, Gregorio v Japan International Cooperation Agency, CSJN Fallos, vol 321, p. 2434; judgment of 4 May 2000, Vallarino, Edelmiro Osvaldo v Japan Embassy regarding Dismissal, CSJN Fallos, vol 323, p 959; judgment of 28 June 2005 CSJN, Silguero Agüero, Felicita v Embassy of Portugal regarding Dismissal, CSJN Fallos, vol 328, p. 2522; judgment of 4 November 2008, CSJN, Mealla, Ester Yolanda v Embassy of France regarding Dismissal M. 787. XLIII; judgment of 4 August 2011, Clementi, Edgar Omar and other v Embassy of the Russian Federation and others regarding Compliance of Contract, CSJN Fallos, vol 334, p. 885.

[52] SCJ of Argentina, judgment of 29 September 1998, Cereales Asunción S.R.L. v National Administration of Navigation and Ports of the Republic of Paraguay regarding damages (breach of contract), CSJN Fallos, vol 321, p. 2594.

[53] SCJ of Argentina, judgment of 9 November 2000, Coronel, Oscar A. and others v National State – Department of Defence regarding accident in the military sphere and security forces, CSJN Fallos, vol 323 p. 3386; judgment of 18 December 2007, Davidoff, Constantino v United Kingdom of Great Britain and Northern Ireland regarding damages, CSJN Fallos, vol 330, p. 5237.

[54] SCJ of Argentina, judgment of 25 September 2001, Ceresole, Norberto v Republic of Venezuela, CSJN Fallos, vol 324, p. 2885.

[55] SCJ of Argentina, judgment of 5 November 2013, Sociedad Italiana de Tiro al Blanco v Italian Republic regarding knowledge process, CSJN Fallos, vol 336, p. 2144.

therefore, is included in Article 1 of Law 24,488.[56] In another case, the Court considered that the activity of Spanish officials at the Barcelona airport border control post cannot be included among the exceptions in Article 2 of Law 24,488 for having been committed within the territory of the respondent state and for being an activity that reflects the exercise of imperium of the state and, therefore, is included in Article 1 of Law 24,488.[57]

6.3 Venezuela

The former SCJ of Venezuela has accepted the restricted theory of immunity from jurisdiction since the judgment *Yrama Rodriguez de Leon v Latin American Economic System* in 1994.[58] The case involved a labour claim against an international organization, however the tribunal also analysed the issue of state immunity. The Court considered that 'international practice admits exceptions to the rule immunity from jurisdiction according to the legal nature of the act' of the subject of international law, and that in general 'it can be said that the principle of immunity from jurisdiction is included in the case of sovereign acts or acts *iure imperii*, while immunity cannot be invoked in the case of commercial or business acts or acta *iure gestionis*'.[59] In subsequent cases, the SCJ considered that diplomatic immunity must proceed in civil, criminal and administrative matters, except for the exceptions established in Article 31 of the VCDR.[60] The successor to the SCJ, the Supreme

[56] SCJ of Argentina, judgment of 10 June 2014, Louge, A. Beltrán and other v His British Majesty's Government, CSJN Fallos, vol 337, p. 731.

[57] SCJ of Argentina, judgment of 15 March 2016, Vergara, Walter Ricardo and other v Kingdom of Spain regarding civil and commercial matters, CSJN Fallos, vol 339, p. 316.

[58] SCJ of Venezuela, Judgment of 5 May 1994, Case No. 305, Political and Administrative Chamber, Yrama Rodriguez de Leon v. Sistema Económico Latinoamericano (SELA). See Bentata, Victor (1996) Estudio de la Sentencia SELA, in RFCIP UCV, No. 98, pp. 223 s. http://www.ulpiano.org.ve/revistas/bases/artic/texto/RDUCV/98/rucv_1996_98_223–256.pdf. Accessed 15 April 2021. The article includes the full text of the decision as an annex. For a complete and updated analisis of inmunities of states and international organizations in Venezuela, see Olivares Hernández and Briceño Laborí (2020).

[59] SCJ of Venezuela, Judgment of 5 May 1994, Case No. 305, Political and Administrative Chamber, Yrama Rodriguez de Leon v. Sistema Económico Latinoamericano (SELA). See Bentata, Victor (1996) Estudio de la Sentencia SELA, in RFCIP UCV, No. 98, pp. 223. http://www.ulpiano.org.ve/revistas/bases/artic/texto/RDUCV/98/rucv_1996_98_223–256.pdf. Accessed 15 April 2021. The article includes the full text of the decision as an annex. For a complete and updated analisis of inmunities of states and international organizations in Venezuela, see Olivares Hernández and Briceño Laborí (2020).

[60] SCJ of Venezuela, Political and Administrative Chamber, Judgment of 17 October 1996, Case No. 677, María Elena Albornoz de Vidal v Ambassador of Spain; Civil Cassation Chamber, Judgment of 18 February 1998, Stephen Louis Olushola v Ambassador of Nigerian Republic in Venezuela; Political and Administrative Chamber, Judgment of 30 July 1998, Case No 505, Lilia Ramírez v United States of America.

Tribunal of Justice (STJ) of Venezuela has also followed a theory of restrictive immunity.[61] From 2001, the STJ considered that when a foreign state is sued, the VCDR, which refers only to the lawsuits attempted against diplomatic agents, does not apply and it proceeded to review this matter under customary rules of immunity from the jurisdiction of the states.[62]

As regards the distinction between acts *iure imperii* and *iure gestionis*, the SCJ considered that the issuance of a passport was related to the official activities of the diplomatic official and, therefore, it was not within the exceptions to the immunity from jurisdiction.[63] The SCJ also ruled that the injuries suffered by a person inside an embassy during the restoration of the building constituted a wrongful act that occurred outside the scope of the sovereign functions of the states, being an act *iure gestionis*.[64] More recently, the STJ has considered that an alleged omission by the foreign state related to the way in which it has administered justice within its territory fell within the sovereign functions of the state,[65] and that a request for recognition of nationality fell also within these functions,[66] being the state covered by state immunity.

6.4 Uruguay

The change in the case-law in Uruguay took place in 1997, in a case involving a Uruguayan national who had worked for the embassy of Mexico in that country. The SCJ of Uruguay, after referring to the main international developments concerning state immunity, considered that 'the principle of absolute immunity of the States to the extent that it admits multiple exceptions does not constitute a rule of general International Law, because it is not practiced in a uniform way and there is no legal

[61] For early examples, see STJ of Venezuela, Political and Administrative Chamber, Judgment of 29 June 2000, Case No 01529, Chaker ELKathib v Embassy of the Republic of Iraq; and Judgment of 6 July 2000, Case No 01972, Bruno García Santos Fernando v Embassy of Republic of Peru. http://www.tsj.gob.ve. Accessed 15 April 2021.

[62] STJ of Venezuela, Political and Administrative Chamber, Judgment of 18 September 2001, Case No 1972, Aurora María Chacón v Republic of Peru.

[63] SCJ of Venezuela, Civil Cassation Chamber, Judgment of 18 February 1998, Stephen Louis Olushola v Ambassador of Nigerian Republic in Venezuela.

[64] SCJ of Venezuela, Political and Administrative Chamber, Judgment of 30 July 1998, Case No 505, Lilia Ramírez v United States of America.

[65] SJT of Venezuela, Political and Administrative Chamber, Judgment of 22 November 2005, Case No 6296, Edwin García Figuera v Unites States of America. http://www.tsj.gob.ve. Accessed 15 April 2021.

[66] SJT of Venezuela, Political and Administrative Chamber, Judgment of 28 February 2018, Case No 00224, José Luis Rodríguez v Kingdom of Spain. Available at http://www.tsj.gob.ve. Accessed 15 April 2021.

conviction about its obligatory nature'.[67] The Court distinguished between acts *iure gestionis* and *iure imperii* and considered that immunity from jurisdiction was exclusively reserved for the latter. From then on, the SCJ took a restrictive view concerning immunity from jurisdiction.

As regards the distinction between acts *iure gestionis* and *iure imperii* among other cases, it is relevant to mention a judgment from 2005 in a case where the claimant promoted an action against Argentina for the payment of sovereign bonds.[68] That country invoked immunity from jurisdiction and the SCJ give rise to the exemption on the grounds that the issuance of bonds and its payment belonged to the category of act *iure imperii* that fell under the immunity from jurisdiction.[69]

6.5 Colombia

For many years, the SCJ of Colombia has been a defender of the absolute immunity of states and the Council of State (*Consejo de Estado*) of Colombia, the highest authority of the jurisdiction in contentious-administrative matters, left the doors open for the Colombian state to respond to the actions or omissions of other states, by virtue of the application of the doctrine of *daño especial* (special damage).[70] Under this doctrine, the holder of a violated right can resort to his or her own state in order to seek reparation for damages suffered. The Council of State, in a judgment of 1998, dealt with the 'patrimonial responsibility of the State for compliance with international treaties' in the context of diplomatic immunities.[71] In that case, Council of State considered that, since the person that was allegedly responsible for the death of a Colombian national was protected by diplomatic immunity, the spouse of the victim had the right to request reparation from the Colombian state. This doctrine supposes that the state of the forum has not fulfilled its obligation to grant an effective remedy to its citizens by virtue of its international and internal obligations, for which it must face the damage derived from the violation.

In 2007 the SCJ changed its previous case-law and considered that there is currently a uniform and repeated practice in some countries which recognizes and accepts the relative immunity of states by virtue of which the sending state must answer before local tribunals of the receiving state for the acts that it has carried out

[67] SCJ of Uruguay, Judgment of 18 April 1997, Diplomatic Case No. 747/95, Martínez García, Susana v Embassy of México.

[68] SCJ of Uruguay, Judgment of 9 December 2005, Diplomatic Case No 1.126/2005, Morresi Castro, Ernesto v Argentine Republic – Embassy of the Argentine Republic in Montevideo.

[69] SCJ of Uruguay, Judgment of 9 December 2005, Diplomatic Case No 1.126/2005, Morresi Castro, Ernesto v Argentine Republic – Embassy of the Argentine Republic in Montevideo.

[70] Quintana Aranguren and Guzmán Carrasco (2006).

[71] Council of State of Colombia, Judgment of 25 August 1998, rad. IJ0001.

as an individual and in labour disputes.[72] In 2012 the SCJ, based on the VCDR, stated that international organizations and foreign states have immunity from jurisdiction for acts *iure imperii* that they carry out in the territory of the receiving state, regardless of whether these acts relate to labour matters.[73]

For its part, the Constitutional Court (CC) of Colombia has consistently upheld the thesis of restricted immunity in its jurisprudence. In 1996, in a case related to immunity from jurisdiction of an international organization, the CC considered that the privileges and immunities granted to foreign states and international organizations are not absolute and that the Colombian state cannot accept absolute immunity from jurisdiction.[74] In 2000, it recalled that under the jurisdictional immunity of states they may not be called to appear before the courts of a foreign nation that intends to prosecute their sovereign acts.[75] In 2009, the CC recalled that state immunity and diplomatic immunity are two different legal institutions and that customary international law recognizes the restricted nature of state immunity in labour matters.[76] In 2010, the CC held that the VCDR does not expressly contemplate diplomatic immunity in relation to labour jurisdiction and that customary international law must continue to govern matters that have not been expressly regulated in the provisions of the said Convention.[77]

6.6 *Chile*

Traditionally, the SCJ of Chile has followed a broad and unrestricted recognition of state immunity. In this vein, in 2013 the Fourth Chamber of the SCJ rendered a judgment of unification of jurisprudence in a labour claim involving the Embassy of the Federal Republic of Germany in Chile.[78] The Court recalled that it had repeatedly decided that labour courts lack jurisdiction to hear labour claims between Chilean nationals and embassies. For the SCJ, by reason of the nature of state immunity and the principles in which it is based, it was inadmissible to restrict its effects in certain cases or matters, beyond the terms established by the VCDR. The SCJ considered that the jurisprudence should be understood as unified in the sense that the labour courts lack jurisdiction to hear a lawsuit filed by national dependents against foreign states settled in Chile.

However, in 2018 the Fourth Chamber of the SCJ accepted the principle of restrictive immunity in a case that related to the execution of a labour judgment,

---

[72] SCJ of Colombia, Labour Chamber, Judgment of 13 December 2007, rad. 32096.

[73] SCJ of Colombia, Labour Cassation Chamber, Judgment of 21 March 2012, Case No 37,637.

[74] CC of Colombia, Plenary, Judgment of 9 April 1996, Case C–137.

[75] CC of Colombia, Plenary, Judgment of 13 September 2000, Case C–1189.

[76] CC of Colombia, Fifth Revision Chamber, Judgment of 15 September 2009, Case T–633.

[77] CC of Colombia, Ninth Revision Chamber, Judgment of 23 November 2010, Case T–932.

[78] SCJ of Chile, Fourth Chamber, Judgment of 13 August 2013, Case No 1.224–2013.

by means of which the Embassy of Mexico in Chile was condemned to the payment of labour benefits.[79] The Chamber determined that immunity from jurisdiction is recognized as a limited prerogative, depending on the nature of the act deployed by the state. In case of acts *jure imperii,* the state enjoys immunity from jurisdiction, while in acts *iure gestioni,* they submit their acts to the jurisdiction of the receiving state. The Chamber ruled that Article 31 of the VCDR should be understood as a precept that must be interpreted restrictively, insofar as it favours with immunity from jurisdiction only diplomatic agents in their personal capacity, but not the state they represent. The Chamber added that it is not possible to extend the prerogative of immunity from jurisdiction enshrined in the VCDR to the obligations arising from the labour relationship that an embassy maintains with a natural person, since it is an act *iure gestionis* excluded from the aforementioned benefit and that, therefore, it is not exempt from the obligation to appear before the jurisdiction of the recipient country and before the Courts of the forum.

6.7 *Paraguay*

In Paraguay, in 2015, the Labour Chamber of Appeals considered that when a foreign state enters into a labour contract with a national or permanent resident of the national territory it performs an act *iure gestionis*, and it must submit itself to the internal labour regulations, given the decline of the thesis of absolute immunity from the jurisdiction of the states in labour matters that gave way to the theory of restricted immunity in that field.[80]

6.8 *Mexico, Central America and the Caribbean*

In the case of El Salvador, in a judgment in 2002, the Constitutional Chamber of the SCJ of that country endorsed a position of a relative immunity in a case related to the Organization of Central American States.[81] The case related to the donation of property for the construction of the offices of that organization. The Court considered that international law does not impose absolute immunity from jurisdiction, but rather allows national courts to attribute territorial jurisdiction, in cases such as that case, and that an interpretation that embraces absolute immunity violates the national constitution.

---

[79] SCJ of Chile, Fourth Chamber, Judgment of 19 June 2018, Case No 8,750–2018.

[80] Labour Chamber of Appeals of Paraguay, First Chamber, Judgment of 21 October 2015, Case No 93, Pedro Antonio Martínez Acosta v Embassy of the U.S.A. regarding Return to work regarding payment of guaranies, Judicial Gazete, 2016 – No 4, pp. 103–113.

[81] SCJ of El Salvador, Constitutional Chamber, Judgment of 20 August 2002, Case 25–S–95.

Moving to Mexico, in 2003, the SCJ of that country issued a criterion that reinforces the adoption of restricted immunity. The Court considered that jurisdictional immunity, that in principle was recognized as absolute, has evolved and at present 'is not an unlimited prerogative'. The Court considered that in those situations where the state acts as a private party, 'as a general rule, it is not granted the referred immunity'.[82]

As regards Costa Rica, the courts of that country in general have followed the criterion of absolute immunity, considering that this immunity is related to the recognition of the sovereignty of the states.[83] The SCJ of Costa Rica, however, in recent cases has given the impression that it could adopt a restrictive criterion in the future. In 2006, it considered that state immunity is based on a functional criterion recognised by customary international law for the protection of the diplomatic functions of the representatives of foreign governments.[84] In another judgment, the SCJ has considered that the enactment of a judgment by the courts of a foreign country constitutes an act *iure imperii*, since they relate to the administration of justice.[85] However, in 2016, in a labour claim against the Embassy of Brazil the Court recognised absolute immunity.[86]

6.9 Peru

The SCJ of Peru appears to continue to apply the theory of absolute immunity, as it is reflected in the case of *Edgar Cristian Tello Rivera v Cooperation Agency of Korea in Peru* rendered in 2017.[87] In that case, the Court considered that Peruvian courts had jurisdiction 'to the extent that the diplomatic representation or the international organization accepts the national jurisdiction'. Among the arguments for adopting a theory of absolute immunity, the Court considered that the theory of relative immunity based on acts *iure imperii* and *iure gestionis* has not been recognised in the VCDR.[88] For the Court, the fact that a labour contract between the Korean international agency and a natural person in Peru implies that the former acted in its

[82] SCJ of Mexico, (Nov 2003) Inmunidad jurisdiccional internacional no es prerrogativa ilimitada, thesis 2a./J. 101/2003, registry No. 182824, Gazette of the Judicial Weekly Paper of the Federation, 9 ep., t XVIII, p. 149.

[83] See Briones (2012), pp. 57–59.

[84] SCJ of Costa Rica, Constitutional Chamber, Judgment of 26 June 2006, Case No 08815–2006.

[85] SCJ of Costa Rica, First Chamber, Judgment of 30 August 2006, Case No 00599–2006.

[86] SCJ of Costa Rica, Second Chamber, Judgment of 24 February 2016, Case No 00201–2016.

[87] SCJ of Peru, Fourth Permanent Labour Chamber, Judgment of 2 October 2017, Edgar Cristian Tello Rivera against the Korean Cooperation Agency in Peru, file 20204–2014–0–1801–JR–LA–15.

[88] SCJ of Peru, Fourth Permanent Labour Chamber, Judgment of 2 October 2017, Edgar Cristian Tello Rivera against the Korean Cooperation Agency in Peru, file 20204–2014–0–1801–JR–LA–15.

private role and not as state, does not exclude the immunity from jurisdiction.[89] The dissenting judge Julio Canales Vidal considered that the most widespread international custom recognizes the restricted nature of the immunity of states in labour matters and this is based on protecting the fundamental right of access to justice and that since there is an employment relationship between an individual with an accrediting state, it is an act *iure gestionis*.[90]

7 Immunity from Execution Before National Courts

As with immunity of jurisdiction, the highest local courts of Latin American countries have historically followed a position of absolute immunity from execution. The situation appears to remain until the present time, although in some countries there appears to be an evolution towards a more restrictive approach as regards state immunity. In the following paragraphs, we will analyse the main cases before the highest courts in each country dealing with immunity from execution.

7.1 Argentina

In the case of Argentina, an important precedent took place in 1958. In *Peru v SIFAR*[91] the state of Peru, as a plaintiff sued an Argentine company before the SCJ of Argentina and the company, in response, submitted a counterclaim. Peru answered the counterclaim with a tacit submission to the jurisdiction of the Court, but there was no specific and separate waiver of immunity from execution. The Court condemned Peru and admitted the execution of a judgment for having mediated 'express agreement of the plaintiff nation for the hearing of this Court in the trial, agreement that includes the necessary procedures for compliance with the Court's ruling, to the extent that they are compatible with the norms and principles of the law of nations'.[92] The Court considered that 'the sole requirement of payment' of the judgment to Peru 'in no way violates the immunities and prerogatives of the former

[89] SCJ of Peru, Fourth Permanent Labour Chamber, Judgment of 2 October 2017, Edgar Cristian Tello Rivera against the Korean Cooperation Agency in Peru, file 20204–2014–0–1801–JR–LA–15.

[90] SCJ of Peru, Fourth Permanent Labour Chamber, Judgment of 2 October 2017, Edgar Cristian Tello Rivera against the Korean Cooperation Agency in Peru, file 20204–2014–0–1801–JR–LA–15.

[91] SCJ of Argentina, judgment of 26 February 1958, Peru, Government of the Republic of v SIFAR, Sociedad Industrial Financiera Argentina SA regarding breach of contract, CSJN Fallos, vol 240, p. 93.

[92] Ibid.

and is, instead, conducive to the adequate realization of justice between the parties'.[93]

More recently, in a judgment rendered in 1999 in *Blasson v Embassy of the Slovak Republic*, the SCJ of Argentina had the opportunity to analyse the matter of immunity from jurisdiction in more detail.[94] The case related to the execution of a judgment in a labour claim, for which a lower court had ordered the seizure of the bank accounts of the embassy of the Slovak Republic in Argentina. The Court noted that Law No. 24,488 only regulates immunity from jurisdiction 'without there being any hint in its articles that allows it to be applied by analogy to immunity from execution' and in such conditions, the Court noted, the case should be resolved according to the applicable rules of international law.[95] The Court considered that enforceable measures against assets of a foreign state seriously affect the sovereignty and independence of that state, so that it is not possible to extend the solutions on immunity from jurisdiction to cases of immunity from execution. The Court noted that the distinction between immunity from jurisdiction and immunity from execution has been made in different legal systems, having established that the waiver of immunity from jurisdiction does not imply the waiver of immunity from execution. The Court considered that international practice with respect to one class of immunity and another differs, adopting the immunity from execution in an absolute manner. It also pointed out that the waiver of immunity from jurisdiction does not imply the waiver of immunity from execution. Even in the face of the conflict between a labour or other claim and immunity from execution, the latter principle prevails.[96] The Court was also of the opinion that it was not proven that the seized bank account had a different destination from meeting the ordinary expenses of its embassy in the country or opened with a specific destination to pay obligations originated in *iure gestionis* activities.

7.2 Brazil

The SFT of Brazil has maintained a position of absolute immunity from execution. In 1987, in a case related to the execution of a judgment in a labour case against Spain, the SFT recalled that it has understood that a foreign state enjoys immunity of jurisdiction not just as a result of customary international law, but by application of the VCDR and in order to remove the immunity of execution, the express renunciation to immunity by the foreign state was necessary.[97] In a case in 1998, related to

---

[93] Ibid.

[94] SCJ of Argentina, judgment of 6 October 1999, in re Blasson, Beatriz Lucrecia Graciela v Embassy of the Slovak Republic, CSJN Fallos, vol 322, p. 399.

[95] Ibid.

[96] Ibid.

[97] SFT of Brazil, judgment of 9 September 1987, Case ACi 9705.

the execution of a fiscal fine against General Consulate of Germany, the SFT considered that immunity from jurisdiction has not changed in view of the new normative framework that was outlined in terms of international law and in the scope of comparative law when the dispute is between the Brazilian state and the foreign state, notably when it comes to execution.[98]

In 2002, in an execution related to a labour claim, the SFT considered that immunity from jurisdiction and immunity from execution, constitute autonomous categories, legally unmistakable, because—although they maintain close relations with each other—they translate into independent and distinct realities.[99] However, the Tribunal considered that the eventual legal impossibility of execution of the condemnatory judgement, due to the immunity from execution, is not sufficient to prevent the initiation, before Brazilian Courts, of proceedings against foreign states, notably when dealing with labour disputes.[100] In 2006, in an execution for lack of payment of fiscal fines filed by the Brazilian government against the Republic of Korea, the SFT considered that from its jurisprudence, unless waived, the immunity of the foreign state to enforceable jurisdiction is absolute.[101] More recently, the SFT recalled that immunity from execution remains absolute in all acts of the sovereign state in foreign territory.[102]

7.3 Colombia

In 2015, the Fifth Chamber of Revision of CC of Colombia analysed the case of a Colombian worker at the Embassy of the United Kingdom.[103] The Court noted that in different cases where it had ruled in favour of the plaintiffs against embassies of different countries, the orders had not been complied with. This was because, even when immunity from jurisdiction is restricted, states still enjoy a wide margin of immunity from the coercive execution of judicial decisions. This means that, even though the forum state can issue judgments against the accredited states in accordance with international law, it does not have the power to request compliance.[104] Consequently, the Chamber ordered the Ministry of Foreign Affairs of Colombia to carry out direct diplomatic negotiations with the representatives of the Embassy of the United Kingdom, in order to find a settlement formula to guarantee the protection of the plaintiff's rights. In the event that these approaches did not succeed, the Chamber ordered the Ministry of Foreign Affairs to advance all administrative and

---

[98] SFT of Brazil, judgment of 16 September 1998, Case ACO 522 AgR.

[99] SFT of Brazil, judgment of 30 April 2002, Case RE 222368 AgR.

[100] Ibid.

[101] SFT of Brazil, judgment of 30 August 2006, Case ACO 543 AgR.

[102] SFT of Brazil, judgment of 11 May 2017, Case ARE 954858 RG.

[103] CC of Colombia, Fifth Chamber of Revision, judgment of 22 July 2015, Case T–462.

[104] Ibid.

judicial procedures on behalf of the plaintiff before the courts of the United Kingdom.

In 2016, the Plenary of CC of Colombia had an opportunity to decide in two accumulated cases that related to two Colombian citizens who worked for the embassies of Lebanon and the United States in Colombia.[105] The CC considered that a restricted immunity from execution cannot be considered as applicable according to customary international law. The CC, following the ICJ in the *Italy v Germany* case, considered that in accordance with customary international law, property belonging to a state is subject to immunity from execution, unless one of the following conditions is met: (1) that the property in question is in use for an activity not pursuing government non-commercial purposes, (2) that the state which owns the property has expressly consented to the taking of a measure of constraint, or (3) that that state has allocated the property in question for the satisfaction of a judicial claim.[106] The CC considered that in the case at issue, there was no request for a seizure of one or more determined or determinable assets and that neither the first nor the third of the conditions established by the ICJ were applicable. As the claimant had not identified an asset on which the execution may fall, it could not be established whether or not it pursued public service purposes. As a result, the Chamber adopted the position outlined in the judgment T-462 of 2015 and ordered the Ministry of Foreign Affairs to advance in the exequatur or any other procedure contemplated in the laws of Lebanon and the United States, in order to execute the decisions issued by the Labour Chamber of the Supreme Court of Justice against the embassies of the aforementioned countries.

7.4 Mexico

In a case related to the execution of a labour claim against an international organization, the SCJ of Mexico in 2014 considered that the immunity from execution of states is instrumental in character, so that it is justified only to the extent that it protects the goods of foreign states that belong to them or are used by them in the exercise sovereign power.[107] When it comes to property of diplomatic mission of the states, the immunity of execution responds to the mutual recognition of the exercise of the sovereign power of foreign states.[108] In its analysis, the Court resorted to the case *Italy v Germany* before the ICJ and to the three situations where a measure of constraint may be taken against property belonging to a foreign state.[109]

[105] CC of Colombia, Plenary, judgment of 18 August 2016, Case SU443/16.

[106] Jurisdictional Immunities of the State (2012) Germany v Italy: Greece intervening, Judgment. ICJ Reports, p. 99, para. 118.

[107] SCJ of Mexico, Second Chamber, Judgment of 15 January 2014, Case 197/2013.

[108] Ibid.

[109] Ibid.

7.5 Uruguay

In 2000, the SCJ refused to execute the eviction judgment of a leased real state property.[110] The SCJ considered that, based on the VCDR, the lifting of immunity from jurisdiction of diplomatic officials does not imply the lifting of immunity from execution, and for that to proceed, the accrediting state should issue a new pronouncement renouncing immunity from execution. Since that was not the case in the proceedings, the Court did not grant the request for the execution of the judgment made by the plaintiff. The SCJ, in a case involving the execution of an award in a labour case against the embassy of Chile, declared in 2017 the immunity from diplomatic execution as absolute and any exception must be clear and express.[111] The Court considered that contemporary international practice clearly exempted the embassy's bank accounts from any enforcement measure. The SCJ pointed out that giving place to the request would imply violating the immunity of execution that the respondent state enjoys and could entail the international responsibility of Uruguay.

7.6 Peru

In 2017, in a claim of a Peruvian airline against the Russian Federation and the Russian Ambassador in Peru, the plaintiff alleged that the Russian Federation had illegally interfered in a contract for the lease of an aircraft where a Russian company was involved.[112] The SCJ resorted to the principle of absolute immunity from jurisdiction and considered that 'a foreign State would not be obliged to appear as a defendant before the courts of another country'. The SCJ noted that in case of a proceeding against a foreign state that reaches the stage of execution, the question of the consent of the foreign state for the execution of the judgment should have to be considered independently from the consent to jurisdiction.

[110] SCJ of Uruguay, Judgment of 30 June 2000, Case No 286/2000, Torrens González, Mario Enrique v Embassy of Republic of Chile, Eviction.

[111] SCJ of Uruguay, Judgment of 8 May 2017, Case No 440/2017, Embassy of the Republic of Chile in Uruguay and other, incident of immunity of execution.

[112] SCJ of Peru, Transitory Civil Chamber, Cassation 004935–2015, Judgment of 8 May 2017, Expresso Aéreo Sociedad Anónima v Russian Federation.

8 Position of National Courts as Regards the UN Convention

National courts have also referred to the work of the ILC that derived in the UN Convention. In *Manauta* the SCJ of Argentina noted that the project on immunity from jurisdiction prepared by the ILC followed the restrictive theory and this was one of the arguments for the Court to move towards a restrictive view of immunity from jurisdiction.[113] The SCJ of Uruguay has resorted to the works of the ILC to sustain the proposition that immunity from jurisdiction is different to immunity from execution.[114]

National courts have also resorted to the UN Convention in order to contrast or support its reasoning. The SFT of Brazil in 2017 stated that in that country the matter of state immunity 'is governed by customary law, given that the country has not yet been bound' by the UN Convention or a similar treaty.[115] The SCJ of Uruguay has reiterated, at least since 2012, that the UN Convention 'even though not yet ratified, is applicable for constituting the most accepted doctrine on the subject'.[116]

The CC of Colombia has considered that the UN Convention provides for legal security and allows the state to fully understand the scope of its obligations and the rights that plausibly will be recognized in terms of immunity from jurisdiction.[117] The SCJ of Colombia, in turn, held in 2016 that customary international law is a primary source of law for matters related to state immunity and that the circumstance that Colombia has not ratified the UN Convention does 'not mean that there is a lagoon or an absence of regulation'.[118] The SCJ of Costa Rica has stated that with respect to the UN Convention that 'in spite of not being subscribed by the country, it deserves a mention', it supports the idea that states can tacitly or expressly renounce immunity from jurisdiction in acts *iure gestionis*.[119]

In other countries, a potential evolution towards recognising the customary nature of some of the provisions of the UN Convention can be identified. The SCJ of Chile in 2013 considered that the UN Convention, which expressly excludes labour contracts from state immunity had not been ratified by Chile, so that it lacked validity for these effects. It concluded that jurisprudence should be understood as unified in the sense that the labour courts lack jurisdiction to hear a lawsuit filed by Chilean national against foreign states settled in the country.[120] In 2017, however, in

[113] SCJ of Argentina, judgments of 22 December 1994, Manauta, Juan José and others v Embassy of the Russian Federation. CSJN, Fallos, vol 317, p 1880. The reference to Manauta was reproduced in judgment by the SCJ of Costa Rica, Judgment of 18 April 1997, Case No 247/1997.

[114] SCJ of Uruguay, judgment of 30 June 1997, Case No 285/2000.

[115] SFT of Brazil, Plenary, judgment of 5 November 2017, Case ARE 954858 RG.

[116] SCJ of Uruguay, Judgment of 23 July 2012, Case No. 1.626/2012.

[117] CC of Colombia, First Revision Chamber, Judgment of 3 December 2013, Case T–901.

[118] SCJ of Colombia, Labour Chamber, Judgment of 20 April 2016, Case No 72569.

[119] SCJ of Costa Rica, Second Chamber, judgment of 21 May 2014, Case No 00457–2014.

[120] SCJ of Chile, Fourth Chamber, judgment of 13 August 2013, Case 1.224–2013.

a case which referred to the privileges and immunities of an international organization, the SCJ considered that what was explained was 'fully consistent with' the UN Charter and Article 11 of the UN Convention.[121] Finally, it is important to overserve that in the case before the SCJ of Peru involving the Korea Cooperation Agency in Peru, the dissenting judge Julio Canales Vidal considered that the UN Convention contains 'the prevailing international custom after the Second World War, which adheres to the thesis of restricted jurisdictional immunity of foreign states in labour matters'.[122]

9 State Immunity and Human Rights

Human rights considerations have played an important role in the evolution towards a theory of restrictive immunity by national courts, since national courts have considered that recognising absolute immunity to foreign representations in labour claims was an impediment to the human right of access to justice.[123]

In *Manauta*, for instance, the SCJ of Argentina considered that accepting absolute immunity would lead to the unfair result of obliging the worker to a chimerical option to resort to the jurisdiction of the foreign state or require the Argentine diplomatic assistance for generally expensive extrajudicial courses.[124] The Court considered that this would lead to a serious risk of the worker's human right to judicial protection, a risk that current international law tends to prevent.[125]

More recently, the CC of Colombia has held that the theory of absolute immunity generates unsustainable tensions with the principles of access to justice and the existence of an effective remedy for the protection of human rights.[126] It considered that eventual conflicts between the different sources of the rules on state immunity

[121] SCJ of Chile, Fourth Chamber, judgment of 14 December 2017, Case 18.264–2017.

[122] SCJ of Peru, Fourth Permanent Labour Chamber, judgment of 2 October 2017, Edgar Cristian Tello Rivera v Korean Cooperation Agency in Peru, file 20204–2014–0–1801–JR–LA–15.

[123] Already in 1974, in a labour claim against the ambassador of South Vietnam, the National Chamber of Labour of Argentina considered that adopting a theory of absolute immunity would imply a negative to the Argentine citizen to the protection of the laws of his own country. The Chamber added that the foreign country could not feel impaired because its embassy is subject to labour jurisdiction, when with this measure 'it is only pursued full compliance with human rights, which the said country recognizes to its nationals under analogous circumstances'. National Chamber of Labour, Chamber IV, judgment of 24 October 1974, Roldán, Segundo Blas v Ambassador of the Republic of South Vietnam, collection of payment, La Ley, t. 1975–B, p. 528.

[124] SCJ of Argentina, judgments of 22 December 1994, Manauta, Juan José and others v Embassy of the Russian Federation. CSJN, Fallos, vol 317, p. 1880.

[125] Ibid., p. 1880.

[126] CC of Colombia, First Revision Chamber, Judgment of 3 December 2013, Case T–901.

should be resolved with due regard to the principle *pro homine*, giving the greatest possible scope to solutions that favour human rights.[127]

Another aspect of the interaction between state immunity and human rights refers to what happens in case of serious violations of such rights. The SFT and the STJ of Brazil had the opportunity to analyse the extent of immunity from jurisdiction in relation to acts *iure imperii* affecting human rights, in particular the deaths related to the sinking of Brazilian fishing vessels in Brazilian waters by German submarines during WWII. In one case before the STJ, Judge Luis Felipe Salomão considered that the dichotomy between acts *iure gestionis* and *iure imperii* was not the only way to face the problem represented by immunity from jurisdiction and that state immunity should not persist in the face of serious violations of international law, and should be relativized in view of the prevalence of peremptory rules that protect humanitarian law and human rights.[128]

In a more recent case, now before the SFT, Judge Edson Fachin considered that in the circumstances under analysis two values that Brazil has undertaken to follow in international relations, the prevalence of human rights and equality between States, were in apparent divergence.[129] At the time of writing, the judges at the SFT were giving their views on the scope on state immunity. One the one hand Judge Edson Fachin (with the support of three other judges) considered that wrongful acts performed by foreign states in breach of human rights do not enjoy immunity from jurisdiction.[130] On the other hand, judges Gilmar Mendes and Marco Aurélio considered that in case of acts *iure imperii,* the SFT should recognise immunity of jurisdiction to the foreign state.

10 State Immunity and Reciprocity

Some legislation and national tribunals in the region have found some basis for state immunity on the principle of reciprocity.[131] As explained previously, in the case of the legislation of Argentina (trough Decree-Law No. 1285/58 and Law No. 26,961) and Chile (trough Decree Law No. 2,349 of 1978) reciprocity plays an important role. The SCJ of Argentina has considered that the principle of absolute immunity was mitigated by Decree-Law No. 9,015/63, which contemplates the possibility that a foreign State could be subject to the jurisdiction of Argentine courts when the Executive Power declares that there is a lack of reciprocity regarding the matter, in

---

[127] Ibid.

[128] STJ of Brazil, Judgment of 21 May 2009, Case No 74 – RJ (2008/0076862–4).

[129] SFT of Brazil, judgment of 5 November 2017, Case ARE 954858 RG.

[130] See, Moraes adia julgamento sobre atos de guerra cometidos no Brasil, Migalhas, 3 March 2021. https://www.migalhas.com.br/quentes/341089/moraes–adia–julgamento–sobre–atos–de–guerra–cometidos–no–brasil with hiperlinks to the relevant opinions. Accessed 15 April 2021.

[131] On the issue of reciprocity see Yang (2012), p. 46.

the sense that this State accepts claims against Argentina before its courts.[132] The SCJ of Chile has considered that immunity from jurisdiction is based on the principles of equality sovereignty and reciprocity[133]

Judges at the STF of Brazil have often resorted to the principle of reciprocity. Judge Celso de Mello has considered that the prerogatives and privileges, including the exemption from taxes provided for in the VCDR and the VCCR, depend on the observance of the principle of reciprocity in the sense that the Brazilian authorities must dispense to foreign countries in Brazil the same treatment that these states dispense in their territories to the Brazilian state.[134] As a consequence, according to Judge de Mello, the Brazilian government should demonstrate that the country to be executed does not provide in its territory to the Brazilian state the same guarantee of immunity from execution.[135] Judge Carlos Ayres Britto, in turn, considered that reciprocity of treatment between sovereign states is none other than the principle of international equality put into action.[136]

The highest tribunals of Colombia have resorted quite often to reciprocity. The CC of Colombia has considered that immunities are not absolute but must be based on principles of independence, sovereignty and reciprocity.[137] The CC has also stated that accepting the absolute nature of immunity in a community of States that has adopted the relative theory of immunity from jurisdiction would be contrary to the principle of reciprocity in international relations, since it would imply that the benefits of absolute immunity that Colombia grants to other countries would not be enjoyed by Colombia in other countries.[138] The SCJ of Colombia, in turn, has considered that, in light of the principle of reciprocity, the foreign state should be not exempted from internal justice, if that state by virtue of its local legislation would not do the same with respect to the Colombian state.[139]

Scholars have often emphasized that the principle of reciprocity has operated as an engine for the development of the restrictive theory of state immunity.[140] Conditioning state immunity to reciprocity could provide some support to the

[132] SCJ of Argentina, judgments of 22 December 1994, Manauta, Juan José and others v Embassy of the Russian Federation. CSJN, Fallos, vol 317, p. 1880.

[133] SCJ of Chile, Fourth Chamber, judgment of 14 November 2007, Case 235–06; judgment of 13 May 2010, Case No 891–2010; judgment of 14 September 2010, Case No 3.493–2010; and judgment of 13 August 2013, Case No 1.224–2013.

[134] SFT of Brazil, judgment of 30 August 2006, Case ACO 543 AgR,. See also SFT of Brazil, Plenary, judgments of 11 April 2007, Cases 633 Agr and ACO 645 Agr.

[135] SFT of Brazil, judgment of 30 August 2006, Case ACO 543 AgR,. See also SFT of Brazil, Plenary, judgments of 11 April 2007, Cases 633 Agr and ACO 645 Agr.

[136] SFT of Brazil, judgment of 30 August 2006, Case ACO 543 AgR,. See also SFT of Brazil, Plenary, judgments of 11 April 2007, Cases 633 Agr and ACO 645 Agr.

[137] CC of Colombia, Plenary, judgment of 9 April 1996, Case C–137.

[138] CC of Colombia, First Revision Chamber, judgment of 3 December 2013, Case T–901.

[139] SCJ of Colombia, Labour Cassation Chamber, judgment of 20 April 2016, Case No 72569.

[140] Badr (1984), p. 35.

argument that States conceive the content of immunity discretionary.[141] At the regional level, reciprocity appears to be used as a shield towards more restrictive views on state immunity applied in other jurisdictions. One question to bear in mind is what the implications are of following the principle of reciprocity, in light of the human right of access to justice.

11 Conclusion

The previous pages have explored how Latin American countries approach state immunity in their regional treaty law, legislation, practice and case-law. The analysis shows that state immunity in the region is to a large extent regulated by customary international law. At the same time, during the twentieth century, Latin American countries have experienced an evolution of the models of state immunity and a movement from a traditional approach of absolute immunity, based on the independence of the state, to a second approach of restrictive immunity, based on the interdependence of states.

From the treaties concluded at the regional level, the Bustamante Code of 1928 is perhaps the most relevant. It adheres to the theory of absolute immunity from jurisdiction, with some limited exceptions, and absolute immunity of execution. The main criteria for the exceptions to the immunity from jurisdiction is when the contracting State acts as an individual or private person. However, the Bustamante Code has a limited application, since it was not ratified by all the states from the region (including Argentina, Colombia, Mexico, Paraguay and Uruguay), and national courts apply exceptions to the principle of absolute immunity that are not contemplated in that treaty, such as the principle of relative immunity in cases of labour claims. Nowadays, references to the Code by the highest courts of Latin American countries is rather limited.

In general, Latin American countries have not enacted local legislation related to State immunity. That means, in practical terms, that national courts apply international rules on state immunity, embodied in customary international law or in treaties (mainly for those countries that have ratified the Bustamante Code and the UN Convention in the case of Mexico). Argentina, one of the few Latin American countries that has regulations on state immunity, applies a principle of relative immunity from jurisdiction and absolute immunity from execution.

Case-law shows that national courts in the region continued to apply for a long time and until the 1990s the doctrine of absolute immunity from jurisdiction, based mainly on customary international law. Nowadays the highest courts in most Latin American countries follow, with some exceptions, the theory of relative immunity from jurisdiction. Case-law from the region includes important decisions dealing with the distinction between acts *iure imperii* and acts *iure gestionis*. National courts

[141] Fox (2008), p. 15.

appear to share the view that waiver of immunity from jurisdiction does not entail waiving immunity from execution. At the same time, national courts appear to apply to a large extent the principle of immunity from execution, although some courts already recognise some exceptions to that principle as it appears to be the case of the CC of Colombia and the SCJ of Mexico and its reliance in the *Italy v Germany* case before the ICJ.

In some countries, given the absence of legislation on the subject, the VCDR has been interpreted extensively, in order to apply by analogy their provisions in the matter of state immunity. But in more recent cases the distinction between diplomatic immunity embodied in the VCDR and state immunity regulated by customary international law, the UN Convention and some regional treaties appear to emerge.

Several courts in the region have understood that the UN Convention reflects an international consensus on state immunity and that some of its provisions codify rules of customary international law. The references to customary international law by national courts, however, have to be taken with caution. They have not always followed an express identification of consistent practice and *opinio iuris* as required by general international law. However, they can have an effect in determining the precise boundaries of state immunity and the evolution of customary international law.

One key aspect that explains in part the position of many countries from the region with respect to state immunity is the fact that Latin American countries have been sued in foreign jurisdictions several times and their immunity in many cases was not recognized. These situations have produced the result that the affected governments resort to diplomatic or legal channels, as it was in the case of Argentina. In 2012, Argentina instituted proceedings before the International Tribunal for the Law of the Sea and an arbitral tribunal constituted under Annex VII of the UN Convention for the Law of the Sea against the Republic of Ghana, due to the detention and court measures adopted by Ghana against the frigate ARA Libertad.[142] The controversy was successfully solved by the interplay of judicial and political methods of dispute settlement. In addition, in 2014, Argentina submitted an application against the United States to the ICJ, where it contended that the United States had 'committed violations of Argentine sovereignty and immunities and other related violations as a result of judicial decisions adopted by US tribunals concerning the restructuring of the Argentine public debt'.[143] No further action was taken in the proceedings, since the United States did not consent to the Court's jurisdiction in the case.

The challenges to state immunity of Latin American countries before foreign courts have also played an important role in the decisions of tribunals from the region when analysing state immunity, and in particular its evolution and the role of reciprocity. In many cases, the position of states or their national courts appears to be

[142]Cabrera Mirassou (2014).

[143]See ICJ, Press release No. 2014/25, 7 August 2014. https://www.icj–cij.org/public/files/press–releases/4/18354.pdf. Accessed 15 April 2021.

based on the concerns that a more flexible approach could impact on the development of state immunity in other countries where they can be sued. Ultimately, there could be a concern that a more flexible approach could contribute to legitimise potential abuses of jurisdiction by other states.

State immunity is in continuing evolution in Latin America and that evolution appears to move into deferent levels. For these reasons, more dialogue between legal doctrine, governmental policymakers and national courts appears to be desirable.

References

Badr GM (1984) State immunity: an analytical and prognostic view. Martinus Nijhoff, The Hague

Briones EB (2012) La Inmunidad de la Jurisdicción Internacional Dentro del Derecho Laboral Interno. Revista de Ciencias Jurídicas No 128:47–72

Cabrera Mirassou M (2014) The ARA libertad. In: Wolfrum R (ed) Max Planck Encycl Public Int Law. OUP, Oxford

Fox H (2008) The law of state immunity, 2nd edn. OUP, Oxford

Goldschmidt W (1974) Derecho Internacional Privado, 2nd edn. Depalma, Buenos Aires

González Napolitano SS, Lozza M (2015) Las Inmunidades de los Estados Extranjeros. In: González Napolitano SS (ed) Lecciones de Derecho Internacional. Erreius, Buenos Aires, pp 725–760

Olivares Hernández A, Briceño Laborí JA (2020) La inmunidad de jurisdicción y su tratamiento por la jurisprudencia venezolana. In: AMDIPC 2020 No 2, pp 299–338

Quintana Aranguren JJ, Guzmán Carrasco G (2006) De Espaldas al Derecho Internacional: Colombia y la Inmunidad de Jurisdicción de los Estados. Revista Colombiana de Derecho Internacional 8:53–102

Reyes Moncayo MA (2017) La inmunidad jurisdiccional de los Estados: diferencias normativas. Revista Mexicana de Política Exterior 109:77–97

Romero F (2010) Inmunidad de Jurisdicción. In: Maekelt T et al (eds) Derecho Procesal Civil Internacional. Academia de Ciencias Políticas y Sociales, Caracas, pp 229–276

Yang X (2012) State immunity in international law. CUP, Cambridge

Facundo Pérez-Aznar is a senior researcher at the Geneva Center for International Dispute Settlement and Associate Professor of international economic law at the University of Buenos Aires. He worked for several years as legal counsel in the Department of International Affairs at the General Attorney's Office of Argentina and previously as legal officer at the Ministry of Foreign Affairs of Argentina.

From Diplomacy to Law: Half-Way in Institutional Transition of China's Regime on State Immunity

Peng Wang

Abstract This chapter maps China's regime on State immunity in general and its nuanced policies and practices on specific issues, such as commercial activities, non-commercial torts, enforcement measures and the case of reciprocity. China's regime on State immunity is a diplomacy-centric approach in transition with manifesting shortcomings: the futile but resilient absolute immunity as well as a principled position with pragmatic manoeuvres. China's laws and practices send a mixed signal on an embedded trajectory to restrictive immunity. China still claims to hold the absolute doctrine of State immunity regarding cases against foreign state, foreign government or its assets despite such absolute immunity could be restricted on the basis of reciprocity. For other privileged persons, the immunity is restrictive to varying degrees without a coherent exception list. The diplomacy-centric regime on State immunity is not enough for a China with comprehensive integrations with the world. China is in an early stage of institutionalizing its regime on State immunity and still need more time to search for a clear and culturalized set of multiple goals with limited and sometimes mutually competing tools.

1 Introduction

China is well known for its insistence on the absolute doctrine of State immunity. Given the recent lawsuits on the Covid-19 pandemic involving China in foreign courts,[1] there are mounting discussions, both domestic and foreign, on China's positions on the State immunity and its implications.

The author thanks Ms. Guannan Qu for her excellent research assistance. The research is supported by a Chinese National Social Science Research Grant (18CFX084). The views expressed in this chapter are those of the author alone.

[1] For example, The State of Missouri v. The People's Republic of China, et al. The United States

P. Wang (✉)
Xi'an Jiaotong University School of Law, Xi'an, PR China

R. Bismuth et al. (eds.), *Sovereign Immunity Under Pressure*,
https://doi.org/10.1007/978-3-030-87706-4_7

State immunity is a lasting issue for China since the very foundation of the People's Republic of China.[2] Existing discussions primarily focus on the historical and cultural explanations on Chinese positions on State immunity. China always bears in mind its bitter days during the era of semi-colonial and semi-feudal with fragmentary sovereignty and thus rather cherishes its sovereignty.[3] Therefore, the People's Republic of China government recognizes no external odious debts incurred by the defunct Chinese governments. The principle of non-interference (as part of the Five Principles)[4] in other states' internal affairs naturally prevents the exercise of jurisdiction of Chinese courts over disputes involving foreign states or governments and equally if not more importantly the exercise of foreign courts over disputes involving Chinese government or its assets.[5]

A handful of literature focuses on explaining China's general position on absolute immunity. The interest-based explanation holds that the restrictive doctrine favors the interests of transnational enterprises and thereby that of their home countries, which are usually more developed countries. The developing countries therefore

District Court for The Eastern District of Missouri Southeastern Division, Case No.1:20-cv-00099, 21 April 2020. The State of Mississippi v. The People's Republic of China, et al. The United States District Court for The Southern District of Mississippi Southern Division, Case No.1:20-cv-00168-LG-RHW, 12 May 2020. Moriah Aharon et al v. Chinese Communist Party et al, United States District Court Southern District of Florida, Case No. 9:20-cv-80604-XXXX, 8 April 2020. Buzz Photos, et al v. The People's Republic of China, et al., The United States District Court for The Northern District of Texas, Case No. 3:20-cv-00656-K, 17 March 2020.

[2]China has been sued in the courts of the United States on a frequent basis. China always claimed absolute immunity and in principle refused to participate in the proceedings. In some cases, China's state immunity had been denied by default judgments by the American courts but later restored due to China's strong diplomatic maneuvers and special appearance in the court to invoke the state immunity. The notable cases are: Jackson v. People's Republic of China (otherwise known as Huguang Railways Bearer Bonds), 550 F. Supp.869 (N.D. Ala. 1982), 22 Int'l Legal. Materials 75; Morris v. People's Republic of China, 478 F. Supp. 2d 561 (S.D.N.Y. 2007); Pons v. The People's Republic of China, 666 F. Supp. 2d 406 (S.D.N.Y. 2009); Covington Marine Corp. et al v. Xiamen Shipbuilding Industry Co., Ltd., et al, 504 Fed.Appx.298(C.A.5(La.),2012); First Inv.Corp.of Marshall Islands et al v. Fujian Mawei Shipbuilding,Ltd., et al, F.3d 742(C.A.5(La.),2012); Walters v. Industrial and Commercial Bank of China, 651 F.3d 280 (2d Cir. 2011).

[3]See Wang (1990), p. 288. China has been the most 'enthusiastic champion' of the principle of sovereignty under international law.

[4]The Five Principles include: '(a) mutual respect for each other's territorial integrity and sovereignty; (b) mutual non-aggression; (c) mutual non-interference in each other's internal affairs; (d) equality and mutual benefit; (e) peaceful co-existence'. The Speech of President XI Jinping at the Conference of the 60th Anniversary of the Five Principles of Peaceful Coexistence. The State Council of the People's Republic of China (28 July 2014) http://www.gov.cn/xinwen/2014-06/29/content_2709613.htm. Accessed 15 April 2021.

[5]Judge Hanqin Xue noted: '[China] holds absolute immunity in case of acts of foreign States from national jurisdiction and execution. It is of the view that the principle of immunity is a right of State under customary international law rather than [of] comity. . .In its judicial practice, Chinese national courts have neither exercised jurisdiction over acts of foreign States, nor have they enforced any decisions involving public property of foreign States'. For details see Xue (2011), pp. 100–101. See also Duan (2011). Law Press, Beijing and The Department of Treaty and Law of the Ministry of Foreign Affairs of China (2018).

should adhere to absolute State immunity in order to protect their national interest.[6] The interaction-based explanation holds that states will become increasingly restrictive when they interact more with the world. 'Some isolated States may or may not still stick to the traditional absolutist position either because they have hardly more than minimum contact with and presence in foreign States (such as North Korea), or because they are regularly sued in foreign courts anyway (such as Cuba in the U.S. courts)'.[7] The identity-based explanation takes the socialist identity, such as the strong role of government played in the market, as a decisive factor underlying China's stance on foreign affairs.[8] However, the above arguments might explain certain but not all the complex dimensions of China's absolute doctrine on State immunity as China is a country with the mixed-identity in transition. From the perspective of developing/developed country, though China claims itself to be a developing country, the rest of the world finds difficulties in lining up China with other typical developing countries. It might also be confusing to understand China as a classical socialist country while it has expanding private interest overseas to protect. And China is certainly not isolated from international communities.

There is not much discussion on the Chinese position on State immunity in the context of the rise of China. This article aims to explain the dilemma between China's growing interests in restrictive immunity with its economic rise and the resilience of absolute immunity on State immunity. This article finds that China is in an early stage of institutionalizing its State immunity regime. The old diplomatic approach does not satisfyingly fit in the new normal of a rising China.

China's regime on State immunity is a diplomacy-centric approach in transition with manifesting shortcomings: the futile but resilient absolute immunity as well as a principled position with pragmatic manoeuvres. China's policies and practices send a mixed signal on restrictive immunity. China follows the general trend of shifting towards codified restrictive immunity but takes its own path sometimes with setbacks. China still claims to hold the absolute doctrine of State immunity regarding cases against foreign state, foreign government or its assets despite the fact such absolute immunity could be restricted on the basis of reciprocity. For other privileged persons, the immunity is restrictive to varying degrees without a coherent exception list. China is rigid in the general principle on State immunity but proves flexible in practical manoeuvres. Fragmentations are also found in the foundations and expressions of State immunity in nuanced issue-specific contexts.

The diplomacy-centric regime on State immunity is not enough for a China which seeks comprehensive integrations with the world. China is in the early stage of institutionalizing its regime on State immunity. China is still and perhaps will in the future also need more time in search for a clear and culturalized set of multiple goals with limited and sometimes mutually competing tools: from prioritizing flexibility in a diplomatic approach to emphasizing the scale effect in a legalized approach.

---

[6] See generally Qi (2008).

[7] Yang (2012), p. 3.

[8] See generally Cai (2019).

The purpose of this article is two-fold: firstly, to describe the Chinese position on State immunity, both the general landscape and the nuances on multifaceted issues; secondly, to provide an institutional explanation on the trajectory of Chinese evolutionary positions on State immunity. The contribution of this article is to contextualize the issue of State immunity in China's unique institutional system and to demonstrate the policy spectrum that State immunity issue might fall in. It also sheds lights on the challenges that China might encounter if it wants to modernize its regime on State immunity to better cope with the new normal of a more open and ambitious China as a major global player.

The rest of the article proceeds as follows. Section 2 maps Chinese positions on international law in general and international dispute settlement in particular. Section 3 makes an overview of China's regime on State immunity at both international and national levels. Section 4 investigates the nuanced policies and practices of China's regime in specific contexts, such as commercial activities, non-commercial torts, enforcement measures and the case of reciprocity. Section 5 summarizes the key features of China's regime as a diplomacy-centric approach with manifesting shortcomings: the futile but resilient absolute immunity as well as a principled position with pragmatic manoeuvres. Section 6 explains China's positions from a perspective of institutional transition.

2 Chinese Position on International Law: A Context

2.1 China and International Law

China is a late-comer to international legal system and for a quite long period of time a rule-taker. With its economic rise, China increasingly finds itself in a somewhat dilemma, a proactive vision with growing ambitions and broadening interests embedded within a conservative institutional set.

China's general attitude to international law has evolved over time. Before the 1970s, China was 'virtually precluded from major international law-making processes'.[9] In line with its diplomatic policy of 'cleaning the house first before the guests are invited' and 'making a fresh start', China's treaty practice focused on 'abrogating the old unequal treaties and concluding new treaties'.[10] Specifically at the beginning of the first period, roughly before the 1960s, China's attitude towards International law had been deeply shaped by the USSR's approach due to the policy of 'leaning to one side'.

After China resumed its seat at the United Nations in the early 1970s, China gradually reconnected itself with major international organizations. China's participation in the international legal system accelerated after China initiated its Reform

[9] Xue (2012), pp. 54–55.
[10] Jia (2019).

and Opening-up policy in late 1970s. A mile stone is China's accession to the WTO which marks the irreversible integration with the world. After the economic crisis in 2008, China's economic rise increasingly manifests. Especially with the Belt and Road Initiative, China takes a more ambitious and constructive approach to international law under the context of a ring China.[11]

2.2 *China and International Dispute Resolution*

Chinese policies on international dispute resolution vary, depending on interests involved from a trinity of national interest. China's national interest could be divided into three categories, namely sovereign interests, security interests and development interests. As a grand principle, China frames its international law policy for different kinds of national interest.

It is a principle for China that all sovereign disputes, especially the territorial disputes, should only be settled by peaceful means directly between the disputing parties. For China, international arbitration or tribunal proceedings are not a welcome means for political issues such as territorial disputes. For the security issues, the disputes should be settled by careful considerations of the interests and concerns of the parties which have a stake in the disputes. For development disputes which typically refer to economic disputes, China gradually adapts to all kinds of international dispute settlement, including the third party dispute settlement, typically arbitration and panel proceedings.

However, the trinity of national interest does not provide much clarity on State immunity. With the economic rise of China, the overlaps between sovereign interest and development interest increasingly manifest. There are increasing economic issues involving sovereign issues. State immunity is one of the typical examples.

3 Chinese Position on the State Immunity: Overview of the Regime

This section maps China's general policies and practices on the State Immunity at both international and domestic levels.

[11] Xi Jinping (President of the People's Republic of China), 'Firmly Pursuing the Rule of Law with Chinese Characteristics and Providing Legal Support for the Comprehensive Construction of a Modern Socialist State', Qiushi, 2021, No.5, http://www.qstheory.cn/dukan/qs/2021-02/28/c_1127146541.htm. Accessed 15 April 2021. ('For unjust and reasonable international rules and regimes that do not cope with the evolution of international order, plans should be proposed to reform the global governance system and construct the Community of Mankind with Shared Destiny'.) See generally Cai (2019).

3.1 General Policy

3.1.1 Current Positions

In *Democratic Republic of Congo v. FG Hemisphere Associates* in 2011,[12] China fully explained the absolute immunity doctrine it held and still holds:

> China firmly adheres to the important legal doctrine of State immunity which protects the normal development of the relations among states. It means that the courts of China have no jurisdiction over, or in practice have they ever entertained, any case in which a foreign state is sued as a defendant or any claim involving the properties of any foreign state. At the same time, China has never accepted any foreign courts having jurisdiction over cases in which the State of China is sued as a defendant, or over any cases involving the properties of the State of China. This position on State immunity adopted by China is usually referred to as absolute immunity.[13]

There are three layers in China's absolute immunity doctrine: absolute jurisdictional immunity and execution immunity; absolute immunity of China and its assets in foreign courts; and absolute immunity of foreign state and its assets in Chinese courts. In the first letter from the Office of the Commissioner of the Ministry of Foreign Affairs of China in Hong Kong ('the OCMFA') on 20 November 2008, China states:

> The consistent and principled position of China is that a state and its property shall, in foreign courts, enjoy absolute immunity, including absolute immunity from jurisdiction and from execution, and has never applied the so-called principle or theory of 'restrictive immunity'. The courts in China have no jurisdiction over, nor in practice have they ever entertained, any case in which a foreign state or government is sued as a defendant or any claim involving the property of any foreign state or government, irrespective of the nature or purpose of the relevant act of the foreign state or government and also irrespective of the nature, purpose or use of the relevant property of the foreign state or government. At the same time, China has never accepted any foreign courts having jurisdiction over cases in which the State or Government of China is sued as a defendant, or over cases involving the property of the State or Government of China. This principled position held by the Government of China is unequivocal and consistent.[14]

---

[12] Democratic Republic of the Congo v. FG Hemisphere Assocs., [2011] 14 H.K.C.F.A.R. 395, pp. 62, 502–12 (C.F.A.) (H.K.).

[13] Li Fei, Deputy Director of the Legislative Affairs Commission of the Standing Committee of the National People's Congress, 'The Explanations on the Draft Interpretation of Paragraph 1, Article 13 and Article 19 of the Basic Law of the Hong Kong Special Administrative Region of the People's Republic of China by the Standing Committee of the National People's Congress, at the 22nd Session of the Standing Committee of the Eleventh National People's Congress on 24 August 2011', para. 3, (27 August 2011) http://www.gov.cn/jrzg/2011-08/27/content_1934211.htm. Accessed 15 April 2021.

[14] Democratic Republic of the Congo, China Railway Group (Hong Kong) Limited, China Railway Resources Development Limited, China Railway Sino-Congo Mining Limited, China Railway Group Limited, Secretary For Justice, v FG Hemisphere Associates, in The Court of Final Appeal of the Hong Kong Special Administrative Region Final Appeal Nos 5, 6 & 7 Of 2010 (Civil) (On Appeal from Cacv Nos 373 Of 2008 And 43 Of 2009), Judgment, 8 June 2011, para. 44.

3.1.2 Foundations of State Immunity and Its Exceptions

Foundations of State Immunity

State immunity derives from the principle of sovereign equality.[15] In the Huguang Railways Bearer Bonds case, China stated that: 'Sovereign immunity is an important principle of international law. It is based on the principle of sovereign equality of all States as confirmed by the Charter of the United Nations'.[16] It was believed by China that '[T]he absolute jurisdictional immunity of States in foreign courts is still a valid rule under international law on the basis of the principle of sovereign equality (*par in parem non habet imperium*, an equal has no power over an equal)'.[17] The restrictive doctrine might jeopardize its very foundation of state equality. As Judge Hanqin Xue put it, 'Albeit a procedural rule, the immunity principle touches ... fundamental principles of international law: sovereign equality...',[18] and 'the principle of sovereignty has been squarely challenged by jurisdictional immunities of States'.[19]

China's regime of State immunity is structured on the basis of a strong notion of sovereignty.[20] China has also 'consistently upheld the principle of State immunity for the maintenance of legal order and the stability of international relations'.[21] Given the tight connection between sovereignty and State immunity, China worried that, easily expanding the application of immunity exceptions forcibly without universal practice will not only fundamentally devalue the immunity principle itself, but also trigger the risk of abusing State immunity for political ends.[22] 'International obligations regarding immunity of States, their property and officials must be honored by States at all times. Violations of these obligations are not in conformity with the principle of sovereign equality of States and may contribute to the escalation of tensions'.[23]

States diverge on exceptions to State immunity. As China claimed in the negotiations of the United Nations Convention on Jurisdictional Immunities of States and

[15] Shan and Wang (2019), p. 61.

[16] Memorandum from China to U.S. on the Case of Huguang Railways Bearer Bonds, 2 February 1983, para. 2, in Duan (2011), pp. 35–36.

[17] Duan (2011), p. 36. 'So far there has not been enough evidence to prove that by State practice and opinio juris, this customary international law rule has changed'.

[18] Xue (2012), p. 103.

[19] Xue (2012), p. 100.

[20] See for instance, Art. 8 Russia-China Joint Declaration on Promotion and Principles of International Law (2016) The Declaration placed the sovereign equality at the primary position of basic principles of International law. To their mutual understanding, the principle of sovereign equality should not only be weakened, but strengthened. In The Department of Treaty and Law of the Ministry of Foreign Affairs of China (2018), p. 5.

[21] Xue (2011), p. 100.

[22] The Department of Treaty and Law of the Ministry of Foreign Affairs of China (2018), p. 15.

[23] Art. 8 Russia-China Joint Declaration on Promotion and Principles of International Law (2016).

Their Property (the UNCSI),[24] the formulation of a codified international legal instrument on State immunities was needed because of 'long-standing differences on the issue of State immunities and conflicting national practices', which 'had adversely affected international exchanges'. Then it was thus of great significance of 'regulating State conduct and harmonizing and defining legal provisions on jurisdictional immunities', and subsequently developing harmonious and stable international relations.[25] Unsurprisingly, in the negotiation of the UNCSI, China had repeatedly emphasized that the principle of jurisdictional immunities of States should firstly be affirmed in general principle on the basis of which specific exceptions could be worked out.[26]

Rationale for the Restrictions on State Immunity

The growing participation of States in international economic activities fundamentally transformed the functions of State and that transformation resulted in different conceptions of the State and State immunity.[27] 'A State engaging in business in competition with private persons or corporations should be answerable in the courts of the country where the business is conducted. The commercial or private law exception is driven by increasing concern for private rights and public morality, coupled with the increasing entry of governments into what had previously been regarded as private pursuits'.[28]

As put by French representatives to the negotiations of the UNCSI, 'The customary rules governing the jurisdictional immunities of States were no longer as relevant as they had been in the past. States were increasingly involved in economic and commercial operations which were largely unrelated to their sovereign functions. Application of the customary rules was resulting distortions and even inequities'.[29]

China acknowledges that 'since the end of the Second World War, the functions of the State had become more complex, and there were more instances of States engaging in international trade and transactions of their own behalf'.[30] However,

[24] United Nations Convention on Jurisdictional Immunities of States and Their Property (2004) (the UNCSI).

[25] UN General Assembly, Summary record of the 13th meeting (A/C.6/59/SR.13), 22 March 2005, p.8

[26] UN General Assembly, Summary record of the 45th meeting (A/C. 6/36//SR.45), 19 November 1981, p. 12. UN, A/47/326/Add.1, 16 July 1992, China, para. 2; UN General Assembly, Summary record of the 25th meeting, (A/C. 6/45/SR. 25), 19 November 1990, p. 4.

[27] Yang (2012), p. 8.

[28] United States, Court of Appeals, Victory Transport Inc. v. Comisaria General, (2d Cir. 1964), 35 ILR 110.

[29] The Statement of Mr. Legal (France) in the Sixth Committee of the UN General Assembly, Summary record of the 33rd meeting(A/C.6/49/SR.33), 14 November 1994, p. 2.

[30] UN General Assembly, Summary record of the 23rd meeting (A/C.6/53/SR.23), 20 November 1998, p. 2.

China does not entirely endorse the dichotomy of public *vis-à-vis* private acts: 'Some of those commercial transactions were for profit, but other sought to promote public welfare. It was obviously inappropriate for a foreign court to exercise jurisdiction over the State when it had not expressly given up immunity beforehand'.[31]

China agreed that it was necessary to envisage exceptions to the jurisdictional immunity of States and thus did not object to include certain reasonable exceptions, but the inclusion shall be restrictive. Since Chinese delegation had complained about introducing 'too many exceptions'[32] to the draft of the UNCSI, they suggested that 'such exceptions must be kept to a minimum that corresponded to real needs arising in practice' and the exceptions shall complement and not negate the principle of jurisdictional immunity of States.[33]

3.2 *International Practices*

3.2.1 UNCSI

During the negotiations on the UNCSI,[34] China clarifies its positions on State immunity in general and on various exceptions in particular. Firstly, China repeatedly emphasized the legal distinction between State and State enterprise:[35] States should not be held responsible for State enterprises and corporations, and that no proceeding could be instituted against a State before court of a foreign State in connection with disputes with those enterprises and corporations, and *vice versa*.[36] Secondly, China opposed the inclusion of human right related exceptions, such as the non-commercial tort,[37] and contract of employment.[38] In this respect, China believes the State practices were too scarce and the disputes could be better solved through diplomatic channels than litigation. Thirdly, China insisted on the inclusion of a purpose test for determining the commercial character of a contract or

---

[31] Ibid., p. 2.

[32] UN General Assembly, Summary record of the 39th meeting (A/C. 6/41/SR. 39), 17 November 1986, p. 6.

[33] UN General Assembly, Summary record of the 23rd meeting (A/C.6/46/SR.23), 13 November 1991, p. 20.

[34] United Nations Convention on Jurisdictional Immunities of States and Their Property (2 December 2004) (the UNCSI).

[35] UN General Assembly, Summary record of the 29th meeting (A/C.6/48/SR.29), 22 December 1993, 17.

[36] UN General Assembly, Summary record of the 25th meeting, (A/C. 6/45/SR. 25), 19 November 1990, 2; UN General Assembly, Summary record of the 32nd meeting (A/C.6/47/SR/32), 3 December 1992, 4; UN General Assembly, Summary record of the 32nd meeting (A/C.6/49/SR.32), 5 December 1994, 6.

[37] UN General Assembly, Report of the Working Group (A/C.6/47/L.10), 3 November 1992, 15.

[38] UN General Assembly, Report of the Working Group (A/C.6/47/L.10), 3 November 1992, 14–15.

transaction. A State may engage in an otherwise commercial transaction in order to promote public welfare[39] and immunity should be given to protect the property of states used for such public purposes.[40]

During the negotiations, China also mentioned multiple times that the process should be more representative. 'The extensive documentation provided by the Special Rapporteur had been mainly drawn from certain countries advocating limited immunity, while the practices of other countries, in particular developing countries, were poorly represented. It would be difficult for any study based on that information to give a full picture of current international practice'.[41] 'The draft articles shall...on the basis of a thorough study of the practice of States, including the socialist and developing countries, pragmatically identifying those exceptions whose necessity and reasonableness are borne out by reality...'.[42] 'International practice in this matter was far from being uniform. However, in no way should the practice of certain States be held up as a universal rule'.[43] 'The commission must therefore seek a balance that would be acceptable to all States, including developing countries, between the two existing doctrines'.[44]

With respect to the effect of UNCSI on China's policy on State immunity, some scholars argue that China has begun to refine its traditional conception of sovereignty.[45] However, China holds that the text of the UNCSI 'was not as satisfactory or perfect as it might have been'. China signed it to express its support of 'the coordination efforts made by the international community'.[46]

---

[39] UN General Assembly, Convention on jurisdictional immunities of States and their property, Report of the Secretary-General (A/56/291), 14 August 2001, 3; UN General Assembly, Summary record of the 23rd meeting (A/C.6/53/SR.23), 20 November 1998, 2; UN General Assembly, Summary record of the 32nd meeting (A/C.6/49/SR.32), 5 December 1994, 6; UN General Assembly, Summary record of the 29th meeting (A/C.6/48/SR.29), 22 December 1993, 17.

[40] UN General Assembly, Convention on jurisdictional immunities of States and their property, Report of the Secretary-General (A/56/291), 14 August 2001, 3. The special interest of a State under exceptional circumstances covers, such as the procurement of food supplies to relieve a famine situation, purchase goods to revitalize an affected area, or supply medicaments to combat a spreading epidemic.

[41] UN General Assembly, Summary record of the 39th meeting (A/C. 6/39/SR. 39), 19 November 1984, para.30.

[42] UN General Assembly, Convention on jurisdictional immunities of States and their property, Comments and observations received from Governments, A/CN.4/410 (28 December 1987), 63, General Comments of China, para. 2.

[43] UN General Assembly, Summary record of the 32nd meeting (A/C.6/49/SR.32), 5 December 1994, para. 17.

[44] UN General Assembly, Summary record of the 39th meeting (A/C. 6/41/SR. 39), 17 November 1986, para. 17.

[45] Cai (2019), p. 258.

[46] The Second Letter from the Office of the Commissioner of the Ministry of Foreign Affairs of China in Hong Kong, in Democratic Republic of the Congo v. FG Hemisphere Assocs., [2011] 14 H.K.C.F.A.R. 395, 62, 502–12 (C.F.A.) (H.K.)., para. 3. UN General Assembly, Summary record of the 13th meeting (A/C.6/59/SR.13), 22 March 2005, p. 8.

3.2.2 Other Treaties

Absolute immunity does not preclude the waiver of state immunity. China has gradually accepted the international investment arbitration. In a classical investment treaty, a foreign investor is entitled to sue the Chinese government before an international tribunal provided other prerequisite conditions are met. The waiver of jurisdictional immunity is also recognized in multilateral treaties, such as in the Convention on the Settlement of Investment Disputes between States and Nationals of Other States (the ICSID Convention).

However, with regard to the enforcement immunity, China takes a more conservative position. The ICSID Convention requires member states to 'enforce the pecuniary obligations imposed by arbitral awards within its territories as if it were a final judgment of a court in that state'[47] but it does not require member states to derogate from the law in force relating to immunity from execution.[48] China also makes a reservation to the New York Convention on Enforcement of Foreign Arbitral Awards (The New York Convention) and precludes the investor-state dispute.

Although international organization immunity and State immunity are two types of immunity, we may nevertheless see some new developments with the increasing number of international organizations seated in China.[49] For example, the Asian Infrastructure Investment Bank (AIIB) adopts a commercial transaction exception to the immunity enjoyed by the AIIB itself.[50] For the immunity enjoyed by employee and personnel of international organizations, exceptions to immunity can be found with regard to tort and commercial transaction.[51]

3.3 *Domestic Practices*

3.3.1 Substantive Rules

State immunity in China's domestic law is more multi-faceted. China remains generally absolute on State immunity while becoming increasingly restrictive on all other forms of immunity.

---

[47] Art. 54 Convention on the Settlement of Investment Disputes Between States and Nationals of Other States (ICSID Convention).

[48] Art. 55 ICSID Convention.

[49] China has signed host agreements with some international organizations, such as the AIIB, the Asia-Pacific Space Cooperation Organization, the international bank for reconstruction and development, the United Nations High Commissioner for Refugees, and the International Committee of the Red Cross.

[50] Art. 46 Asian Infrastructure Investment Bank Articles of Agreement (2015).

[51] Convention on privileges and immunities of the Shanghai Cooperation Organization (2004).

China's policy on absolute State immunity is still under-codified. There is no comprehensive law on the sovereign immunity of foreign State in China. Chinese courts will in principle not entertain jurisdiction over disputes involving foreign State, foreign government or foreign assets as respondent.[52] This position has been consistently reiterated in general by China and there is currently no report on such cases involving a foreign State or its asset. However, State assets may be subject to a narrow reading here, as the assets of foreign central banks may be subject to enforcement measures on the basis of reciprocity or a waiver of immunity in written form.[53] Further, it may be possible for other foreign government assets to be subject to certain constrain measures. For example, foreign military and non-commercial foreign government vehicles passing through on 'the sea area under China's jurisdiction' will be expelled by Chinese authorities if they violate Chinese laws and regulations.[54] The flag state will take international responsibility for any damage or harm caused.[55] But Chinese laws and regulations do not specify the forum, procedure and type of such responsibility.

It is worth mentioning that China has been sued multiple times in foreign courts.[56] In all the cases, China has claimed its absolute immunity and refused to participate in the proceedings except special appearance to defend its immunity in selective cases. It is important to note that in China's readings of absolute State immunity, the immunity of China in foreign courts and immunity of a foreign state in Chinese courts are two sides of one coin. Therefore, the role of reciprocity principle, despite not yet been fully specified in Chinese law should not be underestimated.

3.3.2 Reporting Procedures

In China, there is a special report procedure on cases involving privileged persons. The purpose of the report procedure is 'to strictly enforce the Civil Procedure Law of the People's Republic of China and the relevant international conventions that China has acceded to and ensure the correct acceptance of civil cases involving privilege and immunity'.[57] 'For a civil case filed with the people's court where the defendant

[52] Standing Committee of the National People's Congress, 'Interpretation of the Standing Committee of the National People's Congress on Paragraph 1, Article 13 and Article 19 of the Basic Law of the Hong Kong Special Administrative Region of the People's Republic of China' 2011 (6) Bulletin of the Standing Committee of the National People's Congress of the People's Republic of China 583–585.

[53] Law of the People's Republic of China on Immunity of the Property of Foreign Central Banks from Compulsory Judicial Measures (2005).

[54] Art.21 Law of the People's Republic of China on the Coast Guard (2021).

[55] Art. 10 Law of the People's Republic of China on the Territorial Sea and the Contiguous Zone (1992).

[56] Notably, in the courts of the United States. See the cases listed in footnote 2.

[57] The Supreme People's Court of China, 'Notice on the relevant issues concerning the acceptance by the People's Courts of civil cases involving privileges and immunities', Fa [2007] No 69, ILDC 2756 (CN 2007), 22nd May 2007.

or third party is any of the subjects that enjoys privilege or immunity in China, before deciding to accept it, the people's court shall submit it to the higher people's court with jurisdiction for examination; the higher people's court agreeing on the acceptance shall submit its examination opinions to the Supreme People's Court. Before the Supreme People's Court makes a reply, no acceptance shall be made'.[58] With such a procedure, China could guarantee that a uniform judicial policy regarding immunity will be achieved.

4 Chinese Position on the State Immunity: Multifaceted Rules on Key Issues

This section maps Chinese positions on more nuanced issues, such as commercial transactions, tort, employment, enforcement and the case of reciprocity.

4.1 Commercial Activity Related Exceptions

4.1.1 Test for Commercial Activity

It is widely recognized that when a State engages in a commercial transaction with a foreign entity, the State is not justified to invoke State immunity. However, states diverge on the criteria for determining the commercial character of a contract or transaction.[59]

For example, in the negotiations of the UNCSI, some states propose the nature test as the sole criterion for commerciality of a contract or transaction. Some states, including China, hold 'the purpose of the State for engaging in the transaction must also be considered' because 'if a State engaged in a transaction in order to promote public welfare, it was obviously inappropriate for a foreign court to exercise jurisdiction over the State'.[60] In China's opinion, providing protection for natural or juridical persons involved in the transaction concerning State immunity should

[58] The Supreme People's Court of China, 'Notice on the relevant issues concerning the acceptance by the People's Courts of civil cases involving privileges and immunities', Fa [2007] No 69, ILDC 2756 (CN 2007), 22nd May 2007.

[59] UN General Assembly, Convention on jurisdictional immunities of States and their property, Report of the Secretary-General (A/56/291), 14 August 2001, p. 3.

[60] UN General Assembly, Summary record of the 23rd meeting (A/C.6/53/SR.23), 20 November 1998, p. 2.

not jeopardize the public purpose of the State[61] for engaging in the transaction, which was not the original intention of this clause.[62]

The UNCSI adopts the nature test as the default criterion unless otherwise established: 'In determining … commercial transaction…, reference should be made primarily to the nature of the contract or transaction, but its purpose should also be taken into account if the parties to the contract or transaction have so agreed, or if, in the practice of the State of the forum, that purpose is relevant to determining the non-commercial character of the contract or transaction.[63] Obviously, the 'nature' test prevails as the 'purpose' test only serves as a complementary tool. Therefore, despite China having signed the Convention, the Chinese delegation deemed that, the provisions of the draft Convention did not give as much weight to the purpose of the contract or transaction as those adopted by the International Law Commission (ILC) in defining a 'commercial transaction'.[64]

4.1.2 Scope of Commercial Exceptions to Diplomatic and Consular Immunity

In China, the immunity afforded to diplomats and consular officials may be restricted if they are involved in commercial activities. However, the scope of commercial exceptions to these two types of immunity is different. The commercial exception to diplomatic immunity covers: succession in which the party is involved as a private person and; the professional or commercial activity conducted by the party in China outside the official functions for personal interest.[65] The commercial exception to consular immunity covers disputes: relating to a contract in which the party did not contract expressly as an agent of the sending State; relating to private immovable property situated in the territory of China, unless the party holds it on behalf of the sending State for the purposes of the consular post; relating to succession in which the party is involved as a private person.[66] The scope of commercial exception to

[61] The special interest of a State under exceptional circumstances, such as the procurement of food supplies to relieve a famine situation, purchase goods to revitalize an affected area, or supply medicaments to combat a spreading epidemic.

[62] UN General Assembly, Convention on jurisdictional immunities of States and their property, Report of the Secretary-General (A/56/291), 14 August 2001, p.3; UN General Assembly, Summary record of the 29th meeting (A/C.6/48/SR.29), 22 December 1993, p.17; UN General Assembly, Summary record of the 32nd meeting (A/C.6/49/SR.32), 5 December 1994, p. 6.

[63] Art.2, para. 2 UNCSI (2004).

[64] UN General Assembly, Summary record of the 13th meeting (A/C.6/59/SR.13), 22 March 2005, p. 8.

[65] Art. 14 and 25 Regulations of the People's Republic of China Concerning Diplomatic Privileges and Immunities (1986).

[66] Art. 14 Regulations of the People's Republic of China Concerning Consular Privileges and Immunities (1990).

diplomatic immunity is broader because it covers all non-official professional or commercial acts while that to consular immunity is narrower with an exclusive list.[67]

4.1.3 Legal Personality of State Owned Enterprise

It is the view of China that States should not be held responsible for acts of State enterprises and corporations (SOEs), and that no proceeding could be instituted against a State before a court of a foreign State in connection with disputes with those enterprises and corporations, and *vice versa.*[68] Unless the State explicitly undertakes the guarantee obligation or the SOE is explicitly authorized by the State, the State should not be jointly or severally liable for the actions of SOEs.[69]

If Chinese SOEs were justified to claim State immunity, traders and investors from non-SOE countries would be discouraged from doing business with Chinese SOEs.[70] The Chinese government serves as the shareholder of SOEs, performs its duty of a stakeholder according to law and regulations, and enjoys interests of shareholders without intervening in the daily operations of SOEs.[71]

The UNCSI makes a clear distinction between the legal position of a State and that of a State enterprise with regard to the question of jurisdictional immunities.[72] It helps prevent the abuse of judicial proceedings against the State of nationality of the enterprise concerned and further contribute to the normal development of international relations.[73] China welcomed such a distinction and further held that the

---

[67] See cases for example, Sun Changbao v Bai Songyue. The Beijing Chaoyang District People's Court, Jing0105 Min Chu No.448 [2018]. Richard Philippe Jean Michel v. Arman Darbo. The Beijing First Intermediate People's Court, Yi Zhong Min Chu Zi No.11472 [2008]. Chuangchun yitu Environment Engineering Ltd v. Xu Dawei. The Beijing Third Intermediate People's Court, Jing 03 Min Zhong No.10953 [2018].

[68] UN General Assembly, Summary record of the 25th meeting, (A/C. 6/45/SR. 25), 19 November 1990, 2; UN General Assembly, Summary record of the 32nd meeting (A/C.6/47/SR/32), 3 December 1992, 4; UN General Assembly, Summary record of the 32nd meeting (A/C.6/49/SR.32), 5 December 1994, 6.

[69] Duan (2011), p. 7.

[70] Cai (2019), p. 215.

[71] According to Law of the People's Republic of China on the State-Owned Assets of Enterprises (2008), The State Council and the local people's governments shall in accordance with laws and administrative regulations perform respectively the contributor's functions for state-invested enterprises and enjoy the contributor's rights and interests on behalf of the state, including enjoy the return on assets, participation in major decision-making and selection of managers. The State Council and the local people's governments shall base their operations on the principles of separation of government bodies and enterprises, separation of the administrative functions of public affairs and the functions of the state-owned assets contributor, and non-intervention in the legitimate and independent business operations of enterprises.

[72] Art. 10.3 The UNCSI.

[73] UN, A/47/326/Add.1, 16 July 1992, China, para. 3; UN General Assembly, Convention on jurisdictional immunities of States and their property, Report of the Secretary-General (A/56/291), 14 August 2001, pp. 3–4.

independent legal personality of State enterprise should be determined by the domestic law of the home State concerned.

In the negotiations of the UNCSI, some countries, such as the United Kingdom and the United States, raised the fact that the State may use SOEs to escape the State's responsibilities, and therefore required the application of the principle of 'piercing the corporate veil' by domestic courts. China responded that 'the vast majority of States today, not only developing but also developed, had State enterprises' and the allegation that State enterprises were often undercapitalized reflected a prejudiced or discriminatory way of thinking.[74] Therefore, the general principle of separation of legal personality between the State and SOEs cannot be denied.[75]

4.2 Fundamental Rights related Exceptions

This category covers exceptions on employment, non-commercial tort and *jus cogens*.

Concerning the contracts of employment as an exception to State immunity, China advocated the deletion of such article in the UNCSI. It was the view of China that judicial decisions and State practice were too scarce in this area and that labor disputes could be solved better through diplomatic channels than through litigation,[76] or by mutual agreement or insurance coverage.[77] Of course, a State may waive its immunity concerning employment. It is interesting to note that in a case involving a privileged international organization, the forum Chinese court made

[74] UN, Draft articles on jurisdictional immunities of States and their property. Titles and texts adopted by the Drafting Committee on second reading: articles 1 to 23—reproduced in A/CN.4/SR.2218 to SR.2221 (A/CN.4/L.457), p. 73, para. 69.

[75] Covington Marine Corp. v. Xiamen Shipbuilding Indus. Co., 504 Fed. Appx. 298, 299, 2012 U.S. App. LEXIS 26297, *1, 2013 AMC 294, 2012 WL 6643279. In Covington Marine Corp. v. Xiamen Shipbuilding Indus. Co. the Court held that, because the company was not an alter ego of the PRC, the company could not bind the PRC to an arbitration agreement that the PRC was not a party to, and thus could not bring it within the arbitration exception of the Foreign Sovereign Immunity Act. First Inv. Corp. v. Fujian Mawei Shipbuilding, Ltd., 703 F.3d 742, 744, 2012 U.S. App. LEXIS 26207, *1, 2013 AMC 273. In First Inv. Corp. v. Fujian Mawei Shipbuilding, Ltd., the court holds that the fact that the PRC was the sole shareholder of one of the companies, which was the majority shareholder of the other company, was insufficient to establish an alter ego relationship. The PRC was immune under the Foreign Sovereign Immunities Act as the arbitration exception did not apply; having failed to show an alter ego relationship, the petitioner did not establish that the PRC was bound to the arbitration agreement.

[76] UN General Assembly, Report of the Working Group (A/C.6/47/L.10), 3 November 1992, pp. 14–15.

[77] UN General Assembly, Summary record of the 25th meeting, (A/C. 6/45/SR. 25), 19 November 1990, p. 2.

inquiries on its own initiative on whether or not the international organization would waive its immunity.[78]

The non-commercial tort exception to State immunity is of increasing importance in the context of several Covid-19 related lawsuits in the U.S. courts. In the negotiations of the UNCSI, China objected to the inclusion of the article on personal injuries and damage to property,[79] and held that the issue could also better be solved through diplomatic channels:[80] 'Firstly, according to article 31 of the Vienna Convention on Diplomatic Relations, diplomatic representatives should enjoy immunities from judicial proceedings in tort in the receiving State; it was obviously illogical for the sending State of diplomatic representatives not to be entitled to enjoy those jurisdictional immunities itself; secondly, the article had gone even further than the restrictive doctrine, for it made no distinction between sovereign acts and private law acts; thirdly, the question of a wrongful act or omission attributable to a State was within the scope of the international responsibility of a State'.[81]

The relationship between State immunity and *jus cogens* is unsettled. Albeit the International Court of Justice considered sovereign immunity and *jus cogens* as distinct procedural and substantive rules,[82] 'This dichotomy is not so clear: one distinctly procedural aspect of *jus cogens* is its relationship to universal jurisdiction, while a court's subject-matter jurisdiction cannot be completely divorced from substantive considerations'.[83] As the Nuremburg Tribunal stated, 'the principle of international law which under certain circumstances protects the representatives of a State, cannot be applied to acts which are condemned as criminal by international law'.[84]

---

[78] Zhu Zhu v the International Committee of the Red Cross. The Beijing Third Intermediate People's Court, San Zhong Min Zhong Zi No.06823 [2014].

[79] UN General Assembly, Summary record of the 23rd meeting (A/C.6/46/SR.23), 13 November 1991, p. 20.

[80] UN General Assembly, Report of the Working Group (A/C.6/47/L.10), 3 November 1992, p. 15.

[81] UN General Assembly, Summary record of the 25th meeting, (A/C. 6/45/SR. 25), 19 November 1990, p. 2.

[82] Jurisdictional Immunities of the State (Ger. v. It., Greece Intervening), 2012 IC.J. 1, 93 (Feb. 3); Arrest Warrant of 11 April 2000 (Dem. Rep. Congo v. Belg.), 2002 ICJ. 3, 60 (Feb. 4) ('Immunity from criminal jurisdiction and individual criminal responsibility are quite separate concepts. While jurisdictional immunity is procedural in nature, criminal responsibility is a question of substantive law').

[83] Weatherall (2015).

[84] Goering et al (1946), p. 221. Recent developments have further sharpened the debate on the principle of immunity. For instance, the judgments rendered on 24 March 1999 by the House of Lords in the United Kingdom and on 13 March 2001 by the Court of Cassation in France in the Pinochet and Qaddafi, in which it contends that an exception to the immunity rule was accepted in the case of serious crimes under international law, have invoked more controversial issues on jurisdictional immunities of States and the scope of national jurisdiction. The Pinochet decision recognizes an exception to the immunity rule when Lord Millett stated that '[i]nternational law cannot be supposed to have established a crime having the character of a jus cogens and at the same time to have provided an immunity which is co-extensive with the obligation it seeks to impose', or when Lord Phillips of Worth Matravers said that 'no established rule of international law requires

China has been quite cautious on the issue on *jus cogens* and associated universal jurisdiction. The Chinese Government holds the view that, arbitrarily expanding the exceptions to the State Official immunity brings no benefit to combating crimes and protecting human rights, and reversely, it might be misused as a tool of political abuse of litigation, and further destructs the inter-State relationship.[85] China's focus on *jus cogens* is more on the litigation concerning Japan's behaviour during the World War II. The 1972 Joint Communiqué of the Government of Japan and the Government of the People's Republic of China,[86] specifically in Paragraph 5, stipulates 'the Government of the People's Republic of China declares that in the interest of the friendship between the Chinese and the Japanese peoples, it renounces its demand for war reparation from Japan'.[87]

Some scholars contend that the Communiqué only waives the right of the Chinese government but not that of Chinese nationals.[88] A Chinese citizen has once filed a request to the Ministry of Foreign Affairs of China for making public the details of the China-Japan negotiations on China's waiver of war reparation but the application was dismissed by the Ministry of Foreign Affairs and subsequently by a reviewing Chinese court.[89]

4.3 Enforcement Exceptions

Based on the statements of Chinese representatives in the negotiations of the UNCSI, China's position on the measures of constraint against State property can be summarized to three layers.

Firstly, China held quite negative attitudes on the constraint against State property. From its perspective, 'Immunity from constraint was much more strict than the

state immunity ratione materiae to be accorded in respect of prosecution for an international crime. The French Court of Cassation, in holding that, 'under international law as it currently stands, the crime alleged [acts of terrorism], irrespective of its gravity, does not come within the exceptions to the principle of immunity from jurisdiction for incumbent foreign Heads of State', the Court explicitly recognized the existence of such exceptions.

[85] The Department of Treaty and Law of the Ministry of Foreign Affairs of China (2018), pp. 14–15.

[86] Joint Communiqué of the Government of Japan and the Government of the People's Republic of China, China-Japan (1972). http://www.mofa.go.jp/region/asia-paci/china/joint72.html. Accessed 15 April 2021.

[87] Joint Communiqué of the Government of Japan and the Government of the People's Republic of China, China-Japan (1972). http://www.mofa.go.jp/region/asia-paci/china/joint72.html. Accessed 15 April 2021, para. 5.

[88] See Experts Advise Chinese WWII Laborers to File Class Action, People's Daily Online (Jan. 15, 2002) http://en.people.cn/200201/15/eng20020115_88683.shtml. Accessed 15 April 2021.

[89] Tang Liren v the Ministry of Foreign Affairs of China. The Beijing Third Intermediate People's Court, Jing 03 Xing Chu Zi No.94 [2018].

Zhu Zhu v the International Committee of the Red Cross. The Beijing Third Intermediate People's Court, San Zhong Min Zhong Zi No.06823 [2014].

jurisdictional immunity of States and, from the point of view of international practice,[90] the question of measures of constraint...regarding the property of a foreign State without any distinction would inevitably lead to tensions among States'.[91] Given immunity from measures of constraint is separate from jurisdictional immunity, China deemed that, consent of waiving its immunity to jurisdiction should not imply its consent to the taking of measures of constraint, for which separate consent should be necessary.[92]

Secondly, even if the requirement of consent is met, measures of constraint against the property of a defendant State must fully satisfy the following conditions: '(a) the property is in the territory of the State of the forum; (b) the property is specifically in use or intended for use by the State for other than government non-commercial purposes (the specificity of assets); (c) the property has a connection with the claim which is the object of the proceeding, or with the agency or instrumentality against which the proceeding was directed (the legal connection)'. The condition on the specificity of assets is 'an important criterion for differentiating the property of a State from that of a State enterprise or other entity, and for differentiating the property of the various State enterprises and other entities'. The condition on the legal connection of assets was recognized as of crucial importance.[93] Otherwise, it might cause uncertainty and inconsistency in the implementation of measures of constraint.[94]

Thirdly, it is necessary to distinguish pre-judgment measures of constraint with post-judgment measures of constraint. The Chinese delegation presented that measures of constraint should not be implemented against State property before judgment. Since pre-judgment measures of constraint might lead to the abuse of measures of constraint of national courts, causing harm to the property of a foreign State, the consent of the defendant State is thus required. For post-judgment measures of constraint, China considered that, 'consent of the defendant State is also essential for the execution of such measures, especially in cases in which the defendant State is still contesting the jurisdictional immunity question'.[95]

---

[90] UN General Assembly, Summary record of the 39th meeting (A/C. 6/41/SR. 39), 17 November 1986, p. 7.

[91] UN General Assembly, Summary record of the 32nd meeting (A/C.6/49/SR.32), 5 December 1994, p. 6.

[92] UN General Assembly, Convention on jurisdictional immunities of States and their property, Report of the Secretary-General (A/56/291), 14 August 2001, pp. 4–5.

[93] UN General Assembly, Summary record of the 25th meeting, (A/C. 6/45/SR. 25), 19 November 1990, p. 3.

[94] UN General Assembly, Convention on jurisdictional immunities of States and their property, Report of the Secretary-General (A/56/291), 14 August 2001, pp. 4–5.

[95] Ibid.

4.4 Reciprocity

As a general principle, reciprocity is recognized in both Chinese laws and international practices. The role of reciprocity in China's regime of State immunity could not be underestimated.

4.4.1 Reciprocity in Jurisdictional Immunity

Reciprocity on State Immunity

Reciprocity is an inherent part of China's reading of absolute immunity. The immunity of China in foreign courts and immunity of foreign State in Chinese courts are two sides of one coin of the absolute doctrine held by China.

It is worth mentioning that China has been sued multiple times in foreign courts and in all the cases, China has invoked its absolute immunity and refused to participate in any proceedings except in a special appearance to advocate its immunity. In the special appearance, beyond reiterating the origins and status of absolute immunity, China also made an additional point on countermeasures, for example, in *Huguang Railways Bearer Bonds* in the U.S. court:

> The Chinese Government firmly rejects this practice of imposing US domestic law on China to the detriment of China's sovereignty and national dignity. Should the US side, in defiance of international law, execute the above mentioned judgment and attach China's property in the United States, the Chinese Government reserves the right to take measures accordingly.[96]

Reciprocity on Diplomatic Immunity

Reciprocity is also recognized in Chinese laws on both diplomatic and consular immunity. With regard to diplomatic immunity, China could restrict the immunity given to foreign embassy, embassy working staff and relevant personal if less immunity is granted to China's embassy, embassy working staff and relevant personal.[97] With regard to consular immunity, immunity from jurisdiction of consular officers in respect of acts other than those performed in the exercise of their functions shall be accorded in accordance with the bilateral treaties or agreements concluded between China and other countries concerned, or, in default thereof, on the principle of reciprocity.[98]

---

[96] Memorandum from China to U.S. on the Case of Huguang Railways Bearer Bonds, 2 February 1983, para. 3. Duan (2011), pp. 35–36.

[97] Art. 26 Regulations of the People's Republic of China Concerning Diplomatic Privileges and Immunities (1986).

[98] Art. 14 Regulations of the People's Republic of China Concerning Consular Privileges and Immunities (1990).

In addition, the principle of reciprocity has been recognized in other laws dealing with foreign relationships in China, such as Coast Guard Law (2021), Export Control Law (2020), Foreign Trade Law (2016), State Compensation Law (2012) and especially laws concerning judicial assistance.[99]

4.4.2 Reciprocity in Enforcement Immunity

Reciprocity in Enforcement Against Central Bank Asset

The similar combination of absolute immunity and the principle of reciprocity is also seen in the Law of the People's Republic of China on Immunity of the Property of Foreign Central Banks from Compulsory Judicial Measures adopted by the National People's Congress in October 2005. Subject to the principle of reciprocity, China will, within its jurisdiction, grant immunity to the assets of a foreign central bank from measures of constraint (including an injunction prior to judgment and the enforcement of a final judgment), unless the foreign central bank or its government has expressly waived that immunity in writing.[100]

Reciprocity in Enforcement of Foreign Arbitral Awards and Foreign Judgment

The principle of reciprocity is also one basis for international judicial assistance cooperation and in particular for recognizing and enforcing foreign awards and judgments in China. Previously, the judicial interpretation and application of reciprocity relationship was confined to a strict reading, meaning that established reciprocity had been made on the initiative of the counterparty state.[101]

China is relaxing the requirement of reciprocity from a legal reciprocity to a *de facto* reciprocity. Reciprocity could be established if the courts of the applicant's home State have a record of recognizing and enforcing the awards of Chinese courts.[102] There is no requirement with respect to a formal inclusion of reciprocity on such matters in judicial assistance agreement or treaties alike.

---

[99] See generally Art. 40 State Compensation Law of the People's Republic of China (2012 Amendment); Art. 48 Export Control Law of the People's Republic of China (2020); Art. 6 Foreign Trade Law of the People's Republic of China (2016 Revision); Art.79 Law of the People's Republic of China on the Coast Guard (2021); Art. 2 Provisions of the Supreme People's Court on Handling Requests for Judicial Assistance in Service of Judicial Documents, Investigation and Taking of Evidence in Civil and Commercial Cases in Accordance with International Conventions and Bilateral Treaties on Judicial Assistance (2020 Revision).

[100] Art. 3 Law of the People's Republic of China on Judicial Immunity from Compulsory Measures Concerning the Property of Foreign Central Banks (2005).

[101] The Supreme People's Court of China, 'Reply of the Supreme People's Court on whether the People's Court of my country should recognize and enforce the judgment of the Japanese courts on the content of claims and debts', Min Ta Zi No.17 [1995], 26 June 1995.

[102] Reciprocity could be established if the courts of the applicant's home state have a record on recognizing and enforcing the awards of Chinese courts. There is no requirement on a formal

Furthermore, China moves from an established reciprocity to a presumed reciprocity. China may take the initiative to offer judicial assistance to promote the establishment of a reciprocity relationship if there is evidence that the counterparty state has a good intention with respect to international judicial cooperation or makes a promise on returning the favor of judicial reciprocity in the absence of a formal judicial assistance agreement with China.[103] More importantly, with regard to the Asian states, China will presume the existence of reciprocity relation if there is no record of refusal on the recognition and enforcement of Chinese civil or commercial awards on the basis of absence of reciprocity relation in the counterparty state.[104]

However, there is a public policy review in addition to the reciprocity principle in recognizing and enforcing foreign awards.[105] The enforcement of foreign awards should not violate the basic principles of Chinese laws or be contrary to the national sovereignty, security and social public interest.[106] For now, State immunity of a foreign government or its asset is still read in absolute terms and enforcement measures against them will be probably considered as violating the basic principles of Chinese laws or as being contrary to the national sovereignty, security and social public interest.

Given the potential of reciprocity in restricting and balancing the absolute immunity, the reconstruction of reciprocity relation in the context of recognizing and enforcing foreign judgment is clearly desirable. It enhances the legal entrepreneurship of Chinese courts to manoeuvre in existing legal framework to accommodate the evolving judicial activism in changing contexts.

5 Chinese Position on the State Immunity: Key Features

It is hard to label the Chinese approach to State immunity. There are manifesting tensions, and sometimes self-contradictions in Chinese policies and practices. It sends a mixed signal on restrictive immunity: China follows the general trend of shifting towards codified restrictive immunity but takes its own path. China still

inclusion of reciprocity on such matter in judicial assistance agreement or treaties alike. Kolmar Group AG v. Jiangsu Textile Industry (Group) Import & Export Co., Ltd, The Intermediate People's Court of Nanjing, Su 01 Xie Wai Ren No.3 (2016).

[103] The Supreme People's Court of China, 'Several Opinions of the Supreme People's Court on Providing Judicial Services and Safeguards for the Construction of the Belt and Road by People's Courts', Working Documents of the Supreme People's Court and the Supreme People's Court, Fa No. 9 [2015], 16 June 2015.

[104] Nanning Statement of the 2nd China-ASEAN Justice Forum (8 June 2017), para 7 https://www.chinacourt.org/article/detail/2017/06/id/2891257.shtml. Accessed 15 April 2021.

[105] Kolmar Group AG v. Jiangsu Textile Industry (Group) Import & Export Co., Ltd. The Intermediate People's Court of Nanjing, Su 01 Xie Wai Ren No.3 (2016).

[106] The Civil Procedure Law of the People's Republic of China (2017 Amendment) (27 June 2017), art. 282.

claims to hold the absolute doctrine of State immunity regarding cases against foreign state, foreign government or its assets despite such absolute immunity could be restricted on the basis of reciprocity. For other privileged persons, the immunity is restrictive to varying degrees without a coherent exception list. China still needs more time (and perhaps more importantly, more trial-outs) to transform its regime on State immunity from a diplomatic approach to a legalized approach.

5.1 A Diplomatic Approach to State Immunity

In the absence of a multilateral treaty on State immunity to which China is a party, China adopts a diplomatic approach to State immunity.

Firstly, China upholds the importance of sovereignty. China has persistently endorsed the principles and purposes of the UN Charter, especially the principles of equality, peace and mutual respect, as the core of international order and the basis for its approaches to international law.[107] In the negotiations of the UNCSI, China held that the negotiation should explicitly recognize the principle of sovereign equality of States and fully reflect the international practices taking into account the interests of all parties, thereby making the final work an equitable and reasonable legal instrument with universal applicability.[108]

Secondly, the purpose is to promote international exchange and cooperation.[109] In the negotiations of the UNCSI, China reiterated the importance of international rules on State immunity and its exceptions to facilitate international relations. 'The important and complex issue of jurisdictional immunities of States and their property had a bearing on vital national interests and domestic legal systems'.[110] 'Owing to the numerous lacunae existing in most national legislations, practice differed greatly from one country to another. Moreover, there were also incompatibilities between the practice and the applicable national laws and regulations. Globalization and the intensification of trade and economic cooperation meant that conflicts between legal regimes governing jurisdictional immunities were bound to multiply'.[111] 'The formulation of an international legal instrument on State immunities was therefore highly significant for regulating State conduct and harmonizing and defining legal provisions on jurisdictional immunities, thereby helping to develop harmonious and stable international relations'.[112]

---

[107] Xue (2012), pp. 54–55.

[108] UN General Assembly, Summary record of the 39th meeting (A/C. 6/39/SR. 39), 19 November 1984, p. 10.

[109] Ibid., p. 9.

[110] UN General Assembly, Summary record of the 13th meeting (A/C.6/59/SR.13), 22 March 2005, p. 8.

[111] UN General Assembly, Summary record of the 20th meeting (A/C.6/58/SR.12), 23 October 2003, p. 4.

[112] UN General Assembly, Summary record of the 13th meeting (A/C.6/59/SR.13), 22 March 2005, p. 8.

Thirdly, the process is responsive, thereby to harmonize domestic legislation and State practice concerning State immunity.[113] China takes the absolute doctrine but does not enact a comprehensive law on foreign sovereign immunity. It generates multiple effects: (a) China mainly gained its experience on State immunity from dealing with lawsuits in foreign courts as defendants; (b) China was very much in a defensive position, to settle the disputes while to prevent the abuse of domestic juridical proceedings of the forum State;[114] (c) China has pragmatically applied a dual-track tactic, holding the absolute doctrine in principle while tackling the disputes by diplomatic and legal manoeuvres (making special appearance to invoke State immunity according to the laws of the forum State) in practice.

5.2 The Futile but Resilient Absolute Immunity

The absolute doctrine has been proven futile either in securing China's absolute immunity in foreign courts or retaliating against unfriendly proceedings in foreign courts. Practically speaking, China's position on absolute immunity will not help to secure its actual treatment in foreign courts because the courts of the forum State will firstly and primarily resort to its domestic law rather than the law of the respondent State to determine whether or to what extent the respondent State should be immune. For example, in the cases against China in the United States, the forum courts focused exclusively on the concrete legal issues under the U.S. domestic law.

The absolute doctrine is also insufficient in protecting the interest of China as a forum state. Holding absolute immunity, Chinese courts will not be able to hear and uphold the application from Chinese investors to enforce investment arbitration awards, other foreign arbitral awards or foreign judgments against foreign state, foreign government and/or their assets. Meanwhile, Chinese governments at all levels are answerable in Chinese courts if they infringe the interests or rights of a private party.

To sum up, there is an increasing disparity between China's interests in a more aggressive regime of restrictive immunity and the resilience of the absolute immunity.

---

[113]UN General Assembly, Summary record of the 32nd meeting (A/C.6/47/SR/32), 3 December 1992, p. 4; A/CN.4/410 (28 December 1987), para.1.

[114]UN General Assembly, Summary record of the 25th meeting, (A/C. 6/45/SR. 25), 19 November 1990, p. 4; UN General Assembly, Summary record of the 23rd meeting (A/C.6/46/SR.23), 13 November 1991, p. 19; UN, A/47/326/Add.1, 16 July 1992, China, para. 2; UN General Assembly, Summary record of the 29th meeting (A/C.6/48/SR.29), 22 December 1993; p. 17.

5.3 *The Principled Position and the Pragmatic Manoeuvres*

The absolute doctrine held by China is a formalistic absolute immunity, not entirely absolute in a substantive term. Based on a diplomatic approach, China's regime of State immunity provides necessary flexibilities. It only prevents China from actively restricting the immunity of other States on its own initiative. But it does not prevent China from restricting the immunity of other States on a passive basis, such as a countermeasure against the international wrongful acts of that State. It will certainly not prevent other States from voluntarily giving up their immunity either in a treaty in general or as a waiver in proceedings of a particular dispute.

China's formalistic absolute immunity is also evident in its principled position and pragmatic manoeuvres in dealing specific cases. The formalistic absolute immunity is in nature responsive, focusing on handling the diplomatic effects of the dispute in the courts of other States. China will consider all tools available on a case-by-case basis, ranging from traditional diplomatic consultations, diplomatic protests and unilateral white papers clarifying its positions, to special appearance in proceedings of the forum courts, and finally to retaliations. The actual configuration of the manoeuvres depends on the totality of the circumstances as well as on the perceptions of actual departments dealing with the disputes in China. In the eyes of certain observers, it may be arbitrary and lack the necessary level of predictability.

For example, in *Morris v. People's Republic of China*, China adopted a dual-track combination of diplomatic negotiation and special appearance in court proceedings: in the diplomatic channel, China asserted that the case might likely jeopardize the Sino-U.S. relationship; in the special appearance, China filed a motion to dismiss the complaint on the grounds of the inapplicability of commercial exceptions and the collapse of six-year limitation period in accordance with the U.S. domestic law, which was ultimately upheld by the forum court.[115] In contrast, in recent lawsuits against China on the pandemic in the courts of the United States, China resorted only to diplomatic protests.

6 From Diplomacy to Law: Half-Way in Institutional Transition

Based on the above mapping of key features of China's regime on State immunity, this part demonstrates that the seeming contradiction is actually a sign of China's troubled transition from a diplomatic approach to a legalized approach to State immunity.

[115] Morris v. People's Republic of China, 478 F. Supp. 2d 561, 563, 2007 U.S. Dist. LEXIS 20784, *1.

6.1 A Profound But Slow Transition

With the increasing interactions with the world since its Reform and Opening-up Policy in late 1970s, China follows the general trend of shifting towards codified restrictive immunity but takes its own path.

The first key event is the negotiation of the UNCSI which witnessed the softening of China's attitude (not position) to restrictive doctrine. At the early stage of the UNCSI negotiations in 1980s, China was quite negative on the restrictive doctrine: 'His [Chinese] delegation believed that the main legal basis for the jurisdictional immunities of States was the important principle of respect for national sovereignty. It was essential to proceed from that basic premise and to take fully into account the current international reality and the specific conditions of States. Only then would the articles formulated be more practical, harmonize the interests of all States and promote normal international intercourse and development. Two of the articles drafted by the Special Rapporteur for the topic had been provisionally adopted by the Commission. Article 1, paragraph 1, stipulated that a State was immune from the jurisdiction of another State in accordance with the provisions of the articles. That was tantamount to a negation of the independent existence of a fundamental principle of international law, namely, the immunity of States, and was therefore inappropriate. His delegation believed that the principle of jurisdictional immunities of States should first be affirmed in the General Principles, after which specific provisions could be worked out'.[116]

Although actively participating in the draft of the UNCSI, China was still quite negative even in 1998: 'Nevertheless, there was still no broad consensus on the matter, and the solution of the problem depended on the further development of international practice and the corresponding development of theory. In the view of his delegation, the time had not yet come for the convening of a diplomatic conference to conclude a convention on the matter of jurisdictional immunities of States and their property'.[117]

China's accession to the WTO in 2001 may be one factor underpinning China's signature to the UNCSI which might also indicated the shift of China's attitude.[118] In 2003, China held that '[T]he adoption of an international convention should therefore assist States in regulating and standardizing their practice in the interests of avoiding legal conflicts'.[119] In 2004, China held that '[T]he final text of the draft

[116]UN General Assembly, Summary record of the 45th meeting (A/C. 6/36//SR.45), 19 November 1981, p. 12.

[117]UN General Assembly, Summary record of the 23rd meeting (A/C.6/53/SR.23), 20 November 1998, p. 2.

[118]Ministry of Foreign Affairs, China signed the International Convention for the Suppression of Acts of Nuclear Terrorism and the United Nations Convention on Jurisdictional Immunities of States and Their Property. 16 September 2005, https://www.fmprc.gov.cn/web/wjb_673085/zzjg_673183/t212432.shtml. Accessed 15 April 2021.

[119]UN General Assembly, Summary record of the 20th meeting (A/C.6/58/SR.12), 23 October 2003, p.4.

United Nations Convention on Jurisdictional Immunities of States and Their Property was the product of a compromise achieved through the best efforts of all the parties. His delegation hoped that it would be adopted during the General Assembly's current session'.[120]

The second key event is the Law of the People's Republic of China on Immunity of the Property of Foreign Central Banks from Compulsory Judicial Measures. The legislative process was initiated in 2001 and finalized in 2015. 'The direct reason for enacting this law is to support the urgent need for the Hong Kong Special Administrative Region to maintain its status as an international financial center'.[121] Two points are especially noteworthy: firstly, this law is not just a repetition of its position on absolute immunity, but also expressly includes the principle of reciprocity on State immunity with respect to enforcement measures; secondly, it demonstrates that the factors underlying China's policy on State immunity cover not only the profound values and norms such as sovereign equality, but also some pragmatic considerations of interests, such as maintaining the international financial center of Hong Kong.

The most recent key event is the series of activism judicial entrepreneurship under the Belt and Road Initiative. The establishment of the China International Commercial Court, and the progressive interpretation of reciprocity in recognition of foreign arbitral awards and foreign judgments have demonstrated the potential of Chinese judiciary system on dealing with issues of foreign relations.

6.2 Challenges to the Institutional Transition

China is in early stage of institutionalizing its regime. China is still in search for a clear and coherent set of multiple goals with limited and sometimes mutual competing tools: from prioritizing flexibility in a diplomatic approach to emphasizing the scale effect in a legalized approach. The diplomacy-centric regime on State immunity is not enough for a China with comprehensive integrations with the world. The diplomatic approach is flexible but it demands concentrated diplomatic resources which may be overwhelmed by increasing cases. The legalized approach could process an increasingly number of cases but may lack the sufficient flexibility when it needs to do so. Beyond the tension between flexibility and scale-effects, China may face other institutional and societal challenges.

Institutionally, China needs to relocate State immunity from a political issue to a legal issue and overcome the path dependence of the diplomatic approach. Under the diplomatic approach, State immunity will be firstly and primarily characterized as a

[120] UN General Assembly, Summary record of the 13th meeting (A/C.6/59/SR.13), 22 March 2005, p.8.

[121] Ministry of Foreign Affairs, China enacts its first law on enforcement immunity of foreign state asset, 2 March 2006, https://www.fmprc.gov.cn/web/wjb_673085/zzjg_673183/t238012.shtml. Accessed 15 April 2021.

political issue involving sovereign interests in the Chinese trinity of national interest. Then, it will be the diplomatic department which is usually the Ministry of Foreign Affairs rather than the courts in China to handle the issue diplomatically and flexibly. If State immunity were to be characterized as a legal issue, it would be the courts to firstly and primarily handle the case legally and transparently. The professionalism and legitimacy of the court will downplay the issue, save the increasingly scarce diplomatic resources and provide more rooms for diplomatic manoeuvres.

Besides, the legalized approach will also provide legal tools for political ends for China. With the recent lawsuits against Chinese government and pertinent stakeholders in U.S. and other fora, China is of growing demand of legal instruments to counter the lawsuits in foreign courts. Such demand was responded by the proposals on Chinese comprehensive law on foreign State immunity which made by representatives at National People's Congress of the People's Republic of China in 2020.[122] China also seeks to extend the extraterritorial application of its laws and regulations.[123]

The legalized approach will also need a whole-society switch to embed State immunity into China's legal and cultural system. On the one hand, China is promoting the comprehensive rule of law, in both domestic and foreign affairs. The Chinese governments at all levels will be answerable before Chinese courts if it infringes the interests or rights of a private party, domestic or foreign, in China. It would be a violation of the general principle of rule of law if foreign governments infringe the interests or rights of a private party and are immune from Chinese courts. That also implies that it will still be problematic if China partially switch to restrictive doctrine on a selective basis, for example, recognizing only the principle of reciprocity (to defensively counter unfriendly lawsuits in foreign courts) and the waiver of State immunity in the form of arbitration agreement (to proactively protect China's oversea investments). On the other hand, if China switch wholesale to a comprehensive restrictive immunity, including exceptions on commercial transaction and human rights protection, China will have to develop and perhaps more difficultly to justify its unique delimitation between government and market as well as that between public authority and private rights in China's unique legal and cultural system of strong government tradition. It will probably be a long and incremental process for China to depoliticize the foreign affairs in the mind of both the professionals and the general public, and to reset its strong discourses on multilateralism and sovereignty.

In addition, the U.S.-China relationship might have stimulating effects on China's perception and the institutionalization of its regime on State immunity. After the break of the Covid-19 pandemic, there are several lawsuits against China that will be

[122]NPC Deputies Suggest Enacting a State Immunity Law, Beijing Business Today (28 May 2020). http://finance.sina.com.cn/roll/2020-05-28/doc-iirczymk3909801.shtml. Accessed 15 April 2021.

[123]Zhanshu Li, Chairman of the Standing Committee of the National People's Congress, 'Report on the work of the Standing Committee of the National People's Congress at the third session of the 13th National People's Congress on 25 May 2020' (1 June 2020). http://www.npc.gov.cn/npc/c30834/202006/af401b4c055142179f1cea4a17ebfeb1.shtml. Accessed 15 April 2021.

heard in the U.S. courts. The issue on State immunity becomes unprecedentedly pressing for China. These lawsuits highlight China's defensive interest in State immunity and the insufficiency of its current regime. Firstly, it proves the futility of absolute doctrine as a customary international law in protecting China in foreign courts. Secondly, it provides a reform window. The lawsuits against China promote the awareness of the general public of State immunity issue. Proposals on a Chinese comprehensive law on foreign State immunity have been made by representatives at National People's Congress of the People's Republic of China in 2020.[124] Several Chinese citizens also filed applications against the U.S. governments or the President of the United States with intermediate people's courts in Beijing, Wuhan and Tianjin respectively.[125] Thirdly, China continues to claim the importance of reciprocal State immunity in maintaining international exchanges and needs a more effective approach to achieve *de jure* and *de facto* reciprocity. Given the challenges faced by China in its incremental transition, the role of reciprocity in China's regime of State immunity should not be underestimated, which due to space limitations of the chapter will be the subject of a larger research project in the future.

7 Concluding Remarks

China's regime on State immunity is a diplomacy-centric approach with manifest shortcomings: the futile but resilient absolute immunity as well as a principled position with pragmatic manoeuvres. The seeming contradiction is a sign of China's troubled transition from a diplomatic approach to a legalized approach to State immunity. China is still in search of a clear and coherent set of multiple goals with limited and sometimes mutual competing tools: from prioritizing flexibility in a diplomatic approach to emphasizing the scale effect in a legalized approach. The diplomacy-centric regime on State immunity is not enough for a China which seeks comprehensive integrations with the world. The diplomatic approach is flexible but it demands concentrated diplomatic resources which may be overwhelmed by increasing cases. The legalized approach generates scale effects when dealing with an increasingly number of cases but may lack the sufficient flexibility when needed. Institutionally, China needs to relocate State immunity from being a political issue to a legal issue and overcomes the path dependence of the diplomatic approach. Societally, the legalized approach will also need a whole-society switch to embed State immunity into China's legal and cultural system.

---

[124] NPC Deputies Suggest Enacting a State Immunity Law, Beijing Business Today (28 May 2020). http://finance.sina.com.cn/roll/2020-05-28/doc-iirczymk3909801.shtml. Accessed 15 April 2021.

[125] For example, Wuhan Citizens Sued the U.S. Government, Guancha News (22 March 2020). https://user.guancha.cn/main/content?id=268255. Accessed 15 April 2021.

References

Cai CY (2019) The rise of China and international law taking Chinese exceptionalism seriously. OUP, Oxford

Duan JL (2011) International law in China: cases and practice (中国国际法实践与案例). Law Press, Beijing

Jia GD (2019) New China and international law: practice and contribution in 70 years. Chinese J Int Law 18:727–750

Qi DH (2008) State immunity, China and its shifting position. Chinese J Int Law 7(2):307–337

Shan WH, Wang P (2019) Divergent views on state immunity in the international community. In: Ruys T, Angelet N (eds) and Luca Ferro (ass. ed) Handbook on immunities and international law. OUP, Oxford, pp 61–78

The Department of Treaty and Law of the Ministry of Foreign Affairs of China (2018) International law in China: selected cases and practice (中国国际法实践案例选编), Beijing

Wang TY (1990) International law in China: historical and contemporary perspectives. Collected Courses of the Hague Academy of International Law

Weatherall T (2015) Jus Cogens and sovereign immunity: reconciling divergence in contemporary jurisprudence. Georgetown J Int Law 46:1151–1212

Xue HQ (2011) Chinese Contemporary Perspectives on International Law: History, Culture, and International Law. Collected Courses of the Hague Academy of International Law

Xue HQ (2012) Chinese contemporary perspectives on international law: history, culture and international law. Brill, Leiden

Yang XD (2012) State immunity in international law. CUP, Cambridge

Peng Wang is an Associate professor at Xi'an Jiaotong University School of Law, P.R. China. He teaches international investment law, energy law and policy, and international law and international relations. He has contributed to academic journals such as the ICSID Review, Journal of World Investment and Trade, The Journal of World Energy Law & Business among others.

The Law of State Immunity and the Role of the International Court of Justice: Looking for the Guiding Star

Giulia Bernabei

Abstract This chapter addresses the interpretative imbalances of the law of State immunity through an analysis of the approach of the International Court of Justice to the issue. It draws attention on three aspects: (1) it considers the main features and controversies of the international law of immunities, through an investigation of the elements which characterise this branch of law; (2) it singles out the interpretative trends of the International Court of Justice and determines the extent to which its hermeneutic pattern and posture can be understood as steady; (3) it looks at the future of State immunity law through the lens of the work of the International Court of Justice, identifying the role international courts at large are called to perform within this field of expertise.

1 Introduction

The law of State immunity is an entangled branch of law in which public international law ('PIL') and national laws overlap and, not infrequently, might collide. State immunity originates from the need to protect sovereignty within the international legal sphere but comes into play equally before domestic and international adjudicative *fora*. As to its scope, it 'relates to the grant in conformity with the international law of immunities to States to enable them to carry out their public functions effectively

The original version of this chapter was revised. A correction to this chapter can be found at https://doi.org/10.1007/978-3-030-87706-4_19

The author is profoundly indebted to Professor Philippa Webb for her precious advice and extremely helpful comments on earlier drafts. The author produced this publication prior to the beginning of her current position as Senior Research Fellow at the Max Planck Foundation for International Peace and the Rule of Law in Heidelberg, Germany and her association with the Max Planck Foundation. Unless otherwise stated, sources were up-to-date until 13 January 2020. The author has however updated some case-law and materials until February 2021.

G. Bernabei (✉)
Max Planck Foundation for International Peace and the Rule of Law, Heidelberg, Germany
e-mail: bernabei@mpfpr.de

R. Bismuth et al. (eds.), *Sovereign Immunity Under Pressure*,
https://doi.org/10.1007/978-3-030-87706-4_8

and to the representatives of States to secure the orderly conduct of international relations'.[1] Seen through a magnifying glass, however, it fulfils at least three different functions. State immunity is employed as a method: 'i) [...] to ensure a 'stand-off' between States where private parties seek to enlist the assistance of the courts of one State to determine their claims made against another State; ii) [...] of distinguishing between matters relating to public administration of a State and private law claims; [and] iii) [...] of allocating jurisdiction between States in disputes brought in national courts relating to State activities in the absence of any international agreement by which to resolve conflicting claims to the exercise of such jurisdiction'.[2]

The law of State immunity rests on the interaction of international and municipal laws, subjects and interests. This specific feature, combined with the absence of an enforced treaty law mechanism at present, contributes to determining the instability of this branch of law. When sources of a different nature interact, the role of the interpreter becomes crucial in order to enhance consistency. The present chapter addresses the interpretative imbalances which the International Court of Justice ('ICJ' or 'the Court') has given rise to when confronted with the international law of immunities. It draws attention to three aspects of the law of State immunity.

First, the author considers the main features and controversies of the international law of immunities. The elements which typify this field of PIL are investigated and the value of a case-study on the approach of the ICJ is explained. This first section does not aim to cover all State immunity issues. Rather, its scope is limited to ascertaining the typical elements which can qualify the law of State immunity as an autonomous and proper branch of law.

Second, the author identifies the interpretative trends of the ICJ in this field. The author focuses on the practice of the ICJ and assesses to what extent it can be said to have applied a steady hermeneutic pattern in respect of immunity issues. Through an examination of the *Arrest Warrant of 11 April 2000 (Democratic Republic of the Congo v. Belgium)* case ('*Arrest Warrant* case'),[3] the *Jurisdictional Immunities of the State (Germany v. Italy: Greece intervening)* case ('*Jurisdictional Immunities* case')[4] and also other more recent ICJ judgments such as the *Immunities and Criminal Proceedings (Equatorial Guinea v. France)* case ('*Immunities and Criminal Proceedings* case') and the *Certain Iranian Assets (Islamic Republic of Iran v. United States of America)* case ('*Certain Iranian Assets* case'),[5] the chapter

[1] Fox and Webb (2015), p. 1.

[2] Fox and Webb (2015), p. 1.

[3] Arrest Warrant of 11 April 2000 (Democratic Republic of the Congo v. Belgium), Jurisdiction and Admissibility, Judgment of 14 February 2002, [2002] ICJ Rep. 3.

[4] Jurisdictional Immunities of the State (Germany v. Italy: Greece intervening), Judgment of 3 February 2012, [2012] ICJ Rep. 99.

[5] Immunities and Criminal Proceedings (Equatorial Guinea v. France), Preliminary Objections, Judgment of 6 June 2018, [2018] ICJ Rep. 292; Immunities and Criminal Proceedings (Equatorial Guinea v. France), Merits, Judgment of 11 December 2020, General List No. 163 (not yet published); Certain Iranian Assets (Islamic Republic of Iran v. United States of America), Preliminary Objections, Judgment of 13 February 2019, [2019] ICJ Rep. 7.

uncovers the common stance, if any, underlying the Court's approach to immunity questions. Does the ICJ have a common posture towards State immunity law or does it rather employ individual standards on a case-by-case basis? What consequences result from it? To what extent does this reflect the way it perceives the system of PIL as a whole, and its place within it?

Third, the author looks at the future of State immunity law through the lens of the work of the ICJ. The examples of the 2004 United Nations Convention on Jurisdictional Immunities of States and their Property,[6] not yet in force, and of the ongoing work of the International Law Commission ('ILC') on the subject of 'Immunity of State Officials from Foreign Criminal Jurisdiction'[7] show that efforts are being made to adopt a common understanding of State immunity but that, at least for the time being, this remains a fragmented and heterogeneous topic. Thus, the fourth section of this contribution scrutinises the role the ICJ, and international courts in general, to some extent, are called to perform within this field. These bodies hold a privileged position within the international legal order: unlike national and domestic courts, their judgments can foster or undermine certain interpretative trends, especially in already unstable areas of law. Should such courts pro-actively pursue coherence when addressing the conundrum of State immunity law? If so, how could they function as a hermeneutic model which national judicial bodies could/should be guided by?

2 Preliminary Remarks

Modern English language employs the term *immunity* predominantly in two scenarios: (1) in biology/medicine, to refer to 'protection against a particular disease or illness by particular substances in the blood',[8] and (2) in law, to address 'the condition of being protected from the law'[9] or 'official protection from legal action'.[10] By etymology, *immunity* descends from the combination of two terms: (1) the particle *in*, which implies a negative meaning, and (2) the noun *múnus*, which embraces the idea of obligation, commitment, charge.[11] Unsurprisingly, the whole concept of immunity has a negative nuance, which points at the absence or denial of

---

[6] 2004 United Nations Convention on Jurisdictional Immunities of States and their Property, UN Doc. A/59/508 (2004, not yet in force). https://treaties.un.org/pages/ViewDetails.aspx?src=TREATY&mtdsg_no=III-13&chapter=3&clang=_en. Accessed 24 February 2021.

[7] For the latest developments, see: International Law Commission. http://legal.un.org/ilc/. Accessed 7 February 2021.

[8] Cambridge Dictionary. https://dictionary.cambridge.org/dictionary/english/immunity. Accessed 7 February 2021.

[9] Ibid.

[10] Ibid.

[11] For the origins of the term (in Italian), see: Dizionario Etimologico Online. https://www.etimo.it/?term=immune. Accessed 7 February 2021; for the English translation, see: Latin Dictionary.

a particular duty. Both in its original sense and in contemporary PIL, immunity implies the nonexistence of something, a shortfall to some extent. It frees the beneficiaries from the burden they were originally subject to. It is the exception to the general rule.[12]

The international legal scholarship agrees on such general rule being the exercise of jurisdiction by a State. As highlighted by Judges Higgins, Kooijmans and Buergenthal in their Joint Separate Opinion in the *Arrest Warrant* case, '"[i] mmunity" is the common shorthand phrase for "immunity from jurisdiction". If there is no jurisdiction *en principe*, then the question of an immunity from a jurisdiction which would otherwise exist simply does not arise'.[13] Albeit *jurisdiction* and *immunity* being two distinct concepts,[14] the former remains its natural antecedent and prerequisite, upon which the granting of the latter has to be assessed.[15] Hence, the international law of immunities is made of exceptions which ultimately expunge the exercise of jurisdiction.[16] It also involves immunity from enforcement, which is beyond the scope of this chapter.

The author cannot here discuss at length all issues related to the various meanings and types of jurisdiction[17] and the application of immunity laws which prevent the exercise of jurisdiction. Suffice it to say that jurisdiction is an inherent constituent of

---

https://www.online-latin-dictionary.com/latin-english-dictionary.php?parola=munus. Accessed 7 February 2021.

[12] Arrest Warrant of 11 April 2000 (Democratic Republic of the Congo v. Belgium), Jurisdiction and Admissibility, Judgment of 14 February 2002, [2002] ICJ Rep. 3 (Judges Higgins, Kooijmans and Buergenthal, Joint Separate Opinion), p. 84, para. 71.

[13] Ibid., p. 64, para. 3.

[14] For a survey on the relationship between the concepts of jurisdiction and immunity, see: Fox and Webb (2015), pp. 84–87.

[15] Arrest Warrant of 11 April 2000 (Democratic Republic of the Congo v. Belgium), Jurisdiction and Admissibility, Judgment of 14 February 2002, [2002] ICJ Rep. 3, p. 19, para. 46, (President Guillaume, Separate Opinion), p. 35, para. 1, (Judges Higgins, Kooijmans and Buergenthal, Joint Separate Opinion), p. 64, paras. 4–5; see also: C. Escobar Hernández, Preliminary Report on immunity of State officials from foreign criminal jurisdiction, UN Doc. A/CN.4/654 (2012), p. 43, paras. 10–11; C. Escobar Hernández, Second Report on immunity of State officials from foreign criminal jurisdiction, UN Doc. A/CN.4/661 (2013), p. 42, para. 40; C. Escobar Hernández, Fifth Report on immunity of State officials from foreign criminal jurisdiction, UN Doc. A/CN.4/701 (2016), pp. 63–64, paras. 144–147; R. A. Kolodkin, Preliminary Report on immunity of State officials from foreign criminal jurisdiction, UN Doc. A/CN.4/601 (2008), p. 170, para. 43; S. Sucharitkul, Preliminary Report on the topic of jurisdictional immunities of States and their property, UN Doc. A/CN.4/323 (1979), p. 238, paras. 50–53; Bröhmer (1997), p. 34; Toner (2004), p. 903.

[16] Higgins (2009), p. 376.

[17] On the different concepts of jurisdiction, see e.g.: Reydams (2003), p. 25; Maier (1996), p. 78; Brownlie (2003), pp. 308–310. For some scholars' definition of 'jurisdiction', see: Shaw (2014), pp. 469ff.; Brownlie (2003), pp. 297ff. On the different types of jurisdiction, see, for example: Arrest Warrant of 11 April 2000 (Democratic Republic of the Congo v. Belgium), Jurisdiction and Admissibility, Judgment of 14 February 2002, [2002] ICJ Rep. 3 (Judge *ad hoc* Van den Wyngaert, Dissenting Opinion), p. 168, para. 49; Akehurst (1972–1973), pp. 145–212, 179; Lowe (2006), pp. 338–339; O'Keefe (2004), pp. 735ff.; Reydams (2003), p. 25; Shaw (2014), pp. 472–473; R. A.

the State's sovereign powers[18] and that the way immunity relates to it is by preventing its exercise.

These premises pave the way to a preliminary section where the author discusses the dense and complicated branch of law which falls under the name of *international law of immunities*. This section addresses: (1) the specific features of the law of State immunity; and (2) the reasons why the author decided to restrict the analysis to a case-study on the approach of the ICJ to immunity issues.

Several elements characterise the law of State immunity as a separate branch of international law and differentiate it from other fields of PIL. They can be summarised into five main points:

1. International immunity law is based upon the interplay of international and national laws.

   As curious as it might sound, some international legal matters mainly arise before national courts.[19] This is the case for the norms of immunity law, which remain mainly a product of PIL,[20] but are applied in practice at the level of national law and case-law.[21] In the words of Heß, '[i]t is the special feature of State immunity that it is at the point of intersection of international law and national procedural law'.[22] '[I]t is a doctrine of international law which is applied in accordance with national law in local courts. Its requirements are governed by international law, but the individual national law of the State before whose courts a claim against another State is made determines the precise extent and manner of application'.[23] Inevitably, such interaction gives rise to many conflicts, which exacerbate the tensions of the law of State immunity.[24] Furthermore, the involvement of domestic courts in shaping and applying the law of immunities

Kolodkin, Preliminary Report on immunity of State officials from foreign criminal jurisdiction, UN Doc. A/CN.4/601 (2008), pp. 170–171, para. 45.

[18] See, inter alia: Shaw (2014), pp. 469ff.; Brownlie (2003), pp. 297ff.; Reydams (2003), p. 25; Akehurst (1972–1973), p. 151; Beale (1923), pp. 241–262.

[19] Higgins (1994), p. 208; see also, the same author at p. 218, speaking of a 'decentralized legal order' where 'efforts must be made to overcome a cultural resistance to international law' from the national jurisdictions.

[20] See, in this respect: Fox and Webb (2015), pp. 13–14; Finke (2010), p. 853; Al-Adsani v. UK, Decision of 21 November 2001, [2001] ECHR, Rep. 2001-XI, para. 56; Jones v. Minister of Interior of Kingdom of Saudi Arabia & Ors, Judgment of 14 June 2006, [2006] UKHL 26; Report of the Commission to the General Assembly on the work of its 32nd session, 1980 YILC vol. II (Part 2), p. 147, para. 26; Jurisdictional Immunities of the State (Germany v. Italy: Greece intervening), Judgment of 3 February 2012, [2012] ICJ Rep. 99, p. 123, para. 56; pp. 144–145, para. 106; Report of the Commission to the General Assembly on the work of its 60th session, 2008 YILC vol. II (Part 2), p. 137, para. 281; see also: Webb (2013), p. 64; Jennings and Watts (1996), pp. 342–343.

[21] See, as a reference: van Alebeek (2013), pp. 559–578.

[22] Heß (1993), p. 271.

[23] Fox and Webb (2015), p. 1.

[24] Fox and Webb (2015), p. 1.

aggravates its multifarious nature[25] in at least two different ways. On the one hand, sources may clash one with another and trigger imbalances and uncertainties in an already unstable field. On the other hand, and perhaps less predictably, it could take significant time for international custom (even for State practice, let alone *opinio juris*) to emerge and crystallise on immunity matters.

2. The sources of the international law of immunities are diverse.

   The sources include international and regional conventions and treaties, customary international law ('CIL'), international soft-law instruments, international and domestic case-law and legislation, international scholarship, findings of organs of the United Nations ('UN'), mainly the ILC, or of the *Institut de droit international*, and national laws and practices.[26] This is a common feature of many sub-fields of international law: the international scholar has to confront the variety of such sources and undertake a balancing exercise in order to infer the norms that stand out from all of them. However, this trait is particularly relevant to the field of State immunity whose degree of incertitude, coupled with the absence of a universal treaty regime,[27] implies that each source, whether domestic or international, bears even a more burdensome role when it comes to filling in unanswered gaps.[28]

3. Immunity is procedural in nature with respect to jurisdiction.

   Jurisdiction is the logical antecedent to immunity, that is: there is no immunity in the absence of jurisdiction.[29] Thus, it needs to be determined whether immunity has a substantial or a procedural nature with respect to jurisdiction, *i.e.*: whether, in other terms, it affects the layer of responsibility/accountability of the subject invoking it or whether it simply hinders the triggering of a judicial proceedings but leaves the underlying issues of substantive law unaltered.

   Immunity from jurisdiction only concerns immunity from executive jurisdiction (and also, for those who follow the theory of the tripartite nature of jurisdiction: adjudicative jurisdiction), but certainly not that from legislative jurisdiction.[30] 'Immunity from jurisdiction does not amount to an exemption from the legal order of the territorial State'[31] so that it does not free the individual

[25] Webb (2013), p. 65.

[26] Webb (2013), pp. 2–3; for a review of the sources, see: Webb (2013), pp. 101–132. For a discussion of the interplay of sources in this field, see: Damrosch (2019), pp. 40–60.

[27] Webb (2013), p. 63: the only international treaty on immunity law, the 2004 United Nations Convention on Jurisdictional Immunities of States and their Property, UN Doc. A/59/508 (2004, not yet in force) has not yet entered into force as of 7 February 2021, while most immunity conventions concern specific types of immunities but do not provide for an overriding, and generally applicable, treaty.

[28] See: Webb (2013), p. 100.

[29] See footnotes 13–15.

[30] See, for instance: R. A. Kolodkin, Preliminary Report on immunity of State officials from foreign criminal jurisdiction, UN Doc. A/CN.4/601 (2008), p. 174, para. 64; and also: Sucharitkul (1976), p. 96.

[31] Steinberger (2000), p. 616; R. A. Kolodkin, Preliminary Report on immunity of State officials from foreign criminal jurisdiction, UN Doc. A/CN.4/601 (2008), p. 174, para. 64.

or the State enjoying it from respecting the laws covered by immunity. In practice, the State will be prevented from exercising its executive jurisdiction over such subjects, but these subjects will always be bound to observe those very laws.[32] This is also confirmed by various international treaties, which highlight that individuals enjoying immunity do not give up their observance of substantial laws.[33] Accordingly, the procedural nature of immunity with respect to jurisdiction would have to follow.[34] Interestingly, this also entails that immunity as such could potentially apply to all sorts of substantive legal disputes and that it would have to have been conceived as a flexible and adaptable tool ready to be adjusted to every type of contentious matter the judicial body will be called to adjudge upon.

4. Immunity is not by definition synonymous with impunity.

   As elucidated in the previous point, it is important to underscore the procedural nature of immunity with respect to jurisdiction,[35] which also allows for immunity to be expeditiously decided by a court *in limine litis*.[36] This entails that

---

[32] See some developments concerning the individual criminal liability of individuals remaining unaffected, but this is equally applicable to State responsibility: R. A. Kolodkin, Preliminary Report on immunity of State officials from foreign criminal jurisdiction, UN Doc. A/CN.4/601 (2008), pp. 174–175, para. 66; Parry, Grant et al. (1986, printed in 1988), p. 165, where the possibility to waive immunity is used to demonstrate that immunity does not entail per se that the subject enjoying it is not subject to the law; Tomonori (2001), p. 274.

[33] 1961 Vienna Convention on Diplomatic Relations, 500 UNTS 95, art. 41; 1963 Vienna Convention on Consular Relations, 596 UNTS 261, art. 55; 1969 Convention on Special Missions, 1400 UNTS 231, art. 47.

[34] See: Arrest Warrant of 11 April 2000 (Democratic Republic of the Congo v. Belgium), Jurisdiction and Admissibility, Judgment of 14 February 2002, [2002] ICJ Rep. 3, p. 25, para. 60, where the ICJ developed the issue further to stress that immunity does not mean impunity; Jurisdictional Immunities of the State (Germany v. Italy: Greece intervening), Judgment of 3 February 2012, [2012] ICJ Rep. 99, p. 124, para. 58; p. 140, para. 93; see also: Fox and Webb (2015), pp. 21, 38–39 and 44–49.

[35] A minor position of international scholars pointing at the substantive nature of immunity must, however, be taken into account. See: R. A. Kolodkin, Preliminary Report on immunity of State officials from foreign criminal jurisdiction, UN Doc. A/CN.4/601 (2008), p. 174, para. 65, citing, at ft. 121: 'Stern, "Immunités et doctrine de l'Act of State: Différences théoriques et similitudes pratiques de deux modes de protection des chefs d'État devant les juridictions étrangères", p. 64. [...] Malanczuk, *Akehurst's Modern Introduction to International Law*, p. 118; Khlestova, *op. cit.*, p. 9.'; Kolodkin's Preliminary Report cites these sources in its section on 'Works cited in the present report' (pp. 158–160), as follows: 'Stern, Brigitte "Immunités et doctrine de l'*Act of State*. Différences théoriques et similitudes pratiques de deux modes de protection des chefs d'État devant les juridictions étrangères", *Journal du droit international*, No. 133 (1) (Jan./Feb./March 2006), pp. 63–88'; 'Malanczuk, Peter *Akehurst's Modern Introduction to International Law*, 7th revised ed. London and New York, Routledge, 1997'; 'Khlestova, I.O. "Immunity of a State implies that it is not subject to the jurisdiction of another State", *Problems of the jurisdictional immunity of a foreign State (legislation and practice)*, Moscow, 2002, p. 9 (in Russian).'

[36] R. A. Kolodkin, Preliminary Report on immunity of State officials from foreign criminal jurisdiction, UN Doc. A/CN.4/601 (2008), p. 175, para. 68; Difference relating to immunity from legal process of a Special Rapporteur of the Commission on Human Rights, Advisory Opinion of 29 April 1999, [1999] ICJ Rep. 62, p. 90, para. 67, sub-para. 2), let. b).

immunity acts as an obstacle to the exercise of jurisdiction but it does not affect the substantive legal norms establishing responsibility.[37] The subjects that are granted immunity will be exempt from the executive/adjudicative jurisdiction of the State[38] but they will still be bound to abide by the laws regulating the case at hand. In the words of the ICJ: '*immunity* from jurisdiction [. . .] does not mean that [its beneficiaries] enjoy *impunity* in respect of any crimes they might have committed, irrespective of their gravity. Immunity from criminal jurisdiction and individual criminal responsibility are quite separate concepts. While jurisdictional immunity is procedural in nature, criminal responsibility is a question of substantive law. Jurisdictional immunity may well bar prosecution for a certain period or for certain offences; it cannot exonerate the person to whom it applies from all criminal responsibility'.[39] As a consequence, and not just in principle, the international order does not *waive* its right/duty to prosecute international wrongdoers: its verdict is somehow suspended, but it is not permanently removed. The granting of immunity confines the issue of responsibility *in limbo*: the State/individual cannot be declared innocent nor at fault, immunity prevents the *forum* from adjudicating those very acts, at least for the time being. According to one part of the international legal scholarship, despite immunity and impunity not being synonymous one with another in theory, immunity might lead to *de facto* impunity in practice.[40] However, international treaty law[41] and jurisprudence[42]

[37] See, in this respect, the former ILC Special Rapporteur on immunity of State officials from foreign criminal jurisdiction in: R. A. Kolodkin, Preliminary Report on immunity of State officials from foreign criminal jurisdiction, UN Doc. A/CN.4/601 (2008), p. 174, para. 64 also referring to: 1961 Vienna Convention on Diplomatic Relations, 500 UNTS 95, art. 41; 1963 Vienna Convention on Consular Relations, 596 UNTS 261, art. 55; 1969 Convention on Special Missions, 1400 UNTS 231, art. 47; *Institut de droit international*, Session of Vancouver—2001, Resolution of the Institute of International Law, 26 Aug. 2001, Immunities from Jurisdiction and Execution of Heads of State and of Government in International Law (Thirteenth Commission, Rapporteur: Mr Joe Verhoeven), Preamble.

[38] R. A. Kolodkin, Preliminary Report on immunity of State officials from foreign criminal jurisdiction, UN Doc. A/CN.4/601 (2008), p. 174, para. 64; see also: Sucharitkul (1976), p. 96; Steinberger (2000), p. 616; Parry, Grant et al. (1986, printed in 1988), p. 165; Tomonori (2001), p. 274.

[39] Arrest Warrant of 11 April 2000 (Democratic Republic of the Congo v. Belgium), Jurisdiction and Admissibility, Judgment of 14 February 2002, [2002] ICJ Rep. 3, p. 25, para. 60.

[40] See, for all: Arrest Warrant of 11 April 2000 (Democratic Republic of the Congo v. Belgium), Jurisdiction and Admissibility, Judgment of 14 February 2002, [2002] ICJ Rep. 3 (Judge *ad hoc* Van den Wyngaert, Dissenting Opinion), p. 160, para. 34.

[41] See, for instance: 1961 Vienna Convention on Diplomatic Relations, 500 UNTS 95, fourth preambular para.; 1963 Vienna Convention on Consular Relations, 596 UNTS 261, fifth preambular para.; 1969 Convention on Special Missions, 1400 UNTS 231, seventh preambular para.; also: *Institut de droit international*, Session of Vancouver—2001, Resolution of the Institute of International Law, 26 Aug. 2001, Immunities from Jurisdiction and Execution of Heads of State and of Government in International Law (Thirteenth Commission, Rapporteur: Mr Joe Verhoeven), third preambular para.

[42] Arrest Warrant of 11 April 2000 (Democratic Republic of the Congo v. Belgium), Jurisdiction and Admissibility, Judgment of 14 February 2002, [2002] ICJ Rep. 3, p. 25, para. 60.

have taken an opposite stance, confirming that immunities are granted for the well-being of international relations: they do not free the State/State official from liability but merely 'freeze' (and, where possible, postpone) any substantive investigation on it.

Three main theories have been rationalised to justify the existence of State immunity law: the extraterritoriality,[43] the representative[44] and the functional[45] theories. They purport, respectively: that the premises of a mission or of a sovereign in the receiving State are considered as an extension of the territory of the sending State; that the sending State is embodied by the agents within the borders of the receiving State; and that the State agents or entity perform official functions of the sending State. While it has been claimed that the most-applied rationale combines the latter two theories,[46] all of them rest on the assumption that the State agent/State entity is an extension of/personifies/functions as the sending State. And precisely because they act on behalf of the sending State, these subjects cannot be held responsible for the conduct performed.

5. PIL employs the term *immunity* to refer to State immunity and immunity of State officials alike.

   While immunity covers primarily State entities,[47] the scope of its recipients has gradually expanded so that it could also attach to individuals acting on behalf of a State (including diplomats, consuls, officers on special missions and the so-called troika of Heads of States, Heads of Governments and Ministries for Foreign Affairs), international organisations and their employees and other spe-

[43] Intersessional Meeting of Legal Experts to discuss Matters relating to International Law Commission to be held on 10 April 2012 at Aalco secretariat, New Delhi, Immunity of State Officials from Foreign Criminal Jurisdiction, Background Paper, p. 4. http://www.aalco.int/background%20paper%20ilc%2010%20april%202012.pdf. Accessed 7 February 2021; Westlake (1904), p. 263–264. This theory is now believed to have ceased to exist, see: R. A. Kolodkin, Preliminary Report on immunity of State officials from foreign criminal jurisdiction, UN Doc. A/CN.4/601 (2008), p. 179, para. 87, ft. 157; more broadly, for an in-depth analysis of the notion of extraterritoriality, see also: Strisower (1923), pp. 233ff.

[44] Intersessional Meeting of Legal Experts to discuss Matters relating to International Law Commission to be held on 10 April 2012 at Aalco secretariat, New Delhi, Immunity of State Officials from Foreign Criminal Jurisdiction, Background Paper, p. 4.

[45] Cassese (2002), p. 855; Intersessional Meeting of Legal Experts to discuss Matters relating to International Law Commission to be held on 10 April 2012 at Aalco secretariat, New Delhi, Immunity of State Officials from Foreign Criminal Jurisdiction, Background Paper, p. 4.

[46] R. A. Kolodkin, Preliminary Report on immunity of State officials from foreign criminal jurisdiction, UN Doc. A/CN.4/601 (2008), p. 179, para. 87; see also: Documents of the 10th Session, including the report of the Commission to the General Assembly, A/CN.4/SER.A/1958/Add.1, Yearbook of the International Law Commission, 1958, Volume II at 95, General Comments to Section II, Diplomatic Privileges and Immunities, para. 3; Arrest Warrant of 11 April 2000 (Democratic Republic of the Congo v. Belgium), Jurisdiction and Admissibility, Judgment of 14 February 2002, [2002] ICJ Rep. 3, p. 22, para. 53.

[47] See, as a reference: Fox and Webb (2015), p. 1.

cial regimes.[48] In line with this approach, the immunity of State officials has also been understood as 'a corollary of the rule of state immunity'[49] or even as a residual type of immunity.[50]

As a consequence, and in abstract terms, immunity has to be applicable to both civil and criminal jurisdiction.[51] According to the traditional position, while State officials may be prosecuted for their civil and/or criminal liability, such distinction does not apply to the international responsibility of States, which cannot be classified according to the binomial civil/criminal jurisdiction.[52] However, the international law of immunities is evolving at an incredibly fast pace, as might be proven by the recent shifts from a traditional stance according to which a State cannot commit crimes under international or domestic law to a more flexible approach.[53] For the purpose of this chapter, it is sufficient to underline that immunity as it stands today is a broad term, that can be adjusted to the type of jurisdiction before which it is invoked.

The law of State immunity should be understood as having a tripartite nature, as follows: (1) State immunity (immunity pertaining to the State entity); (2) State officials' immunity *ratione personae* (immunity belonging to the so-called troika of Heads of State, Heads of Governments and Ministries for Foreign Affairs, covering all acts performed by the those officials, temporary in nature—as long as the official is on duty); and (3) State officials' immunity *ratione materiae* (immunity pertaining to all State officials, for acts carried out in the exercise of official functions, permanent in nature—even after the official's office has ceased).[54] Specific regimes of immunity (those granted to diplomats, consuls, officials on special missions, officials of international organisations) will have to be added to such categories, even though, for the purpose of this categorisation, they can be considered under the cloak of immunity of State officials. In light of the above, and for the sake of clarity, it would be beneficial for the international legal community to distinguish between immunity of States and State officials rather than subsuming both of them under an all-inclusive label of 'State immunity'.

---

[48] For a comprehensive study, see: Fox and Webb (2015), pp. 543–614; a special regime is, for instance, the one which applies to visiting armed forces, see: Fox and Webb (2015), pp. 577, 601–611.

[49] van Alebeek (2008), p. 103.

[50] Gaeta (2013), p. 537.

[51] For an in-depth discussion, see: Fox and Webb (2015), pp. 87–98.

[52] ILC Draft Articles on the Responsibility of States for Internationally Wrongful Acts, UN Doc. A/56/10 (2001) art. 12 with commentary, p. 55, para. 5.

[53] Fox and Webb (2015), pp. 91–98. Cf., for instance: J. Crawford, Fourth Report on State responsibility, UN Doc. A/CN.4/517 and Add.1 (2001), p. 12, para. 46.

[54] For an analysis on the two types of State officials' immunity, see, as representative examples: Cassese (2002), pp. 862ff.; Frulli (2008), pp. 6ff.; Luzzatto and Queirolo (2006), pp. 209ff. See also this tripartition as adopted by: Webb (2013), pp. 62–102.

These features of the law of State immunity illustrate that a close examination of this specific branch of law offers an opportunity to review the structure of international law as a whole. As it has been noted by commentators,[55] the international law of immunities is a fruitful case-study of the PIL system, of its interplay of sources and of the creation of new rules. Of course, this chapter cannot disentangle the approach of all types of international and regional courts to immunity issues (it would take a whole volume, if not more, to carry out a study of this proportion). On the contrary, a focus on the principal judicial organ of the UN, the ICJ, allows for a closer and more detailed analysis. The ICJ has a special position in the international legal arena: it is the principal judicial organ of one of its main subjects, the UN, but it is also mandated with the scrutiny of other subjects' acts under PIL. It is one ship sailing the waters of international law; but it is also the lighthouse keeper. The author attempts to unravel this area of law gazing at the blue waters of the sea: at how they appear under the shadows of the night and at how they change under the intermittent rays of light.

3 The Influence Played by the ICJ on the International Law of Immunities to Date

The ICJ has been confronted with immunity issues in various cases.[56] This section will first address some cases where the ICJ dealt with the merits of immunities and will then turn to instances where the Court considered immunity matters to the extent that they impacted on the Court's jurisdiction.

Two of the Court's most relevant judgments on the merits are: the *Arrest Warrant* case[57] and the *Jurisdictional Immunities* case.[58] Clearly, the stance of the Court in respect of immunity cannot be assessed solely by reference to two judgments, however important they might be. Those rulings can, however, serve the purpose of this chapter: to identify the recent posture of the ICJ towards immunity issues and to highlight how the Court's approach has been influenced by and has impacted upon the international legal system. Additionally, the *Immunities and Criminal Proceedings* case[59] will be analysed in two respects: the judgment on the merits will be

[55] Fox and Webb (2015), pp. 7–8.

[56] See, for instance, even if not dealt with in this chapter: Certain Questions of Mutual Assistance in Criminal Matters (Djibouti v. France), Judgment of 4 June 2008, [2008] ICJ Rep. 177; Difference relating to immunity from legal process of a Special Rapporteur of the Commission on Human Rights, Advisory Opinion of 29 April 1999, [1999] ICJ Rep. 62.

[57] Arrest Warrant of 11 April 2000 (Democratic Republic of the Congo v. Belgium), Jurisdiction and Admissibility, Judgment of 14 February 2002, [2002] ICJ Rep. 3.

[58] Jurisdictional Immunities of the State (Germany v. Italy: Greece intervening), Judgment of 3 February 2012, [2012] ICJ Rep. 99.

[59] Immunities and Criminal Proceedings (Equatorial Guinea v. France), Preliminary Objections, Judgment of 6 June 2018, [2018] ICJ Rep. 292; Immunities and Criminal Proceedings (Equatorial

appreciated, albeit to a limited extent, in the merits sub-section while the judgment on the preliminary objections will be tackled in so far as this affected the assessment of the Court's jurisdiction. From this latter perspective, some consideration will also be given to another recent ICJ judgment: the *Certain Iranian Assets* case.[60]

3.1 Selected ICJ Judgments Covering the Merits of Immunity Issues

3.1.1 The *Arrest Warrant* Case

This dispute[61] concerned the issuance of an international arrest warrant by a Belgian judge against the then incumbent Minister for Foreign Affairs ('MFA') of the Congo, Mr. Yerodia, in relation to which the Congo asked the Court to declare Belgium's breach of PIL particularly with regard to the immunity of its Minister.[62] The international arrest warrant was issued by an investigating judge of the Brussels *Tribunal de première instance* on 11 April 2000 and it charged Mr. Yerodia 'with offences constituting grave breaches of the Geneva Conventions of 1949 and of the Additional Protocols thereto, and with crimes against humanity'.[63] As regards the immunity claim, with the dissenting votes of Judges Oda, Al-Khasawneh and Judge *ad hoc* Van den Wyngaert, the ICJ found that Belgium had violated Mr. Yerodia's immunities and inviolabilities.[64] The findings of the Court can be synthesised as follows:

Guinea v. France), Merits, Judgment of 11 December 2020, General List No. 163 (not yet published).

[60] Certain Iranian Assets (Islamic Republic of Iran v. United States of America), Preliminary Objections, Judgment of 13 February 2019, [2019] ICJ Rep. 7. As of 7 February 2021, the latest developments of this case have been the following: by an Order of 15 August 2019, the President of the ICJ extended the time-limit for the filing of the Counter-Memorial of the United States to 14 October 2019 (see: Certain Iranian Assets (Islamic Republic of Iran v. United States of America), Order of 15 August 2019, I.C.J. Reports 2019, p. 552); by an Order of 15 November 2019, the Court fixed the time-limit for the filing of written pleadings (see: Certain Iranian Assets (Islamic Republic of Iran v. United States of America), Order of 15 November 2019, I.C.J. Reports 2019, p. 680); on 26 November 2019 the Court authorised the submission of a Reply by the Islamic Republic of Iran and a Rejoinder by the United States of America and fixed 17 August 2020 and 17 May 2021 as the respective time-limits for the filing of those written pleadings (see: ICJ, Certain Iranian Assets (Islamic Republic of Iran v. United States of America), Press Release No. 2019/51, 26 November 2019). For the latest developments, see: https://www.icj-cij.org/en/case/164. Accessed 7 February 2021.

[61] Arrest Warrant of 11 April 2000 (Democratic Republic of the Congo v. Belgium), Jurisdiction and Admissibility, Judgment of 14 February 2002, [2002] ICJ Rep. 3.

[62] Ibid., p. 6, para. 1.

[63] Ibid., p. 9, para. 13.

[64] Ibid., p. 33, para. 78, sub-para. 2.

- Jurisdiction naturally precedes immunity and questions on the latter can only be assessed once the former has been ascertained (however, in the given case, the Court decided to address immunity matters on the assumption that Belgium had jurisdiction);[65]
- Within the limited scope of immunity from criminal jurisdiction and the inviolability of an incumbent MFA,[66] immunity has to be assessed on the basis of customary, rather than treaty, law[67] and independently of conventions which require States to extend their criminal jurisdiction to certain acts;[68]
- By virtue of their office, MFAs represent the State, like the Heads of States and Heads of Governments: their immunities are not granted for their personal benefit but for the effective and efficient performance of their duties;[69]
- While in office, MFAs enjoy full immunity from criminal jurisdiction and inviolability, irrespective of the distinction between private or official acts and of the moment in time when the acts were performed, *i.e.* before or throughout the duration of the office;[70]
- The analysis of State practice, national and international case-law leads to exclude the existence of exceptions to such immunity and inviolability in case of performance of international crimes (war crimes and crimes against humanity, in this case);[71]
- Immunity does not imply impunity: it is procedural in nature and cannot affect the substantive law.[72] MFAs can be prosecuted in the following cases: (1) in their own States; (2) if the State waives their immunity and inviolability; (3) once their time in office has ceased, for acts performed before or after the term of office and for acts performed in private capacity even during the term of office; (4) before certain international criminal tribunals.[73]

Eleven judges (including the President) appended declarations, separate and dissenting opinions.[74] The author singles out the joint Separate Opinion and the three dissenting opinions, with their remarks on immunity issues.

---

[65] Ibid., p. 19, para. 46.

[66] Ibid., p. 21, para. 51.

[67] Ibid., p. 21, para. 52.

[68] Ibid., pp. 24–25, para. 59.

[69] Ibid., pp. 21–22, para. 53.

[70] Ibid., p. 22, paras. 54–55.

[71] Ibid., p. 24, para. 58.

[72] Ibid., p. 25, para. 60.

[73] Ibid., pp. 25–26, para. 61.

[74] Arrest Warrant of 11 April 2000 (Democratic Republic of the Congo v. Belgium), Jurisdiction and Admissibility, Judgment of 14 February 2002, [2002] ICJ Rep. 3 (President Guillaume, Separate Opinion; Judge Oda, Dissenting Opinion; Judge Ranjeva, Declaration; Judge Koroma, Separate Opinion; Judges Higgins, Kooijmans and Buergenthal, Joint Separate Opinion; Judge Rezek, Separate Opinion; Judge Al-Khasawneh, Dissenting Opinion; Judge *ad hoc* Bula-Bula, Separate Opinion; Judge *ad hoc* Van den Wyngaert, Dissenting Opinion).

In their Joint Separate Opinion, Judges Higgins, Kooijmans and Buerghental reiterated their agreement with the main findings of the Court on immunity matters, however they underscored that the approach of the Court lost sight of the nature of jurisdiction as the natural antecedent of immunity, which can only be claimed when jurisdiction has already been ascertained.[75] They looked at recent trends in the evolution of State immunity in civil law matters and in international criminal law to restate, specifically for the latter ones, the effort of the international community to avoid impunity for the most heinous crimes behind the shield of immunity.[76] The three judges highlighted that the circumstances mentioned by the Court to prove that immunity does not equate with impunity are not feasible pathways in practice.[77] Additionally, they affirmed that those immunities have to be granted with restraint, particularly in the event of heinous crimes,[78] and they emphasised that immunities of Heads of State and MFAs are not the same.[79] They were also uncertain as to the scope of MFAs immunities for private acts but clearly expressed that they endure during the MFAs term of office and also after it, only for official acts.[80]

Noting that the Congo changed the subject-matter from mere diplomatic immunity to immunity from criminal proceedings,[81] Judge Oda did not answer the question whether MFAs enjoy diplomatic immunity[82] but wondered whether it was necessary for the Court to 'conclude that [MFAs] enjoy absolute immunity'.[83] He questioned the Court's finding at para. 3 of the operative part of the ICJ judgment (whereby the Court ordered Belgium to cancel the Arrest Warrant)[84] and impugned its practical significance at a time when Mr. Yerodia had become a *former* MFA.[85] While pointing out that immunities of MFAs cannot be assimilated to those of

---

[75] Arrest Warrant of 11 April 2000 (Democratic Republic of the Congo v. Belgium), Jurisdiction and Admissibility, Judgment of 14 February 2002, [2002] ICJ Rep. 3, (Judges Higgins, Kooijmans and Buergenthal, Joint Separate Opinion), p. 84, para. 71.

[76] Ibid., pp. 84–85, paras. 72–75.

[77] Ibid., p. 86, para. 78.

[78] Ibid., pp. 86–87, para. 79.

[79] Ibid., p. 87, para. 81.

[80] Ibid., pp. 88–89, paras. 84–85.

[81] Arrest Warrant of 11 April 2000 (Democratic Republic of the Congo v. Belgium), Jurisdiction and Admissibility, Judgment of 14 February 2002, [2002] ICJ Rep. 3 (Judge Oda, Dissenting Opinion), pp. 49–50, paras. 8–9.

[82] Ibid., pp. 52–53, para. 14.

[83] Ibid., p. 52, para. 14.

[84] Ibid., p. 33, para. 78, sub-para. 3.

[85] Ibid., p. 53, para. 15. See an excerpt of para. 15 for the exact terms employed by Judge Oda: 'I find little sense in the Court's finding in paragraph (3) of the operative part of the Judgment, which in the Court's logic appears to be the consequence of the finding set out in paragraph (2) (Judgment, para. 78). Given that the Court concludes that the violation of international law occurred in 2000 and the Court would appear to believe that there is nothing in 2002 to prevent Belgium from issuing a new arrest warrant against Mr. Yerodia, this time as a former Foreign Minister and not the incumbent Foreign Minister, there is no practical significance in ordering Belgium to cancel the arrest warrant of April 2000.'.

diplomats,[86] nor to those of Heads of State,[87] Judge Al- Khasawneh challenged the judgment in its 'attempt at proving that immunity and impunity are not synonymous'[88] -which ultimately allows for absolute immunity of MFAs-[89] and favored a restrictive approach to immunity, mainly based on the *jus cogens* character of grave crimes.[90] Judge Van den Wyngaert's Dissenting Opinion offers a comprehensive scrutiny of the topic of immunity. She argued that: (1) no rule of CIL grants full immunity to MFAs;[91] and (2) international law encourages States to prosecute international crimes, irrespective of the official capacity of the perpetrator.[92] In addition to this, she downplayed the importance of the distinction between immunity as procedural or substantive defense for the given issue[93] and stressed that, in practice, the application of immunity leads to a *de facto* impunity.[94]

Also in light of its *obiter dicta*, the decision of the ICJ has attracted much comment and criticism since its delivery.[95] This sub-section investigates the Court's reasoning, focusing on the Court's rationale and final determination on immunity issues. The author makes two main arguments.

First, scholars can discuss which avenues the Court could have, should have and has in fact taken to get to its conclusions. However, this is only possible when the grounds upon which the final decision was made are disclosed. It seems that, in the present case, the Court could not root its adjudication upon firm bases or, at least, it did not explain them to the general public. Apart from the already-mentioned functional analogy,[96] the ICJ generally mentioned 'State practice'[97] and CIL[98] but did not expressly identify the examples and norms it was referring to.[99] Since the

[86] Arrest Warrant of 11 April 2000 (Democratic Republic of the Congo v. Belgium), Jurisdiction and Admissibility, Judgment of 14 February 2002, [2002] ICJ Rep. 3 (Judge Al-Khasawneh, Dissenting Opinion), pp. 95–96, para. 1.

[87] Ibid., p. 96, para. 2.

[88] Ibid., pp. 97–98, para. 6.

[89] Ibid., p. 98, para. 8 (a).

[90] Ibid., p. 98, para. 7; pp. 98–99, para. 8, let. b.

[91] Arrest Warrant of 11 April 2000 (Democratic Republic of the Congo v. Belgium), Jurisdiction and Admissibility, Judgment of 14 February 2002, [2002] ICJ Rep. 3 (Judge *ad hoc* Van den Wyngaert, Dissenting Opinion), pp. 142–151, paras. 10–23.

[92] Ibid., pp. 142–143, para. 10; pp. 152–157, paras. 24–28.

[93] Ibid., pp. 157–159, paras. 29–33.

[94] Ibid., pp. 159–163, paras. 34–38.

[95] See: Bates (2007), p. 680; Sands (2002), p. 545; Gaeta (2003), pp. 186–196; Spinedi (2002), pp. 895–899; Wirth (2002), pp. 877–893; Boister (2002), pp. 293–314.

[96] See, for instance: Arrest Warrant of 11 April 2000 (Democratic Republic of the Congo v. Belgium), Jurisdiction and Admissibility, Judgment of 14 February 2002, [2002] ICJ Rep. 3, pp. 20–22, paras. 51–55.

[97] Ibid., p. 24, para. 58.

[98] Ibid., pp. 21, 24 and 25, paras. 52, 53, 58, 59.

[99] In one passage of the judgment, the ICJ mentioned to have 'carefully examined State practice, including national legislation and those few decisions of national higher courts, such as the House

position of the Court contradicted what seemed to be an emerging trend of CIL towards greater accountability for allegations of grave human rights abuses,[100] it should have at least provided for some solid grounds to justify its stance. And even when the Court's posture was intelligible (*e.g.* on the procedural nature of immunity)[101] it did not engage in any dialogue with other courts which had previously dealt with the *jus cogens* nature of some crimes.[102] In addition to that, it might also be useful to recall that the Court dealt with immunity before addressing the issue of jurisdiction, while logically it should have first determined the matter of jurisdiction.[103]

Second, and more importantly, the ICJ seems to have adopted a formalistic and minimalistic approach to immunity issues:[104] it confined itself to addressing the immunity issue as if it was detached from other inextricably related topics (*i.e.* jurisdiction) and somehow lost sight of the implications that the solution of immunity questions would have had on the whole system of international law. In the attempt to focus on the detail, it might have neglected the broader picture. It bypassed other interdependent matters[105] or, worse, it provided for implied answers

---

of Lords or the French Court of Cassation' (Arrest Warrant of 11 April 2000 (Democratic Republic of the Congo v. Belgium), Jurisdiction and Admissibility, Judgment of 14 February 2002, [2002] ICJ Rep. 3, p. 24, para. 58) presumably alluding to the Pinochet and Qaddafi cases quoted by the parties (p. 23, paras. 56–57).

[100] See: Arrest Warrant of 11 April 2000 (Democratic Republic of the Congo v. Belgium), Jurisdiction and Admissibility, Judgment of 14 February 2002, [2002] ICJ Rep. 3 (Judge *ad hoc* Van den Wyngaert, Dissenting Opinion), p. 151, para. 23; (Judges Higgins, Kooijmans and Buergenthal, Joint Separate Opinion), pp. 84–85, paras. 72–75; du Plessis and Bosch (2003), pp. 255, 262; Skordas (2002) p. 58; Wirth (2002), pp. 890–893; Cassese (2002), pp. 870–874.

[101] Arrest Warrant of 11 April 2000 (Democratic Republic of the Congo v. Belgium), Jurisdiction and Admissibility, Judgment of 14 February 2002, [2002] ICJ Rep. 3, p. 25, para. 60.

[102] To name a few examples available at the time when the Court rendered its judgment: Al-Adsani v. UK, Decision of 21 November 2001, [2001] ECHR, Rep. 2001-XI; Prosecutor v. Furundžija, Judgment, Case No. IT-95-17/1-T, T. Ch., 10 December 1998; Prosecutor v. Blaškić, Judgement On The Request Of The Republic Of Croatia For Review Of The Decision Of Trial Chamber II Of 18 July 1997, Case No. IT-95-14-A, App. Ch., 29 October 1997; Prosecutor v. Kunarac et al., Judgment, Case No. IT-96-23-T & IT-96-23/1-T, T. Ch., 22 February 2001; Prefecture of Voiotia v. Federal Republic of Germany (Distomo Massacre Case), Greece, Court of Cassation (Areios Pagos), 4 May 2000 (Case No. 11/2000) 129 ILR 513.

[103] Arrest Warrant of 11 April 2000 (Democratic Republic of the Congo v. Belgium), Jurisdiction and Admissibility, Judgment of 14 February 2002, [2002] ICJ Rep. 3, pp. 19–26, paras. 46–61.

[104] Arrest Warrant of 11 April 2000 (Democratic Republic of the Congo v. Belgium), Jurisdiction and Admissibility, Judgment of 14 February 2002, [2002] ICJ Rep. 3 (Judge *ad hoc* Van den Wyngaert, Dissenting Opinion), pp. 153–157, paras. 27–28. For the contrary position see Arrest Warrant of 11 April 2000 (Democratic Republic of the Congo v. Belgium), Jurisdiction and Admissibility, Judgment of 14 February 2002, [2002] ICJ Rep. 3 (Judge Koroma, Separate Opinion), p. 62, para. 11.

[105] E.g.: the status of the principle of international accountability, the relationship between international jus cogens crimes and immunity, see: Arrest Warrant of 11 April 2000 (Democratic Republic of the Congo v. Belgium), Jurisdiction and Admissibility, Judgment of 14 February 2002, [2002] ICJ Rep. 3 (Judge *ad hoc* Van den Wyngaert, Dissenting Opinion), pp. 155–157, para. 28.

to such problems. This can be observed, for instance, in relation to the Court's assessment of the absence of any customary norm allowing for an exception to incumbent MFAs' immunity from criminal jurisdiction.[106] The Court considered the immunity question from the outside, however it did not engage in the discussion of the consequences that its finding could determine from the inside. As pinpointed by Judge Wyngaert,[107] this strictly formalistic approach enabled the ICJ to avert a more substantial analysis on the level of international criminal responsibility and accountability, which remained unanswered.

3.1.2 The *Jurisdictional Immunities* Case

On 3 February 2012, the ICJ delivered its judgment[108] in the case involving the jurisdictional immunities that Germany was entitled to enjoy before Italian domestic courts.[109] Italy's position, predicated on two main arguments, was that Germany was not entitled to immunity before Italian courts.[110] As far as State immunity was concerned, the *dispositif* of the Court established that: (1) by allowing civil claims related to international humanitarian law ('IHL') violations occurred during World War II to be brought against Germany before its own courts and by taking enforcement measures against Villa Vigoni ('"German State property used for government non-commercial purposes"')[111] Italy violated Germany's immunity;[112] and (2) by declaring the enforceability in Italy of Greek decisions based on IHL violations committed by Germany during World War II, Italy infringed Germany's immunity.[113] The view espoused by the Court can be summarised as follows:

[106] Arrest Warrant of 11 April 2000 (Democratic Republic of the Congo v. Belgium), Jurisdiction and Admissibility, Judgment of 14 February 2002, [2002] ICJ Rep. 3, p. 24, para. 58. For the precise wording of the ICJ, see an excerpt of para. 58: '[The Court] has been unable to deduce from this practice that there exists under customary international law any form of exception to the rule according immunity from criminal jurisdiction and inviolability to incumbent Ministers for Foreign Affairs, where they are suspected of having committed war crimes or crimes against humanity. [...] It finds that these rules likewise do not enable it to conclude that any such an exception exists in customary international law in regard to national courts.'.

[107] Arrest Warrant of 11 April 2000 (Democratic Republic of the Congo v. Belgium), Jurisdiction and Admissibility, Judgment of 14 February 2002, [2002] ICJ Rep. 3 (Judge *ad hoc* Van den Wyngaert, Dissenting Opinion), p. 156, para. 28.

[108] Jurisdictional Immunities of the State (Germany v. Italy: Greece intervening), Judgment of 3 February 2012, [2012] ICJ Rep. 99.

[109] Ibid.

[110] Ibid., pp. 126–145, paras. 62–108.

[111] Ibid., p. 107, para. 15.

[112] Ibid., pp. 154–155, para. 139, sub-paras. 1–2.

[113] Ibid., p. 155, para. 139, sub-para. 3.

- Immunity is a matter of international law, not of comity[114] and, in the absence of treaty law, its applicability must be assessed on the basis of CIL;[115]
- The distinction between *acta jure gestionis* and *acta jure imperii* characterises State immunity so that only the latter can be protected by it;[116]
- There is no territorial tort exception to State immunity for acts performed by armed forces abroad during an armed conflict;[117]
- State immunity applies even where it bars the exercise of jurisdiction over acts originating from serious IHL violations;[118]
- The *jus cogens* nature of the rules does not trump the applicability of State immunity;[119]
- The 'last resort' argument -according to which: 'the Italian courts were justified in denying Germany the immunity to which it would otherwise have been entitled, because all other attempts to secure compensation for the various groups of victims involved in the Italian proceedings had failed'[120]- cannot prevent the application of State immunity;[121]
- Measures of constraint cannot be enforced over State properties used for governmental purposes;[122]
- The application for *exequatur* of a foreign judgment against a third State violates the immunity that the respondent State enjoys before the courts of the State in which *exequatur* proceedings have been instituted.[123]

Six judges voiced their concurring or discordant positions in their separate and dissenting opinions.[124] Judge Cançado Trindade was particularly vocal in expressing his dissent from the Court's overall methodology and assessment; with core arguments on the factual context of the *cas d'espèce* and on (what can be distilled as) the prevailing interests of justice over immunity, he strongly opposed the

[114] Ibid., p. 122, para. 53.

[115] Ibid., p. 122, para. 54.

[116] Ibid., pp. 124–125, paras. 59–61.

[117] Ibid., pp. 127–135, paras. 64–79.

[118] Ibid., pp. 136–139, paras. 81–91; pp. 144–145, paras. 105–108.

[119] Ibid., pp. 140–142, paras. 92–97; pp. 144–145, paras. 105–108. For a critique of the Court's analysis of the distinction between substantive and procedural law, see: Jervis (2019), pp. 105–128.

[120] Jurisdictional Immunities of the State (Germany v. Italy: Greece intervening), Judgment of 3 February 2012, [2012] ICJ Rep. 99, p. 142, para. 98.

[121] Ibid., pp. 142-144, paras. 99–104; pp. 144–145, paras. 105–108.

[122] Ibid., pp. 145–148, paras. 109–120.

[123] Ibid., pp. 149–152, paras. 121–133.

[124] Jurisdictional Immunities of the State (Germany v. Italy: Greece intervening), Judgment of 3 February 2012, [2012] ICJ Rep. 99 (Judge Koroma, Separate Opinion; Judge Keith, Separate Opinion; Judge Bennouna, Separate Opinion; Judge Cançado Trindade, Dissenting Opinion; Judge Yusuf, Dissenting Opinion; Judge *ad hoc* Gaja, Dissenting Opinion).

majority of the Court in a lengthy opinion.[125] In the same vein, and in another detailed opinion, Judge Yusuf questioned the reasoning of the ICJ, he disapproved its analysis of issues of reparations for IHL violations and of the role of domestic courts in the determination of CIL and, more generally, he distanced himself from the Court's conclusions on State immunity and its scope.[126] The Dissenting Opinion of Judge *ad hoc* Gaja was founded on a less restrictive scope of application of the territorial tort exception, which, he stipulated, should have led the Court to adjudge in favor of Italy.[127]

Similarly to the *Arrest Warrant* case, this judgment echoed far and wide.[128] The author's focal point in the next two arguments is the rationale *per curiam* of immunity issues.

First, if compared to the *Arrest Warrant* case, the inquiry of the ICJ in *Jurisdictional Immunities* was more complete, itemised and three-dimensional. The Court relied on diverse examples of international and domestic State practice (including its own) and legislation to reach its final ruling.[129] Nonetheless, it did not look at more recent, contrary trends according to which, for instance, political and inter-State reasons shall give way to the protection of the individual, such as those in support of the human rights exception.[130]

Even so, and as a second point, the reasoning of the ICJ remained quite formalistic and slightly mechanical since it did not weigh the consequences that its decision might have triggered even beyond the parties to the case. The Court held that it found 'unnecessary [...] to consider a number of questions which were discussed at some length by the Parties', including 'whether [...] international law confers upon the individual victim of a violation of the law of armed conflict a directly enforceable right to claim compensation [or] whether [...] Article 77, paragraph 4, of the Treaty of Peace or the provisions of the 1961 Agreements amounted to a binding waiver of the claims which are the subject of the Italian proceedings'.[131] It honoured its primary mandate to pursue international stability[132] and confirmed its conservative

[125] Jurisdictional Immunities of the State (Germany v. Italy: Greece intervening), Judgment of 3 February 2012, [2012] ICJ Rep. 99 (Judge Cançado Trindade, Dissenting Opinion).

[126] Jurisdictional Immunities of the State (Germany v. Italy: Greece intervening), Judgment of 3 February 2012, [2012] ICJ Rep. 99 (Judge Yusuf, Dissenting Opinion).

[127] Jurisdictional Immunities of the State (Germany v. Italy: Greece intervening), Judgment of 3 February 2012, [2012] ICJ Rep. 99 (Judge *ad hoc* Gaja, Dissenting Opinion).

[128] See, for example: Boudreault (2012), pp. 1003–1012; De Santis di Nicola (2016), pp. 107–121; Menkes (2012), pp. 173–196; Najandi-Manesh and Abedini (2014), pp. 73–104; Shah (2012), pp. 555–573; Souresh (2017), pp. 15–36.

[129] See, for instance: Jurisdictional Immunities of the State (Germany v. Italy: Greece intervening), Judgment of 3 February 2012, [2012] ICJ Rep. 99, pp. 121–143, 147, 148, 150–154, paras. 53–56, 58, 59, 61–64, 66–77, 83, 85–90, 93, 95, 96, 100, 116–118, 127, 129, 130, 137, 138.

[130] Orakhelashvili (2012), pp. 612–616.

[131] Jurisdictional Immunities of the State (Germany v. Italy: Greece intervening), Judgment of 3 February 2012, [2012] ICJ Rep. 99, p. 145, para. 108.

[132] Botchway (2014), p. 270.

and State-centric approach.[133] For example, the Court examined the rule of State immunity and the principle of sovereign equality of States in broad terms[134] and assessed them from the general perspective of CIL.[135] It concluded that '[t]he question whether Germany still has a responsibility towards Italy, or individual Italians, in respect of war crimes and crimes against humanity committed by it during the Second World War does not affect Germany's entitlement to immunity. Similarly, the Court's ruling on the issue of immunity can have no effect on whatever responsibility Germany may have'.[136] Yet, it overlooked that it is the role of the judge to also flexibly apply the rule, so to stave off that its slavish application overturns the ultimate 'interest of justice' for which it was created in the first place.

Those remarks are not to say that the ICJ should have necessarily taken an alternative route. However, bringing back the metaphor of the end of Sect. 2, instead of lighting up the darkness of the high waters from the solidity of mainland, the ICJ chose to be one of the many vessels, and just went with the tide.

3.1.3 The *Immunities and Criminal Proceedings* Case: Judgment on the Merits

As explained at the beginning of this section, the *Immunities and Criminal Proceedings* case is worth to be examined from a two-tiered perspective: the judgment on the merits in the present sub-section, and the judgment on the preliminary objections in the next one.

In this case, the Court has been called to adjudge a dispute over the immunity from criminal jurisdiction of the Second Vice-President of the Republic of Equatorial Guinea and the legal status of the Embassy of Equatorial Guinea,[137] which had arisen between the Republic of Equatorial Guinea and France. The dispute arose from France's exercise of criminal jurisdiction over offences allegedly perpetrated by the Second Vice-President of Equatorial Guinea and from France's order of attachment of a building belonging to the Republic of Equatorial Guinea and used for the purposes of that country's diplomatic mission in France.[138] In particular, the investigations concerned 'the methods used to finance the acquisition of movable and immovable assets in France by several individuals, including Mr. Teodoro Nguema Obiang Mangue, the son of the President of Equatorial Guinea, who was

[133] Calisto (2012), pp. 330–335; see also: Francioni (2012), pp. 1129, 1132.

[134] Jurisdictional Immunities of the State (Germany v. Italy: Greece intervening), Judgment of 3 February 2012, [2012] ICJ Rep. 99, pp. 123–124, paras. 57.

[135] See, for instance: Ibid., pp. 122–123, paras. 53–56; p. 135, para. 78; p. 139, para. 91; p. 142, para. 97; p. 143, para. 101; p. 145, paras. 107–108.

[136] Ibid., p. 145, para. 108.

[137] Immunities and Criminal Proceedings (Equatorial Guinea v. France), Preliminary Objections, Judgment of 6 June 2018, [2018] ICJ Rep. 292, p. 297, para. 1.

[138] Ibid., pp. 299–300, para. 18. For a recent detailed discussion of the law on diplomatic immunity, see: Webb (2019), pp. 634–650.

at the time *Ministre d'Etat* for Agriculture and Forestry of Equatorial Guinea'.[139] Following the issuance of an arrest warrant by the French courts, which Mr. Teodoro Nguema Obiang Mangue unsuccessfully challenged,[140] Equatorial Guinea accepted France's request for mutual legal assistance on criminal matters and he was eventually indicted by the French authorities.[141] Proceedings before the French judiciary continued even after Equatorial Guinea filed its Application before the ICJ and Mr. Teodoro Nguema Obiang Mangue was found guilty of money laundering offences, for which he was sentenced to a prison term and a fine.[142] At the time when the ICJ delivered its judgment on Preliminary Objections, Mr. Mangue had appealed his conviction before French courts, which had a suspensive effect on the enforcement of his sentence.[143]

On 11 December 2020, the ICJ delivered its judgment on the merits in the case,[144] by which it held that the building at 42 avenue Foch in Paris had not acquired the status of 'premises of the mission' under the Vienna Convention on Diplomatic Relations ('VCDR') and that, as a result, France had not breached its obligations under the VCDR.[145] Undeniably, the issue of the premises' status, inviolability and immunity are, by their very nature, intertwined.[146] While immunity from enforcement remains outside the scope of this chapter, as does the issue of inviolability, and, for this reason, this judgment on the merits is tackled only to a limited extent in this chapter,[147] selected aspects of the judgment are nonetheless taken into account below for their significance within the present analysis.[148]

The ICJ briefly commented on the privileges and immunities granted to diplomatic personnel and staff of the mission, stating that these 'broad immunities' are balanced by the receiving State's power to declare such individuals *personae non gratae*,[149] in order to highlight the difference with the mission premises, for which there is 'no equivalent to the *persona non grata* mechanism'.[150] The Court grounded

[139] Immunities and Criminal Proceedings (Equatorial Guinea v. France), Preliminary Objections, Judgment of 6 June 2018, [2018] ICJ Rep. 292, p. 303, para. 24.

[140] Ibid., p. 305, para. 30.

[141] Ibid., pp. 305–306, paras. 31–33.

[142] Ibid., pp. 306–307, paras. 34–40.

[143] Ibid., p. 307, para. 41. For a recollection of the proceedings before the ICJ, see: Immunities and Criminal Proceedings (Equatorial Guinea v. France), Merits, Judgment of 11 December 2020, General List No. 163 (not yet published), pp. 5–7, paras. 1–21.

[144] Immunities and Criminal Proceedings (Equatorial Guinea v. France), Merits, Judgment of 11 December 2020, General List No. 163 (not yet published).

[145] Ibid., p. 36, para. 126, sub-paras. 1–2.

[146] See, for all: Fox and Webb (2015), pp. 509–534, particularly pp. 515–520.

[147] For some early reactions on the merits' judgment, see, e.g.: Etkin (2020); Flasch (2021); Moiseienko (2020).

[148] For an analysis, see: Etkin (2020).

[149] Immunities and Criminal Proceedings (Equatorial Guinea v. France), Merits, Judgment of 11 December 2020, General List No. 163 (not yet published), p. 20, para. 64.

[150] Ibid., pp. 20–21, para. 65.

its decision upon the privileges and immunities' rationale under the VCDR, (that is: 'the objective of fostering friendly relations among nations'[151] rather than the individuals' benefits[152]) and explained that the premises status cannot be imposed unilaterally by the sending State.[153]

A relevant novelty worth remarking is the three-pronged test the Court developed in the interpretation of the notion of 'premises of the mission' under the VCDR. At para. 74 of the judgment, the Court reached the conclusion that if the receiving State objects the sending State's characterisation of some property as 'premises of the mission' and such an objection is: (1) communicated in a timely fashion, (2) not arbitrary, and (3) not discriminatory, then such premises do not fall under the definition of arts. 1, para. *(i)* and 22 of the VCDR. Regrettably, the judgment did not elucidate these cumulative criteria: the Court made a broad reference to its own case-law on States' exercise of discretionary powers in accordance with reasonableness and good faith and to arts. 21 and 47 of the VCDR[154] but the sources from which the three requirements above stem remain unspecified. Ultimately, the Court found that France had met the three-step test[155] and determined that the premises did not qualify as 'premises of the mission' under art. 1, para. *(i)* of the VCDR.[156]

Several opinions and a declaration were appended to the judgment.[157] A holistic examination of the dissenting and separate opinions attests the individual judges' views, in disagreement with the ICJ, as to how the VCDR's interpretation of the privileges and immunities' rationale should be applied in order to determine the status of the premises at stake in the case.[158]

In particular, President Yusuf and Judges Gaja and Sebutinde all considered that the property had become 'premises of the mission' as of 27 July 2012 (the date of the Note Verbale sent by Equatorial Guinea to France and notifying that the Embassy's offices were located at 42 avenue Foch and used for the performance of diplomatic

[151] Ibid., p. 21, para. 66.

[152] Ibid., p. 21, paras. 66–67.

[153] Ibid., p. 21, para. 67.

[154] Ibid., p. 23, para. 73.

[155] Ibid., mainly p. 28, para. 92; p. 33, para. 110; p. 34, paras. 115–116.

[156] Ibid., p. 35, paras. 117–118.

[157] Immunities and Criminal Proceedings (Equatorial Guinea v. France), Merits, Judgment of 11 December 2020, General List No. 163 (not yet published) (President Yusuf, Separate Opinion; Vice-President Xue, Dissenting Opinion; Judge Bhandari, Dissenting Opinion; Judge Gaja, Declaration; Judge *ad hoc* Kateka, Dissenting Opinion; Judge Robinson, Dissenting Opinion; Judge Sebutinde, Separate Opinion).

[158] See, for some illustrative passages: Immunities and Criminal Proceedings (Equatorial Guinea v. France), Merits, Judgment of 11 December 2020, General List No. 163 (not yet published) (President Yusuf, Separate Opinion), pp. 1–2, paras. 1–4; pp. 16–17, paras. 59–61; (Vice-President Xue, Dissenting Opinion), pp. 3–4, paras. 13–15; (Judge Bhandari, Dissenting Opinion), p. 19, para. 78; (Judge *ad hoc* Kateka, Dissenting Opinion), p. 1, para. 1; p. 2, paras. 3–4; p. 9, para. 35; (Judge Robinson, Dissenting Opinion), pp. 6–7, paras. 23, 26; pp. 18–20, para. 76; (Judge Sebutinde, Separate Opinion), p. 1, para. 1; p. 9, para. 31.

functions)[159] but that, since the relevant facts of the case covered a time-span that forerun the critical date, France had not breached the VCDR.[160] Through different avenues and rationales, the three of them rejected the criterion of consent as a solid base upon which to ground the assessment of the premises' status.[161]

The dissenting judges voiced their unanimous opposition to the majority's conclusions and reasoning also through varying modalities. Vice-President Xue criticised the Court's restriction of its jurisdictional scope by effect of which it evaded an opportunity to shed light on 'the issue of the rights and obligations of a State under international law in handling criminal cases concerning a foreign State and its property'[162] and questioned the practical application of the three criteria laid down by the ICJ.[163] Noting that the building in question had acquired the status of 'premises of the mission' since 27 July 2012, that he qualified as 'the date of its actual use',[164] Judge Bhandari disagreed with the Court's newly-fabricated test warning that this might unjustifiably render consent the final determinant of the premises' status.[165] Judge *ad hoc* Kateka was also disapproving of the decisive role the majority attributed to consent[166] and suggested that, pursuant to the application of the condition of 'use',[167] the critical date should have been considered to be the date of 4 October 2011,[168] *i.e.* the date when Equatorial Guinea sent a Note Verbale to France stating that the building at 42 avenue Foch had been at the disposal of the Embassy and used for the performance of diplomatic functions for many years.[169]

---

159 Immunities and Criminal Proceedings (Equatorial Guinea v. France), Merits, Judgment of 11 December 2020, General List No. 163 (not yet published), p. 14, para. 32.

160 Immunities and Criminal Proceedings (Equatorial Guinea v. France), Merits, Judgment of 11 December 2020, General List No. 163 (not yet published) (President Yusuf, Separate Opinion), pp. 15–16, paras. 54–58; (Judge Gaja, Declaration), p. 3, para. 14; (Judge Sebutinde, Separate Opinion), p. 7, para. 22; pp. 8–9, paras. 28–31.

161 Particularly: Immunities and Criminal Proceedings (Equatorial Guinea v. France), Merits, Judgment of 11 December 2020, General List No. 163 (not yet published) (President Yusuf, Separate Opinion), p. 9, para. 25; (Judge Gaja, Declaration), pp. 1–2, paras. 4–7; also pp. 2–3, paras. 10–12; (Judge Sebutinde, Separate Opinion), p. 2, para. 6; p. 7, paras 23–26.

162 Immunities and Criminal Proceedings (Equatorial Guinea v. France), Merits, Judgment of 11 December 2020, General List No. 163 (not yet published) (Vice-President Xue, Dissenting Opinion), p. 3, para. 12.

163 Ibid., pp. 5–7, paras. 19–28.

164 Immunities and Criminal Proceedings (Equatorial Guinea v. France), Merits, Judgment of 11 December 2020, General List No. 163 (not yet published) (Judge Bhandari, Dissenting Opinion), p. 19, para. 78.

165 Ibid., p. 1, para. 1.

166 Immunities and Criminal Proceedings (Equatorial Guinea v. France), Merits, Judgment of 11 December 2020, General List No. 163 (not yet published) (Judge *ad hoc* Kateka, Dissenting Opinion), pp. 1–2, paras. 1–2; pp. 4–6, paras. 10–19; p. 6, para. 21; p. 7, para. 25.

167 Ibid., pp. 6–7, paras. 20–25.

168 Ibid., pp. 7–9, paras. 26–34.

169 Immunities and Criminal Proceedings (Equatorial Guinea v. France), Merits, Judgment of 11 December 2020, General List No. 163 (not yet published), p. 13, para. 27.

He also deplored that the Court had left the matter of the fate of the premises 'when the appeal against the judgment of the *Cour d'appel* of 10 February 2020 comes to an end' unresolved.[170] Distancing himself from the majority's interpretation,[171] Judge Robinson suggested a diverging approach to the VCDR, based upon a discussion of the intended and actual uses of the premises,[172] as a result of which he argued that the critical date should have been determined to be that of 4 October 2011.[173]

Clearly the extent to which the Court's findings and reasoning on immunity issues in this case will affect the developments of the law of State immunity can only be fully appreciated in an extended time-frame. An exhaustive and definitive survey on the consequences the decision triggered upon the international arena cannot be yielded at present. However, the limited analysis carried out at the time being in this chapter seems to confirm that the posture of the Court on immunity issues is still in line with the approach it adopted in the other two ICJ cases on the merits addressed above: it certainly reached a conclusion in order to settle the dispute at hand but provided scarce guidance as to the rationale behind its findings and, hence, as to the application of the criteria it developed, *e.g.* the three-pronged test discussed above, in future scenarios.

3.2 ICJ Judgments on Whether Immunity Is Within the Scope of the Court's Jurisdiction

Particularly with regard to its jurisdiction, the Court has adopted a narrow view on whether immunity falls within the scope of its jurisdiction in the preliminary objections' phase of two recent cases,[174] namely: the *Immunities and Criminal Proceedings* case[175] and the *Certain Iranian Assets* case.[176] Considerations on these two judgments are drawn jointly at the end of this sub-section. The discussion

[170] Immunities and Criminal Proceedings (Equatorial Guinea v. France), Merits, Judgment of 11 December 2020, General List No. 163 (not yet published) (Judge *ad hoc* Kateka, Dissenting Opinion), p. 9, para. 35.

[171] Immunities and Criminal Proceedings (Equatorial Guinea v. France), Merits, Judgment of 11 December 2020, General List No. 163 (not yet published) (Judge Robinson, Dissenting Opinion), pp. 1–9, paras. 3–37.

[172] Ibid., pp. 10–15, paras. 38–57; pp. 19–20, para. 76, sub-paras. (vi), (viii), (ix).

[173] Ibid., p. 15, para. 56; p. 19, para. 76, sub-para. (vi).

[174] For the latest developments, see: https://www.icj-cij.org/en/pending-cases. Accessed 7 February 2021.

[175] Immunities and Criminal Proceedings (Equatorial Guinea v. France), Preliminary Objections, Judgment of 6 June 2018, [2018] ICJ Rep. 292.

[176] Certain Iranian Assets (Islamic Republic of Iran v. United States of America), Preliminary Objections, Judgment of 13 February 2019, [2019] ICJ Rep. 7.

will commence with the former case, whose merits phase has recently concluded before the ICJ, as described in the previous sub-section.

3.2.1 The *Immunities and Criminal Proceedings* Case: Judgment on the Preliminary Objections

While the facts of this case and the judgment on the merits have been elaborated above in this section, the analysis will now focus on the Preliminary Objections judgment, where the Court established that it had jurisdiction to entertain the Application in so far as it concerned the status of the building located at 42, Avenue Foch in Paris as premises of the mission.[177]

Particularly with regard to the issue at hand, the Court found that art. 4 of the 2000 United Nations Convention against Transnational Organized Crime ('Palermo Convention')[178] does not enclose the customary international norms on State immunity.[179] In light of the above, the ICJ concluded that the immunity dispute in the given case did not concern the interpretation or application of the Palermo Convention and that it lacked jurisdiction in that respect.[180] By interpreting the provision in accordance with the rules of arts. 31 and 32 of the Vienna Convention on the Law of Treaties ('VCLT'),[181] the Court observed that the wording of the article[182] refers to the principle of sovereign equality, but not to the rules that can be derived from such principle.[183] Moreover, the ICJ added that neither art. 4, interpreted in context and in light of the object and purpose of the Convention, nor the Palermo Convention as a whole concern immunity issues,[184] as also confirmed by the *travaux préparatoires* of the Convention.[185] The Court corroborated its view through a comparative

[177] Immunities and Criminal Proceedings (Equatorial Guinea v. France), Preliminary Objections, Judgment of 6 June 2018, [2018] ICJ Rep. 292, p. 338, para. 154, sub-para. 4.

[178] 2000 United Nations Convention against Transnational Organized Crime, 2225 UNTS 209, art. 4.

[179] Immunities and Criminal Proceedings (Equatorial Guinea v. France), Preliminary Objections, Judgment of 6 June 2018, [2018] ICJ Rep. 292, p. 323, para. 102. For some illustrative discussions of various aspects of the judgment, see: Baetens (2019); Paparinskis (2019), pp. 1–2.

[180] Immunities and Criminal Proceedings (Equatorial Guinea v. France), Preliminary Objections, Judgment of 6 June 2018, [2018] ICJ Rep. 292, p. 323, para. 102.

[181] 1969 Vienna Convention on the Law of Treaties, 1155 UNTS 331, arts. 31 and 32.

[182] Art. 4 of the Palermo Convention reads as follows: '1. States Parties shall carry out their obligations under this Convention in a manner consistent with the principles of sovereign equality and territorial integrity of States and that of non-intervention in the domestic affairs of other States. 2. Nothing in this Convention entitles a State Party to undertake in the territory of another State the exercise of jurisdiction and performance of functions that are reserved exclusively for the authorities of that other State by its domestic law'.

[183] Immunities and Criminal Proceedings (Equatorial Guinea v. France), Preliminary Objections, Judgment of 6 June 2018, [2018] ICJ Rep. 292, p. 321, para. 93.

[184] Ibid., pp. 321–322, paras. 94–95.

[185] Ibid., p. 322, paras. 96–98.

analysis of art. 4[186] and art. 2, para. 2[187] of the Convention against Illicit Traffic in Narcotic Drugs and Psychotropic Substances of 1988.[188] Amongst the various dissenting and separate opinions and declarations appended to the judgment,[189] Vice-President Xue, Judges Sebutinde and Robinson and Judge *ad hoc* Kateka expressed their dissatisfaction on the point in their Joint Dissenting Opinion, by reference to an interpretation of the principle of sovereign equality which inextricably links it to State immunity and by concluding that the core meaning of art. 4, para. 1 of the Palermo Convention is to oblige a State party to respect the rules of State immunity as a manifestation of the principle of sovereign equality.[190]

---

[186]This provision reads as follows: '1. Each Party: (a) Shall take such measures as may be necessary to establish its jurisdiction over the offences it has established in accordance with article 3, paragraph 1, when: (i) The offence is committed in its territory; (ii) The offence is committed on board a vessel flying its flag or an aircraft which is registered under its laws at the time the offence is committed; (b) May take such measures as may be necessary to establish its jurisdiction over the offences it has established in accordance with article 3, paragraph 1, when: (i) The offence is committed by one of its nationals or by a person who has his habitual residence in its territory; (ii) The offence is committed on board a vessel concerning which that Party has been authorized to take appropriate action pursuant to article 17, provided that such jurisdiction shall be exercised only on the basis of agreements or arrangements referred to in paragraphs 4 and 9 of that article; (iii) The offence is one of those established in accordance with article 3, paragraph 1, subparagraph (c)(iv), and is committed outside its territory with a view to the commission, within its territory, of an offence established in accordance with article 3, paragraph 1.2. Each Party: (a) Shall also take such measures as may be necessary to establish its jurisdiction over the offences it has established in accordance with article 3, paragraph 1, when the alleged offender is present in its territory and it does not extradite him to another Party on the ground: (i) That the offence has been committed in its territory or on board a vessel flying its flag or an aircraft which was registered under its law at the time the offence was committed; or (ii) That the offence has been committed by one of its nationals; (b) May also take such measures as may be necessary to establish its jurisdiction over the offences it has established in accordance with article 3, paragraph 1, when the alleged offender is present in its territory and it does not extradite him to another Party.3. This Convention does not exclude the exercise of any criminal jurisdiction established by a Party in accordance with its domestic law'.

[187]Para. 2 of art. 2 provides that: 'The Parties shall carry out their obligations under this Convention in a manner consistent with the principles of sovereign equality and territorial integrity of States and that of non-intervention in the domestic affairs of other States'.

[188]1988 United Nations Convention against Illicit Traffic in Narcotic Drugs and Psychotropic Substances, 1582 UNTS 95, art. 2, para. 2; Immunities and Criminal Proceedings (Equatorial Guinea v. France), Preliminary Objections, Judgment of 6 June 2018, [2018] ICJ Rep. 292, pp. 322–323, paras. 99–101.

[189]Immunities and Criminal Proceedings (Equatorial Guinea v. France), Preliminary Objections, Judgment of 6 June 2018, [2018] ICJ Rep. 292 (Vice-President Xue, Judges Sebutinde and Robinson and Judge *ad hoc* Kateka, Joint Dissenting Opinion; Judge Owada, Declaration; Judge Abraham, Separate Opinion; Judge Donoghue, Dissenting Opinion; Judge Gaja, Declaration; Judge Crawford, Declaration; Judge Gevorgian, Separate Opinion).

[190]Immunities and Criminal Proceedings (Equatorial Guinea v. France), Preliminary Objections, Judgment of 6 June 2018, [2018] ICJ Rep. 292 (Vice-President Xue, Judges Sebutinde and Robinson and Judge *ad hoc* Kateka, Joint Dissenting Opinion), pp. 346–354, paras. 18–44.

3.2.2 The *Certain Iranian Assets* Case

This case tackled Iran's claim that the United States had violated the Treaty of Amity, Economic Relations, and Consular Rights ('the Treaty')[191] to which the two States were parties.[192] In particular, the case concerned the United States' treatment of Iranian companies, including Bank Markazi, and also Iran's and Iranian State-owned companies' entitlement to immunity from the United States' jurisdiction and in respect of enforcement proceedings in the United States.[193] The case originates from plaintiffs bringing action against Iran before courts of the United States for 'damages arising from deaths and injuries caused by acts allegedly supported, including financially, by Iran'[194] in the late 1990s and from the President of the United States issuing Executive Order 13599 in 2012 which blocked all Iranian assets within the territory of the United States or '"within the possession or control of any United States person [...]"'.[195] Also in the same year, the United States adopted the Iran Threat Reduction and Syria Human Rights Act, Section 502 in order to make sure that the assets of Bank Markazi were subject to execution.[196] As a result, many United States courts have entered default judgments and substantial damages awards against Iran and, in some cases, against Iranian State-owned entities; accordingly, enforcement proceedings targeting Iranian assets have been carried out.[197]

In its operative clause, while upholding the United States' second preliminary objection on immunity issues, the Court found that it had jurisdiction to rule on the application and declared it admissible.[198] The Court upheld the second objection of the United States, according to which the ICJ had no jurisdiction to rule upon the alleged violation of rules of international law on sovereign immunities.[199] The ICJ examined all the relevant provisions of the Treaty[200] and denied its jurisdiction in relation to them. The Court explained that: (1) the reference to the 'require[ments of] international law'[201] of art. IV, para. 2 is not broad enough to allow the

---

[191] 1955 Treaty of Amity, Economic Relations, and Consular Rights between Iran and the United States.

[192] Certain Iranian Assets (Islamic Republic of Iran v. United States of America), Preliminary Objections, Judgment of 13 February 2019, [2019] ICJ Rep. 7, p. 13, para. 1. For a thorough discussion see: Franchini (2020), pp. 433–483. For some reactions see also: Hosseinnejad and Askary (2019); Keitner (2019); Paddeu (2019).

[193] Certain Iranian Assets (Islamic Republic of Iran v. United States of America), Preliminary Objections, Judgment of 13 February 2019, [2019] ICJ Rep. 7, pp. 15–16, para. 13.

[194] Ibid., p. 20, para. 22.

[195] Ibid., p. 21, para. 25.

[196] Ibid., p. 21, para. 26.

[197] Ibid., p. 21, para. 27.

[198] Ibid., pp. 44–45, para. 126, sub-paras. 2, 5.

[199] Ibid., pp. 25–35, paras. 48–80.

[200] 1955 Treaty of Amity, Economic Relations, and Consular Rights between Iran and the United States.

[201] Ibid., art. 4, para. 2.

incorporation, by reference, of the customary rules on sovereign immunities;[202] (2) while art. XI, para. 4[203] leaves intact the State immunity for *acta jure imperii*, this does not entail that it incorporates that type of immunity into the Treaty;[204] (3) art. III, para. 2[205] concerns the obligation to grant Iranian companies freedom of access to United States courts and cannot be interpreted as imposing an obligation to uphold the immunities allegedly accorded by CIL to some of those entities;[206] (4) for reasons similar to those elaborated with respect to art. IV, para. 2, also art. IV, para. 1[207] does not provide for an obligation to respect the sovereign immunities of the State and those of its entities invoking such immunities under CIL;[208] (5) as already established in the ICJ *Oil Platforms* judgment,[209] the freedom of commerce and navigation referred to in art. X, para. 1 cannot be extended so as to include activities with no or little connection with the commercial relations of the parties to the Treaty, such as sovereign immunities.[210] Consequently, the Court denied its jurisdiction on the matter, holding that 'Iran's claims based on the alleged violation of the sovereign immunities guaranteed by customary international law do not relate

[202] Certain Iranian Assets (Islamic Republic of Iran v. United States of America), Preliminary Objections, Judgment of 13 February 2019, [2019] ICJ Rep. 7, pp. 27–28, paras. 53–58.

[203] The provision reads as follows: 'No enterprise of either High Contracting Party, including corporations, associations, and government agencies and instrumentalities, which is publicly owned or controlled shall, if it engages in commercial, industrial, shipping or other business activities within the territories of the other High Contracting Party, claim or enjoy, either for itself or for its property, immunity therein from taxation, suit, execution of judgment or other liability to which privately owned and controlled enterprises are subject therein'.

[204] Certain Iranian Assets (Islamic Republic of Iran v. United States of America), Preliminary Objections, Judgment of 13 February 2019, [2019] ICJ Rep. 7, pp. 29–30, paras. 59–65.

[205] The article states that: 'Nationals and companies of either High Contracting Party shall have freedom of access to the courts of justice and administrative agencies within the territories of the other High Contracting Party, in all degrees of jurisdiction, both in defense and pursuit of their rights, to the end that prompt and impartial justice be done. Such access shall be allowed, in any event, upon terms no less favorable than those applicable to nationals and companies of such other High Contracting Party or of any third country. It is understood that companies not engaged in activities within the country shall enjoy the right of such access without any requirement of registration or domestication'.

[206] Certain Iranian Assets (Islamic Republic of Iran v. United States of America), Preliminary Objections, Judgment of 13 February 2019, [2019] ICJ Rep. 7, pp. 30–32, paras. 66–70.

[207] The article provides that: 'Each High Contracting Party shall at all times accord fair and equitable treatment to nationals and companies of the other High Contracting Party, and to their property and enterprises; shall refrain from applying unreasonable or discriminatory measures that would impair their legally acquired rights and interests; and shall assure that their lawful contractual rights are afforded effective means of enforcement, in conformity with the applicable laws'.

[208] Certain Iranian Assets (Islamic Republic of Iran v. United States of America), Preliminary Objections, Judgment of 13 February 2019, [2019] ICJ Rep. 7. pp. 32–33, paras. 71–74.

[209] Oil Platforms (Islamic Republic of Iran v. United States of America), Preliminary Objection, Judgment of 12 December 1996, [1996] ICJ Rep. 803.

[210] Certain Iranian Assets (Islamic Republic of Iran v. United States of America), Preliminary Objections, Judgment of 13 February 2019, [2019] ICJ Rep. 7, pp. 33–34, paras. 75–79.

to the interpretation or application of the Treaty of Amity and, as a result, do not fall within the scope of the compromissory clause in Article XXI, paragraph 2'.[211]

Various separate opinions and a declaration were appended to the judgment.[212] Judges Robinson, Gevorgian and Judge *ad hoc* Momtaz voiced their dissent with regard to the Court's denial of jurisdiction in the second preliminary objection relying, respectively: on the interpretation of art. XI, para. 4 of the Treaty in accordance with art. 31, para. 1 of the VCLT[213] and an *a contrario* reading;[214] on an analysis of art. III, para. 2 and art. X, para. 1 of the Treaty;[215] and on the interpretation of art. XI, para. 4 in light of the object and purpose of the Treaty, consistent with art. 31, para. 3, let. c, of the VCLT[216] and according to an *a contrario* reading.[217] Turning to the detail: Judge Robinson held that a consistent interpretation of the above-mentioned provisions yields the conclusion that the Treaty covers sovereign immunity for *acta jure imperii* and inferred from such analysis that, since the Treaty only excludes immunity for *acta jure gestionis*, it has to be understood as covering acts of governmental nature;[218] Judge Gevorgian contended that the Court had disregarded the procedural and preliminary nature of immunities when it established that art. III, para. 2 did not cover the very substantive and procedural rights a Party's national or company might claim before domestic authorities and added that its limitation of jurisdiction under art. X, para. 1, was

---

[211] Ibid., pp. 34–35, para. 80; it might also interesting to note that Judge *ad hoc* Brower also provided for additional ground upon which to uphold the second preliminary objection raised by the United States, see: Certain Iranian Assets (Islamic Republic of Iran v. United States of America), Preliminary Objections, Judgment of 13 February 2019, [2019] ICJ Rep. 7 (Judge *ad hoc* Brower, Separate Opinion), pp. 70–75, paras. 13–23.

[212] Certain Iranian Assets (Islamic Republic of Iran v. United States of America), Preliminary Objections, Judgment of 13 February 2019, [2019] ICJ Rep. 7 (Judges Tomka and Crawford, Joint Separate Opinion; Judge Gaja, Declaration; Judge Robinson, Separate Opinion; Judge Gevorgian, Separate Opinion; Judge *ad hoc* Brower, Separate Opinion; Judge *ad hoc* Momtaz, Separate Opinion).

[213] 1969 Vienna Convention on the Law of Treaties, 1155 UNTS 331, art. 31, para. 1.

[214] Certain Iranian Assets (Islamic Republic of Iran v. United States of America), Preliminary Objections, Judgment of 13 February 2019, [2019] ICJ Rep. 7 (Judge Robinson, Separate Opinion), pp. 54–58, paras. 1–14.

[215] Certain Iranian Assets (Islamic Republic of Iran v. United States of America), Preliminary Objections, Judgment of 13 February 2019, [2019] ICJ Rep. 7 (Judge Gevorgian, Separate Opinion), pp. 61–64, paras. 3–13.

[216] 1969 Vienna Convention on the Law of Treaties, 1155 UNTS 331, art. 31, para. 3, let. c.

[217] Certain Iranian Assets (Islamic Republic of Iran v. United States of America), Preliminary Objections, Judgment of 13 February 2019, [2019] ICJ Rep. 7 (Judge *ad hoc* Momtaz, Separate Opinion), pp. 83–90, paras. 8–27.

[218] Certain Iranian Assets (Islamic Republic of Iran v. United States of America), Preliminary Objections, Judgment of 13 February 2019, [2019] ICJ Rep. 7 (Judge Robinson, Separate Opinion), pp. 54–57, paras. 3–11.

unjustified;[219] Judge *ad hoc* Momtaz argued that the violation of Bank Mazari's immunities on acta *jure imperii* deprived the Treaty of its object and scope, that the VCLT required a systematic integration between the Treaty and CIL on immunities and also that an *a contrario* interpretation of art. XI, para. 4, would be in line with the Treaty's object and purpose and with its provisions.[220]

In both preliminary objections' judgments discussed above, once again, the Court had the occasion to demystify the concept of State immunity, at least with regard to its jurisdictional scope and, possibly, also with regard to the link between immunity, on the one hand, and the principles of sovereign equality and non-intervention, on the other hand, to the conceptual distinction between substantive and procedural rules and, more broadly, to the width of immunity law and its limits. However, the Court decided to adopt a narrower approach and did not seize the opportunity. If anything, and in line with its case-law on the merits addressed earlier in this chapter, this suggests some high degree of caution in the Court's attitude towards immunity matters.

In conclusion, through its case-law the ICJ has made findings on various immunity-related issues, spanning immunities of MFAs, the relationship between the law of immunity and IHL violations, immunities of the premises of the mission, immunity and *acta jure imperii*. The following section and the conclusions offer an evaluation of the Court's stance on such issues.

4 The Future of the International Law of Immunities: The Role of the ICJ and International Courts

One phenomenon of international law, 'which runs against the classic view of international law being made by states alone'[221] is that, in practice, judicial decisions contribute to the making of PIL.[222] While courts generally tend to disprove to have taken on that role,[223] their work plays a part (a significant one) in the development of international law. This holds true for 'proper' judicial decisions but also for other less authoritative sources such as, for instance, advisory opinions, *obiter dicta* and dissenting and separate opinions. Emanating from international judicial bodies, these sources give a voice to those courts' understanding, interpretation and application of

[219] Certain Iranian Assets (Islamic Republic of Iran v. United States of America), Preliminary Objections, Judgment of 13 February 2019, [2019] ICJ Rep. 7 (Judge Gevorgian, Separate Opinion), pp. 62–63, paras. 7–9; pp. 63–64, paras. 10–12.

[220] Certain Iranian Assets (Islamic Republic of Iran v. United States of America), Preliminary Objections, Judgment of 13 February 2019, [2019] ICJ Rep. 7 (Judge *ad hoc* Momtaz, Separate Opinion), pp. 83–85, paras. 8–12; pp. 85–87, paras. 13–16; pp. 87–89, paras. 17–22.

[221] Webb (2013), p. 1.

[222] See Webb (2013), pp. 204–209.

[223] Webb (2013), p. 2.

international law. Once they are made available to the public, they constitute the basis which new international legal norms will be construed and accrued upon.

As a system which rejects the traditional hierarchical structure of domestic orders, PIL is, *per defitionem*, a field of cross-fertilisation of various actors. Today more than yesterday, this is particularly true for international courts and, even more so, for the law of immunities.[224] Even if immunity law is applied differently by the ICJ, international criminal courts and tribunals and other adjudicative bodies, these bodies influence each other and they also condition the posture of other non-judicial bodies upon immunity issues. When one realises that precisely such latter bodies[225] contribute to the development of international law themselves, it is possible to discern the vicious or virtuous cycle that international *fora* can elicit.

Hence, what role should international courts, and the ICJ in particular, play when dealing with questions of immunity in order to foster the coherence and consistency of the international legal order? Does this role differ from the tasks that such courts are required to perform on a daily basis? If so, to what extent? Eminent scholars have appreciated the Court's contribution to the development of international immunities law on several occasions[226] but the law of State immunity evolves at a fast pace and updated considerations might offer new insights.

Amongst traditional adjudicative functions that are typical of every judicial body, international courts are also vested with a mission to support the PIL norms[227] and regime,[228] in order to strengthen the international rule of law. This is particularly true for the ICJ,[229] whose function, as it has been claimed,[230] can also extend to the advancement and development of international law. The Court is entrusted with the role of guardian of international law, for it must ensure that PIL is correctly comprehended and utilised in the international arena.

Speaking of guardians, and in line with the effort to visualise courts' functions and personify them with familiar images, there is one God in the ancient Roman mythology, not appearing yet amongst the Greek religion, called *Janus*. *Janus* was conceived as a God who looked after passages, both in their material and immaterial meaning: the caretaker of new starts and changes in all of their acceptations.[231] He was worshipped for his ability to preside over journeys, births, trades and wars, to

[224] For a complete study on how the multiplicity of international courts contributes to the development of international law, see: Webb (2013), particularly, on the law of immunities, pp. 62–102.

[225] E.g.: the ILC or the *Institut de Droit International*.

[226] See, for instance: O'Keefe (2013), pp. 107–148.

[227] Shany (2014), pp. 38–40.

[228] Shany (2014), pp. 43–44.

[229] For a comprehensive study, see Thirlway (2016).

[230] Shany (2014), pp. 167–168.

[231] The term *Janus* is etymologically linked to the nouns *janua* (door) and *janus* (covered passage) and it is an eponym of the month of *Januarius* (January), the traditional inception of the year. The English term 'janitor' derives from this root and indicates exactly the doorkeeper. See, for a short introduction (in Italian): Enciclopedia Treccani. http://www.treccani.it/enciclopedia/giano/. Accessed 7 February 2021.

name a few. So it does not come as a surprise to learn that he was commonly addressed as *Janus Bifrons* (two-faced) and traditionally depicted as bicephalous, with one head gazing at the past, the other head looking at the future and both heads overseeing the shift between the two. To some extent, the law of State immunity can be pictured as the Roman deity of *Janus*: it brings together the international and the national, the public and the individual limbs in one figure and synthesises the continuous swing between them. And like *Janus*, immunity is inherently dual in essence and it is the role of courts, particularly the ICJ, to guard the oscillation between the two heads.

'*Sed quis custodiet ipsos custodes?*'[232] Who will guard the guardians? Since the keepers' function is to watch that everything runs smoothly, such keepers are usually not an object of scrutiny themselves. Because of their highly selective designation methodology and because they remain the system's final resource, there is (and, there must be) an implied presumption that the custodians will carefully perform their duties.

The author argues that the role of international courts, mostly the ICJ, in the field of the law of State immunity in no way deviates from the functions that these bodies have to fulfill in other branches of law. Each one of these *fora* should be as active as it is on other issues when it comes to immunity law. What differentiates the operational system of the law of immunities before international courts and tribunals is not the obligation that such bodies carry towards it. What makes immunity law different is the consequence that will arise from the courts' compliance or non-compliance with such very functions, as proven below.

The stability of international law is built upon the clarity and robustness of all of its branches. It is logical that international courts have to operate as guardians in all areas of international law. But, while a lot of international legal matters pertain to the PIL domain only, immunity law does not. As already mentioned in this chapter, the international law of immunities is a place of interaction of national and international actors. When seen under this light, the role of non-domestic courts becomes pivotal. They are required to engage proactively with immunity issues for the harmony of PIL. Yet, this harmony is also ensured through the correct application of immunity laws by national judicial bodies, which (have to) rely on the stance of their international counterparts. How is a domestic court of any State to be blamed for disrespecting or misapplying the international law of immunities when international courts' stances clash one with another and also within themselves? The ICJ and other

[232]The sentence is an excerpt from Juvenal's Satires (Juvenal, Satire VI, lines 346–348) whose full quote runs: '*Audio quid veteres olim moneatis amici, 'pone seram, cohibe'. Sed quis custodiet ipsos custodes? Cauta est et ab illis incipit uxor*' (Juvenal, Satire VI, lines 346–348) ('I understand, old friends, what you often warn me about, 'bolt the door, constrain her'. But who will guard the guardians? The wife is astute and she starts from them'). The citation evokes Plato's verse: '*Γελοῖον γάϱ, ἦ δ' ὅς, τόν γε φύλακα φύλακος δεῖσθαι*' (Plato, Πολιτεία, The Republic, III, 403e) ('It would certainly be ridiculous, he said, if the guardian needed a guardian'). Translations into English are the author's own. For the original Latin and Greek quotes, with texts translated into Italian, see: Dotti (2013), pp. 150–151; Vegetti (2018), pp. 494–495.

international courts have to embrace their guiding function: to explain the current state of international law, to illustrate it with examples, to interpret murky rules in accordance with the PIL principles, especially when it comes to intricate matters. They are not asked to (and they should not) distort their primary dispute settlement role and turn it into a legislator's mandate. A court is a court, whose primary function remains to settle disputes. But a court, especially the ICJ, should seize the moment and make use of every opportunity to clarify upon extremely complex international legal matters like international immunity law. All PIL should expect these courts to do is to understand the cases submitted to them as opportunities to clarify the substance of international law. To step in, not back.

If this holds true for all courts of the international legal order, it is definitely much more so for the case of the ICJ. '[I]t is common knowledge that the jurisprudence of the International Court forms a rich resource for the definition and elucidation of many areas of law'.[233] This leads to wider questions on the extent to which the ICJ contributes to the evolution of international law through its contentious judgments and advisory opinions despite the acceptance that they, respectively, do not operate as precedents nor carry directly binding effects. The present analysis is not concerned with the specific weight and substantial consequences of ICJ decisions and opinions. What it does confront, however, is the unchallenged impact that all ICJ's manifestations have onto domestic and international systems alike. Hence, and precisely because of this, the Court should honour its privileged function and assist with a correct and consistent interpretation of international law. Because it is the only subject entrusted with this tremendous power and because its voice is going to reach all corners of the world with the same strength and relevance. But also, and more importantly, because such voice will likely be echoed by national and municipal courts, in their own administration and quest for justice.

5 Conclusions

'In some ways, the law on immunities has been in transition for almost as long as it has existed'.[234] The shift from absolute to restrictive doctrine[235] is a prime example of the change immunity law has been, and still is, subject to. The law of State immunity is vibrant, vivid and dynamic and it offers a practical example to test the current state of PIL as a whole.

Through a case-study on the response of the ICJ to questions on immunities of States and State officials, this chapter explored some common issues that this area of law gives rise to. It considered the results of the Court's enquiry, not so much for

[233] Thirlway (2016), Preface.

[234] Webb (2013), p. 69.

[235] Webb (2013), p. 69; see also: Bröhmer (1997), pp. 141, 222–223; Fox and Webb (2015), pp. 32–38.

their substantive reach but mainly for the role the ICJ has been playing within its search for answers. The goal has been to qualify the function that the Court embodies within the international law of immunities and the extent to which this mirrors the way it conceives PIL.

While the results of the ICJ investigation have been different in the case-law addressed, it is here submitted that, in all such scenarios, the Court endorsed a cautious yet reticent conduct towards some problems of international law and, more specifically, towards immunity issues. It did not always engage with manifold international legal dilemmas and, when it did so, it was chiefly responsive to the bare minimum questions, without necessarily taking into account consequential matters which arose in practice. This behavior, the author suggests, can be detrimental to the whole system and to the branch of the law of State immunity even to a greater extent.

The international law of immunities remains a very topical issue to-date. *Inter alia*, the Special Rapporteur of the ILC on 'Immunity of State officials from foreign criminal jurisdiction' delivered her eighth report in 2020[236] with the hope that the ILC will adopt the draft articles in the near future.[237] As this chapter has tried to highlight, this area of law features many pitfalls and snares. It poses a lot of interrelated questions that cannot always be solved with case-by-case answers. It involves issues spanning, *ex multis*: State responsibility, international criminal accountability and the relationship between domestic and international law. There is an emerging need 'for an organizing principle that allows us to discern and justify the differences between immunities in a systematic way. This approach would yield the least fragmentation in outcomes, but would not subsume differences for the sake of uniformity'.[238] Today more than ever, international lawyers urge the international adjudicators to pursue the goal of consistency, rather than that of uniformity; to set some minimum standards all States should abide by, but also leave room for appreciation of every system's peculiar structure.

At a time of bewilderment where even the most diligent disciple could not easily discern the legal rules in this area, we need a guiding star more than ever. It is on international courts, especially on its supreme agent, the ICJ, that this role of guiding the international community falls. Not only for the pursuit of justice in the individual cases at hand, but also for the certainty and stability of international law. Not just for the present but also for the future. For all those sailors who will navigate these troubled waters at night.

[236] C. Escobar Hernández, Eighth Report on immunity of State officials from foreign criminal jurisdiction, UN Doc. A/CN.4/739 (2020).

[237] Ibid., p. 19, para. 62. The topic is indeed in the provisional agenda of the ILC 72nd session, see: Provisional agenda for the 72nd session To be convened in Geneva on Monday, 26 April 2021, at 3 p.m., UN Doc. A/CN.4/733/Rev.1 (2021) and International Law Commission, https://legal.un.org/ilc/. Accessed 24 February 2021.

[238] Webb (2018), p. 21.

References

Akehurst M (1972–1973) Jurisdiction in international law. Br Yearb Int Law 46:145–257

Baetens F (2019) Abuse of process and abuse of rights before the ICJ: ever more popular, ever less successful? EJIL:Talk! 15 October 2019. https://www.ejiltalk.org/abuse-of-process-and-abuse-of-rights-before-the-icj-ever-more-popular-ever-less-successful/. Accessed 23 Feb 2021

Bates E (2007) State immunity for torture. Hum Rights Law Rev 7:651–680

Beale JH (1923) The jurisdiction of a sovereign state. Harv Law Rev 36:241–262

Boister N (2002) The ICJ in the Belgian arrest warrant case: arresting the development of international criminal law. J C S L 7:293–314

Botchway FN (2014) The immunity conundrum. Afr J Int Comp Law 22:258–272

Boudreault F (2012) Identifying conflicts of norms: the ICJ approach in the case of the jurisdictional immunities of the state (Germany v. Italy: Greece Intervening). LJIL 25:1003–1012

Bröhmer J (1997) State immunity and the violation of human rights. Martinus Nijhoff, The Hague

Brownlie I (2003) Principles of public international law, 6th edn. Clarendon Press, Oxford

Calisto M (2012) Jurisdictional immunities of the state: Germany v. Italy before the ICJ from an Italian perspective. Ger Yearb Int Law 55:319–344

Cassese A (2002) When may senior state officials be tried for international crimes? Some comments on Congo v Belgium Case. EJIL 13:853–875

Damrosch LF (2019) The sources of immunity law – between international and domestic law. In: Ruys T, Angelet N, Ferro L (eds) The Cambridge handbook of immunities and international law. CUP, Cambridge, pp 40–60

De Santis di Nicola F (2016) Civil actions for damages caused by War Crimes vs. State Immunity from jurisdiction and the political act doctrine: ECtHR, ICJ and Italian Courts. Int Comp Jurisprud 2:107–121

Dotti U (a cura di) (2013) Giovenale. Satire. Testo originale a fronte. Giangiacomo Feltrinelli Editore, Universale Economica, Classici, Milano

du Plessis M, Bosch S (2003) Immunities and universal jurisdiction – the World Court steps in (or on). S Afr Yearb Int Law 28:246–262

Etkin B (2020) An analysis of the ICJ's judgment on the merits of the immunities and criminal proceedings (equatorial Guinea v. France) case: all for nothing? EJIL:Talk!, 21 December 2020. https://www.ejiltalk.org/an-analysis-of-the-icjs-judgment-on-the-merits-of-the-immunities-and-criminal-proceedings-equatorial-guinea-v-france-case-all-for-nothing/. Accessed 7 Feb 2021

Finke J (2010) Sovereign immunity: rule, comity or something else? EJIL 21:853–881

Flasch O (2021) ICJ equatorial Guinea ruling could alter diplomatic relations. Signature Litigation, 14 January 2021. https://www.signaturelitigation.com/icj-equatorial-guinea-ruling-could-alter-diplomatic-relations-olivia-flasch/. Accessed 11 Feb 2021

Fox H, Webb P (2015) The law of state immunity, 3rd edn. OUP, Oxford

Franchini D (2020) State immunity as a tool of foreign policy: the unanswered question of certain Iranian assets. Va J Int Law 60:433–483

Francioni F (2012) From Utopia to disenchantment: the ill fate of 'Moderate Monism' in the ICJ judgment on the jurisdictional immunities of the state. EJIL 23:1125–1132

Frulli M (2008) Sull'Immunità dalla Giurisdizione Straniera degli Organi Statali sospettati di Crimini Internazionali. In: Bardusco A, Cartabia M, Frulli M et al (a cura di) Immunità costituzionali e crimini internazionali: Atti del Convegno Milano, 8 e 9 febbraio 2007. Giuffrè Editore, Milano, pp 3–60

Gaeta P (2003) Ratione Materiae immunities for former heads of state and international crimes: the Hissène Habré Case. JICJ 1:186–196

Gaeta P (2013) Extraordinary Renditions e Giurisdizione Italiana nei confronti degli Agenti Statunitensi coinvolti nel c.d. caso Abu Omar. Riv Dir Intern 96:530–537

Heß B (1993) The International Law Commission's Draft Convention on the jurisdictional immunities of states and their property. EJIL 4:269–282

Higgins R (1994) Problems and process: international law and how we use it. Clarendon Press, Oxford

Higgins R (2009) Themes and theories: selected essays, speeches, and writings in international law. OUP, Oxford

Hosseinnejad K, Askary P (2019) Interpretation of implication: some observations on the recent ICJ decision in the case of certain Iranian assets. OpinioJuris, 1 March 2019. https://opiniojuris.org/2019/03/01/interpretation-of-implication-some-observations-on-the-recent-icj-decision-in-the-case-of-certain-iranian-assets/. Accessed 22 Feb 2021

Jennings R, Watts A (eds) (1996) Oppenheim's international law: Volume 1: Peace, 9th edn. Longman, London

Jervis CEM (2019) Jurisdictional immunities revisited: an analysis of the procedure substance distinction in international law. EJIL 30:105–128

Keitner C (2019) World Court rules on Iran challenge to US suits for acts of terrorism: an explainer. Just Security, 19 February 2019. https://www.justsecurity.org/62604/unpacking-icj-judgment-certain-iranian-assets/. Accessed 22 Feb 2021

Lowe V (2006) Jurisdiction. In: Evans MD (ed) International law, 2nd edn. OUP, Oxford, pp 335–360

Luzzatto R, Queirolo I (2006) Sovranità territoriale, 'Jurisdiction' e regole di immunità. In: Carbone SM, Luzzatto R, Santa Maria A (a cura di) Istituzioni di diritto internazionale, 3rd edn. G. Giappichelli Editore, Torino, pp 203–242

Maier HG (1996) Jurisdictional rules in customary international law. In: Meessen KM (ed) Extraterritorial jurisdiction in theory and practice. Kluwer Law International, London, pp 64–102

Menkes M (2012) Sovereign immunity and the ICJ's ruling in Ferrini. Polish Rev Int Eur Law 1: 173–196

Moiseienko A (2020) When no diplomatic immunity is good news: equatorial Guinea v France in the International Court of Justice. Commentary, Royal United Services Institute, 21 December 2020. https://rusi.org/commentary/when-no-diplomatic-immunity-good-news-equatorial-guinea-v-france-international-court. Accessed 11 Feb 2021

Najandi-Manesh H, Abedini A (2014) Struggle between state immunity and jus cogens at the International Court of Justice. Int Stud J 10:73–104

O'Keefe R (2004) Universal jurisdiction: clarifying the basic concept. JICJ 2:735–760

O'Keefe R (2013) Jurisdictional immunities. In: Tams CJ, Sloan J (eds) The development of international law by the International Court of Justice. OUP, Oxford, pp 107–148

Orakhelashvili A (2012) Jurisdictional immunities of the state. AJIL 106:609–616

Paddeu F (2019) Non-precluded measures clause: substance or procedure? A comment on certain Iranian assets. EJIL:Talk!, 6 March 2019. https://www.ejiltalk.org/non-precluded-measures-clause-substance-or-procedure-a-comment-on-certain-iranian-assets/. Accessed 22 Feb 2021

Paparinskis M (2019) Immunities and criminal jurisdiction (Equatorial Guinea v. France): preliminary objections (I.C.J.). Int Leg Mater 58:1–70

Parry C, Grant JP et al (1986, printed in 1988) Encyclopaedic dictionary of international law. Oceana Publications, Dobbs Ferry

Reydams L (2003) Universal jurisdiction: international and municipal legal perspectives. OUP, Oxford

Sands P (2002) What is the ICJ for. R B D I 35:537–545

Shah S (2012) Jurisdictional immunities of the state: Germany v Italy. Hum Rights Law Rev 12: 555–573

Shany Y (2014) Assessing the effectiveness of international courts. OUP, Oxford

Shaw MN (2014) International law, 7th edn. CUP, Cambridge

Skordas A (2002) ICJ: guardian of sovereignty or catalyst for integration. Int Leg Theory 8:49–74

Souresh A (2017) Jurisdictional immunities of the state: why the ICJ got it wrong. Eur J Leg Stud 9: 15–36

Spinedi M (2002) State responsibility v individual responsibility for international crimes: Tertium Non Datur. EJIL 13:895–899
Steinberger H (2000) State immunity. In: Rudolf B (ed) Encyclopedia of public international law, vol IV. North Holland, Amsterdam, pp 615–638
Strisower L (1923) L'Extraterritorialité et ses Principales Applications. R C A D I 1:229–288
Sucharitkul S (1976) Immunities of foreign states before national authorities. R C A D I 149:87–215
Thirlway H (2016) The International Court of Justice. OUP, Oxford
Tomonori M (2001) The individual as beneficiary of state immunity: problems of the attribution of ultra vires conduct. Denv J Int Law Policy 29:261–287
Toner PJ (2004) Competing concepts of immunity: revolution of the head of state immunity defense. Penn State Law Rev 108:899–927
van Alebeek R (2008) The immunity of states and their officials in international criminal law and international human rights law. OUP, Oxford
van Alebeek R (2013) Domestic courts as agents of development of international immunity rules. LJIL 26:559–578
Vegetti M (a cura di) (2018) Platone. La Repubblica. Testo Greco a fronte, dodicesima edizione BUR Classici greci e latini: maggio 2020. Mondadori Libri S.p.A., Milano, pubblicato per BUR Rizzoli
Webb P (2013) International judicial integration and fragmentation. OUP, Oxford
Webb P (2018) How far does the systemic approach to immunities take us? AJIL Unbound 112:16–21
Webb P (2019) Judicial review of qualifications made by receiving states and host states of international organisations. In: Ruys T, Angelet N, Ferro L (eds) The Cambridge handbook of immunities and international law. CUP, Cambridge, pp 634–650
Westlake J (1904) International law, Part I: Peace. The University press, Cambridge
Wirth S (2002) Immunity for core crimes? The ICJ's judgment in the Congo v Belgium Case. EJIL 13:877–893

Giulia Bernabei is a Senior Research Fellow at the Max Planck Foundation for International Peace and the Rule of Law in Heidelberg, Germany. She produced this publication prior to the beginning of her current position and her association with the Max Planck Foundation. She has previously researched and also taught public international law and international human rights law in various capacities. She holds a Dottorato di Ricerca in Discipline Giuridiche (PhD in Legal Disciplines) from Università degli Studi Roma Tre and a Master of Laws in Public International Law from Queen Mary University of London.

Part II
International Customary Law of Sovereign Immunity, Human Rights and Counter-Terrorism

Can Human Rights Overcome State Immunity? National Courts at the Crossroads

Anna Wyrozumska

Abstract The purpose of this Chapter is to explore the extent to which a human rights exception (a *jus cogens* exception) to State immunity is recognised by domestic courts. To this end, it examines the practice of the United States, Canadian, Greek and Italian courts, and, in particular, the developments taking place after the *Judgment 238/2014* of the Italian Constitutional Court, which opposed the ruling of the ICJ in the *Jurisdictional Immunities of the State* case. The main issue is whether a national court can depart from customary law on State immunity, when the ICJ has clearly established its limits. Such a departure would undermine the authority of international adjudication, but on the other hand it could lead to elaboration of a new standard. Consequently, this Chapter will focus on the obligation of national judges to comply with international law and their right to participate in the creation of customary law.

1 Introduction

The considerable part of international law on State immunity was developed by national courts by balancing the relevant values and societal interests in exempting foreign States from local jurisdiction. The most significant manifestation of this exercise was shaping the 'commercial' exception to the absolute jurisdictional immunity of a foreign State by the Italian, Belgian and Egyptian courts in the late nineteenth century due to the development of international trade.[1] In the twentieth century, the jurisdictional immunity was designed as covering only the State's governmental actions (*acta de jure imperii*), including the acts of their armed

[1]For reference to the court's decisions see Yearbook of the ILC 1991, vol. II, part 2, p. 36, fn 111–113. Cf. Amnesty International Publications 2011, Germany v. Italy, The Right to Deny State Immunity When Victims Have No Other Recourse, pp. 1–23.

A. Wyrozumska (✉)
University of Lodz, Faculty of Law and Administration, Lodz, Poland
e-mail: awyrozumska@wpia.uni.lodz.pl

R. Bismuth et al. (eds.), *Sovereign Immunity Under Pressure*,
https://doi.org/10.1007/978-3-030-87706-4_9

forces.[2] Immunity was not, however, applicable to acts of a foreign State having commercial or private law character (*acta de jure gestionis*).

The on-going erosion of State immunity is primarily associated with changes taking place in international law, which ceases to be understood as referring only to obligations between States, due to recognition of peremptory norms of international law[3] and the development of human rights protection. In particular, it results from the acceptance by courts or law of some States that an individual harmed by acts *de jure imperii* of a foreign State constituting grave violations of international law (e.g. violation of the prohibition of war crimes, genocide or torture) may claim damages without the intermediary of his or her State, directly in national court.

The problem of *jus cogens* violations was not reflected in main treaties on State immunity: the European Convention on State Immunity of 1972[4] or the UN Convention on Immunity from Jurisdiction of States and their Property of 2004.[5] However, in the course of work on the UN Convention, the Working Group on Jurisdictional Immunities of States and Their Property appointed by the International

---

[2]Some restrictions on immunity do not correspond to the strict division into acta de jure imperii and de jure gestionis, e.g. the expropriation exception in the Foreign Sovereign Immunities Act, vol. II, 28 U.S.C. § 1605(a)(3)) or the tort exception (for the first time the exception was recognized by an Austrian court in a case concerning the collision with a government car (decision of the Supreme Court of Austria of 10 February 1961, ILR 1970, vol. 40, p. 73). The tort exception is justified on the grounds of territorial jurisdiction of the State. See commentary to Art. 12 of the 2004 UN Convention on Immunity from Jurisdiction of States and their Property of 2004, Yearbook of the ILC 1991, part II, p. 46, para. 8.

[3]Norms accepted and recognized by the international community of States as a whole as not derogable. For definition see Art. 53 of the Vienna Convention of the Law of Treaties of 1969. For an overview see e.g. Mik (2013), pp. 27–93, especially pp. 71–73 on immunity of a State and its officials and enforcement of jus cogens.

[4]The European Convention of State Immunity, Basle 16 May 1972, European Treaty Series – No. 74.

[5]War crimes, genocide or crimes against humanity are mainly committed by the armed forces. Art. 31 of the 1972 Convention clearly indicates that the Convention does not apply to acts of armed forces: 'Nothing in this Convention shall affect any immunities or privileges enjoyed by a Contracting State in respect of anything done or omitted to be done by, or in relation to, its armed forces when on the territory of another Contracting State'. The similar provision was not inserted in the UN Convention. But such conclusion may be drawn from its travaux préparatoires. G. Hafner, Chairman of the Ad Hoc Committee on Jurisdictional Immunities of States and Their Property, while introducing in October 2004 the draft Convention to the UN Sixth Committee declared that a 'general understanding had always prevailed' to the effect that military activities were not covered by the Convention (Statement Chairman of the Ad Hoc Committee 6, para. 36). He added in this regard that the reference should be made to the ILC commentary to Art. 12 of the Convention (tort exception) which indicates that Art. 12 did not apply to 'situations involving armed conflicts' (see Yearbook of the ILC 1991, vol. II, part II, p. 46, para10) and that: 'It had to be born in mind that the preamble Stated that the rules of customary international law continued to govern matters not regulated by the provisions of the Convention' (Statement, para. 36). He also explained that the general approach of the Convention was that it did not apply where there was a special immunity regime, including immunities ratione personae and that '(s)ometimes that was expressly stated in the text, sometimes not'. (Statement, para. 37). The UN Convention has not yet achieved the required number of thirty ratifications (Art. 31).

Law Commission noted with great attention examples of practice of States and changes in legislation relating to rejection of State immunity in the event of violations of peremptory norms of international law, in particular the violation of the prohibition of torture, indicating that this development cannot be ignored.[6]

A *jus cogens* exception is usually justified by the need to combat impunity, the right of access to a court and the right to compensation for damage. This is how e.g. the Italian courts have started invoking an exception in recent years. They refused to grant immunity to Germany in a number of cases for compensation submitted by the victims, or their heirs, of hideous war crimes committed by German armed forces during World War II. The refusal was grounded on the existence of peremptory norms of international law protecting fundamental individual rights, which, in the opinion of the courts, prevail over law on State immunity. Italian courts decisions were found contrary to international customary law in the International Court of Justice (ICJ) judgment in the *Jurisdictional Immunities of the State* case.[7] Moreover, the ICJ held that the emergence of *jus cogens* protecting individuals may not affect rules on State immunity.[8] In return, the Italian Constitutional Court found the norms of customary law on State immunity as determined by the ICJ not applicable in Italy as contrary to human rights enshrined in the Italian Constitution.[9]

Human rights arguments appear thus in two different settings, firstly, they address the substance of State act which cannot be shielded (war crimes, genocide or torture—violations of fundamental individual rights). Secondly, the balance which has to be attained between competing norms, of State immunity and human rights—the right of access to a court and the right to compensation for damages (property rights).

The purpose of this Chapter is to explore the extent to which a human rights exception or a *jus cogens* exception is accepted by domestic courts. To this end, it examines the practice of the United States, Canadian, Greek and Italian courts. Since the Italian Constitutional Court may find its followers, e.g. in the Polish Constitutional Court, it is worth to ask, if a national court may depart from customary law, when the ICJ has clearly established its limits. Such a departure would undermine the authority of international adjudication, but on the other hand it could lead to elaboration of a new standard. Consequently, this Chapter will focus on the obligation of national judges to comply with international law and their right to participate in the creation of customary law.

[6] Report of the ILC's Working Group on Jurisdictional Immunities of States and their Property, Yearbook of the ILC 1999, vol. II, part 2, s. 172, para. 13.

[7] Jurisdictional Immunities of the State (Germany v. Italy: Greece Intervening), 2 February 2012, [2012] ICJ Rep., para. 107.

[8] Ibid., para. 93.

[9] See Sect. 7 of this chapter.

2 US Courts Practice on State and State Officials Immunity

First judicial decisions recognizing domestic jurisdiction in relation to acts *de jure imperii* of a foreign State or its officials if they were contrary to international law, in particular seriously violating human rights (universally accepted international law norms), appeared in the United States in the 1980s. They were based on interpretation of US legislation, especially the Foreign Sovereign Immunities Act of 1976 (FSIA)[10]—the first domestic regulation on State immunity.

The FSIA is based on the general presumption of foreign State immunity in section 1603(a) subject to a number of listed exceptions in section 1605(a) such as e.g. waiver of immunity, commercial activity, rights in property taken in violation of international law,[11] rights in property in the United States, tortious acts occurring in the United States, and actions brought to enforce arbitration agreements with a foreign State. Besides, State immunity can be overridden in case of extraterritorial breaches involving either US citizens or foreign citizens affected by an act of a foreign State or its officials—this could be done i.a. pursuant to the Civil Rights Act 1964 (Title VII),[12] the Alien Tort Claims Act (ATCA),[13] or the Torture Victims Protection Act (TVPA).[14] But it should be added that US courts strictly distinguish between State immunity and State officials immunity. The first one is governed by legislation (FSIA), while the second one is governed both by legislation (e.g. ATCA, TVPA) and common law.[15]

---

[10] 28 U.S.C. §§1602ff.

[11] I.a. on this ground the Supreme Court based its ruling in the Republic of Austria et al. v Altmann case, 541 US 677 (USA 2004) where the Court found that the FSIA applies retroactively. The case involved a claim by the descendants of owners of famous Gustav Klimt paintings against the Austrian government for return of those paintings, which were allegedly seized during the Nazi era. As a consequence of the Altmann case, the FSIA applies to all suits filed after 1976, even where the conduct took place prior to its enactment.

[12] The Civil Rights Act of 1964, Pub.L. 88-352, 78 Stat. 241, enacted July 2, 1964.

[13] The Alien Tort Claims Act, 28 U.S.C. § 1350. Originally enacted as section 9 of the Judiciary Act of 1789. Since 1980, the ATCA has been held to apply to human rights violations by agents of foreign nations or individuals and corporations occurring outside the United States. It can only be applied in cases where US courts have jurisdiction under the FSIA. Moreover, due to fear of being overburdened by international tort claims, the ATCA exception is now interpreted narrowly, i.a. as relating only to the most serious international crimes. See the Sosa v Alvarez-Machain case (542 US 692 (USA 2004)) where the court held that the ATCA applies only to violations of international norms that are 'specific, universal, and obligatory', and it determined that general prohibitions against arbitrary arrest and detention did not meet that standard. In 2013 the court ruled in the Kiobel v Royal Dutch Petroleum Co. case (133 S Ct 1659 (USA 2013)) regarding a foreign petroleum corporation's alleged complicity in human rights abuses in Nigeria, that the ATCA generally does not apply to torts committed in foreign countries, though exceptions are possible in cases 'where the claims touch and concern the territory of the United States' with 'sufficient force'. Cf. Potesta (2010), pp. 571–576; Chukwuemeke Okeke (2018), pp. 227–231.

[14] The Torture Victim Protection Act (Pub.L. 102–256, H.R. 2092, 106 Stat. 73), enacted 12 March 1992.

[15] See e.g. Keitner (2016), pp. 10–12.

The argument of *jus cogens* exception came up in parallel with regard to the immunity of the State and the immunity of State officials. We will first briefly refer to the case law on State officials immunity as it contributed to clarifying the definition of State immunity, although it did not confirm the *jus cogens* exception. According to this case law, the acts of State officials acting within their official capacity are covered by State immunity.

In several important decisions American courts recognized that acts committed in serious violation of human rights (*jus cogens* norms) do not constitute official acts, and State officials may incur an individual civil liability, as e.g. the *Filártiga v Peña-Irala* case,[16] the *Kadic v Karadžić* case[17] or the *Yusuf-Samantar* saga.[18] In 2012 in the *Yousuf v Samantar* case the Fourth Circuit Court has found that *jus cogens* violations are not shielded by *ratione materiae* immunity under the federal common law, noting that '(t)here has been an increasing trend in international law to abrogate foreign official immunity for individuals who commit acts, otherwise attributable to the State, that violate *jus cogens* norms'.[19] The Court further emphasized that 'under

[16] In the Filártiga v Peña-Irala case US court interpreted the ATCA as establishing US jurisdiction of any civil action by an alien for a tort committed by agents of foreign States in violation of the law of nations or a treaty of the United States. The Court held that 'an act of torture committed by a State official against one held in detention violates established norms of international law of human rights, and hence the law of nations' (Filartiga v Peña-Irala 630 F 2d 876 (USA 1980)). The case concerned the liability for damages for torture with the outcome of Filártiga death. The civil suit was brought by the relatives of the deceased Paraguayan against the Chief Police Inspector of Paraguay, Peña-Irala. The incident took place outside of the US, while all parties to the proceedings were at the time of adjudication in the US (no argument of immunity was raised in the case). In consequence the deceased's family was awarded high compensation.

[17] Kadic v Karadžić, 70 F 3d 232 (USA 1996).

[18] In the decision of 2010 the Supreme Court held that the FSIA does not apply to foreign officials and noted that the distinction between acts committed in an official capacity and those committed beyond the scope of authority 'may well be correct as a matter of common-law principles'. (Samantar v Yousuf, 130 S Ct 2278 (USA 2010)). In the decision of 2 November 2012, in the Yousuf et al. v Samantar case (Case No 11-14792 (USA 2012)) the Court of Appeals of the Fourth Circuit distinguished between head of State immunity and official acts immunity. The Court observed that Samantar (the Minister of Defense at the time of instituting of the proceedings and later Prime Minister of Somalia) is alleged to have committed acts of torture, summary execution and prolonged arbitrary imprisonment, acts which are in violation of universally agreed upon norms, or norms of *jus cogens*. Whilst *jus cogens* violations may be committed under the guise of the law and in that sense constitute acts performed in the course of the official's duties, both international and domestic law recognizes that such violations are acts not officially recognized by the Sovereign of the State. American courts have generally followed the trend of international law to abrogate foreign official immunity for individuals who commit violations of *jus cogens* norms. This does not affect head of State immunity which is of an absolute nature and applies even against *jus cogens* claims (pp. 19–21). The Court concluded that Samantar is not entitled to immunity for official acts in light of the violations of *jus cogens* he is alleged to have committed, even if the acts were performed in his official capacity. This is supported by the TVPA which created an express private right of action for victims of torture and extrajudicial killing against perpetrators (p. 22). Finally, Samantar accepted liability as a superior for the crimes perpetrated by his subordinates in the Somali Armed Forces and the affiliated national intelligence services.

[19] Yousuf v Samantar, 699 F 3d 763 (USA 2012), p. 773.

international and domestic law, officials from other countries are not entitled to foreign official immunity for *jus cogens* violations, even if the acts were performed in the defendant's official capacity'.[20] The other US courts refused to recognize an exception to the rule of immunity for alleged *jus cogens* violations and preferred not to decide on immunity of foreign officials without deference to the determinations of the State Department.[21] This case law is not uniform and revolves around territorial jurisdiction.[22]

State immunity, as distinct from any personal immunities, is governed by the FSIA. In several cases US courts attempted to interpret the FSIA exceptions to foreign State immunity as covering 'action that is clearly contrary to the precepts of humanity as recognized in both national and international law',[23] acts manifestly

---

[20] Ibid., p. 777.

[21] See e.g. the Doğan v Barak case in which the Court of Appeals was to decide whether the parents of a US citizen killed during a military operation conducted by a foreign nation abroad may, i.a. under the TVPA, sue the Israel's Minister of Defense responsible for the operation in a situation in which the acts were performed in his official capacity, where the sovereign government has ratified his conduct, and where the US Department of State has asked the judiciary to grant him foreign official immunity. The Court affirmed the district court's grant of immunity. It refused to recognize a jus cogens exception and the reading of the Yousuf case (2012) suggested by the Doğan. The Court observed that: 'Although the court ultimately held that foreign officials are not immune for jus cogens violations, it did not have occasion to consider whether that should be the case where the foreign sovereign has ratified the defendant's conduct and the State Department files a Suggestion of Immunity on his behalf. Yousuf v Samantar, 699 F 3d 763 (USA 2012), p. 776. ('However, as a matter of international and domestic law, jus cogens violations are, by definition, acts that are not officially authorized by the Sovereign'.) (citing Siderman, 965 F.2d at 718). Thus, the court in Yousuf had no occasion to consider whether jus cogens violations should be an exception to foreign official immunity because, as in the Marcos cases, the defendant was never given immunity in the first place. As far as we can tell, no court has ever carved out an exception to foreign official immunity under the circumstances presented here. We also decline to do so'. Doğan v Barak No 16–56704 DC No 2:15–cv–08130– ODW–GJS (9th Cir) (USA 2019), pp. 18–19.

[22] Cf. conclusions and cases cited by Keitner (2016), pp. 11–12.

[23] In the Letelier v Republic of Chile case US District Court for the District of Columbia noted: 'Whatever policy options may exist for a foreign country, it has no 'discretion' to perpetrate conduct designed to result in the assassination of an individual or individuals, action that is clearly contrary to the precepts of humanity as recognized in both national and international law. Accordingly there would be no 'discretion' within the meaning of section 1605(a) (5) (A) to order or to aid in an assassination and were it to be demonstrated that a foreign State has undertaken any such act in this country, that foreign State could not be accorded sovereign immunity under subsection (A) for any tort claims resulting from its conduct. As a consequence, the Republic of Chile cannot claim sovereign immunity under the Foreign Sovereign Immunities Act for its alleged involvement in the deaths of Orlando Letelier and Ronni Moffitt'. (488 F Supp 665 (USA 1980), p. 673).

violating international law[24] or *jus cogens* norms.[25] But in none of these decisions did the courts recognize a *jus cogens* exception (or a manifest violation of international law exception) under the FSIA. An exception for manifest violation of international law was denied in the unanimous decision of the Supreme Court of 1989, in the *Argentine Republic v Amerada Hess Shipping Corp* case, in which this court held that the only basis of jurisdiction against a foreign State is the FSIA which do not provide for the lifting of State immunity in case of violations of international law.[26] The court observed that none of the exceptions enumerated in the FSIA applied to the facts of this case. Especially, the exception for non-commercial torts is limited by its terms to cases in which the damage to or loss of property occurs in the US.[27] Consequently, it does not cover petitioner's attack on the high seas.

In the 1994 decision in the *Princz v Germany* case[28] the US Court of Appeals expressly rejected a *jus cogens* exception. The court based on the lack of retroactive effect of the FSIA but nevertheless examined the application of the exceptions, which were provided for by the FSIA. H. Princz, the US citizen, a Holocaust survivor, brought an action to recover monetary damages for having been put through slave labour and for injuries he suffered as a prisoner in Nazi Germany concentration camp during World War II. The Court of Appeal observed that even if the FSIA applied retroactively to the period of 1942–1945, none of the statutory exceptions to the foreign sovereign immunity under the FSIA would apply to the

[24] In the Von Dardel v USSR case (623 F Supp 246 (USA 1985)), the Court rejected the immunity of the USSR, assuming that the FSIA provides for an exception to sovereign immunity in case of a manifest violation of international law. The Court also referred to the principle of universal jurisdiction in relation to violations of jus cogens or international law norms of the erga omnes effect. According to the Court, the violation of diplomatic immunity by unlawful detention in 1945 and the imprisonment of the Swedish diplomat (Wallenberg) by the USSR constituted such a violation. But this judgment was later reversed relying on the Argentine Republic v Amerada Hess Shipping Corp. case, see the Von Dardel v USSR case, 736 F Supp 1 (USA 1990).

[25] In the Siderman de Blake v. Republic of Argentina case the District Court found that the prohibition of torture reached the status of jus cogens under international law but it held that the fact that there had been violation of jus cogens did not confer jurisdiction under the FSIA. However, by accepting an implied waiver exception, the Court of Appeals finally decided that the District Court had erred in dismissing Siderman's torture claims. The Court of Appeals concluded that 'the Sidermans have presented evidence sufficient to support a finding that Argentina has implicitly waived its sovereign immunity with respect to their claims for torture. The evidence indicates that Argentina deliberately involved United States courts in its efforts to persecute Jose Siderman. If Argentina has engaged our courts in the very course of activity for which the Sidermans seek redress, it has waived its immunity as to that redress'. (965 F 2d 699 (USA 1992)), p. 722.

[26] Argentine Republic v Amerada Hess Shipping Corp., 488 US 428 (USA 1989), p. 434. A crude oil tanker chartered to Amerada Hess Corp., Liberian corporation, was severely damaged when it was attacked in international waters by Argentine military aircraft during the war between Great Britain and petitioner Argentine Republic over the Falkland Islands (Malvinas) off the Argentine coast. The respondents brought previously the suits for the damage they sustained in the attack.

[27] Argentine Republic v Amerada Hess Shipping Corp., 488 US 428 (USA 1989), p. 434, pp. 439–441.

[28] Hugo Princz v Federal Republic of Germany, 26 F 3d 1166 (USA 1994).

case. Princz's claim does not fall into the commercial activity exception because the Nazi's leasing of Princz's force did not have a 'direct effect' in the US. The treaty provision exception is not applicable because no treaty stipulated that Germany had to pay compensation for the war crimes. Princz raised also an argument that section of the FSIA on waiver of immunity by a foreign State should be read as granting jurisdiction against foreign State violating *jus cogens* norm against genocide since violation of such norm implies a waiver of immunity.[29] The Court rejected this reading.[30] Since then there have been a number of other courts cases rejecting an implied waiver exception, i.e. reaffirming the *Princz* decision.[31]

The decision of 2019 in genocide and expropriation case—*Rukoro v Federal Republic of Germany*—does not bring any change. The case concerned the German empire's genocide and brutal expropriations of thousands of Ovaherero and Nama people in South West Africa (now Namibia) between 1885 and 1909. Plaintiffs, descendants of the Ovaherero and Nama that were excluded from recent discussions on reparations between Germany and Namibia, brought a putative class action against Germany in which they invoked the commercial activity exception and the takings exception under the FSIA. Judge Swain began the consideration of the arguments of the parties observing that: 'As other courts in this circuit have noted in similar circumstances, "strong moral claims are not easily converted into successful legal causes of action"'.[32] The plaintiffs in the present case were not successful either. They were not able to assert exceptions under the FSIA.

The picture of the relation between State immunity and significant violations of human rights in the US practice would be incomplete without mentioning of the terrorism exception introduced to the FSIA in 1996 (so called 'Flatow amendment')[33] to allow US nationals to sue foreign States if the State has been designated as a State sponsor of terrorism (SST) and if the plaintiff's injury has been caused by the State's support of a terrorist organization.[34] According to the subsequent

[29] See Caplan (2003), pp. 767, 774.

[30] Eg. Hugo Princz v Federal Republic of Germany, 26 F 3d 1166 (USA 1994); See also Potesta (2010), pp. 578–579.

[31] Smith v Libya, 101 F 3d 239 (USA 1996); Hirsh v State of Israel, 962 F Supp 377 (USA 1997); Sampson v Federal Republic of Germany, No. 96 C 6242, 1997 WL 583069 (USA 1997).

[32] Rukoro v Federal Republic of Germany, 17 CV 62-LTS, March 6, 2019, Opinion of Judge Swain, p. 6. Judge Swain cited the court in Garb v Republic of Poland, 440 F 3d 579 (USA 2006).

[33] The amendment was named after Stephen Flatow, an American lawyer, whose daughter Alisa Flatow, temporarily studding in Israel, was killed in 1995 in a suicide bombing attack carried out by militants belonging to the Islamic Jihad Movement in Palestine. Flatow lobbied congress to amend the FSIA. The amendment allowed him to commence a series of lawsuits against the Iranian government, the sponsor of terrorism.

[34] The terrorism exception has been introduced by section 221 of the Antiterrorism and Effective Death Penalty Act of 1996 (Pub L No 104–132, 110 Stat 1214).

amendment,[35] a designated State sponsor of terrorism has no immunity in case 'in which money damages are sought for personal injury or death that was caused by an act of torture, extrajudicial killing, aircraft sabotage, hostage taking, or the provision of material support or resources for such an act if such act or provision of material support or resources is engaged in by an official, employee, or agent of such foreign State while acting within the scope of his or her office, employment, or agency'.[36] This provision allows suits against a foreign State for the enumerated acts if the State has been designated SST at the relevant time, and if the act injured a US national, member of the US armed forces, or US government employee. Following these amendments, numerous cases have been filed against the States designated sponsors of terrorism, particularly Iran.

The FSIA was once again amended in 2016 by the Justice Against Sponsors of Terrorism Act (JASTA).[37] The most important change is that previously, US citizens were permitted to sue a foreign State if such State was designated as a State sponsor of terrorism by the US Department of State and if they were harmed by that State's aid for international terrorism. The JASTA authorizes federal courts to exercise subject matter jurisdiction over any foreign State's support for acts of international terrorism against a US national or property regardless of whether such State is designated as a State sponsor of terrorism or not. The JASTA is specifically designed to allow suits arising after 9/11 attacks (it has retroactive effect) against Saudi Arabia. However, the JASTA exception is narrowed by a formal procedure allowing the US government to intervene in cases asserting 'JASTA claims' for the purpose of seeking a stay 'if the Secretary of State certifies that the United States is engaged in good faith discussions with the foreign State defendant concerning the resolution of the claims against the foreign State'.[38] The stay lasts 180 days, but is renewable.[39]

Moreover, the Congress decided (for the first time in 2002)[40] to restrict the scope of the immunity from execution to allow judgments to be enforced against certain frozen assets of SSTs as well as paid from certain US funds appropriated for that purpose.[41] Special law was also enacted to lift enforcement immunity of Iran in

[35] The National Defense Authorization Act for Fiscal Year 2008, Pub L No 110–181, 122 STAT 3.

[36] 28 USC § 1605A(a)(1) (2010).

[37] The Justice Against Sponsors of Terrorism Act, Pub L 114–222.

[38] JASTA §5(c)(1)).

[39] JASTA §5(c)(2)A and (B)(ii). See also the Anti-Terrorism Clarification Act 2018, which removes obstacles to certain lawsuits related to terrorism against the Palestinian Authority (PL 115–253). The law amended the Anti-Terrorism Act (18 USC 2334) by stating that a defendant consents to personal jurisdiction in US federal court for lawsuits related to international terrorism if the defendant accepts certain types of US foreign aid after the law has been in effect for 120 days.

[40] Prior to 2002, if a judgment was awarded against a foreign State, only assets of the foreign State that were located in the US and 'used for commercial activity' could have been seized to satisfy the judgment. The Terrorism Risk Insurance Act of 2002 (TRIA) allowed judgments to be executed against 'the blocked assets of terrorist party'. Blocked assets include assets that may be seized by the President pursuant to his authority granted by Congress.

[41] See 28 U.S.C. §1610 (2018).

relation to a specific case, identified by a docket number.[42] The case concerned victims of Iranian sponsored terrorism, particularly the 1983 Beirut barracks bombings and 1996 Khobar Towers bombing, who sought execution against a bank account in New York held, through European intermediaries, on behalf of Bank Markazi, the State-owned Central Bank of Iran. In 2016 in the *Bank Markazi v Peterson* case[43] the Supreme Court found the law constitutional. It did not examine whether the statutory waiver of immunity was in accordance with international law.

Two months later Iran instituted the proceedings before the ICJ against the United States under the 1955 Iran-US Treaty of Amity. Iran questioned i.a. the legality of the exercise of jurisdiction over it by US courts and the seizure of assets of Iranian State-owned companies to satisfy those court's judgments. Regrettably, the ICJ did not comment on this matter. In the decision of 2019 in the *Certain Iranian Assets* case, the court concluded that the question of sovereign immunities does not fall within the scope of the Treaty of Amity.[44] Therefore the ICJ did not adjudicate, whether the terrorism exceptions to immunity from jurisdiction or enforcement under US law violate international law.

To sum up, when adjudicating on State immunity from jurisdiction or execution, US courts strongly rely on domestic law. They have disallowed broad interpretation of the FSIA exceptions both on the argument of the superiority of *jus cogens* norms over the jurisdictional immunity of the State (the normative hierarchy argument), and the argument of the implied waiver of immunity in the event of violation of *jus cogens*. Challenges to immunity based on the right to access to a court or the right to property, unlike in European courts, did not appear in the US.[45] The terrorism exception to immunity from jurisdiction goes for the moment contrary to existing customary international law. As the enforcement immunity is concerned, the US law allowed, in exceptional cases of terrorism, to attach or otherwise seize foreign sovereign assets located in the United States even if the property is used or intended for use by the State for government non-commercial purposes what is contrary to customary international law and the rules enshrined in the 2004 UN Convention on Jurisdictional Immunities of States and Their Property, i.a. in Art. 19 (c) and Art. 21 (1)(c). The latter explicitly enumerates property of the central bank as property,

---

[42] 22 U.S. Code § 8772. Interests in certain financial assets of Iran. The law applied to the judgment of the District Court for the Southern District of New York of 9 July 2013 in the Peterson et al v Islamic Republic of Iran et al case, No 10 Civ 4518 (BSJ) (USA 2013) and the subsequent court orders. It eliminated all of the defenses one party had raised during the court proceedings.

[43] Bank Markazi, a.k.a. the Central Bank of Iran v Deborah Peterson et al, 578 US 136 S Ct 1310 (USA 2016).

[44] See the judgment of the ICJ of 13 February 2019 in the Certain Iranian Assets (Islamic Republic of Iran v. United States of America) Preliminary Objections case, [2019] ICJ Rep, paras 48–80. In Jurisdictional Immunities of the State (op.cit.), Italy referred to Flatow amendment to the US FSIA, adopted in 1996. In that regard the ICJ noted only that 'this amendment has no counterpart in the legislation of other States. None of the States which has enacted legislation on the subject of State immunity has made provision for the limitation of immunity on the grounds of the gravity of the acts alleged' (para. 88).

[45] Keitner (2016), p. 12.

which 'shall not be considered specifically in use or intended for use by the State for other than government non-commercial purposes under article 19, subparagraph (c)'.

3 Canadian Law and Practice: A Terrorism Exception

In Canada like in the other common law countries, the principle of State immunity is reflected in the statutory law—the State Immunity Act (SIA).[46] The Act is recognized by the Canadian courts as giving effect to customary international law and viewed as exhaustive and trumping countervailing doctrines of any exceptions that may exist elsewhere under common law or international law. Moreover, the Canadian courts emphasize that State immunity represents important issues of comity and mutual respect between nations.[47] The Canadian courts refused to interpret the SIA broadly, especially as allowing an exception for the violation of *jus cogens*. In a well-known decision in the *Bouzari v Islamic Republic of Iran* case of 2004, the Ontario Court of Appeal held that the existing Canadian law—the SIA—precludes claims against foreign State based on the allegations of torture.[48] More recently, the Supreme Court in the *Estate of Kazemi v Islamic Republic of Iran* case[49] repeated these findings referring broadly for justification *i.a.* to the ICJ judgment in the *Jurisdictional Immunities of the State* case and the decisions of the European Court of Human Rights (ECtHR).

In 2012 Canada amended the SIA and introduced the terrorism exception. The Justice for Victims of Terrorist Act (JVTA)[50] allowed victims of terrorism to sue perpetrators and supporters of terrorism, including foreign States formally listed by Canadian government as supporters of terrorism (subsection 6.1(1) et seq., the SIA).

---

[46] State Immunity Act, R.S.C. 1985, as amended 2012. c. S1–18.

[47] Akthar (2018), p. 227.

[48] Bouzari v Ismalic Republic of Iran, Ontario Court of Appeal, No C38295 (Canada 2004), paras 42–59. The court refused to interpret the SIA as providing civil redress for grave human rights abuses and observed that neither Canada's treaty obligations nor the rules of customary international law binding Canada accord to the appellant the civil remedy he seeks. 'Both under customary international law and international treaty there is today a balance struck between the condemnation of torture as an international crime against humanity and the principle that States must treat each other as equals not to be subjected to each other's jurisdiction. It would be inconsistent with this balance to provide a civil remedy against a foreign State for torture committed abroad. In the future, perhaps as the international human rights movement gathers greater force, this balance may change, either through the domestic legislation of States or by international treaty. However, this is not a change to be effected by a domestic court adding an exception to the SIA that is not there, or seeing a widespread State practice that does not exist today'. (para. 95). The case was brought by an Iranian immigrant who was tortured by government officials in Iran. See also Arar v Syrian Arab Republic et al, Superior Court of Justice, Ontario, No 03–CV–259270CM2 (Canada 2005).

[49] Estate of Kazemi v Islamic Republic of Iran [2014] SCC 62 (Canada 2014).

[50] The Justice for Victims of Terrorist Act, SC 2012, c 1, s. 1.

Under subsection 6.1(11) of the SIA if the judgment is given against a foreign State by the court of another foreign State, the judgment may be recognized in Canada if the State concerned is on the list referred to in subsection 6.1(2) of the SIA. That provision allowed US victims of terrorist attacks to bring group cases to enforce their US judgments by seizing Iranian non-diplomatic assets in Canada. In 2016 in the *Tracy v Iranian Ministry of Information and Security* case,[51] the Ontario Superior Court of Justice had recognized a series of American judgments rendered against Iran in favour of American victims of terrorist acts, which Iran was found to have sponsored. The court held that Iran was not immune from the enforcement proceedings and that accordingly the American judgments were enforceable against certain non-diplomatic properties and various bank accounts of Iran in Ontario.

Both US and Canadian terrorism exceptions to State immunity, however morally justified, are criticized[52] and deviate from international customary law.

4 The European Courts Practice Based on International Law

In the case law of the European courts, the rulings of the Greek Supreme Court in the *Prefecture of Voiotia v Germany* (*Distomo*) case of 2000[53] and the Italian Court of Cassation of 2004 in the *Ferrini v Germany* case[54] are particularly noteworthy. They relate strictly to State immunity of Germany and its responsibility for serious crimes committed during World War II.

The decision of the Supreme Court in the *Distomo* case appeared only six years after the judgment in the *Princz* case, and more importantly, it took over the arguments rejected by US courts (argument of alleged waiver of immunity and argument of normative hierarchy). The Greek Supreme Court upheld the decision of the court in *Livadia*, rejecting the immunity of Germany in the action for damages brought by the families of the victims of the massacre carried out in the Greek town of Distomo by the German armed forces during World War II. The Supreme Court acknowledged that a State that had committed a serious violation of international law waived immunity. The Court awarded victims the damages, stating that the violation of *jus cogens* norms of international law cannot be regarded as *acta jure imperii*, since the gravity of those violations requires redress. However, Germany refused to

[51] Tracy v Iranian Ministry of Information and Security, 2016 ONSC 3759 (Canada 2016).

[52] See e.g. Holcombe (2017). See especially the arguments that JASTA dangerously disrupts the principle of sovereign immunity and the separation of power doctrine by limiting the executive's control over foreign policy, pp. 380–387.

[53] Judgment of the Greek Supreme Court (Areios Pagos), No 11/2000 (Distomo massacre) (Greece 2000), ILR 2007, vol 129, p. 514. The Court upheld the decision of the First Instance Court in Livadia of 30 October 1997, No 137/1997.

[54] Ferrini v Federal Republic of Germany, No 5044 (Italy 2004), ILR 2006, vol 128, p. 659.

pay compensation and the plaintiffs failed to enforce the decision in Greece, especially they failed to seize the building of the German cultural centre in Athens—the Goethe Institute—against compensation. The enforcement proceedings lacked consent of the Greek Minister of Justice required by Art. 923 of the Greek Code of Civil Procedure.[55] The judgment in the *Distomo* case proved to be a single incident. In subsequent cases, the Greek courts declined the argument of *jus cogens* exception to State immunity.[56]

The *Ferrini* case concerned the compensation for an Italian citizen for imprisonment, deportation and forced labour in Germany during World War II. The Court of Cassation rejected the position of the lower courts, lifted the immunity of Germany and awarded damages. The Court grounded its decision not on an implied waiver of immunity (the Court criticized the reasoning in the *Distomo* case),[57] but on the seriousness of violations of *jus cogens* norms protecting human rights. Granting jurisdictional immunity in these cases would impede the protection of the values that must be recognized as fundamental to the international community of States as a whole.[58] In the *Ferrini* case, the cardinal argument was therefore the supremacy of peremptory norms of international law over procedural norms of international customary law on jurisdictional immunity in relation to the acts *de jure imperii* of a foreign State. In the opinion of the Court, the peremptory norms are at the top of the normative hierarchy of the international legal order and therefore prevail over any other treaty norms or customary law.

The ruling in the *Ferrini* case was confirmed by the Court of Cassation in subsequent cases. In 2008, in the *Germany v Giovanni Mantelli et al* case, the Court of Cassation openly admitted that by refusing immunity to Germany against violations of *jus cogens*, the Court no longer applied customary law, but rather contributed to its creation.[59] The Court cited the argument of the normative hierarchy, but its conclusions were not based on the purely formal supremacy of *jus cogens*, but on the systemic interpretation of the international legal order in the light

[55] See e.g. Biehler (2008), pp. 115–116. The applicants in Distomo lodged a complaint with the ECtHR, accusing Greece of violating Art. 6(1) ECHR (right to access to court) and Art. 1 of Protocol No 1 (property right). The ECtHR held that the grant of immunity in this case was not contrary to the ECHR (Kalogeropoulou and Others v Greece and Germany, Application No 59021/00, decision of 12 December 2002). Enforcement of the judgment of the Livadia Court, upheld by the Greek Supreme Court in 2000, was refused by a court in Germany in the Greek Citizens v Federal Republic of Germany, No III ZR 245/98 (Germany 2003). Subsequently, the applicants attempted to execute the judgment in Italy. Italian courts have allowed the execution. This became the subject of proceedings by the ICJ in Jurisdictional Immunities of the State.

[56] I.a. Margellos v Federal Republic of Germany No 6/2002 (Italy 2002), ILR 2002, vol 129, p. 525.

[57] Ferrini v Federal Republic of Germany, No 5044 (Italy 2004), ILR 2006, vol 128, p. 659, para. 8.2.

[58] Ferrini v Federal Republic of Germany, No 5044 (Italy 2004) para. 9.1. Criticized by Caplan (2003), pp. 771–776. For comments see also e.g. De Sena and De Vittor (2005), pp. 89–112.

[59] See Federal Republic of Germany v Giovanni Mantelli et al, No 14199 and Nos 14200–14212 (Italy 2008), Rivista di diritto internazionale privato e processuale 2009, p. 651. See Potesta (2010), pp. 654–655.

of its fundamental values. The Court also took into account the lack of alternative means of redress, as Germany refused compensation in many similar cases. In the judgment of 2009, the Court of Cassation recognized the *jus cogens* exception to State immunity as binding case law.[60]

5 The ICJ's Rejection of the *Jus Cogens* Exception to State Immunity

The Italian example shows what may happen when national courts depart from customary law. When it comes to judicial assessment of the legality of initial deviations from the customary norm,[61] international courts consider them to be contrary to international law (as e.g. the Permanent Court of International Justice did in the *Lotus* case).[62] This happened exactly in the case of Italy. Germany brought the case against Italy to the ICJ on the basis of the jurisdiction clause contained in Art. 1 of the European Convention on the Peaceful Settlement of Disputes of 1957.[63]

The practice of Italian courts was critically assessed by the ICJ in its judgment of 2012 in the *Jurisdictional Immunities of the State*. One of the reasons for Germany's complaint to the ICJ were the Italian court rulings authorizing the execution in Italy of a judgment issued by a Greek court against Germany in the *Distomo* case by seizing German property—Villa Vigoni—the seat of the Goethe Institute branch (the case was suspended due to the proceedings before the ICJ).[64] The ICJ recognized the practice of Italian courts as isolated, which could not yet produce customary law. The Court opposed it to 'the substantial body of State practice from other countries which demonstrates that customary international law does not treat a State's entitlement to immunity as dependent upon the gravity of the act of which it is accused or the peremptory nature of the rule which it is alleged to have violated'.[65] After

[60] Judgment of the Italian Court of Cassation of 13 January 2009, No 1072 (Italy 2009); Rivista di diritto internazionale 2009, vol. 92, pp. 619 and 626.

[61] The State is responsible for all its organs, including courts, and cannot rely on its internal law (even the Constitution) or internal practice to justify non-compliance with international obligations, see Art. 4 Articles on Responsibility of States for Internationally Wrongful Acts, annex to General Assembly resolution 56/83 of 12 December 2001 and Art. 27 of the Vienna Convention of the Law of Treaties.

[62] Judgment of the PCIJ of 7 September 1927, SS Lotus (France v Turkey), PCIJ 1927, Series A, No 1.

[63] European Treaty Series No 23.

[64] Jurisdictional Immunities of the State (Germany v. Italy: Greece Intervening), 2 February 2012, [2012] ICJ Rep., paras 33–35.

[65] Ibid., para. 84. The Court widely cites various court's rulings rejecting a jus cogens exception, i.a. the Polish Supreme Court decision in the Natoniewski case (see para. 85).

reviewing national and international courts judgments,[66] the ICJ found that Italian courts violated international customary law by denying Germany both jurisdictional immunity and enforcement immunity. The ICJ concluded that 'under customary international law as it presently stands, a State is not deprived of immunity by reason of the fact that it is accused of serious violations of international human rights law or the international law of armed conflict'.[67]

The Court continued that even on the assumption 'that the rules of the law of armed conflict which prohibit the murder of civilians in occupied territory, the deportation of civilian inhabitants to slave labour and the deportation of prisoners of war to slave labour are rules of *jus cogens*, there is no conflict between those rules and the rules on State immunity. These two sets of rules address different matters'.[68] The norms regulating State immunity refer only to the determination whether the courts of one State may exercise jurisdiction over another State in a given case. They are of a procedural character and cannot serve to determine whether the conduct at issue in the main proceedings was legal or illegal. Consequently, there can be no conflict between procedural and substantive rules. They operate at different levels.[69] There is thus no conflict between State immunity and the rule prohibiting the original wrongful act or the duty to make reparation.[70]

Moreover, the ICJ addressed the argument submitted by Italy to justify its courts decisions—lack of other means of redress for the victims (last resort argument). Citing, among others the case law of the ECtHR, the ICJ Stated that national and international practice indicates that international law does not currently make the right to immunity conditional on the existence of effective alternative means of securing redress.[71]

[66]Jurisdictional Immunities of the State (Germany v. Italy: Greece Intervening), 2 February 2012, [2012] ICJ Rep., para. 90. The ICJ referred i.a. to the ECtHR decisions of 21 November 2001 in the Al-Adsani v United Kingdom case (Application No 35763/97); of 12 December 2002 in the Kalogeropoulou and Others v Greece and Germany case (Application No 59021/00).

[67]Jurisdictional Immunities of the State (Germany v. Italy: Greece Intervening), 2 February 2012, [2012] ICJ Rep., para. 91.

[68]Ibid., para. 93.

[69]Ibid., paras 92–97.

[70]Ibid., para. 94. The ICJ continued: 'Moreover, against the background of a century of practice in which almost every peace treaty or post-war settlement has involved either a decision not to require the payment of reparations or the use of lump sum settlements and set-offs, it is difficult to see that international law contains a rule requiring the payment of full compensation to each and every individual victim as a rule accepted by the international community of States as a whole as one from which no derogation is permitted'.

[71]Jurisdictional Immunities of the State (Germany v. Italy: Greece Intervening), 2 February 2012, [2012] ICJ Rep., para. 101. See also paras. 98–100.

6 Chilling Effect of the ICJ Ruling

Taking into consideration the authority of the ICJ, the ruling in the *Jurisdictional Immunities of the State* case, despite criticism,[72] should end or at least cool the process of judicial law-making. Italy implemented the judgment of the ICJ, changed the law to allow the resumption of proceedings ended with a final decision and to ensure the execution of the judgment in proceedings that have not yet ended (Act No 5 of 14 January 2013).[73] However, even before the law entered into force, some courts, using various legal arguments, managed to resolve disputes in accordance with the ruling of the ICJ.[74]

In one of these rulings—a decision delivered on appeal by the First Criminal Section of the Court of Cassation in the *Criminal Proceedings against Albers et al* case of 2012, the Court, although revoked the lower court's decision and accorded jurisdictional immunity to Germany, but nevertheless recalled the controversy, and repeated its conviction of the hierarchical supremacy of *jus cogens* rules regarding international crimes violating human rights over a rule of customary law on State immunity for acts *de jure imperii* (e.g. conduct of the armed forces).[75] The primacy of *jus cogens* cannot apply only to the substantive rules or material phase of the dispute, but must as well apply to the procedural phase. The Court of Cassation further explained that the judges are perfectly aware that their opinion is not shared by the courts of other States and that customary law on *jus cogens* exception to State immunity has not yet developed. This fact and the indisputable authority of the ICJ's judgment prompted them to take into account the ICJ's judgment and, in accordance with Italy's international obligations, they decided to allow Germany's appeal and reconsider the lower court decision.[76]

Unlike other decisions of Italian courts of that period, the *obiter dictum* of the judgment of the Court of Cassation, may have a persuasive effect. But speaking on the 'chilling effect' of the ICJ judgment, a better example than that of the courts of the State bound by the ruling is the example of the decision of 10 October 2014 of

[72] See e.g. Germany v. Italy, The Right to Deny State Immunity When Victims Have No Other Recourse, Amnesty International Publications 2011, pp. 1–23; Orakhelashvili (2012), pp. 612–616; McGregor (2013), pp. 125–139; Souresh (2017), pp. 15–35.

[73] Act No 5 of 14 January 2013, Accession by the Italian Republic to the United Nations Convention on Jurisdictional Immunities of States and their Property, signed in New York on 2 December 2004 (Adesione della Repubblica italiana alla Convenzione della Nazioni Unite sulle immunità giurisdizionali degli Stati e dei loro beni, fatta a New York il 2 dicembre 2004).

[74] E.g. Fontanelli (2013), p. 635 refers to Manfredi v. Repubblica federale di Germania, Trib. Firenze, 28 marzo 2012 (Italy 2012), 95 Rivista di diritto internazionale 583 (2012); Repubblica federale di Germania v. De Guglielmo, App. Torino, 3 maggio 2012 (Italy 2012), 95 Rivista di diritto internazionale 916 (2012).

[75] Judgment of the Court of Cassation of 9 August 2012, No 32139/2 (Italy 2012), 95 Rivista di diritto internazionale 1196 (2012), see e.g. Fontanelli (2013), pp. 632–638.

[76] Judgment of the Court of Cassation of 9 August 2012, No 32139/2 (Italy 2012), 95 Rivista di diritto internazionale (2012), pp. 1204–1205; Fontanelli (2013), pp. 634–635.

the Canadian Supreme Court in the *Estate of Kazemi v Islamic Republic of Iran* case, mentioned above, in which the Court found that Canada's State Immunity Act shields both the State of Iran and its officials from civil claims for torture. Referring for support to the ICJ in the *Jurisdictional Immunities of the State* case and the ECtHR in the *Jones and others v United Kingdom* case which 'reviewed judicial decisions from around the world',[77] including the ICJ decision, the Canadian Supreme Court concluded that an exception to immunity for *jus cogens* violation had not yet crystallized. Consequently, since 'Canada is not obliged by the *jus cogens* prohibition on torture to open its courts so that citizens may seek redress for torture committed abroad',[78] the SIA does not violate principles of fundamental justice protected by section 7[79] of the Canadian Charter of Rights and Freedoms.[80] On the argument that the SIA is unconstitutional to the extent that it prevents access to an effective remedy for gross human rights violations, the Court observed that remedies are by no means automatic or unlimited and that 'there is no societal consensus that an effective remedy is always guaranteed to compensate for every rights violation'.[81]

7 The Judgment 238/2014 of the Italian Constitutional Court—State Immunity Versus National Constitution

Surprisingly, almost at the same time, on 22 October 2014, in the judgment in the case No 238/2014 (*Judgment 238/2014*)[82] the Italian Constitutional Court decided to oppose the ruling in the *Jurisdictional Immunities of the State* case. The Constitutional Court found Art. 3 of the Italian law implementing the ICJ's decision[83] unconstitutional. The provision obliged Italian courts to reject jurisdiction in cases of compensation for war crimes and crimes against humanity committed on Italian territory by German armed forces during World War II. The Constitutional Court,

[77] Estate of Kazemi v Islamic Republic of Iran [2014] SCC 62 (Canada 2014), para. 155.

[78] Estate of Kazemi v Islamic Republic of Iran [2014] SCC 62 (Canada 2014), para. 157.

[79] The provision reads: 'Everyone has the right to life, liberty and security of the person and the right not to be deprived thereof except in accordance with the principles of fundamental justice'.

[80] Estate of Kazemi v Islamic Republic of Iran [2014] SCC 62 (Canada 2014), para. 157. The Court cited the ICJ agreeing that 'individuals have a right to be free from torture, but State immunity is procedural bar which prevents an individual from bringing a civil claim against foreign State. State immunity regulates a State's exercise of jurisdiction over another foreign State, which is a procedural matter. This regulation is distinct from the substantive law which would determine whether the alleged acts of torture were lawful (...)', para. 61.

[81] Estate of Kazemi v Islamic Republic of Iran [2014] SCC 62 (Canada 2014), para. 159.

[82] Judgment of the Constitutional Court of 22 October 2014, No 238/2014 (Italy 2014), unofficial translation by A. Gracis, http://italyspractice.info/judgment-238-2014. The case was broadly commented, see i.a. positive reaction of Longobardo (2015), pp. 1–15.

[83] Act No 5 of 14 January 2013.

without questioning the ICJ's determination of international customary law, underlined that the rule recognized by the ICJ affording to a foreign State the absolute immunity for acts *de jure imperii* is not allowed to enter the Italian legal order. It conflicts with its basic principles, in particular with Art. 24 of the Constitution (the right of access to a court) and Art. 2 of the Constitution (the principle of protection of fundamental rights of individuals). Finally, the Constitutional Court found as unconstitutional Art. 1 of Act No 848 of 17 August 1957[84] introducing the United Nations Charter in Italian legal order, in the scope in which it made effective its Art. 94 that obliged Italy to comply with the decision of the ICJ of 2012. The choice of the Italian Constitutional Court to disregard the ICJ's judgment was conscious. The Court noted that its ruling could contribute to the 'desired – and expected by many – evolution of international law', similar to that which took place in the early nineteenth century by decisions of national courts (initially Italian and Belgian) in the case of the rule of absolute State immunity and later the immunity restricted to *de jure imperii* acts.[85]

7.1 Impact on Other Courts: General Remarks

The exception to State immunity recognized by the Italian courts has some support in academia.[86] The exception does not question the existence of traditional theory of State immunity, but attempts to redefine the concept of *de jure imperii* acts by dividing them into legitimate and illegitimate ones.[87] On the other hand, the ICJ judgment is criticized by some authors as conservative,[88] but at the same time considered to correctly identify existing customary law.[89] It is emphasized that the Italian exception serves to strengthen the rule of law in international relations, to avoid impunity for the most severe crimes, and is formulated in a reasonable way—i.e. narrowly. Limitation of immunity recognized by Italian courts only takes place if

[84]Esecuzione dello Statuto delle Nazioni Unite, firmato a San Francisco il 26 giugno 1945, § 72.2.15 – L. 17 agosto 1957, n. 848 (GU 25 settembre 1957, n. 238, SO). www.edizionieuropee.it/LAW/HTML/39/zn72_02_015.html. *Accessed 15 April 2021.*

[85]Judgment No 238/2014 (Italy 2014), para. 3.3.

[86]I.a. Bothe (2015), pp. 99–115; see also Amnesty International Publications (2011) Germany v. Italy, The Right to Deny State Immunity When Victims Have No Other Recourse, pp. 1–23; Saputo (2012), pp. 5–36; De Santis di Nicola (2016), pp. 107–121; Ekpo (2017), pp. 151–164, especially pp. 163–164; Wojcikiewicz Almeida (2018), pp. 61–64. In defense of immunity see Tomuschat (2011), pp. 1105–1140; Kranz (2015), pp. 116–127.

[87]Dominelli (2016), p. 6.

[88]I.a. Nagan and Root (2013), pp. 379–383; Bothe (2015), pp. 101–107; Boggero (2016), p. 210.

[89]van Alebeek (2012), pp. 282–283, 313; McMenamin (2013), pp. 207–209; Dickinson (2013), pp. 147–166; Blanke and Falkenberg (2013), p. 1842. See also Talmon (2012), pp. 2–30. The author convincingly defends the main argument of the ICJ based on the distinction between procedural and substantive norms.

the claim relates to serious violations of international humanitarian law or crimes against humanity and there are no alternative means of redress.

On the other hand, Italian judgments, in particular the *Judgment 238/2014*, may be criticized[90] as violating the balance of interests achieved in the twentieth century and a source of unforeseen difficulties.[91] Moreover, after few years the 'Italian exception' has ceased to be narrowly cut.

The Italian Constitutional Court may find the followers. New cases against foreign States for *jus cogens* violations, including against Germany for crimes committed during World War II, are still possible. The example is an attempt in 2017 in Poland to use a court decision as an instrument of a political game. To get measurable benefits in the following elections, governing political party, the Law and Justice (PiS), has resumed the issue of World War II reparations owed by Germany to Poland. The PiS questioned the validity of renunciation of reparations made by Polish communist government in 1953 and formulated new financial demands. Part of this policy was to encourage bringing individual claims for compensation against Germany before Polish courts. To this end, the PiS wanted to reverse the position taken previously by the Supreme Court. In 2017 a group of the deputies to the Polish Parliament, the members of the PiS, sought from the Constitutional Court a declaration that granting State immunity in such cases is incompatible with human rights provisions of the Constitution: the right to property and the right of access to a court (case *K 12/17).*[92] The similarity of arguments between the application of the Polish MPs and the decision of the Italian Constitutional Court is not accidental.

Moreover, at the same time Art. 89(1) of the Polish Act on the Supreme Court of 2017 introduced a new mechanism to question final courts' decisions delivered after October 1997—an extraordinary complaint which may be lodged e.g. by Prosecutor General or Ombudsman, if it is necessary to ensure the rule of law and social justice and the judgment violates the principles or freedoms and human and citizen rights set out in the Constitution, and if the judgment may not be set aside or amended by other extraordinary measures of appeal. A new Supreme Court chamber was even established for these purposes. The procedure may also be used to reverse a judgment in the *Natoniewski* case (the time limit to bring the case to the Supreme Court is April 2021).[93] Meanwhile, due to termination of the parliamentary term at the end of 2019, the case *K 12/17* was discontinued and has not yet been renewed by the new elected Parliament. However, considering the strong support of the case by

---

[90] See e.g. Boggero (2016), pp. 203–224; De Sena (2014), pp. 17–31.

[91] Kolb (2014), p. 6—calls the judgment 'a murder of international law through municipal law'; Chechi regards the Italian court as 'jeopardising the coherence of international law' (2015), p. 472.

[92] Request of a group of Members of the Parliament to the Constitutional Court of 26 October 2017 (the Code of Civil Procedure—obligations for compensation due from a foreign State for war crimes, genocide and crimes against humanity), registered in the Polish Constitutional Court, No K 12/17. Available in Polish at K_12_17_wns_2017_10_26_ADO.pdf. Accessed 15 April 2021.

[93] Act of 8 December 2017 on the Supreme Court (Journal of Laws of 2018, item 5).

the Polish Sejm[94] and the Prosecutor General,[95] it cannot be ruled out that the issue will not return. For this reason alone, it is worth considering the role of national courts in the current situation.

National judges may take part in the development of customary law. Judgments of national courts can express both the practice of the State and its *opinio juris*.[96] They can also indirectly influence the law-making process by the persuasiveness of the reasoning and the values on which they were based. The law-making role of the court decision cannot sometimes be performed without violation of current international law, so it seems obvious from the very beginning that courts should use this option in exceptional and well-founded cases, considering the inevitable consequences of the derogation.

The Polish Supreme Court in 2010 faced, like the Greek or the Italian courts, with the liability of Germany for crimes of its armed forces during the World War II preferred to take the path of the majority of national courts understanding State immunity as covering all the acts of *jure imperii* character. In the *Natoniewski* case it took restrictive stance on the role of judges in creating international law. The Court observed that '(i)t is not for the national court to 'develop' international law by unilaterally giving it such content that, however desirable and in line with the values inherent in imperative norms of international law, is not accepted by other States. While such activism in the field of national law falls within the limits of judicial functions, it cannot be accepted in the field of international law, which is based on the common consent of States. Therefore, in a situation where there is no evidence that States, by way of exception to the principle of immunity, accept the jurisdiction of national courts in cases pending against foreign States arising from violations of the norms of *juris cogentis*, the principle of immunity of foreign States should apply'.[97] The court seemed to leave it to the executive or the legislator to deviate from customary law.

---

[94] Opinion of the Sejm in case K 12/17 of 26 July 2018, available in Polish at K_12_17_sjm_2018_07_26_ADO.pdf. Accessed 15 April 2021.

[95] Opinion of the Prosecutor General in case K 12/17 of 8 October 2018, available in Polish at K_12_17_pg_2018_10_08_ADO.pdf. Accessed 15 April 2021.

[96] Traditionally, national courts' decisions were considered merely facts (see Certain German Interests in Polish Upper Silesia (Merits), PCIJ 1926, Series A, No 7, p. 19). Many authors recognize that courts' decisions may be an expression of the practice of States, e.g. Lauterpacht (1929), pp. 65–95; Akehurst (1975), pp. 8–10; Moremen (2006), pp. 261–309; Brownlie (2008), p. 6. For different opinion see Oppenheim (1908), pp. 336–341. The ILC recognized that the practice of States should be found in a combination of national law, decisions of national courts, executive practice, diplomatic practice and treaty practice. See Formation and evidence of customary international law, Memorandum by the Secretariat, dok. A/CN.4/659, 14 March 2013, p. 14. See also Nollkaemper (2011), p. 267.

[97] Decision of the Supreme Court of 29 October 2010 r., No IV CSK 465/09 (Poland 2010), upheld the immunity of Germany under international customary law in matters relating to compensation for damages resulting from violation of international law of jus cogens nature (prohibition of war crimes, genocide and crimes against humanity). The Supreme Court rejected the arguments based on human rights. Natoniewski was cited by the ICJ in Jurisdictional Immunities of the State.

Customary law is still an important source of international law and it may evolve. Paradoxically, if the common position of the national courts were such as in the *Natoniewski* case, they would probably seriously restrict or even cease to participate in the creation of customary law. To evolve customary law needs an initial error to occur somewhere in practice, be it a court judgment or a parliament bill. Otherwise, the courts would have nothing to refer to in the process of determination of customary law. But if this 'error' is corrected by the decision of international court, especially the ICJ, it is risky to oppose it, including by invoking national constitution.

7.2 Consequences for Internal Legal Order

The judgments opposing customary law on the ground of the conflict with the State constitution may have systemic consequences for internal legal order. For instance, the *Judgment 238/2014* was seen in Italy as the shift to dualism and return to the tendency to perceive the systemic difference between national law and international law.[98] E. Cannizzaro noted that even the deference to the ICJ in the *Judgment 238/2014* was 'offset by the strict dualist approach in the subsequent parts of the judgment. Once the Constitutional Court accepted the determination of international law made by the ICJ, it went on to assess the lawfulness of these rules in the light of a purely domestic standard of review. The implications of this choice are perverse. From theoretical viewpoint, it has created a deep cleavage between international law, considered as the realm of interstate interests, and the constitutional legal order, where human rights concerns take priority over other consideration'.[99] From a judicial policy perspective, the choice can have rendered more difficult to attain the objective stated by the Constitutional Court—to promote the development of customary law. E. Cannizzaro is probably right arguing that the same result could be more easily attained if presented as the outcome of a process of change already pending at the international level.[100]

If a similar court decision were made in Poland, the consequences would be comparable. In particular, that the applicants requested to reinterpret Art. 9 of the Constitution which reads: 'The Republic of Poland shall respect international law binding upon it'. So far the provision has been understood as imposing an obligation on State organs to comply with all the sources of international obligations, including international customary law both on internal and external levels. The Constitutional

[98] See interesting analysis of the Judgment 238/14 in the light of European and American approach to the review of compliance of international law with national law, (Notes) Constitutional Courts and International Law: Revisiting the Transatlantic Divide, Harvard Law Review 2016, vol. 129, p. 1362.

[99] Cannizzaro (2015), pp. 127–128.

[100] Cannizzaro (2015), p. 128.

Court would have to narrow this reading to external relations, since otherwise the decision would not only violate customary international law but also the Constitution.[101] This shift would severely limit the application of international law in Poland. Given the current politicization of the Polish Constitutional Court[102] and assuming the resumption of the proceedings mentioned above, such a scenario is not impossible. The Court may want to support the government either in internal political campaign or in diplomatic attempts, if they were real, in obtaining war reparations from Germany.[103] In such a 'game' costs for the international legal order may not count.

7.3 *The Right to Oppose International Law Which Violates Fundamental Constitutional Principles*

Internal law implications do not yet contradict the right of Polish courts (or any other national court), especially the Constitutional Court as the guardian of the Constitution, to oppose international law when this law violates fundamental constitutional principles or domestic core values.[104] This right, in the case of Poland, could be even drawn from the Constitution itself (Art. 8 of the Constitution expressly provides for its supremacy) and the ensuing case law of the Constitutional Court on the relation

[101] The applicants urged the Polish Constitutional Court to confirm that Art. 9 refers only to external relations (Request of 26 October 2017, K 12/17, pp. 8–9).

[102] See i.a. Sadurski (2018), pp. 1–72; Sadurski (2019); Wyrzykowski (2019), pp. 417–422.

[103] After World War II Poland received part of reparations from Germany (from the territory occupied by the Soviet Union, but renounced the rest in 1953. Later on, Poland had obtained ex gratia payments for the compensation of certain individual claims. These processes have been well described and documented. See e.g. Barcz (2017), pp. 18–32.

[104] In the judgment of 11 May 2005, No K 18/04 (Poland 2005), on the constitutionality of the Accession Treaty to the EU, the Polish Constitutional Court clearly stated the primacy of the Constitution over international law. The Court highlighted that '(t)he norms of the Constitution in the field of individual rights and freedoms set a minimum and impassable threshold that cannot be lowered or challenged as a result of the introduction of Community law. The Constitution performs its guarantee role in this respect, from the point of view of the protection of rights and freedoms clearly defined in it, and in relation to all entities active in the sphere of its application'. (Para. 6.5.). It is interesting to note that in 2015 the German Constitutional Court uphold an amendment to the Income Tax Act that violated a German–Turkish dual taxation treaty (BVerfG, Order of the Second Senate of 15 December 2015 – 2 BvL 1/12). The Court held that there is no an unreserved constitutional duty to comply with all rules of international law. The legislature is bound only by constitutional law and has the right 'to enact legislation that diverges from what was agreed under international law'. (Para. 55). Moreover, 'the Basic Law seeks to integrate Germany into the legal community of peaceful and democratic States, it does not relinquish sovereignty in relation to the final authority that ultimately belongs to the Constitution'. (Para. 68). See Peters (2016).

between EU law and Polish law, which strongly emphasised this supremacy.[105] Neither an Italian judgment nor a feasible Polish one are or would be groundbreaking in this field.[106] It is enough to mention a famous *Solange I* decision of the German Federal Constitutional Court of 1974, as the first attempt to limit the supremacy of EU law over national constitutional law, shadowed later by other European courts.[107] The Italian Constitutional Court followed exactly the *controlimiti* doctrine applied earlier to EU law when it reiterated that the basic principles of constitutional order and inalienable human rights create a restriction on the introduction into national law of universally recognized norms of international law.[108] Moreover, similar conduct of some courts (including the Court of Justice of the EU in the *Kadi* saga[109] in this group) led to positive adjustments in international law,[110] in other cases, to compromise solutions.[111]

---

[105] As in many other countries, the Polish Constitution provides for primacy of the Constitution over international law. Under Art. 8 the Constitution is the supreme law of Poland and under Art. 178—judges are 'subject only to the Constitution and statues'.

[106] Judgment 238/2014 is compared to Avena Medellín v Texas (552 US 491 (USA 2008)) rejecting to enforce the ICJ judgment. But in contrast to that ruling, it explicitly contests the decision of the ICJ. In Medellín, the US court questioned rather the direct effect of the ICJ judgment in US law, what meant federal law was needed to make the judgment enforceable.

[107] Solange I, BVerfGE 37, 271 (Germany 1974). In the judgment No 2 BvR 859/15 (Germany 2020) the Federal Constitutional Court found for the first time the judgment of the Court of Justice of the European Union to be contrary to the German Constitution (the case concerned Public Sector Purchase Programme of the ECB). See below footnote 112.

[108] Judgment No 238/2014 (Italy 2014), para. 3.2.

[109] I.a. the judgment of the CJEU of 3 September 2008, Joined cases C-402/05 P and C-415/05 P CJEU, Kadi and Al Barakaat International Foundation v Council of the European Union and Commission of the European Communities, ECLI:EU:C:2008:461, paras 281–286.

[110] Solange I has resulted in the development of protection of fundamental rights in the EU. The CJEU ruling in Kadi refusing to implement without any reflection UN Security Council smart sanctions, induced changes in the UN to establish UN ombudsman and, moreover, modified the standard of protection of fair trail rights. This standard was accepted by the ECtHR in Al-Dulimi when the Strasbourg court admitted that the national implementation of UN Security Council decisions should be subjected to scrutiny regarding its compliance with human rights. See the judgment of the ECtHR of 26 November 2013, *Al-Dulimi and Montana Management Inc v Switzerland*, Application No 5809/08, paras 145–149.

[111] In several cases, the ECtHR adapted its case-law to the position of the opposing national courts. E.g. judgment of the Grand Chamber of 15 December 2011, Al-Khawaja and Tahery v the United Kingdom, Applications Nos 26766/05 and 22228/06. See also the ECtHR Grand Chamber judgment in Moreira Ferreira v Portugal (no 2) of 11 July 2017, Application No 19867/12. The case concerned the ruling of the Portuguese Supreme Court rejecting a request for revision of criminal conviction following the judgment of the ECtHR of 2011 in which the Court found that a reopening of proceedings at the applicant's request would constitute an appropriate means of redressing the violation found. In that regard it noted that the Portuguese Code of Criminal Procedure allowed domestic proceedings to be reopened where the Court had found a violation of the applicant's rights and fundamental freedoms. The Grand Chamber considered that the Supreme Court's refusal to reopen the proceedings had not distorted or misrepresented that judgment and that the grounds on which it was based fell within the domestic authorities' margin of appreciation.

However, this does not have to happen with other decisions of national courts refusing to comply with international courts judgments. The phenomenon may turn out to be dangerous if it grows.[112] Even if the black scenario does not work, those who warn that the resistance of national courts can only take place in exceptional and justified cases are right.[113] But there is no guarantee that the national courts will want to hear these voices.

Admittedly, there is a growing support for conditional supremacy of domestic constitutional law over international law in the academia.[114] As early as at the end of 1990s some authors began to argue that international norms, which disregard fundamental rights and suffer from democratic deficiencies, should be unenforceable in the domestic legal order. They spoke even of a 'constitutional right to resistance' and found that right necessary for the States to be able to accept the supremacy and direct applicability of international law.[115] They suggested that contemporary relationship between international law and domestic law should not be conceived as a hierarchal one, but rather as a 'communicative' relationship.[116] These views highlighted the complexity of the current relations between international law and

[112] E.g. recent cases of challenging CJEU or ECtHR rulings by the Constitutional Courts may be worrying. See the Federal Constitutional Court judgment of 5 May 2020—2 BvR 859/15 (Germany 2020) and the Constitutional Court decisions of 20 April 2020 (U 2/20) (Poland 2020) and of 21 April 2020 (Kpt 1/20) (Poland 2020)—the last one clearly finding the CJEU judgment contrary to the Polish Constitution and ultra vires. As the ECtHR is concerned, the Italian Constitutional Court held on 26 March 2015 that only 'settled case law' of the ECtHR is binding upon Italian ordinary courts (Judgment No 49/2015 (Italy 2015)). The Russian Constitutional Court openly refused to obey the ECtHR's rulings. See the Constitutional Court judgment of 14 July 2015 No 21–П/2015 (Russian Federation 2015) in which to back up its position the Court referred i.a. to Judgment 238/14), and the judgment of 19 April 2016 No 12– П /2016 (Russian Federation 2016) in which the Court ruled that enforcement of the ECtHR decision in Anchugov and Gladkov v Russia is impossible because it is contrary to the Russian Constitution. In 2017 the Russian Constitutional Court declared non-executable the ECtHR decision in OAO Neftyanaya Kompaniya Yukos v Russia (Judgment of 19 January 2017, No 1– П /2017). For further examples see Martinico (2016), pp. 177–198. Cf. Kosar and Petrov (2019), pp. 270–271.

[113] See e.g. Kunz (2018), p. 15, who argues that Judgment 238/14 cannot be considered as an example of legitimate opposition to the ICJ decision.

[114] For example von Bogdandy (2008), p. 412, while referring to Kadi, notes that: 'There should always be the possibility, at least in liberal democracies, to limit, legally, the effect of a norm or an act under international law within the domestic legal order if it severely conflicts with constitutional principles. This corresponds to the state of development of international law and the sometimes debatable legitimacy of international legal acts—just recall the listing of suspected terrorists by the UN Security Council'.; see also Nollkaemper (2010), pp. 83–85; Peters (2009), p. 195, ft. 134; Palombino (2015), p. 527; Lando (2015), pp. 1037–1041.

[115] Peters (2009), p. 194, noted that the reasonable resistance 'probably constitutes an 'emergency brake' and thereby one condition for the opening-up of States' constitutions towards the international sphere. On the long run, reasonable resistance by national actors might compel the international law-makers and appliers to engage in democratization and improve human rights protection against international actors themselves. It might thereby promote the progressive evolution of international law in the direction of a system more considerate of human rights and democracy'.

[116] Cottier and Woger (1999), pp. 241–281, 263–264. Cited after Peters (2009), p. 195.

national law, which cannot be defined by a simple dichotomy of dualism and monism. They indicated rather the plurality of legal orders, plurality of legal actors claiming ultimate authority and a plurality of rules of conflict. In this pluralistic world there is no formal hierarchy of norms and courts necessarily belong to one of the various orders, they speak from their own perspective and apply the rule of conflict belonging to the order in which they operate. Conflicts can therefore not be decided by legal argument, but must be solved politically.[117] Anne Peters, for example, laid emphasis on 'ordered pluralism'. The term illustrates the process, mutual adjustment, harmonization, cooperation, not hierarchical ordering. In this environment, national courts are one of the most important actors. On the other hand, as she explained, 'the international bodies should grant a margin of appreciation to national decision-makers with a strong democratic legitimation'.[118]

The vision of a world based on the 'communicative' relationship between international law and national law seems idealistic if one considers institutional bias of national courts, or their predisposition to serve national interests. Any opposition to the binding decision of international court threatens the authority of the court and the effectiveness of international law.[119] That is why those scholars who advocate for the 'judicial disobedience' or 'judicial non-compliance' make it dependent primarily on the 'serious' nature of the conflict. The conflict between the norms of international law and constitutional law has to concern the constitutional norm of a certain gravity (norm important in terms of 'substance' or the 'constitutional core value').[120]

The severity of the conflict can be seen differently by different courts. It may be argued that the condition is not satisfied in the conflict between the customary law on State immunity for acts *de jure imperii* and the constitutional principle of protection of human rights. Firstly, neither the right to compensation (property right) nor the right to access to court are absolute rights.[121] The ECtHR has consistently held that the right of access to a court is not absolute and may be subject to limitations. In the

---

[117]Peters (2009), p. 196.

[118]Peters (2009), p. 198.

[119]Cannizzaro (2015) emphasized that '(d)isrespect with a binding decision of the ICJ has the effect of disrupting the confidence in the principal judicial organ of the UN and, more in general, in the judicial settlement of disputes' (p. 131) and that it 'can seriously imperil the authority of international law' (p. 133).

[120]Peters (2009), pp. 197–198, observes: '(i)t must be acknowledged that national courts are under a bona fide obligation to take into account international law, must interpret domestic constitutional law as far as possible consistently with international prescriptions, and must give reasons for non-compliance. Moreover, any refusal to apply international law based on domestic constitutional arguments must be strictly limited to constitutional core values, and may be permissible only 'as long as' the constitutional desiderata have not been even in a rudimentary fashion incorporated into international law itself'. Cf. von Bogdandy (2008), pp. 412–413; Palombino (2015), pp. 527–529; Lando (2015), pp. 1037–1041.

[121]E.g. De Sena (2014), pp. 29–31, denies that international law have developed to such a point where the State could invoke its constitutional principles regarding the right to a court to justify non-compliance with international obligations.

Jones and others v United Kingdom case[122] the ECtHR decided that the grant of immunity to foreign State officials in cases concerning civil claims for torture did not amount to a violation of Art. 6 of the ECHR.[123] Secondly, also the right to compensation is not absolute. Moreover, in international law it is left to the interested States (the State which has committed the breach and the State acting in diplomatic protection) to agree on the form and scope of the satisfaction. They can agree to compensate individuals partially, or even transfer one another the duty to compensate.[124] Thirdly, it may also be said that the argument on the absence of any alternative means of redress is not convincing. Enzo Cannizzaro rightly noted that every State has a duty to act for the benefit of its citizens at international level, and proposed as it seems, a remedy of last instance, the possibility to have the individuals injured compensated by the forum State, 'in order to safeguard its space for manœuvring at the diplomatic level'.[125] In the case of State immunity, it is particularly fair.

There are also some other conditions that should be put together. National courts which would like to oppose international law or which aspire to take part in the development of customary law must act in good faith (not burdened with specific national interests, or worse, the interests of the governing party)[126] and in a spirit of international cooperation.[127] They have to be able to reliably assess legal arguments at stake, the seriousness of the conflict of norms, and convincingly motivate their decision. Certainly, in a long run, as it is put by Stefano Dominelli, they 'should not be blind to the issue of sovereignty and to what the international community will look like if States will no longer be sovereigns, especially if the de-construction of the Westphalian model follows a case by case approach adopted by domestic courts under the focal lenses of domestic constitutional provisions'.[128]

[122] Applications nos 34356/06 and 40528/06.

[123] Cannizzaro (2015), p. 130, noted that '(t)he right to compensation does not necessarily have the same normative value as the fundamental right which it is designed to replace'.

[124] Cannizzaro (2015), p. 130.

[125] Cannizzaro (2015), p. 131.

[126] Like in the case of the Polish Constitutional Court decisions of April 2020 (U 2/20 and Kpt 1/20), see above fn 112.

[127] See in this regard Peters (2014). 'In the long run, reasonable resistance by national actors – if it is exercised under respect of the principles for ordering pluralism, notably in good faith and with due regard for the overarching ideal of international cooperation – might build up the political pressure needed for promoting the progressive evolution of international law in the direction of a system more considerate of human rights'.

[128] Dominelli (2016), p. 31.

7.4 Infringement of International Customary Law

It is true that the decision the Constitutional Court (likewise the *Judgment 238/2014*) adopted under the abstract control procedure, in which the court does not resolve the dispute against a foreign State but merely answers the questions on law, cannot in itself infringe international law. But one may expect the decisions of common courts following the Constitutional Court judgment. There are already the Italian examples.[129] In 2016, the Italian Court of Cassation did not recognize Germany's immunity in case for compensation for deportation and forced labour that took place during World War II.[130] Moreover, the *Judgment 238/2014* encouraged further exceptions to immunity. In 2015, an Italian court ruled that it was competent in a case against Serbia, rejecting its immunity for *acta jure imperii*.[131] The case concerned joined actions, criminal and civil proceedings, concerning the death of several members of the European monitoring mission as a result of the downing of a helicopter by the Yugoslav Army in Podrute in 1991. The court allowed an action of the relatives of victims for damages against the successor State of Yugoslavia. The court interpreted the *Judgment 238/2014* as authorizing the denial of State immunity also in a situation where there is an alternative means of redress (i.e. in a situation in

[129] See also the cases cited by Oellers-Frahm (2016), pp. 197–201 and Boggero (2016), pp. 216–221. These authors noted that the Italian courts tried to reconcile the ICJ judgment with the Italian law and the Judgment 238/2014 in various ways, also by referring to EU law, including the Charter of Fundamental Rights (as a newborn European constitutional framework, neonato quadro constitutzionale europeo) to argue that in relations between EU member States, a State is not liable internationally if it gives priority to human rights over State immunity (see judgment No 2468 of 6 May 2015 of the Florence Court). As a result the judgments of these courts are not fully compatible with either the judgment of the ICJ, the Judgment of 238/2014 or EU law, especially with the ruling of the CJEU in the judgment of 15 February 2007 in C-292/05 Lechouritou et al v Federal Republic of Germany (ECLI:EU:C:2007:102, see paras 27–46) or the order of 12 July 2012 in C-466/11 Gennaro Currà et al v Federal Republic of Germany (ECLI:EU:C:2012:465, see paras 12–27). The last case is the aftermath of Ferrini. Following that judgment, the applicants in the main proceedings before the Italian court sought from Germany fair compensation for the forced labour and deportation during the World War II. The referring court asked the CJEU i.a. whether the objection of State immunity deriving from international law which Germany invoked before the court is contrary to EU Treaties and Arts. 17, 42 and 52 of the Charter. The CJEU found that this situation does not come within the scope of EU law (para. 19) and recalled in para. 20 that 'as regards the interpretation and application of the principle of State immunity in an application for compensation brought by citizens of one State against another State in respect of events which took place during the Second World War, the two Member States at issue brought proceedings before the International Court of Justice without challenging the jurisdiction of that latter court. That court declared that it had jurisdiction and delivered a judgment on the merits of the case on 3 February 2012'. Cf. Boggero (2016), pp. 222–224.

[130] Della Fina (2016), pp. 24–25.

[131] Judgment of 14 September 2015, No. 43696, Cassazione, Prima sezione penale (Italy 2015). In: Rivista di diritto internazionale 2016, p. 629 et seq. See Dominelli (2016), p. 21, ft. 76.

which the waiver is not necessary).[132] The Italian exception has therefore been extended.

Another breakthrough may concern the immunity from enforcement. To date, however, it seems that there are no Italian judgments repealing enforcement immunity. Moreover, Italian courts tried to reconcile the ICJ decision with the *Judgment 238/2014*. They followed the Constitutional Court in regard to jurisdictional immunity of a foreign State, but at the same time they noted that their ruling was only declaratory, since it cannot be enforced.[133]

The decisions of other domestic courts consistent with the Constitutional Court judgment, as e.g. cited above the Italian Court of Cassation decision of 2016 violate international law. They give rise to international responsibility of the State. In the event of further violations of Germany's immunity by Italy, Germany could once again lodge a complaint with the ICJ. However, this does not solve the problem. The parties should rather seek a satisfactory solution through negotiation as proposed by the ICJ. The Court noted that it 'is not unaware that the immunity from jurisdiction of Germany in accordance with international law may preclude judicial redress for the Italian nationals concerned'.[134] For this reason, the claims, which have not been settled, could be the subject of further negotiation between the two States concerned. To date, however, the negotiations have not been undertaken, but the Italian courts decisions rendered after 2012 did not force them either.

7.5 *Enforcement Immunity Endangered?*

The pursuit of claims against a foreign State brings finally the question what is a merit undertaking the effort of long and costly domestic court proceedings, if it turns out that the judgment awarding damages cannot be enforced due to the immunity from execution of the foreign State. The enforcement immunity still has a wide scope in international law. The customary law that was enshrined in the 2004 UN Convention, protects State property which is in use or intended for use by the State for governmental purposes.[135] Enforcement is permissible only on State assets in use or intended for use for State commercial purposes, i.e. *de jure gestionis*, or if the State expressly consents to it or specifically allocated the assets to satisfy the claim. This scope of enforcement immunity was confirmed by the ICJ in the *Jurisdictional*

[132] Judgment of 14 September 2015, No. 43696 (Italy 2015), In: Rivista di diritto internazionale 2016, p. 651ff.

[133] See judgment of the Florence Court of 6 May 2015, No. 2468 (Italy 2015), cited by Boggero (2016), p. 220.

[134] Judgment of the Florence Court of 6 May 2015, No. 2468 (Italy 2015), para. 104.

[135] See part IV of the Convention.

Immunities of the State case.[136] The Court noted that Villa Vigoni, German property seized by Italy as compensation, was used as cultural centre that is for governmental purposes that were entirely non-commercial and that Germany had in no way consented to the registration of the legal charge in question, nor had allocated that property for the satisfaction of the claims which were the object of the proceedings before Italian courts. Accordingly, the ICJ found that Italy had violated the obligation to respect Germany's immunity from enforcement.[137] As the result, the legal charge on Villa Vigoni was removed.[138]

This leads to the conclusion that even if the compensation was awarded by the court decision, it may not be enforceable because there are no assets or not enough property of a foreign State in use or intended for use for governmental commercial purposes located on the territory of a forum State and the search for property in other States may appear not successful either. Besides it is time consuming and costly, especially if the applicant is a natural person and not a reach company.

It does not seem that States would easily give up immunity from enforcement, what is not only demonstrated by Germany's complaint to the ICJ after the seizure of Villa Vigoni but also e.g. by the Russian Federation strong action taken with connection to the launch of attachment and enforcement proceedings in Belgium and France following the Permanent Court of Arbitration awards in three Energy Charter Treaty arbitrations under which Russia was required to pay high compensation to former stockholders of the Yukos oil company. The Belgian and French courts decisions offering less protection to property of foreign States risked Belgium and France incurring international responsibility and facing significant diplomatic consequences. The result was that a few months after the freezing of Russia's assets in Belgium, the Parliament decided to reinforce law on State immunity from execution by inserting in the Belgian Code of Civil Procedure a new 'Article 1412*quinquies*'.[139] A similar provision was adopted by the French Parliament in

---

[136] Jurisdictional Immunities of the State (Germany v. Italy: Greece Intervening), 2 February 2012, [2012] ICJ Rep., para. 118.

[137] Ibid., paras 119–120.

[138] In the judgment of 27 January 2015, No. 1278 the Appellate Court in Milan (Italy 2015) refused to apply an enforcement measure against Villa Vigoni noting that Judgment 238/2014 of the Constitutional Court concerned only immunity from jurisdiction and that jurisdictional immunity and enforcement immunity were two distinct institutions. See Boggero (2016), p. 220, ft. 40.

[139] Loi insérant dans le Code judiciaire un article 1412quinquies régissant la saisie de biens appartenant à une puissance étrangère ou à une organisation supranationale ou internationale de droit public, 23 août 2015 (the so-called 'Yukos Act'). Yukos together with an American hedge fund holding debt securities against Argentina (*NML Capital Limited*) brought a complaint against the Act before the Belgian Constitutional Court. They claimed that the law breached the principle of equality and non-discrimination (Arts. 10 and 11 of the Constitution) by imposing disproportionate burdens on creditors of foreign States as compared to other types of creditors. The case was dismissed (Decision No. 48/2017 of 27 April 2017, Moniteur 12/06/2017 (Belgium 2017)). The Court considered that the difference in treatment relied on an objective criterion (i.e. the nature of the debtor), was legitimated by the Act's aim of fostering international comity and was proportionate since it reflects customary international law. The Court did, however, found unconstitutional the

December 2016.[140] Both provisions draw from the 2004 UN Convention. Moreover, they provide for a new safeguard mechanism requiring judicial prior authorisation for interim and post-judgment measures of constraint, under which creditor can no longer go directly to the bailiff to perform a seizure. The Russian Federation has also decided to regulate State immunity introducing the Law on Jurisdictional Immunity of a Foreign State and a Foreign State's Property in the Russian Federation generally based on the 2004 UN Convention but additionally providing for reciprocity.[141]

The problem is also noticed by the Italian legislator who decided to reinforce the immunity from enforcement. The Italian Parliament adopted a provision protecting foreign States against execution from bank or postal accounts of embassies and consulates. The Italian law provides that enforcement from a bank or postal account of a foreign State is not possible if the foreign State had expressly indicated that the money accumulated on these accounts is intended for diplomatic or consular use.[142]

It is not easy to find not only the property suitable for seizure elsewhere but also a foreign court that would enforce a judgment granting damages. The ICJ found that the decisions of the Italian courts declaring enforceable in Italy the civil judgments rendered against Germany by Greek courts in proceedings arising out of the Distomo massacre constituted a violation by Italy of its obligation to respect the jurisdictional immunity of Germany.[143]

---

requirement that the waiver of immunity must be not only express but also 'specific', finding that this went too far as compared to customary international law.

[140] Loi n° 2016–1691 relative à la transparence, à la lutte contre la corruption et à la modernisation de la vie économique, 9 Décembre 2016. French law was the answer also to NML Capital Ltd litigations against Argentina. The Law amended the French Code of Civil Enforcement Procedures. Article L. 111–1–3 of the Code reinforces the immunity of diplomatic property by requiring a special and express waiver to implement an enforcement measure. The provision contradicts the decision of the Court of Cassation that did away with the requirement of a 'special waiver' in favour of an 'express waiver' (1st Civil chamber, Decision No 13–17.751, 13 May 2015 (France 2015)). The law was approved by the decision of the Constitutional Council (Decision No 2016–741 DC of 8 December 2016 (France 2016)).

[141] Federal Law No. 297–FZ (3 November 2015). The Law declares reciprocity to be the main principle under which Russian courts will consider the scope of jurisdictional immunity of a foreign State. Reciprocity will be determined on the bases of the opinion of the Russian Ministry of Foreign Affairs (Art. 5). If Russian property has limited or no immunity in a particular country, Russia shall be empowered to establish similar restrictions on that country's property located in the Russian Federation. Immunity does not apply to measures taken to secure a claim or to execute a court ruling (arts. 15 and 16). Any property of a foreign State located in Russia can be used to secure the execution of a court ruling if this property is not used and/or supposed to be used for the purpose of performing sovereign functions (Art. 17(3)).

[142] Art. 19–bis, l. 10 novembre 2014 no 132 decreto–legge 12 settembre 2014, n. 132 (in Gazzetta Ufficiale – serie generale – n. 212 del 12 settembre 2014), coordinato con la legge di conversione 10 novembre 2014, n. 162 (in questo stesso supplemento ordinario alla pag. 1), recante: 'Misure urgenti di degiurisdizionalizzazione ed altri interventi per la definizione dell'arretrato in materia di processo civile'. (14A08730). See Dominelli (2016), p. 22.

[143] Jurisdictional Immunities of the State (Germany v. Italy: Greece Intervening), 2 February 2012, [2012] ICJ Rep, para. 131. The ICJ observed that a court seised of an application for exequatur of a foreign judgment rendered against a third State had to ask itself whether, in the event that it had

However, it must be emphasized that the ICJ decision did not prevent the enforcement of the Distomo judgment in Italy. In 2019 in *Deutsche Bahn Ag v Regione Stereá Ellada* case, the Court of Cassation relied strongly on the Constitutional Court *Judgment 238/2014,* that the ICJ ruling is not directly binding on Italian courts and that there is jurisdiction, in Italy, over acts of a foreign State consisting of war crimes and crimes against humanity affecting fundamental rights of the person.[144] The Court of Cassation read the judgment of the Constitutional Court as referring both to the proceedings on the merits and the enforcement process and granted the request to seize German assets located in Italy, in particular, the sums owed to Deutsche Bahn by the Italian railway and train companies. Unlike the Villa Vigoni, the assets were not allocated for the performance of public functions.[145]

Obstacles may also be of a different nature. The example is the long struggle of Flatow to enforce the US court judgment of 1998[146] against the Iranian government and several of its entities under the State-sponsored terrorism exception to the FSIA he had won earlier.[147] Flatow tried to enforce the judgment i.a. in Italy. In the decision of 2015 the Court of Cassation, however, affirmed that jurisdictional immunity of the State does not apply to violations of *jus cogens* norms, in this case terrorist attack, i.e. crime committed in violation of inalienable human rights,[148]

---

itself been seized of the merits of a dispute identical to that which was the subject of the foreign judgment, it would have been obliged under international law to accord immunity to the respondent State. See para. 128.

[144] The judgment of the Italian Court of Cassation of 3 September 2019, Deutsche Bahn Ag v Regione Stereá Ellada, No. 21995 (Italy 2019), part of Distomo saga. The German railway company Deutsche Bahn, a private joint–stock company whose single shareholder is the Federal Republic of Germany, lodged an appeal asking the Court of Cassation to set aside a judgment of the Rome Tribunal (enforcing the Greek judgment). See case note of Mariottini (2020), pp. 486–493.

[145] Mariottini (2020), p. 492 gives another example: in 2017 the Italian court of first instance assigned the municipality of Roccaraso and the successors of victims the compensation for the massacre of 128 residents by the German armed forces in Pietransicri (Comune di Roccaraso and Others v. Germany and Ministry of Foreign Affairs of Italy, Judgment No. 20 (Sulmona Tribunal , 2 November 2017) (Italy 2017). In November 2019, the applicants obtained a judicial lien on some fields that are part of the park enclosure surrounding Villa Vigoni (which may not be allocated exclusively for public functions).

[146] Flatow v Islamic Republic of Iran, 999 F Supp 1 (USA 1998).

[147] See footnotes 33, 44.

[148] The Court noted that 'the principle of jurisdictional immunity is not applicable to the defendant State where compensation for damage has been requested and granted following a terrorist incident that can be counted among the international crimes committed in violation of the inviolable human rights. The immunity of the foreign State, in fact, is not a right, but a prerogative that cannot be ensured in the face of delicta imperii, of crimes, that is, committed in violation of international norms of ius cogens, as such damaging universal values that transcend the interests of individual State communities. And from the US ruling subject to the proceeding deliberation it follows that the terrorist attack that cost Alisa Michelle Flatow's life can be traced back to the crimes against humanity, as it was a criminal act perpetrated in the context of a systematic and conscious attack of the defenseless civilian population, inspired by reasons of racial, ethnic, political and religious hatred and seriously dangerous for international security and order'. Flatow v Islamic Republic of Iran, Cass. Civ. 20 October 2015, No 21964 (Italy 2015), para. 5.

but refused to enforce the judgment (i.a. because the unlawful conduct—the terrorist attack—and the harmful event—the death of Flatow's daughter—occurred entirely outside of the US). According to the Court, to be enforceable in Italian courts, a foreign judgment must have been based on criteria established by the Code of Civil Procedure for territorial jurisdiction while the US court judgment was based on the premises not recognized in Italian law.[149]

8 Final Conclusions

There is still little practice confirming an exception to immunity from jurisdiction of a foreign State regarding its acts *de jure imperii*. In the case of the US and Canada, it concerns only the terrorism exception established by the legislator, and not by the courts. At the moment only Italian courts formulate *jus cogens* exception but they derive it now from national law. The reaction of the States to attempts by their courts to relax immunity from enforcement was to strengthen it by the means of legislation. While there are strong moral grounds for the State's liability towards individuals for damages caused by *jus cogens* violations, the question arises whether redress before national court, which at some point comes to a halt, interfering with the State's immunity from enforcement, is an appropriate and effective tool. Apart from the hundreds or even thousands of lawsuits that may arise in connection with mass violations in the event of armed conflict, which show the impracticality of this method, the key question is to find a reasonable balance between the protection of State sovereignty and the condemnation of *jus cogens* violations.

Hugo Princz, when his case was dismissed by the US court by granting immunity to Germany, sought an alternate route to obtain compensation. He was suing the German companies for whom he was forced to work while he was a prisoner at Auschwitz. He also lost in these cases. His lawsuits, however, drew attention to a vital issue and contributed to the conclusion of the agreement between the United States and Germany, under which he and other American citizens in comparable situation were finally compensated. Moral, political and diplomatic pressure, of which the *Princz* cases[150] were one of the elements, led relevant German companies to establish special compensation fund and, moreover, to the decision of the German government to create the Foundation Remembrance, Responsibility and Future with the purpose of making financial compensation available 'to former forced laborers and to those affected by other injustices from the National Socialist period'.[151] The court litigation may help even if not successful. But this is not always the case. The

---

[149]Flatow v Islamic Republic of Iran, Cass. Civ. 20 October 2015, No 21964 (Italy 2015), paras 6.4–6.7.

[150]See e.g. Hayes (2015), p. 855.

[151]The Law on the Creation of a Foundation 'Remembrance, Responsibility and Future' of 2 August 2000 (Federal Law Gazette I 1263), Section 2(1).

'ball' in a game between State immunity and human rights, responsibility for *jus cogens* violations and justice, is rather with governments.[152] If they don't take up the challenge, the Italian saga may go on.[153]

References

Akehurst M (1975) Custom as a source of international law. BYIL 47(1):1–53

Akthar Z (2018) Acts of state, state immunity, and judicial review in the United States. Br J Am Leg Stud 7(1):205–234

Barcz J (2017) Odszkodowania wojenne od Niemiec dla Polski po upływie 70 lat od zakończenia II wojny światowej w świetle prawa międzynarodowego. Państwo i Prawo 11:18–32

Biehler G (2008) Procedures in international law. Springer

Blanke H-J, Falkenberg L (2013) Is there state immunity in cases of war crimes committed in the forum state: on the decision of the International Court of Justice (ICJ) of 3 February 2012 in jurisdictional immunities of the state (Germany v. Italy: Greece Intervening). German Law J 14 (9):1817–1850

Boggero G (2016) The legal implications of Sentenza Nr 238/2014 by Italy's Constitutional Court for Italian municipal judges: is overcoming the 'Triepelian approach' possible? ZaöRV 76:203–224

Bothe M (2015) Remedies of victims of war crimes and crimes against humanity: some critical remarks on the ICJ's judgment on the jurisdictional immunity of states. In: Peters A, Lagrange E, Oater S, Tomuschat C (eds) Immunities in the age of global constitutionalism. Brill, pp 99–115

Brownlie I (2008) Principles of public international law. OUP, Oxford

Cannizzaro E (2015) Jurisdictional immunities and judicial protection: the decision of the Italian Constitutional Court No. 238 of 2014. Rivista Di Dirito Internazionale 98(1):126–134

Caplan L (2003) State immunity, human rights, and Jus Cogens: a critique of the normative hierarchy theory. AJIL 97:741–781

Chechi A (2015) Introductory Note to Judgment No. 238/2014. ILM 54:471–473

Chukwuemeke Okeke E (2018) Jurisdictional immunities of states and international organizations. OUP, Oxford

Cottier T, Woger D (1999) Auswirkungen der Globalisierung auf das Verfassungsrecht: Eine Diskussionsgrundlage. In: Sitter-Liver B (ed) Herausgeforderte Verfassung: Die Schweiz im globalen Konzert. Universitatsverlag Freiburg

[152] See the opinion of Hofmann (2013). He advocates for changes in international humanitarian law to provide for an international law right to reparation for individual victims but emphasises 'that the recognition of such a right does not per se imply that victims might sue the responsible State in whatever forum they might wish to choose. There are still strongly convincing arguments, both of a legal and a political nature, to continue to apply the rules of State immunity as concerns acta iure imperii—also with regard to violations of ius cogens norms. (. . .) Therefore, such claims might—and should—only be made before the courts of the State responsible for the relevant violations of international humanitarian law, or competent international courts' (para. E (34)).

[153] In Jones and others v United Kingdom (Applications nos 34356/06 and 40528/06) the ECtHR decided on Saudi Arabia immunity against the allegations of torture but the Court also observed that 'in light of the developments currently under way in this area of public international law, this is a matter which needs to be kept under review'. para. 215.

De Santis di Nicola F (2016) Civil actions for damages caused by war crimes vs. state immunity from jurisdiction and the political act doctrine: ECtHR, ICJ and Italian courts. Int Comp Jurisprud 2:107–121

De Sena P (2014) The judgment of the Italian Constitutional Court on state immunity in cases of serious violations of human rights or humanitarian law: a tentative analysis under international law. Questions of International Law, Zoom out II, pp 17–31

De Sena P, De Vittor F (2005) State immunity and human rights: the Italian Supreme Court decision on the Ferrini case. EJIL 16(1):89–112

Della Fina V (2016) Correspondents' Reports, Judgment No 15812 of 3 May 2016 the Court of Cassation, Civil United Sections. Yearb Int Humanit Law 19:24–25

Dickinson A (2013) Germany v. Italy and the territorial exception. Walking the tightrope. J Int Crim Justice 11(1):147–166

Dominelli S (2016) Immunity from civil jurisdiction: where do we go from here? Assessing the relevance of recent opposing trends in the conceptualization of state immunity. ESIL Conf Pap Ser 8(2):1–32

Ekpo S (2017) Jurisdictional immunities of the state (Germany v. Italy): the debate over state immunity and Jus Cogens norms. Queen Mary Law J 8:151–164

Fontanelli F (2013) Case note: criminal proceedings against Albers. AJIL 107:632–638

Hayes P (ed) (2015) How was it possible? A Holocaust reader. University of Nebraska Press, Lincoln London

Hofmann R (2013) Compensation for personal damages suffered during World War II, Max Planck Encyclopedia of Public International Law

Holcombe K (2017) JASTA Straw Man? How the Justice Against Sponsors of Terrorism Act undermines our security and its stated purpose. Am Univ J Gend Soc Policy Law 25(3):359–390

Keitner Ch (2016) Authority and dialogue: state and official immunity in domestic and international courts, Draft of 8/2016. In: Giorgetti Ch, Verdiame G (eds) Concepts of international law in Europe and the United States. CUP (forthcoming), pp 1–23

Kolb R (2014) The relationship between the international and the municipal legal order: reflections on the decision no. 238/2014 of the Italian Constitutional Court, Questions of International Law, Zoom out II, pp 5–16

Kosar D, Petrov J (2019) The domestic judiciary in the architecture of the Strasbourg system of human rights. In: Ulrich G, Ziemele I (eds) How international law works in times of crisis. OUP, Oxford, pp 255–271

Kranz J (2015) L'affaire Allemagne contre Italie ou les dilemmes du droit et de la justice. In: Peters A, Lagrange E, Oeter S, Tomuschat C (eds) Immunities in the age of global constitutionalism. Brill, pp 116–127

Kunz R (2018) Teaching the world court makes a bad case, revisiting the relationship between domestic courts and the ICJ. MPIL Res Pap 12:1–17

Lando M (2015) Intimations of unconstitutionality: the supremacy of international law and Judgment 238/2014 of the Italian Constitutional Court. Mod Law Rev 78(6):1028–1041

Lauterpacht H (1929) Decisions of municipal courts as a source of international law. BYIL 10:65–95

Longobardo M (2015) The Italian Constitutional Court's ruling against state immunity when international crimes occur: thoughts on Decision No 238 of 2014. Melb J Int Law 16:1–15

Mariottini CM (2020) Case note: DEUTSCHE BAHN AG V. REGIONE STEREÁ ELLADA. Judgment No. 21995 (IT:CASS:2019:21995CIV). Corte di Cassazione (III Division), September 3, 2019. AJIL 114(3):486–493

Martinico G (2016) National courts and judicial disobedience to the ECtHR: a comparative overview. In: Arnardóttir OM, Buyse A (eds) Shifting centers of gravity in human rights protection. Routledge, pp 177–198

McGregor L (2013) State immunity and human rights, is the future after Germany v. Italy? J Int Crim Justice 11:125–145

McMenamin M (2013) State immunity before the International Court of Justice. Vic Univ Wellingt Law Rev 44:189–219

Mik C (2013) Jus Cogens in contemporary international law. Polish Yearb Int Law 33:27–93
Moremen PM (2006) National court decisions as state practice: a transnational judicial dialogue? N C J Int Law Commerc Regul 32:259–309
Nagan WP, Root JL (2013) The emerging restrictions on sovereign immunity: peremptory norms of international law, the U.N. Charter, and the application of modern communications theory. N C J Int Law Commerc Regul 38:375–471
Nollkaemper A (2010) Rethinking the supremacy of international law. ZaöRV 65(1):65–85
Nollkaemper A (2011) National courts and the international rule of law. OUP, Oxford
Oellers-Frahm K (2016) A never-ending story: the International Court of Justice – The Italian Constitutional Court – Italian Tribunals and the question of immunity. ZaöRV 76:193–202
Oppenheim L (1908) The science of international law: its task and method. AJIL 2(2):313–356
Orakhelashvili A (2012) Jurisdictional immunities of the state. AJIL 106:609–616
Palombino FM (2015) Compliance with international judgments: between supremacy of international law and national fundamental principles. ZaöRV 75:503–529
Peters A (2009) Supremacy lost: international law meets domestic constitutional law. Vienna Online J Int Const Law 3:170–198
Peters A (2014) Let not triepel triumph – how to make the best out of sentenza no. 238 of the Italian Constitutional Court for a global legal order, EJIL: Talk! (December 22)
Peters A (2016) New German Constitutional Court decision on "Treaty Override": Triepelianism continued, EJIL: Talk! (February 29)
Potesta M (2010) State immunity and Jus Cogens violations: the Alien Tort Statute against the backdrop of the latest developments in the law of nations. Berkeley J Int Law 28(2):571–586
Sadurski W (2018) How democracy dies (in Poland): a case study of anti-constitutional populist backsliding. Sydney Law School Res Pap 1:1–72
Sadurski W (2019) Poland's constitutional breakdown. OUP, Oxford
Saputo NM (2012) The Ferrini Doctrine: abrogating state immunity from civil suits for Jus Cogens violations. Univ Miami Natl Secur Armed Conflict Law Rev 2:4–36
Souresh A (2017) Jurisdictional immunities of the state: why the ICJ got it wrong. Eur J Leg Stud 9 (2):15–35
Talmon S (2012) Jus Cogens after Germany v. Italy: substantive and procedural rules distinguished. Bonn Res Pap Public Int Law 4:1–30
Tomuschat C (2011) The international law of state immunity and its development by national institutions. Vanderbilt J Transnatl Law 44:1105–1140
van Alebeek R (2012) Jurisdictional immunities of the state (Germany v Italy): on right outcomes and wrong terms. GYIL 55:281–317
von Bogdandy A (2008) Pluralism, direct effect and the ultimate say. On the relationship between international and domestic constitutional law. Int J Const Law 6(3&4):397–413
Wojcikiewicz Almeida P (2018) L'affaire des immunités juridictionnelles de l'Etat (Allemagne c. Italie): la Cour Internationale de Justice à contre-sens de l'évolution du droit international. Anuario Colombiano de Derecho 11:21–70
Wyrzykowski M (2019) Experiencing the unimaginable: the collapse of the rule of law in Poland. Hague J Rule Law 11:417–422

Anna Wyrozumska is a Professor of public international law and European Union law at the Faculty of Law and Administration of the University of Lodz, Poland—head of the Department of European Constitutional Law. Her research interests include the law of treaties, state immunity, application of international law and EU law in domestic law.

Shrinking of Jurisdictional Immunities and Victims' Rights: From Separation to Synergy

Elisa Ruozzi

Abstract One of the major challenges faced by the effective realization of international human rights is State immunity, whose recognition is capable of undermining, in particular, the right to access to justice, from both a procedural and a substantial point of view. The aim of the chapter is to explore the extent to which the rise and development of victims' rights can contribute to a progressive shrinking of State immunities, especially in the light of the consolidation of the right to individual compensation. This latter will be taken into account, looking in particular at 'burden sharing' mechanisms conveying the idea that serious human rights violations may entail the subsidiary liability of the whole international community. If this is true, resort to immunity by responsible States might become harder, given that the viability of judicial action works as an essential prerequisite of any contribution by innocent States to the reparation of human rights breaches.

1 Introduction

Though clashing with the customary rule establishing States' sovereign immunities, the conflict between the latter and the objective to guarantee access to justice and respect of victims' rights is nowadays increasingly acknowledged. As effectively stated by the UN Committee against Torture: '[G]ranting immunity, in violation of international law, to any State or its agents or to non-State actors for torture or ill-treatment, is in direct conflict with the obligation of providing redress to victims. When impunity is allowed by law or exists *de facto*, it bars victims from seeking full redress as it allows the violators to go unpunished and denies victims full assurance of their rights'.[1]

[1] Committee against Torture, General Comment no 3 (2012), para. 42.

E. Ruozzi (✉)
University of Turin, Turin, Italy
e-mail: elisa.ruozzi@unito.it

R. Bismuth et al. (eds.), *Sovereign Immunity Under Pressure*,
https://doi.org/10.1007/978-3-030-87706-4_10

The rule establishing the jurisdictional immunity of States is, as is known, one of the most ancient customary norms, whose origin can be traced back to as early as the fourteenth century, in close connection with the notion of State sovereignty.[2] While, on one side, immunity from jurisdiction guarantees States' independence, on the other side, it can entail a compression of individual rights, stemming from the impossibility of subjecting a State's conduct to adjudication. Aside from the traditional limitation stemming from the distinction between *acta jure imperii* and *acta jure gestionis*, doctrine and jurisprudence are increasingly faced with the challenges jurisdictional immunities pose to the protection of individual rights, including the right to redress and, more precisely, to compensation. Notwithstanding some uncertainties, the existence—or, at least, the progressive consolidation—of such rights is, nowadays, generally accepted by the majority of doctrine, raising doubts about the compatibility between the right of victims of human rights abuses to receive compensation for the harm suffered and the preservation of States' independence.

The most frequent approach adopted in this respect is based on the progressive emergence, in international law, of peremptory norms protecting the core values of the international community and prohibiting breaches of fundamental human rights. Those breaches, mainly identified by means of international crimes, call for aggravated international responsibility, the consequences of which may include the shrinking of immunity and, possibly, the granting of compensation to victims. At the same time, the increased attention devoted to the notion of victim, calling for compliance with the right to redress, constitutes a further avenue to advocate a limitation of the rule on sovereign immunity.

Given this premise, the aim of this paper is to explore the relationship between the law of international responsibility and the protection of victims' rights having regard to a specific effect of the shrinking of State immunities, i.e. the granting of monetary compensation. More precisely, the analysis will focus on whether compensation can act as an effective driver for this shrinking, in light of a specific feature of reparation mechanisms, *i.e.* the participation of non-responsible entities in the compensation effort. After having outlined how the law of international responsibility and the victimological approach contribute to the consolidation of an individual right to compensation, attention will firstly be focused on the possibility of granting it, at least partially, through State funds on the basis of solidarity with the victim, thus sharing the burden between the perpetrator and an innocent entity. This analysis will then be elevated to a superior level by enquiring whether such sharing can occur with the State, which, pursuant to national or international legislation, is required to provide reparation, along with the rest of the international community. The existence of this possibility will be explored not only in the area of State responsibility and in the context of victims' rights, but also considering the practice of international and hybrid criminal tribunals, given their widespread use of external funding to finance

[2] Stoll (2011), para. 4. On the general features of State immunity see, among others: Chukwuemeke Okeke (2018), pp. 22ff; Fox and Webb (2013); Van Alebeek (2008), pp. 12ff; Yang (2012); Ronzitti (2008); Panebianco (1967).

reparations. In light of these elements, the paper will address the question as to whether a further, and perhaps more solid, foundation exists for holding States accountable for serious human rights breaches—thus waiving jurisdictional immunity—allowing, at the same time, for a subsidiary role to be played by other States. Such a foundation can be found in the notion of *erga omnes* obligations, whose breach may justify a collective reaction, the main purpose of which is not inspired by a retributive intention but, rather, by the need to guarantee that the situation of victims of human rights violations is not aggravated by the impossibility to obtain redress.

Before entering into the merits of the problem, and as a form of background to the entire analysis, some preliminary remarks on the existence of an individual right to compensation, seen as a form of 'substantial'[3] reparation, would be helpful. While the obligation for States to adopt interstate reparation measures following breaches of human rights obligations is nowadays generally accepted and forms part of a customary norm,[4] the same is not necessarily true for the individual right to receive compensation. Even though most authors tend to support the progressive creation of a customary norm[5] in this regard, it is still underlined that an individual right to reparation can be hindered by institutional, procedural or economic factors,[6] with few examples of such an individual right being established on a treaty basis.[7] In this evolving landscape, the statement, in the *Code on Crimes against Humanity*,

[3] Authoritative doctrine distinguishes between substantial reparation (in the form of restitution, compensation and satisfaction, as set out by Art. 34 of the ILC Draft Articles on Responsibility of States for Internationally Wrongful Acts) and procedural reparation, consisting of the obligation, for States, to provide individuals with effective internal remedies. See Committee against Torture, General Comment no. 3, para. 5. The Draft Articles were adopted by the International Law Commission in 2001.

[4] Francioni (2007), pp. 10ff.

[5] In favour of a 'slow' development of an individual right to reparation, see, among others: Pisillo-Mazzeschi (2003), p. 347. More optimistic views are expressed by Evans (2012), p. 39; Cançado Trindade (2011), pp. 197ff., 209; Francioni (2007), pp. 33ff. An opposite opinion is expressed by Tomuschat, who emphasises the difficulty generally encountered by individuals in enjoying rights stemming from customary norms, often due to jurisdictional obstacles (Tomuschat 1999, pp. 14ff.). In a sense favourable to an individual right to compensation, see also the Report of the International Commission of Inquiry on Darfur to the United Nations Secretary-General Pursuant to Security Council Resolution 1564 of 18 September 2004, paras. 593ff. The same paragraph recalls that the international obligation to pay compensation was first laid down in Article 3 of the 1907 Hague Convention on Land Warfare and restated in each of the 1949 Geneva Conventions (footnote no. 213). It is not within the scope of this paper to discuss compensation issues in the context of armed conflict. On this theme see, from the many, Ronzitti (2007), pp. 95ff.

[6] Pisillo-Mazzeschi (1999), p. 165; Shelton (2015), pp. 96ff.

[7] Examples of a direct obligation for States to provide reparations to 'the injured party' are found in the European Convention on Human Rights (Rome, 4 November 1950; entry into force 3 September 1953; Art. 41), in the American Convention on Human Rights (San José, 22 November 1969; entry into force 18 July 1978; Art. 63 para. 1) and in the Protocol to the African Charter on Human and Peoples' Rights on the Establishment of an African Court on Human and Peoples' Rights (Maputo, 10 June 1998; entry into force 25 January 2004; Art. 27 para. 1). On the issue of reparation measures prescribed by international tribunals and organs, see Bartolini (2009).

recently drafted by the International Law Commission,[8] of the obligation for States to ensure that victims obtain reparation, including compensation, can only reinforce the idea of the progressive consolidation of a customary norm in this regard.

2 State Immunity and Responsibility for Breach of Fundamental Human Rights

Before analysing the relationship between the shrinking of jurisdictional immunities and the protection of human rights, it is worth recalling, albeit briefly, the main developments underpinning the theme of State immunity and, in particular, the transition from the absolute doctrine to the restricted doctrine of immunity. The immunity of States from other States' jurisdiction stems from the principle of sovereign equality and independence of States: the State of the forum is obliged to set and to accept limitations to the exercise of its sovereign functions in order to respect other States' competences.[9] Since ancient times, jurisdictional immunity consisted of a set of procedural privileges that States mutually grant to each other in order to avoid any interference with sovereign functions.

Since the beginning of the last century, the subject matter—currently codified by the United Nations Convention on Jurisdictional Immunities of States and Their Property[10]—has undergone dramatic changes: the growing intervention of the State in economic and commercial activities prompted jurisprudence to affirm the idea that jurisdictional immunity shall be granted only with respect to acts performed by States in the exercise of their sovereign activities and, therefore, to those acts performed *jure gestionis*. Conversely, activities carried out by States acting as private entities—*jure imperii*—will not benefit from the exemption from jurisdiction, as the essential prerequisite of such an exemption, i.e. the exercise of sovereign functions, is absent.

[8] Draft Articles on Prevention and Punishment of Crimes Against Humanity; the Code was adopted by the International Law Commission in 2019.

[9] As explicitly stated by Art. 6 of the United Nations Convention on Jurisdictional Immunities of States and Their Property (New York, 2 December 2004), 'A State shall give effect to State immunity [. . .] by refraining from exercising jurisdiction in a proceeding before its courts against another State and to that end shall ensure that its courts determine on their own initiative that the immunity of that other State [. . .] is respected'. The Convention was adopted by the General Assembly Resolution 59/38 of 16 December 2004 and is not yet in force.

[10] A previous attempt to codify the law of State immunity was made by the Council of Europe, through the adoption of the European Convention on State Immunity (Basel, 16 May 1972, entry into force 11 June 1976). The Convention has only been ratified by three States.

The UN Convention is based upon the presumption of State immunity,[11] which can be renounced by the State by way of express consent[12] or, implicitly, by its participation in a proceeding.[13] Beyond circumstances where immunity is set aside by its *titulaire*, there are cases where the impossibility to invoke immunity stems from the nature of the activity performed, presumed not to constitute an expression of a State's public functions. These cases, listed by the Convention under Part III, entitled 'Proceedings in which State immunity cannot be invoked', lie at the heart of the effort to codify emerging norms of international law in this field.[14] These include the so-called 'tort exception', enshrined in Article 12 of the Convention: as clarified by the Commentary, the rationale of the 'tort exception' is to provide the possibility of obtaining justice for individuals who have suffered personal injury in situations where the applicable law would be the *lex loci commissii delicti* and the most convenient court is that of the State where the delict was committed.[15] According to the text of the Convention, the tort exception is therefore the main legal instrument for shrinking State immunity based on human rights considerations.

However, the growing recognition of the role and value of *jus cogens* norms prompted national courts and doctrine to take into consideration—and, in some cases, to advocate—a further avenue to protect individual rights from the negative effects of State immunity. When serious human rights breaches are committed, implying the violation of peremptory norms of international law, it is argued that invoking State immunity would contradict the very idea of *jus cogens*, as it would allow its violation by excluding any consequence for the responsible State.

As is well known, this position was strongly supported in the *Ferrini* case, concerning judicial proceedings initiated against Germany by some Italian citizens who were victims of forced labour during the Second World War. More specifically, limitations on State immunity were advocated on two different grounds: the

[11] United Nations Convention on Jurisdictional Immunities of States and Their Property, Art. 5: 'A State enjoys immunity, in respect of itself and its property, from the jurisdiction of the courts of another State subject to the provisions of the present Convention'.

[12] United Nations Convention on Jurisdictional Immunities of States and Their Property, Art. 7; the consent of the State can be expressed by international agreement, in a written contract, or by a declaration before the court or by a written communication in a specific proceeding (para. 1).

[13] United Nations Convention on Jurisdictional Immunities of States and Their Property, Art. 8 para. 1; however, consent will not be considered to have been given if the State takes part in the proceeding only to invoke immunity or to assert a right in property involved in the proceeding (Art. 8 para. 2). Nor can immunity be invoked in relation to counterclaims arising out of the same legal relationship which is the object of a proceeding instituted before the court of another State (Art. 9 para. 1). The same applies if the State merely intervenes to present a claim (Art. 9 para. 2).

[14] Part III includes commercial transactions (Art. 10), employment contracts (Art. 11), State rights or interests in ownership, possession and use of property (Art. 13), intellectual and industrial property (Art. 14), participation in companies or other collective bodies (Art. 15), the operation of ships for non-commercial purposes (Art. 16), disputes relating to a commercial arbitration agreement entered into by the State (Art. 17).

[15] Draft Articles on Jurisdictional Immunities of States and Their Property, with Commentaries, 1991, p. 44.

prevalence of *jus cogens* norms (notably the prohibition of slave labour) against general international law norms (State immunity)[16] and the impossibility for the domestic legal order to incorporate a customary norm granting immunity to a State responsible for this kind of breach.[17] As far as the first ground is concerned, the Court of Cassation, while not questioning the sovereign nature of the activities performed by Germany in the case in question,[18] raises the issue of whether sovereign immunity can be invoked in relation to international crimes, *i.e.* acts that, by virtue of an international customary norm, damage universal values which transcend the interests of individual national communities.[19] Also in light of the ILC Draft Articles on States Responsibility, Article 41 of which attaches 'particular consequences' to the breach of peremptory norms of international law,[20] the court notes that the granting of immunity would conflict with the need for a 'qualitatively different reaction' to the breach of these norms.[21] Allowing a State to escape from a foreign State jurisdiction would, according to the Italian judge, hinder the protection of values that are fundamental for the whole international community[22] and what is ultimately framed as a conflict of norms can only be solved by granting primacy to the peremptory norm at issue—the norm prohibiting anybody being subjected to forced labour—with regard to the customary norm on State immunity.[23]

Such line of reasoning was not accepted by the International Court of Justice in the dispute between Italy and Germany, the latter acting as complainant due to the denial of jurisdictional immunity by the former. According to the ICJ, neither the hierarchy between sources of international law nor the protection of constitutional values can justify a waiver of the norm prescribing immunity, the latter being of procedural nature and 'confined to determining whether or not the courts of one State may exercise jurisdiction in respect of another State'.[24] Norms on immunity, the Court claimed, are not related to the lawfulness or unlawfulness of State conduct and, as a consequence, their application does not impinge upon the question of the breach of another norm, even when the latter is of peremptory nature.[25]

---

[16] Italian Supreme Court, 11 March 2004, no. 5044/04.

[17] Italian Constitutional Court, 22 October 2014, no. 238.

[18] Italian Supreme Court, 11 March 2004, no. 5044/04, p. 11.

[19] Italian Supreme Court, 11 March 2004, no. 5044/04, p. 12.

[20] According to Article 41 of the Draft, States shall cooperate to bring to an end violations of peremptory norms (para. 1), they shall not recognise as lawful a situation created by such a breach nor render aid or assistance in maintaining that situation (para. 2).

[21] Italian Constitutional Court, 22 October 2014, no. 238, p. 20.

[22] Ibid., p. 20.

[23] Ibid., p. 21.

[24] Jurisdictional Immunities of the State (Germany v. Italy), Judgment, ICJ Reports 2012, p. 99, para. 93.

[25] Jurisdictional Immunities of the State (Germany v. Italy), Judgment, ICJ Reports 2012, p. 99. Among the considerable number of works published on this issue, see: De Sena and De Vittor (2013), pp. 89ff; Gattini (2005), pp. 224ff; Boudreault (2012), pp. 1003ff; Francioni (2012),

Notwithstanding the court's position, the idea that serious crimes call for a waiver of State immunity is far from being set aside; such a perspective finds further impetus when considering the breach of human rights not from the perspective of the law of international responsibility but, rather, from the viewpoint of the victims.

3 State Immunity and Victims' Rights

The theme of victims' rights is inextricably linked to the issue of the international legal personality of the individual which, as it is known, has obtained growing consensus in doctrine[26] as well as in jurisprudence starting, in particular, from the second half of the last century.[27] Although it is not the purpose of this paper to explore this theme in detail, and despite the fact that doctrine remains divided on the individual having fully reached the status of subject of international law,[28] the role of the individual must be considered as one of the roots of the so-called 'victimological revolution'. As a paradigm shift focusing attention on the victim's 'need to repair',[29] such an approach offers a further avenue for immunity shrinking, especially in the case of gross violations.

In a nutshell, the victimological approach is premised on the victims' right to reparation and redress, including restitution, compensation, rehabilitation, satisfaction and guarantees of non-repetition.[30] At national level, such an approach has inspired, for example, national schemes for the compensation of victims of very diverse phenomena, ranging from organised crime to motor accidents.[31]

---

pp. 1125ff; Orakhelashvili (2012), pp. 609ff; Pisillo-Mazzeschi (2012), pp. 310ff; Salerno (2012), pp. 350ff; Frulli (2011), pp. 1129ff; Iovane (2004), pp. 165ff; Focarelli (2005), pp. 951ff.

[26] In this respect see for all Peters (2016), p. 551.

[27] The role of the individual has strongly emerged in the LaGrand case, where the ICJ stated that Art. 36, paragraph 1, of the Vienna Convention on consular relations 'creates individual rights' (LaGrand (Germany v. United States of America), Judgment, I.C.J. Reports 2001, p. 466, para. 77). The statement has been recalled by the Court in the Avena case (Avena and Other Mexican Nationals (Mexico v. United States of America), Judgment, I. C. J. Reports 2004, p. 12, para. 40).

[28] Nowadays, the majority of doctrine tends to recognise individual legal personality (Shaw 2017, pp. 204–205); however, Crawford defines the classification of the individual as a subject as 'unhelpful', given the lack of some capacity and notes that the norms of human rights law are not yet regarded as applying horizontally and international law provides no means for their enforcement (Brownlie 2012, p. 121).

[29] Van Boven (2012), p. 694.

[30] Committee against Torture, General Comment no. 3 (2012), para. 2. See also UN Basic Principles and Guidelines on the Right to a Remedy and Reparation for Victims of Gross Violations of International Human Rights Law and Serious Violations of International Humanitarian Law, General Assembly resolution 60/147, 16 December 2005, Chapter IX (Reparation for harm suffered).

[31] Examples of this kind of legislation are, with reference to the Italian legal system, the law establishing a national fund for victims of motor accidents, guaranteeing compensation to victims

At international level, the victims' perspective has found egregious expression, firstly, in the adoption of the UN Basic Principles and Guidelines on the Right to a Remedy and Reparation for Victims of Gross Violations of International Human Rights Law and Serious Violations of International Humanitarian Law in 2005 (henceforth UN Basic Principles).[32] The UN Basic Principles 'represent the first comprehensive codification of the rights of victims of international crimes to reparations, remedies, and access to systems of justice'.[33] Despite the lack of any reference to the theme, the right to access to justice[34] and the right to reparation,[35] including compensation,[36] for all victims of gross violations inevitably call into question the issue of immunity, given the fact that, from a victim's viewpoint, the main consequence of granting immunity is the denial of justice. The same is even truer when looking at compensation, considering that other forms of reparation (e.g. rehabilitation and satisfaction) are more easily granted in those cases where judicial action has not been taken. Finally, the granting of jurisdictional immunity would appear to be at least incoherent with a number of specific obligations imposed by the UN Basic Principles in relation to international crimes, including the duty to submit to prosecution the author of the crime and to punish him or her,[37] as well as the prohibition on applying statutes of limitations.[38]

On a parallel and related path, earlier that year the UN Commission on Human Rights has adopted the Updated Set of Principles for the Protection and Promotion of Human Rights through Action to Combat Impunity (henceforth Updated Principles).[39] Designed in a period when the international community witnessed a number of mass atrocities, often perpetrated by the State, the Principles to Combat Impunity can be considered as part of a 'global anti-impunity discourse' and a reflection of a

---

if the vehicle is not covered by insurance or the liable person has not been identified (Italian Law 24-12-1969 no. 990, Assicurazione obbligatoria della responsabilità civile derivante dalla circolazione dei veicoli a motore e dei natanti, Official Journal of 3 January 1970, no. 2). Victims of organised crime can apply for compensation based on different funds, one of which is specifically devoted to victims of the Mafia (Italian Law 22 December 1999, no. 512, Istituzione del Fondo di rotazione per la solidarietà alle vittime dei reati di tipo mafioso, Official Journal of 10 January 2000, no. 6). On the establishment of the Victims' Rights Movement and on the first examples of the related legislation, see Daigle (2013), pp. 7ff.

[32] Adopted and proclaimed by General Assembly resolution 60/147 of 16 December 2005.

[33] McCracken (2005), p. 77. The adoption of the Principles is the outcome of a long process that began with the transfer, in 1950, to the United Nations, of the functions of the International Penal and Penitentiary Commission ('IPPC'). The IPPC was an international body created to promote cooperation in the development of international crime policies (https://legal.un.org/avl/pdf/ha/dbpjvcap/dbpjvcap_ph_e.pdf. Accessed 15 April 2021).

[34] Basic Principles, no. 12-14.

[35] Basic Principles, no. 15-23.

[36] Basic Principles, no. 20.

[37] Basic Principles, no. 4.

[38] Basic Principles, no. 6, 7.

[39] Updated Set of Principles for the Protection and Promotion of Human Rights through Action to Combat Impunity, E/CN.4/2005/102/Add.1, 8 February 2005.

'trend towards accountability'.[40] The adoption of a victimological perspective clearly emerges when looking at the very structure of the document, where principles are organised under the right to know (Part II), the right to justice (Part III) and the right to reparation and to guarantees of non-recurrence (Part IV). At the same time, the close link between these principles and the legacy of transitional justice is expressed in the decision to insert, within Part II, a set of articles specifically devoted to the institution and functioning of inquiry commissions, as well as in the attention devoted to reparation programmes.[41] Compensation is, of course, included as one of the different available methods of reparation.[42] The contrast between the granting of immunity and the aspiration to restore victims' rights is quite explicit when considering that, according to the Updated Principles, impunity is defined as 'the impossibility, *de jure* or *de facto*, of bringing the perpetrators of violations to account [...] since they are not subject to any inquiry'[43] and that this conduct amounts to a 'failure to meet [States'] obligations', including that of ensuring that victims receive reparation for the harm suffered.[44] The need to fight against impunity and the potential clash with immunity further emerges from the invitation, addressed to States, to endow their courts with universal jurisdiction when dealing with international crimes,[45] as well as from the provisions allowing 'restrictive measures', i.e. 'safeguards against any abuse of rules',[46] including the prescription of prosecution or penalty. The latter is particularly targeted by Principle no. 23, barring it completely when international crimes are at stake and, in any case, allowing it only to the extent that effective remedy is not compromised.

Neither the UN Basic Principles nor the Updated Set of Principles contain any reference to the issue of immunity;[47] this shows how, notwithstanding the evident link that this latter displays with both international responsibility for serious violations of human rights and victims' rights, it has generally been considered in the context of the first one. On one side, such a lack of attention can be attributed to the rationale of these instruments, which are not aimed at 'entailing new international or domestic legal obligations but [at] identifying mechanisms, modalities, procedures and methods for the implementation of existing legal obligations under international human rights law and international humanitarian law'.[48] On the other side, and given

[40] Haldemann and Unger (2018), pp. 4–5.

[41] Updated Principles, no. 32; reparation programmes can be addressed to individuals and communities and they should be implemented with the participation of victims and civil society, attempting to ensure the contribution of women and minority groups.

[42] Updated Principles, no. 34.

[43] Updated Principles, Definitions, letter A.

[44] Updated Principles, no. 1.

[45] Updated Principles, no. 21.

[46] Updated Principles, no. 22.

[47] See, in particular, the 'Restrictions on rules of law justified by action to combat impunity', set out by the Updated set of principles, where State immunity is not listed (Part III, letter c).

[48] UN Basic Principles, Preamble.

that the original version of the UN Basic Principles of which the Updated Set of Principles are an evolution was drafted in the aftermath of mass atrocities committed by State authorities, such an explanation does not give account of the difficulties inherent in the reconciliation between right to redress and respect for sovereign immunity. As has been underlined,[49] the question of impunity appeared for the first time on the Agenda of the UN Sub-commission on Prevention of Discrimination and Protection of Minorities following a report on amnesties prepared by the Special Rapporteur Joinet. In analysing the purpose and scope of amnesty laws, the author raised the problem of international crimes as examples of situations where such laws should not apply, referring *inter alia* to mass atrocities occurred in some Latin American countries experiencing at those times the transition from tyrannical *régimes* to democracy.[50]

4 Compensation as a Form of Reparation vs. 'Welfare Measures'

In many instances where the issue of State immunity has been raised, compensation had already been granted to victims not as a form of reparation following judicial actions but, rather, through the allocation of funds on an individual or collective basis. This was the case, for example, for the so-called Holocaust litigation: as resulting from the *Germany v. Italy* case mentioned above, compensation for victims of the Holocaust was provided by Germany to the Remembrance, Responsibility and Future Foundation, established in 2000.[51] A similar approach was adopted by the Compensation Commission set up by the UN Security Council in the aftermath of the First Gulf War, aimed at compensating citizens who had suffered harm stemming from the illegal occupation of Kuwait by Iraq. The Commission allocated compensation directly provided by Iraq, based on the assessment of claims and not on a formal legal proceeding.[52] Any use of collective schemes is based on the assumption

[49] Haldemann and Unger (2018), p. 7.

[50] Study on Amnesty Laws and Their Role in the Safeguard and Promotion of Human Rights, E/CN.4/Sub.2/19, 21 June 1985, para. 51. In 1997, the same Author issued a Report, including the first version of the Updated Principles and introducing the same structure adopted by these latter (Question of the Impunity of Perpetrators of Human Rights Violations (Civil and Political), E/CN.4/Sub.2/1997/20, 26 June 1997).

[51] Jurisdictional Immunities of the State (Germany v. Italy), cit., para. 26. The Foundation did not provide compensation directly to individuals, but rather to 'partner organisations' such as the International Organisation for Migration. However, many Italian internees never had access to compensation, given their military status.

[52] The UN Compensation Commission was established by Security Council resolution 687/1991. The Commission was charged with the task of administering the Fund (para. 18). The processing of claims was concluded in 2005 and payments ceased in 2007. For reference, see: Mensah (2011); Gattini (2002), pp. 161ff; Frigessi di Rattalma and Treves (1999).

of their capacity to deal with a large number of claims more appropriately, which also explains their frequent use in the context of transitional justice.[53] Given the frequent obstacles encountered by individuals in submitting claims at international level, collective reparation schemes can offer undeniable advantages, consisting *inter alia* of non-discriminatory and equitable treatment of victims.[54]

The 'welfare' approach is not, however, a prerogative of mass claims: similar schemes also exist at domestic level, often as a result of the implementation of international human rights conventions. Under these instruments, monetary compensation must be granted by the (even innocent) State with the sole purpose of restoring damage suffered and as part of its duty of solidarity towards citizens.[55] Examples in this sense are the European Convention on the Compensation of Victims of Violent Crimes,[56] which Article 2 sets out States' obligation to contribute to compensating victims and their dependants, when compensation is not fully available from other sources. Similar provisions are enshrined in the Declaration of Basic Principles of Justice for Victims of Crime and Abuse of Power[57] and in the Draft UN Convention on Justice and Support for Victims of Crime and Abuse of Power.[58]

Taking into account instruments targeting specific categories of victims, it is worth mentioning the Convention on Preventing and Combating Violence against Women and Domestic Violence,[59] stating that 'Adequate State compensation shall be awarded to those who have sustained serious bodily injury or impairment of health, to the extent that damage is not covered by other sources such as the perpetrator, insurance or State-funded health and social provisions'.[60] Similarly,

[53] Institut de droit international, Universal Civil Jurisdiction with Regard to Reparation for International Crimes, 2015, para. 144. On the choice, by the responsible State, between administrative compensation and the tort approach, including the case where the former is not even available (so-called 'judicial closure'), see Malamud-Goti and Sebastián Grosman (2006), pp. 546–547.

[54] Institut de droit international, Universal Civil Jurisdiction with Regard to Reparation for International Crimes, 2015, para. 146.

[55] See, in this sense, Groenhuijsen (2014), pp. 37–38.

[56] European Convention on the Compensation of Victims of Violent Crimes, Strasbourg, 24 November 1983, entry into force 1 February 1988. The Convention has so far received only three ratifications.

[57] General Assembly resolution 40/34, 29 November 1985. According to point no. 12 'When compensation is not fully available from the offender or other sources, States should endeavour to provide financial compensation'. On the Principles, see, among others: Bassiouni (1987); Fattah (1992), pp. 401ff.

[58] Draft UN Convention on Justice and Support for Victims of Crime and Abuse of Power, 8 February 2010, Art. 11.1. See Groenhuijsen (2008), pp. 121ff.

[59] Council of Europe Convention on Preventing and Combating Violence against Women and Domestic Violence, Istanbul, 11 May 2011, entry into force 1 August 2014. The resolution encourages States to create national funds for compensation (point no. 13).

[60] Council of Europe Convention on Preventing and Combating Violence against Women and Domestic Violence, Istanbul, 11 May 2011, entry into force 1 August 2014, Art. 30, para. 2. See, also, the Nairobi Declaration on Women's and Girls' Right to a Remedy and Reparation (2007),

the Convention on Action against Trafficking in Human Beings[61] sets out States' obligation to adopt legislative or other measures to guarantee compensation for victims, for instance, through the establishment of a fund.[62] Though not mentioning the creation of national funds, the idea that compensation should be ensured by the State also emerges from the text of the Protocol against Trafficking in Persons supplementing the United Nations Convention against Transnational Organized Crime,[63] according to which the parties shall ensure that their domestic legal system contains measures that offer victims of trafficking the possibility of obtaining compensation for the damage suffered.[64]

In the same vein is the provision, contained in the EU Directive Relating to Compensation to Crime Victims,[65] establishing the responsibility of the State in which the crime was committed and the creation of national compensation schemes.[66] Notwithstanding the absence, in the Convention against Torture, of a similar provision, it is interesting to note the Statement, made by the Committee against Torture, according to which Article 14[67] of the Convention requires States to acknowledge the principle of 'subsidiary liability' and the request, by the same Committee, for reparation schemes to be set up at national level.[68] Though not binding, the 2007 Paris Principles on Children Associated with Armed Forces[69] note the need for adequate funding to support actions aimed at protecting and

stating 'That national governments bear primary responsibility to provide remedy and reparation' (point 6).

[61] Council of Europe Convention on Action against Trafficking in Human Beings, Warsaw, 16 May 2005, entry into force 1 February 2008. The Convention has thus far been ratified by ten States.

[62] Ibid., Art. 15 para. 4. According to the same provision, compensation 'could be funded' through sanctions against the offender.

[63] United Nations Convention against Transnational Organized Crime, New York, 15 November 2000, entry into force 29 September 2003.

[64] Protocol to Prevent, Suppress and Punish Trafficking in Persons, Especially Women and Children, supplementing the United Nations Convention against Transnational Organized Crime, New York, 15 November 2000, entry into force 25 December 2003, Art. 6 para. 6. See Van Dijk (2002), pp. 15ff.

[65] Council Directive 2004/80/EC of 29 April 2004 relating to compensation to crime victims, OJ L 261, 6 August 2004, pp. 15–18, Art. 2.

[66] Ibid., Art. 12 para. 2.

[67] The text of Art. 14 reads as follows: 'Each State Party shall ensure in its legal system that the victim of an act of torture obtains redress and has an enforceable right to fair and adequate compensation, including the means for as full rehabilitation as possible'.

[68] Committee against Torture, Decision adopted by the Committee under article 22 of the Convention, concerning Communication No.854/2017, para. 7, 9 letter d). In the case at issue, compensation based on domestic law had already been granted to the complainant, a victim of rape during the armed conflict in Bosnia and Herzegovina (para. 4.4.).

[69] Principles and Guidelines on Children Associated with Armed Forces or Armed Groups, 2007. The Principles were adopted by the United Nations at the international conference 'Free children from war' held in Paris in 2007.

reintegrating children, irrespective of any formal or informal peace process,[70] including 'an appeal for the necessary funding'.[71]

A somehow weaker idea emerges, finally, from the Draft Articles on Prevention and Punishment of Crimes Against Humanity recently adopted by the International Law Commission, which, as seen previously, establishes the obligation for States to ensure that, in their legal systems, victims have the right to obtain reparation. On one side, such an obligation is incumbent not only upon the State to which the acts are attributable, but also upon the State in the territory of which the acts were committed,[72] coherently with the idea of the 'subsidiary liability' of an innocent entity. However, the wording adopted seems to refer more to the existence of effective domestic avenues than to the obligation for the State involved to provide compensation.

If, therefore, compensation in the form of 'welfare measures' often exists for victims of violence and crimes, one may wonder why there is an impetus to obtain the acknowledgment of State responsibility. The answer is twofold: on one side, the amount of compensation granted on the basis of national compensation schemes is often lower than the amount fixed by the judge as a form of reparation.[73] Moreover, as can clearly be seen from the instruments cited above, national compensation schemes are often conceived as complementary sources that should come into play, in particular, when the liable person is unwilling or unable to meet its obligations—which could also concern a part of the amount. In some cases, this complementary function is reflected in the obligation, for the liable person, to reimburse the State if the latter has already compensated the victim.[74]

However, the strongest argument for instituting proceedings against a State, waiving, when necessary, its sovereign immunity, lies in the judicial response being part and parcel of the right to access justice to which victims are entitled. More precisely, access to compensation plays an essential role in the context of remedial justice, whose aim is to rectify the wrong done to a victim[75] and where the 'right to know' goes hand in hand with the 'right to reparation'.[76] Such a view is reflected in the fact that, under classical international law categories, the punishment

---

[70] Ibid., para. 3.23.

[71] Ibid., para. 7.2.

[72] Draft Articles on Prevention and Punishment of Crimes Against Humanity, 2019, Art. 12 para. 3.

[73] Administrative compensation has been defined as an approach where: 'victims are defined in standardized terms in a statute that provides a relatively fixed, tabulated amount of compensation for all' (Malamud-Goti and Sebastián Grosman 2006, p. 540).

[74] See, in particular, Art. 30 para. 2 of the Convention on Preventing and Combating Violence against Women and Domestic Violence: 'Adequate State compensation shall be awarded to those who have sustained serious bodily injury or impairment of health, to the extent that the damage is not covered by other sources such as the perpetrator, insurance or State-funded health and social provisions'.

[75] Shelton (2015), p. 19.

[76] Van Boven (2012), p. 695.

of authors of illicit acts is considered as a form of satisfaction.[77] As effectively argued by the complainant in the case submitted to the Committee against Torture mentioned above, compensation granted on the basis of national schemes can be qualified as an administrative welfare measure that differs from the compensation to which the individual is entitled following the verdict of a court and which can 'complement, but not replace' fair and adequate compensation.[78]

The elements gathered so far allow it to be said that, while 'welfare measures' can be considered as a second-best solution when compared to compensation, a trend undeniably exists, consisting of imposing some kind of liability on the State—even when the latter is innocent—as a part of its duty to guarantee redress. As a consequence, also given the broad language used by these instruments, it becomes difficult to draw a clear-cut distinction between so-called 'welfare measures' and compensation: on one side, administrative schemes somehow imply an acknowledgement of the author's responsibility and, on the other, reparation might result in an innocent entity being held liable, even in the context of judicial proceedings. One difference might lie, as has been already mentioned, in the amount of compensation; but as far as the origin of financial resources is concerned—in terms of an entity other than the author of the crime—in all these cases it is not the latter who actually bears the burden of redress.

In order to analyse the implications of these elements in the context of immunity, it is useful to examine if and to what extent the instruments mentioned so far, as well as the practice of international criminal tribunals, contemplate some form of involvement of States other than the one actually responsible.

5 Reparation as a Shared Burden?

In the context of victims' protection, State's 'subsidiary liability' often translates—or should be translated—into a requirement on the territorial State (or on the victim's State of nationality) to set up national compensation schemes, which, in turn, are not exclusively financed by that State, but also by other States.

This kind of possibility can be seen, for instance, in the UN Basic Principles. Unlike other instruments, the latter do not explicitly impose the reparation burden on a predefined State and generally refer to 'States'. That being said, and even assuming

[77] See, as an example, the Rainbow Warrior case, where declarations of material breaches by France of its obligations were considered sufficient satisfaction for New Zealand by the arbitral tribunal (Case Concerning the Difference Between New Zealand and France Concerning the Interpretation or Application of Two Agreements, Concluded on 9 July 1986 Between the Two States and Which Related to the Problems Arising from the Rainbow Warrior Affair, 30 April 1990, para. 123).

[78] Committee against Torture, Decision adopted by the Committee under article 22 of the Convention, concerning Communication No.854/2017, para. 5.3.

that the territorial State is the one required to provide compensation,[79] the application of universal jurisdiction,[80] advocated by the UN Basic Principles as a form of cooperation in the prosecution of crimes,[81] would inevitably shift the burden onto the State instituting proceedings, irrespective of the place where the violation occurred. Moreover, the possible involvement of non-responsible States in the context of this instrument was contemplated by a report by the High Commissioner for Human Rights: after mentioning solidarity as the basis of the State's effort in facilitating redress,[82] the report suggests the possibility of replacing the establishment of 'national funds' with a reference to 'programmes' encompassing a much broader range of possible support mechanisms.[83]

A similar idea resounds in the Declaration of Basic Principles of Justice for Victims of Crime and Abuse of Power which, while assuming the reparation burden as generally falling on the State of nationality of the victim, foresees the creation of 'other funds' when the latter is not in a position to compensate.[84] The Updated Principles on Impunity are more explicitly in favour of international participation in the reparation burden, according to which 'Reparations may also be provided through programs, based upon legislative or administrative measures, funded by national or international sources'.[85]

Though not directly related to the theme of State immunity—with the perpetrators generally being State officials and, therefore, natural persons—the area of international criminal justice offers several interesting insights in this regard, as the idea of internationalising the reparation burden often affects the structure and functioning of judicial bodies. This applies, firstly, to the Trust Fund for Victims set up by the Rome Statute establishing the International Criminal Court. According to Article 79 of the Statute,[86] the Fund is managed according to criteria to be determined by the

[79] In this regard, the approach taken by the Council of Europe Convention on Action against Trafficking in Human Beings consists of setting out grounds for jurisdiction (Art. 31 para. 1) and of generically establishing States' duty to ensure compensation (Art. 15 para. 1,3). The same approach is followed by the Council of Europe Convention on Preventing and Combating Violence against Women and Domestic Violence (Art. 44 para. 1; Art. 30 para. 1). Grounds for jurisdiction refer to State territory, as well as to the nationality of the perpetrator and of the victim.

[80] The topic of universal jurisdiction was analysed in particular by the Institut de droit international in its report Universal Civil Jurisdiction with Regard to Reparation for International Crimes, 2015.

[81] UN Basic Principles, no. 4, 5.

[82] The Right to a Remedy and Reparation for Victims of Violations of International Human Rights and Humanitarian Law, Note by the High Commissioner for Human Rights, E/CN.4/2004/57, 10 November 2003, p. 9.

[83] Ibid., p. 10.

[84] Principle 13. Similar language is found in the Draft UN Convention on Justice and Support for Victims of Crime and Abuse of Power (Art. 11.6).

[85] Updated Principles, no. 32.

[86] Rome Statute of the International Criminal Court, Rome, 17 July 1998, entry into force 1 July 2002.

Assembly of States Parties[87] and the Court can order money and other property collected through fines or forfeiture to be transferred to it.[88]

Part II of the Regulations[89] of the Trust Fund, named 'Receipt of funds', lists the sources through which the Fund is financed, including voluntary contributions from governments, international organisations, individuals, corporations and 'other entities'.[90] According to the Regulations, the Board presents an annual appeal for voluntary contributions to the Fund[91] and establishes contact with governments, international organisations, individuals, corporations and other entities to solicit them.[92] The intermediary[93] function assigned to the Trust Fund in the handling of compensation arises from the wording of Article 75 of the Statute, according to which 'the award for reparations [is] made through the Trust Fund'; however, such a strict mandate will be overridden if the perpetrator is indigent and therefore unable to fund reparation.[94] A similar mechanism is envisaged in the context of the Special Panels for Serious Crimes in East Timor: Regulation no. 2000/15 adopted by the United Nations Transitional Administration in East Timor sets out the possibility of establishing a Trust Fund for the benefit of victims of crimes and their families.[95] The Fund may be financed through money and other property collected through fines, forfeiture, foreign donors or other means.[96]

Similarly, in the system of the Extraordinary Chambers in the Courts of Cambodia (ECCC), where only collective and moral reparations can be awarded,[97] assistance to victims in obtaining compensation is provided by the Victims Support

[87] Ibid., Art. 79 para. 3.

[88] Ibid., Art. 79 para. 2.

[89] Regulations of the Trust Fund for Victims, 3 December 2005.

[90] Regulations of the Trust Fund for Victims, 3 December 2005, Art. 21 letter. a); the Regulations also mention 'other sources': money and other property collected through fines or forfeiture, resources collected through awards for reparations ordered by the Court and such resources, other than assessed contributions, as the Assembly of States Parties may decide to allocate (Art. 21 letters b), c) and d)).

[91] Regulations of the Trust Fund for Victims, 3 December 2005, Art. 22.

[92] Ibid., Art. 23.

[93] Dannebaum (2010), pp. 258–259. The same expression is found in Article 98 of the Rules of Evidence of the Court (para. 3), mentioning the case where a collective award is deemed more appropriate. According to that provision, individual awards for reparations shall be made directly against a convicted person (para. 1) and can be deposited with the Trust Fund only when it is impossible to make individual awards directly to each victim. In this case, they shall be separated from other resources of the Trust Fund and shall be forwarded to each victim as soon as possible (para. 2). On the Trust Fund for Victims see, also, Rombouts and Parmentier (2009), pp. 149ff; Davidovic (2015), pp. 217ff.

[94] Balta et al. (2019), pp. 233–234.

[95] Regulation no. 2000/15 on the Establishment of Panels with Exclusive Jurisdiction over Serious Criminal Offences, Art. 25.1.

[96] Ibid., Art. 25.2.

[97] Extraordinary Chambers in the Courts of Cambodia—Internal Rules (rev.9) as revised on 16 January 2015, Rule 23(5).

Section. After it became clear that reparation from the accused would be impossible due to their indigence, and after the ECCC declined the possibility of seeking reparations from the Cambodian State,[98] the Courts' Rules were amended in order to consider, subject to court approval, some externally funded projects as reparations.[99] According to the Guidebook to Judicial Reparations issued in 2004 by the Civil Party Lead of the Co-Lawyers' Section, civil parties must choose between one of the two modes of implementation: in the event of a reparation award, the costs will be borne by the convicted person, whereas reparation projects will be funded externally.[100] The Guidebook further specifies that externally funded reparation projects must have secured funding; this can occur through a funding agreement with the project partner or through an agreement with the Victims Support Section. Upon submission of a reparation project, it will be therefore up to the victims to show to the Chamber, through Verification of Secured Funding, that the project can be properly funded.[101] In order to fulfil its task, the Victims Support Section organises 'fundraising meetings' at which potential donors and relevant stakeholders are informed of the projects and of the opportunities to fund them.

Further examples come from the African continent: the Statute of the Extraordinary African Chambers within the courts of Senegal[102] sets out the establishment of a Trust Fund 'for the benefit of victims of crimes within the jurisdiction of the Extraordinary African Chambers, and of the beneficiaries of such victims', financed by voluntary contributions from foreign governments, international institutions, non-governmental organisations and other entities wishing to support victims.[103] The Special Tribunal for Lebanon receives external donors' contributions through a Management Committee, established in 2007[104] and the same applies to the (now Residual) Special Court for Sierra Leone (SCSL).[105]

---

[98] Prosecutor v Kaing Guek Eav, Appeal Judgment, 3 February 2012, para. 654ff.

[99] Killean (2017), p. 484. An example of an externally funded reparation project is the one set up in Case 002/02; on this point, see Balta (2018). See, also, Sperfeldt (2012), pp. 257ff.

[100] Guidebook to Judicial Reparations in Case 02/02 before the ECCC, p. 3.

[101] Ibid., p. 7.

[102] The Chambers were created to prosecute international crimes committed in Chad between 7 June 1982 and 1 December 1990. The Agreement on the Establishment of the Extraordinary African Chambers within the Senegalese Judicial System between the Government of the Republic of Senegal and the African Union was signed on 22 August 2012; the Chambers were inaugurated in February 2013.

[103] Statute of the Extraordinary African Chambers, Art. 28 para. 1.

[104] The Special Tribunal for Lebanon was set up under UN Resolution 1757(2007) to deal with claims relating to terrorist attacks occurring in Lebanon since 2004. The Agreement between the United Nations and the Lebanese Republic on the establishment of the Tribunal was signed by the Government of Lebanon and the United Nations respectively on 23 January and on 6 February 2007. Unlike the other tribunals mentioned so far, compensation claims must be addressed to national tribunals or 'other competent institutions' (Art. 25 para. 3 of the Statute).

[105] The SCSL was established by an agreement between the UN and the Government of Sierra Leone (Agreement Between the United Nations and the Government of Sierra Leone on the Establishment of a Special Court for Sierra Leone; Freetown, 16 December 2002) to prosecute

Finally, at the crossroad between international criminal justice and State responsibility, the International Commission of Inquiry on Darfur encouraged the creation of a Compensation Commission dealing with compensation claims for any international crime perpetrated in Darfur.[106] The report—which, interestingly, draws the notion of victim from the Declaration of Basic Principles of Justice for Victims of Crime and Abuse of Power mentioned above[107]—proposes a double track for funding compensation. Whereas Sudanese authorities would fund compensation for crimes committed by government forces or *de facto* agents of the government, a Trust Fund to be established on the basis of international voluntary contributions would fund compensation relating to acts committed by rebels.[108] As stated by the report, the Commission should rule on compensation claims whether or not the perpetrator has been identified and brought to trial,[109] coherently with the idea, underscored by the UN High Commissioner for Human Rights, of legal principles of accountability and social principles of solidarity calling for victims' protection beyond cases where the perpetrator could be held accountable.[110]

What is therefore peculiar in the instances illustrated above is that the right to financial compensation, established by courts as a form of redress, is conditional upon 'crowdfunding' activity carried out, if not by the court itself, by a related structure. Such a system has two main consequences: on one side, the right to compensation is not absolute, but rather contingent on a set of external circumstances and, if it is true that such a risk is inherent in any legal proceeding, in the examples illustrated above, it appears to be embedded in the very structure of the system. Secondly, the link between compensation and the responsible person or entity is weakened, which risks affecting the rationale of the compensation itself.

6 Back to the Theme: Why Shrinking Immunity?

In light of the elements highlighted thus far, some reflections can now be developed on the theme of State immunity and, more precisely, on the drivers of its shrinking, considering whether the need and the right to receive compensation—as a form of

---

persons who bear the greatest responsibility for serious violations of international humanitarian law and Sierra Leonean law committed in the territory of Sierra Leone since 30 November 1996. Following the termination of the Courts' activities in 2013, the Residual Court was established, dealing with the remaining legal obligations of the SCSL.

[106]Report of the International Commission of Inquiry on Darfur to the United Nations Secretary-General Pursuant to Security Council Resolution 1564 of 18 September 2004, para. 601.

[107]Ibid., para. 595.

[108]Ibid., para. 595.

[109]Ibid., para. 601.

[110]The Right to a Remedy and Reparation for Victims of Violations of International Human Rights and Humanitarian Law, Note by the High Commissioner for Human Rights, E/CN.4/2003/63, 27 December 2002, para. 13.

reparation of human rights breaches—is actually a 'good' driver of this phenomenon. As a preliminary consideration, as we have seen, if the aim is compensation *per se*, instituting legal proceedings and therefore engaging State responsibility is not always necessary, as compensation can be granted under administrative schemes. However, if those schemes are not available, or the amount awarded is not considered to be satisfactory, or the victims are not willing to replace proper compensation with 'welfare measures', the waiving of immunity is actually a prerequisite.

That being said, the experience drawn from international human rights law as well as international criminal law shows us that, in several cases, compensation for serious breaches is often found to be problematic and that, also in the context of judicial proceedings, the reparation burden tends to shift to actors that are unrelated to the perpetrator. This can apply to the relationship between the individual responsible for the breach and the State in which the violation took place, but also to the relationship between the responsible State and the entire international community.

Assuming that compensation—intended as a form of reparation—is the driver of judicial action, this trend may well discourage victims from bringing responsible States to trial, as burden sharing mechanisms make the availability of compensation contingent upon external sources, not only jeopardising the enjoyment of the right to redress, but also watering down the very idea of international responsibility. From a practical point of view, compensation based on projects funded by voluntary contributions gathered in a 'crowdfunding style' may ultimately be frustrating for the victims. As has been highlighted in the context of transitional justice, donors should not assume the cost of reparations as the latter 'should be concrete expressions of an individual State's responsibility and an important form of acknowledgment; they would lose much of their reparative effect if other governments should take on the burden *in lieu* of the individual State'.[111]

Adopting the opposite point of view, good reasons exist for seeking compensation (also) through a judicial avenue, and thus for waiving immunity when necessary, which mainly relate to the right to redress as an individual fundamental right. Notwithstanding the perplexities shown by some of doctrine on the existence of such a right (as opposed to the obligation of inter-state compensation), it is reasonable to assume that a trend exists, in international human rights law, towards the recognition of the right of victims to be compensated. Such a trend is rooted in the so-called victimological approach as well as in the consolidation of the right to justice as a fundamental right, while being coherent with the progressive strengthening of the individual's international legal personality. Moreover, the participation of the international community in the reparation effort, as limited as it may be, could find a further basis in fundamental rights being protected by *erga omnes* norms, whose breach—according to Article 48, par. 1 (b) of the ILC Draft Principles on State

[111] International Centre for Transitional Justice, Reparation and the Darfur Peace Process: Ensuring Victims' Rights, November 2007, p. 42. The text also notes how international assistance may be more appropriate to peace-building measures. A similar opinion has been expressed by Segovia (2006), p. 659.

Responsibility—entitles 'other States than the injured State' to invoke responsibility. The latter may claim, under paragraph 2 of the same provision, the performance of the obligation of reparation in the interest of the injured State or of the beneficiaries of the obligation breached.[112] As underlined by the Commentaries to the Articles,[113] Article 48 'intends to give effect to the Statement by ICJ in the Barcelona Traction case, where the Court drew 'an essential distinction' between obligations owed to particular States and those owed 'towards the international community as a whole'. With regard to the latter, the Court went on to state that '[i]n view of the importance of the rights involved, all States can be held to have a legal interest in their protection; they are obligations *erga omnes*'.[114]

What is argued is that, in the case of reparations for serious human rights breaches, the right of other States of the international community to invoke responsibility would translate into a right to replace the responsible State if the latter is not willing or able to offer financial redress. As underlined by the resolution on Universal Civil Jurisdiction with Regard to Reparation for International Crimes adopted by the Institut de Droit international, the breach of *erga omnes* obligations would also imply the right of other States to react, and therefore to adopt measures to guarantee implementation of the individual right.[115] Such a right would expand into an 'individual and collective obligation' to adopt measures in this regard, as the duty of solidarity entails obligations to 'facilitate and support'.[116] The idea is further supported, albeit recognising the difficulties that a translation into a legal obligation would entail, by recalling the notion of responsibility to protect.[117]

The Institut de droit international further underlines the need to maintain the distinction between injured States and other States, reiterating the idea according to which, whereas the injured State is entitled to the full array of countermeasures, other

[112] Draft Articles on Responsibility of States for Internationally Wrongful Acts, Art. 48 para. 2 letter b). According to letter a), such States are also entitled to request cessation of the internationally wrongful act, and assurances and guarantees of non-repetition.

[113] Draft Articles on Responsibility of States for Internationally Wrongful Acts, with commentaries, 2001, p. 127.

[114] International Court of Justice, Barcelona Traction, Light and Power Company, Limited, Judgment, I.C.J. Reports 1970, pp. 3, 32.

[115] Universal Civil Jurisdiction with Regard to Reparation for International Crimes, 2015, para. 107.

[116] Ibid., para. 108. The duty of solidarity was also mentioned by the Institute in the resolution on The Protection of Human Rights and the Principle of Non-intervention in Internal Affairs of States, 1989, Art. 1.

[117] Universal Civil Jurisdiction with Regard to Reparation for International Crimes, para. 108. As is known, the notion of 'responsibility to protect' was first formulated in 2001 by the International Commission on Intervention and State Sovereignty, set up by the Canadian Government, in its report 'The Responsibility to Protect'. It was later endorsed by the High-Level Panel on Threats, Challenges and Change formed by experts appointed by the UN Secretary General. In its report, adopted in 2004, the panel submits that Chapter VII of the UN Charter allows military intervention in case of disasters or mass atrocities occurring within States' borders (para. 201). The idea was re-stated by the UN Secretary General in its report 'In Larger Freedom: Towards Development, Security and Human Rights for All', adopted in 2005. (para. 132).

States can only require 'performance of the obligation of reparation [...], in the interest of the injured State or of the beneficiaries of the obligation breached'.[118] This implies the possibility for any State of the international community harmed by the breach of an *erga omnes* obligation to authorise its own tribunals to repress the violation of the right to receive compensation, giving priority, at the same time, to the injured State.[119] Such an allocation of functions would imply that, in the absence of any initiative by the injured State, any other State will be entitled to claim compensation by the State author of the crime, so as to guarantee compliance with the right to redress. Such an obligation, although *subsidiary*, is, according to the report, a fully-fledged one.[120]

Considering, further, the peremptory nature of the norms prohibiting gross violations of human rights, the States' obligation to cooperate to bring the breach to an end through lawful means, set out by the Draft Articles,[121] also comes into play. The point was considered by the Institut de droit international in the report mentioned above, raising the question as to whether the obligation of the responsible State to ensure the right to reparation to victims is only incumbent on the latter State or if an obligation can arise for other States. The answer provided is somewhat ambiguous: despite recognising that, in principle, nothing opposes such an idea, the report reverts to a more conservative stance by adding that in the event of a default by the author of the crime, other States are not supposed to replace it, as such a rule, similar to a guarantee of the performance of acts due by the perpetrator, is not supported by international law.[122]

The recently adopted Draft Articles on Prevention and Punishment of Crimes Against Humanity appear to be silent on the matter of State immunity and do not give much credence to the possibility of participation, by innocent entities, in the reparation effort. It is nevertheless interesting to note the emphasis given to victims' rights, more than to the law of State responsibility, as emerges from the title of the provision on reparation ('Victims, witnesses and others').[123] While, on one side, this can be explained through the fact that crimes mostly entail, by definition, a breach of human rights, the reference to the Basic Principles and Guidelines on a Right to a

---

[118]Draft Articles on Responsibility of States for Internationally Wrongful Acts, Art. 48 para. 2 letter b). Such a provision must be read in conjunction with Article 54, confirming the right of any State, entitled under Article 48, para. 1 to invoke the responsibility of another State to take lawful measures against that State to ensure cessation of the breach and reparation in the interest of the injured State or of the beneficiaries of the obligation breached.

[119]Draft Articles on Responsibility of States for Internationally Wrongful Acts, paras. 115–116.

[120]Ibid., para. 117.

[121]Ibid., Art. 41 para. 1.

[122]Universal Civil Jurisdiction with Regard to Reparation for International Crimes, 2015, paras. 110–111. The report focuses its attention on other States' obligation not to hinder compliance with the obligation to provide redress, i.e. by preventing the transfer of funds deposited in its banks to the responsible State (para. 112). Under these terms, according to the Institut, States would actually be bound by the obligation to compensate.

[123]Draft Articles on Prevention and Punishment of Crimes Against Humanity, Art.12 para. 3.

Remedy[124] made by the Commentaries to Article 12 is a clear testimony to the link existing between the law of international responsibility and the victimological approach.

Notwithstanding the difficulties that the elements highlighted above, and in particular enforcement of *erga omnes* obligations, actually raise, it is submitted that they confirm the progressive consolidation of the individual right to compensation and point towards a rationale for sharing the burden between the members of the international community while enforcing State responsibility. A remarkable role is played by the notion of subsidiarity, recurring in different contexts as a legal tool to guarantee that the right to receive compensation is not deprived of its content. As we have seen, such a notion can support the adoption of welfare measures but also, and perhaps more importantly, the intervention of States 'other than the injured one' in the context of *erga omnes* norms. The case recently brought before the ICJ by The Gambia against Myanmar[125] shows, for the first time, how, in the absence of any intervention by an injured State, other States can actually step in and demand the performance of the obligatio, - as already arises from the granting, by the court, of provisional measures.[126] It is therefore clear that an effective implementation of subsidiarity can act as an additional ground for waiving immunity, as such an idea requires, by definition, the acknowledgment of the responsibility of a perpetrator and, secondly, the intervention of the international community to ensure that victims' right to compensation is respected.

7 Concluding Remarks

Based on the elements gathered so far, some preliminary conclusions on the future perspectives of financial compensation as a driver for the shrinking of State immunity can be outlined. An initial observation concerns the very existence of the right to compensation that, as can be seen from the relevant legal instruments, is gradually acquiring individual nature. In light of this development, it is reasonable to claim that the artificiality of any rigid separation between the law of international responsibility and the victims' perspective when dealing with the issue of immunity is an obstacle

[124] Draft articles on Prevention and Punishment of Crimes Against Humanity, with Commentaries, p. 107, footnote no. 541.

[125] Application of the Convention on the Prevention and Punishment of the Crime of Genocide (The Gambia v. Myanmar). The complaint was brought by The Gambia in relation to acts performed by the Government of Myanmar against members of the Rohingya group, allegedly victims of genocidal acts. The jurisdiction of the Court is based on Article IX of the Convention against Genocide, ratified by both The Gambia and Myanmar. The Convention on the Prevention and Punishment of the Crime of Genocide, adopted in Paris on 9 December 1948, entered into force on 12 January 1951.

[126] Application of the Convention on the Prevention and Punishment of the Crime of Genocide (The Gambia v. Myanmar), Order, 23 January 2020.

to compensation. On the contrary, the individual right to receive compensation is a necessary complement of the interstate obligation of reparation while, at the same time, lying at the heart of the 'need to repair' which is typical for the victimological approach. The connection between these two areas of law implies, firstly, that the decision to waive immunity is a prerequisite for both establishing State responsibility and guaranteeing victims' rights. Secondly, as underlined by the International Commission of Inquiry on Darfur: 'the universal recognition and acceptance of the right to an effective remedy cannot but have a bearing on the interpretation of the international provisions on State responsibility for war crimes and other international crimes'.[127] In other words, from a human rights perspective, it is particularly the law of international responsibility that is likely to benefit from such a relationship: the centrality granted to the right to redress by the protection of victims' rights can indeed help limit the most state-centric aspects of international responsibility and reduce the obstacles, including jurisdictional immunity, which hinder access to justice.

Building on these premises, the right to receive compensation has been tackled from the angle of the possibility—or, albeit with less likelihood, the obligation—for entities unrelated to the breach to participate in the compensation effort, on the basis of solidarity with the victim and of the duty to ensure that the latter receives compensation, regardless of the perpetrator's financial situation. The analysis carried out on a broad array of legal instruments, as well as on the practice of international criminal tribunals, revealed that such a subsidiary liability might apply not only at domestic level but also at international level and, at the same time, revealed the problematic aspects of considering compensation to be a 'welfare measure', leading to the question as to whether compensation might actually act as a good driver for the shrinking of immunity.

Such a question was answered in the affirmative by considering, especially in light of the works of the International Law Commission and of the Institut de Droit international, how the categories of *erga omnes* obligations—of which the right to redress is no doubt part—and, to some extent, of peremptory norms of international law are able to support the idea of a subsidiary liability of the international community or, at least, of the possibility for the latter to act in replacement of the liable State in order to ensure compliance with the right to redress. Given that such a possibility is contingent upon a State being subjected to judicial proceedings and, therefore, upon the shrinking of immunity, it is submitted that compensation can actually act as an incentive in this regard. In other words, the international legal environment appears to be supportive of a process that, although admitting the cooperation of

[127] Report of the International Commission of Inquiry on Darfur to the United Nations Secretary-General Pursuant to Security Council Resolution 1564 of 18 September 2004, para. 597. See, also, the Final Award rendered by the Eritrea-Ethiopia Claims Commission, where it notes that: 'The size of the Parties' claims raised potentially serious questions involving the intersection of the law of State responsibility with fundamental human rights norms' (Final Award, Ethiopia's Damages Claims between The Federal Democratic Republic of Ethiopia and The State of Eritrea, 17 August 2009, para. 19).

external entities, can only function if States' acts are subjected to judicial scrutiny. Once again, such a conclusion is coherent with the need to hold States accountable for particularly serious breaches of international law and, at the same time, to guarantee that victims are not denied the right to redress. That being said, future judicial developments will confirm such a hypothesis or will reveal if the victims' right to repair can be better served through simple 'welfare measures'.

References

Balta A (2018) Extraordinary chambers in the Courts of Cambodia, regulation of marriage, and reparations: judgment in case 002/02 under review. Opinio Juris. http://opiniojuris.org/2018/11/20/extraordinary-chambers-in-the-courts-of-cambodia-regulation-of-marriage-and-reparations-judgment-in-case-002-02-under-review/. Accessed 15 Apr 2021

Balta A, Bax M, Letschert R (2019) Trial and (potential) error: conflicting visions on reparations within the ICC system. Int Crim Just Rev 29:221–249

Bartolini G (2009) Reparation for violations of human rights: possible co-ordination in the case-law of international supervisory bodies. Federalism. https://federalismi.it/nv14/articolo-documento.cfm?artid=13780. Accessed 15 Apr 2021

Bassiouni C (1987) Introduction to the United Nations resolution and declaration of basic principles of justice for victims of crime and abuse of power. De Paul University, Chicago

Boudreault F (2012) Identifying conflicts of norms: the ICJ approach in the case of the jurisdictional immunities of the state (Germany v. Italy: Greece intervening). Leiden J Int Law 25:1003–1012

Brownlie I (2012) Public international law, 8th edn. OUP, Oxford

Cançado Trindade AA (2011) The access of individuals to international justice. OUP, Oxford

Chukwuemeke Okeke E (2018) Jurisdictional immunities of states and international organizations. OUP, Oxford

Daigle LE (2013) Victimology: the essentials. Sage, Los Angeles

Dannebaum T (2010) The International Criminal Court, Article 79, and transitional justice: the case for an independent trust fund for victims. Wisconsin Int Law J 28:234–298

Davidovic J (2015) International Criminal Court, the trust fund for victims, and victim participation. In: Edenberg E (ed) Jus Post Bellum and transitional justice. CUP, Cambridge, pp 217–243

De Sena P, De Vittor F (2013) State immunity and human rights: the Italian Supreme Court decision on the Ferrini case. Eur J Int Law 16:89–113

Evans E (2012) The right to reparation in international law for victims of armed conflict. CUP, Cambridge

Fattah EA (1992) Towards a critical victimology. ST.Martin's Press, New York

Focarelli C (2005) Denying foreign state immunity for commission of international crimes: the Ferrini decision. Am J Int Law 54:951–958

Fox H, Webb P (2013) The law of state immunity, 3rd edn. OUP, Oxford

Francioni F (2007) The rights of access to justice under customary international law. In: Access to justice as a human right. OUP, Oxford, pp 1–55

Francioni F (2012) From Utopia to disenchantment: the ill fate of 'Moderate Monism' in the ICJ judgment on the jurisdictional immunities of the state. Eur J Int Law 23:1125–1132

Frigessi Di Rattalma M, Treves T (1999) The United Nations Compensation Commission: a handbook. The Kluwer Law International, Hague

Frulli M (2011) 'The Times they are A-Changing' – the Italian Court of Cassation denies Germany immunity from execution to allow compensation to war crimes' victims. J Int Crim Just 9:1129–1143

Gattini A (2002) The UN Compensation Commission – old rules, new procedures on war reparations. Eur J Int Law 13:161–181
Gattini A (2005) War crimes and state immunity in the Ferrini Decision. J Int Crim Just 3:224–242
Groenhuijsen M (2008) The Draft UN Convention on justice and support for victims of crime, with special reference to its provisions on restorative justice. Int Ann Criminol 46:121–137
Groenhuijsen M (2014) The development of international policy in relation to victims of crime. Int Rev Victimol 20:31–49
Haldemann F, Unger T (2018) Introduction. In: The United Nations principles to combat impunity – a commentary. OUP, Oxford
Iovane M (2004) The Ferrini Judgment of the Italian Supreme Court: opening up domestic courts to claims of reparation for victims of serious violations of fundamental human rights. Italian Yearb Int Law 14:165–193
Killean R (2017) Pursuing retributive and reparative justice within Cambodia. In: Lawther C, Moffett L, Jacobs D (eds) Research handbook on transitional justice. Edward Elgar, Cheltenham, pp 466–487
Malamud-Goti JE, Sebastián Grosman L (2006) Reparations and civil litigations: compensations for human rights violations in transitional democracies. In: De Greiff P (ed) The handbook of reparations. OUP, Oxford, pp 539–559
Mccracken K (2005) Commentary on the basic principles and guidelines on the right to a remedy and reparation for victims of gross violations of international human rights law and serious violations of international humanitarian law. Revue internationale de droit pénal 76:77–79
Mensah TA (2011) United Nations Compensation Commission (UNCC). In: Wolfrum R (ed) Max Planck Encyclopedia of Public International Law. OUP, Oxford
Orakhelashvili A (2012) Jurisdictional immunities of states. Am J Int Law 106:609–616
Panebianco M (1967) Giurisdizione interna e immunità degli Stati stranieri. Jovene, Naples
Peters A (2016) Beyond human rights – the legal status of the individual in international law. CUP, Cambridge
Pisillo-Mazzeschi R (2003) Reparation claims by individuals for state breaches of humanitarian law and human rights: an overview. J Int Crim Just 1:339–347
Pisillo-Mazzeschi R (1999) International obligations to provide for reparation claims? In: Randelzhofer A, Tomuschat C (eds) State responsibility and the individual. Martinus Nijhoff, The Hague, pp 149–172
Pisillo-Mazzeschi R (2012) Il rapporto fra norme di ius cogens e la regola sull'immunità degli Stati: alcune osservazioni critiche sulla sentenza della Corte internazionale di giustizia del 3 febbraio 2012. Diritti umani e diritto internazionale 6:310–326
Rombouts H, Parmentier S (2009) The International Criminal Court and its trust fund are coming of age: towards a process approach for the reparation of victims. Int Rev Victimol 16:149–182
Ronzitti N (2007) Access to justice and compensation for violations of the law of war. In: Francioni F (ed) Access to justice as a human right. OUP, Oxford, pp 95–134
Ronzitti N (2008) Le immunità giurisdizionali degli Stati e degli altri enti internazionali. Cedam, Padua
Salerno F (2012) Gli effetti della sentenza internazionale nell'ordinamento italiano: il caso Germania c. Italia. Diritti umani e diritto internazionale 6:350–370
Segovia A (2006) Financing reparations programs. In: De Greiff P (ed) The handbook of reparations. OUP, Oxford, pp 650–675
Shaw MN (2017) International law. CUP, Cambridge
Shelton D (2015) Remedies in international human rights law. OUP, Oxford
Sperfeldt K (2012) Collective reparations at the extraordinary chambers in the courts of Cambodia. Int Crim Law Rev 12:457–491
Stoll PT (2011) State immunity. In: Wolfrum R (ed) Max Planck Encyclopedia of Public International Law. OUP, Oxford

Tomuschat C (1999) Individual reparation claims in instances of grave human rights violations: the position under general international law. In: Randelzhofer A, Tomuschat C (eds) State responsibility and the individual. Martinus Nijhoff, The Hague, pp 1–25
Van Alebeek R (2008) The immunity of states and their officials in international criminal law and international human rights law. OUP, Oxford
Van Boven T (2012) The need to repair. Int J Hum Rights 16:694–697
Van Dijk JJM (2002) Empowering victims of organized crime: on the concurrence of the Palermo Convention with the UN declaration on basic principles of justice for victims. Int Rev Victimol 9:15–30
Yang X (2012) State immunity in international law. CUP, Cambridge

Elisa Ruozzi is an Associate Professor of international law at the University of Turin (Italy). She holds a Ph.D in international economic law from Bocconi University (Milan) and a DEA in international economic law from Université Paris I - Panthéon-Sorbonne. She currently teaches international law and international environmental law.

Assessing State Jurisdictional Immunities Through the Lenses of the European Court of Human Rights: Embassy Employment Disputes as Test Bench for Restrictive Immunity

Giovanni Ardito

Abstract Over the last 20 years, the European Court of Human Rights has played a pivotal role in shaping the understanding of State jurisdictional immunities in the European continent. Taking into account its case-law on embassy employment disputes, this chapter will analyse State jurisdictional immunities in light of Article 6 of the Convention for the Protection of Human Rights and Fundamental Freedoms. When in *Fogarty* the European Court of Human Rights first addressed the issue, it concluded that lacking a settled practice, no violation of the right of access to courts had occurred. However, since the adoption of the United Nations Convention on Jurisdictional Immunities of States and Their Property, the approach of the Court has changed. In fact, from *Cudak* on, the European Court of Human Rights largely relied on Article 11 of the abovementioned convention, as codification of customary international law by which employment-related disputes are out of the scope of State immunity, with some exceptions. While the conclusions of the Court are acceptable in principle, its arguments are debatable to some extent. It did not undergo any examination of the practice in the field and apparently underestimated the approaches taken by domestic courts. This chapter will dwell on the risks to domestically replicate the European Court of Human Rights' reasoning, which could result in an interpretation of State jurisdictional immunity that is less restrictive than that generally accorded at the national level.

1 Introduction

Over the last 20 years, the European Court of Human Rights (ECtHR or the Court) has played a pivotal role in shaping the current understanding of State jurisdictional immunity in the European continent, alternatively favouring an absolute and a

G. Ardito (✉)
Sapienza University, Rome, Italy
e-mail: giovanni.ardito@uniroma1.it

R. Bismuth et al. (eds.), *Sovereign Immunity Under Pressure*,
https://doi.org/10.1007/978-3-030-87706-4_11

restrictive approach. This chapter will analyse the case-law of the ECtHR to assess its attitude towards State jurisdictional immunity in embassy employment disputes.

Since the beginning of the new millennium, the Court coped with a number of proceedings related to nationals of receiving countries working in foreign embassies and prevented to sue the employer State on the ground of jurisdictional immunity. Deprived of any access to justice in the domestic legal orders, applicants have filed a case in the Court for an alleged violation of Article 6 §1 of the Convention for the Protection of Human Rights and Fundamental Freedoms (ECHR).[1]

In delivering its judgments, the Court has relied on Article 11 of the United Nations Convention on Jurisdictional Immunities of States and Their Property (the UNJISP)[2]—which is not yet in force—as codification of customary international law and has elaborated a legitimacy and proportionality test for copying with such disputes.

With the aim to not incur declarations of violation with respect to Article 6 §1, and in the spirit of cooperation with the ECtHR, domestic courts are redefining their jurisprudence to meet the arguments and criteria laid down by the Court. While there is a general tendency towards the limitation of State immunity in employment-related disputes, sticking to the Court's *dicta* could result in the weakening of the human rights' protection. In order to ascertain such trend, this chapter firstly deals with how the Court has matched the granting of jurisdictional immunity with Article 6 §1 of the ECHR.[3] It will then focus on its jurisprudence, with peculiar regard to the *Fogarty*[4] and *Cudak*[5] cases. The latter will offer the chance to outline the test applied by the Court in deciding recent embassy employment disputes.

In light of the State practice, this chapter will question some arguments elaborated by the Court, namely that Article 11 reflects *in toto* customary international law and that the texts of the UNJISP and the Draft Articles on Jurisdictional Immunities of

[1]Convention for the Protection of Human Rights and Fundamental Freedoms, 213 UNTS 221 (entered into force 3 September 1953). Article 6 §1 reads: 'In the determination of his civil rights and obligations or of any criminal charge against him, everyone is entitled to a fair and public hearing within a reasonable time by an independent and impartial tribunal established by law. Judgment shall be pronounced publicly but the press and public may be excluded from all or part of the trial in the interests of morals, public order or national security in a democratic society, where the interests of juveniles or the protection of the private life of the parties so require, or to the extent strictly necessary in the opinion of the court in special circumstances where publicity would prejudice the interests of justice'.

[2]United Nations Convention on Jurisdictional Immunities of States and Their Property, annexed to A/RES/59/38. As of November 2020, the Convention has not entered into force, since the minimum number of ratifications (30) required by Article 30 has not been reached yet. Only Austria, the Czech Republic, Equatorial Guinea, Finland, France, Iran, Iraq, Italy, Japan, Kazakhstan, Latvia, Lebanon, Liechtenstein, Mexico, Norway, Portugal, Romania, Saudi Arabia, Slovakia, Spain, Sweden and Switzerland have, in fact, ratified the Convention.

[3]For a commentary of the Article with regard to employment-related disputes, see Shabas (2015), pp. 274–287.

[4]ECtHR, Fogarty v. United Kingdom, 37112/97, Judgment, 21 November 2001.

[5]ECtHR, Cudak v. Lithuania, 15869/02, Judgment, 23 March 2010.

States and Their Property (the Draft Articles on Jurisdictional Immunities),[6] of the International Law Commission (the ILC) can be considered interchangeably.

Finally, the ripple effects of the ECtHR jurisprudence on the Contracting Parties will be investigated to underscore the risks associated to the replication, at the national level, of the very same Court's arguments.

2 The Delicate Balance Between State Jurisdictional Immunity and Article 6 of the ECHR: The Legitimacy and Proportionality Test

A glance at the practice in the field of jurisdictional immunity reveals that employment-related disputes concerning embassy and consulate staff are increasingly growing and count for the most challenging to deal with.[7] Indeed, in such disputes, domestic courts address the jurisdictional immunity of foreign States through a number of different and sometimes inconsistent criteria, with some always accepting the plea of jurisdictional immunity raised by the sending State, and most of the others adopting a restrictive approach.

In the European continent, the attitude towards State jurisdictional immunity in embassy employment disputes has been shaped by the adoption of the ECHR, the 1972 European Convention on State Immunity (the Basel Convention),[8] and a number of European Union legal instruments,[9] which have consistently limited the operation of immunity.

With regard to the ECHR, State jurisdictional immunity is addressed through the gate of Article 6 §1 on the right of access to court. By its constant case-law, the ECtHR has determined that this provision is procedural in nature. Indeed, the Court has maintained that Article 6 §1 does not in itself guarantee any particular content for rights and obligations in substantive law of the State parties to the ECHR.[10]

[6]Draft Articles on Jurisdictional Immunities of States and Their Property with Commentaries (1991), pp. 13–62.

[7]See Fox and Webb (2013), p. 440; Yang (2012), p. 169; Hafner et al. (2006), p. 77.

[8]European Convention on State Immunity (ECSI), 1495 UNTS 181 (entered into force 11 June 1976).

[9]See, among the others, Charter of the Fundamental Rights of the European Union, O.*J. C 326 (2012)*; and European Union Regulation No. 44/2001 on jurisdiction and the recognition and enforcement of judgments in civil and commercial matters, *O. J. L 12 (2001)* articles 18–21. See also Garnett (2015), pp. 808–817; Rodgers (2015), pp. 55–60.

[10]ECtHR, Z and Others v. The United Kingdom, 29392/95, Judgment, 10 May 2001, para. 87; see also ECtHR, Fayed v. The United Kingdom, 17101/90, Judgment, 21 September 1994, para. 25; ECtHR, James and Others v. The United Kingdom, 8793/79, Judgment, 21 February 1986, para. 81; ECtHR, Lithgow and others v. The United Kingdom, 9006/80; 9262/81; 9263/81; 9265/81; 9266/81; 9313/81; 9405/81, Judgment, 8 July 1986, para. 192.

Furthermore, the ECtHR has acknowledged that the right of access to court is not absolute and can be subject to limitations. Bearing in mind that the access shall not be restricted in a way that would prejudice the very essence of the right,[11] States are entitled to a certain margin of appreciation. However, it is for the Court to finally determine whether such discretion has not resulted in an impairment of Article 6 §1.[12] To this extent, the Court relies on two parameters, namely the legitimacy of and the proportionality to the aim.[13]

As a matter of fact, the ECtHR always showed a certain deference towards State jurisdictional immunity and never questioned the legitimacy of its recognition,[14] since it reflects a well-established principle of international law, whose ultimate goal is 'to promote comity and good relations among States through the respect of another State sovereignty'.[15] The Court is instead to evaluate that 'the degree to which the legitimate aim [can] be lawfully' pursued does not 'impair the essence of a conventional right'.[16] Generally speaking, the Court relies on a strong presumption of proportionality between Article 6 §1 and State jurisdictional immunity. As it was made clear in the *Al-Adsani* case, in fact, 'measures taken by a High Contracting Party which reflect generally recognised rules of public international law on State immunity cannot in principle be regarded as imposing a disproportionate restriction on the right of access to a court as embodied in Article 6 §1'.[17]

As such, the test based on legitimacy and proportionality serves the purpose to apply a logic of reconciliation between Article 6 §1 of the ECHR and the principle of State jurisdictional immunity. In fact, given that the latter is not *per se* incompatible with the right of access to court, the ECtHR is mainly called to establish if jurisdictional immunity was mandated by international law and whether domestic tribunals have correctly interpreted its content, so to 'reconcile general international

[11] ECtHR, Affaire de Geouffre de la Pradelle v. France, 12964/87, Judgment, 16 December 1992, para. 28.

[12] See ECtHR, Waite and Kennedy v. Germany, 26083/94, Judgment, 18 February 1999, para. 59.

[13] ECtHR, Waite and Kennedy v. Germany, 26083/94, Judgment, 18 February 1999, para. 59.

[14] From this perspective, it seems that the ECtHR applies to State jurisdictional immunity the very same reasoning to which it resorts when ascertaining whether a specific national law or policy pursues a legitimate aim. See, in this respect, ECtHR, Gillow v. The United Kingdom, 9063/80, Judgment, 23 October 1986, paras. 53–54; ECtHR, Campbell v. The United Kingdom, 3590/88, Judgment, 28 February 1993, paras. 39–41; ECtHR, Barthold v. Germany, 8734/79, Judgment, 25 February 1985, para. 51; ECtHR, Vogt v. Germany, 17851/91, Judgment, 2 September 1995, paras. 49–51; ECtHR, Cingilli Holding A.S. and Cingillioğlu v. Turkey, 31833/06 and 37538/06, Judgment, 21 July 2015, paras. 47–51.

[15] ECtHR, Al-Adsani v. United Kingdom, 35763/97, Judgment, 21 November 2001, para. 54; see also ECtHR, Fogarty v. United Kingdom, 37112/97, Judgment, 21 November 2001, para. 34; ECtHR, McElhinney v. United Kingdom, 31253/96, Judgment, 21 November 2001, para. 35.

[16] Voyakis (2003), p. 312. See also James and Others v. The United Kingdom, 8793/79, para. 51.

[17] ECtHR, Al-Adsani v. United Kingdom, 35763/97, Judgment, 21 November 2001, para. 56. Emphasis added.

law with the right of access to court'[18] by eventually safeguarding the individual right of the applicant.

Jurisdictional immunity in employment disputes was first addressed by the European Commission of Human Rights (the Commission) and later on by the ECtHR.[19] In the 1988 *Spaans* case,[20] the Commission was required to settle a dispute concerning an employee of the Iran-United States of America (US) Claims Tribunal based in The Hague, who was denied access to the Dutch courts for ascertaining the validity of the termination of his contract. The Commission, while concluding that the application was not admissible, since it was incompatible *ratione personae* with the ECHR, nonetheless maintained that, in so doing, the local courts had correctly applied a restraint of sovereignty to facilitate the aims of the international body.

Ten years later, in the *Waite and Kennedy* case, the Court found that it had jurisdiction in reviewing the compatibility between the general rules on immunities of international organisations and Article 6 §1 of the ECHR. As the case related to an employment dispute between the European Space Agency and two of its employees before a German court, the ECtHR concluded that a limitation of the right of access to court was necessary to avoid the 'thwart[ing of] the proper functioning of international organizations',[21] possibly resulting in the dilution of the international cooperation to which States are committed.

However, it was only in 2001 that the Court developed its jurisprudence on embassy employment disputes. In *Fogarty v. UK*, Mrs. Fogarty, an administrative assistant at the US embassy in London, had been fired on alleged sex discrimination. The applicant filed a case for unlawful dismissal with the North London Industrial Tribunal, which ascertained that she had been victim of sexual harassment. While the proceeding was still pending, Mrs. Fogarty applied for and obtained a 12-months job as administrative assistant at the same embassy. When the contract was about to expire, she unsuccessfully applied for two other positions and decided to lodge the case in the labour tribunal, on the ground that the refusal to employ her was due to the decision of the same court in the previous suit. In this case, pursuant to the 1978 UK State Immunity Act,[22] the US government claimed immunity from jurisdiction. When Mrs. Fogarty was informed that she could not seek remedy in the domestic judicial system, she applied to the Court for an alleged breach of Article 6 §1 of the ECHR. It admitted that whenever the granting of State immunity is consistent with

[18] Bonafe' (2010), p. 64. See also ECtHR, Al-Adsani v. United Kingdom, 35763/97, Judgment, 21 November 2001, para. 53; ECtHR, Fogarty v. United Kingdom, 37112/97, Judgment, 21 November 2001, para. 33; ECtHR, McElhinney v. United Kingdom, 31253/96, Judgment, 21 November 2001, para. 34.

[19] See Klerk (1996), pp. 35–46. The only exception is ECtHR, Pellegrin v. France, 28541/95, Judgment, 8 December 1999.

[20] See European Commission of Human Rights, Spaans v. The Netherlands, 12516/86, Decision on Admissibility, 12 December 1988.

[21] ECtHR, Waite and Kennedy v. Germany, 26083/94, Judgment, 18 February 1999, para. 72.

[22] State Immunity Act 1978, UK Public General Acts, 1978 c. 33.

the principles of international law, no violation of Article 6 might occur,[23] and that 'there appears to be a trend in international and comparative law towards limiting State immunity in respect of employment-related disputes. However, where the proceedings relate to employment in a foreign mission or embassy, international practice is divided on the question whether State immunity continues to apply and, if it does so apply, whether it covers disputes relating to contracts of all staff or only more senior members of the mission'.[24] The Court, hence, concluded that there had not been any breach of the right of access to court, since the recruitment of staff relates to the organisational duties of a foreign country in respect to which no relaxation of the immunity rule could be found. In other terms, as further elaborated in the concurring opinion of Judges Caflisch, Costa and Vajić, the ECtHR found that the UK did not act beyond the limits imposed by any recognised international standard, and thus it lawfully exercised its margin of appreciation in limiting the access to court to Mrs. Fogarty.

3 *Cudak v. Lithuania*: The UNJISP as a Parameter to Assess State Jurisdictional Immunity

From 2010 the ECtHR delivered some judgements which reverted its previous findings with regard to the correct determination of the scope and content of State jurisdictional immunity in the field of embassy employment disputes. The first of them related to Mrs. Cudak, a Lithuanian national who worked for the Polish embassy in Vilnius as secretary and switchboard operator, according to the duties specified under Article 1 of her contract of employment. The applicant alleged to have suffered sexual harassment by one of her male colleagues—also resulting in psychological disorders—as the Ombudsman later on ascertained. Mrs. Cudak was no longer authorised to enter the premises of the embassy and was finally dismissed for failing to go to work. The applicant did not request reinstatement by the local courts, but she only asked for compensation for wrongful dismissal. As the Polish plea of immunity was upheld, she was deprived of any effective judicial remedy and decided to apply to ECtHR. Having rejected the responding State's argument that Mrs. Cudak could have instituted proceedings before the Polish courts, the Strasbourg judges applied the legitimacy and proportionality test to evaluate the alleged violation of Article 6 §1.[25] The Court did not question the legitimacy of the granting of State jurisdictional immunity[26] and once again admitted that there was a trend under international and comparative law towards limiting State immunity in respect

[23] See ECtHR, Fogarty v. United Kingdom, 37112/97, Judgment, 21 November 2001, paras. 32–33.
[24] ECtHR, Fogarty v. United Kingdom, 37112/97, Judgment, 21 November 2001, para. 37.
[25] See ECtHR, Cudak v. Lithuania, 15869/02, Judgment, 23 March 2010, paras. 60–61.
[26] Ibid.

of employment-related disputes.[27] Such convincement was based on the recent evolutions of the State practice and was also testified by the adoption of the UNJISP. It is precisely on its relevant provisions and the Draft Articles on Jurisdictional Immunities prepared by the ILC, on which the former is modelled, that the ECtHR developed its arguments. The Court recalled that the most pertinent norm in the field is Article 11 of this convention—on contracts of employment—which is the outcome of the mediation between two opposing needs: while, in fact, each foreign State is understandably interested in preserving its organisational autonomy and in managing the labour relations with the employees of the receiving country by applying its own national legislation, the latter is willing to retain jurisdiction in disputes concerning its nationals employed in foreign embassies.

In line with the restrictive approach to immunity pursued by the UNJISP,[28] the first paragraph of Article 11 reads that State immunity cannot be invoked in disputes relating to a contract of employment between the foreign country and the national of the receiving State for a job to be performed in its territory.[29] Having set the general rule, the following paragraph is devoted to the identification of six exceptions to this general rule under which State jurisdictional immunity is restored.

The first one, letter (a),[30] acknowledges the admissibility of the plea of immunity when the employee has been recruited to perform functions of governmental authority. According to the Commentary of the ILC to the Draft Articles on Jurisdictional Immunities (the Commentary), it was intended to apply to 'private secretaries, code clerks, interpreters, translators, and other persons entrusted with functions related to State security or basic interests of the State':[31] the same Gerhard Hafner, Chairman of the United Nations Working Group which drafted the final version of the UNJISP, excluded that the provision applied to administrative, technical and service staff.[32]

As far as the reach of governmental authority is concerned, in *Vilho Eskelinen v. Finland*,[33] the ECtHR admitted that the right of access to court should always be granted unless two conditions are satisfied: 'firstly, the State in its national law must have expressly excluded access to a court for the post or category of staff in question. Secondly, the exclusion must be justified on objective grounds in the State's interest'.[34] In other terms, 'the mere fact that the applicant is in a sector or

---

[27] Ibid., paras. 63 and 66.

[28] See Stewart (2005), p. 194.

[29] Article 11 §1 reads: 'Unless otherwise agreed between the States concerned, a State cannot invoke immunity from jurisdiction before a court of another State which is otherwise competent in a proceeding which relates to a contract of employment between the State and an individual for work performed or to be performed, in whole or in part, in the territory of that other State'.

[30] Article 11 §1 (a) reads: 'Paragraph 1 does not apply if: (a) the employee has been recruited to perform particular functions in the exercise of governmental Authority'.

[31] Draft Articles on Jurisdictional Immunities of States and Their Property with Commentaries (1991), p. 42. See also Stewart (2005), p. 210; Gaja (1991), p. 921.

[32] See Hafner (2010), paras. 26–27.

[33] ECtHR, Vilho Eskelinen and others v. Finland, 63235/00, Judgment, 19 April 2007.

[34] Ibid., para. 62.

department which participates in the exercise of power conferred by public law is not in itself decisive'.[35] The Strasbourg judges, hence, excluded that the mere special bound of trust and loyalty was sufficient to pose a limit to Article 6 §1[36] and also held that the *onus probandi* of the exercise of governmental functions rests with the respondent: it is for the Contracting Party to satisfactorily demonstrate that the right of access to court finds a limitation in its own domestic legal system on the ground of the job of the applicant and that the restraint is based on the existence of such a national interest to require a peculiar relation of trust between the foreign State and the employee.[37]

Letter (b) of the second paragraph of Article 11 foresees the restoration of the plea of immunity whenever the employee is '(i) a diplomatic agent, as defined in the Vienna Convention on Diplomatic Relations of 1961; (ii) a consular officer, as defined in the Vienna Convention on Consular Relations of 1963; (iii) a member of the diplomatic staff of a permanent mission to an international organization or of a special mission, or is recruited to represent a State at an international conference; or (iv) any other person enjoying diplomatic immunity'.

This exception has understandably generated interpretative issues with peculiar regard to (b) (iv) on 'any other person enjoying diplomatic immunity'. From this formulation, it follows that, for the plea of immunity to be restored, it is first necessary to ascertain whether the individual who initiates a proceeding before a Court enjoys diplomatic immunity under general international law, as codified by the 1961 Vienna Convention on Diplomatic Relations.[38] Under its Article 37, immunity varies according to the category of worker. In particular, members of the diplomatic staff, including those having administrative and technical functions, who are not national or permanent residents of the receiving States, are entitled to immunity.[39] By jointly reading Article 37 of the Vienna Convention and Article 11 §2 (b) (iv) of the UNJISP, one could *prima facie* conclude that, when it comes to

[35] ECtHR, Vilho Eskelinen and others v. Finland, 63235/00, Judgment, 19 April 2007.

[36] See ECtHR, Pellegrin v. France, 28541/95, Judgment, 8 December 1999, para. 66.

[37] See Lanciotti and Panetta (2012), p. 349.

[38] Vienna Convention on Diplomatic Relations, 500 UNTS 95 (entered into force on 24 April 1964). Article 37 §2 and 3 of the Vienna Convention on Diplomatic Relations states: '2.Members of the administrative and technical staff of the mission, together with members of their families forming part of their respective households, shall, if they are not nationals of or permanently resident in the receiving State, enjoy the privileges and immunities specified in articles 29 to 35, except that the immunity from civil and administrative jurisdiction of the receiving State specified in paragraph 1 of article 31 shall not extend to acts performed outside the course of their duties. They shall also enjoy the privileges specified in article 36, paragraph 1, in respect of articles imported at the time of first installation. 3.Members of the service staff of the mission who are not nationals of or permanently resident in the receiving State shall enjoy immunity in respect of acts performed in the course of their duties, exemption from dues and taxes on the emoluments they receive by reason of their employment and the exemption contained in article 33'.

[39] See Court of Justice of the European Union, Mahamdia v. Algeria, C-154/11, Judgment, 19 July 2012, para. 15. Germany confers immunity on all members of foreign diplomatic mission, notwithstanding their nationality.

employment-related disputes, a plea of immunity could bar proceedings initiated by the workers of the embassy having the prescribed requisites, and thus enjoying diplomatic immunity.

It is nonetheless to be acknowledged that such conclusion would run contrary to the general spirit and scope of the UNJISP—aiming at restricting State immunity—as well as its *traveaux préparatoires*. Indeed, when drafters had to determine whether a State should be entitled to immunity in employment disputes regarding the technical and administrative staff of an embassy, they denied such possibility 'so as to keep to a minimum the range of employment proceedings involving nationals or permanent residents of the forum State (and, indeed, of third States) in respect of which a foreign employer State would remain immune'.[40]

If this were not the case—and so immunity was to be recognised in suits concerning diplomats and administrative personnel alike—after all there would be little purpose in making a distinction between the two categories, since—should an employment dispute arise—the sole fact that an individual enjoys diplomatic immunity would restore the plea of the State. For this reason, it seems that the exception referred to in (b) (iv) is not to be read as referring to the staff, but rather to the eventual residual category of people performing diplomatic functions who have not been included in the same provision.

This line of reasoning has also been upheld in the recent *Benkharbouche* case decided by the English courts.[41] The dispute at stake dealt with a cleaner and a cook, members of the diplomatic staff of the Sudanese and Libyan diplomatic missions in London, who were third State nationals, and thus entitled to diplomatic immunity under Article 37 of the Vienna Convention. This could, in turn, have triggered State jurisdictional immunity. However, in determining the case, the English Court of Appeal recognised that the combined reading of the two conventions could result in outcomes which are clearly in contrast with the aim of the UNJISP. In particular, it held that it cannot be subsumed that all members of the non-diplomatic staff are included under Article 11 §2 (b) (iv) of the UNJISP, since—for the reasons which have been presented—it 'would be inconsistent with the scheme, purpose and *travaux préparatoires* of that provision taken as a whole'.[42]

The English Supreme Court, which in turn analysed the dispute, went further in stating that if Article 11 §2 (b) (iv) was to be interpreted as admitting the plea of jurisdictional immunity in employment disputes regarding the administrative and technical staff of the embassy, it would be 'legislative rather than declaratory of existing international law. It may one day bind states qua treaty. It may come to represent customary international law if and when the Convention attracts sufficient

---

[40] Foakes and O'Keefe (2013), p. 201.

[41] See United Kingdom Court of Appeal (civil division), Benkharbouche and Janah v. Embassy of the Republic of Sudan, A2/2013/3062, Judgment, 5 February 2015.

[42] ECtHR, Fogarty v. United Kingdom, 37112/97, Judgment, 21 November 2001, para. 38. See also Pavoni (2018), p. 274.

support. But it does not do either of these things as matters presently stand'.[43] It also added that 'in a practical sense, it might be thought reasonable that a contract between a State and one of its own nationals should have to be litigated in the courts of that State under its laws, but unreasonable that the same should apply to locally recruited staff'.[44]

The third exception to Article 11 §1 is referred to in §2 (c),[45] relating to disputes whose subject matter is the recruitment of an employee or renewal of a contract of employment. As recalled in the Commentary, this provision 'is designed to confirm the existing practice in support of the rule of immunity in the exercise of the discretionary power of appointment or non-appointment by the State of an individual to any official post or employment position'.[46] However, Article 11 §2 (c) does not prevent employees from seeking redress for any damage they could have suffered as a consequence of a wrongful dismissal: this has also been largely confirmed by the ECtHR's jurisprudence so far.

Article 11 §2 (d) introduces a rather controversial exception: foreign countries can plead immunity on the ground that the proceeding interferes with the security interests of the employer State as determined by its competent authorities.[47] The interests referred to are only ambiguously detailed in the understanding attached to the UNJISP, which holds that 'to the security interests of the employer State is intended primarily to address matters of national security and the security of diplomatic missions and consular posts'.[48] This entails a certain degree of interpretative autonomy that should be in any case carefully contextualised within the restrictive approach to immunity pursued by Article 11 of this convention.

With regard to the last two exceptions listed at letter (e) and (f), according to the former[49] immunity can be invoked whenever the employee is a national of the employer State and is not a permanent resident in the State of forum at the time when the proceeding is instituted. In other terms, any employment dispute, which arises between a State and its nationals, although in a foreign country, shall be

---

[43] United Kingdom Supreme Court, Benkharbouche v. Secretary of State for Foreign and Commonwealth Affairs, Judgment, [2017] UKSC 62, 18 October 2017, para. 72.

[44] Ibid., para. 59.

[45] Article 11 §2 (c) reads: 'Paragraph 1 does not apply if: [...](c) the subject-matter of the proceeding is the recruitment, renewal of employment or reinstatement of an individual'.

[46] Draft Articles on Jurisdictional Immunities of States and Their Property with Commentaries (1991), p. 13.

[47] Article 11 §2 (d) states: 'Paragraph 1 does not apply if: [...] (d) the subject-matter of the proceeding is the dismissal or termination of employment of an individual and, as determined by the head of State, the head of Government or the Minister for Foreign Affairs of the employer State, such a proceeding would interfere with the security interests of that State'.

[48] United Nations Convention on Jurisdictional Immunities of States and their Property, Annex to the Convention, Understanding with respect to Article 11 of the Convention.

[49] Article 11 §2 (e) reads: 'Paragraph 1 does not apply if: [...] (e) the employee is a national of the employer State at the time when the proceeding is instituted, unless this person has the permanent residence in the State of the forum'.

decided by the competent judicial authorities of the sending country, since 'the State of the forum lacks the essential ground for claiming priority for the exercise of its applicable labour law'.[50] A similar provision is also contained in Article 5 §2 (a) of the Basel Convention (which was used by the ILC as a reference for its Draft Articles on Jurisdictional Immunities)[51] to restore the plea of immunity when the individual is a national of the employing State.[52]

Finally, according to letter (f)[53] immunity can be pleaded if the employer and the employee have so agreed in light of policy considerations, which would confer exclusive jurisdiction to the forum State's courts.[54]

As mentioned, when deciding the *Cudak* case, the ECtHR made extensive reference to the UNJISP, the Draft Articles on Jurisdictional Immunities and its Commentary. In particular, relying on a passage from the latter which holds that the norms contained in the Draft are consistent with the emerging trend in the State practice,[55] the Court concluded that its Article 11—on which the same provision of the UNJISP was elaborated—applied under customary international law. As Lithuania had not ratified the UNJISP, it also added that 'it is a well-established principle of international law that, even if a State has not ratified a treaty, it may be bound by one of its provisions in so far as that provision reflects customary international law, either codifying it or forming a new customary rule'.[56]

Without further elaborating on the assumed correspondence between the texts of the Draft Articles on Jurisdictional Immunities and of the UNJISP, the Court concluded that 'it is possible to affirm that Article 11 of the ILC's 1991 Draft Articles, [...] applies to the respondent State under customary international law'.[57] As a consequence, in deciding whether Article 6 of the ECHR had been breached, it had to evaluate if the exceptions provided by the second paragraph of Article 11

---

[50] Draft Articles on Jurisdictional Immunities of States and Their Property with Commentaries (1991), p. 16.

[51] It shall also be noticed that the date from which the nationality is relevant for the plea of State immunity is coherent with that identified by the International Court of Justice, Jurisdictional immunities of the State, Judgment, Reports 2012, p. 99, in which it recognized that 'the compatibility of an act with international law can be determined only by reference to the law in force at the time when the act occurred' (para. 58).

[52] ECSI, Article 5 §2 (a).

[53] Article 11 §2 (f) reads: 'Paragraph 1 does not apply if: [...] (f) the employer State and the employee have otherwise agreed in writing, subject to any considerations of public policy conferring on the courts of the State of the forum exclusive jurisdiction by reason of the subject-matter of the proceeding'.

[54] See Fox and Webb (2013), p. 459.

[55] See Draft Articles on Jurisdictional Immunities of States and Their Property with Commentaries (1991), p. 44.

[56] ECtHR, Cudak v. Lithuania, 15869/02, Judgment, 23 March 2010, para. 66. By referring to the dictum of the International Court of Justice in North Sea Continental Shelf the ECtHR maintained that although Lithuania was not a Party to the UN Convention, it had neither voted against its adoption by the General Assembly of the United Nations.

[57] ECtHR, Cudak v. Lithuania, 15869/02, Judgment, 23 March 2010, para. 67.

found application in the case at stake. It concluded that Mrs. Cudak was neither a diplomatic agent nor a consular officer, had not the Polish nationality and did not perform any function connected to the exercise of governmental authority. In particular, with regard to this last requirement, the Court recalled that Mrs. Cudak was a switchboard operator, whose main duties were recording telephone conversations, typing, photocopying and assisting with the organisation of events. It thus found that Lithuania had failed to preserve a reasonable relationship of proportionality in granting immunity to Poland and that accordingly Article 6 §1 had been breached.[58]

4 Towards Restrictive Immunity: The Court's Case-Law from *Cudak* on

The legal arguments developed in *Cudak* to determine a breach of Article 6 §1 for the failure of domestic courts to correctly apply jurisdictional immunity as mandated under international law is a model to which the ECtHR resorted in its following case-law on embassy employment disputes. Its most salient feature lies in declaring a violation of Article 6 of the ECHR for lack of proportionality only when none of the exceptions enumerated in Article 11 §2 of the UN Convention—which in the Court's understanding apply under customary international law—find application.

This was the case in *Sabeh el Leil v. France*.[59] The suit concerned a French national, Mr. Sabeh el Leil, working since 1980 as accountant at the Kuwaiti embassy in Paris and also unofficially holding the position of staff representative. In 2000, he was dismissed on the ground that Kuwait needed to restructure the embassy's departments and hence lodged the case in the Paris Employment Tribunal asking for compensation. It found that the claimant was entitled to reparation, but since Mr. Sabeh el Leil disagreed with the awarded sum, he appealed the decision. The plea of immunity raised by Kuwait was considered admissible under the general principles of international law by the Court of Appeal and the Court of Cassation and the claimant finally applied to the ECtHR for an alleged violation of Article 6 §1 of the ECHR. The Court first clarified that 'it is possible to affirm that the provisions of the 2004 Convention apply to the respondent State under customary international law'.[60] Indeed, as far as contracts of employment were concerned, France had not behaved as a persistent objector,[61] and had also signed the UN Convention, whose ratification procedures were ongoing. In applying the test developed in *Cudak*, the Court particularly focused on the exception of Article 11 §2 (d), relied upon also in the domestic proceeding. It highlighted that although the applicant's functions

[58] Ibid., para. 74.

[59] ECtHR, Sabeh El Leil v. France, 34869/05, Judgment, 29 June 2011.

[60] Ibid., para. 58.

[61] See Marchisio (2017), p. 61.

entailed wider responsibilities if compared to those of Mrs. Cudak, the proceeding was not at risk of colliding with the Kuwaiti security interests: in fact, nor the Head of State, nor the Head of Government or the Minister for Foreign Affairs had ever claimed the existence of such risk. The Court assumed, without offering any explanation for such restrictive choice that 'the exceptions enumerated therein [in Article 11] [. . .] must be strictly interpreted',[62] and it concluded that the competent French judiciary authorities had failed to apply State jurisdictional immunity in the correct way, so to preserve a reasonable relationship of proportionality.[63]

In 2016 the ECtHR dealt with two other cases: *Radunović and others v. Montenegro*[64] and *Naku v. Lithuania and Sweden*.[65] The three applicants in *Radunović* were employees at the US embassy in Montenegro. Two of them worked as security guards and a third one as a protocol specialist and translator, and they all had Montenegrin nationality. Between 2009 and 2012 they were informed of their dismissal and instituted separate proceedings claiming compensation and (only two of them) reinstatement.

The Court of First Instance in Podgorica highlighted that reinstatement was a very sensitive issue that attains to the organization of a foreign State and it accordingly upheld the US plea of immunity. When they lodged constitutional appeals, the Court concluded that, in granting immunity to the US, there had been no violation of Article 6 §1 of the ECHR. Hence, deprived on any judicial remedy, the applicants filed the case in the ECtHR. It maintained that 'Article 6 §1 of the Convention must be construed in light of the principle of the rule of law, one of the fundamental aspects of which is the principle of legal certainty, which requires that all litigants should have an effective judicial remedy enabling them to assert their civil rights'.[66] With regard to the criterion of proportionality, the Court stated that 'reinstatement falls under an exception which allows for an application of the rule of immunity. However, [. . .] it does not prevent an employee from bringing action against the employer State in the State of the forum to seek redress for damage arising from wrongful dismissal'.[67] With respect to the request for compensation, the Court maintained that by rejecting the applicants' claim on the ground of State jurisdictional immunity, the Montenegrin authorities failed to stick to the customary norms codified by Article 11 of the UNJISP. In particular, as none of the exceptions provided in the second paragraph of the Article were of a relevance for the case

[62] ECtHR, Sabeh El Leil v. France, 34869/05, Judgment, 29 June 2011, para. 66. This approach has been questioned by Pavoni (2018), p. 274.

[63] ECtHR, Sabeh El Leil v. France, 34869/05, Judgment, 29 June 2011, para. 67.

[64] ECtHR, Radunović and others v. Montenegro, 45197/13, 53000/13 and 73404/13, Judgment, 25 October 2016.

[65] ECtHR, Naku v. Lithuania and Sweden, 26126/07, Judgment, 8 November 2016.

[66] ECtHR, Radunović and others v. Montenegro, 45197/13, 53000/13 and 73404/13, Judgment, 25 October 2016, para. 61.

[67] Ibid., para. 76.

under review, the ECtHR concluded that the local courts did not ensure a reasonable relationship of proportionality.[68]

Only few days later, the fourth section of the Court dealt with the case of Mrs. Naku, a Lithuanian national who worked as receptionist and translator, later promoted to cultural, information and press officer, at the Swedish embassy in Vilnius. In 2005 a Swedish diplomat, Mr. T.S. held the post of counsellor for cultural affairs and became the superior of Mrs. Naku. After some quarrels on the respective competences, the ambassador sent the applicant a letter of caution, stating that—due to the difficulties she encountered in cooperating with the rest of the personnel—she was given 2 days to resign. Consequently, when the day after she went to work, Mrs. Naku was not allowed to enter the building. In the following days, the applicant suffered an ischemic neurological deficit and took sick leave. On the ground that the embassy did not receive any sick leave certificate from 5 to 30 December 2005, she was finally dismissed. Before the request of reinstatement and compensation, the local courts upheld the plea of immunity raised by Sweden, since 'from the title of the applicant's job description (head of culture and information projects) it was already possible to conclude that the duties which were assigned to her contributed to a certain extent to the Kingdom of Sweden's implementation of its sovereign functions'.[69] Lacking access to domestic remedies, Mrs. Naku applied to the ECtHR. The Court did not find any reason to deviate from the test elaborated in *Cudak*: it recalled that the applicant was required to act in consultation with the diplomatic personnel and concluded that 'by plainly considering that everyone who worked in a diplomatic representation of a foreign State [. . .] by virtue of that employment alone in one way or another contributed to the meeting of sovereign goals of a represented State, and [. . .] dismissing the applicant's claim without giving relevant and sufficient reasons that the applicant in the instant case in reality performed specific duties in the exercise of governmental authority, the Lithuanian courts impaired the very essence of the applicant's right of access to a court'.[70]

Finally, early in 2019 the Court also decided the *Ndayegamiye-Mporamazina v. Switzerland* case.[71] The applicant, a national of the Republic of Burundi living in France, worked as secretary at the Burundi Permanent Mission to the United Nations in Geneva. While the ambassador was absent, she also used to manage the current business of the mission under the approval of the government. Without any further clarification, in 2007 Burundi decided not to renovate her contract of employment. As Article 8 of such contract established that any employment dispute had to be settled by Switzerland, the applicant initiated proceedings before the local courts. Despite the inconsistent decisions of the various tribunals, the Court of Justice finally accepted the governmental plea of immunity, recognizing—as also held by

[68] Ibid., para. 81.

[69] ECtHR, Naku v. Lithuania and Sweden, 26126/07, Judgment, 8 November 2016, para. 38.

[70] Ibid., para. 95.

[71] ECtHR, Ndayegamiye-Mporamazina v. Switzerland, 16874/12, Judgment, 5 February 2019, para. 66.

Burundi—that the applicant could still lodge the case in the judiciary of her country of origin.

Questioning the effectiveness of such remedy, the claimant applied to the ECtHR, alleging a violation of Article 6 §1. In deciding the case, the Court took into account three main elements. First, it considered that—although not entered into force yet—Switzerland had ratified the UNJISP. Second, the Court took note of the applicant's claim that—through Article 8 of her contract of employment —Burundi had waived its jurisdictional immunity in case of disputes. Lastly, the Court took note of the different wording of Article 11 (2) (e) in the Draft Articles on Jurisdictional Immunities and in the final version of the UN Convention, but it held that such exception nonetheless found application under general international law. Since the applicant was clearly a national of Burundi at the time of the proceeding and had no permanent residence in the forum State, 'la Cour est d'avis que les tribunaux suisses ne se sont pas écartés des principes de droit international généralement reconnus en matière d'immunité des États et que l'on ne saurait considérer la restriction au droit d'accès à un tribunal comme disproportionnée en l'espèce.'[72] Hence, the Court concluded that no violation of Article 6 §1 of the ECHR had taken place.[73]

5 The ECtHR and State Jurisdictional Immunity: Open Issues on Article 11 of the UNJISP

Generally speaking, the recalled jurisprudence of the ECtHR seems consistent with the decisions of most European national courts insomuch as they have—with different methods and arguments—mainly endorsed a restrictive interpretation of State jurisdictional immunity in embassy employment disputes.

However, there are two main issues emerging from the Court's decisions that, legally speaking, seem questionable.

The first one, which also underwent criticism by many commentators and by the judges of the highest jurisdictions in Europe,[74] relates to the asserted *in toto*

[72] Ibid., para. 66.

[73] It shall be noted that in this circumstance the Court has not extensively elaborated on the clause included in article eight of the applicant's contract of employment. For such clause to take effects, under Article 7 of the UNJISP, it is required that the willingness of the government of Burundi to waive immunity should be clearly expressed. This was not the case, as reflected in the very different conclusions reached by the Switzerland courts. However, the Court only relied on such discrepancy to dismiss the relative argument of the applicant, without offering any additional explanation.

[74] In her concurring opinion in Naku, Judge Motoc also admitted that 'The Cudak decision was an example of the ECtHR applying international law without really assessing whether it is appropriate to completely defer legal matters to this sphere. In this light, it is also argued that if the ECtHR had decided to take account of the international norms, it would also have been useful to examine the origin, quality and reliability of the customary norms in question'. (ECtHR, Naku v. Lithuania and Sweden, 26126/07, Judgment, 8 November 2016, p. 42.) See also Babu (2007), pp. 469–502; Köhler (2004), pp. 191–215; Fox (1995), pp. 97–176; Pavoni (2007), pp. 211–223.

correspondence of Article 11 of the UNJISP to customary international law. In this respect, in the *Benkharbouche* case, the English Supreme Court considered that the '[European] Court [of Human Rights]'s assertion on the general character of Article 11 have simply served to sow confusion'.[75] Similarly, the Advocate General of the European Court of Justice Mengozzi in the *Mahamdia v. Algeria* case held that the reasoning of the Court regarding the breach of Article 6 of the ECHR in embassy employment disputes failed to offer 'a [...] convincing answer'.[76]

As highlighted, according to the ECtHR, the provisions contained in Article 11 apply under customary law since they 'appear to be consistent with the emerging trend in the recent legislative and treaty practice of a growing number of States'.[77] However, the same Commentary to which the Court refers does not provide full evidence of this kind, since it only recalls a limited State practice, mostly related to Italy, the Netherlands and Belgium and mainly referred to the exception in Article 11 (2) (c), on the renewal of a contract or reinstatement of an employee.[78] Nor, in asserting the customary nature of Article 11, the ECtHR makes any reference to its material (*repetitio facti)* and psychological (*opinio juris sive necessitates*) elements.[79] In particular, it does not conduct any autonomous investigation on the State practice with regard to embassy employment disputes to assess the general character of the rule in question. Equally, it also seems to disregard the two requirements that the International Court of Justice (ICJ) identified in the *North Sea Continental Shelf* case to find that a certain treaty rule has attained the status of a customary norm.[80] Indeed, the UNJISP cannot be said to have gained a very widespread and representative participation nor the practice developed since its adoption has been extensive and virtually uniform and has occurred in such a way to show a general recognition that a rule of law or legal obligation is involved.

---

[75] United Kingdom Supreme Court, Benkharbouche v. Secretary of State for Foreign and Commonwealth Affairs, Judgment, [2017] UKSC 62, 18 October 2017, para. 29.

[76] Mahamdia v. Algeria, Opinion of Advocate General Mengozzi, 24 May 2012, para. 25.

[77] Draft Articles on Jurisdictional Immunities of States and Their Property with Commentaries (1991), p. 44. See also ECtHR, Cudak v. Lithuania, 15869/02, Judgment, 23 March 2010, paras. 63 and 66; ECtHR, Sabeh El Leil v. France, 34869/05, Judgment, 29 June 2011, paras. 57–58; ECtHR, Radunović and others v. Montenegro, 45197/13, 53000/13 and 73404/13, Judgment, 25 October 2016, paras. 69 and 73; ECtHR, Naku v. Lithuania and Sweden, 26126/07, Judgment, 8 November 2016, para. 89; ECtHR, Ndayegamiye-Mporamazina v. Switzerland, 16874/12, Judgment, 5 February 2019, paras. 53 and 61.

[78] See, for instance, Italian Court of Cassation, Console generale britannico in Napoli v. Ferraino, Case No. 283, Judgment, 17 January 1986 (the text is reported in ItYIL 7:298–299); The Hague Sub-District Court, M.K. v. Republic of Turkey, Case No. R 2569, Judgment, 1 August 1985 (the text is reported in NYIL 19:435–438); and Tribunal du Travail de Bruxelles, Castanheira v. Office commercial du Portugal, Judgment, 1 February 1980 (the text is reported in RBDI 19(2):339–368). For an overview of the Italian case-law in the field, see Pavoni (2008), pp. 29–44.

[79] See Treves (2006), paras. 7–9.

[80] International Court of Justice, North Sea Continental Shelf Cases, Judgment, 20 February 1969, ICJ Report 1969, para. 73.

In line with a method widely adopted by the ICJ in its judgments,[81] known as assertion, the Court has shared the former's attitude to mainly rely on codification conventions, draft articles and their comments adopted by the ILC, as evidence of the customary character of a certain norm.[82] While it is accepted that assertion has often supplanted the most traditional inductive and deductive approaches, the ECtHR should nonetheless have used particular care in distinguishing the fields in which the ILC operated a codification or progressive development of the rules on State jurisdictional immunity. In particular, to fully assess the existence of a customary norm of international law, it should have at least demonstrated that the criteria national courts employ to limit their jurisdiction *vis-à-vis* the plea of State jurisdictional immunity are homogenous and constitute a general practice.

By contrast, as more exhaustive studies in the field have demonstrated,[83] there are at least four different criteria used by national courts when deciding on the granting of immunity in embassy employment disputes.[84]

The first one takes into account the activities carried out by the employees and their linkage to the exercise of sovereign authority. Because of the incompatible positions taken by States during the drafting of the UNJISP, this convention does not mention the circumstances and the conditions under which the duties performed by the employee can be considered of a sovereign character. This standard is certainly the most used by national courts, even though some countries—like Austria and Italy up to 2014[85]—considered it irrelevant excepting for the circumstances when diplomatic or consular functions were at stake. The uncertainties arising from this criterion as a guidance to decide on the granting of State immunity have been highlighted by a large part of the doctrine,[86] which admitted that it is always possible to argue that every employee works for the fulfilment of the institutional aims of a State.

The second criterion emphasizes the place where the employee performs his or her functions. In fact, if the applicant works in an embassy, consulate or in a military base, the acceptance of the respondent's plea of immunity can change accordingly.[87] This is not the case for most of the common law countries, which extend

[81] See the International Court of Justice, Jurisdictional immunities of the State, Judgment, Reports 2012, p. 99, paras. 64–65.

[82] On the methods used by the International Court of Justice to identify the norms belonging to customary international law, with particular regard to assertion, see Tomka (2013), pp. 195–215; Alvarez-Jimenez (2011), pp. 681–712; Iovane (2018), pp. 2–23; Talmon (2015), pp. 417–443; Petersen (2017), pp. 357–385; Roberts (2001), pp. 757–791; Worster (2014), pp. 445–521. For a similar trend in the identification of customary law by some other international courts, see Van Den Herik (2016), pp. 230–252; Tan (2018), pp. 92–110; Casolari (2008), pp. 72–160; Besson (2017), pp. 106–129; Giannelli (2012), pp. 93–110; Ziemele (2013), pp. 243–252.

[83] See Yang (2012).

[84] See Ryngaert and Hora Siccama (2018), pp. 1–25.

[85] See Rossi (2019), p. 23.

[86] See Conforti (2018), p. 277; Cannizzaro (2016), p. 349; Cassese (2017), p. 121.

[87] See Garnett (1997), p. 81.

jurisdictional immunity to disputes concerning all the employees of foreign States[88] since—as held in the *Sengupta* case before the United Kingdom Employment Appeal Tribunal—they all 'participate in the public acts of the foreign sovereign'.[89] In the same vein, the finding that the actual employer is not a State but one of its agencies can result in the immunity not to apply. This conclusion was reached, *inter alia*, by an Italian court in the case of a citizen employed as a cashier at the recreation center created by the United States of America Navy in Naples. Since the claimant worked for the internal services of the club, had no military responsibility and was not carrying out activities of a sovereign nature, the US was prevented from invoking immunity.[90]

The *petitum* is the third criterion taken into account by national courts. In particular, and in line with the UNJISP, there is a trend to uphold the plea of immunity in disputes concerning reinstatement or renewal of a contract of employment, whilst it is generally rejected for compensation claims.[91]

Finally, the nationality of the worker can be of a certain relevance. If in some legal orders—like that of the US—it does not seem to be discriminating,[92] in the European continent this criterion has also been included in the Basel Convention.[93]

Before such a variety of approaches considered by domestic courts, it is legitimate to wonder whether a clear-cut customary rule on the granting of immunity in the field of employment disputes does exist and requires the forum State to exercise or to abstain from exercising its jurisdiction, in accordance with the exceptions mentioned in Article 11 §2. Some of them, as it is the case for Article 11 §2 (b) (iv) and (d) could even end up recognizing to foreign countries a degree of immunity which is higher than that currently granted by domestic courts, as the *Benkharbouche* case showed.[94]

The customary nature of the rules in the field of embassy employment disputes are thus far less clear than the ECtHR maintained from *Cudak* on. All that can be inferred is that Article 11 certainly corresponds to customary law in the kernel of State jurisdictional immunity, when referring to disputes involving diplomatic and consular personnel *stricto sensu* or when the claims relate to the recruitment, renewal of employment or reinstatement of a worker.

The second arguable issue emerging from the Court's jurisprudence, which is also evidently connected to the first, is the alleged correspondence of the Draft

---

[88] See Garnett (2005), pp. 705–718.

[89] United Kingdom Employment Appeal Tribunal, Sengupta v. Republic of India, Judgment, 17 November 1982, pp. 228–229.

[90] See Tribunal of Naples, Novaco v. United States Navy, Judgment, 2 December 1957 (the text of the decision is reported in RivDirInt 41(3):452).

[91] See Rossi (2019), p. 25.

[92] See Yang (2012), p. 162.

[93] ECSI, Article 5 §2 (a).

[94] In this regard, see, among the others, Köhler (2004), p. 215. However, other authors, like Garnett (2015), p. 796, hold that the conclusion 'that Article 11 (2) (a) of the United Nations Convention represents customary international law is correct'.

Articles on Jurisdictional Immunities to the final version of the UN Convention. Indeed, the ECtHR seems at least dismissive of the existing divergences between the two documents, which do not allow for an overlapping reading.[95]

This is particularly true for Article 11 of the UNJISP, which gave rise to prolonged debates in the various stages of the negotiations.[96] It is known that the topic of contracts of employment was included among the five outstanding substantive issues in respect to which States were in disagreement and which had to be reconsidered by the Working group of the ILC. In particular, the most evident divergences relate to letter (a) and (e) of the article of the UNJISP, which do not find correspondence in the Draft Articles on Jurisdictional Immunities.

As for letter (a), while the final text refers to an employee recruited to perform 'functions in the exercise of governmental authority', the correspondent ILC provision dealt with 'functions *closely* related to the exercise of governmental authority'. Arguably, the different wording implies that also the administrative and technical staff would be prevented from suing, with the consequence that the provision of the UNISP enlarges the degree of immunity enjoyed by the foreign State.

Similarly, letter (e) on the requirement of nationality has been differently addressed during the negotiations. Any reference to the permanent residence of the individual—as endorsed by the Basel Convention—was considered discriminatory and thus not included in the Draft Articles on Jurisdictional Immunities, which in this respect was instead modelled on the common law practice.

This is but one example of the evidence that the UNJISP is the outcome of mediations and revisions on the ILC text, which do not allow—contrary to what the Court held—an interchangeable reading of Article 11 of the Draft Articles on Jurisdictional Immunities and the same provision of the UN Convention.

6 From the ECtHR to Domestic Courts: The Ripple Effects of the Court's Case-Law

The competence of the Court is related to the observance of the engagements undertaken by the Contracting parties in the ECHR.[97] However, when arguing in support of its decisions, it also sheds light on the most opportune and correct ways

[95] See Pavoni (2018), p. 269. With the Resolution 46/55 of 9th December 1991, the United Nations General Assembly created an open-ended working group of its Sixth Commission, with the aim to examine 'issues of substance arising out of the draft articles, in order to facilitate a successful conclusion of a convention'. The Commission has then created its own Working group in 1999. With resolution 55/150 of 12th December 2000, the General Assembly also instituted an ad hoc committee, 'with a view to elaborating a generally acceptable instrument based on the draft articles on jurisdictional immunities of States and their property adopted by the International Law Commission'.

[96] See, in this regard, Hafner (2013), pp. 1–12.

[97] ECHR, Article 19.

for a State to deal with similar situations in the future, with a view to avoid incurring, if any, in the very same breaches.[98]

Such compliance and *ultra partes* effect of the Court's judgments is particularly relevant in the field of embassy employment disputes, as in so-doing the ECtHR can indirectly trigger the harmonization of the Sate practice, one of the two constitutive elements of a customary international norm.[99] This happens as national courts, in deciding whether to grant immunity to foreign States, could end up strictly applying the criteria and arguments laid down in ECtHR judgments.

The application of Article 11 of the UNJISP as interpreted by the Court could produce positive and negative ripple effects. On the one hand, positive consequences have already been experienced in the field of claims for compensation for unlawful dismissals. The Italian tribunals, for instance, have accordingly changed their jurisprudence, by replacing their *in dubio pro immunitate* approach[100] with the rejection of the plea of immunity for compensation claims.[101]

But on the other hand, a number of negative effects can arise if States fully stick to the legal arguments developed by the Court. Among them, the risk of 'imposing the UNJISP *qua* purported customary law on ECHR Parties through the back door of the ECHR obligation'[102] is certainly the most evident. Those countries that for the time being will not be part to the UNJISP, could nonetheless find themselves obliged to apply some of its provisions in domestic proceedings, as the Court admitted that they reproduce customary international law in the field. For instance, apart from the diplomatic immunity exception, the national security clause as contained in Article 11 §2 (d)—which is rarely reflected in the international practice as a criterion restoring immunity in employment disputes—would allow States to enjoy a much wider jurisdictional immunity.[103]

Other negative consequences of the acceptance of Article 11's customary nature can relate to the importance attributed to the tasks performed by employees as well as to their citizenship in the exceptions enumerated at the second paragraph. While some legal orders do not attach any relevance to the issue when deciding on the granting of immunity, others have interpreted the notion of 'exercise of governmental authority' in a much restrictive way.[104] Lacking a specific framework for determining the circumstances under which certain tasks could be considered as

[98] See Cataldi (2010), p. 565.

[99] See Nigro (2012), p. 845, arguing that through its jurisprudence the ECtHR is attempting to promote as much as possible State compliance with the UNJISP. It is however debatable whether this can be pursued through the interpretation of Article 11 as representative of customary law. See also Draft conclusions on identification of customary international law (2018), p. 119.

[100] See Nigro (2012), p. 840.

[101] See Italian Court of Cassation, Académie de France à Rome v. Galamini di Recanati, Order No. 19674, 18 September 2014 (the text is reported at https://opil.ouplaw.com/view/10.1093/law:ildc/2437it14.case.1/law-ildc-2437it14) and more in general Sciso (2011), p. 1206.

[102] Pavoni (2018), p. 282.

[103] See Pavoni (2018), p. 283.

[104] See Rossi (2019), p. 37.

jure imperii, the coordination with the findings of the ECtHR about the customary nature of the provision could result in a broader interpretation of governmental functions and State interests, at detriment of the individual human rights' protection.

Additionally, some perplexities arise with regard to the nationality exception. As the *Ndayegamiye* case reveals, the ECtHR excludes that, in accordance with Article 11 §2 (e), claims of applicants having the nationality of the employer embassy can be brought before the forum State's courts unless the plaintiff is a permanent resident of that State with no other exception. From the perspective of the protection of human rights, this seems rather curious as full compliance with the ECtHR *dicta* could even leave some individuals to be totally deprived of any access to a judicial remedy. In this case, the Contracting Parties should enjoy a much wider margin of appreciation in deciding how to handle the case on the basis of the factual circumstances,[105] by even waiving the full application of Article 11 §2 (e), which is in fact not uniformly accepted in the State practice.

In sum, it is debatable at best whether reference to Article 11 of the UNJISP as a codification of customary rules of international law is fit for the purpose of engaging in a restrictive interpretation of State immunity in the interest of human rights' protection. This is certainly the main goal of the Court, but it could have been better pursued through other argumentative tools.

The conviction that the ECtHR could have endorsed a restrictive interpretation of State jurisdictional immunity through a different path—which did not unduly overestimate the customary character of Article 11 of the UN Convention—has also been expressed by the UK Supreme Court in the abovementioned *Benkharbouche* case.[106]

As the Court of Appeal had already noticed in the same dispute: 'it is questionable whether Article 11 of the ILC Draft Articles [...] or Article 11 of the UN Convention [...] can be taken to be a definitive statement of the extent of State immunity required by international law on embassy employment disputes'.[107] Based on such assumption, the Court of Appeal held that the Article only codifies customary law in the sense that it endorses a restrictive approach to State immunity, as generally confirmed by the State practice. Hence, in reviewing the compatibility of the right of access to court granted by the ECHR with the provisions of the UK State Immunity Act, the UK Court of Appeal refused to stick to the ECtHR's findings and autonomously underwent an analysis of the practice of States and the existing international instruments, of which the UNJISP is only one among those to be taken into account. As a result, the UK court denied that Article 11 §2 (b) (iv) of the UNJISP—at risk of

[105] See Foakes and O'Keefe (2013), p. 205.

[106] See United Kingdom Supreme Court, Benkharbouche v. Secretary of State for Foreign and Commonwealth Affairs, Judgment, [2017] UKSC 62, 18 October 2017, para. 29.

[107] United Kingdom Court of Appeal (civil division), Benkharbouche and Janah v. Embassy of the Republic of Sudan, A2/2013/3062, Judgment, 5 February 2015, para. 30.

enlarging the enjoyment of State immunity[108]—apply under customary international law. In so doing, it inaugurated an alternative, more coherent and effective methodology which, while balancing jurisdictional immunity and the right of access to court, does not rest on the asserted and controversial general character of Article 11 of the UN Convention.

In light of the foregoing, it is evident that—although both the jurisprudence of the Court and the practice of the Contracting Parties to the ECHR seem to support a restrictive interpretation of immunity—imposing on the latter to consider Article 11 and its exceptions as codification of customary international law could represent a drawback. Since some national courts have already noticed that the area of immunity provided under Article 11 is broader than that they generally recognize, forcing them to stick to the very wording of the provision could result in domestic tribunals applying under customary international law the exceptions contained in Article 11 of the UNJISP, and thus recognising a much broader application of State jurisdictional immunity.

7 Conclusion

To date, the solution of disputes related to embassy employment disputes for unfair dismissal is one of the most difficult judicial exercises, mainly because State practice is neither clear nor uniform. As the above-mentioned case-law of the ECtHR since *Cudak* demonstrates, the Strasbourg judges have supported a restrictive interpretation of State jurisdictional immunity in the field of embassy employment disputes. However, although guided by the prominent interest of safeguarding the respect of human rights, the arguments developed by the Court to ascertain a breach of Article 6 §1 of the ECHR seem to be methodologically questionable.

By upholding the customary nature of Article 11 of the UN Convention without thoroughly taking into account the practice of, at least, European countries, the Court's arguments are at risk of—and in some cases have already—produced negative ripple effects at the domestic level. With a view to effectively reinforce the protection of human rights *vis-à-vis* the granting of jurisdictional immunity to foreign countries, the Court should offer solutions which do not recognize the sending States—under customary law—a degree of immunity which is broader than that generally accorded by domestic courts.[109]

[108] United Kingdom Supreme Court, Benkharbouche v. Secretary of State for Foreign and Commonwealth Affairs, Judgment, [2017] UKSC 62, 18 October 2017, para. 72.
[109] See in this regard Rossi (2019), pp. 33–34.

References

Alvarez-Jimenez A (2011) Methods for the identification of customary international law in the International Court of Justice's jurisprudence: 2000–2009. ICLQ 60(3):681–712

Babu R (2007) Foreign state immunity in contract of employment with particular reference to Indian state practice. J Ind Law Inst 49:469–502

Besson S (2017) General principles and customary law in the EU legal order. In: Voganauer S, Weatherill S (eds) General principles of law: European and comparative perspectives. Hart, London, pp 106–129

Bonafe' BI (2010) The ECHR and the immunities provided by international law. ItYIL 20:55–71

Cannizzaro E (2016) Diritto internazionale, 3rd edn. Giappichelli, Torino

Casolari F (2008) L'incorporazione del diritto internazionale nell'ordinamento dell'Unione Europea. Giuffrè, Milano

Cassese A (2017) Diritto internazionale, 3rd edn. Il Mulino, Bologna

Cataldi G (2010) La natura self-executing delle norme della Convenzione europea dei diritti umani e l'applicazione delle sentenze della Corte europea negli ordinamenti nazionali. In: Caliguri A et al (eds) La tutela dei diritti umani in Europa tra sovranità statale e ordinamenti sovranazionali. CEDAM, Padova, pp 565–594

Conforti B (2018) Diritto internazionale, 11th edn. Editoriale scientifica, Napoli

Foakes J, O'Keefe R (2013) Article 11. In: O'Keefe R et al (eds) The United Nations Convention on jurisdictional immunities of states and their property. OPIL, Oxford, pp 183–208

Fox H (1995) Employment contracts as an exception to state immunity: is all public service immune? BYIL 66(1):97–176

Fox H, Webb P (2013) The law of state immunity. OUP, Oxford

Gaja G (1991) Quale immunità degli Stati esteri per le controversie di lavoro? RivDirInt 74 (1):920–946

Garnett R (1997) State immunity in employment matters. ICLQ 46(1):81–124

Garnett R (2005) The precarious position of embassy and consular employees in the United Kingdom. ICLQ 54(3):705–718

Garnett R (2015) State and diplomatic immunity and employment rights: European law to the rescue? ICLQ 64(4):783–827

Giannelli A (2012) Customary international law in the European Union. In: Cannizzaro E et al (eds) International law as the law of the European Union. Martinus Nijhoff, Leiden, pp 93–110

Hafner G (2010) United Nations Convention on jurisdictional immunities of states and their property. In: Wolfrum R (ed) Max Planck Encyclopedia of Public International Law. OUP, Oxford

Hafner G (2013) Historical background of the convention. In: O'Keefe R et al (eds) The United Nations Convention on jurisdictional immunities of states and their property. OPIL, Oxford, pp 1–12

Hafner G, Kohen M, Breau S (2006) State practice regarding state immunities. Martinus Nijhoff, Leiden

Iovane M (2018) Some reflections on identifying custom in contemporary international law. federalism.it, 09/2018

Klerk Y (1996) Protocol No. 11 to the European Convention for Human Rights: a drastic revision of the supervisory mechanism under the ECHR. NQHR 14(1):35–56

Köhler U (2004) Contracts of employment under the UN Convention on jurisdictional immunities of states and their property. ARIEL 9(1):191–215

Lanciotti A, Panetta A (2012) L'immunità dello Stato straniero dalla giurisdizione e il diritto dell'individuo di accesso alla giustizia per violazione dei suoi diritti fondamentali. In: Cassetti L (ed) Diritti, principi e garanzie sotto la lente dei giudici di Strasburgo. Jovene editore, Napoli, pp 335–353

Marchisio S (2017) Corso di diritto internazionale, 2nd edn. Giappichelli, Torino

Nigro R (2012) Immunità degli Stati esteri e diritto di accesso al giudice: un nuovo approccio nel diritto internazionale? RivDirInt 95(3):812–846
Pavoni R (2007) La jurisprudence italienne sur l'immunité des États dans les différends en matière de travail: tendances récentes à la lumière de la convention des Nations Unies. AFDI 53:211–223
Pavoni R (2008) L'immunità degli Stati nelle controversie di lavoro. In: Ronzitti N, Venturini G (eds) Le immunità giurisdizionali degli Stati e degli altri enti internazionali. CEDAM, Padova, pp 29–44
Pavoni R (2018) The myth of the customary nature of the United Nations Convention on state immunity: does the end justify the means? In: Van Aeken A, Motoc I (eds) ECHR and general international law. OUP, Oxford, pp 264–284
Petersen N (2017) The International Court of Justice and the judicial politics of identifying customary international law. EJIL 28(2):357–385
Roberts AE (2001) Traditional and modern approaches to customary international law: a reconciliation. AJIL 95:757–791
Rodgers L (2015) Immunity and public/private boundary in EU employment law. ELLJ 6(1):48–71
Rossi P (2019) Controversie di lavoro e immunità degli Stati esteri: tra codificazione e sviluppo progressivo del diritto consuetudinario. RivDirInt 102(1):5–44
Ryngaert CM, Hora Siccama DW (2018) Ascertaining customary international law: an inquiry into the methods used by domestic courts. NILR 65:1–25
Sciso E (2011) Italian Judges' point of view on foreign States' immunity. Vand J Transnatl Law 44 (5):1201–1231
Shabas W (2015) The European Convention on Human Rights: a commentary. OUP, Oxford
Stewart DP (2005) The UN Convention on jurisdictional immunities of states and their property. AJIL 99(1):194–211
Talmon S (2015) Determining customary international law: the ICJ's methodology between induction deduction and assertion. EJIL 26(2):417–443
Tan Y (2018) The identification of customary rules in international criminal law. UtrJIEL 34:92–110
Tomka P (2013) Custom and the International Court of Justice. LPICT 12(2):195–215
Treves T (2006) Customary international law. In: Wolfrum R (ed) Max Planck Encyclopedia of Public International Law. OUP, Oxford
Van Den Herik L (2016) The decline of customary international law as a source of international criminal law. In: Bradley C (ed) Custom's future: international law in a changing world. CUP, Cambridge, pp 230–252
Voyakis E (2003) Access to Court v. State Immunity. ICLQ 52(2):297–332
Worster WT (2014) The inductive and deductive methods in customary international law analysis: traditional and modern approaches. GJIL 45:445–521
Yang X (2012) State immunity in international law. CUP, Cambridge
Ziemele I (2013) Customary international law in the case law of the European Court of Human Rights: the method. LPIJ 12(2):243–252

Giovanni Ardito is PhD candidate in international law and human rights at Sapienza University of Rome (Italy). He is also Teaching assistant in international law at LUISS University in Rome and member of the Italian delegation to the International Seabed Authority. His main fields of research are international human rights law, international law of the sea and international environmental law.

Terrorism Exception to State Immunity: An Emerging Customary Norm of International Law?

Magdalena Matusiak-Frączczak

Abstract The terrorism exception to State immunity is a relatively new method of combatting terrorism, introduced so far by the United States and Canada. Moreover, its aim is to force State sponsors of terrorism to compensate victims of terrorist attacks. After presenting the US and Canadian regulations and case-law on terrorism exception, the exception will be analysed from the point of view of international custom, whether the exception is or might eventually become a new rule of customary international law. The emphasis will be placed on the judgment of the International Court of Justice in the case *Jurisdictional Immunities of the State* (Germany v. Italy, Greece Intervening). Finally, the deliberations will concentrate on finding some solutions that would help to deal with the problems that terrorism exceptions are currently raising in the international community.

1 Introduction

At the beginning of this chapter, it should be pointed out that it concerns only State immunity in civil cases and the *status quo* of the terrorism exception. State immunity in penal proceedings is not the subject matter of this chapter. The aim of this text is to analyse the terrorism exception to State immunity on the national level of the United States and Canada (the only States that have this exception to immunity in their legislation) as well as from the point of view of international law. The chapter will be divided into three parts. The first substantial part will be devoted to a profound analysis of the legislation and case-law on the terrorism exception in the United States and Canada. Then, in the second part, I will focus on deliberations on the current state of customary international law, with reference to exceptions on State immunity concerning tortious acts of a State. In particular, it will be examined whether currently terrorism exceptions can be considered to be a part of customary international law. Answering this question in negative, in the final part it will be

M. Matusiak-Frączczak (✉)
University of Łódź, Łódź, Poland
e-mail: mfracczak@wpia.uni.lodz.pl

R. Bismuth et al. (eds.), *Sovereign Immunity Under Pressure*,
https://doi.org/10.1007/978-3-030-87706-4_12

assessed whether terrorism exceptions might nonetheless become a customary law exception to State immunity. This part will contain conclusions and remarks on the future of terrorism exceptions in international law, and indicate which possible solutions may be adopted against State sponsors of terrorism.

2 Terrorism Exception to State Immunity in National Law of the United States and Canada

The terrorism exception to State immunity is directed against two categories of States. First, these are States alleged to have committed certain acts of terrorism, like torture, extrajudicial killing, aircraft sabotage or hostage taking. The second category encompasses States that allegedly have sponsored terrorism. Sponsoring terrorism, on its part, means providing safe havens, funding, training, supplying weaponry, medical assistance, false travel documentation and similar support.[1]

2.1 The United States

The US legislation in the area of terrorism exceptions presents a constant erosion of both immunity from jurisdiction and immunity from enforcement. This part will be devoted to the development of the US law and case-law.

2.1.1 The US Legislation

The terrorism exception to State immunity is regulated in the United States by 28 U. S. Code §1605A. The regulation on foreign States immunities was introduced to the US legislation in 1976 by the FSIA,[2] however, it gave very few rights to individuals to act before US courts. The FSIA applies not only to foreign States themselves, but also to individual officials of foreign governments in their official capacities.[3] The terrorism exception was included in the FSIA by the AEDPA[4] and the Flatow Amendment.[5] However, it permitted suits and the awarding of punitive damages

[1] In re Islamic Republic of Iran Terrorism Litigation, 659 F. Supp. 2d 31 (D.D.C. 2009). In re: Terrorist Attacks on September 11, 2001, 538 F.3d 71, 75 (2d Cir. 2008).

[2] Foreign Sovereign Immunities Act, 21.10.1976, s. 2891 (94th)—(FSIA).

[3] Estate of Botvin v. Islamic Republic of Iran, 873 F. Supp. 2d 232 (D.D.C. 2012). In re: Terrorist Attacks on September 11, 2001.

[4] Antiterrorism and Effective Death Penalty Act, 24.4.1996, s. 1214 (104th)—AEDPA.

[5] Civil Liability for Acts of State Sponsored Terrorism (the Flatow Amendment), a part of Omnibus Consolidated Appropriations Act, 30.9.1996, 110 Stat. 3009 (104th).

only against individual officials, employees and agents of a foreign State, but not against a foreign State itself.[6] It is worth mentioning that ever since its enactment, the terrorism exception has had a retroactive effect.[7] The situation changed in 2008, when the US legislator introduced a new § 1605A US Code and decided definitely that the terrorism exception permits individuals to sue before US courts and foreign States themselves by creating a private right of action against foreign States. Moreover, it allowed the awarding of punitive damages to plaintiffs.[8] These provisions could also be applied retroactively, even in cases that had already ended with a final judgment and US courts did not find this solution as violating *res judicata*[9] or collateral estoppel[10] defences, which protect the finality of judgments.[11]

In general, currently a foreign State shall not be immune from the jurisdiction of courts of the United States or of the federal States in any case not otherwise covered by the relevant US Code chapter in which money damages are sought against a foreign State for personal injury or death that was caused by an act of torture, extrajudicial killing, aircraft sabotage, hostage taking, or the provision of material support or resources for such an act if such act or provision of material support or resources is engaged in by an official, employee, or agent of such foreign State, while acting within the scope of his or her office, employment, or agency.[12]

A State is considered to be a terrorism sponsor if the US Secretary of State designates that State as a terrorism sponsor.[13] To be able to file a claim before one of

---

[6]Campuzano v. Islamic Republic of Iran, 281 F. Supp. 2d 258 (D.D.C. 2003). Cicippio-Puelo v. Islamic Republic of Iran, 353 F. 3d 1024. In re Islamic Republic of Iran Terrorism Litigation. Case Concerning Certain Iranian Assets (Islamic Republic of Iran v. United States of America), Memorial of the Islamic Republic of Iran, 1.2.2017, p. 26. Keller (2005), pp. 1029, 1031–1032.

Contrary view: Cronin v. Islamic Republic of Iran, 238 F. Supp. 2d 222 (D.D.C. 2002). Yet, this opinion was criticised and did not meet with general acceptance. Keller (2005), pp. 1036–1054.

[7]Cicippio v. Islamic Republic of Iran, 18 F. Supp. 2d 62 (D.D.C. 1998).

[8]Section 1083 National Defense Authorization Act for Fiscal Year 2008, 28.1.2008, H.R. 4986 (110th)—(NDAA 2008). Luxembourg Tribunal d'Arrondissement, civil judgment of 27.3.2019 n° 2019TALCH/00116, n°177266 du role, 3.2.2.2.2.1. In re Islamic Republic of Iran Terrorism Litigation. European Parliament Research Service (2016) Justice Against Sponsors of Terrorism. JASTA and its international impact. Briefing October, pp. 4–5. Certain Iranian Assets (Islamic Republic of Iran v. United States of America), Memorial of the Islamic Republic of Iran, 1.2.2017, pp. 4, 15, 24. Gartenstein-Ross (2002), pp. 496, 502–503.

[9]The doctrine of res judicata precludes parties to courts' disputes from relitigating claims when parties previously litigated them or could have litigated them in prior civil action that ended up in a final judgment on the merits. US courts found out that new regulations permitted new actions that were not available to terrorism victims before, therefore they are not covered by res judicata, because the previous judgments did not concern the same claims.

[10]Parties may be precluded from litigating any issue of fact or law that was previously resolved by a court in the course of reaching a final judgment in another action between those parties.

[11]In re Islamic Republic of Iran Terrorism Litigation.

[12]28 U.S. Code § 1605A(a)(1). Czapliński and Wyrozumska (2014), p. 316.

[13]28 U.S. Code § 1605A(h)(6). E.g. Iran is a designated State sponsor of terrorism as, according to the US administration, it provided material resources and support, in the form of funding, training and direction to Hezbollah. The US State Department has classified Iran as one of the most active

the US courts, an individual should be a US national, a member of the US armed forces or otherwise an employee of the US Government, or of an individual performing a contract awarded by the US Government, acting within the scope of the employee's employment. In a case in which the act occurred in the foreign State against which the claim has been brought, the individual must have afforded the foreign State a reasonable opportunity to arbitrate the claim in accordance with the accepted international rules of arbitration.[14] The result is that at the time of the introduction of these regulations, the aim of the US legislator was not the protection of human rights of any individual from injuries suffered in the territory of third States. The real objective of this regulation is to protect human rights of the US citizens who are either in the US territory or abroad and who are victims of terrorism.[15]

Another major improvement to the US legislation was made in 2016, when the Congress overrode the presidential veto to pass JASTA.[16] Until that date, there were four unsuccessful attempts to pass different versions of JASTA in the US Congress (in 2009, 2011, 2013 and 2015).[17] Before JASTA, US courts had jurisdiction only if a foreign State was designated at the time the act of terrorism was committed, or it was listed as a result of such act and remained designated when the claim is filed or was designated within the 6-month period before the claim is filed.[18] After JASTA, on the basis of 28 U.S. Code § 1605B, any foreign State, designated or not by the

and dangerous the State sponsors of terrorism: Tracy v. Islamic Republic of Iran slip.op. (D.D.C. 2003).

[14] 28 U.S. Code § 1605A(a)(2)(A)(ii). In re Islamic Republic of Iran Terrorism Litigation.

[15] Ferrer Lloret (2007), pp. 29, 48.

[16] Justice Against Sponsors of Terrorism Act, 13.9.2016, s. 2040 (114th)—JASTA. Obama B (2016) Veto to the Justice Against Sponsors of Terrorism Act (JASTA), Congressional Record, 114th Congress, Vol. 162, 26.9.2016, Washington.

During his 8 years of office, Barack Obama was faced only once with overriding his veto by the US Congress—in the case of the JASTA. Kohan (2017), pp. 1515, 1552. In the US Senate 97 senators voted against the veto, 1 voted for it and 2 senators were absent. One of the reasons of this result was that the JASTA was voted shortly before the Parliamentary elections in the United States and the representatives did not want to vote against victims of terrorism, as it could be negatively regarded by Americans. Hancock (2018), pp. 1293, 1318–1319.

[17] Kohan (2017), p. 1516.

[18] 28 U.S. Code § 1605A(a)(2)(A)(i). European Parliament Research Service (2016) Justice Against Sponsors of Terrorism. JASTA and its international impact. Briefing October, pp. 7–8. Bettis v. Islamic Republic of Iran, 315 F. 3d 325.

Since 1976 among the designated States were: Cuba, Iran, Iraq, Libya, North Korea, Sudan and Syria. Afghanistan was never listed as a State sponsor of terrorism because the United States never recognized the Taliban as Afghanistan's legal government. Gartenstein-Ross (2002), p. 498. Currently there are four States designated as sponsors of terrorism: North Korea (since 20.11.2017), Iran (since 19.1.1984), Sudan (since 12.8.1993), Syria (since 29.12.1979). See: U.S. Department of State (2020) State Sponsors of Terrorism https://www.State.gov/State-sponsors-of-terrorism/. Accessed 15 April 2021. Certain Iranian Assets (Islamic Republic of Iran v. United States of America), Memorial of the Islamic Republic of Iran, 1.2.2017, p. 18. Cicippio v. Islamic Republic of Iran.

executive branch, might be sued before US courts for physical injury to person or property or death occurring in the United States and caused by an act of international terrorism in the United States and a tortious act or acts of the foreign State, or of any official, employee, or agent of that foreign State while acting within the scope of his or her office, employment or agency, regardless where the tortious act or acts of the foreign State occurred.[19] This wording still limits categories of individuals who may seek civil redress from State sponsors of terrorism to US nationals, members of the US armed forces or employees of the US Government. Nevertheless, a foreign State will not be subject to US courts' jurisdiction if the tortious act being the subject-matter of the case constitutes mere negligence.[20]

JASTA was a subject of a lively debate in the United States, including, as was mentioned above, the presidential veto of Barack Obama. Section 2 of the JASTA (Findings and Purpose) indicated that State sponsored terrorism threatens the security of US nationals or the national security, foreign policy or economy. State sponsors of terrorism direct their conduct at the United States, so they should reasonably anticipate being brought to court in the US to answer for such activities.[21] On the other hand, the United States has a vital interest in providing victims of terrorism with full access to the court system in order to pursue civil claims against State sponsors of terrorism.[22] The purpose of the JASTA is to provide victims of terrorism with the broadest possible basis to seek relief against foreign States, wherever acting and wherever they may be found, that have provided material support, directly or indirectly, to terrorists.[23]

In his Statement to the US Congress on the veto to JASTA, the US President Barack Obama emphasized his deep sympathy to the victims of the attacks of September 11, 2001. Nevertheless, there were essential legal and political reasons behind the presidential veto to JASTA. The first of them was that the JASTA might reduce the effectiveness of the US response to indications that a foreign State had provided material support to terrorism. The evaluation of these indications was moved, by JASTA, from the executive to the private litigants and courts. Yet, it is the executive, including all intelligence professionals, that is capable and has all necessary information to determine, whether a foreign State sponsored terrorism or

[19] 28 U.S. Code § 1605B (1) and (2). European Parliament Research Service (2016) Justice Against Sponsors of Terrorism. JASTA and its international impact. Briefing October, pp. 7–8. Justice Against Sponsors of Terrorism Act, 13.9.2016, s. 2040 (114th)—JASTA. Obama B (2016) Veto to the Justice Against Sponsors of Terrorism Act (JASTA), Congressional Record, 114th Congress, Vol. 162, 26.9.2016, Washington. Hancock (2018), p. 1309.

[20] 28 U.S. Code § 1605B(d). Also: In re Islamic Republic of Iran Terrorism Litigation. European Parliament Research Service (2016) Justice Against Sponsors of Terrorism. JASTA and its international impact. Briefing October, pp. 1–2.

[21] Section 2 (a)(6) JASTA.

[22] Section 2 (a)(7) JASTA.

[23] Section 2 (b) JASTA.

not.[24] It was due to intelligence information that Saudi Arabia was never listed as a State sponsoring terrorism, despite the fact that most of the September 11th, 2001 attackers were of Saudi Arabian nationality.

The second reason for vetoing JASTA was that it would have serious implications for the US national interests. The United States is probably a State that has the largest international presence. Sovereign immunity also protects the US from attempted trials and seizures by private litigants abroad. Taking into consideration the role of reciprocity in international relations, JASTA could trigger reciprocal foreign States' responses, resulting in suits against the United States before foreign courts and, as a consequence, seizure of US assets situated abroad.[25]

Thirdly, JASTA could create complications with US relationships with foreign States, including US close allies. Even the minimal allegations would suffice to permit a litigation and waive State immunity. As a result, the US partners in combatting terrorism could limit their cooperation with the United States on key national security issues.[26] Despite these arguments, the presidential veto was outvoted and JASTA became binding law in the US.

After presenting the law on immunity from adjudication, it is indispensable to discuss immunity from execution in the US. Immunity from enforcement is broader than immunity from jurisdiction. As a general rule, a foreign State shall be immune from attachment, arrest and execution.[27] However, the terrorism exception also brings restrictions to immunity from execution. On the basis of 28 U.S. Code § 1610 (g)(1) the property, especially of a commercial character, of a foreign State, against which a judgment is entered under § 1605A, is subject to attachment in aid of execution, an execution, regardless of the level of economic control over the property by the government of the foreign State, of whether the profits of the property go to that government, of the degree to which officials of that government manage the property or otherwise control its daily affairs, of whether that government is the sole beneficiary in interest of the property, or of whether establishing the property as a separate entity would entitle the foreign State to benefits in the United States courts while avoiding its obligations.[28] On the other hand, notwithstanding the provisions of § 1610 the property of a foreign State shall be immune from attachment and from execution, if the property is that of a foreign central bank or

[24] Justice Against Sponsors of Terrorism Act, 13.9.2016, s. 2040 (114th)—JASTA. Obama B (2016) Veto to the Justice Against Sponsors of Terrorism Act (JASTA), Congressional Record, 114th Congress, Vol. 162, 26.9.2016, Washington. Similarly: In re Islamic Republic of Iran Terrorism Litigation. Hancock (2018), pp. 1316–1317.

[25] Justice Against Sponsors of Terrorism Act, 13.9.2016, s. 2040 (114th)—JASTA. Obama B (2016) Veto to the Justice Against Sponsors of Terrorism Act (JASTA), Congressional Record, 114th Congress, Vol. 162, 26.9.2016, Washington. Hancock (2018), pp. 1312–1313.

[26] Justice Against Sponsors of Terrorism Act, 13.9.2016, s. 2040 (114th)—JASTA. Obama B (2016) Veto to the Justice Against Sponsors of Terrorism Act (JASTA), Congressional Record, 114th Congress, Vol. 162, 26.9.2016, Washington.

[27] 28 U.S. Code § 1609.

[28] Gartenstein-Ross (2002), pp. 499–500, 517.

monetary authority held for its own account, unless such bank or authority, or its parent foreign government, has explicitly waived its immunity from attachment in aid of execution, or from execution, notwithstanding any withdrawal of the waiver which the bank, authority or government may purport to effect except in accordance with the terms of the waiver or the property is, or is intended to be, used in connection with a military activity and is of a military character, or is under the control of a military authority or defense agency.[29]

These are general rules of US law on State immunity from enforcement. However, in the case of the terrorism exception, the US legislator kept introducing further limits to State immunity. General rules still applied after 1996, when the terrorism exception was first introduced, until 2002. There were legislative attempts to introduce exceptions to immunity from enforcement,[30] however President Bill Clinton used waivers contained in those acts to make them totally ineffective.[31]

Then, in 2002, US law[32] permitted successful plaintiffs to attach the blocked property of Iran as well as the property of Iranian State-owned companies (agencies, instrumentalities), although they have separate judicial status from the State of Iran, provided they were blocked assets. Yet, enforcement on property subjected to two Vienna conventions on diplomatic and consular relations[33] was not allowed under TRIA.[34] Section 1083 NDAA 2008 further expanded the scope of enforcement against foreign State companies.[35]

In the case of Iran, US President Barack Obama also issued Executive Order 13599[36] and blocked all property and interests in property of the Government of Iran, including the Central Bank of Iran, or of any Iranian financial institution, provided it is situated in the United States. This Order permitted limiting immunity from attachment and from execution of property of a foreign central bank or

[29]28 U.S. Code § 1611 (b).

[30]Treasury and General Government Appropriations Act 1999, 31.8.1998, H.R. 4104 (105th).

[31]In re Islamic Republic of Iran Terrorism Litigation; Hancock (2018), p. 1306.

[32]Terrorism Risk Insurance Act, 26.11.2002, s. 2322 (116th)—(TRIA).

[33]Convention on diplomatic relations, Vienna, 18.4.1961. Convention on consular relations, Vienna, 22.4.1963.

[34]Rubin v. Islamic Republic of Iran, *2005 WL 670770 (D.D.C. 2005)*. In re Islamic Republic of Iran Terrorism Litigation. Certain Iranian Assets (Islamic Republic of Iran v. United States of America), Memorial of the Islamic Republic of Iran, 1.2.2017, pp. 15, 19–21. Hancock (2018), p. 1308.

[35]28 U.S. Code § 1605A (g)(1) permitted enforcement from property of Iranian companies regardless of: (A) the level of economic control over the property by the government of the foreign State; (B) whether the profits of the property go to that government; (C) the degree to which officials of that government manage property or otherwise control its daily affairs; (D) whether that government is the sole beneficiary in interest of the property; or (E) whether establishing the property as a separate entity would entitle the foreign State to benefits in United States courts while avoiding its obligations.

[36]Executive Order 13599 Blocking Property of the Government of Iran and Iranian Financial Institutions, 5.2.2012, Federal Register Vol. 77, No. 26—(Executive Order 13559).

monetary authority as described by § 1610, mentioned above.[37] As a 'blocked asset' of the alleged 'terrorist party,' the property of Iranian Central Bank or other Iranian financial institutions could be subjected to section 201 TRIA, permitting enforcement proceedings against it.[38] Here it should also be emphasized that in the current state of customary international law, immunity of a central bank persists regardless of whether it is a separate judicial person from the State or not,[39] so US law is contrary to international law.

Moreover, in 2012 the US Congress adopted the Iran Threat Reduction and Syria Human Rights Act[40] that introduced further exceptions to State immunity from execution. According to 22 U.S. Code § 8772 (1), a financial asset that is held in the United States for a foreign securities intermediary doing business in the United States, a blocked asset (whether or not subsequently unblocked) and equal in value to a financial asset of Iran, including an asset of the central bank (Bank Markazi) or monetary authority of the Government of Iran or any agency or instrumentality of that government, that such foreign securities intermediary or a related intermediary holds abroad, shall be subject to execution or attachment in aid of execution in order to satisfy any judgment to the extent of any compensatory damages awarded against Iran for damages for personal injury or death caused by an act of torture, extrajudicial killing, aircraft sabotage, or hostage-taking, or the provision of material support or resources for such an act.[41] As Iran pointed out in its Memorandum to the ICJ, all these legislative changes were aimed at guaranteeing that the American plaintiffs would win in their cases against Iran.[42]

The application of the above mentioned exception requires a court's decision. As it is regulated in 22 U.S. Code § 8772 (2) in order to ensure that Iran is held accountable for paying the judgments described in paragraph 1 and in furtherance of the broader goals of this Act to sanction Iran, prior to an award turning over any asset pursuant to execution or attachment in aid of execution with respect to any judgments against Iran described in paragraph 1, the court shall determine whether Iran holds equitable title to, or the beneficial interest in, these assets and that no other person possesses a constitutionally protected interest in these assets under the Fifth Amendment to the Constitution of the United States. To the extent that the court determines that a person other than Iran holds equitable title to, or a beneficial interest in, these assets (excluding a custodial interest of a foreign securities intermediary or a related intermediary that holds the assets abroad for the benefit of Iran); or a constitutionally protected interest in the assets, such assets shall be available

[37] Certain Iranian Assets (Islamic Republic of Iran v. United States of America), Memorial of the Islamic Republic of Iran, 1.2.2017, pp. 4–5, 15–16.

[38] Ibid., pp. 30–33.

[39] Ibid., pp. 54, 58–59.

[40] Iran Threat Reduction and Syria Human Rights Act, 10.8.2012, H.R. 1905 (112th).

[41] Certain Iranian Assets (Islamic Republic of Iran v. United States of America), Memorial of the Islamic Republic of Iran, 1.2.2017, pp. 5, 30–33.

[42] Ibid., p. 34.

only for execution or attachment in aid of execution to the extent of Iran's equitable title or beneficial interest therein and to the extent such execution or attachment does not infringe upon such constitutionally protected interest.

Despite the restrictions on immunities from enforcement, the victims are not compensated by the States designated as terrorism sponsors. Therefore the United States introduced funds permitting at least partial compensation to some of terrorism victims on the basis of the Victims of Trafficking and Violence Protection Act (VTVPA) of 2000[43] and later on the basis of the Justice for United States Victims of State Sponsored Terrorism Act (JUSVSSTA) of 2015.[44] As a result, the victims receive compensation from US taxpayers and not from State sponsors of terrorism.

As is clear from the above-mentioned provisions and their development, the main aim of introducing the terrorism exception was to provide to victims of terrorism a possibility of filing civil lawsuits against State sponsors of terrorism. Since 1996, foreign States' right to immunity has been constantly limited whereas private claimants have been granted more and more procedural possibilities of acting against foreign States before US courts.

2.1.2 The US Judiciary

Immunity from Adjudication

Until 1952 (the Tate Letter), foreign States enjoyed absolute immunity before the US courts. Since 1952, the US courts apply the 'restrictive' theory of sovereign immunity, which means that they recognize sovereign immunity with regard to sovereign public rights, but not for private acts.[45] This development stays in conformity with changes to State immunity worldwide, in that period.

This 'restrictive' theory of State immunity was codified by the FSIA and was designed to move resolution of foreign sovereign immunity issues from the executive branch to the judiciary of the US and to promote 'uniformity in decision' in matters related to foreign State immunity. Ever since the adoption of the FSIA, US courts have considered it to be the sole and exclusive standard to be used in resolving questions of sovereign immunity raised by foreign States before US courts.[46] Since

---

[43] Victims of Trafficking and Violence Protection Act, 28.10.2000, s. 1464 (106th)—(VTVPA).

[44] Justice for United States Victims of State Sponsored Terrorism Act, 18.12.2015, s. 3007 (114th)—(JUSVSSTA).

[45] Letelier v. the Republic of Chile, 488 F. Supp. 665 (D.D.C. 1980). Olsen and Sanchez v. the Republic of Mexico, 729 F. 2d 641. Frolova v. Union of Soviet Socialist Republics, 761 F.2d 370. Saudi Arabia v. Nelson, 507 U.S. 349 (1993) 113 S. Ct. 1571. Hugo Princz v. Federal Republic of Germany, 26 F. 3d 1166. Rubin v. Islamic Republic of Iran, 408 F. Supp. 2d 549 (N.D. Ill. 2005). Rubin and others v. Islamic Republic of Iran, 830 F. 3d 470 (7th Cir. 2016). Rubin and others v. Islamic Republic of Iran, 583 U.S. (2018). Syed (2016), pp. 251, 258.

[46] Letelier v. the Republic of Chile. Saudi Arabia v. Nelson. In re Islamic Republic of Iran Terrorism Litigation. McKeel v. Islamic Republic of Iran, 722 F. 2d 582 (9th Cir. 1983). Frolova v. Union of

that time, these courts refrain from referring to international customary law on State immunity and decide on that subject-matter solely on the basis of domestic law—the FSIA.

In the US a foreign State is therefore entitled to immunity, unless the FSIA provides an exception thereto. However, if the case falls within the narrow limits shaped by the FSIA, US courts exercise jurisdiction over foreign States, regardless of international custom in that area.[47] It is worth noticing that in *McKeel* the Court of Appeals, Ninth Circuit emphasized that by enacting the FSIA the Congress would make US law on sovereign immunity consistent with international law.[48] This conclusion is based on the wording of 28 U.S. Code § 1602:

> The Congress finds that the determination by United States courts of the claims of foreign States to immunity from the jurisdiction of such courts would serve the interests of justice and would protect the rights of both foreign States and litigants in United States courts. Under international law, States are not immune from the jurisdiction of foreign courts insofar as their commercial activities are concerned, and their commercial property may be levied upon for the satisfaction of judgments rendered against them in connection with their commercial activities. Claims of foreign States to immunity should henceforth be decided by courts of the United States and of the States in conformity with the principles set forth in this chapter.

This wording has an essential implication for the subject of this research. US courts fully apply domestic legislation on the terrorism exception to State immunity, either in relation to terrorist attacks occurring in the US territory, or without geographic limitations, as long as the victim is a US national.[49] They emphasize that the aim of the regulation is also to promote the safety of US citizens travelling overseas.[50]

What is typical for US jurisprudence is the analysis of the terrorism exception solely from the point of view of the domestic legal system. The interpretation of 28 U.S. Code § 1605(A) is made on the basis of referral to national judgments as well as legislative works of the US Congress,[51] as depicting Congressional intent to permit the federal courts to create national standards to support the protection of victims of terrorism. One of the aims of this regulation was to promote uniformity of determinations with respect to the liability of foreign State sponsors of terrorism

Soviet Socialist Republics. Liu v. the Republic of China, 892 F. 2d 1419. Rubin and others v. Islamic Republic of Iran, 583. Shaw (2008), p. 715. Kohan (2017), p. 1536.

[47] Perez v. the Bahamas, 482 F. Supp. 1208 (D.D.C. 1980). Letelier v. the Republic of Chile. McKeel v. Islamic Republic of Iran. Olsen and Sanchez v. the Republic of Mexico. Frolova v. Union of Soviet Socialist Republics. Liu v. the Republic of China. Hugo Princz v. Federal Republic of Germany. Rubin and others v. Islamic Republic of Iran, 830.

[48] McKeel v. Islamic Republic of Iran.

[49] Tracy v. Islamic Republic of Iran. Doe v. Usama bin Laden et al., Islamic Emirate of Afghanistan, 663 F.3d 64 (2d Cir. 2011).

[50] Tracy v. Islamic Republic of Iran. In re Islamic Republic of Iran Terrorism Litigation.

[51] Doe v. Usama bin Laden et al., Islamic Emirate of Afghanistan.

acts.[52] It is pointed out that the US Congress has the prerogative to alter foreign State's immunity and to render the alteration dispositive of judicial proceedings in progress.[53]

This interpretation is not new, as it was applied in earlier cases of US courts on State immunity. According to the US case-law, it was the intention of the US Congress that the FSIA be the sole basis for obtaining jurisdiction over foreign States. Therefore it is the FSIA, and not international customary law, that governs the scope of State immunity in the United States and the exceptions thereto.[54]

US courts underline that if a foreign State's agent, official or employee provides material support and resources to terrorists or terrorist organisations, such provision will be considered to be the execution of the State's sovereign powers. However, to waive State immunity, the foreign State's government must have engaged in the wrongful conduct either deliberately or permissively as a matter of policy or custom. This requirement will be fulfilled when the foreign State's officials routinely provide material resources or support to terrorist organisations. However, plaintiffs need not establish that material support or resources provided by a foreign State for a terrorist attack contributed directly to the act from which their claims arise.[55]

According to US courts, international terrorism is subject to universal jurisdiction.[56] Therefore, US courts can exercise jurisdiction over foreign State sponsors of terrorism, because it is required by fair play and substantial justice for victims of terrorism.[57]

Immunity from Enforcement

First of all, the basic criteria of enforcement proceedings against a foreign State in the United States are: (1) the property must be owned by that foreign State and (2) the property must be within the territorial jurisdiction of the United States. Neither the US legislation, nor its case-law permit enforcement proceedings against foreign State property located anywhere in the world.[58]

As was indicated above, successful plaintiffs have problems with execution of judgments entered against State sponsors of terrorism. In most cases, the States

[52] Tracy v. Islamic Republic of Iran.

[53] Bank Markazi, aka Central Bank of Iran v. Peterson et. al, 578 U.S. __ (2016).

[54] Argentine Republic v. Amerada Hess Shipping (1989) 488 U.S. 428 (1989). In re: Terrorist Attacks on September 11, 2001.

[55] Cicippio v. Islamic Republic of Iran. Tracy v. Islamic Republic of Iran. In re Islamic Republic of Iran Terrorism Litigation.

[56] Tracy v. Islamic Republic of Iran.

[57] Ibid.

[58] According to the Court of Appeals, Seventh Circuit, permitting enforcement from foreign State's property located anywhere in the world would constitute a 'breath-taking assertion of extraterritorial jurisdiction': Rubin and others v. Islamic Republic of Iran, 830.

against which US courts deliver judgments, do not have property located in the United States that can be the subject of enforcement proceedings.

These difficulties can be illustrated with the *Rubin* saga concerning enforcement proceedings against Iran. The saga had its beginning in a terrorist attack committed by Hamas in Jerusalem on September 4, 1997. Eight US citizens were injured in the attack, therefore they and their relatives filed a civil action against Iran for its role in providing material support to terrorists. Iran was ordered to pay to the plaintiffs a US $71.5 million. They tried to enforce the judgment by an attempt to execute or attach various collections of Persian artefacts that were in the possession of, inter alia, the University of Chicago, the Museum of Fine Arts (Boston) and Harvard University, and also by execution against bank accounts.[59]

One of the plaintiffs' legal arguments was a reference to 28 U.S. Code § 1610 (a) (1) permitting execution of the property of a foreign State used for commercial activity in the United States. As was already stated, Iran did not appear before US courts to raise the issue of its immunity. At the beginning of the proceedings, in its judgment of 2005, the District Court, N.D. Illinois, Eastern Division concluded that only Iran and not the US museums, being only third party respondents, may raise State immunity as a defence from enforcement. If Iran did not appear before the court, the objection of State immunity from enforcement would not be applied.[60]

However, the final outcome of the *Rubin* saga was the denial of execution from the Iranian artefacts. The US courts concluded, that the exceptions to State immunity from execution are narrow. The plaintiffs referred to several of them, for example, to 28 U.S. Code §1610(a) permitting enforcement from State's property used for a commercial activity in the United States. The plaintiffs' argument was that the University of Chicago and Chicago's Field Museum of Natural History were using the artefacts also for commercial activity. Nevertheless, according to US case-law, this exception requires commercial use by the foreign State itself and not by a third party.[61]

Another exception referred to by the plaintiffs was 28 U.S. Code § 1610(g), which permits the execution not only from property of the foreign State itself, but also from the one owned by its juridically separate instrumentality. However, US courts concluded that this section is not a self-standing exception to State immunity from execution, permitting enforcement from any property of the foreign State (or its

[59] Campuzano v. Islamic Republic of Iran. Rubin v. Islamic Republic of Iran, 408. Rubin v. Islamic Republic of Iran, 349 F. Supp. 2d 1108 (N.D. Ill. 2004). Rubin v. Islamic Republic of Iran. Rubin v. Islamic Republic of Iran, 810 F. Supp. 2d 402 (D. Mass. 2011). Rubin v. Islamic Republic of Iran, 709 F. 3d 49 (1st Cir. 2013). Rubin v. Islamic Republic of Iran, 33 F. Supp. 3d 1003 (2014). Rubin and others v. Islamic Republic of Iran, 830. Rubin and others v. Islamic Republic of Iran, 583.

[60] Rubin v. Islamic Republic of Iran, 408. However, we may find case-law that emphasizes that it is the plaintiff who has the burden of proof that immunity should not be granted under the exceptions to the FSIA. In re: Terrorist Attacks on September 11, 2001.

[61] Rubin v. Islamic Republic of Iran, 349. Rubin v. Islamic Republic of Iran, 33. Rubin and others v. Islamic Republic of Iran, 830. In re Terrorist Attacks on September 11, 2001, 295 F. Supp.3d 416 (2018).

instrumentality) provided that the executed judgment was delivered within the limits of the terrorism exception. Application of 28 U.S. Code § 1610(g) requires an existence of one of exceptions to State immunity from enforcement listed in subsections 28 U.S. Code § 1610 (a) and (b) which was not the case in these proceedings.[62]

The last exception mentioned by the plaintiffs was section 201 of the TRIA. This section permits holders of judgments issued on the basis of the terrorism exception to execute on assets blocked (seized or frozen) by executive order under certain international sanctions provisions. That was not the case in any of the artefacts with respect to which the plaintiffs wanted to enforce judgment against Iran.[63]

The plaintiffs could not institute enforcement proceedings regarding artefacts in the possession of the Museum of Fine Arts and Harvard University, as they did not prove that those artefacts were owned by Iran. The only reason that the plaintiffs presented, namely that the artefacts in question come from ancient ruins of Persepolis, was not in itself enough to validly claim that Iran was their owner.[64]

The problem with enforcement from bank accounts in the *Rubin* saga was that these accounts were titled ‘Consulate General of the Islamic Republic of Iran’ and ‘Consulate General Iran’. Therefore US courts needed to decide, whether TRIA applies or not and whether these accounts can be considered to be blocked for the purposes of execution proceedings. It was concluded that bank account cannot be treated as ‘premises of the missions’ as those premises include solely buildings and land. However, Vienna conventions on diplomatic and consular relations mention also ‘property’ which contains bank accounts. In the *Rubin* saga, US courts found that the bank accounts in question could be blocked as they were dormant accounts, so they were not actively in use and Vienna conventions require an active use of property to fall into categories of property protected by the conventions. This success of the *Rubin* plaintiffs did not bring them relief, however, as they did not find in these accounts money permitting them to satisfy their claims.[65]

In the *Bennet* decision, the Court of Appeals for the District of Columbia underlined that enforcement proceedings cannot be initiated against consular and diplomatic premises of a foreign State. As the Court noticed, even during periods in which the US is experiencing extremely strained or outright hostile relationship with a foreign nation, it remains obligated to protect that nation’s diplomatic properties.[66]

[62] Rubin and others v. Islamic Republic of Iran, 830. Rubin and others v. Islamic Republic of Iran, 583.

[63] Rubin and others v. Islamic Republic of Iran, 830.

[64] Rubin v. Islamic Republic of Iran, 810. Rubin v. Islamic Republic of Iran, 709.

[65] Rubin v. Islamic Republic of Iran, 2005.

[66] Bennett v. Islamic Republic of Iran, 604 F. Supp. 2d 152 (D.D.C. 2009).

This reasoning is compatible with art. 50 (2)(b) of the ILC's *Draft Articles*[67] and the texts of two Vienna conventions mentioned previously.

Lastly, it can be noticed that the US Supreme Court in its judgment from 2016 in *Bank Markazi v. Peterson*[68] decided that 22 U.S. Code § 8772 permitting certain limits to State immunity from enforcement may be applied retroactively. Moreover, according to the court, this section does not violate the constitutional separation of powers as it constitutes an exercise of congressional authority regarding foreign affairs. Therefore it cannot be regarded as an encroachment on the federal courts' jurisdiction.[69] The result was that US courts accepted enforcement proceedings against foreign central banks.

On the basis of the US legislation and case-law, it can be concluded that private civil plaintiffs are granted a wide variety of possible lawsuits against State sponsors of terrorism. US courts are sympathetic towards plaintiffs and award them very elevated compensations, including punitive damages. Yet these judgments might bring to plaintiffs only a partial psychological relief. They face very serious problems with enforcing these judgments and getting financial compensation for their injuries and damages. What is the most important, ever since enacting the FSIA in 1976, State immunity has been treated by the United States, especially by US courts, as a concept of domestic law without reference to international law, as according to these courts the national codification of customary international law deprived State immunity of its international law character and made it a subject of solely national law, regulated by laws passed by the US Congress.

2.2 *Canada*

The Canadian legislation and case-law is not as developed as the US ones. Yet, as Canada is the only State that followed the US pattern on terrorism exception to State immunity, its solutions are worth mentioning.

2.2.1 Canadian Legislation

In Canada, the issue of terrorism exception to State immunity is regulated by the SIA.[70] A foreign State is not immune from the jurisdiction of a court in proceedings

[67] International Law Commission, Draft Articles on Responsibility of States for Internationally Wrongful Acts, 2001, annex to General Assembly Resolution 56/83 of 12.12.2001 and corrected by document A/56/49 (Vol. 1)/Corr.4.

[68] Bank Markazi, aka Central Bank of Iran v. Peterson et al.

[69] Similar retroactive effect was confirmed regards the TRIA in: Bennett v. Islamic Republic of Iran, 927 F. Supp. 2d 833 (N.D. Cal. 2013). Bennett v. Islamic Republic of Iran, 799 F. 3d (9th Cir. 2015).

[70] State Immunity Act, R.S.C., 1985, c. S-18—(SIA).

against it for its support of terrorism on or after January 1, 1985.[71] The list of States considered to support terrorism is created by the Governor in Council, on the recommendation of the Minister of Foreign Affairs, made after consulting with the Minister of Public Safety and Emergency Preparedness. Once this recommendation is made, the Governor in Council is satisfied that there are reasonable grounds to believe that the foreign State supported or supports terrorism.[72] To be removed from the list, a foreign State shall submit a written application. The Minister of Foreign Affairs may decide, after consulting with the Minister of Public Safety and Emergency Preparedness, whether there are reasonable grounds to recommend the delisting to the Governor in Council.[73] Moreover, the list is also periodically reviewed.[74] Just as in the case of the United States, creating the list is a political decision of the executive branch. Canada did not decide to introduce a possibility of law-suits, regardless of the prior designation of a foreign State as a State sponsor of terrorism by the executive.

2.2.2 Canadian Jurisprudence

The Canadian courts consider State immunity to be a rule of customary international law, and they notice the international content of State immunity, yet the role of the national Parliament is decisive. According to Canadian case-law, State immunity reflects, as well, domestic choices made for policy reasons. That is why the precise extent and manner of the application of State immunity is determined by the State of the forum and in Canada the SIA is intended to be an exhaustive and complete codification of Canadian law on State immunity. The Canadian Parliament shapes international relations by making a choice on State immunity and exceptions thereto.[75] It means that in Canada the general rule is that a foreign State is entitled to immunity, except for the express exceptions provided for in the SIA. Even if there appears a new exception to State immunity in customary international law, it is up to the Canadian Parliament to include this exception in the domestic legal acts. Until this is done by the Parliament, the exception is not applicable in Canada.[76]

The existence and legality of the terrorism exception seems to be accepted by the Canadian jurisprudence. The amendment of the SIA in 2012 by the introduction of the terrorism exception shows that the Canadian Parliament can and does take active steps to redress and pre-empt emergent international challenges.[77] Here the Canadian case-law shows similarities with the US case-law. It is aware of international

[71] Section 6.1 (1) SIA.

[72] Section 6.1 (2) SIA. Kazemi Estate v. Iran [2014] 3 S.C.R. 176, at 44.

[73] Section 6.1 (4) SIA.

[74] Section 6.1 (7)(8)(9) SIA.

[75] Kazemi Estate v. Iran, at 44–46.

[76] Section 3 (1) SIA. Kazemi Estate v. Iran at 54, 56, 58, 60–61, 170.

[77] Kazemi Estate v. Iran, at 44.

law and foreign courts' decisions on State immunity, yet it accepts the decisive role of the Canadian Parliament.

After deliberations on the terrorism exception in national laws and case-law of the United States and Canada, the next part will constitute their confrontation with customary international law on State immunity. The main part of the discussion will be devoted to indicating whether the terrorism exception can achieve the status of a norm of customary international law.

3 Terrorism Exception and Customary International Law

At the beginning of this part, it needs to be underlined that the terrorism exception will be a subject of the scrutiny of the ICJ in *Certain Iranian Assets (Islamic Republic of Iran v. United States of America)*. Currently the case is awaiting a filing of a reply by the Islamic Republic of Iran and a rejoinder by the United States of America.[78] Nevertheless, the aim of this chapter is not a prognosis of the outcome of the ICJ's deliberations. It presents the author's opinion on the actual state of customary international law on State immunity and conclusions resulting thereof for terrorism exception.

As State immunity is regulated by international custom, the determination of the existence of an eventual new exception thereto must be based on the analysis of customary international law in this area. A relevant pattern to be followed was presented by the ICJ in 2012 in *Jurisdictional Immunities of the State* concerning State immunity and a serious violation of human rights laws amounting even to a violation of *jus cogens*.[79]

To identify international custom meaning 'evidence of a general practice accepted by law'[80] the following criteria should be applied: a settled practice and *opinio juris*.[81] The presence of only one of the above-mentioned constituent elements does not suffice for the identification of a rule of customary international law. In assessing

[78] International Court of Justice (2020) Certain Iranian Assets (Islamic Republic of Iran v. United States of America).

[79] Art. 53 Convention on the Law of Treaties, Vienna, 23.5.1969: a peremptory norm of general international law is a norm accepted and recognized by the international community of States as a whole as a norm from which no derogation is permitted and which can be modified only by a subsequent norm of general international law having the same character.

[80] Art. 38 (1)(b) ICJ Statute.

[81] Areios Pagos, case no. 11/2000 Distomo, judgment of 4.5.2000, 129 ILR 513. Jurisdictional Immunities of the State (Germany v. Italy: Greece Intervening), Judgment, ICJ Reports 2012, p. 99 at 55. North Sea Continental Shelf Cases (Federal Republic of Germany v. Denmark, Federal Republic of Germany v. Netherlands), Judgment I.C.J. Reports 1969, p. 44 at 74, 77. Case Concerning the Continental Shelf (Libyan Arab Jamahiriya v. Malta), Judgment, I.C.J. Reports 1985, p. 13 at 27. Luxembourg Tribunal d'Arrondissement, civil judgment of 27.3.2019 at 1.1.2.2.1. Sąd Najwyższy, case no. IV CSK 465/09 Natoniewski, order of 29.10.2010. Kazemi Estate v. Iran at 38, 102. International Law Commission, Draft conclusions on identification of

evidence of existence of these two elements, regard must be taken to the overall context, the nature of the rule and particular circumstances in which evidence in question is to be found.[82]

The pragmatic, external element of custom, namely the settled practice of States, should be constant and uniform (although a complete consistency is not required), repetitive and general (widespread and representative).[83] The element of time must be taken into consideration as long duration shows consistency in application and confirmation of the value of the customary law.[84] Nevertheless, there might be cases in which a long period of practice is not necessary for the formation of international practice.[85] The settled practice is to be looked for in States' legislation, the ratification of international conventions and in their courts' judgments, in works and opinions of international bodies and organisations as well as in works of legal doctrine.[86]

Nevertheless, the mere practice itself does not suffice. It has to be carried out in such a way as to be evidence of a belief that this practice is rendered obligatory by the existence of a rule of law requiring it, so there needs to be this subjective element, namely, that a State feels that it is conforming to a legal obligation and not a mere usage, habit, comity, political expediency or convenience (*opinio juris vel necessitatis*).[87] A failure to react over time to a practice may serve as evidence of acceptance as law.[88]

As international custom evolves and might change over time, to determine whether a terrorism exception to State immunity exists in customary international

customary international law with commentaries, 2018, A/73/10, Conclusion 2, p. 124; Barcik and Srogosz (2017), p. 144. Czapliński and Wyrozumska (2014), pp. 98–99. Shaw (2008), p. 74.

[82] International Law Commission, Draft conclusions on identification of customary international law with commentaries, 2018, A/73/10, Conclusion 2, Conclusion 3, p. 126.

[83] Barcik and Srogosz (2017), pp. 144–146. Shaw (2008), pp. 76 84.

[84] Sąd Najwyższy Natoniewski.

[85] Barcik and Srogosz (2017), p. 146.

[86] Areios Pagos, Distomo. Bundesverfassungsgericht, case no. 2 BvM 1/60, judgment of 30.10.1962. Bundesverfassungsgericht, case no. 2 BvM 1/62, judgment of 30.4.1963. Constitutional Court of the Republic of Slovenia, case Up-13/99, judgment of 8.3.2001, at 12. Jones v. Saudi Arabia [2006] UKHL 26, at 46. Jurisdictional Immunities of the State (Germany v. Italy: Greece Intervening), Judgment, ICJ Reports 2012, p. 99, p. 55. Luxembourg Tribunal d'Arrondissement, civil judgment of 27.3.2019, at 1.1.2.2.1. Sąd Najwyższy Natoniewski. International Law Commission, Draft conclusions on identification of customary international law with commentaries, 2018, A/73/10, Conclusion 4, Conclusion 5, Conclusion 8, pp. 130, 132, 135–137. Scherr (2012), pp. 139, 147. Barcik and Srogosz (2017), pp. 144–146. Shaw (2008), pp. 76–84.

[87] Areios Pagos Distomo. North Sea Continental Shelf Cases, at 77. Luxembourg Tribunal d'Arrondissement, civil judgment of 27.3.2019, at 1.1.2.2.1. Sąd Najwyższy, Natoniewski. Kazemi Estate v. Iran, at 102. International Law Commission, Draft conclusions on identification of customary international law with commentaries, 2018, A/73/10, Conclusion 9, Conclusion 10, at 138–140. Barcik and Srogosz (2017), pp. 144, 146. Czapliński and Wyrozumska (2014), pp. 99–100. Shaw (2008), pp. 84–89.

[88] Czapliński and Wyrozumska (2014), pp. 99–100.

law, one needs to look for relevant and up-to-date State practice on this matter in the States' legislation, ratified conventions and courts' judgments on State immunities, especially in matters concerning State sponsored terrorism.[89] To analyse the existence of the *opinio juris,* the following criteria should be applied:

> *Opinio juris* [. . .] is reflected in particular in the assertion by States claiming immunity that international law accords them a right to such immunity from the jurisdiction of other States; in the acknowledgement, by States granting immunity, that international law imposes upon them an obligation to do so; and [. . .] in the assertion by States in other cases of a right to exercise jurisdiction over foreign States.[90]

Despite a high level of legal deliberations, decisions of international courts, including the ICJ, as well as national courts and also publications of legal doctrine concerning the existence and content of rules of customary international law are only a subsidiary means for the determination of such rules.[91]

The ICJ in *Jurisdictional Immunities of the State*, basing itself on numerous judgments of national courts, concluded that the actions of the German armed forces during the Second World War could not be a reason to deprive Germany of State immunity from jurisdiction. In the proceedings, Italy raised three types of arguments, allegedly permitting the overpowering of State immunity: territorial tort exception, the subject-matter and circumstances of the claims and the 'last resort' argument. The ICJ rejected all of them. This part of the paper will focus on analysing whether the reasoning of the ICJ in *Jurisdictional Immunities of the State* on the acts of Germany can be eventually applied to terrorism exception.

It needs to be indicated that recently, on March 27, 2019, the Luxembourg District Court refused to grant enforceability in Luxembourg of several judgments of the United States courts directed against Iran, its enumerated ministries and its Central Bank. The American judgments were based on the recognition that Iran was the State sponsor of the September 11, 2001 attacks on the World Trade Center. The Luxembourg District Court established that the present state of customary international law refuses to accept the terrorism exception as one of the exceptions to State immunity.[92]

The American scholars notice that the terrorism exception, especially after the JASTA amendment, might lack both—State practice and *opinio juris*,[93] therefore it might be impossible for the terrorism exception to become customary international law.

[89] Jurisdictional Immunities of the State (Germany v. Italy: Greece Intervening), Judgment, ICJ Reports 2012, p. 99, p. 55. Luxembourg Tribunal d'Arrondissement, civil judgment of 27.3.2019, at 1.1.2.2.1.

[90] Ibid., p. 55.

[91] International Law Commission, Draft conclusions on identification of customary international law with commentaries, 2018, A/73/10, Conclusion 13, Conclusion 14, at 149–151.

[92] Luxembourg Tribunal d'Arrondissement, civil judgment of 27.3.2019.

[93] Kohan (2017), p. 1517.

3.1 *Territorial Tort Exception and Terrorism Exception*

As gross violations of human rights that were the subject of the ICJ's decision in *Jurisdictional Immunities of the State* were committed by armed forces during armed conflicts, they are considered by States to be *acta de jure imperii*.[94] The will of international community of States was to exclude these acts of armed forces from the exception to State immunity relating to territorial tort exception. Therefore, in the texts of the conventions on immunities, States underline expressly that these military acts are not covered by the conventions and exceptions provided therein.[95] Lichtenstein, Sweden and Switzerland in their written reservations to United Nations Convention on Jurisdictional Immunities of States and their Property (UNCJIS)[96] emphasized that activities of armed forces fall outside the scope of the application of the Convention.[97]

Acts committed by armed forces during armed conflict, constituting serious violations of human rights laws, should not be covered either by Art. 12 of the UNCJIS, or by Art. 11 of the European Convention on State Immunity (ECSI). This was confirmed by the ICJ expressly in *Jurisdictional Immunities of the State*.[98] This conclusion was reached after a detailed scrutiny of national laws,[99] judgments of

---

[94] Jurisdictional Immunities of the State (Germany v. Italy: Greece Intervening), Judgment, ICJ Reports 2012, p. 99, p. 60. Finke (2011), p. 860.

[95] Art. 31 European Convention on State Immunity, Basle, 16.5.1972—ECSI.

[96] United Nations Convention on Jurisdictional Immunities of States and their Property, New York, 2.12.2004.

[97] United Nations Treaty Collection (2020) United Nations Convention on Jurisdictional Immunities of States and their Property. https://treaties.un.org/Pages/ViewDetails.aspx?src=IND&mtdsg_no=III-13&chapter=3&lang=en. Accessed 15 April 2021.

[98] Jurisdictional Immunities of the State (Germany v. Italy: Greece Intervening), Judgment, ICJ Reports 2012, 65–79. Contrary: Areios Pagos, Distomo. Nevertheless this decision was not reached unanimously. It needs to be pointed out that four members of the Greek Court (President Matthias and Judges Rigos, Bakas and Vardavakis) in their dissenting opinion emphasized that torts arising from armed conflicts fall outside the scope of application of territorial tort exception. An interesting analysis was presented by Finke, who expressed the view that art. 12 UNCJIS does not exclude activities of armed forces from the application of territorial tort exception. Accenting art. 32 of the Vienna convention on the law of treaties, this author underlined that referral to insurable risks in the preparatory works on UNJIS could be invoked only if the interpretation of art. 12 UNCJIS was obscure, ambiguous or if it led to a result which is manifestly absurd or unreasonable. Including personal injuries caused by armed forces in the territory of the State of the forum in the area of the application of art. 12 UNCJIS cannot be, however, seen as such. Finke (2011), p. 863.

[99] Art. 12 UNCJIS; art. 11 ECSI; § 1605(a)(5) U.S. Code; section 6, section 16 (2) SIA; section 13 Foreign States Immunities Act 1985,196, 16.12.1985; section 5 State Immunity Act 1978, 20.7.1978; section 7, section 19(2)(a) Singapore State Immunity Act; art. 2 (e) Ley N° 24.488 Inmunidad jurisdiccional de los estados extranjeros antes los tribunales argentinos, 31.5.1995; section 5 Foreign States Immunity Law 5769-2008; art. 10 Act on the Civil Jurisdiction of Japan with respect to a Foreign State, etc., act N° 24, 24.4.2009; section 6 Foreign States Immunities Act 1981, 6.10.1981, Act No. 87, 1981.

national courts declining their jurisdiction,[100] as well as courts' judgments refusing to enforce judgments delivered by foreign courts in violation of State immunity.[101] However, the mere referral to the outcome of the judgment of the ICJ and national courts is not sufficient in the case of terrorism exception, as there are serious differences between State military activities and sponsoring terrorism.

First, armed activities are expressly excluded from the application of the provisions of the mentioned conventions, whereas none of the analysed provisions refer *expressis verbis* to terrorism. Second, the exclusion of armed activities concerns acts committed during armed conflict. Sponsored acts of terrorism were and may be committed outside any armed conflict, in territories that are considered to be safe.[102] Finally, although terrorists often use military methods and equipment, they are not members of armed forces, they are criminals supposedly sponsored by some States. Therefore, to exclude terrorism exceptions from territorial tort exceptions, one needs to indicate other reasoning than that adopted by the ICJ in *Jurisdictional Immunities of the State.*

In the works of the International Law Commission, it was mentioned that territorial tort exception is essential for an injured individual, because otherwise this individual would be without recourse to justice if a foreign State were entitled to immunity from jurisdiction. Moreover, the applied law should be the law of the State of the forum (*lex loci delicti commissi*), so the most convenient court of the scene of the delict.[103] This argumentation can be applied as well to terrorism exceptions. Both the United States and Canada claim that the aim of the act is to permit victims of terrorism to bring an effective claim before a court.

On the other hand, the ILC in its report underlined that the will of States was to cover by territorial tort exceptions mostly insurable risks, mainly concerned with accidental injuries and damages caused by traffic accidents, irrespective of the means of transport. Nevertheless, it is also emphasized that the wording of the Art. 12 of the UNCJIS is wide enough to cover also intentional physical harm, including homicide, although there were members of the ILC who expressed their reservations about too broad understanding of this article.[104] Terrorist attacks are intentional killings,

---

[100] Jurisdictional Immunities of the State (Germany v. Italy: Greece Intervening), Judgment, ICJ Reports 2012, 65–74. Sąd Najwyższy Natoniewski.

[101] Jurisdictional Immunities of the State (Germany v. Italy: Greece Intervening), Judgment, ICJ Reports 2012, 75. Bundesgerichtshof, case no. III ZR 245/98, judgment of 26.6.2003.

[102] Kohan (2017), pp. 1559, 1565–1566.

[103] International Law Commission, Draft Articles on Jurisdictional Immunities of States and Their Property, with commentaries, 1991, p. 44.

[104] Ibid., pp. 45–46. Bundesgerichtshof, case no. III ZR 245/98. Constitutional Court of the Republic of Slovenia, case Up-13/99:13. McElhinney v. Ireland App No 31253/96 [2001] ECHR 763, at 38. Ferrer Lloret (2007), pp. 30, 45. Fox and Webb (2013), pp. 468, 470.

The US Courts, deciding on cases falling within the scope of the 28 U.S. Code 1605(a)(5), that has the same wording as art. 12 UNCJIS, consider that this section covers all tort actions for damages not otherwise encompassed by other sections of the FSIA, as it casts in general text as applying to all tort actions, not only the ones resulting from traffic accidents. Letelier v. the

therefore this argument supports the view that territorial tort exceptions might cover terrorism exceptions.

What is decisive in the exclusion of terrorism exceptions from the area of the application of territorial tort exceptions is the fact that terrorist attacks are conducted by individuals directly present in the territory of the forum State, whereas the State benefiting from State immunity and being at the same time the State sponsor of terrorism has no presence in that territory connected to the terrorist attack at issue. The relevant texts of international conventions refer to the presence of the author of the injury or damage in the territory of the forum State and it is interpreted narrowly. Therefore in case of terrorism exceptions, the State or its agents should be present in the territory of the forum State and their presence should be connected to the execution of the wrongful act itself. In most cases the link between a State and direct authors of a terrorist attack will be too vague to fulfil this requirement and a mere general presence of representatives of the foreign State on the territory of the forum State unconnected to carrying out of a terrorist attack is not enough to induce responsibility of that foreign State.[105]

Moreover, in judgments relating to territorial tort exceptions, US courts themselves indicated, that although the relevant section of the FSIA refers in general to all tort actions for money damages, the condition of its application are not tortious acts committed anywhere in the world, but within the jurisdiction of the United States, so in the US territory.[106] It is worth noticing, that in *McKeel* the Court of Appeals, Ninth Circuit stated that the opposite interpretation would not be consistent with the prevailing practice in international law.[107] Therefore territorial tort exceptions cannot refer to terrorist acts committed outside the territory of the State of the forum.

This interpretation is also confirmed by the report of the ILC that emphasizes that the requirement of the presence of the author of the injury or damage in the territory of the State of the forum was inserted into the text of the UNCJIS to exclude transboundary injuries or trans-frontiers tort or damage from the application of

---

Republic of Chile. McKeel v. Islamic Republic of Iran. Frolova v. Union of Soviet Socialist Republics. Liu v. the Republic of China.

However, in Olsen and Sanchez the US Court of Appeals, Ninth Circuit presented an opinion that a foreign State remains largely immunized from torts committed in its governmental capacity. Olsen and Sanchez v. the Republic of Mexico.

[105] Al-Adsani v. the United Kingdom App No. 35763/97 [2001] ECHR 761 at 57. Luxembourg Tribunal d'Arrondissement, civil judgment of 27.3.2019 at 1.1.2.2.2.3, 2.1.2.2.2.3. Smith v. Socialist People's Libyan Arab Jamahiriya, 101 F. 3d 239, 65 USLW 2374. International Law Commission, Draft Articles on Jurisdictional Immunities of States and Their Property, with commentaries, 1991, p. 45. Council of Europe (1972) Explanatory Report to the European Convention on State Immunity, p. 12. Ferrer Lloret (2007), pp. 30, 33. Fox and Webb (2013), pp. 471–474.

[106] Perez v. the Bahamas. McKeel v. Islamic Republic of Iran. Olsen and Sanchez v. the Republic of Mexico. Frolova v. Union of Soviet Socialist Republics.

[107] McKeel v. Islamic Republic of Iran.

territorial tort exception.[108] Even if we assume that terrorists are in fact sponsored by a foreign State, a terrorist attack in question would be a case of a transboundary injury not covered by a territorial tort exception. Therefore acts of terrorism committed outside the US and Canada fall outside territorial tort exceptions.

On the other hand, it is highly doubtful that terrorists can be recognised as State's servants or agents. Art. 2 (1)(b)(iv) defines as 'State' representatives of the State acting in their capacity. A State may claim immunity for any act of its servant or agent, for which it is responsible under international law. Moreover, international law does not require that this agent or servant should have been acting in accordance with his instructions or authority. The mere fact that the conduct itself is unlawful or objectionable is not of itself a ground for refusing State immunity.[109] Despite the fact of alleged terrorism sponsoring, it cannot be validly claimed that terrorists are empowered, under national law, to exercise elements of the governmental authority. It is hardly imaginable that executing acts of terrorism constitutes acting in the capacity of State officials.[110] It also needs to be underlined that acts of State officials acting in their capacity are not attributable to them personally but only to the State.[111] The possible outcome thereof, if applied to a terrorism exception, would be the exemption of terrorists themselves from their own responsibility for terrorist acts.

Nevertheless, this position might be disputable, at least from the point of view of US courts. Starting from the decision in *Letelier*, US courts concluded that intentional killings perpetrated in the US territory by another State's officers or agents do

[108] International Law Commission, Draft Articles on Jurisdictional Immunities of States and Their Property, with commentaries, 1991, p. 45.

[109] Jones v. Saudi Arabia. Kazemi Estate v. Iran at 86–90.

In this place it is indispensable to refer also to works of the ILC: International Law Commission, Draft Articles on Jurisdictional Immunities of States and Their Property, with commentaries, 1991.

Art. 4 (1) The conduct of any State organ shall be considered an act of that State under international law whether the organ exercises legislative, executive, judicial or any other functions, whatever position it holds in the organization of the State, and whatever its character as an organ of the central Government or of a territorial unit of the State.

(2) An organ includes any person or entity which has that status in accordance with the internal law of the State.

Art. 5 The conduct of a person or entity which is not an organ of the State under article 4 but which is empowered by the law of that State to exercise elements of the governmental authority shall be considered an act of the State under international law, provided the person or entity is acting in that capacity in the particular instance.

Art. 8 The conduct of a person or group of persons shall be considered an act of a State under international law if the person or group of persons is in fact acting on the instructions of, or under the direction or control of, that State in carrying out the conduct.

[110] In Jones v. Saudi Arabia the House of Lords indicated, in reference to acts of torture, that 'torture cannot constitute an official act. It is so illegal that it must fall outside the scope of official activity': Jones v. Saudi Arabia at 72. The gravity of illegality of acts of terrorism is comparable to that of acts of torture.

Syed (2016), p. 253. Kohan (2017), pp. 1563–1564.

[111] Jones v. Saudi Arabia at 66. Wheatherall (2015), p. 404.

not constitute acting within a State's discretionary powers, as there is no discretion in committing an illegal act. Assassinations of individuals are contrary to both domestic and international law. That is why, if assassination is committed in the US territory, a foreign State cannot be accorded sovereign immunity for any tort claims resulting from its conduct in committing an assassination.[112] This logic could be applied to terrorism exceptions, once it is proven that terrorists were acting on behalf of a foreign State while committing a specific act of terrorism. It is doubtful whether general allegations of supporting terrorism suffice to conclude that terrorists executed a specific attack on behalf of an alleged State sponsor of terrorism, as its agents.

Lastly, even the States that introduced a terrorism exception to their legislation consider it to be separated from territorial tort exceptions. The territorial tort exception is, in the United States, regulated shortly in 28 U.S. Code § 1605 (a)(5), together with other exceptions to State immunity. The entire sections 28 U. S. Code § 1605A and § 1605B concentrate solely on terrorism exception. In Canada, the territorial tort exception is regulated by section 6 SIA, whereas the terrorism exception is covered by section 6.1 SIA. In legal doctrine, we may also find opinions separating territorial tort exceptions and terrorism exceptions.[113] This interpretation is confirmed by the case-law of US courts that excludes the application of territorial tort exceptions to situations covered by terrorism exceptions.[114]

On the contrary, Eric T. Kohan tries to incorporate *de novo* terrorism exception into territorial tort exception, accenting that Art. 12 of the UNCJIS was always understood broadly as encompassing also *acta de jure imperii* or even intentional killings of foreign nationals in foreign territories. Therefore, he opposes a narrow interpretation of territorial tort exceptions with the exclusion of terrorist attacks therefrom.[115] This argumentation could be correct, if the United States and Canada did not decide on their own that the terrorism exception is a category that falls outside the territorial tort exception. The present State of the relevant legislation stands against Kohan's interpretation.

Taking all the above-mentioned arguments into consideration, it can be concluded that the terrorism exception is not covered by the territorial tort exception. Terrorists are not agents of a State and the terrorism exception includes also acts of terrorism committed abroad, whereas the aim of the territorial tort exception is to apply the principle of *lex loci delicti commissi.* Although there might be some reasoning supporting the opposite view, actions of the United States and Canada themselves excluded the terrorism exception from the scope of application of one of approved exceptions to State immunity.

---

[112]Letelier v. the Republic of Chile. Liu v. the Republic of China.

[113]Finke (2011), pp. 874–875.

[114]In re: Terrorist Attacks on September 11, 2001.

[115]Kohan (2017), pp. 1555, 1560.

3.2 The Subject-Matter and Circumstances of the Claims

In *Jurisdictional Immunities of the State,* the ICJ concluded that the particular nature of the acts, being the subject-matter of the claims and the specific circumstances of the claims, did not suffice to deprive Germany of the right to State immunity. It needs to be stressed that the ICJ did not dispute the fact that Germany's actions during the Second World War constituted serious violations of the principles of international law applicable to the conduct of armed conflicts, amounting to war crimes and crimes against humanity, and thus contravening even peremptory norms (*jus cogens*).[116]

The ICJ underlined that immunity from jurisdiction is not only a mere immunity from being subject to the trial process, as the State is entitled to immunity even before a national court of a foreign State can hear the merits of the case brought before it and before the facts of the case have been established. Assuming that the gravity of the allegations could deprive a State of the right to State immunity would lead to a simple conclusion that the national court would have to make an inquiry into the merits in order to determine whether the alleged violation of law was serious enough to deprive a foreign State of its immunity, whereas immunity protects the foreign State from any consideration of the claim based on a balance or comparison of the loss to the individual and of sovereign interests of the foreign State. Once again, forming its opinion on the basis of State practice as well as of judgments of numerous national courts, the ICJ acknowledged that State immunity does not depend on the gravity of the alleged wrongful act. Moreover, none of the conventions enumerated in this chapter support a thesis that State immunity can be waived because of the gravity of the act.[117]

This part of deliberations of the ICJ was also devoted to *jus cogens,* meaning peremptory norms of international law prevailing over any inconsistent rule of international law.[118] According to the ICJ, no conflict between *jus cogens* prohibiting committing certain acts (e.g. crimes against humanity) and State immunity exists, as these two sets of rules address different matters. The rules of State immunity, being procedural in nature, are not connected with the question whether or not the conduct of a State concerned was lawful or unlawful, so the immunity is not an exemption from material law. Recognizing State immunity does not mean a

---

[116] Jurisdictional Immunities of the State (Germany v. Italy: Greece Intervening), Judgment, ICJ Reports 2012, 80–81.

[117] Bundesgerichtshof case no. III ZR 245/98. Fang and Ors. v. Jiang and Ors. [2007] NZAR 420, at 27–71. Jones v. Saudi Arabia at 33. Jurisdictional Immunities of the State (Germany v. Italy: Greece Intervening), Judgment, ICJ Reports 2012, 82–91. Sąd Najwyższy, Natoniewski. Kazemi Estate v. Iran at 34, 105, 118. Fox and Webb (2013), pp. 368–369.

Contrary opinion: Areios Pagos, Distomo. Von Dardel v. Union of Soviet Socialist Republics, 623 F. Supp. 246 (D.D.C. 1985).

[118] Al-Adsani v. the United Kingdom at 57–60. Hugo Princz v. Federal Republic of Germany.

The status of jus cogens norms and doubts they raise is not the subject of this article, it might be even disputed whether State sovereignty is or is not a jus cogens norm. Finke (2011), pp. 867–868.

recognition of the legality of the acts in question and it constitutes neither aid nor assistance in maintaining the unlawful situation. A breach of *jus cogens* does not suffice to confer jurisdiction and it does not constitute an implied waiver of State immunity. Therefore a State that would respect State immunity of other State would not violate international customary rule reflected in Art. 41 of the International Law Commission's Draft Articles obliging States to cooperation in bringing to an end to any serious breach of international law. This ICJ's view was also supported by numerous references to judgments on relations between State immunity and violations of fundamental human rights or *jus cogens*[119] and approved subsequently by judgments of other courts.[120] This interpretation is not contradicted by the text of the resolution of the UN General Assembly no. 60/147,[121] as this resolution requires the existence of access to justice and effective remedy for victims of gross human rights violations, however the text is ambiguous and it cannot be deduced thereof that it means granting of jurisdiction over foreign States to domestic courts.[122]

This reasoning is fully applicable to terrorism exceptions. Acts of terrorism are serious violations of human rights laws, in some cases even amounting to crimes

[119] Bundesgerichtshof case no. III ZR 245/98. Constitutional Court of the Republic of Slovenia, case Up-13/99 at 14. Cour de cassation, case no. 02-45961, judgment of 16.12.2003. Cour de cassation, case no. 03-41851, judgment of 2.4.2004. Cour de cassation, case no. 04-47504, judgment of 3.1.2006. Bouzari v. Islamic Republic of Iran (2004) 2004 CanLII 87 (ON CA), at 84–94. Al-Adsani v. the United Kingdom at 63, 66. Kalogeropoulou and others v. Greece and Germany App No 59021/00 [2002] 129 ILR 537. However it needs to be underlined that six ECHR judges (Rozakis, Caflisch, Wildhaber, Costa, Cabral Barreto and Vajić) in their dissenting opinion expressed the view that a violation of jus cogens deprives the rule of sovereign immunity of all its legal effects. Grosz v. France App No 14717/06, 16 June 2009. Fang and Ors. v. Jiang and Ors. at 26–71. Kuwait Airways Corporation v. Iraqi Airways Company and Others [2002] UKHL 19 at 24. Jones v. Saudi Arabia at 24. Jurisdictional Immunities of the State (Germany v. Italy: Greece Intervening), Judgment, ICJ Reports 2012, 92–97. Hugo Princz v. Federal Republic of Germany. Siderman de Blake v. Republic of Argentina, 965 F. 2d 699 (9th Cir. 1992). Smith v. Socialist People's Libyan Arab Jamahiriya. Finke (2011), pp. 868–869. Scherr (2012), pp. 148–149. European Parliament Research Service (2016) Justice Against Sponsors of Terrorism. JASTA and its international impact. Briefing October, p. 4. Czapliński and Wyrozumska (2014), p. 303. Kohan (2017), pp. 1543–1544. Cf. Areios Pagos, Distomo. Also: Judge Patricia Wald, dissenting opinion in: Hugo Princz v. Federal Republic of Germany. The procedural nature of State immunity in civil proceedings is consistent with case-law on the procedural nature of immunities in criminal proceedings, separating issues relating to immunities from material law on individual criminal responsibility: Case Concerning the Arrest Warrant of 11 April 2000 (Democratic Republic of the Congo v. Belgium), Judgment, I.C.J. Reports 2002, pp. 3, 58–60.

[120] X v. the Attorney General of New Zealand, Ministry of Defence (United Kingdom) [2017] NZHC 768, at 40–47. Luxembourg Tribunal d'Arrondissement, civil judgment of 27.3.2019, 1.1.2.2.2.4, 2.1.2.2.2.4. Sąd Najwyższy, case no. II CSK 548/18, order of 9.5.2019. Kazemi Estate v. Iran at 61, 101–103, 157–161.

[121] UN General Assembly, resolution no. 60/147 Basic Principles and Guidelines on the Right to a Remedy and Reparation for Victims of Gross Violations of International Human Rights Law and Serious Violations of International Humanitarian Law, 16.12.2005, A/RES/60/147.

[122] Contrary view: Supreme Court of Canada, case Kazemi Estate v. Iran, R.S. Abella (dissenting opinion), at 198.

against humanity. Sponsoring them by States could be considered to be a participation in these crimes and even a violation of *jus cogens*.[123] Yet the determination of whether a terrorist attack being the subject-matter of the dispute at stake was grave enough to consider it to be a crime against humanity or other serious violation of international law attributable to the alleged State sponsor requires a detailed scrutiny of the merits of the dispute. State immunity, as it has been just mentioned, makes it impossible for a court to enter into the merits. Even the ICJ itself notices in *Jurisdictional Immunities of the State* that apart from the United States (and up-to-date also Canada) there are no other States that would enact similar legislation based on the gravity of terrorist crimes. This isolation of the United States is considered by the ICJ to be an indication that customary international law in that area protects immunity.[124] The ECtHR emphasized in *Al-Adsani* that terrorism exception even in the United States was very limited and restricted at that time to recognize it as an evidence of international custom.[125]

3.3 The 'Last Resort' Argument

In *Jurisdictional Immunities of the State,* Italy argued that depriving Germany of its right to State immunity was necessary, because there were no other ways to secure compensation for various groups of victims of Germany's actions during the Second World War. Also, in that case, the ICJ concluded that the issue of State immunity must be separated from whether the international responsibility of a State is engaged and whether it has an obligation to make reparation for injuries and damages suffered by individuals.[126]

This conclusion leads to deliberations about the relationship between State immunity and the right to a fair trial. State immunity is not a disproportional limitation of the right to a fair trial,[127] even in the case relating to terrorism

[123] Cour de cassation, case no. 09-14743, judgment of 9.3.2011.
Whether terrorism is a jus cogens violation is disputable (see: Syed 2016, pp. 271–286. Kohan 2017, pp. 1541–1542. Tel-Oren v. Libyan Arab Republic, 726 F. 2d 774, 233 U.S.App.D.C. 384). For the purposes of this paper it will be assumed that it is a breach of a jus cogens norm.

[124] Jurisdictional Immunities of the State (Germany v. Italy: Greece Intervening), Judgment, ICJ Reports 2012, 88.

[125] Al-Adsani v. the United Kingdom, p. 64.

[126] Jurisdictional Immunities of the State (Germany v. Italy: Greece Intervening), Judgment, ICJ Reports 2012, 98–101.

[127] Waite and Kennedy v. Germany App No 26083/94 [1999] ECHR 13, at 50. Beer and Reagan v. Germany App No 28934/95 [1999] ECHR 6, at 40. Fogarty v. the United Kingdom App No 37112/97 [2001] ECHR 762 at 32. McElhinney v. Ireland at 33. Kalogeropoulou and others v. Greece and Germany. Al-Adsani v. the United Kingdom at 52. Grosz v. France. Jones v. Saudi Arabia at 39.

exception.[128] As was stated by the House of Lords in *Jones v. Saudi Arabia*, international law cannot be established solely on the basis of the sympathy that one must feel for the victims.[129] It is indisputable that victims of State sponsored terrorism suffered immense injuries and that it might be impossible for them to institute proceedings before the courts of the State sponsoring terrorism. Yet all these circumstances do not suffice to overcome State immunity and to grant jurisdiction to courts of other States.

Taking all the above-mentioned arguments into consideration, a conclusion can be drawn that a rule accepting terrorism exception to State immunity has not been crystallized in the form of customary international law. It does not mean that in the future such a rule will not become an international custom, as it all depends on developments in public international law.[130] Nevertheless, an isolated practice of the United States and Canada is not enough to ascertain an appearance of a new rule of customary international law, it is rather a violation of customary international law.

In this part, however, some additional arguments can be indicated. In its Memorial in *the Certain Iranian Assets* case Iran alleged that the terrorism exception breaches not only customary international law, but also the 1955 Treaty of Amity.[131] Iran referred the ICJ to *United States Diplomatic and Consular Staff in Teheran*[132] and emphasized that despite hostilities between the US and Iran since 1979,[133] the 1955 Treaty of Amity was still considered to be in force.[134] According to Iran the US violates inter alia.:

1. the most favourable treatment clause (Art. II);
2. recognition of separate judicial status of Iranian companies and freedom of access to courts of nationals of the other Party (Art. III). Iranian companies are deprived of possibility of defending their rights properly before US courts as their assets are seized and they are forced to satisfy judgment debts in cases against Iran, not being even parties to those cases;[135]

[128] Luxembourg Tribunal d'Arrondissement, civil judgment of 27.3.2019 at 1.1.2.2.3, 2.1.2.2.3.

[129] Jones v. Saudi Arabia, p. 34.

[130] Grosz v. France.

[131] Treaty of Amity, Economic Relations, and Consular Rights, Teheran, 15.8.1955.

[132] Case Concerning United States Diplomatic and Consular Staff in Teheran, Judgment, I.C.J. Reports 1980, p. 3, 54.

[133] On 4.11.1979 the US embassy in Teheran was overrun and its nationals taken hostage.

[134] It was confirmed in 2019 by the ICJ: Case Concerning Certain Iranian Assets (Islamic Republic of Iran v. United States of America) Preliminary Objections, Judgment, not reported, at 114. Certain Iranian Assets (Islamic Republic of Iran v. United States of America), Memorial of the Islamic Republic of Iran, 1.2.2017, pp. 1, 45–50.

[135] Certain Iranian Assets (Islamic Republic of Iran v. United States of America), Memorial of the Islamic Republic of Iran, 1.2.2017, pp. 2, 6, 15, 64–95. Bennett v. Islamic Republic of Iran, 927. Bennett v. Islamic Republic of Iran, 799.

3. fair and equitable treatment to nationals and companies of the other Party (Art. IV);[136]
4. protection of property right of nationals and companies of the other Party (Art. V);[137]
5. freedom from restrictions on the making of payments and other transfers of funds to or from the territory of the United States (Art. VII);[138]
6. freedom of commerce between the territories of Iran and the United States (Art. X).[139]

Whether this is the case will be decided by the ICJ. Here it is worth noticing that the terrorism exception might constitute also a violation of the United States—Iran international agreement. Other bilateral or multilateral agreements concluded by the US and Canada with foreign States may contain similar provisions possibly contravening the terrorism exception.

As was stated above, currently the terrorism exception is not a part of customary international law. The next part of this chapter represents deliberations concerning possible future improvements of customary international law in the area of terrorism exception.

4 Perspectives of Terrorism Exception in International Law

It is natural that one feel sympathy towards victims of terrorism and support them in search for justice for injuries and damages they suffered. Nevertheless, legal disputes should be decided on the basis of law,[140] especially international legal disputes should be resolved with reference to international law, including customary law, and not on the basis of feelings or sentiments like compassion.

First of all, the terrorism exception to State immunity is an isolated practice of the United States and Canada ('unilateral exercise of the function of guardian of international values[141]'), therefore it is considered to be discriminatory and contrary to customary international law.[142] Of course, the States against which US courts'

---

[136]Certain Iranian Assets (Islamic Republic of Iran v. United States of America), Memorial of the Islamic Republic of Iran, 1.2.2017, pp. 96–107.

[137]Ibid., pp. 108–109.

[138]Ibid., pp. 111–112.

[139]Ibid., pp. 112–117.

[140]In re Islamic Republic of Iran Terrorism Litigation. Rubin v. Islamic Republic of Iran, 349.

[141]Jones v. Saudi Arabia, p. 99.

[142]Jones v. Saudi Arabia, p. 99. Certain Iranian Assets (Islamic Republic of Iran v. United States of America), Memorial of the Islamic Republic of Iran, 1.2.2017, p. 55. Ferrer Lloret (2007), p. 56.

Bennett v. Islamic Republic of Iran, 799 we may read that 'there's nothing unreasonable, discriminatory or in violation of international law about waiving sovereign immunity for terrorism-based judgments'.

judgments are delivered, do not accept the US jurisdiction and they are absent at those trials. Moreover, they do not recognize these judgments and refuse to pay the compensations entered by the US courts.[143]

However, objections to this exception were expressly raised by third parties, including States or their organs. We may find among them the Luxembourg District Court,[144] the European Parliament, as well as representatives of the following States: Saudi Arabia, Russia, France, the Netherlands and the United Kingdom.[145] The Ministry of Foreign Affairs of the Russian Federation called the JASTA a 'complete disregard of international law', a 'megalomania and tendency to establish extraterritorial jurisdiction' as 'any American citizen can now sue any country and accuse it, without proof, of any possible wrongdoing'.[146] The EU Delegation to the United States of America in its letter of 9.9.2016 emphasized that the JASTA would be in conflict with fundamental principles of international law.[147] The Dutch Parliament expressed an opinion that the JASTA is a 'gross unwarranted breach of Dutch sovereignty' which could result in 'astronomical damages'.[148]

On the other hand, it is worth mentioning that the French *Cour de cassation* accepted that under certain conditions the terrorism exception may limit State immunity. The court emphasized that the fact of complicity in execution of a terrorist attack does not constitute the exercise of sovereign powers of State. Referring to judgments of the ECtHR, the Court concluded that there exists neither legitimate aim nor a reasonable relation of proportionality in protecting a foreign State with State immunity if the responsibility of the State is sought on the basis of committed acts of terrorism. Yet, the responsibility covers only cases of active participation of a State in terrorist attack. A mere moral responsibility for a terrorist attack, for example a lack of persecution of perpetrators thereof, does not suffice to waive State's immunity.[149] However, it is not clear from this judgment, whether the *Cour de cassation* would equate the responsibility for State's complicity in a terrorist attack with alleged sponsoring of terrorist attacks.

---

[143] Bank Markazi, aka Central Bank of Iran v. Peterson et al. International Court of Justice, Case Concerning Certain Iranian Assets (Islamic Republic of Iran v. United States of America), Memorial of the Islamic Republic of Iran, 1.2.2017, p. 55. Ferrer Lloret (2007), p. 48. Gartenstein-Ross (2002), pp. 498–499.

[144] Luxembourg Tribunal d'Arrondissement, civil judgment of 27.3.2019.

[145] European Parliament Research Service (2016) Justice Against Sponsors of Terrorism. JASTA and its international impact. Briefing October, pp. 8–10.

[146] Ministry of Foreign Affairs of the Russian Federation (2020) Comment by the Information and Press Department on the US passing the Justice Against Sponsors of Terrorism Act with extraterritorial jurisdiction. http://www.mid.ru/en/foreign_policy/news/-/asset_publisher/cKNonkJE02Bw/content/id/2479122. Accessed 15 April 2021.

[147] European Union Delegation to the United States of America (2019) Letter of 9.9.2016. https://www.washingtonpost.com/gdpr-consent/?destination=%2fnews%2fpowerpost%2fwp-content%2fuploads%2fsites%2f47%2f2016%2f09%2fEU-on-JASTA.pdf%3f. Accessed 15 April 2021.

[148] Hancock (2018), p. 1295.

[149] Cour de cassation (France), case no. 09-14743.

Moreover, it needs to be pointed out that even the classical territorial tort exception is considered to not be supported by State practice, as many States do not apply it.[150] The terrorism exception is recognized by even fewer States than the territorial tort exception. Therefore the opinion of US legal doctrine that there is persuasive support for terrorism exception as no court has found that it lacked jurisdiction in a terrorism exception suit[151] cannot be accepted, as it refers only to US courts, but it lacks a worldwide approval.

The acceptance of the terrorism exception by United States courts has some importance, yet it is not decisive. It needs to be borne in mind that although US courts are aware of international implications of State immunity, they consider it appropriate to decide on State immunity solely on the basis of the national law. According to United States courts, the degree to which a foreign State is entitled to immunity under the FSIA is determined by the procedures set forth by the US Congress.[152] According to *Kohan,* even if the terrorist exception does violate international law (as US courts operate under the assumption that the US law does not violate international law unless the Congress expressly indicates that it wants to deviate from international law), it would have no effect on the way it is treated in US courts, as they probably would enforce the exception without considering the international implications thereof.[153] That is why the US jurisprudence reflects the current state of State immunity in the United States and not customary international law on State immunity, despite the fact that in some instances US courts emphasized that the FSIA, enacted by the US Congress, reflects the modern realities of the interdependence of nations.[154] It was so in 1976 when the FSIA was first enacted, but it is not the case anymore.

A different attitude is applied in the Canadian case-law. Canadian courts notice and analyse judgments of international and foreign courts on State immunity. However, according to the Canadian jurisprudence, international customary law gives only a general shape to State immunity in civil matters. The precise scope of State immunity and accepted exceptions is a subject-matter of domestic law based on domestic choices of the Canadian Parliament made for policy reasons in matters of international relations.[155] Both US and Canada courts seem to overlook the international implications of the terrorism exception.

The aim of State immunity, that reflects current political realities and relationships, is to promote comity and good relations between States through respect of

---

[150] European Parliament Research Service (2016) Justice Against Sponsors of Terrorism. JASTA and its international impact. Briefing October, p. 3.

[151] Gartenstein-Ross (2002), pp. 498–499.

[152] McKeel v. Islamic Republic of Iran. Olsen and Sanchez v. the Republic of Mexico. Von Dardel v. Union of Soviet Socialist Republics. Tracy v. Islamic Republic of Iran. Rubin v. Islamic Republic of Iran, 408. Kohan (2017), pp. 1563–1564.

[153] Kohan (2017), pp. 1563–1564.

[154] Olsen and Sanchez v. the Republic of Mexico.

[155] Kazemi Estate v. Iran, pp. 44–46, 170.

another State's sovereignty.[156] The terrorism exception contradicts this aim, as the United States and Canada unilaterally decide to recognize foreign States as terrorism sponsors and deprive them of their right to State immunity. It is not unimaginable that States listed as terrorism sponsors, as a countermeasure, may unilaterally adopt similar laws permitting them, or their judicial organs, to ignore State immunity of the United States and Canada and accept civil claims against those States.[157] This might be especially risky for the United States as it is a State with a very large global presence with remarkable property situated abroad, therefore it could be subjected to jurisdiction of foreign courts and to enforcement proceedings from that property. It needs to be remembered here that 28 U.S. Code § 1605A(a)(1) waives State immunity of foreign States before US courts in case of extrajudicial killings considered to be acts of terrorism and the United States have their own targeted killing program.[158] It is not unimaginable that some States, in a mirror legislation, might declare the US to be a State supporting terrorism due to its extrajudicial killing program. The same could apply to cases of extraordinary rendition as the United States adopted universal jurisdiction in cases of torture. Other States could permit lawsuits against the US for cases of extraordinary rendition[159] by applying the same reasoning and logic as the US did.

And in fact, there appear to be attempts to introduce grounds for lawsuits against the United States abroad. For example, in Iraq a group called the 'Arab Project' requested the Iraqi Parliament to file a suit against the US for the involvement of the United States in Iraq in 2003.[160] Ferrer Lloret writes even about a possible situation

---

[156] Fogarty v. the United Kingdom at 34. McElhinney v. Ireland, at 35. Al-Adsani v. the United Kingdom at 54. Grosz v. France. Kuwait Airways Corporation v. Iraqi Airways Company and Others at 138. Jones v. Saudi Arabia at 18. McKeel v. Islamic Republic of Iran. Theo Garb and Others v. Republic of Poland *2006* WL 515500 (2d. Cir. *2006*). In re: Terrorist Attacks on September 11, 2001. Rubin and others v. Islamic Republic of Iran, 830. Rubin and others v. Islamic Republic of Iran, 583. European Parliament Research Service (2016) Justice Against Sponsors of Terrorism. JASTA and its international impact. Briefing October, p. 4. Wheatherall (2015), p. 402.

[157] As in fact Cuba did: Ferrer Lloret (2007), p. 48.

It was also one of the reasons why the President Barack Obama vetoed the JASTA: Justice Against Sponsors of Terrorism Act, 13.9.2016, s. 2040 (114th)—JASTA. Obama B (2016) Veto to the Justice Against Sponsors of Terrorism Act (JASTA), Congressional Record, 114th Congress, Vol. 162, 26.9.2016, Washington.

This risk was also previously noted also by the US Courts: McKeel v. Islamic Republic of Iran.

This view was also presented by representatives of other States: Ministry of Foreign Affairs of the Russian Federation (2020); Kohan (2017), p. 1558. Hancock (2018), p. 1311. Keller (2005), pp. 1051–1052.

[158] White House (2019) U.S. Policy Standards and Procedures for the Use of Force in Counterterrorism Operations Outside the United States and Areas of Active Hostilities, 23.5.2013. https://obamawhitehouse.archives.gov/the-press-office/2013/05/23/fact-sheet-us-policy-standards-and-procedures-use-force-counterterrorism. Accessed 15 April 2021.

[159] Al Nashiri v. Poland App No 28761/11 [2012] ECHR 2028.

[160] Hancock (2018), pp. 1312–1313.

of extraterritorial judicial anarchy (*anarquía judicial extraterritorial*).[161] The unilateral application of the terrorism exception can therefore lead to unnecessary tensions and conflicts between States. However, in legal literature we may find authors who pose a question whether individual rights should not be disregarded to protect interstate interests.[162]

Another argument that contravenes the recognition of terrorism exceptions as customary international law in the future is the principle according to which exceptions should be subjected to a restrictive interpretation. State immunity is a general customary rule of international law so in case of any doubts it should be interpreted extensively.[163] This interpretation can only lead to a denial of the existence of terrorism exceptions in customary international law.

The next important issue concerns the application of the principle of universal jurisdiction to civil proceedings against States sponsors of terrorism. In that area it needs to be pointed out at the beginning that international law accepts universal jurisdiction in criminal matters. As it was stated already in the *Lotus* decision,[164] a State may exercise extraterritorial criminal jurisdiction unless there exists a rule of international law limiting this freedom of States. One of the main reasons thereof is that usually a perpetrator of an international crime is present in the State of the forum.[165]

Also judgments on civil claims related to acts of torture committed by foreign States can serve, *per analogiam,* as a source of inspiration for conclusions in that area. The jurisprudence is currently unanimous that international law permits for universal jurisdiction in criminal matters for acts of torture.[166] This view is based on the wording of Art. 4 and 5 of the United Nations Convention against Torture and Other Cruel, Inhuman or Degrading Treatment or Punishment (UNCAT)[167] that constitutes an obligation for States to ensure that all acts of torture are offences under their criminal law. On the contrary, the same cannot be said about Art. 14 of the UNCAT that requires the introduction of forms of civil redress for acts of torture, which is read as obliging States only to provide a civil remedy for torture committed within their own jurisdiction, but not abroad.[168] However, it needs to be mentioned

---

[161] Ferrer Lloret (2007), p. 59.

[162] Ferrer Lloret (2007), pp. 36–37.

[163] Luxembourg Tribunal d'Arrondissement, civil judgment of 27.3.2019, pp. 1.1.2.2.2.1.

[164] The Case of the S.S. Lotus', Judgment of 7.9.1927, Collection of Judgments, Series A.—No. 10.

[165] Ryngaert (2015), pp. 126–127.

[166] Bouzari v. Islamic Republic of Iran, pp. 71–72.

[167] United Nations Convention against Torture and Other Cruel, Inhuman or Degrading Treatment or Punishment, New York, 10.12.1984, UN General Assembly resolution no. 39/46—(UNCAT).

[168] Bouzari v. Islamic Republic of Iran at 74, 78, 83. Kazemi Estate v. Iran at 50, 103, 139–145, 153, 157.

However, the Committee Against Torture is of a contrary opinion and considers that art. 14 UNCAT requires States to introduce civil redress for acts of torture committed also abroad: Committee Against Torture, General comment no. 3: Implementation of article 14 by State Parties, 13.12.2012, CAT/C/GC/3, pp. 22, 42.

that the legislation of the United States—the Torture Victims Protection Act (TVPA)[169]—introduced also a universal civil jurisdiction against a foreign individual who subjects another individual to torture, provided that the US courts' jurisdiction remains the 'last resort' jurisdiction.[170]

As was mentioned above, US courts consider terrorism to be subjected to universal jurisdiction, including in civil matters.[171] It is contrary to the previous judgments of US courts on the territorial tort exception. In *McKeel* the Court of Appeals, Ninth Circuit excluded jurisdiction over a foreign State for a tort that occurred in the territory of that foreign State, as otherwise the FSIA would have almost unlimited geographic scope and it would lead to an unprecedented assertion of jurisdiction over foreign States.[172]

Therefore, it cannot be said that the principle of universal jurisdiction also applies to civil proceedings against State actors. However, in due course the acceptance of universal criminal jurisdiction over certain criminal offences by State officials may lead to an acceptance of a similar tort jurisdiction in the future,[173] yet it still has not happened in current international law.

The question of universal jurisdiction in civil matters deals only with acts of terrorism committed abroad. Yet, also acts of terrorism committed within the jurisdiction of the State of the forum need to deliberated. As was stated in *Letelier,* by exercising jurisdiction for such acts, a State deals with the consequences of unlawful acts on its own territory.[174] The principle of territoriality may stand in favour of granting jurisdiction over State sponsors of terrorism if an attack occurs within the territory of the State of the forum. On the other hand, in *Letielier* the assassination was committed by State agents, officially employed by Chile. Terrorists are not formal employees of a State sponsor of terrorism. Their only connection with that State is an alleged sponsoring. Therefore the above-mentioned principle of territoriality does not seem decisive. Moreover, it needs to be emphasized that State immunity means that a State relinquishes the jurisdiction it naturally possesses due to

---

[169]Torture Victims Protection Act, 12.3.1992, H.R. 2092, 106 Stat. 73 (102nd).

[170]Section 2 (a) An individual who, under actual or apparent authority, or color of law, of any foreign nation "(1) subjects an individual to torture shall, in civil action, be liable for damages to that individual; or (2) subjects an individual to extrajudicial killing shall, in a civil action, be liable for damages to the individual's legal representative, or to any person who may be a claimant in an action for wrongful death".

(b) A court shall decline to hear a claim under this section if the claimant has not exhausted adequate and available remedies in the place in which the conduct giving rise to the claim occurred.

(c) No action shall be maintained under this section unless it is commenced within 10 years after the cause of action arose.

[171]Tracy v. Islamic Republic of Iran. A similar approach was adopted by Silberman Abella in her dissenting opinion in Kazemi Estate v. Iran, Silberman Abella R (dissenting opinion), pp. 174, 215–216, 228–230.

[172]McKeel v. Islamic Republic of Iran.

[173]Bouzari v. Islamic Republic of Iran. Jones v. Saudi Arabia at 22, 26, 33, 98.

[174]Letelier v. the Republic of Chile. Controller and Auditor-General v. Sir Ronald Davison [1996] 2 NZLR 278.

the concept of territorial jurisdiction.[175] Therefore there exist some circumstances that permit making a distinction between the *Letelier* case and territorial tort exception cases based on a too vague connection between a foreign State and terrorists.

Terrorism is a gross violation of human rights law, it might be even considered to be a violation of *jus cogens* or a crime against humanity. However, rejecting jurisdiction on the basis of State immunity does not mean that the actions of the State sponsoring terrorism were or are legal.[176] It only means that the dispute might not be decided by the court of the forum State, notwithstanding the gravity of the allegations. As Jasper Finke rightly points out, the existence of a rule of international law and its enforcement are two different set of problems and one of the weaknesses of the international legal system is the lack of centralised enforcement mechanisms.[177]

That is why the argumentation of US courts that Iran (or other State sponsor of terrorism) knew it was violating the law therefore it should have foreseen the possible consequences thereof, including suits by private actors,[178] is flawed. Customary international law provides for possible countermeasures in case of violations of international law and a waiver of State immunity is not among them. Therefore, as Iran could reasonably expect international sanctions directed against it, including actions by the UN Security Council, it could not have predicted that it will be denied immunity in civil cases instituted by individuals, as this development is not supported by general practice of States forming an international community.

Lastly, the terrorism exception gives a deceiving hope to victims of terrorist acts. They are able to receive a judgment against a foreign State, yet they never receive payments resulting from this judgment, as foreign States do not recognize these decisions and refuse to execute them. Usually these States neither have any (or sufficient) property in the territory of the United States, nor have any economic or commercial relations with the US. These foreign States do not even appear at trials, therefore the United States decided to pay to the victims an alternative compensation on the basis of the VTVPA and the JUSVSSTA. As a matter of fact, terrorism victims that engage their emotions, time and money into a process, receive a judgment, some of them even get compensated by the American taxpayers, but they do not get justice.[179] As was rightly pointed out by the President of the

[175] Letelier v. the Republic of Chile. Controller and Auditor-General v. Sir Ronald Davison [1996] 2 NZLR 278.

[176] Jurisdictional Immunities of the State (Germany v. Italy: Greece Intervening), Judgment, ICJ Reports 2012, 58. Wheatherall (2015), p. 403.

[177] Finke (2011), pp. 869–870.

[178] Bennett v. Islamic Republic of Iran, 799.

[179] Bennett v. Islamic Republic of Iran, 604. In re Islamic Republic of Iran Terrorism Litigation. Rubin v. Islamic Republic of Iran, 349. European Parliament Research Service (2016) Justice Against Sponsors of Terrorism. JASTA and its international impact. Briefing October, pp. 4, 7. Ferrer Lloret (2007), pp. 49–50. Gartenstein-Ross (2002), pp. 499, 501, 512–513. Hancock (2018), pp. 1306–1307.

United States Barack Obama in his veto to the JASTA, enacting this act would neither protect Americans from terrorist attacks nor improve the effectiveness of the US response to such attacks.[180]

Even US courts regard the terrorism exception as a failed policy and call upon the US Congress and the US Executive, including the President, to reconsider the matter.[181] They called terrorism exception judgments 'Pyrrhic victories', 'lies', even amounting to violation of the rule of law, as on one hand plaintiffs are allowed to file suits against foreign States, whereas on the other they are refused to initiate an effective execution thereof.[182] As Iran does not participate in the proceedings, issues of State immunity are raised before US courts by the Federal Government that in fact becomes an adversary of victims in litigations. This situation increases the victims' frustration as they get contrary signals from the US Government. On one hand they are being assured of the governmental support in their fight for compensation, on the other they are opponents of their own Government in litigations against Iran. As judge *Lamberth* rightly emphasized in *In re Islamic Republic of Iran Terrorism Litigation*:

> if Congress and the President are serious about finding redress of the injustices suffered by these terrorism victims, then they should pull together to find meaningful, workable solutions, rather than finding new and creative ways to push these tragic claims back onto the Courts. [. . .] Frankly, these measures are politically superficial and overly simplistic solutions to much deeper problems. These measures are empty political gestures that offer no justice for so many victims who – whether intentionally or not – have been exploited by the politics of these terrorism lawsuits.[183]

Moreover, the terrorism exception makes it less possible that relations between the United States and Iran become less hostile, as it creates a psychological obstacle. Due to the fact that number of judgments rendered against Iran in US courts increases and on their basis Iran owes terrorism victims over US$60 billion,[184] Iran is not that inclined to change its policy and enter into negotiations on resolving its conflict with the United States and it still remains one of the most significant State sponsors of terrorism.[185]

However, in order to present a complete study on the terrorism exception, it must be noticed that there are also arguments presented with the aim of justifying an opinion that this exception to State immunity does not contravene customary

---

[180] Justice Against Sponsors of Terrorism Act, 13.9.2016, s. 2040 (114th)—JASTA. Obama B (2016) Veto to the Justice Against Sponsors of Terrorism Act (JASTA), Congressional Record, 114th Congress, Vol. 162, 26.9.2016, Washington.

[181] In re Islamic Republic of Iran Terrorism Litigation.

[182] Eisenfeld v. Islamic Republic of Iran, 172 F. Supp. 2d 1 (2000).

[183] Eisenfeld v. Islamic Republic of Iran, 172 F. Supp. 2d 1 (2000). Isenfeld v. Islamic Republic of Iran. Bennett v. Islamic Republic of Iran, 604.

[184] The amount on 1.2.2017—the date on which Iran filed to the ICJ its Memorandum. Certain Iranian Assets (Islamic Republic of Iran v. United States of America), Memorial of the Islamic Republic of Iran, 1.2.2017, p. 35.

[185] In re Islamic Republic of Iran Terrorism Litigation. Keller (2005), p. 1051.

international law and permits US courts to proceed to the merits. One of them is a reference to the International Law Commission's Draft Articles on Responsibility of States for Internationally Wrongful Acts,[186] especially those on serious breach of obligations under peremptory norms of international law.[187]

Eric T. Kohan starts his deliberations on Draft Articles by indicating that as countermeasures for violations of international law, States are entitled to temporary suspension of their obligations towards the responsible State (Art. 49 (2) of the Draft Articles). As respecting other State's immunity is an obligation towards that State, he concludes that it is possible to suspend it.[188] Then Kohan indicates that the ILC Articles permit a State to take countermeasures against another one that refuses to comply with its obligations to remedy an international wrongful act. This author emphasizes that the Articles enumerate actions States can never take as countermeasures,[189] yet the denial of State immunity is not on that list. According to Kohan, a denial of State immunity is not a disproportional response (Art. 51 of the Draft Articles) to terrorism sponsoring.[190]

Nevertheless, Art. 41 (1) of the Draft Articles underlines that States shall cooperate to bring an end to any serious breach of international law through lawful means. Depriving another State of its immunity regardless of customary international law in that area might not be considered to be lawful. Art. 50 (1)(d) provides that countermeasures shall not affect *jus cogens* norms, yet customary international law on State immunity might be considered to be peremptory norms. Terrorism exception can be also regarded as avoidance of the application of Art. 50 (2)(a) that stipulates that countermeasures cannot violate obligations under any dispute procedure applicable between States. If the US Government sued Iran before its courts for terrorism sponsoring, it would mean an obvious violation of this obligation, therefore the United States could have placed the right to bring a claim to a court in hands of private actors.

Moreover, Kohan even criticised the ICJ for its judgment in *Jurisdictional Immunities of the State* for not taking into consideration the evolutionary process from absolute to restrictive State immunity. In this author's opinion, *jus cogens* violations should not be protected by State immunity and it was a mistake of the ICJ to separate these two concepts.[191] In this area it needs to be pointed out that, in my

[186] International Law Commission, Draft Articles on Responsibility of States.

[187] Kohan (2017), pp. 1519, 1548, 1559, 1563.

[188] Kohan (2017), pp. 1519–1563.

[189] Art. 50 (1) enumerates: the obligation to refrain from the threat or use of force as embodied in the Charter of the United Nations, obligations for the protection of fundamental human rights, obligations of a humanitarian character prohibiting reprisals, other obligations under peremptory norms of general international law.

On the basis of art. 50 (2) a State taking countermeasures is not relieved from fulfilling its obligations under any dispute settlement procedure applicable between it and the responsible State and to respect the inviolability of diplomatic or consular agents, premises, archives and documents.

[190] Kohan (2017), p. 1549.

[191] Kohan (2017), pp. 1551–1552, 1566.

view, the ICJ was correct and properly justified its decision. Deciding whether a case concerns a breach of a *jus cogens* norm or not requires a court to enter into the merits of the case. Yet the aim of State immunity is to protect a foreign State from a submission to a process before the court of the State of the forum and a necessity of deliberating the merits. Waiving State immunity in this case would deprive State immunity of its very essence.

5 Conclusion

All the above-mentioned deliberations mean that the international community should find another way to react to State sponsored terrorism. Definitely State sponsors of terrorism should bear consequences of terrorist attacks, including ones of an economic character. Nevertheless, the response should not be applied unilaterally by the United States or Canada with a violation of State immunity.

Therefore in international law a more appropriate way of regulating compensations from States supporting terrorism should be a friendly settlement of disputes between States, for example in the form of an agreement.[192] Another proposal is the creation of *ad hoc* or permanent tribunal whose task would be to decide on claims brought by victims of terrorism.[193] The drawback of this solution is that it requires a political will and bilateral agreement between the State victim of a terrorist attack and the State sponsor of terrorism. This way of friendly settlement of terrorism disputes may never take place or may come into play after many years, even decades. For individual victims of terrorism this solution seems rather too unrealistic and ineffective, as it is dependent on the will of the State that sponsors terrorism.

These States should look for a political support within the system of international collective peace and security mechanism, especially within the framework of the UN Security Council. It was done with targeted sanctions in the aftermath of the September 11, 2001 attacks. It would be an appropriate forum for the United States to look for political support in its search for redress for victims of terrorism.

References

Barcik J, Srogosz T (2017) Prawo międzynarodowe publiczne, 3rd edn. CH Beck, Warsaw

Czapliński W, Wyrozumska A (2014) Prawo międzynarodowe publiczne, 3rd edn. CH Beck, Warsaw

Ferrer Lloret J (2007) La inmunidad de juridicción del estado ante violaciones graves de los derechos humanos. REDI LIX:29–63

Finke J (2011) Sovereign immunity: rule, comity or something else? EJIL 21:853–881

[192] Sąd Najwyższy Natoniewski.

[193] Ferrer Lloret (2007), pp. 57–58. Gartenstein-Ross (2002), pp. 521–525.

Fox H, Webb P (2013) The law of state immunity. OUP, Oxford
Gartenstein-Ross D (2002) Resolving outstanding judgments under the terrorism exception to the Foreign Sovereign Immunities Act. N Y Univ Law Rev 77:496–535
Hancock RE (2018) 'Mob-Legislating': JASTA's addition to the terrorism exception to foreign sovereign immunity. Cornell Law Rev 103:1293–1328
Keller J (2005) The Flatow Amendment and state-sponsored terrorism. Seattle Univ Law Rev 28:1029–1055
Kohan ET (2017) A natural progression of restrictive immunity: why the JASTA Amendment does not violate international law. Geo Wash Law Rev 92:1515–1569
Ryngaert C (2015) Jurisdiction in international law. OUP, Oxford
Scherr D (2012) Jurisdictional immunities of the state (Germany v Italy: Greece Intervening): a case note. NZYIL 10:139–151
Shaw MN (2008) International law, 3rd edn. CUP, Cambridge
Syed SG (2016) Sovereign immunity and *Jus Cogens*: is there a terrorism exception for conduct-based immunity? Columbia J Law Soc Probl 49:251–293
Wheatherall T (2015) Jus Cogens. International law and social contract. CUP, Cambridge

Magdalena Matusiak-Frączczak is an assistant professor in the Department of European Constitutional Law (Faculty of Law and Administration/University of Łódź, Poland) and an attorney at law (adwokat). Her main field of research and expertise are terrorism combating, human rights, state immunity and legal professional privilege.

The United States Hegemony and Reshaping the Norms of State Immunity for International Crimes

Rana M. Essawy

Abstract Since 1996, the United States (US) has made several changes to its laws on State immunity. *Prima facie*, this indicates that the US is trying to reshape the international norms of State immunity, especially in the case of international crimes. However, this chapter argues that the US is not exerting any hegemonic effort to change the norms of State immunity for international crimes but is rather using its hegemony to preserve a privileged position, giving itself the right to dismiss the immunity of States and their officials in case of international crimes while denying other States the right to take a similar path.

> Ce n'est que si le droit international lui-même, ou plus exactement les Etats qui instituent les règles spécifiques concernant les immunités, limite dès l'origine celles-ci au profit de la protection de certain droits de l'homme, que ces immunités se verront retreintes (Salmon 2009, p. 25)

1 Introduction

In 2012, the International Court of Justice (ICJ) indicated, in the case concerning the *Jurisdictional Immunities of the State,*[1] that the amendment to the United States Foreign Sovereign Immunities Act in 1996 (FSIA1605A) has no counterpart in the

I am deeply indebted to my husband, Amr El Attar, without whom this article would not exist. I would also like to thank my father and mother for their continuous support and encouragement. Special thanks to Professor Anne Lagerwall for her comments on an early draft proposal of this contribution. All opinions and errors remain the author's alone.

[1] ICJ, Jurisdictional Immunities of the State (Germany v. Italy: Greece intervening), Judgment, ICJ Reports 2012, p. 99.

R. M. Essawy (✉)
Faculty of Law, Alexandria University, Alexandria, Egypt
e-mail: dr.rana.mostafa.law@alexu.edu.eg

R. Bismuth et al. (eds.), *Sovereign Immunity Under Pressure*,
https://doi.org/10.1007/978-3-030-87706-4_13

legislation of other States and thus decided, among other reasons, the absence of a customary rule that deprives States of immunity based on the gravity of the act attributable to it.[2]

However, the ICJ's finding regarding the uniqueness of this piece of legislation is no longer an actual fact. The United States FSIA1605A had an effect on the Canadian Coalition Against Terror,[3] which in turn pushed the Canadian legislature to adopt a similar piece of legislation that deprives a State (listed by the Canadian Government as a sponsor of terrorism) of immunity in case of its support to an act of terrorism, wherever this act occurs.[4]

What must be noted is that neither the FSIA1605A, nor the Canadian terrorism exception witnessed international protests upon their adoption.[5] Even when the United States District of Columbia Court deprived Iran of its immunity in *Flatow v. Islamic Republic of Iran (1998)*,[6] no opposition was raised. On the contrary, protests arose when the Congress adopted the 'Terrorism Risk Insurance Act 2002' (TRIA) and the 'Iran Threat Reduction and Syria Human Rights Act 2012' (ISA), both of which deprive States of their immunity from execution. Not only did Iran express its concern through a letter to the UN,[7] it also instituted proceedings against the United States before the ICJ, particularly after the United States Supreme Court applied the ISA in the case of *Bank Markazi, aka Central Bank of Iran v. Peterson (2016)*.[8] Similarly, the Non-Aligned Movement strongly expressed rejection of the US practice in the context of State immunity.[9]

Despite this, in September 2016, the United States took a further step when the Congress overrode President Obama's veto and adopted the Justice against Sponsors of Terrorism Act (JASTA). This Act allows raising claims by Americans against foreign States, not necessarily designated by the State department as a State sponsor of terrorism, for aiding and abetting in the commission of acts of terrorism in the

---

[2]ICJ, Jurisdictional Immunities of the State (Germany v. Italy: Greece intervening), Judgment, ICJ Reports 2012, p. 99, paras. 81–91. This is the latest decision in which the ICJ discussed State immunities knowing that it refused to tackle the status of State immunity under customary international law in the Iranian assets case. See Certain Iranian Assets (Islamic Republic of Iran v. United States of America), Preliminary Objections, Judgment ICJ Reports 2019, p. 7. This part of the judgment is criticized. See Hosseinnejad (2019).

[3]See more on this coalition at www.c-catcanada.org. Accessed 15 April 2021.

[4]Article 6.1, State Immunity Act. This article States that 'A foreign State that is set out on the list referred to in subsection (2) is not immune from the jurisdiction of a court in proceedings against it for its support of terrorism on or after Jan 1, 1985'.

[5]See, at the national level, Kim (2004), pp. 513ff.

[6]Flatow v. Islamic Republic of Iran (1998) United States District Court, District of Columbia, March 1998, 1999 F.Supp.1.

[7]United Nations (2008) Letter dated 24 September 2008 from the Permanent Representative of the Islamic Republic of Iran to the United Nationals addressed to the Secretary General, A/C.6/63/2.

[8]Bank Markazi Aka Central Bank of Iran v. Peterson (2016), Supreme Court of the United States No. 14-770.

[9]Daugirdas (2016), p. 561; Grandaubert (2016).

United States.[10] Although the JASTA is narrower than the FSIA1605A, as it requires the act of terrorism to occur in the United States, this Act has triggered a lot of criticism, not only at the national level[11] but also at the international level. It has been reported that Saudi Arabia told President Obama's administration and members of the Congress that it would be forced to sell up to $750 billion in assets in the United States if the Congress passes the JASTA.[12] Although the JASTA does not point towards Saudi Arabia's responsibility for the 9/11 events, it must be noted that this act was only passed after the Congress issued a 28-page report, which manifested the probability that 'charities with significant Saudi government sponsorship diverted funds to Al Qaeda'.[13] In support of Saudi Arabia's stance, the Gulf Co-operation Council expressed its concern towards JASTA as a bill contradicting the principle of sovereign immunity and establishing 'a flagrant precedent in international relations...'.[14]

The European Union delegation to the United States, on its part, expressed its concern that 'the possible adoption and implementation of JASTA would be in conflict with the fundamental principles of international law and in particular the principle of State immunity'.[15] Similarly, Russia described the JASTA as reflecting the persisting United States policy in disregarding international law and stated that the JASTA is considered a violation of one of the fundamental norms of international law.[16]

[10]28 U.S.C. §1605B.

[11]See Obama B (2016) Veto message from the President. https://obamawhitehouse.archives.gov/the-press-office/2016/09/23/veto-message-president-s2040. Accessed 15 April 2021. Cf. Pass JASTA (2016) Response to the message of the President accompanying his veto of the Justice Against Sponsors of Terrorism Act (2016). http://passjasta.org/2016/09/response-message-president-accompanying-veto-justice-sponsors-terrorism-act/. Accessed 15 April 2021.

[12]Mazzetti (2016) Saudi Arabia warns of economic fallout if Congress passes 9/11 bill. https://www.nytimes.com/2016/04/16/world/middleeast/saudi-arabia-warns-ofeconomic-fallout-if-congress-passes-9-11-bill.html?_r=0. Accessed 15 April 2021. See also Gordon J and Gillman O (2016) Saudi Arabia threatens to pull $750 billion in US assets if Congress passes bill makings its government liable for 9/11-related lawsuits. http://www.dailymail.co.uk/news/article-3543702/Saudi-Arabia-threatens-pull-750-billion-U-S-assets-Congress-passes-bill-making-government-liable-9-11-related-lawsuits.html.

[13]The 9/11 Commission Report (2004), p. 171. https://www.9-11commission.gov/report/911Report.pdf. Accessed 15 April 2021.

[14]Saudi Press Agency (2016) GCC expresses concern over a US Congress bill contradicting the principles of equality and sovereign immunity of countries of the world. www.spa.gov.sa/viewstory.php?lang=en&newsid=1537574. Accessed 15 April 2021. Saudi Press Agency (2016a) Official at Ministry of Foreign Affairs: JASTA great concern to community of nations objecting to erosion of principle of sovereign immunity. www.spa.gov.sa/viewstory.php?lang=en&newsid=1543953. Accessed 15 April 2021.

[15]Cîrlig and Pawlak (2016) Justice Against Sponsors of Terrorism Act: The JASTA and its implications. http://www.europarl.europa.eu/RegData/etudes/BRIE/2016/593499/EPRS_BRI(2016)593499_EN.pdf. Accessed 15 April 2021.

[16]Russian Foreign Ministry (2016) Comment by the information and press department on the US passing the Justice Against Sponsors of Terrorism Act with extraterritorial jurisdiction. http://www.mid.ru/en/web/guest/kommentarii_predstavitelya/-/asset_publisher/MCZ7HQuMdqBY/content/id/2479122. Accessed 15 April 2021.

China expressed concern as well regarding the JASTA. It confirmed opposing 'all forms of terrorism and supports the international community in conducting counter-terrorism cooperation'.[17] Nevertheless, it believed 'that the international endeavour against terrorism should bring into full play the leading role of the UN, conform to purposes and principles of the UN Charter, and follow international law and norms governing international relations, including sovereign equality and other international law principles. Countries must not put their domestic laws above international law, nor link terrorism with specific countries, nations or religions'.[18]

Prima facie, it appears that the United States—through the FSIA1605A, TRIA, ISA, and JASTA—is attempting to reshape the international rules of State immunity, be it immunity from jurisdiction or execution. Therefore, it is the purpose of this paper to examine the possible effect of the United States hegemony on reshaping the norms of State immunity, particularly in the case of international crimes. The research question is, whether the hegemonic position of the United States will have an eventual role in changing the aforementioned opposing views of States and modifying the norms of State immunity for international crimes.

It is no new observation that a powerful State such as the United States can play a role in changing the customary rules of international law;[19] however, this does not always work for the United States as clearly witnessed, for example, in the field of the *jus ad bellum.*[20] This owes to two main reasons. Firstly, the process of the creation or evolution of international customary rules is a complex one,[21] it not only requires a uniform practice from the generality of States but also demands—as the ICJ stated in the *North Sea Continental Shelf* case—that this practice:

> . . .be such; or be carried out in such a way, as to be evidence of a belief that this practice is rendered obligatory by the existence of rule of law requiring it. The need for such a belief, i.e., the existence of a subjective element, is implicit in the very notion of the *opinio juris sive necessitatis*. The States concerned must therefore feel that they are conforming to what amounts to a legal obligation.[22]

Apart from this complex nature of changing customary rules of international law, the unwarranted role of the United States in this context owes to the nature of

[17] Chinese Foreign Ministry (2016) Foreign Ministry Spokesperson Remarks on JASTA. http://sa.china-embassy.org/eng/gdxw/t1404794.htm. Accessed 15 April 2021.

[18] Ibid.

[19] Helfer and Wuerth (2016), pp. 584–590. See also Corten (2009), pp. 171–175. See, on the role of power in international law, Byers (1999). See also Schachter (1999), pp. 200–205; Vagts (2001), pp. 873–888; Koskenniemi (2004), pp. 197–218; Alvarez JE (2003), pp.873-888.

[20] See, on this topic, Marcelo and Kohen (2003), pp. 197–231, Roth (2003), pp. 232–63. See also Byers (2003), pp. 171–190. See, more generally, on the prohibition of the use of force, Corten (2012).

[21] See Salmon (2014), p. 314, 'Son changement ne pouvait s'effectuer que par la conjonction d'une nouvelle opinio juris accompagnée d'une pratique concordante de tous s'agissant de la coutume générale. C'était là, on le mesure, des conditions extrêmement lourdes'.

[22] International Court of Justice, North Sea Continental Shelf Cases, Judgment, ICJ Report 1969, paras. 76–77.

international politics. The international community is composed of States with different ideological, sociological, political backgrounds; this diversity of States has been described by Stephen Toope as 'a bastion against the overpowering influence of any single State or group of States'.[23] Therefore, unless the United States uses its power to persuade other States of the importance of change and its legality, this change will not be achieved. To summarize this situation, one finds it perfectly suitable to quote Jean Salmon: '*Le système de droit international est dominé par le jeu des contradiction'*.[24]

So, the question raised in this paper is: Will the United States hegemony be able to overcome these complexities and reshape the norms of State immunity for international crimes? Two points should be clarified before addressing this research question. Firstly, international crimes are defined in this paper as those 'serious crimes under international law as reflected in relevant treaties and the statutes and jurisprudence of international courts and tribunals'.[25] Secondly, this paper examines the effect of the United States hegemony on the rule of State immunity in the wider context of international crimes and not merely in the context of terrorism because the JASTA and FSIA1605A have been approached by the ICJ and other domestic courts[26] as examples of national laws that deprive States of their immunity on the grounds of the gravity of the act attributed to it. Further, there is a growing tendency to view acts of terrorism as serious crimes under international law reflected in the elaboration of 12 conventions criminalizing certain acts of terrorism.[27] After the 9/11 events, the UN Security Council unanimously adopted Resolution 1373, which manifested a growing tendency to criminalize all forms of assistance provided to terrorist groups and obliging States themselves to refrain from providing any form of support to these groups.[28] Moreover, with the rise of the terrorist group called Da'esh in Syria and Iraq, terrorism rose at the forefront of the international political agenda and the UN Security Council issued a number of resolutions urging States to ensure that their domestic laws and regulations establish 'serious criminal offences sufficient to provide the ability to prosecute and to penalize in a manner duly reflecting the seriousness of the offence'.[29] In light of this, it seems to be suitable

[23] Toope (2003), p. 289.

[24] Salmon (2014), p. 9. See also Chaumont (1975), pp. 32–37.

[25] Institute of International Law (2009) Resolution on the immunity from jurisdiction of the State and of persons who act on behalf of the State in case of international crimes. Third Commission, Annuaire de l'Institut de droit international-Session de Naples 73:228.

[26] See for example, le Tribunal d'arrondissement de et à Luxembourg, première chambre (2019). Jugement civil 2019TALCH01/00116. See also Report of the International Law Commission on the Work of Its 51st session, A/54/10 (1999), Appendix, p. 172, para. 8.

[27] A list of the international instruments adopted in the fight against terrorism is available at https://www.unodc.org/documents/terrorism/Publications/Int_Instruments_Prevention_and_Suppression_Int_Terrorism/Publication_-_English_-_08-25503_text.pdf. Accessed 15 April 2021.

[28] S/RES/1373 (2001).

[29] See, for example, S/RES/2178 (2014).

to examine the possible effect of the US legislative acts on State immunity in the wider context of international crimes.[30]

To that end, this research is divided into five sections. In the first place, the methodology selected to assess the impact of the United States hegemony on the rules of State immunity will be delineated (Sect. 2). This paper will next examine the historical role of the United States in the context of State immunity (Sect. 3). Following this, the paper turns to contextualizing the United States recent practice (Sect. 4). The reactions of States to this practice will be analyzed afterwards (Sect. 5). Finally, the role of reciprocity in the evolution of the customary rules on State immunity for international crimes will be examined (Sect. 6).

2 Methodological Approach

For the purpose of assessing the impact of United States hegemony on the rules of State immunity, it is necessary to clarify my intention in using the term 'hegemonic impact' as distinguished from the term 'role modelling'. By 'hegemonic impact', I refer to the influence exerted by a hegemonic State over other States to take similar actions. This influence depends primarily on the will of the hegemonic State to produce this effect. As Stephen Toope indicates, 'hegemony requires not only material resources but the willingness to use them to maintain the "essential rules governing inter-State relations"'.[31] If the hegemonic State is not willing to enforce a change in the international norms, then one cannot speak of any 'hegemonic influence' but rather about 'role modelling'. 'Role modelling' refers to the imitation of the actions of another State,[32] yet this process of 'role modelling' does not depend on any will on the part of the role-model State but rather depends on the motivation generated by observing its behaviour.[33]

In light of this differentiation, the impact of the United States hegemony on the rules of State immunity will be analysed primarily by examining whether it is willing to enforce a change in the rules of State immunity, particularly those related to international crimes. However, the evaluation of the hegemonic impact of the United States does not stop at this point. The research also extends to analyse the reaction of

[30]It is interesting to note that the United States District Court for the District of Columbia determined in the Flatow case that 'Terrorism has achieved the status of almost universal condemnation, as have slavery, genocide, and piracy and the terrorist is the modern era's hosti humani generis—an enemy to all mankind', Flatow v. Islamic Republic of Iran, p. 23.

[31]Toope (2003), p. 292 quoting Keohane (1984).

[32]This definition is built on the definition of the term role model in the Oxford Dictionary of Sociology. Role-model is defined as 'A significant other, upon which an individual patterns his or her behavior in a particular social role, including adopting appropriate similar attitudes'. See Scott and Marshall (2009), p. 99.

[33]See Morgenroth (2015), p. 84. He indicates that 'Role aspirant motivation is central to the main outcomes of role modelling - goal adoption, goal reinforcement, and achievement'.

other States towards the effort exerted by the United States to induce a change. International relations jurists, save realists, generally agree that hegemony is a 'characteristic relationship between the 'will' (or attitude) of the leading State and the 'will' (or attitude) of those which it leads'.[34]

Nevertheless, this twofold analysis is not an easy task. While it is relatively easy to evaluate the United States hegemony in the realm of treaties by reviewing the various stages of the negotiations that preceded the conclusion of a specific treaty,[35] it is difficult to assess the hegemonic impact in the process of generating customary international law. This is because of the fact that the emergence of a customary rule does not involve formal negotiations[36] or is least described to be 'created by conduct of members of the international community which constantly 'negotiate' with each other by means of actual deeds, statements, and other acts'.[37] Accordingly, it is difficult to identify a 'cause and effect' type of link between the conduct of States, making it difficult to verify whether the behaviour of certain States is a result of hegemonic impact.

In addition, it is difficult to identify a causation relationship between the conduct of a powerful State and the conduct of other States, because powerful States do not usually prefer to resort to their material capabilities to enforce a change in customary international law,[38] but are rather willing to use a non-tangible power known as 'soft power'. Soft power is identified by Joseph Nye, the 'intellectual father' of this term,[39] as the ability of a State to obtain the outcome it wants by non-coercive means.[40] Wielding soft power rather than hard power to stimulate a change in customary international law raises methodological hurdles when analysing the impact of the United States hegemony on customary rules. It has been argued that 'it is difficult or impossible to establish a causal relationship between inputs and outcomes',[41] since the adoption of a certain behaviour is mostly a result of overlapping factors.[42] In light of this, one must proceed with caution when analysing the hegemonic impact of the United States on the rules of State immunity for international crimes.

With this in mind, the following sections proceed to analyse the historical and future role of the United States hegemony on the rules of State immunity by

[34] Nolte (2003), p. 493, citing Triepel (1938). See also Clark (2011), pp. 18–23.

[35] See Klein (2003), pp. 363–391.

[36] Helfer and Wuerth (2016), pp. 575–580.

[37] Danilenko (1993), p. 75.

[38] Byers (1999), p. 6.

[39] Hall (2010), p. 191.

[40] Nye (2004), pp. 1–33.

[41] Seiichi (2008), pp. 189–211; Patalakh (2016), pp. 85–112. See also Schachter (1999), p. 202. He states that 'its (the power) utility depends on context and the specific factors that affect the power relationship'.

[42] For example, see what Helfer and Wuerth (2016) called 'custom's overlapping domain', pp. 594–596.

primarily questioning whether the United States has been willing to induce a change in the customary rules of State immunity because, as previously mentioned, without the willingness of the hegemonic State to use its resources of power, one cannot speak of hegemonic impact. In ascertaining this intention, the analysis will be based on the instruments of soft power identified by Joseph Nye—namely persuasion and public diplomacy, where persuasion refers to moving others by arguments and public diplomacy refers to communicating a decision to internal and external audiences.[43] Therefore, the official statements made by the US representatives in the domestic and international foras with respect to State immunity will be relied upon to deduce whether the US was willing to use its hegemonic power to induce a change in the rules of State immunity.

Having clarified the methodology followed throughout this paper, the question of whether the United States had previously played any role in the evolution of the rules of State immunity will now be examined.

3 The Historical Role of the United States in the Context of State Immunity

It is contended that the Tate letter issued by the State Department of the United States was the turning point in the shift from the rule of absolute State immunity to the rule of restrictive immunity.[44] Yet, this contention does not appear to be agreed upon. Xiaodong Yang argued that changes in the rules of State immunity are not due to the predominance of any ideological approach,[45] nor has 'the so-called 'developed countries/developing countries' division been seriously determinative of the shaping of the rules of State immunity'.[46] That being said, this section focuses on determining whether the United States had any historical role in the evolution of the rules of State immunity.

It is generally accepted that the United States was not the first country to shift from the rule of absolute immunity to the rule of restrictive immunity, which provides for the dismissal of State immunity in case of commercial activities. Belgium, Italy, the Netherlands, Switzerland, Greece, and Egypt earlier allowed their courts to exercise jurisdiction against foreign States in case those States were involved in commercial activities.[47] Then, in 1952, the United States expressly announced

[43] This is one of the three dimensions of public diplomacy as put forward by Joseph S. Nye. See Nye (2008), pp. 94–109.

[44] Skordas (2003), p. 339, Verdier and Voeten (2015); Donner (2001), p. 28.

[45] Yang (2012), pp. 23–25.

[46] Yang (2012), pp. 25–26.

[47] See Verdier and Voeten (2015), pp. 4, 15, Annex 1. See also Bankas (1999), p. 132. Further, there are a number of inter-governmental initiatives to restrict State immunity in specific areas. For an account of these initiatives, see Hafner (2013), pp. 1–4.

abandoning the rule of absolute immunity through the 'Tate Letter'. The State Department's legal advisor Jake B. Tate indicated the increasing tendency in State practice of denying State immunity in relation to commercial acts and clarified that the adoption of restrictive immunity in that context was justified by the increasing role of States in commerce, which made it necessary to 'enable persons doing business with them to have their rights determined in the courts'.[48] The United States' stance was subsequently codified in 1976 when the Congress enacted the Foreign Sovereign Immunities Act (FSIA).

Ever since, it has been recorded that the number of States adopting restrictive immunity has increased dramatically.[49] The question, which then arises, is 'Did the United States hegemony play a role in the increase in the number of States abandoning the rule of absolute immunity?'

As mentioned earlier, assessing the hegemonic impact of the United States necessitates determining, in the first place, whether the United States had the intention to change the customary rules of State immunity. It can be argued that this intention existed. Such an intention could be deduced from the act of announcing the rule of restrictive immunity as part of the United States foreign policy, thereby communicating this policy change not only to the internal audience but also to the external audience. Although the rule of restrictive immunity was earlier adopted by other States, the Tate Letter was the first official Statement of change of policy, which indicated the will of the United States to induce a certain change in the customary rules of State immunity.[50]

This intention could also be deduced from the persuasive discourse included in the Tate Letter. The letter focused on two primary issues. Firstly, it emphasized that the customary rules of State immunity are evolving towards the restrictive rule. Secondly, it indicated the importance of shifting to the restrictive rule being the achievement of justice for businessmen engaging in commercial activities with governments. By this, knowing that most States grant immunity according to the principles of international law,[51] the United States brought to their attention the customary nature of the restrictive rule of immunity in order to drive them to make a similar shift.[52] It also revealed the practical necessity of shifting from the rule of absolute immunity to that of restrictive immunity. Therefore, this persuasive discourse reveals the intention of the United States to induce a change in the customary rules of State immunity.

---

[48] Tate (1952), pp. 984–985.

[49] Verdier and Voeten (2015), p. 14. See also Byers (1999), pp. 113–114. He noticed that States belonging to the common-law family adhered to the restrictive immunity rule after the United States adopted the FSIA.

[50] The FSIA is also claimed to be the first statute on State immunity. See Bankas (1999), p. 139; Donner (2001), p. 28.

[51] See States' answers to the questionnaire submitted by the International Law Commission on the subject of State immunity: A/CN.4/343 (1981), pp. 30–35.

[52] The customary nature of the rule of restrictive immunity is also highlighted in the finding and declaration of the purpose section. See 28 U.S. Code § 1602.

This is further confirmed by reviewing the political context of the Tate Letter and the FSIA. The United States was willing to change the rules of State immunity to the detriment of the communist sphere where the State participated increasingly in trading. It is well-known that during the cold war, the Soviet Union declared an economic war on the United States.[53] This war involved an increasing participation of the State in trading activities. Therefore, the United States adhered to restrictive immunity and had the intention of making others follow its lead, because the continued expansion of State trading places an unfair burden on businessmen if they cannot bring suit against those States, which will drive them to avoid transactions with foreign governments and 'thus hamper the expansion of foreign trade which is concomitant of international peace'.[54] This is reflected in the Tate Letter, in which it was stated that 'the reasons which obviously motivate state-trading countries in adhering to the theory (of absolute immunity) with perhaps increasing rigidity are most persuasive that the United States should change its policy'. From this, one may deduce the intention of the United States to change the international rules governing State immunity to face the potential Soviet economic expansion.

Having deduced a positive intention to induce a change in the customary rules of State immunity, the following question remains: Was the United States hegemony the main factor in shifting States towards the restrictive rule of State immunity? It is really difficult to provide a definite answer to this question because studying the effect of the United States hegemony on other States requires examining mainly the political and economic background of each State to understand its actual motive behind shifting to the restrictive rule of immunity, an analysis which cannot be performed due to the insufficiency of data and the limited space assigned to this chapter. Nevertheless, based on the data collected by Pierre-Hugues Verdier & Erik Voeten from 121 States, the increasing shift to the restrictive rule of State immunity was arguably influenced by the Tate Letter and the arguments therein. According to this analysis, the shift from absolute immunity to restrictive immunity has a 'significant correlation' with the economic status of a State.[55] Therefore, the arguments in the Tate Letter relating to the protection of individuals engaged in commercial activities with States convinced non-trading States with the importance of abandoning the rule of absolute immunity and adopting the rule of restrictive immunity.

With the intention of the United States to induce a change in the rules of State immunity and the correlation between that will and the change occurring in other States, this section concludes that the hegemony of the United States played a role in the emergence of the rule of restrictive immunity. This article turns now to question whether the United States hegemony will similarly induce a change in the customary rules of State immunity for international crimes. To that end, the following section focuses on assessing the intention of the United States in that context.

---

[53] Fensterwald (1959), p. 382.

[54] Fensterwald (1959), p. 396.

[55] Verdier and Voeten (2015), p. 23.

4 Contextualizing the United States' Practice

The question is, whether FSIA and its amendments (FSIA1605A and the JASTA) reflect an *opinio juris* that accepts only a terrorism exception to State immunity or one that accepts an exception that extends to all international crimes? Given that the *opinio juris* of a State can be deduced from the decisions of its national courts and discussions taking place upon the introduction of a draft legislation before the legislature,[56] this section focuses on the decisions of the US national courts on the subject of State immunity—more specifically those decisions which have tackled the immunity of States in the case of international crimes. It will also refer to the debates, which took place in the Congress on the occasion of the adoption of the different legislations on State immunity.

4.1 FSIA

In 1976, the Congress codified the rules governing State immunities in FSIA. This legislation stipulated that foreign States are immune from the jurisdiction of the United States' courts, except in the case:

> (1) in which the foreign State has waived its immunity either explicitly or by implication...; (2) in which the action is based upon a commercial activity...; (3) in which rights in property taken in violation of international law are in issue...; (4) in which rights on property in the United States acquired by succession or gift or rights on immovable property situated in the United States are in issue; (5) not otherwise encompassed in paragraph (2) above, in which money damages are sought against a foreign State for personal injury, death, or damage to or loss of property occurring in the United States and caused by the tortious act or omission of that foreign State or of any official or employee of that foreign State while acting within the scope of his office or employment...[57]

The claim that State immunity is dismissed under FSIA in case of international crimes was raised several times before the national courts. In the *Siderman v. Argentina* case, Siderman, a Jewish American tortured by men acting under the direction of Argentine military officials, argued that the United States' courts had jurisdiction over his claim because Argentina did not enjoy immunity under FSIA in case of violations of *jus cogens* norms. However, the Court of Appeals (Ninth Circuit) replied that:

> Nothing in the text or legislative history of the FSIA explicitly addresses the effect violations of jus cogens might have on the FSIA's cloak of immunity... Clearly, the FSIA does not

---

[56] See International Law Commission Draft conclusions on the identification of customary international law with commentaries, A/73/10 (2018), pp. 140–141. See also ICJ, Jurisdictional Immunities of the State (Germany v. Italy: Greece intervening), Judgment, ICJ Reports 2012, p. 99 p. 135, para. 77.

[57] 28 U.S.C. §1605.

> specifically provide for an exception to sovereign immunity based on jus cogens. . . . The fact that there has been a violation of jus cogens does not confer jurisdiction under the FSIA.[58]

This decision was upheld by the Court of Appeals for the District of Columbia Circuit in the *Princz v. Germany* case.[59] In this case, Hugo Princz—a Jewish American tortured and subjected to slave labour in Nazi concentration camps—argued that the United States' courts had jurisdiction over his claim because Germany did not have immunity against violations of peremptory norms. Nevertheless, the Court rejected this claim because FSIA did not provide for the dismissal of immunity in case of violations of peremptory norms. Similarly, in the *Smith v. Libya* case, the United States' District Court for the Eastern District of New York rejected the contention that FSIA provides for the dismissal of immunity whenever a State commits a violation of peremptory norms.[60]

Again, in the *Cabiri v. Ghana* case,[61] the Court of Appeals Second Circuit dismissed the claim that FSIA shall be construed as to allow the waiver of State immunity in case of violations of *jus cogens* norms. Further, in the *Sampson v. Germany* case,[62] Jacob Sampson sued Germany for being imprisoned in Nazi concentration camps. However, the United States Court of Appeals Seventh Circuit affirmed the non-jurisdiction of United States' courts for claims made against States in cases of violations of peremptory norms since 'Congress did not create an exception to foreign sovereign immunity under the FSIA for violations of *jus cogens* norms'. This decision was upheld again in the *Hwang Geum Joo v. Japan* case, in which 15 females filed a suit against Japan for being victims of sexual slavery and torture by the Japanese military.[63] On the occasion of tackling the immunity of State officials, the Court of Appeals for the District of Columbia Circuit affirmed that FSIA does not provide for the dismissal of State immunity in case of violations of peremptory norms.[64]

Taking the above decisions into consideration, the national judicial decisions concerning the application of FSIA before the 1996 amendment reflect that the United States did not believe in its right under international law to dismiss State immunity in case of international crimes as long as they occur outside the United States.

On the other hand, the national courts appear to adopt a different approach with respect to international crimes committed within the United States. In the *Letelier v. Republic of Chile*,[65] Isabelle demanded compensation from the Republic of Chile for aiding and directing the killing of her husband, Mr. Letelier, in the District of

---

[58] Siderman de Blake v. Republic of Argentina (1992), 965 F.2d 699, 9th Cir.

[59] Hugo Princz v. Federal Republic of Germany (1994), 26 F.3d 1166, DC Cir.

[60] Smith v. Socialist People's Libyan Arab Jamahiriya (1995), 886 F. Supp. 306, EDNY.

[61] Cabiri v. Government of the Republic of Ghana (1999), 165 F.3d 193, 202, 2nd Cir.

[62] Sampson v. Federal Republic of Germany (2001), 250 F.3d 1145, 7th Cir.

[63] Hwang Geum Joo v. Japan (2003), 332 F.3d 679, DC Cir.

[64] Belhas v. Ya'alon (2008), 07-7009, DC Cir.

[65] Letelier v. Republic of Chile (1980), 488 F. Supp. 665, DDC.

Columbia. In response, the United States District Court for the District of Columbia stated that it had jurisdiction under the tort exception to immunity stipulated in paragraph 5 of the FSIA. The court denied that Chile actions could be subsumed under any of the exceptions to the application of paragraph 5[66] because:

> whatever policy options may exist for a foreign country, it has no 'discretion' to perpetrate conduct designed to result in the assassination of an individual or individuals, action that is clearly contrary to the precepts of humanity as recognized in both national and international law. Accordingly there would be no 'discretion' within the meaning of section 1605 (a) (5) (A) to order or to aid in an assassination and were it to be demonstrated that a foreign State has undertaken any such act in this country, that foreign State could not be accorded sovereign immunity under subsection (A) for any tort claims resulting from its conduct.[67]

This judgment has been interpreted to reflect the conviction of the national courts that FSIA denies the immunity for States involved in international crimes committed within the United States.[68] Yet, this does not appear to be an interpretation shared by the executive organ of the United States. It was emphasized, during the negotiations of the UN Convention on Jurisdictional Immunities, that Article 12 of this convention:

> on jurisdiction over non-commercial torts, must be interpreted and applied consistently with the time-honoured distinction between *acts jure imperii* and *acts jure gestionis*. It was entirely appropriate for States to be held accountable—not to be able to invoke immunity—with regard to their tortious acts or omissions in circumstances where private persons would be. Domestic law in the United States and in many other countries provided for that eventuality.[69]

In light of this clash of opinions between both organs, it is difficult to distil an *opinio juris* on part of the United States that reflects its legal conviction that States are not immune, under international law, in case of international crimes committed within the territory of the United States. Accordingly, the FSIA barely shows that the United States puts forward an exception to State immunity in the case of international crimes, whether committed within the United States or abroad.

4.2 *The 1996 Amendment (FSIA Section 1605A)*

In 1996, the congress added section (1605A) to the FSIA, which stipulates that a foreign State designated as a State sponsor of terrorism:

---

[66] It is stipulated in § 1605(5) that the tort exception shall not be applicable to (a) any claim based on the exercise or performance or the failure to exercise or perform a discretionary function regardless of whether the discretion be abused, or (b) any claim arising out of malicious prosecution, abuse of process, libel, slander, misrepresentation, deceit, or interference with contract rights.

[67] Letelier v. Republic of Chile (1989) This paragraph has been recited in Liu v. Republic of China (1989), 892 F.2d 1419, 9th Cir.

[68] Pavoni (2011), p. 153. See also Schnably (2017), pp. 310–312.

[69] A/C.6/59/SR.13 (2005), para. 63.

> shall not be immune from the jurisdiction of Courts of the United States or of the States in any case ... in which money damages are sought against a foreign State for personal injury or death caused by an act of torture, extrajudicial killing, aircraft sabotage, hostage taking, or the provision of material support or resources for such an act if such an act or provision is engaged in by an official, employee, or agent of such foreign State while acting within the scope of his or her office, employment, or agency.[70]

As previously mentioned,[71] the ICJ and other national courts consider section 1605A as one of the national legislations that put forward a wider exception to State immunity—one that dismisses State immunity based on the gravity of the act attributable to the State. However, reviewing the text of section 1605A and the manner in which the different organs of the United States presented this amendment, one can argue that the United States considers section 1605A as a countermeasure against States designated as sponsors of terrorism.[72] Thus, the 1996 amendment does not reflect the United States *opinio juris* in the sense of its legal conviction of having the right, under international law, to dismiss State immunity on the grounds of the gravity of the act in question.

The text of section 1605A reflects that this section is adopted as a countermeasure, as it links the dismissal of State immunity to the acts that caused enlisting the State as a State sponsor of terrorism or those acts that occurred following its enlistment.[73] By this, section 1605A shares the main characteristic of countermeasures—that is, being adopted in response to an internationally wrongful act.[74]

Further, judicial decisions reflect that section 1605A is a countermeasure. On several occasions, courts have described section 1605A as a remedy taken in response to internationally wrongful acts attributable to the State designated as a sponsor of terrorism. For example, in *Daliberti v. Iraq*, the United States District Court (District of Columbia) stated that 'those nations that operate in a manner inconsistent with international norms should not expect to be granted the privilege of immunity from suit that is within the prerogative of Congress to grant or withhold'.[75] In addition, the Supreme Court of the United States decided—after President Bush waived section 1605A with respect to Iraq—that courts have no jurisdiction over claims pending against Iraq, even those claims related to acts that occurred prior to the waiver.[76] This demonstrates that the Supreme Court views section 1605A as a

---

[70] 28 U.S.C. §1605A.

[71] Le Tribunal d'arrondissement de et à Luxembourg, première chambre (2019).

[72] Given that the purpose of (Sect. 4) is only to contextualize the US opinio juris, it is beyond the scope of this section to tackle the legality of denying State immunity as a countermeasure. On this topic, see Franchini (2019); Moser (2012), pp. 809–852. See also Fox and Webb (2013), p. 16.

[73] §1605A (2)(a)(i)(I). See also Franchini (2017), p. 9.

[74] Senator Arlen Specter Statement (1994), Hearing before the Subcommittee on Court and Administrative Practice of the Committee on the Judiciary for Consideration on S.835. Hrg 103-1077, quoted in Cooper-Hill (2006), pp. 130–131. He emphasized that the denial of State immunity is a response to an act of terrorism.

[75] Daliberti et al. v. Republic of Iraq (2000) 97 F.Supp.2d 38. See also Flatow v. Iran (1999).

[76] Republic of Iraq v. Beaty (2009), 556 U.S. 848.

countermeasure which 'may not be taken, and if already taken must be suspended if the internationally wrongful act has ceased'.[77]

Moreover, in the *Certain Iranian Assets,* section 1605A has been presented before the ICJ as one of the measures taken to address Iran's sponsorship of terrorism.[78] In other words, the United States presented section 1605A as a countermeasure taken in response to an internationally wrongful act in order to induce the responsible State (Iran in that case) to abide by its international obligations.

Therefore, the 1996 amendment to the FSIA can be qualified as a countermeasure against States sponsoring terrorism and, thus, does not reflect any *opinio juris* on the part of the United States.[79] Therefore, it must be excluded when examining the effect of the United States hegemony on the evolution of customary law related to State immunity.

4.3 JASTA

Following successive failures to sue Saudi Arabia for the 9/11 events[80] and after the issuance of the 28-page report, which revealed that Al Qaeda received funds from charities funded by the Saudi Government,[81] the Congress adopted JASTA in 2016, which provided that States do not enjoy immunity:

> in any case in which money damages are sought for physical injury to persons or property or death occurring in the United States and caused by (1) an act of terrorism in the United States and (2) a tortious act or acts of the foreign State, or of any official, employee, or agent of that foreign State while acting within the scope of his or her office, employment, or agency, regardless where the tortious act or acts of the foreign State occurred.[82]

Thus far, US courts have not directly tackled the issue of whether JASTA provides a legal basis for dismissing State immunity in the broader case of international crimes. Cases brought before the courts concern allegations against Saudi Arabia for its involvement in the 9/11 events, which undisputedly constitute acts of terrorism.[83]

---

[77] Articles on the Responsibility of States for Internationally Wrongful Acts (2001), A/56/10, Article 52(3)(a).

[78] Preliminary objections submitted by the United States of America (2017), pp. 31–32, https://www.icj-cij.org/files/case-related/164/164-20170501-WRI-01-00-EN.pdf. Accessed 15 April 2021.

[79] See also Grandaubert (2016).

[80] Fed. Ins. Co. v. Qaida (2015) In: re Terrorist attacks on Sept. 11, 2001, 134 F. Supp. 3d 774, SDNY, Fed. Ins. Co. v. Qaida (2008) In: re Terrorist Attacks on Sept. 11, 2001, 538 F.3d 71, 83, 2d Cir.

[81] The 9/11 Commission Report (2004), p. 171.

[82] 28 U.S.C. §1605B.

[83] Ashton v. Al Qaeda Islamic Army (2018) In: Terrorist attacks on 11 September 2001, 298 F. Supp. 3d 631, SDNY. A new case has been brought against Turkey for violence committed by the Turkish security officials during protests that took place on 16 May 2017 in front of the

Nevertheless, this chapter argues that JASTA provides an exception to State immunity in the case of international crimes. In JASTA, the term 'international terrorism' is widely defined by referring to the definition found in §2331 of the United States' code.[84] International terrorism is defined under this section as those activities that (A) involve violent acts or acts dangerous to human life that are a violation of the criminal laws of the United States or of any State, or that would be a criminal violation if committed within the jurisdiction of the United States or of any State (B) appear to be intended (1) to intimidate or coerce a civilian population; (2) to influence the policy of a government by intimidation or coercion; or (3) to affect the conduct of a government by mass destruction, assassination, or kidnapping.[85] This definition is sufficiently broad to comprise other international crimes because they all involve 'violent acts or acts dangerous to human life' and are 'intended to coerce a civilian population'. International crimes also fit in this definition because they are considered a 'violation of the criminal laws of the United States'.[86]

Furthermore, the legislative history of JASTA shows that the Congress did not intend to limit JASTA to the 9/11 events but rather sought to extend its reach to similar acts in the future. This is reflected in the purpose section of this act where it is stipulated that 'the purpose of this Act is to provide civil litigants with the broadest possible basis, consistent with the Constitution of the United States, to seek relief against persons, entities, and foreign countries, wherever acting and wherever they

---

residence of the Turkish ambassador in Washington. However, no judicial decision has been adopted on the matter. See Usoyan et al. v. Turkey (2018), Docket No. 1_18-cv-01141, DDC, Court Docket. Although this case does not raise the question of whether State immunity is dismissed in case of international crimes, it will be interesting to view the court's interpretation of the term 'international terrorism' and whether it follows a wide or strict interpretation.

[84] See also Stewart (2019), n. 99. It is noteworthy that there are several other definitions for terrorism in the United States Code. On this subject, see Perry (2004), pp. 249–274.

[85] 18 U.S.C. § 2331—U.S. Code.

[86] See Genocide: 18 U.S.C §1091; Torture: 18 U.S.C 2340A; War Crimes 18 U.S.C Chapter 118.

However, the crime against humanity is not expressly codified in the United States criminal laws. Nevertheless, it is difficult to say that this implies that crimes against humanity are excluded from the aforementioned definition of international terrorism, given that most of the forms of crimes against humanity are already crimes in the United States. Furthermore, there is no comprehensive convention on crimes against humanity that resolves the uncertainty surrounding the scope of these crimes. Bearing this in mind, it is difficult to generally state that crimes against humanity are not included in the definition of international terrorism. A bill was introduced at the Congress, yet not in force, on crimes against humanity. See https://www.congress.gov/bill/111th-congress/senate-bill/1346. Accessed 15 April 2021. However, it is beyond the scope of this article to tackle the necessity of a separate codification of crimes against humanity. On that topic, see Elise Keppler (2008) From Nuremberg to Darfur: Accountability for Crimes Against Humanity—Testimony of Elise Keppler, International Justice Program senior counsel, before the Senate Judiciary Subcommittee on Human Rights and the Law. https://www.hrw.org/news/2008/06/24/nuremberg-darfur-accountability-crimes-against-humanity. Accessed 15 April 2021. See also Van Schaack (2019); Aceves and Hoffman (2003), pp. 237–267. See also Murphy (2015) First report on crimes against humanity, A/CN.4/680. p. 29, para. 55.

may be found, that have provided material support, directly or indirectly, to foreign organizations or persons that engage in terrorist activities against the United States'.[87] This is further confirmed by the inaction of the Congress upon the proposed act presented by Mr. Issa and named 'Safeguarding America's Armed Forces and Effectiveness Act' which limits the JASTA to the 9/11 events only.[88] This in its turn reflects that JASTA serves as a legal basis for dismissing State immunity in case of international crimes in general as long as they occur in the territory of the United States.

Yet the question that arises is whether JASTA reflects an *opinio juris* on part of the United States in the sense of its legal conviction that international law accords it the right to dismiss State immunity in case of international crimes?[89] It is hard to ascertain whether JASTA could be considered to reflect an *opinio juris* against the uncertainty surrounding the nature of the rules of State immunity in the United States. While the Government characterizes those rules as customary rules of international law,[90] the judiciary refers to the rules on State immunity as comity.[91] Further, the legislative history of JASTA[92] and the absence of any reference in the purpose and finding section to international law[93] reflect that this piece of legislation was merely enacted for serving the interests of the United States. Taking this into consideration, it is unclear whether JASTA reflects an *opinio juris* in the sense of the

[87] 28 U.S.C. §1605B Section 2(b).

[88] (2016) H.R. 6223 (IH): Safeguarding America's Armed Forces and Effectiveness Act. This bill was intended 'to amend title 28, United States Code to provide that a national of the United States may only bring a claim against a foreign State for an injury which was caused by international terrorism and which occurred on 11 September 2001'.

[89] See ICJ, Jurisdictional Immunities of the State (Germany v. Italy: Greece intervening), Judgment, ICJ Reports 2012, p. 99, para. 55, where the court explained that an opinio juris 'is reflected in particular in the assertion by States claiming immunity that international law accords them a right to such immunity from the jurisdiction of other States; in the acknowledgment, by States granting immunity, that international law imposes upon them an obligation to do so; and, conversely, in the assertion by States in other cases of a right to exercise jurisdiction over foreign States'.

[90] See the United States (2005) Statement, A/C.6/59/SR.13, para. 63.

[91] Altmann v. Republic of Austria (2005), 541 US 677, where the United States Supreme court stated that 'the principal purpose of foreign sovereign immunity has never been to permit foreign States and their instrumentalities to shape their conduct in reliance on the promise of future immunity from suit in United States courts. Rather, such immunity reflects current political realities and relationships, and aims to give foreign States and their instrumentalities some present 'protection from the inconvenience of suit as a gesture of comity' (quoting the Supreme Court's decision in Dole Food Co. v. Patrickson (2003), 538 U.S. 468). See, on the nature of the rules of State immunity in general, Finke (2010), pp. 853–881. See also Fox (2006), pp. 403–406. See generally on the topic of comity in American law: Dodge (2015), pp. 2071–2141.

[92] See United States Senate (2016) Justice against sponsors of terrorism act, Congressional Record vol. 162, no. 78.

[93] This is unlike the finding and declaration of purpose section of the FSIA 1976, which revealed that the restrictive rule of immunity was codified to bring the United States practice to conformity with the rules of international law. See 28 U.S. Code § 1602.

United States' legal conviction that international law accords it the right to dismiss State immunity in case of international crimes.[94]

Even if JASTA arguably reflects an *opinio juris* that accepts dismissing immunity in the case of international crimes, JASTA advances a limited exception to State immunity; thus, its effect on the evolution of customary international law in the context international crimes shall not be exaggerated.[95] Firstly, the JASTA, unlike the FSIA1605A, dismisses State immunity in relation to acts of terrorism that occur only within the territory of the United States.[96] Further, JASTA requires a high threshold for proving the link between the acts of a State and the act of terrorism that occurred in the United States.[97]

To return to the main question of this article, which is, if the JASTA reflects that the United States accepts an exception to State immunity in case of international crimes, will the US hegemony affect the evolution of customary international law in that direction. It is necessary to recall that assessing the hegemonic influence on the rules of international law depends on the intention of the hegemonic State. Accordingly, the answer to the aforementioned question is a negative one, for the United States does not seem to have any intention on changing the rules of State immunity in case of international crimes. The United States has not exerted any effort in getting involved in any persuasive discourses with other States; rather President Obama[98] and other senators[99] have expressed their fear that other States may adopt similar

[94] See also Pavoni (2011), p. 146, where he states that the ICJ in the Jurisdictional Immunities case 'highlights the absence of opinio juris when States grant immunities more extensively than required by international law'. In Pavoni's view, 'this reasoning equally applies when States accord immunities less extensively than those imposed by international law, regardless of the latter's requirements and only as a matter of domestic law and policy'.

[95] See also House Judiciary Committee (2016) Written testimony of Jimmy Gurule, Hearing before the House Judiciary Committee Subcommittee on the Constitution and Civil Justice Washington, D.C. https://republicans-judiciary.house.gov/wp-content/uploads/2016/07/Gurule-Testimony-07142016-1.pdf. Accessed 15 April 2021. United States Senate (2016) Justice against sponsors of terrorism act, Congressional Record vol. 162, no. 78.

[96] The territory of the United States has been narrowly interpreted by United States' courts to only include 'the continental United States and those islands that are part of the United States or its possessions'. Argentine Republic v. Amerada Hess Shipping Corp., 488 U.S. 428; Smith v. Socialist People's Libyan Arab Jamahiriya (1995), 886 F. Supp. 306, EDNY.

[97] The purpose and finding section of the JASTA states that 'the decision of the United States Court of Appeals for the District of Columbia in Halberstam v. Welch (1983), 705 F.2d 472, DC Cir, provides the proper legal framework for how such liability should function in the context of chapter 113B of title 18, United States Code'. Halberstam identified the following elements for an aiding and abetting claim: (1) the party whom the defendant aids must perform a wrongful act that causes an injury; (2) the defendant must be generally aware of his role as part of an overall illegal or tortious activity at the time he provides the assistance; and (3) the defendant must knowingly and substantially assist the principal violation.

[98] Obama B (2016) Veto message from the President. https://obamawhitehouse.archives.gov/the-press-office/2016/09/23/veto-message-president-s2040. Accessed 15 April 2021.

[99] See United States Senate (2016a) Congressional Record vol. 162, no. 178 (2016). See in particular Graham and McCain (2016) Senators Graham and McCain discuss amendment to

legislations that may lead to prosecuting the American military forces located abroad. This undesirability of generalizing the practice of the United States among other States reflects the unwillingness of the United States to induce a change in the customary rules of State immunity for international crimes—the expected costs exceed the excepted benefits.[100] In light of this, the lack of intention to induce a change negates the existence of any hegemonic impact in changing the rules of State immunity for international crimes.

Nonetheless, the story of the United States hegemony in the context of State immunity for international crimes does not end at this point. As the threat of international terrorism is spreading everywhere and the danger of State-sponsored terrorism is growing, two new questions arise: Is it likely that States will follow the United States and adopt a legislation similar to JASTA? Should that be the case, will the US hegemony have a role in preventing the development of the rules of State immunity in that direction?

5 State Reactions to the United States' Practice: Persistent Objection or Role-Modelling

This section aims to determine the probability that other States will follow the United States' practice by enacting legislations that dismiss the immunity of foreign States that aid and abet in acts of terrorism committed on its territory, with terrorism broadly defined—as in JASTA—to encompass other international crimes. For this purpose, it is necessary to understand the reaction of third States towards JASTA, because, as it was shown in the previous section, it is the only piece of legislation that can serve as a legal basis for denying State immunity in the case of international crimes.

It has been earlier highlighted that JASTA has been criticized for violating the principle of State immunity and, thus, violating one of the fundamental norms of international law—namely the principle of sovereign equality of States. This implies that the probability of a change in States' opinion regarding the rules of State immunity relies mainly on the probability that they change their approach to the principle of sovereign equality within the context of international terrorism.[101] In this section, it will be clarified that it is very probable that States adopt legislations similar to the JASTA because their objection to JASTA is not mainly legally based,

JASTA law. https://www.c-span.org/video/?c4633606/user-clip-jasta-amendment&fbclid=IwAR3_VuZefJAStxfpRtkUyTGfkIo90Edvq9Eo8AtTzWj7Q97KBfdMbpQakZg. Accessed 15 April 2021.

[100] Giblin has stated that 'a State will attempt to change the international system if the expected benefits exceed the expected costs (i.e., if there is an expected net gain)'. See Gilpin (1981), pp. 9–10.

[101] Data collected by Verdier and Voeten (2015), p. 24, reveals that normative changes to the notion of sovereignty contribute to the change of the customary rules of State immunity.

given that their conception of the principle of sovereign equality is rather similar to that of the United States in the specific context of international terrorism occurring within the territorial boundaries of a State.[102]

To begin with, it is necessary to recall that rules on State immunity with respect to acts occurring on the territory of the forum State reflect a direct confrontation between the forum State's sovereignty and the principle of sovereign equality of States. In the *Jurisdictional Immunities* case, the ICJ clarified that the rule of State immunity:

> . . .derives from the principle of sovereign equality of States, which, as Article 2, paragraph 1, of the Charter of the United Nations makes clear, is one of the fundamental principles of the international legal order. This principle has to be viewed together with the principle that each State possesses sovereignty over its own territory and that there flows from that sovereignty the jurisdiction of the State over events and persons within that territory. Exceptions to the immunity of the State represent a departure from the principle of sovereign equality. Immunity may represent a departure from the principle of territorial sovereignty and the jurisdiction which flows from it.[103]

This implies that when States grant other States jurisdictional immunity, they overweigh the principle of sovereign equality. *A contrario*, this means that States overweigh their territorial sovereignty when they decide to dismiss the immunity of other States with respect to acts occurring on its territory. Accordingly, in deciding to dismiss the immunity of States sponsoring terrorist acts occurring on its territory, the United States accords primacy to its territorial sovereignty over the principle of sovereign equality. Such an approach of prioritizing one's territorial sovereignty over others' sovereignty is upheld by States in the context of fighting terrorist attacks occurring on their territory. This reveals that objections raised by States to JASTA were not legally based.

It makes sense to begin with Russia, as it is widely argued that one of the greatest controversies between Russia and the United States is the principle of sovereignty.[104] Russia proclaims that is has a different approach to the principle of sovereignty than that advanced by the United States.[105] It is claimed that Russia supports the 'Westphalian' edition of the principle of sovereignty, one that emphasizes the primacy of the sovereignty of States and the sovereign equality between

---

[102]The reason for focusing on this specific context and not the wider context of international terrorism lies in the fact that the JASTA is concerned with State immunity with respect only to terrorism within the United States.

[103]ICJ, Jurisdictional Immunities of the State (Germany v. Italy: Greece intervening), Judgment, ICJ Reports 2012, p. 99, para. 57. The relationship between the principle of sovereign equality and territorial sovereignty was earlier laid down by Chief Justice Marshall in Schooner Exchange v. Mcfaddon (1812), 11 U.S. 116, 136.

[104]Deyermond (2016), pp. 967–984; Silaeva et al. (2016); Bershidsky (2015). See also Smith (2000).

[105](2016) The Declaration of the Russian Federation and the People's Republic of China on the promotion of international law. For an analysis of this declaration, see Mälksoo (2016). See also (2000) The foreign policy concept of the Russian Federation, https://fas.org/nuke/guide/russia/doctrine/econcept.htm. Accessed 15 April 2021.

States.[106] Accordingly, Russia has criticized the United States' foreign policy for violating these two fundamental norms of international law. It has rejected the United States' doctrines of humanitarian intervention, pre-emptive self-defence against terrorist groups located in other States without the latter's consent, the United States' extraterritoriality and, evidently, the United States' legislations on State immunity.

Still, it has been argued that Russia has on its part violated the sovereignty of other States and the principle of the sovereign equality of States. This is evident in its recognition of South Ossetia and Abkhazia in 2008[107] and its annexation to Crimea in 2014.[108] Therefore, Russia's approach to the principle of sovereignty is qualified as inconsistent.

However, Ruth Deyermond rejects this description and provides a convincing explanation for the variance in applying the principle of sovereignty by Russia.[109] She argues that Russia adopts a dual approach to State sovereignty; a 'Westephalian' sovereignty is applied outside the region of the former Soviet Union and a 'post-Westephalian' sovereignty—one assimilated to that advanced by the United States and other Western States—is applied within the region of the former Soviet Union. She explains that this dual approach to sovereignty serves three functions in Russian foreign policy: 'Firstly, it helps to secure Russian national interests at domestic, regional, and international levels; secondly, it acts as a form of balancing against the United States and its allies...; and thirdly, it acts as a marker of 'non-Western' power identity in an emergent multipolar order'.[110] Thus, according to Deyermond, Russia's approach to the principle of sovereignty is 'instrumental' and not 'ideational'.[111]

Based on this explanation, it becomes evident that Russia violates the sovereignty of other States when there is a direct threat to its national sovereignty. This clarifies the reason why Russia violates the sovereignty of States located in the region of the former Soviet Union; changes in this region are considered a potential direct threat to the sovereignty of Russia. Therefore, Georgia's membership of the NATO and Ukraine's potential membership of the NATO constituted a direct threat to Russia's national sovereignty and arguably justified Russia's interventions in these States.[112]

On the other hand, the situation in the States outside the region of the former Soviet Union does not usually constitute a direct threat to its sovereignty. Therefore,

[106] Silaeva et al. (2016); Bershidsky (2015).

[107] See, on the legality of Russia's behavior towards South Ossetia and Abkhazia, Gray (2018), pp. 712–728.

[108] See, on the legality of the Russian annexation of Crimea, O'Connel (2018), pp. 855–873. See also A/RES/68/262 (2014).

[109] Deyermond (2016), p. 958.

[110] Deyermond (2016), pp. 958–959.

[111] Deyermond (2016), p. 958.

[112] Deyermond (2016), p. 974.

Russia prefers to uphold the principle of sovereignty and the sovereign equality of States against United States actions as 'a practical mechanism for the exercise of resistance to United States global leadership'.[113] This implies that Russia would violate the sovereignty of States outside the region of the former Soviet Union if the situation in any of those States had a direct implication on Russia's national sovereignty. This is confirmed by Russia's support to the United States' invasion of Afghanistan after the 9/11 terrorist attacks, despite its alleged illegality.[114] Al-Qaeda has been arguably providing financial support to terrorists in Chechnya;[115] thus, the threat in Afghanistan was linked to a threat to the Russian sovereignty in Chechnya, driving the Russian government to support the United States invasion in Afghanistan.[116]

Taking the aforementioned aspects into consideration, it can be argued that Russia and the United States similarly believe in their right to give supremacy to their national sovereignty over the sovereignty of others when their sovereignty is faced with a direct threat. Thus, Russia's main objection to JASTA cannot, in reality, be legally principled because terrorism within the boundaries of a State constitutes a direct threat to the State's national sovereignty.

This is also true for Arab States who have previously expressed concern to JASTA. The fight against terrorism has revealed that Arab States give supremacy to their national sovereignty over the sovereignty of other States. This is reflected in their support to the US-led coalition in Syria against the terrorist group (Da'esh) which have been conducting attacks on their territory or against their nationals. Even more, Bahrain, Jordan, Saudi Arabia, and the United Arab Emirates launched several strikes against Da'esh in 2014,[117] without the consent of Syria.[118] In addition, one could also refer to measures adopted by Arab States—namely Saudi Arabia,[119]

[113] Deyermond (2016), p. 975.

[114] See, on the legality of the Unites States invasion of Afghanistan, Byers (2018), p. 625ff. Cf. Greenwood (2002), pp. 301–317. See, on the topic of self-defense, Corten (2012), pp. 401–494.

[115] (2011) Task force on Russia and U.S national interests report, Russia and U.S national interests: Why should Americans care? p. 30. https://cdn.cfr.org/sites/default/files/pdf/2011/10/Russia_US_nationalinterests_report.pdf?_ga=2.982451.323003478.1579708961-888287984.1579708961. Accessed 15 April 2021.

[116] See Deyermond (2016), p. 963.

[117] Anti-ISIL Airstrikes Continue in Syria, Iraq, 14 August 2015, https://archive.defense.gov/news/newsarticle.aspx?id=129469. Accessed 15 April 2021.

[118] See United Nations (2015) Identical letters dated 17 September 2015 from the Permanent Representative of the Syrian Arab Republic to the United Nations addressed to the Secretary-General and the President of the Security Council, S/2015/719.

[119] (2017) The Kingdom of Saudi Arabia severs diplomatic and consular relations with Qatar, 6 May 2017. https://www.mofa.gov.sa/sites/mofaen/ServicesAndInformation/news/MinistryNews/Pages/ArticleID201765134958689.aspx. Accessed 15 April 2021.

United Arab Emirates,[120] Egypt,[121] and Bahrain,[122]—against Qatar. The fact that Qatar was—in the opinion of those States—a State sponsor of terrorism, justified the adoption of a series of actions against Qatar, ranging from expelling Qatari diplomats to closing their land, naval, and aerial borders for travel and transport to and from Qatar and ordering Qatari citizens to leave their country. It has been argued that the majority of these measures constitute a violation of the principle of sovereign equality of States and the principle of non-intervention.[123]

Against this background, one can argue that Arab States give supremacy to their national sovereignty over the sovereignty of other States in the context of the fight against terrorism. Therefore, their approach does not appear to differ from that adopted by the United States in this context. Accordingly, their objection to JASTA is not mainly principled on its violation to the principle of the sovereign equality of States.

In its fight against the Kurdish Workers Party (PKK), Turkey has also revealed its commitment to its national sovereignty at the expense of the sovereignty of other States. Since 2011, Turkey has launched several strikes against the PKK, which is considered in its view a terrorist group, in Iraq and Syria without the consent of both States undermining their sovereignty.[124] In light of that, it is hard to believe that Turkey's objection to JASTA was legally principled on its violation of the principle of sovereign equality of States.

Similarly, it is barely convincing that the objection of European States to JASTA is mainly based on its violation of the principle of sovereignty and the sovereign equality of States. European States have shared the United States' conception of State sovereignty. Their intervention in Syria against the terrorist group Da'esh revealed the commitment of European States to their national sovereignty at the expense of the sovereignty of other States. The terrorist attacks in France in 2015 and in Belgium in 2016 have driven not only these States, but numerous other European States to expand the scope of their military operations to the Syrian territory against Da'esh, irrespective of Syria's objection to those military strikes. In other words, since Da'esh represented a threat to the national sovereignty of the European States that conducted military strikes in Syria, these States did not consider the principle of the sovereign equality as an obstacle to their intervention in Syria. In light of this, the objection of the European States to the JASTA is not mainly based on its violation of

[120](2017) UAE: Measures against Qatar came after long patience. https://www.mofaic.gov.ae/MediaHub/News/2017/9/12/12-09-2017-UAE-Qatar. Accessed 15 April 2021.

[121](2017) Cairo breaking off relations came as a result of Qatari rule insistence against Egypt http://www.sis.gov.eg/Story/113332?lang=en-us. Accessed 15 April 2021.

[122](2017) Statement of the Kingdom of Bahrain on the severance of diplomatic relations with the State of Qatar, 5 June 2017, https://www.mofa.gov.bh/Default.aspx?tabid=7824&language=en-US&ItemId=7474. Accessed 15 April 2021.

[123]See Hofer and Luca Ferro (2017).

[124]Those strikes have been condemned by Iraq and Syria; see Letter dated 11 December 2015 from the Permanent Representative of Iraq to the United Nations addressed to the President of the Security Council, UN Doc. S/2015/963 (2015). See also SC/13994 (2019).

the principle of sovereign equality because these States have displayed a disregard of this principle when their national sovereignty was violated.

To summarize, State practice has revealed that States that have previously rejected the JASTA are, akin to the United States, willing to violate the principles of sovereignty and sovereign equality if their national sovereignty was breached or was under an imminent threat by acts of terrorism.[125] Therefore, the objection of States to JASTA is not primarily based on the legal argument that it violates the principle of sovereign equality.

However, this objection may be understood as an instrument of self-protection. As previously mentioned, the JASTA does not specify the States against which it could apply, unlike the FSIA1605A which is only applicable to States designated as sponsors of terrorism by the State Department of the United States. Further, JASTA has a wide scope of application, given that it refers to the broadly defined term of 'international terrorism'. Therefore, other States probably consider that the JASTA gives the United States an extended leeway in their internal affairs and on their assets. It is claimed that the United States has used the term 'terrorism' and 'acts of terror' as a 'catchall term' to pursue its political agenda.[126] A popularly cited example is the invasion of Iraq by the United States in 2003. The United States is accused to have used the term 'war against terror' to conceal its main purpose of controlling the 'world's fifth-largest proved crude oil reserves'.[127] Similarly, the United States is blamed for using the term 'war on terror' to justify its continuing intervention in Syria to conceal the intention to pursue a regime change.[128] Accordingly, given the lack of an accepted definition of terrorism, States appears to be threatened by JASTA. This is confirmed further by the limited protests to the FSIA1605A and the Canadian terrorism exception to State immunity. The FSIA1605A and the Canadian terrorism exception are only applicable to States that are designated as sponsors of terrorism by governments. Therefore, States who maintained a secure alliance with the United States government did not fear FSIA1605A and stopped short of protesting it, while expressing concern towards JASTA that contained no similar safeguards.

---

[125] See also Nagan and Hammer (2004), p. 170 in which the authors highlighted that 'States targeted by terrorists acts are reluctant to accept that their responses to such attacks are constrained by principles of sovereignty in international law'. Nevertheless, it must be emphasized that States do not justify their responses by the same legal arguments presented by the United States.

[126] Gupta (2004), p. 558.

[127] (2019) Iraq: Analysis-Energy Sector Highlights https://www.eia.gov/international/overview/country/IRQ. Accessed 15 April 2021. On the main purpose behind the Iraq invasion: Rogers (2003); Juhasz A (2013) Why the war in Iraq was fought for big oil. https://edition.cnn.com/2013/03/19/opinion/iraq-war-oil-juhasz/index.html. Accessed 15 April 2021. See also Abizaid (2008).

[128] Defense Intelligence Agency (2017) Russia military power: building a military to support great power aspirations, p. 15. https://www.dia.mil/portals/27/documents/news/military%20power%20publications/russia%20military%20power%20report%202017.pdf. Accessed 15 April 2021. See also Depetris (2018).

Having concluded that the objection of the States to the JASTA cannot be considered legally principled, it is probable that they may follow the lead of the United States and adopt similar legislations that deny State immunity in case of international terrorism—widely defined to comprise other international crimes—occurring on its territory. With the increasingly voiced concern towards State-sponsored terrorism[129] and the growing tendency towards the importance of compensating victims of terrorism,[130] it becomes highly expected that the States will adopt reciprocal legislations dismissing State immunity for international terrorism. This brings us to our last question: Will the hegemony of the United States stand against reciprocity?

6 The Reciprocal Character of the Law of Immunity: Any Role Against Hegemony

It is generally acknowledged that international law is based on reciprocity in the sense that a State claiming a right under international law is expected to accord that right to all other States.[131] In this regard, Michael Byers has argued that the principle of reciprocity qualifies 'the application of power in the process of customary international law'.[132] The powerful States 'will only claim rights which they are prepared to see generalized'.[133]

This limiting role of the principle of reciprocity explains President Obama's veto of the JASTA[134] and the European Union's Statement on this piece of legislation.[135] Concern was expressed that adopting the JASTA will enable other countries to enact similar legislations against the United States and other European States for allegations of participation either in the supply of military equipment, training, financing to third parties involved in the commission of war crimes, crimes against humanity, or

[129] See, for example, (2019) India's Statement, SC/13963; (2019) Cuba's Statement, S/PV.8496, pp. 55–56, Ukraine's Statement, pp. 67–68, (2019) Democratic People's Republic of Korea's Statement, GA/L/3594 and (2017) Pakistan's Statement, GA/11950.

[130] See Stewart (2019), pp. 652–653.

[131] See Virally (1967), pp. 48–51; Byers (1999), pp. 88–90; Simma (1984), pp. 400–404. See also Paulus (2011), pp. 113–137.

[132] Byers (1999), p. 90.

[133] Byers (1999), pp. 90–101. See also Verdier and Voeten (2014), pp. 389–434. The authors claim that powerful States comply with international law in order to avoid setting a precedent that undermines a norm whose continued existence they value.

[134] Obama (2016) Veto message from the President. https://obamawhitehouse.archives.gov/the-press-office/2016/09/23/veto-message-president-s2040. Accessed 15 April 2021.

[135] Cîrlig and Pawlak (2016) Justice Against Sponsors of Terrorism Act: The JASTA and its implications. http://www.europarl.europa.eu/RegData/etudes/BRIE/2016/593499/EPRS_BRI(2016)593499_EN.pdf. Accessed 15 April 2021.

genocide, which will consequently erode the principle of State immunity and the underlying principle of sovereign equality.

Discussing the role of reciprocity in the process of custom generation in the context of State immunity, one should distinguish two types of reciprocity. The first type is referred to as 'negative reciprocity', where States enact legislations that provide for the dismissal of State immunity only with respect to those States who violate its immunity. The second type of reciprocity could be referred to as 'positive reciprocity' where States enact legislations that provide for the dismissal of State immunity with respect to all States.

It is generally accepted that 'negative reciprocity' does not lead to a change in the customary rules of international law, because the dismissal of State immunity in this case does not reveal an *opinio juris* but merely reflects the rejection of the act of dismissing its immunity by another State.[136] On the other side, Bruno Simma has highlighted that negative reciprocity may 'weaken established standards or even lead to their non-application'.[137] Therefore, legislations based on negative reciprocity can truly lead to the erosion of the rule of State immunity and the principle of sovereign equality.

Notwithstanding, the dismissal of State immunity on the basis of reciprocity is a rare practice. Based on data collected by Pierre-Hugues Verdier & Erik Voeten, it appears that State immunity is rarely dismissed by domestic courts based on reciprocity arguments.[138] In addition, a questionnaire submitted by the International Law Commission in 1981,[139] on which the Commission's work was based, showed that States were reluctant to accept that the law of State immunity is applied on reciprocity grounds.

On the other hand, 'positive reciprocity' signals the State's own conviction regarding the existence of an international norm, as it provides for the dismissal of the immunity of any State—without discrimination among States—if proven responsible for a specific action. Thus, adopting general legislations that provide for the jurisdiction of domestic courts against foreign States for particular acts will be considered as relevant State practice for the emergence of a new customary rule. Therefore, the concern that the JASTA will create a precedent that may induce other States to adopt similar legislations—thereby resulting in the erosion of the customary rules of State immunity for international crimes—is valid.

However, the following question arises in this context: Will the hegemonic position of the United States impede this type of reciprocity? Will the hegemony of the United States play a role in preserving a privileged position in the application of an emerging rule of State immunity for international crimes?

---

[136] Lauterpacht (1951), p. 228; Verdier and Voeten (2014), p. 398.

[137] Simma (1984), p. 402.

[138] Verdier and Voeten (2015), pp. 16–17. Cf. Guerra (2016) Cuba. In: Laws lifting sovereign immunity in selected countries. The Law Library of Congress, pp. 2–5. https://www.loc.gov/law/help/sovereign-immunity/lifting-sovereign-immunity.pdf. Accessed 15 April 2021.

[139] A/CN.4/343, pp. 48–52 (1981); A/CN.4/.343/ADD.3, p. 3 (1981).

Charles De Visscher emphasized that 'great powers after imprinting a definite direction upon a usage make themselves its guarantors and defenders'.[140] Nevertheless, this image of great powers as 'guarantors' of a new norm—in the sense that the great powers' acceptance of a new rule is a condition for effective implementation of this new rule—'must be judged in the context of specific conditions and the play of forces in the particular case'.[141] It is not always that a powerful State's objection to a specific rule will impede its emergence as a customary international law, or even impede its effective implementation. This is verified by the failure of the objections raised by the United States to prevent the emergence of a new customary rule that extends the territorial waters of a State to 12 nautical miles.[142] One may also mention the failure of the United States to impede a change in the customary rules related to the standard of compensation upon the expropriation of foreign-owned property.[143] It now becomes interesting to examine whether the hegemony of the United States is expected to fail or succeed in preventing a change in the customary rules of State immunity after initiating, unintentionally, such a change.

Firstly, it is necessary to recall that JASTA does not only concern State immunity but is also relevant to the immunity of State officials. As established in Sec. 4.3, JASTA provides for the jurisdiction of the national courts against foreign State officials who aid or abet in committing acts of terrorism within the United States.[144] Therefore, if all the States follow the lead of the United States, it is expected that their laws will also provide for a similar exception to the immunity of State officials. This would allow national courts, as feared by President Obama, to have jurisdiction over claims against American military officials for providing support to groups involved in international crimes.

However, bringing American forces before foreign criminal courts or even international tribunals has been a pain in the neck for the United States to which it has reacted strongly. The United States has delayed the ratification of the 1948 United Nations Convention on the Prevention and Punishment of the Crime of Genocide[145] for almost 40 years. One of the reasons for this delayed ratification was the fear that this treaty will enable the automatic prosecution of American

[140] De Visscher (1957), pp. 149–150.

[141] Schachter (1999), p. 203.

[142] See Toope (2003), pp. 310–311.

[143] Toope (2003), pp. 312–313.

[144] See Stewart (2019), pp. 665–666. Cf. Hancock (2018), p. 1310; Pass JASTA (2016a) JASTA poses no risk of suits against our military personnel. http://passjasta.org/2016/09/jasta-poses-no-risk-suits-military-personnel/. It is argued that the JASTA does not tackle the immunity of State officials, citing in this context the Samantar decision where the Supreme Court decided that the FSIA does not concern the immunity of State officials. Nevertheless, it must be recalled that the Samantar decision was adopted before the enactment of the JASTA, which implies that it did not address whether or not the JASTA provides for an exception to the immunity of State officials. See Samantar v. Yousuf, 560 U.S. 305 (2010).

[145] United Nations (1951) Treaty series vol. 78, p. 277.

military forces before an anticipated international criminal court.[146] Expectedly, the United States also refused to sign the Rome Statute for the establishment of the International Criminal Court (ICC). The US even demanded other States to sign agreements, stating that it would not hand over to the ICC any American nationals who might be accused of genocide and threatened to terminate military assistance to countries that refused to sign such agreements.[147] Moreover, it threatened to stop financing the United Nations peacekeeping missions if its forces, that were participating in these missions, were not excluded from the ICC jurisdiction in the case of a Security Council referral.[148] The United States also threatened the ICC judges that it will deny their requests for visas and even arrest them if they prosecute any of its military forces.[149] Apparently, these threats and measures have succeeded in keeping officials from being prosecuted by the ICC or any other court.[150] In September 2020, those threats materialized as the Trump administration imposed assets freeze against the then ICC Prosecutor Ms Fatou Bensouda and other ICC officials and imposed travel bans against their family members.[151]

It is similarly expected that the United States will also react forcefully to any attempt to bring civil actions against it or its State military officials. Civil suits, as rightly highlighted by José Alvarez, will enable victims to expose the involvement of the United States in the commission of international crimes to 'public scrutiny',[152] degrading the reputation of the United States and its military forces. Further, 'litigation fatigue' will seriously impede the functioning of these military forces. In addition, the emergence of a customary rule denying States and State officials of their immunity in the case of international crimes may facilitate pursuing American assets, not only in the forum State but in other jurisdictions willing to enforce immunity decisions.[153] Thus, given that President Trump and others have sworn to the protection of Americans and American security, it is highly expected that the

---

[146] Pfaff (2001), p. 50. For other reasons, see Korey (1997), pp. 271–290; LeBlanc (2012), pp. 73–186.

[147] See Bolton (2018). See also Wind (2009), p. 82 and references included therein.

[148] See Amnesty International (2003) International Criminal Court: The unlawful attempt of the security council to give US citizens permanent impunity against international justice. https://www.amnesty.org/download/Documents/108000/ior400062003en.pdf. Accessed 15 April 2021.

[149] See Bolton (2018).

[150] See also Amnesty International (2019) Afghanistan: ICC refuses to authorize investigation, caving into USA Threats. https://www.amnesty.org/en/latest/news/2019/04/afghanistan-icc-refuses-to-authorize-investigation-caving-into-usa-threats/. Accessed 15 April 2021.

[151] Human Rights Watch (2020), US sanctions International Criminal Court prosecutor. https://www.hrw.org/news/2020/09/02/us-sanctions-international-criminal-court-prosecutor. Accessed 15 April 2021.

[152] Alvarez (1998), pp. 2101–2103. See also Murphy (1999), pp. 47–48.

[153] A tribunal in Luxembourg has refused to enforce a judgment issued in the United States because the terrorism exception in the FSIA1605A was not part of customary international law. See le Tribunal d'arrondissement de et à Luxembourg. On the contrary, courts will be more willing to enforce foreign judgments if the international crime exception to State immunity was part of customary international law.

United States will take aggressive measures against those States that adopt legislations that are similar to JASTA, if there is a threat of applying them against its military forces.

The fear of retaliation could be the main reason why no further step is taken in the process of enacting an act similar to JASTA in Iraq. Calls for denying immunity for American troops began in 2011, when Iraqi political leaders agreed that there was no need to grant immunity to the American military troops.[154] This in turn led to the failure of any agreement between the Iraqi and American sides to retain a residual force after the designated date for the withdrawal of all American military forces.[155] When the terrorist group Da'esh targeted Iraq, President Obama agreed to send military forces in response to the request of the Iraqi government only after the Iraqi government sent a diplomatic note accepting the immunity of American military forces.[156] In 2016, an Iraqi lobby group called 'The Arab Project', requested the government to file a lawsuit against the United States seeking compensation for violations of international law committed by its military forces during the 2003 invasion.[157] Since then, calls of immunity denial disappeared into thin air until the killing of the Head of Iran's Quds force, Major-General Qassem Soleimani in January 2020. Calls in the Iraqi parliament for removing the immunity of American forces escalated once more, but President Trump reacted by threatening severe sanctions if American forces were expelled or denied immunity.[158]

With this in mind, it can be concluded that the United States hegemony will allow it a privileged position in the application of an emerging customary exception to the rules of State immunity, given that States affected by terrorism[159] and, thus, more likely to adopt similar legislations JASTA, are financially dependent on the United States.[160]

[154] Arango and Schmidt (2011) Iraq denies legal immunity to US troops after 2011. https://www.nytimes.com/2011/10/05/world/middleeast/iraqis-say-no-to-immunity-for-remaining-american-troops.html. Accessed 15 April 2021.

[155] Jakes and Santana (2011) Iraq Prime Minister: immunity issue scuttled us troop deal. https://www.washingtontimes.com/news/2011/oct/22/iraq-pm-immunity-issue-scuttled-us-troop-deal/. Accessed 15 April 2021.

[156] Baker (2014) Diplomatic note promises immunity from Iraqi law for U.S. advisory troops. https://www.nytimes.com/2014/06/24/world/middleeast/us-advisory-troops-get-immunity-from-iraqi-law.html. Accessed 15 April 2021.

[157] Samuel (2016) Families of victims killed during US-led invasion of Iraq demand compensation. https://www.independent.co.uk/news/world/middle-east/iraqis-demand-compensation-from-us-for-victims-of-invasion-a7343996.html. Accessed 15 April 2021.

[158] BBC (2020) Trump threatens Iraq with sanctions if us troops are expelled https://www.bbc.com/news/world-middle-east-51003159. Accessed 15 April 2021.

[159] For the 2019 list of States affected by terrorism, see The Institute for Economics and Peace (2019) Global terrorism index 2019. http://visionofhumanity.org/app/uploads/2019/11/GTI-2019web.pdf. Accessed 15 April 2021.

[160] For the 2019 list of States receiving military aid from the United States, see http://www.foreignassistance.gov/explore. Accessed 15 April 2021.

7 Conclusion

It becomes apparent that the United States does not have the intention to induce any change to the rules of State immunity in case of international crimes but rather seems to preserve itself an exceptional right to deny States of their immunity in that context. Nevertheless, the reciprocal character of international law, 'as a legal consequence of the formal equality of States',[161] stands against this perceived exceptionalism by giving States the right to adopt similar legislations that dismiss State immunity in the case of international crimes. Therefore, the United States legislations on State immunity, in particular the JASTA, may have the unintentional effect of changing the rules of State immunity for international crimes.

Nonetheless, it is noteworthy that the United States, 'where it could not secure the legalization of inequality, it opted for unequal legalization–other States became subject to new rules, while the United States did not'.[162] This chapter has shown that rules of State immunity is another field of international law where the United States will seek to have a privileged position, giving itself the right to deny States and their State officials of their immunity in case of international crimes but denying those States the right to apply their legislations in order to bring lawsuits against it or any of its military forces. To what extent this privileged position will be resisted by States remains to be assessed in further studies.

References

International Courts and Tribunals Decisions

Certain Iranian Assets (2019) Islamic Republic of Iran v. United States of America. Preliminary Objections, ICJ Reports

Jurisdictional Immunities of the State (2012) Germany v. Italy: Greece Intervening. Judgment. ICJ Reports

North Sea Continental Shelf Judgment (1969) Judgment. ICJ Reports

National Court Decisions

Altmann v. Republic of Austria (2005) 541 US 677

Argentine Republic v. Amerada Hess Shipping Corp. (1989), 488 U.S. 428

Ashton v. Al Qaeda Islamic Army (2018) In: re Terrorist attacks on 11 September 2001, 298 F. Supp. 3d 631, SDNY

---

[161] Byers (1999), p. 90.

[162] Krisch (2003), p. 154.

Bank Markazi Aka Central Bank of Iran v. Peterson (2016) Supreme Court of the United States No. 14-770, https://www.supremecourt.gov/opinions/15pdf/14-770_9o6b.pdf. Accessed 25 Jan 2020
Belhas v. Ya'alon (2008) 07-7009, DC Cir
Cabiri v. Government of the Republic of Ghana (1999) 165 F.3d 193, 202, 2nd Cir
Daliberti et al. v. Republic of Iraq (2000) 97 F.Supp.2d 38
Fed. Ins. Co. v. Qaida (2008) In: re Terrorist Attacks on Sept. 11, 2001, 538 F.3d 71, 83, 2d Cir
Fed. Ins. Co. v. Qaida (2015) In: re Terrorist attacks on Sept. 11, 2001, 134 F. Supp. 3d 774, SDNY
Flatow v. Islamic Republic of Iran (1998) United States District Court, District of Columbia, March 1998, 1999 F.Supp.1
Halberstam v. Welch (1983) 705 F.2d 472, DC Cir
Hugo Princz v. Federal Republic of Germany (1994) 26 F.3d 1166, DC Cir
Hwang Geum Joo v. Japan (2003) 332 F.3d 679, DC Cir
le Tribunal d'arrondissement de et à Luxembourg, première chambre (2019) Jugement civil 2019TALCH01/00116. https://justice.public.lu/dam-assets/fr/actualites/2019/Jgt20190327-exequatur-anonyme.pdf. Accessed 25 Jan 2020
Letelier v. Republic of Chile (1980) 488 F. Supp. 665, DDC
Liu v. Republic of China (1989), 892 F.2d 1419, 9th Cir
Republic of Iraq v. Beaty (2009) 556 U.S. 848
Samantar v. Yousuf (2010) 560 U.S. 305
Sampson v. Federal Republic of Germany (2001) 250 F.3d 1145, 7th Cir
Schooner Exchange v. Mcfaddon (1812) 11 U.S. 116, 136
Siderman de Blake v. Republic of Argentina (1992) 965 F.2d 699, 9th Cir
Smith v. Socialist People's Libyan Arab Jamahiriya (1995) 886 F. Supp. 306, EDNY
Usoyan et al. v. Turkey (2018) Docket No. 1_18-cv-01141, DDC

Books

Aceves W, Hoffman W (2003) Pursuing crimes against humanity in the United States: the need for a comprehensive liability regime. In: Lattimer M, Sands P (eds) Justice for crimes against humanity. Hart, Oxford, pp 237–267
Byers M (1999) Custom, power and the power of rules: international relations and customary international law. Cambridge University Press, Cambridge
Byers M (2018) The Intervention in Afghanistan—2001. In: Ruys T, Corten O, Hofer A (eds) The use of force in international law: a case-based approach. Oxford University Press, Oxford, pp 625 et seq
Clark I (2011) Hegemony in international society. Oxford University Press, Oxford
Cooper-Hill J (2006) The law of sovereign immunity and terrorism. Oceana Publications, New York
Corten O (2009) Le discours du droit international pour un positivisme critique. Editions A. Pedone, Paris
Corten O (2012) The law against war. Hart, Oxford
Danilenko GM (1993) Law-making in the international community. Martinus Nijhoff, The Netherlands
De Visscher C (1957) Theory and reality in public international law. Princeton University Press, New Jersey
Fox H, Webb P (2013) The law of state immunity, 3rd edn. Oxford University Press, Oxford
Gilpin R (1981) War and change in world politics. Cambridge University Press, Cambridge
Gray C (2018) The conflict in Georgia—2008. In: Ruys T, Corten O, Hofer A (eds) The use of force in international law: a case-based approach. Oxford University Press, Oxford, pp 712 et seq

Hafner G (2013) Historical background to the Convention. In: O'Keefe R, Tams CJ, Tzanakopoulos A (eds) The United Nations Convention on jurisdictional immunities of states and their property: a commentary. Oxford University Press, Oxford, pp 1–12

Juhasz A (2013) Why the war in Iraq was fought for big oil. https://edition.cnn.com/2013/03/19/opinion/iraq-war-oil-juhasz/index.html

Klein P (2003) The effects of US predominance on the elaboration of treaty regimes and on the evolution of the law of treaties. In: Byers M, Nolte G (eds) United States hegemony and the foundations of international law. Cambridge University Press, Cambridge, pp 363–391

Krisch N (2003) More equal than the rest? Hierarchy, equality and US predominance in international law. In: Byers M, Nolte G (eds) United States hegemony and the foundations of international law. Cambridge University Press, Cambridge, pp 135–175

LeBlanc L (2012) The United States and the genocide convention: the sovereignty package in perspective. In: van der Wilt H, Sluiter G, Vervliet J, Houwink ten Cate J (eds) The Genocide Convention: the legacy of 60 years. Martinus Nijhoff, Leiden, pp 173–186

Marcelo G, Kohen MG (2003) The use of force by the United States after the end of the Cold War and its impact on international law. In: Byers M, Nolte G (eds) United States hegemony and the foundations of international law. Cambridge University Press, Cambridge, pp 197–231

Nolte G (2003) Conclusion: a historical question and contemporary responses. In: Byers M, Nolte G (eds) United States hegemony and the foundations of international law. Cambridge University Press, Cambridge, pp 491–514

Nye JS (2004) Soft power: the means to success in world politics. Public Affairs, New York

O'Connel M (2018) The crisis in Ukraine 2014. In: Ruys T, Corten O, Hofer A (eds) The use of force in international law: a case-based approach. Oxford University Press, Oxford, pp 855 et seq

Paulus A (2011) Reciprocity revisited. In: Fastenrath U, Geiger R, Khan D-E, Paulus A, von Schorlemer S, Vedder C (eds) From bilateralism to community interest: essays in honour of Bruno Simma. Oxford University Press, Oxford, pp 113–137

Roth BR (2003) Bending the law, breaking it, or developing it? The United States and the humanitarian use of force in the post-cold war era. In: Byers M, Nolte G (eds) United States hegemony and the foundations of international law. Cambridge University Press, Cambridge, pp 232–263

Salmon J (2014) Droit International et Argumentation. Bruylant, Bruxelles

Scott J, Marshall G (2009) A dictionary of sociology, 3rd edn. Oxford University Press, Oxford, p 99 (online numbering). https://www.oxfordreference.com/view/10.1093/acref/9780199533008.001.0001/acref-9780199533008. Accessed 25 Jan 2020

Seiichi K (2008) Wielding soft power: the key stages of transmission and reception. In: Yasushi W, McConnell D (eds) Soft power superpowers: cultural and national assets of Japan and the United States. Routledge, pp 191–206

Simma B (1984) Reciprocity. In: Bernhardt R (ed) Encyclopedia of public international law. Elsevier Science Publishers, Amsterdam, pp 400–404

Skordas (2003) Hegemonic custom? In: Byers M, Nolte G (eds) United States hegemony and the foundations of international law. Cambridge University Press, Cambridge, pp 317–347

Stewart D (2019) Immunity and terrorism. In: Ruys R, Angelet N, Ferro L (eds) The Cambridge handbook of immunities and international law. Cambridge University Press, Cambridge, pp 651–669

Toope S (2003) Powerful but unpersuasive? The role of the United States in the evolution of customary international law. In: Byers M, Nolte G (eds) United States hegemony and the foundations of international law. Cambridge University Press, Cambridge, pp 287–316

Yang X (2012) State immunity in international law. Cambridge University Press, Cambridge

Articles

Alvarez JE (2003) Hegemonic international law revisited. AJIL 97:873–888
Chaumont C (1975) Methode d'analyse du droit international. Revue Belge de Droit International XI:32–37
Finke J (2010) Sovereign immunity: rule, comity or something else? EJIL 21:853–881
Fox H (2006) Defense of State immunity: why the UN Convention on state immunity is important. ICLQ 55:399–406
Hall T (2010) An unclear attraction: a critical examination of soft power as an analytical category. Chinese J Int Polit 3:189–211
Lauterpacht H (1951) The problem of jurisdictional immunities of foreign states. Br Yearb Int Law 28:220
Pavoni R (2011) An American anomaly? On the ICJ's selective reading of United States practice in jurisdictional immunities of the state. Ital Yearb Int Law XXI:143–159
Tate J (1952) Letter from Jack B. Tate, Acting Legal Adviser, U.S. Dept. of State, to Acting U.S. Attorney General Philip B. Perlman. Dep State Bull 26:984–985
Vagts DF (2001) Hegemonic international law. AJIL 95:843–848
Verdier P, Voeten E (2014) Precedent, compliance and change in customary international law: an explanatory theory. AJIL 108:389–434
Virally M (1967) Le principe de réciprocité dans le droit international contemporain. Recueil de Cours 122:5–105

Electronic References

(2000) The foreign policy concept of the Russian Federation, 28 June 2000. https://fas.org/nuke/guide/russia/doctrine/econcept.htm
(2011) Task force on Russia and U.S national interests report, Russia and U.S national interests: Why should Americans care?. https://cdn.cfr.org/sites/default/files/pdf/2011/10/Russia_US_nationalinterests_report.pdf?_ga=2.982451.323003478.1579708961-888287984.1579708961
(2015) Anti-ISIL Airstrikes Continue in Syria, Iraq, 14 August 2015. https://archive.defense.gov/news/newsarticle.aspx?id=129469
(2016) H.R. 6223 (IH): Safeguarding America's Armed Forces and Effectiveness Act. https://www.govinfo.gov/app/details/BILLS-114hr6223ih
(2016) Senators Graham and McCain discuss amendment to JASTA law. https://www.c-span.org/video/?c4633606/user-clip-jasta-amendment&fbclid=IwAR3_VuZefJAStxfpRtkUyTGfkIo90Edvq9Eo8AtTzWj7Q97KBfdMbpQakZg
(2016) The Declaration of the Russian Federation and the People's Republic of China on the promotion of international law. https://www.mid.ru/en/foreign_policy/position_word_order/-/asset_publisher/6S4RuXfeYlKr/content/id/2331698
(2017) Cairo breaking off relations came as a result of Qatari rule insistence against Egypt. http://www.sis.gov.eg/Story/113332?lang=en-us
(2017) Statement of the Kingdom of Bahrain on the severance of diplomatic relations with the State of Qatar. https://www.mofa.gov.bh/Default.aspx?tabid=7824&language=en-US&ItemId=7474
(2017) The Kingdom of Saudi Arabia severs diplomatic and consular relations with Qatar. https://www.mofa.gov.sa/sites/mofaen/ServicesAndInformation/news/MinistryNews/Pages/ArticleID201765134958689.aspx
(2017) UAE: Measures against Qatar came after long patience. https://www.mofaic.gov.ae/MediaHub/News/2017/9/12/12-09-2017-UAE-Qatar
(2019) Iraq: Analysis-Energy Sector Highlights. https://www.eia.gov/international/overview/country/IRQ

Abizaid J (2008) Of course it's about oil, we can't really deny that. https://www.huffpost.com/entry/abizaid-of-course-its-abo_n_68568 (unless indicated otherwise, all URLs cited were last accessed on 25 Jan 2020)
Alvarez JE (1998) Rush to closure: lessons of the Tadić judgment. Mich Law Rev 96:2031–2112. https://repository.law.umich.edu/cgi/viewcontent.cgi?article=2014&context=mlr
Amnesty International (2003) International Criminal Court: the unlawful attempt of the Security Council to give US citizens permanent impunity against international justice. IOR40/006/2003. https://www.amnesty.org/download/Documents/108000/ior400062003en.pdf
Amnesty International (2019) Afghanistan: ICC refuses to authorize investigation, caving into USA threats. https://www.amnesty.org/en/latest/news/2019/04/afghanistan-icc-refuses-to-authorize-investigation-caving-into-usa-threats/
Arango T, Schmidt MS (2011) Iraq denies legal immunity to U.S. troops after 2011. https://www.nytimes.com/2011/10/05/world/middleeast/iraqis-say-no-to-immunity-for-remaining-american-troops.html. Accessed 25 Jan 2020
Baker P (2014) Diplomatic note promises immunity from Iraqi law for U.S. advisory troops. https://www.nytimes.com/2014/06/24/world/middleeast/us-advisory-troops-get-immunity-from-iraqi-law.html
Bankas E (1999) International law: state immunity and the controversy of private suits against sovereign states in domestic courts. Dissertation, Durham University, p 132. http://etheses.dur.ac.uk/4793/
Bershidsky L (2015) Nature of sovereignty a key issue in Russia–U.S. divide. https://www.japantimes.co.jp/opinion/2015/09/21/commentary/world-commentary/nature-sovereignty-key-issue-russia-u-s-divide/#.XfnHcC2B1p9
Bolton J (2018) Bolton's remarks on the International Criminal Court. https://www.justsecurity.org/60674/national-security-adviser-john-bolton-remarks-international-criminal-court/
British Broadcast Corporation (2020) Trump threatens Iraq with sanctions if US troops are expelled. https://www.bbc.com/news/world-middle-east-51003159
Byers M (2003) Preemptive self-defense: hegemony, equality and strategies of legal change. J Polit Philos 11:171–190. https://doi.org/10.1111/1467-9760.00173
Chinese Foreign Ministry (2016) Foreign Ministry Spokesperson Remarks on JASTA. http://sa.china-embassy.org/eng/gdxw/t1404794.htm
Cîrlig C, Pawlak P (2016) Justice against sponsors of terrorism act: the JASTA and its implications. http://www.europarl.europa.eu/RegData/etudes/BRIE/2016/593499/EPRS_BRI(2016)593499_EN.pdf
Daugirdas K (2016) Contemporary practice of the United States relating to international law. University of Michigan Law School Scholarship Repository. http://repository.law.umich.edu/cgi/viewcontent.cgi?article=2808&context=articles
Defense Intelligence Agency (2017) Russia military power: building a military to support great power aspirations, p 15 https://www.dia.mil/portals/27/documents/news/military%20power%20publications/russia%20military%20power%20report%202017.pdf
Depetris D (2018) The Trump administration is pursuing a regime change in Syria under the guise of fighting terrorism. https://reason.com/2018/03/19/the-trump-administration-is-pursuing-reg-2/
Deyermond R (2016) The uses of sovereignty in twenty-first century Russian foreign policy. Europe-Asia Stud 68:957–984. https://doi.org/10.1080/09668136.2016.1204985
Dodge WS (2015) International comity in American law. Columbia Law Rev 115:2071–2141. https://papers.ssrn.com/sol3/papers.cfm?abstract_id=2558175
Donner R (2001) The Tate letter revisited. Willamette J Int Law Disp Resolut 9:28. www.jstor.org/stable/26211177
Fensterwald B (1959) United States policies towards state trading. Law Contemp Probl 24:369–397. https://www.jstor.org/stable/1190450?seq=1

Franchini D (2017) Suing foreign states before US courts: non-recognition of state immunity as a response to internationally wrongful acts. https://papers.ssrn.com/sol3/papers.cfm?abstract_id=3073429

Franchini D (2019) State immunity as a tool of foreign policy: the unanswered question of certain Iranian assets. https://papers.ssrn.com/sol3/papers.cfm?abstract_id=3449086

Gordon J, Gillman O (2016) Saudi Arabia threatens to pull $750 billion in US assets if Congress passes bill makings its government liable for 9/11-related lawsuits. http://www.dailymail.co.uk/news/article-3543702/Saudi-Arabia-threatens-pull-750-billion-U-S-assets-Congress-passes-bill-making-government-liable-9-11-related-lawsuits.html

Grandaubert V (2016) Is there a place for sovereign immunity in the fight against terrorism? The US Supreme Court says 'no' in *Bank Markazi v. Peterson*. https://www.ejiltalk.org/is-there-a-place-for-sovereign-immunity-in-the-fight-against-terrorism-the-us-supreme-court-says-no-in-bank-markazi-v-peterson/

Greenwood C (2002) International law and the 'war against terrorism'. Int Aff 78:301–317. https://academic.oup.com/ia/article/78/2/301/2434742

Guerra G (2016) Cuba. In: Laws lifting sovereign immunity in selected countries. The Law Library of Congress, pp 2–5. https://www.loc.gov/law/help/sovereign-immunity/lifting-sovereign-immunity.pdf

Gupta S (2004) The changing dimensions of international terrorism and the role of the United States: a comprehensive and multilateral approach to combat global terrorism. Indian J Polit Sci LXV:558. https://www.jstor.org/stable/41856077?seq=1

Gurule J (2016) Written testimony of Jimmy Gurule, Hearing before the House Judiciary Committee Subcommittee on the Constitution and Civil Justice Washington, D.C. https://republicans-judiciary.house.gov/wp-content/uploads/2016/07/Gurule-Testimony-07142016-1.pdf

Hancock RE (2018) Mob-legislating: JASTA's addition to the terrorism exception to foreign sovereign immunity. Cornell Law Rev 103:1293–1328. https://scholarship.law.cornell.edu/cgi/viewcontent.cgi?article=4766&context=clr

Helfer LR, Wuerth IB (2016) Customary international law: an instrument choice perspective. Mich J Int Law 37:584–590. http://repository.law.umich.edu/cgi/viewcontent.cgi?article=1340&context=mjil

Hofer A, Ferro L (2017) Sanctioning Qatar: coercive interference in the States Domain-reserve? https://www.ejiltalk.org/sanctioning-qatar-coercive-interference-in-the-States-domaine-reserve/

Hosseinnejad K (2019) Interpretation of implication: some observations on the recent ICJ decision in the case of certain Iranian assets. http://opiniojuris.org/2019/03/01/interpretation-of-implication-some-observations-on-the-recent-icj-decision-in-the-case-of-certain-iranian-assets/

Human Rights Watch (2020) US sanctions International Criminal Court prosecutor. https://www.hrw.org/news/2020/09/02/us-sanctions-international-criminal-court-prosecutor

Institute of International Law (2009) Resolution on the immunity from jurisdiction of the state and of persons who act on behalf of the state in case of international crimes. Third Commission, Annuaire de l'Institut de droit international- Session de Naples 73:228. https://www.idi-iil.org/app/uploads/2017/06/Lady-Fox.pdf

Jakes L, Santana R (2011) Iraq Prime Minister: immunity issue scuttled U.S. troop deal. https://www.washingtontimes.com/news/2011/oct/22/iraq-pm-immunity-issue-scuttled-us-troop-deal/. Accessed 22 Jan 2020

Keppler E (2008) From Nuremberg to Darfur: accountability for crimes against humanity—testimony of Elise Keppler, International Justice Program senior counsel, before the Senate Judiciary Subcommittee on Human Rights and the Law. https://www.hrw.org/news/2008/06/24/nuremberg-darfur-accountability-crimes-against-humanity

Kim J (2004) Making state sponsors of terrorism pay: a separation of powers discourse under the foreign sovereign immunities act. Berkeley J Int Law 22:513 et seq. https://berkeleylawir.tind.io/record/1119257?ln=en

Korey W (1997) The United States and the genocide convention: leading advocate and leading obstacle. Ethics Int Aff 11:271–290. https://doi.org/10.1111/j.1747-7093.1997.tb00032.x
Koskenniemi M (2004) International law and hegemony: a reconfiguration. Camb Rev Int Aff 17:197–218. https://doi.org/10.1080/0955757042000245852
Mälksoo L (2016) Russia and China challenge the Western hegemony in the interpretation of international law. https://www.ejiltalk.org/russia-and-china-challenge-the-western-hegemony-in-the-interpretation-of-international-law/
Mazzetti M (2016) Saudi Arabia warns of economic fallout if Congress passes 9/11 bill. https://www.nytimes.com/2016/04/16/world/middleeast/saudi-arabia-warns-ofeconomic-fallout-if-congress-passes-9-11-bill.html?_r=0
Morgenroth T (2015) How role models affect role aspirants' motivation and goals. Dissertation, University of Exeter. https://www.researchgate.net/publication/284515013_The_Motivational_Theory_of_Role_Modeling_How_Role_Models_Influence_Role_Aspirants%27_Goals
Moser PT (2012) Non-recognition of state immunity as a judicial countermeasure to Jus Cogens violations: the human rights answer to the ICJ decision on the Ferrini case. Goettingen J Int Law 4:809–852. https://www.gojil.eu/issues/43/43_article_moser.pdf
Murphy JF (1999) Civil liability for the commission of international crimes as an alternative to criminal prosecution. Harv Hum Rights J 12:1–56. https://harvardhrj.com/wp-content/uploads/sites/14/2020/06/12_Murphy_Civil-Liability-For-the-Commission-of-International-Crimes.pdf
Murphy S (2015) First report on crimes against humanity, A/CN.4/680. p 29, para 55. https://scholarship.law.gwu.edu/cgi/viewcontent.cgi?article=2371&context=faculty_publications
Nagan W, Hammer C (2004) The changing character of sovereignty in international law and international relations. Columbia J Transnatl Law 43:141–187. https://scholarship.law.ufl.edu/cgi/viewcontent.cgi?article=1592&context=facultypub
Nye JS (2008) Public diplomacy and soft power. Ann Am Acad Polit Soc Sci 616:94–109. https://www.jstor.org/stable/25097996?read-now=1&seq=1
Obama B (2016) Veto message from the President. https://obamawhitehouse.archives.gov/the-press-office/2016/09/23/veto-message-president-s2040
Pass JASTA (2016a) JASTA poses no risk of suits against our military personnel. http://passjasta.org/2016/09/jasta-poses-no-risk-suits-military-personnel/.
Pass JASTA (2016b) Response to the message of the President accompanying his veto of the Justice Against Sponsors of Terrorism Act (2016) http://passjasta.org/2016/09/response-message-president-accompanying-veto-justice-sponsors-terrorism-act/
Patalakh A (2016) Assessment of soft power strategies: towards an aggregative analytical model for country-focused case study research. Croat Int Relat Rev 76:85–112. https://doi.org/10.1515/cirr-2016-0007
Perry NJ (2004) The numerous federal legal definitions of terrorism: the problem of too many grails. J Legis 30:249–274. http://scholarship.law.nd.edu/jleg/vol30/iss2/3
Pfaff W (2001) Judging ear crimes. Survival 42:46–58. https://doi.org/10.1093/survival/42.1.46
Rogers P (2003) The myth of a clean war and its real motive. https://www.opendemocracy.net/en/article_1041jsp/
Russian Foreign Ministry (2016) Comment by the information and press department on the US passing the Justice Against Sponsors of Terrorism Act with extraterritorial jurisdiction. http://www.mid.ru/en/web/guest/kommentarii_predstavitelya/-/asset_publisher/MCZ7HQuMdqBY/content/id/2479122
Salmon J (2009) Jean Salmon's comments regarding the fundamental rights of the person and the immunity from jurisdiction in international law. Annuaire de l'Institut de droit international - Session de Naples 73:228. https://www.idi-iil.org/app/uploads/2017/06/Lady-Fox.pdf
Samuel G (2016) Families of victims killed during US-led invasion of Iraq demand compensation. https://www.independent.co.uk/news/world/middle-east/iraqis-demand-compensation-from-us-for-victims-of-invasion-a7343996.html

Saudi Press Agency (2016a) Official at Ministry of Foreign Affairs: JASTA great concern to community of nations objecting to erosion of principle of sovereign immunity. www.spa.gov.sa/viewstory.php?lang=en&newsid=1543953

Saudi Press Agency (2016b) GCC expresses concern over a US Congress bill contradicting the principles of equality and sovereign immunity of countries of the world. http://www.spa.gov.sa/viewstory.php?lang=en&newsid=1537574

Schachter O (1999) The role of power in international law. Proc Annu Meet ASIL 93:200–205. www.jstor.org/stable/25659290

Schnably SJ (2017) The transformation of human rights litigation: the alien tort statute, the anti-terrorism act, and JASTA. Univ Miami Int Comp Law Rev 24:285–440. http://repository.law.miami.edu/umiclr/vol24/iss2/5

Silaeva V, Kazakova A, Loshkaryov I, Chernyavskaya K (2016) State sovereignty in the US Russian, European interpretations. Paper presented for the Annual Conference Student Webinar '"Conceptual Conversations": Exploring Russian, European & American Understandings of Core Concepts Underpinning Russia-West Relations', Higher School of Economics, Moscow, 30 September–1 October 2016. https://www.sant.ox.ac.uk/sites/default/files/university-consortium/files/chernyavskaya_kazakova_loshkayrov_silaeva_State_sovereignty_in_the_us_russian_and_european_interpretations_2016.pdf

Smith GB (2000) Russian exceptionalism? Putin's assertion of sovereignty at home and abroad. https://www.law.upenn.edu/live/files/1882-gordon-smith-russian-exceptionalismpdf. Accessed 25 Jan 2020

The 9/11 Commission Report (2004). https://www.9-11commission.gov/report/911Report.pdf

United States Senate (2016a) Congressional Record vol. 162, no. 178 (2016) https://www.congress.gov/congressional-record/2016/12/09/senate-section/article/S7005-2

United States Senate (2016b) Justice against sponsors of terrorism act, Congressional Record vol. 162, no. 78. https://www.congress.gov/congressional-record/2016/05/17/senate-section/article/S2845-1

Van Schaack B (2019) Crimes against humanity: repairing Title 18's blind spot. https://www.justsecurity.org/wp-content/uploads/2019/06/Arcs-of-Global-Justice-The-Need-for-a-US-CAH-Statute.pdf

Verdier P, Voeten E (2015) How does customary international law change? The case of state immunity. Int Stud Q. https://papers.ssrn.com/sol3/papers.cfm?abstract_id=2106627

Wind M (2009) Challenging sovereignty? The USA and the establishment of International Criminal Court. Ethics Glob Polit 2:83–108. https://doi.org/10.3402/egp.v2i1.1973

U.N. Documents

United Nations (1981) A/CN.4/.343/ADD.3

United Nations (1981) A/CN.4/343

United Nations (1981) States' answers to the questionnaire submitted by the International Law Commission on the subject of State immunity, A/CN.4/343

United Nations (1999) Report of the International Law Commission on the work of its fifty-first session, A/54/10, Appendix

United Nations (2001) Articles on the Responsibility of States for Internationally Wrongful Acts, A/56/10

United Nations (2001) S/RES/1373

United Nations (2005) A/C.6/59/SR.13

United Nations (2005) The United States Statement, A/C.6/59/SR.13

United Nations (2008) Letter dated 24 September 2008 from the Permanent Representative of the Islamic Republic of Iran to the United Nationals addressed to the Secretary General, A/C.6/63/2

United Nations (2014) A/RES/68/262
United Nations (2014) S/RES/2178
United Nations (2015) Identical letters dated 17 September 2015 from the Permanent Representative of the Syrian Arab Republic to the United Nations addressed to the Secretary-General and the President of the Security Council S/2015/719
United Nations (2015) Letter dated 11 December 2015 from the Permanent Representative of Iraq to the United Nations addressed to the President of the Security Council, S/2015/963
United Nations (2017) GA/11950
United Nations (2018) International Law Commission Draft conclusions on the identification of customary international law with commentaries, A/73/10 (2018)
United Nations (2019), GA/L/3594
United Nations (2019), S/PV.8496
United Nations (2019), SC/13963

Rana M. Essawy is an assistant professor of public international law at Alexandria University (Egypt). Her thesis 'The Doctrine of Implied Powers in International Law' was awarded the Boutrous Boutrous-Ghali prize for the second-best PhD in Egypt for the years 2018–2019. She recently published two COVID-19 related posts with EJIL: Talk! (the blog of the European Journal of International Law).

Part III
Sovereign Immunity of States and Their Financial Obligations

Sovereign Debt and State Immunity: Towards a Loss of Dissonance Between Public and EU Private International Law?

Stefano Dominelli

Abstract A juxtaposition of theories and relevant concepts in public and private international law shows that the coexistence of such branches of laws has encouraged the development of comparable methodologies and results. The result is that courts and scholars (usually) reason on common yet separate grounds. Whilst the relationship between public and private international law has often been studied to explore if there are principles and rules in public international law to which rules on jurisdiction and applicable law must abide, the aim of the work is to dwell on the effects of the application of EU law on international civil procedure over relevant public international law concepts. The case of sovereign debt and the international law of State immunity is taken here as a case study to explore the relevance and effects of a reversed influence, i.e. to what extent the application and enforcement of the Brussels Ibis Regulation of the European Union shape traditional theories and concepts of public international law.

The present work has been written in the framework of the of the Research Project 'Enhancing Enforcement under Brussels Ia'—EN2BRIa, European Union Justice Programme 2014-2020, JUST-JCOO-AG-2018 JUST 831598. The work represents the views of the author only, and the European Commission, nor any other institution, accepts responsibility for its content or the use it can be made of.

S. Dominelli (✉)
University of Genoa, Genova, Italy
e-mail: stefano.dominelli@unige.it

R. Bismuth et al. (eds.), *Sovereign Immunity Under Pressure*,
https://doi.org/10.1007/978-3-030-87706-4_14

1 State Immunity in Public and Private International Law: Divided But Coherent Approaches

It has long been debated whether private international law is 'part' of public international law.[1] If one assumes so, the principles and rules developed in the context of public international law would have direct and automatic effects in the field of conflict of jurisdictions and conflicts of laws. Even though, from a continental perspective, a 'unity' of the two branches of law is typically not accepted, practitioners generally adopt consistent theories and approaches in such different unities of law.[2] In matters concerning immunity, fundamental concepts of public and private international law have traditionally been somewhat consistent despite the formalistic autonomy between the two fields. As framed by the Permanent Court of International Justice, the territorial understanding of 'jurisdiction'[3] bears the consequence that 'the first and foremost restriction imposed by international law upon a State is that - failing the existence of a permissive rule to the contrary - it may not exercise its power in any form in the territory of another State'.[4] According to such a judgment, jurisdiction is territorial.[5] 'Enforcement jurisdiction' abroad requires a permissive rule, whilst prescriptive jurisdiction and adjudicative jurisdiction within the territory of the State can be exercised[6] even in respect to conducts that take place abroad under exorbitant heads of jurisdiction.[7] Foreign State immunity becomes a limit to both the jurisdiction to adjudicate and to enforce.[8] Here, legal concepts in public and private international law related to the possibility to adjudicate conducts of foreign States should be consistent (otherwise, exercise of jurisdiction might amount to international wrongdoing).[9]

---

[1]See Morelli (1971), p. 12 f; Mills (2009), p. 211ff; Michaels (2008), p. 121; Muir Watt and Fernández Arroyo (2014); Corneloup et al. (2017); Mankowski (2018b), p. 45; Balladore Pallieri (1950), p. 95; Vitta (1972), p. 10; Hess (2016), p. 71ff.

[2]This can be seen with regard to the definition of 'State' for both the purposes of statehood and for the purposes of applicable law. Public and private international law generally rely on an effectiveness test, rather than on mere formal political recognition of a territorial unit as 'sovereign State'. See ex multis Basedow (2018/2019), p. 1; Dickinson (2015), p. 69.

[3]Ryngaert (2015).

[4]SS Lotus (France v Turkey) (1927) PCIJ Series A, No. 10, p. 4, p. 18.

[5]Verheul (1983), p. 199 quoting van Bynkershoek (1721), p. 7 ('extra territorium ius dicentis non pareri'). Cf. South Africa Supreme Court, State v. Ebrahim, 16.2.1991, in 95 International Law Reports, 1994, p. 417, p. 431.

[6]Hertogen (2015), p. 907.

[7]Giuliano (1970), p. 9ff, where the Author noted how limits on jurisdiction imposed by way of international conventions, *a contrario*, confirmed how States were free to determine the content of their heads of jurisdiction under general public international law. See also Morelli (1938), p. 145ff.

[8]This being the most addressed field by international law which has given rise to customs; cfr. Koh (1996), p. 132.

[9]Which might be intentional to promote given internal values, as is the case for Italy, whose Constitutional court developed the principle that Article 10 of the Constitution cannot operate

1.1 State Immunity and the 'Commercial Exception' Under Public International Law

'Absolute immunity' is generally[10] abandoned in public international law.[11] Even though it remains difficult, in practical terms, to exactly determine the content of the rule of State immunity,[12] the 'commercial exception' to immunity is amongst those mostly accepted in the international community. In principle, a State does enjoy immunity from foreign jurisdiction unless it enters a 'commercial activity'.[13] States have developed different techniques to qualify foreign conducts for the purposes of exception to immunity at hand. Some follow the 'list approach',[14] where exceptions to immunity are listed in statutory law; others[15] leave the matter of qualification to domestic courts. In spite of different methodological approaches, and competing

---

where the custom is contrary to certain fundamental and non-renounceable values of the constitution. This, without contesting the content of international customary law as reconstructed by the International Court of Justice in Jurisdictional Immunities of the State (Germany v. Italy: Greece intervening), Judgment of 3 February 2012, available online. On Judgment n. 238/2014 of the Italian Constitutional court, see *ex multis* in the scholarship Cannizzaro (2015), p. 126; Francioni (2014), p. 1; Pisillo Mazzeschi (2014), p. 9; Cataldi (2014), p. 37; Palchetti (2014), p. 53; Palombino (2012), p. 187; Pavoni (2016), p. 573; Frulli (2016), p. 587; Palombella (2016), p. 607; Francioni (2016), p. 629.

[10] Of course, such a position is not unanimous, as some States still adhere to an absolute immunity theory (cf Hong Kong Court of Final Appeal 8 June 2011 and 8 September 2011, Democratic Republic of the Congo and others v FG Hemisphere Associates LLC, respectively in (2011) 147 ILR, p. 376, and (2011) 150 ILR, p. 684), or have it subject to reciprocity (on this point, see Fox and Webb 2013, p. 14 f).

[11] Corte d'Appello Lucca, 1887, Hamspohn contro Bey di Tunisi, in Foro it., 1887, I, p. 474, and Tribunal civil of Brussels, Societe pour la fabrication de cartouches v Colonel Mutkuroff, Ministre de la guerre de la principaute de Bulgarie, in Pandectes periodiques, 1889, p. 350. Under the 2004 New York Convention, a three-pronged test is adopted to identify a 'commercial transaction'; either there are contracts or transactions—thus not necessarily requiring the existence of a contract—for sales of goods or supply of services, a wording suggesting that 'activities' do not fall within the scope of application of the provision, and that sales or services are never immune, regardless of the goal of the contract (in these terms, Wittich 2013, pp. 61–63); either contracts for a loan or of financial nature, or any other contract or transaction of a commercial, industrial, trading or professional nature.

[12] Nino (2014), p. 822; Adinolfi (2014), p. 892.

[13] United Nations Convention on Jurisdictional Immunities of States and Their Property, New York, 2 December 2004, art. 2, and art. 10.

[14] Cf. 28 U.S. Code §1604, §1605(a)(2), and §1603(d). See also in the United Kingdom, State Immunity Act 1978, Part 1, art. 1, and art. 3(3), according to which 'commercial transaction' means any contract for the supply of goods or services; any loan or other transaction for the provision of finance and any guarantee or indemnity in respect of any such transaction or of any other financial obligation; and any other transaction or activity (whether of a commercial, industrial, financial, professional or other similar character) into which a State enters or in which it engages otherwise than in the exercise of sovereign authority. In the scholarship, cf Bröhmer (1997), p. 51ff.

[15] Such as a number of European continental States; cf Queirolo and Dominelli (2013), p. 160, for references in State practice.

legal narratives, at least in respect to this exception to State immunity[16] it is generally accepted that the exercise of domestic jurisdiction to adjudicate or enforce over a foreign State is only forbidden when said foreign State has acted *jure imperii*. Jurisdiction can—and must—be exercised when the State has acted *jure privatorum*. The fact that a 'contract' or an 'activity' lacks authoritative (sovereign) powers usually constitutes the *discrimen* for the recognition of foreign immunities.[17]

1.2 EU International Civil Procedure in 'Civil Matters' and State Immunity: Non-Applicability as a (Necessary and Indirect) Way of Coordination

The *discrimen* between *acta jure imperii* and *acta jure gestionis* is relevant for EU international civil procedure as well. EU regulations on conflict of jurisdictions,[18] as well as instruments on judicial cooperation—such as cross-border service of documents[19]—are only applicable in 'civil and commercial matters' (as per art. 81 TFEU). This means, from the EU law perspective, an *acta jure imperii* will 'simply' fall outside the scope of application of EU international civil procedure. Domestic courts will thus turn to domestic law to determine the same conduct for the purposes of immunities under international law. Notwithstanding the different purpose of the same classification, the Court of Justice of the European Union (CJEU) has traditionally defined the scope of application of EU law in such a way that domestic courts had comparable legal reasoning to follow for the subsequent assessment of immunities. The court argued for example that

[16] Less consensus is to be found on emerging exceptions to State immunity, as is the case for the terrorism exception adopted in some countries, such as the United States of America and Canada. Reference is made not only to the US Justice Against Sponsors of Terrorism Act (Pub.L. 114–222), which has found sensitive opposition, but also to judgments that have found little room in political debate, such as a judgment of the Italian Supreme court that allowed, in principle, the recognition and enforcement of the US decision—as no immunity for terrorism is to be granted (yet, denying in practice enforcement as the State of origin was not competent on the merit of the claim according to heads of jurisdiction contained in Italian law, which still adopts rules for recognition and enforcement as indirect heads of international jurisdiction; cf. Cassazione sezioni unite, sentenza 21964/2015).

[17] However, 'international public law itself has yet to establish unequivocal criteria to distinguish *acta jure imperii*' (Vischer 1992, p. 192).

[18] See ex multis Regulation (EU) No 1215/2012 of the European Parliament and of the Council of 12 December 2012 on jurisdiction and the recognition and enforcement of judgments in civil and commercial matters, in OJ L 351, 20.12.2012, p. 1 (Brussels Ibis Regulation), art. 1(1).

[19] Regulation (EC) No 1393/2007 of the European Parliament and of the Council of 13 November 2007 on the service in the Member States of judicial and extrajudicial documents in civil or commercial matters (service of documents), and repealing Council Regulation (EC) No 1348/2000, in OJ L 324, 10.12.2007, p. 79, art. 1(1).

> Although certain judgments given in actions between a public authority and a person governed by private law may fall within the area of application of the Convention, this is not so where the public authority acts in the exercise of its powers. Such is the case in a dispute which ... concerns the recovery of charges payable by a person governed by private law to a national or international body governed by public law for the use of equipment and services provided by such body, in particular where such use is obligatory and exclusive. This applies in particular where the rate of charges, the methods of calculation and the procedures for collection are fixed unilaterally in relation to the users.[20]

This criterion resembles approaches followed in public international law to determine the existence of State immunity as, in private international law as well, an investigation on the use of authoritative powers by the foreign State is necessary.[21] From a methodological perspective, the case-by-case analysis requires an investigation on the basis and the detailed rules governing the bringing of the action.[22] Yet, such an approach appears residual in the case law of the Court of Justice of the European Union. Where actions for damages were connected to war crimes,[23] jurisdiction over the subsequent claim for redress—civil in nature—was excluded without any specific investigation. Conducts that are (or which are connected with) the typical expression of sovereign powers, such as the use of force, are 'exempted' from any other verification about the 'equal powers' between private parties and foreign States.[24] With the consequence that the proper qualification of the foreign conduct as *acta jure imperii* or *acta jure gestionis* appears necessary only so far as the foreign State has not acted in an *icto oculi* exercise of sovereign powers.

[20] Judgment of the Court of 14 October 1976, LTU Lufttransportunternehmen GmbH & Co. KG v Eurocontrol, Case 29-76, in Reports of Cases, 1976, p. 1541, p. 1551. Consistently with such case law, actions for payment of parking spots have been qualified as 'contracts', due to the lack of authoritative powers on the public or delegated private body managing parking areas (Judgment of the Court (Second Chamber) of 9 March 2017, Pula Parking d.o.o. v Sven Klaus Tederahn, Case C-551/15, in Electronic reports; but see differently, AG München, 30 September 2015 - 412 C 18198/15).

[21] Cf, Nejvyšší soud 30 October 2012 - 33 Cdo 3015/2011, in unalex CZ-61.

[22] In these terms, Opinion of the Advocate general Bot delivered on 9 December 2014, Joined Cases C-226/13, C-245/13, C-247/13 and C-578/13, in Electronic report, para. 53.

[23] Judgment of the Court (Second Chamber) of 15 February 2007, Eirini Lechouritou and Others v Dimosio tis Omospondiakis Dimokratias tis Germanias, Case C-292/05, in Electronic reports, para. 36ff ('The legal action for compensation brought by the plaintiffs in the main proceedings against the Federal Republic of Germany derives from operations conducted by armed forces during the Second World War. As the Advocate General has observed ..., there is no doubt that operations conducted by armed forces are one of the characteristic emanations of State sovereignty, in particular inasmuch as they are decided upon in a unilateral and binding manner by the competent public authorities and appear as inextricably linked to States' foreign and defence policy. It follows that acts such as those which are at the origin of the loss and damage pleaded by the plaintiffs in the main proceedings and, therefore, of the action for damages brought by them before the Greek courts must be regarded as resulting from the exercise of public powers').

[24] Opinion of the Advocate general Bot delivered on 9 December 2014, Joined Cases C-226/13, C-245/13, C-247/13 and C-578/13, in Electronic report, para. 57.

What emerges from the above is a convergence between public and EU private international law regarding the interpretation of *acta jure imperii*, which leads to a theoretical and practical consistency: where a foreign conduct does not fall within the scope of application of the European rules on international jurisdiction, domestic courts will also likely declare their lack of jurisdiction due to the recognition of immunities.

Nonetheless, this (not absolute) convergence is currently under a stress test, and public and private international law approaches might take different paths. Also, the interrelations between the diverse and diverging areas seem to impose a reflection on their indirect cross-fertilisation in the qualification of *acta jure imperii* and *acta jure privatorum*.

2 Unilateral Changes of State Bonds and a Cross-Fertilization Between Public and Private International Law

Many recent cases in the field of State immunity are connected to State liability for the performance of bonds, either following a suspension of payment or a cut in the original nominal value.

The performance of the original contract has raised issues both in terms of immunity from adjudication and of immunity from enforcement, since it is quite likely that the foreign debtor has only military assets in the State of the forum, or assets reserved for diplomatic functions, as the case of bank accounts could be.[25] It is in respect of the first of these issues, in particular, that consistency seems challenged today, as approaches in public and EU private international law might diverge.

2.1 State Immunity and Unilateral Changes of State Bond Terms

State practice shows that different solutions have been followed so far as per the recognition of State immunity connected to unilateral changes of State bond terms

[25] Reference is made to ITLOS, "ARA Libertad" (Argentina v. Ghana), Provisional Measures, Order of 15 December 2012, ITLOS Reports, 2012, p. 332, and to the arbitral proceedings closed by conjunct request for termination in Permanent Court of Arbitration, PCA 104115, In the matter of The Ara Libertad Arbitration between The Argentine Republic and The Republic of Ghana, Termination order 11 November 2013. In the scholarship, see and Queirolo (2013), p. 179. In the case law, see also European Court of Human Rights, NML Capital LTD v France, application no. 23242/12, 5 February 2015, available online, in French only, and on sovereign debt restructuring and property rights, see Frigo (2013), p. 144ff.

previously sold on the secondary market (rather than per bonds acquired by international organizations).

Although some may argue differently, 'sovereign bonds' should fall within the commercial exception to State immunity. As noted in the scholarship, the attribute of 'sovereign' does suggest that bonds are privileged as they stem from a sovereign authoritative act. On the contrary, the attribute refers to the State as one of the parties to the contract.[26] State bonds should fall within the commercial exception to State immunity[27] according to art. 2(1)(c)(ii) UN convention ('*contract*[s] *for a loan or other transaction of a financial nature...*'). Their contractual nature is not disputed here, and, in some circumstances, such contracts also contain express waiver of immunity as well as choice of court clauses and *optio legis*.[28] A survey of different State bonds shows that similar clauses are not always included. Waiver of immunities, exclusive choice of foreign courts, and choice of foreign applicable law are, all in all, elements that should contribute in the sale of a State title.[29] Titles that may be perceived as 'weak' can be accompanied by waiver of immunity (even though immunity is not granted for contracts),[30] to ensure buyers that the State will not try to make recourse to immunity at later stages. Along the same line of argument, the choice of exclusive jurisdiction in favor of courts that are not those of the 'selling' State may also be perceived by buyers as an element of reassurance when it comes to weak titles.

State practice however shows that one relevant question is whether a subsequent sovereign act overrules the contractual nature of bonds already sold. The case law has followed different approaches on the matter. On the one side, defences on the merits have been quashed by domestic courts. International law principles on the state of necessity have been deemed not applicable to private contracts. This was (re)confirmed in 2019 by the German Constitutional[31] court, which has argued that a 'general rule of international law which entitles a State to temporarily refuse to meet private-law payment claims due towards private individuals by invoking State necessity declared because of an inability to pay cannot currently be ascertained'.[32] On the other side, some courts have excluded that a subsequent sovereign act

[26] In these terms, Bröhmer (2015), p. 182.

[27] Specifically on sovereign debt, see Bonafè (2006), p. 165; Bordoni (2006), p. 1031; Bordoni (2007), p. 140; Delaume (1985), p. 319; Dolzer (1989), p. 531; Dorigo (2002), p. 958; Francioni (2009), p. 729; Gathii (2006), p. 251; Lauterpacht (1951), p. 224; Megliani (2009); Pustorino (2008), p. 142; Sacerdoti (1972); Sinclair (1980), p. 117; Tomz (2007); Unzicker (2003), p. 5. In the case law, Court of Appeal, Twycross c. Dreyfus, (1877) 5 Ch.D. 605. In the scholarship, see Phillimore (1882), p. 18, writing that 'English courts have decided that bonds payable to bearer issued by the government cannot be enforced by any foreign tribunal nor by the tribunal of the borrowing State itself, unless with the consent of its government'.

[28] Villata (2013b), p. 107ff.

[29] Choi et al. (2012), p. 151.

[30] Queirolo (2013), p. 171ff.

[31] BVerfG, Beschluss der 3. Kammer des Zweiten Senats, 3 July 2019 - 2 BvR 824/15.

[32] Wagner (2019).

suspending payments or unilaterally changing the contract 'reinstalls' immunities. The contract remains commercial in nature, and jurisdiction can be exercised over it—in particular when the seised court is identified by the contract as exclusively competent under a choice of court agreement that pre-dates the suspension of the contract.[33] A position, this last one, that is not unanimous. On the same question, Italian courts have reached the opposite solution.[34] The Supreme Court extended the immunity of the sovereign act (the moratorium) to the pre-existing contract given the predominance of the foreign State's interests in protecting its existence and avoiding default. Thus, Italian courts have excluded the exercise of jurisdiction over the foreign contracts *jure privatorum.*[35]

2.2 EU International Civil Procedure and Unilateral Changes of State Bond Terms

Investors started proceedings against Greece, an 'EU domiciled' sovereign defendant,[36] which triggers the potential applicability of EU international civil procedure. Such claims followed the adoption of law 4050/2012 (Rules on the modification of titles issued or guaranteed by the Greek State with the Bondholders' agreement). Such a law provided for the application of English law to titles, and introduced collective action clauses, by which the proposal to substitute instruments accepted

[33] Cf Republic of Argentina v. Weltover, Inc., 504 U.S. 607 (1992), p. 620; Lightwater Corp. v. Republic of Argentina, No. 02 Civ. 3804 (TPG), 2003 WL 1878420 (S.D.N.Y.) 14 April 2003; Anye Salinovich et al. v. Rep. Argentina, 7 June 2012; United States Court of Appeals for the Second Circuit, NML Capital, Ltd. v. Republic of Argentina, August Term, 2011, Decided October 26, 2012; Landgericht Frankfurt am Main 14 March 2003, n. 294/02, in Zeitschrift für Wirtschafts- und Bankrecht, 2003, p. 783; OLG Frankfurt, 13 June 2006 - 8 U 107/03, in Zeitschrift für Wirtschafts- und Bankrecht, 2007, p. 929; United States District Court for the District of Columbia, Salah Turkmani v. The Republic of Bolivia, 193 f. supp. 2d 165, and Morgan Guaranty Trust Co. of New York v. Republic of Palau, 702 F.Supp. 60 (S.D.N.Y.1988). On the role of the waiver of immunity, cf also the reconstruction of the domestic case law in Republic of Argentina v. NML Capital, Ltd., 573 U.S. (2014); Koutsoukou and Askotiris (2014), p. 285.

[34] Denying immunity, Giudice di Pace Brescia 13 August 2004, Bellitti e Donati c. Rep. Argentina, decreti ingiuntivi n. 1816 e 1817, quoted in Bordoni (2007), p. 145, *passim*; Trib. Roma 22 July 2002, Mauri et al. c. Rep. Argentina, in Rivista di diritto internazionale privato e processuale, 2003, p. 174; Trib. Roma 22 March 2005, in Dir. e giust., 2005, 29, 42. Granting immunity; Trib. Milano 11 March 2003, Gallo c. Rep. Argentina, in Foro it., 2004, I, p. 293; Trib. Milano 11 March 2003, Goldoni et al. C. Rep. Argentina, in Rivista di diritto internazionale privato e processuale, 2005, p. 1102; Trib. Roma 31 March 2003, Gallo c. Rep. Argentina, in Giuri. Romana, 2003, p. 271.

[35] Cass. civ. sez. un., ordinanza 27 May 2005 n. 11225, Borri c. Repubblica Argentina, in Rivista di diritto internazionale, 2005, p. 856, para. 4.2ff of the reasoning in law. On immunities and moratoriums, cf also Corte costituzionale sentenza 329/1992.

[36] On the applicability of the uniform rules in civil and contractual matters against defendants domiciled in a Member State of the European Union, see for all Vlas (2016), p. 106.

by the majority of bondholders, the Greek Central Bank, had binding effects in respect to all bondholders.[37]

2.2.1 The First Phase: Service of Writs of Summons

As per the change of old titles with new ones, the qualification of the conduct as *acta jure imperii* rather than *acta jure gestionis* for the purposes of the application of EU law already arose at a moment of cross-border service in civil and commercial matters.[38] German courts[39] raised a preliminary question as per the applicability of the service of documents regulation, asking whether unilateral changes of bonds were *acta jure imperii* for the purposes of EU law. Advocate General Bot offered a solution,[40] not followed by the Court. The Advocate General sought to determine whether a subsequent action could be qualified as the expression of sovereign powers.[41] In other words, the Advocate General was not in principle adherent to the idea '*once a trader, always a trader*'.[42] Where the unilateral change of contracts follows the adoption of laws, as was in the case at hand, the Advocate General develops a progressive test. In the first place, *acta jure imperii* must be recognised where the change is the indirect effect of a general law, such as taxation laws, i.e. when the law is not specifically aimed at changing the pre-existing contracts (and thus the contracts are indirectly affected by the new law). There still remains a distinction between the sovereign State and the contracting State.[43] On the contrary, where the law expressly and directly wishes to change the contract, and thus the lines between the 'investor' and 'sovereign' State blur, the scrutiny follows based on whether the conduct is the expression of a 'sovereign power'. Based on his reasoning, the solution is rather straightforward; as '*in that situation the contracting State avails itself of its sovereign power with direct regard to the contract*',[44] the conduct is *acta jure imperii* and EU law should not be applied.

Nonetheless, the CJEU stressed the specific function of the Service of Documents Regulation, and considered that this is applied at a preliminary stage of proceedings,

---

[37] Villata (2013a) bis, p. 325.

[38] Regulation (EC) No 1393/2007, cit., art. 1(1). In the scholarship, see Franzina (2009), p. 219ff; Heiderhoff (2015), p. 781.

[39] The potential jurisdiction was based on the place of performance of the contract under the Brussels I regime; declining jurisdiction under the special heads of jurisdiction in EU uniform law, OLG Oldenburg, 18 April 2016 - 13 U 43/15.

[40] Advocate General Bot, 9 December 2014, joined Cases C-226/13, C-245/13, C-247/13 and C-578/13, Stefan Fahnenbrock et al. v Hellenische Republik, para. 61ff.

[41] Ibid., para. 63.

[42] On the expression, see Geimer (2017), p. 344.

[43] Advocate General Bot, 9 December 2014, joined Cases C-226/13, C-245/13, C-247/13 and C-578/13, Stefan Fahnenbrock et al. v Hellenische Republik, para. 64.

[44] Ibid., para. 65.

i.e. before trial by (most likely) an administrative body.[45] To ensure the fullest application of EU law, the court has focused on whether the legal relationship was characterized by an exercise of public powers beyond the scope of the ordinary legal rules applicable to private individuals.[46] In the Court's eye, issuance and management of bonds, i.e. the legal basis of the action, do not necessarily presuppose the exercise of sovereign powers.[47]

Additionally, the Court adopts a 'direct effect theory' to break the chain of causation between the contract and the subsequent unilateral change in bond terms, so as to avoid a spill-over effect of the *acta jure imperii* qualification from such laws to pre-existing contracts. The intermediation by the bondholder in the primary market, i.e. the Greek Central Bank, and so the acceptance of this institute of the new bonds in substitution of the former, leads to the conclusion that the public debt has not been unilaterally changed by the State in the exercise of its sovereign powers, but was rather a negotiated solution.[48]

2.2.2 Domestic Reaction to the First Phase: From Applicability of EU Law to State Immunity

Under the CJEU judgment on the Service of Documents Regulations, domestic courts still retain the possibility to come to opposite solutions when starting proceedings and addressing their jurisdiction.[49] The German *Bundesgerichtshof* dissented with the Court of Justice, and argued that civil actions for the enforcement of contracts changed by the Greek State were indeed actions related to *acta jure imperii*, thus falling outside the scope of application of EU law.[50]

This bears two consequences. In the first place, service of documents against a foreign State are not governed by the EU Regulation but must follow traditional channels to be valid.[51] In the second place, the qualification of the conduct as *acta jure imperii* made by the domestic court also serves the purposes of recognition of

---

[45] Judgment of the Court (First Chamber) of 11 June 2015, Stefan Fahnenbrock and Others v Hellenische Republik, Case C-226/13, para. 48. Other than the already quoted scholarship, see on the judgment Mankowski (2015), p. 495; Wagner (2015), p. 636.

[46] Judgment of the Court (First Chamber) of 11 June 2015, Stefan Fahnenbrock and Others v Hellenische Republik, Case C-226/13, para. 51.

[47] Ibid., para. 53.

[48] Ibid., para. 54ff.

[49] Ibid., para. 46.

[50] BGH, Urteil vom 8 March 2016 – VI ZR 516/14, in Neue Juristische Wochenschrift, 2016, p. 1659, with note by Müller. See also van Calster (2016).

[51] See Ministero di Grazia e Giustizia 10-1215/2062(56), 18 April 1956, recently invoked by Italian bailiffs for notification of a payment order against Libya, according to which notifications against foreign States are governed by public international law that only allows for diplomatic service.

State immunity.[52] Greece is immune from German civil jurisdiction in the matter of bond-cuts, even though the CJEU qualified, for a different purpose, the very same conduct as not being *acta jurejure imperii.*

2.2.3 The Second Phase: From the Place of Performance of Bonds Under the Brussels Ibis Regulation to Acta Jure Imperii

From the above, it emerges how the question of the applicability of EU law, and the underlying matter of qualification of *acta jure imperii*, was unsettled in the European judicial space. With some notable exceptions,[53] German courts were instructed by the *Bundesgerichtshof,*[54] whose vision was differing from that of the CJEU. Other domestic courts were more in line with the interpretation and qualification developed by the CJEU, and thus took for granted that actions against the Greek State where not *acta jure imperii*. Rather, Austrian courts were unsure if they were competent under the Brussels Ibis Regulation. As the instrument grants international jurisdiction and territorial competence to the courts of the place of performance of the obligation, this place—of payment—was debated (the State of the final client or the place where the Greek Central Bank receives the first payment from the Greek State).

Following a preliminary request of Austrian courts, Advocate General Bot, again, sought to exclude such actions from the scope of application of EU international civil procedure, suggesting a distinguishing from the previous case law specifically developed in the specific context of the cross-border service of documents.[55] Taking into account the legal basis of the proceedings, the Advocate General has stressed the non-contractual nature of the retroactive insertion of CAC clauses (whereby the acceptance of new titles by the majority of bondholders—the Greek Central Bank—is biding upon everyone), so to support the view that such actions fall outside the scope of application of the Brussels Ibis Regulation.[56]

On its side, the CJEU,[57] in a rather succinct judgment, shared the conclusion of the Advocate General in this instance, in that the unilateral change of the applicable law, thus the retroactive insertion of CAC clauses, exceeds the '*scope of the ordinary*

[52] BGH, Urteil vom 8 March 2016 – VI ZR 516/14, in Neue Juristische Wochenschrift, 2016, para. 7.

[53] Opening to jurisdiction, but declaring the lack of international jurisdiction and territorial competence under EU rules on international civil procedure, OLG Oldenburg, 18 April 2016 - 13 U 43/15.

[54] Cf OLG Schleswig, 7 July 2016 - 5 U 84/15; OLG Köln, 12 May 2016 - I-8 U 44/15; BGH, 19 December 2017 - XI ZR 796/16; BGH, 19 December 2017 - XI ZR 217/16; BGH, 19 December 2017 - XI ZR 247/16; OLG Oldenburg, 26 May 2017 - 6 U 1/17, and LG Bonn, 20 April 2016 - 1 O 72/13.

[55] Opinion of Advocate General Bot delivered on 4 July 2018, Case C-308/17, Hellenische Republik v Leo Kuhn, para. 48ff.

[56] Ibid., para. 65ff.

[57] Judgment of the Court (First Chamber) of 15 November 2018, Hellenische Republik v Leo Kuhn, Case C-308/17, in Electronic reports. See Mankowski (2019), p. 193.

legal rules applicable to relationships between private individuals'.[58] That also means such a change has direct effect on the substitution of titles. The acceptance of the new contract by the majority of bondholders against the minority does not interrupt the chain of 'liability' between the private investors and the State.

In turn, the Court also argues that actions based on the unilateral change of the original conditions of titles are the expression of sovereign powers, thus *acta jure imperii*, with the (mere) consequence that jurisdiction must be assessed not under EU law, but under domestic rules on international civil procedure.

2.2.4 Domestic Reaction to the Second Phase: From Non-Applicability of EU Law to State Immunity

Austrian courts thus received clear indications: the unilateral retroactive insertion of CACs is the expression of sovereign powers, whose related actions fall outside the scope of application of EU law. Austrian courts still had the possibility to declare their jurisdiction to maintain the diverse qualification of the act for the purposes of jurisdiction, deny State immunity and open a complaint to national exorbitant heads of jurisdiction.[59] Evidently, the coexistence of two different understandings of *acta jure imperii* is not a desirable result. The same conduct and the very same legal claim is, for the purposes of application of EU international civil procedure, *acta jure imperii*, and for the purposes of the international law of State immunity, *acta jure gestionis*. As the respect of immunities is considered by some authors a pre-condition for the movement judgments within the European judicial space,[60] this 'dissonance' might pave the way to problems at the later stage of recognition and enforcement abroad of the decision.

With little surprise, the reaction of the domestic courts was to change their public international law understanding of *acta jure imperii*. Following the non-application of EU law to *acta jure imperii*, courts have maintained the same qualification for the purposes of immunities and have thus changed their first approach to declare lack of jurisdiction.[61] In other words, courts have sought to safeguard a certain parallelism between public and private international law notions.

Where traditionally the law of State immunity has offered a first methodological framework to develop and interpret heads of jurisdiction, the Greek saga has shown how the interpretation of the scope of application of EU law can indirectly affect the domestic interpretation and application of international law.

---

[58] Ibid., para. 35ff.

[59] Mankowski (2018a) bis.

[60] For all, see Franq (2016), p. 868.

[61] OGH 10 Ob 103/18x. See Walter (2019).

3 The Contribution of the Non-Application of EU Law to Public International Law: Towards a New Customary Approach?

Provided that the substantial effect of CJEU case law on the applicability of EU international civil procedure has been that of (indirectly) reshaping domestic approaches to State immunity, the question is whether and to what extent this case law might contribute to the emergence of a new rule of customary law. It seems likely that, for the time being, EU Member States' courts will, in the end, recognize immunity to all EU Member States for cases of unilateral and retroactive cuts in State bonds. However, it seems unlikely that such an approach could foster a clear customary rule in public international law in the short term.

Non-EU Member States are unlikely to contest the shift towards immunity experienced by Austrian courts so long as the new trend inhibits the jurisdiction of Member States to adjudicate in favor of other Member States only. If this new trend does not impair the possibility for non-EU courts to assess their jurisdiction against the backdrop of international law, and eventually start proceedings against EU Member States in said third country for a unilateral change in bond terms, the European solution does not seem destined to be contested by third States themselves.

From the perspective of EU Member States, it seems unlikely that States will oppose this approach and thus contest it as a generally accepted practice of international law. More importantly, it seems—from a general perspective—that only EU Member States are in substance granted a better treatment in terms of immunity when it comes to unilateral changes in bond terms. The above-mentioned German Constitutional court decision concerning the enforcement of the Argentinian *Tango Bonds*[62] postdated and coexisted, in fact, with the more favorable approach reserved to Greece. Argentina contested the violation of the German Constitution, in particular section 25 which is the transposing of general public international law into domestic law. Argentina argued that domestic courts erred in not recognizing and not applying a customary rule on the state of necessity including that of suspending payments in contractual matters. The court excluded the existence of such a rule under public international law, and has not taken the chance to return to the matter of the correct application of customary law on State immunity via section 25 of the Constitution.

Even if the CJEU case law seems unlikely at this point in time to indirectly promote a new understanding of *acta jure imperii* in terms of international customary law, some passages of the Court's decision must be highlighted. In the Court's eye, the 'unprecedented reliance on the retroactive inclusion of a CAC and the resulting amendment to the financial terms took place in an exceptional context, in the circumstances of a serious financial crisis. They were namely dictated by the

[62] BVerfG, Beschluss der 3. Kammer des Zweiten Senats vom 3 July 2019 - 2 BvR 824/15. See Wagner (2019).

necessity, within the framework of an intergovernmental assistance mechanism, to restructure the Greek State's public debt'.[63] Usually, the non-application of EU law for *acta jure imperii* is determined by the private nature of the action[64] (unless the conduct is the immediate expression of sovereign powers).[65] In this sense, domestic courts have stressed that the public aim underlying a contract concluded by the State bears no role in the qualification of the commercial activity.[66] Contrary to this line of argument, in its latest commented case law, the CJEU seems to make recourse to an *ex abundantiam cautela* reasoning revolving around the *necessity* following the exceptional financial context and intergovernmental assistance.

The *obiter* of the CJEU on the aim of the State contract might still argued to be consistent with those decisions on State immunity if the reasoning at hand is understood as a mere discursive reinforcement of conclusions already reached—as the use of 'furthermore' in the text suggests.

However, the *obiter* of the CJEU might have a greater impact in the future. Rather than introducing a 'public aim' test in the evaluation of *acta jure imperii* for determining the scope of application of EU law, it seems more likely that the Court pursued another goal. As it is structured, the passage at hand seems already destined to offer domestic courts future guidance for possible human rights complaints following declination of jurisdiction (if courts of Member States align EU law and public international law understandings of *acta Jure imperii*). As fundamental rights can be limited provided that a number of conditions are met,[67] amongst which necessity and proportionality, the Court seems to suggest that limitations to the right of access a court of law imposed upon individual investors needs to be balanced with the interest to avoid the default of a State, and its possible spill-over effects in the Eurozone.

---

[63] Judgment of the Court (First Chamber) of 15 November 2018, Hellenische Republik v Leo Kuhn, Case C-308/17, para. 40.

[64] On the double approach adopted by the Court, Opinion of the Advocate general Bot delivered on 9 December 2014, Joined Cases C-226/13, C-245/13, C-247/13 and C-578/13, para. 57.

[65] Judgment of the Court (Second Chamber) of 15 February 2007, Eirini Lechouritou and Others v Dimosio tis Omospondiakis Dimokratias tis Germanias, Case C-292/05.

[66] Republic of Argentina v. Weltover, Inc., 504 U.S. 607 (1992), p. 616. *Contra*, before this ruling of the Supreme Court, De Sanchez v. Banco Central de Nicaragua, 770 F. 2d 1385 (1985).

[67] Specifically, on the right to property and bond cuts made by the Greek State, see European Court of Human Rights, Mamatas and Others v. Greece, 21 July 2016, application nos. 63066/14, 64297/14 and 66106/14.

4 Can the Brussels Ibis Regulation 'Connect' to the International Law of State Immunity?

Assuming that the trends following the Leo Kuhn judgment are so far unlikely to contribute to the emergence of a new clear customary rule concerning the qualification of commercial activities for the purposes of recognition of State immunity, it can also be questioned whether the Brussels Ibis Regulation should *directly coordinate* with the law of State immunity. This would mean that the Regulation, in cases of *acta jure imperii*, would oblige domestic courts to *directly* declare their lack of jurisdiction—differently from what happened before Austrian courts.

The Brussels Ibis Regulation contains a number of provisions aimed at solving conflicts between concurring legal regimes. Article 71 prescribes the prevalence of pre-existing international treaties in special matters to which Member States are parties that overlap *ratione materiae* with the regulation.[68] As recently confirmed by Advocate General Szpunar,[69] Article 71 'sits ill with the evolving nature of customary international law which, moreover, is binding both on the Member States and on the European Union'. For this reason, the provision at hand is not considered adequate in terms of coordination between EU law and general public international law.

At the same time, Article 67 prescribes the prevalence of other heads of jurisdiction contained in EU law acts.[70] Amongst these, there are other regulations or directives, but possibly also decisions of the Council on the accession of the European Union to international treaties, where this is possible.[71]

Even though rules on State immunity might be considered to be a 'negative head of jurisdiction' imposed by public international law upon EU law, which are thus binding upon the Union and part of EU law, it does not seem possible for the Brussels Ibis Regulation to 'connect' and coordinate itself with customary law. Notwithstanding that international customary rules are under some conditions a parameter of validity of EU secondary law,[72] international customary law should

[68] In the scholarship, see Carbone (2017), p. 17; Tuo (2017), p. 33; Carpaneto (2017), p. 63; Espinosa Calabuig (2017), p. 107; Puetz (2017), p. 141; Soleti (2017), p. 181; Celle (2017), p. 215; Carrea (2017), p. 237; Borrás and De Maestri (2012), p. 928.

[69] Opinion of Advocate General Szpunar, delivered on 14 January 2020, Case C-641/18, LG v Rina SpA, Ente Registro Italiano Navale, in Electronic Reports, para. 134. In the same case, the CJEU concluded that the principle of customary international law concerning the jurisdictional immunity of States does not preclude the application of the Brussels I(bis) Regulation in proceedings relating to actions for damages brought against private-law bodies in respect of classification and certification activities carried out by those bodies as delegates of a third State, on behalf of that State and in its interests (Judgment of the Court (First Chamber) of 7 May 2020, LG v Rina SpA and Ente Registro Italiano Navale, Case C-641/18, in electronic Reports, para. 60).

[70] See Mankowski (2016b), p. 1215; Mankowski (2016a) bis, p. 1020.

[71] Cf Kropholler and von Hein (2011), p. 719; Puetz (2018), p. 125.

[72] Cf Judgment of the Court of 16 June 1998, A. Racke GmbH & Co. v Hauptzollamt Mainz, Case C-162/96.

not trigger the EU disconnection clause, as customs are not '*contained in instruments of the Union*'.

De lege lata, Article 67 Brussels Ibis Regulation is destined to be applied in favor of heads of jurisdiction contained in other '*instruments of the Union*'. Should some successfully argue that international customs are more than a simple parameter of validity of EU secondary law, such an improbable connection to public international law would require the existence of a more or less certain customary rule. In light of the current practice, this might be difficult for the Court of Justice to reconstruct.

Additionally, the coordination of the Brussels Ibis Regulation with the law of State immunity seems unlikely *de lege ferenda* as well. If the EU lawmaker wanted to promote a direct coordination between these two, a change in the wording of Article 67 of the regulation would not be sufficient. The legal basis for EU judicial cooperation, so the provisions in EU treaties, is limited to 'civil and commercial matters'. The direct coordination of the regulation with the law of State immunity, so the duty for domestic courts to declare their lack of jurisdiction in application of EU law, would make the instrument applicable to sovereign acts, thus beyond the competence of the Union as *acta jure imperii* are intrinsically not 'civil and commercial matters'.

As the task of coordination of concepts in public and private international law seems destined to remain set on the current parallel tracks approach, the mission to ensure consistency of notions will remain upon domestic courts who will be encouraged to follow characterizations of specific conducts as *acta jure imperii* made by the Court of Justice at times for the additional purposes of granting State immunity.

References

Adinolfi G (2014) Sovereign wealth funds and state immunity: overcoming the contradiction. Rivista di diritto internazionale privato e processuale 50:885–930

Balladore Pallieri G (1950) Diritto internazionale privato. Giuffré, Milano

Basedow J (2018/2019) Non-recognised states in private international law. Yearb Priv Int Law XX:1–14

Bonafè BI (2006) State immunity and the protection of private investors: the Argentine bonds case before Italian courts. Ital Yearb Int Law 16:165–185

Bordoni M (2006) Default nel debito pubblico ed immunità dello Stato estero dalla giurisdizione civile. Rivista di diritto internazionale 89:1031–1060

Bordoni M (2007) Bonds argentini, immunità degli Stati esteri dalla giurisdizione civile e stato di necessità: orientamenti giurisprudenziali a confronto. Comunicazioni e studi 23:140–203

Borrás A, De Maestri ME (2012) Articolo 67. In: Simons T, Hausmann R, Queirolo I (eds) Regolamento Bruxelles I. Commento al Regolamento (CE) 44/2001 e alla Convenzione di Lugano. IPR Verlag, Monaco di Baviera, p 928

Bröhmer J (1997) State immunity and the violation of human rights. Brill, The Hague

Bröhmer J (2015) State immunity and sovereign bonds. In: Peters A, Lagrange E, Oeter S, Tomuschat C (eds) Immunities in the age of global constitutionalism. Brill Nijhoff, Leiden, pp 182–208

Cannizzaro E (2015) Jurisdictional immunities and judicial protection: the decision of the Italian Constitutional Court No. 238 of 2014. Rivista di diritto internazionale 98:126–134
Carbone SM (2017) From speciality and primacy of uniform law to its integration in the European judicial area. In: Carbone SM (ed) Brussels Ia and conventions on particular matters. The case of transports. Aracne, Rome, pp 17–31
Carpaneto (2017) On collisions and interactions between EU law and international transport conventions. In: Carbone SM (ed) Brussels Ia and conventions on particular matters. The case of transports. Aracne, Rome, pp 63–104
Carrea S (2017) Brussels Ia and the arrest of ships: from the 1952 to the 1999 Arrest Convention. In: Carbone SM (ed) Brussels Ia and conventions on particular matters. The case of transports. Aracne, Rome, pp 237–282
Cataldi G (2014) A historic decision of the Italian Constitutional Court on the balance between the Italian legal order's fundamental values and customary international law. Ital Yearb Int Law 24:37–52
Celle P (2017) Jurisdiction and conflict of laws issues between contracts of transport and insurance. In: Carbone SM (ed) Brussels Ia and conventions on particular matters. The case of transports. Aracne, Rome, pp 215–235
Choi S, Gulati M, Posner E (2012) The evolution of contractual terms in sovereign bonds. J Leg Anal 4:131–179
Corneloup S, Heiderhoff B, Honorati C, Jault-Seseke F, Kruger T, Rupp C, van Loon H, Verhellen J (2017) Private international law in a context of increasing international mobility: challenges and potential. European Union Parliament, Brussels
Delaume GR (1985) Economic development and sovereign immunity. Am J Int Law 79:319–346
Dickinson A (2015) Territory in the Rome I and Rome II Regulations. In: Basedow J, Magnus U, Wolfrum R (eds) The Hamburg Lectures on Maritime Affairs 2011–2013. Springer, Heidelberg, pp 69–125
Dolzer R (1989) Staatliche Zahlungsunfähigkeit: Zum Begriff und zu den Rechtsfolgen im Völkerrech. In: Jekewitz J, Heinz Klein K, Detlef Kühne J, Petersmann H, Wolfrum R (eds) Des Menschen Recht zwischen Freiheit und Verantwortung. Festschrift für Karl Josef Partsch zum 75. Geburtstag. Dunker & Humbolt, Berlin, pp 531–554
Dorigo S (2002) Il debito pubblico argentino dinanzi ai giudici italiani. Rivista di diritto internazionale 85:958–961
Espinosa Calabuig R (2017) Brussels Ia Regulation and Maritime Transport. In: Carbone SM (ed) Brussels Ia and conventions on particular matters. The case of transports. Aracne, Rome, pp 107–140
Fox H, Webb P (2013) The law of state immunity. OUP, Oxford
Francioni F (2009) Access to justice, denial of justice and international investment law. Eur J Int Law 20:729–747
Francioni F (2014) From deference to disobedience: the uncertain fate of Constitutional Court Decision No. 238/2014. Ital Yearb Int Law 24:1–8
Francioni F (2016) Access to justice and its pitfalls: reparation for war crimes and the Italian Constitutional Court. J Int Crim Just 14:629–636
Franq S (2016) Article 45. In: Magnus U, Mankowski P (eds) Brussels Ibis Regulation. Otto Schmidt, Köln, p 864
Franzina P (2009) La notificazione degli atti giudiziari e stragiudiziali in ambito comunitario. In: Bonomi A (ed) Diritto internazionale privato e cooperazione giudiziaria in materia civile e commerciale. Giappichelli, Torino, p 217
Frigo (2013) Le operazioni di ristrutturazione del debito obbligazionario alla luce delle norme CEDU in materia di diritto di proprietà. In: Adinolfi G, Vellano M (eds) La crisi del debito sovrano degli Stati dell'area euro. Profili giuridici. Giappichelli, Torino, pp 135–149
Frulli M (2016) Time will tell who just fell and who's been left behind': on the clash between the International Court of Justice and the Italian Constitutional Court. J Int Crim Just 14:587–594

Gathii JT (2006) The sanctity of sovereign loan contracts and its origins in enforcement litigation. George Wash Int Law Rev 38:251–325
Geimer R (2017) Vertragsbruch durch Hoheitsakt: 'Once a trader, not always a trader?' – Immunitätsrechtlicher Manövrierspielraum für Schuldnerstaaten? Praxis des Internationalen Privat– und Verfahrensrechts 37:344–347
Giuliano M (1970) La giurisdizione civile italiana e lo straniero. Giuffré, Milano
Heiderhoff B (2015) Art 1 EG-ZustVO 2007. In: Rauscher T (ed) Europäisches Zivilprozess- und Kollisionsrecht EuZPR/EuIPR, Band II, EG-VollstrTitelVO, EG-MahnVO, EG-BagatellVO, EU-KPfVO, HProrogÜbk 2005, EG-ZustVO 2007, EG-BewVO, EG-InsVO. Otto Schmidt, Köln, p 780
Hertogen A (2015) Letting Lotus Bloom. Eur J Int Law 26:901–926
Hess B (2016) The private–public divide in international dispute resolution. Recueil des cours 388:49–266
Koh HH (1996) International business transactions in United States courts. Recueil des cours 261:13–242
Koutsoukou G, Askotiris N (2014) Tightening the scope of general waivers of sovereign immunity from execution. Rivista di diritto internazionale privato e processuale 50:285–316
Kropholler J, von Hein J (2011) Europäisches Zivilprozessrecht: Kommentar su EuGVO, Lugano–Übereinkommen 2007, EuVTVO, EuMVVO und EuGFVO. Verlag Recht und Wirtschaft, Frankfurt am Main
Lauterpacht H (1951) The problem of jurisdictional immunities of foreign states. Br Yearb Int Law 28:220–272
Mankowski P (2015) Zustellung der von Privatpersonen erhobenen Klagen wegen des Zwangsumtauschs von griechischen Staatsanleihen an Griechenland nach EuZustVO ('Fahnenbrock'). Entscheidungen zum Wirtschaftsrecht 31:495–496
Mankowski P (2016a) *bis*, Article 67. In: Magnus U, Mankowski P (eds) Brussels Ibis Regulation. Otto Schmidt, Köln, p 1020
Mankowski P (2016b) Art. 67 Brüssel Ia–VO. In: Rauscher T (ed) Europäisches Zivilprozess– und Kollisionsrecht, Band I, Brüssels Ia–VO. Otto Schmidt, Köln, p 1215
Mankowski P (2018a) The saga of the Greek State bonds and their haircut: Hellas Triumphans in Luxemburg. Really?. Conflictoflaws.net [published on 22 November 2018]
Mankowski P (2018b) Das Verhältnis von Internationalem Privatrecht und Völkerrecht in der Entwicklung. In: Dethloff N, Nolte G, Reinisch A (eds) Rückblick nach 100 Jahren uns Ausblick – Migrationsbewegungen. C.F. Müller, Heidelberg, pp 45–124
Mankowski P (2019) Griechische Staatsanleihen und der griechische Schuldenschnitt vor dem EuGH (Folge Zwei). Zeitschrift für Wirtschaftsrecht 38:193–202
Megliani M (2009) Debitori Sovrani e obbligazionisti esteri. Giuffré, Milano
Michaels R (2008) Public and private international law: German views on global issues. J Priv Int Law 4:121–138
Mills A (2009) The confluence of public and private international law. CUP, Cambridge
Morelli G (1938) Il diritto processuale civile internazionale. CEDAM, Padova
Morelli G (1971) Elementi di diritto internazionale privato italiano. Jovene, Napoli
Muir Watt H, Fernández Arroyo DP (eds) (2014) Private international law and global governance. OUP, Oxford
Nino M (2014) State immunity from civil jurisdiction in labor disputes: evolution in international and national law and practice. Rivista di diritto internazionale privato e processuale 50:819–848
Palchetti (2014) Can state action on behalf of victims be an alternative to individual access to justice in case of grave breaches of human rights? Ital Yearb Int Law 24:53–62
Palombella G (2016) German war crimes and the rule of international law. J Int Crim Just 14:607–613
Palombino FM (2012) Italy's compliance with ICJ decisions vs. constitutional guarantees: does the 'counter–limits' doctrine matter? Ital Yearb Int Law 22:187–200

Pavoni R (2016) How broad is the principle upheld by the Italian Constitutional Court in Judgment No. 238? J Int Crim Just 14:573–585

Phillimore R (1882) Commentaries on international law, vol I. T. & J. W. Johnson, London

Pisillo Mazzeschi R (2014) Access to justice in constitutional and international law: the recent judgment of the Italian Constitutional Court. Ital Year Int Law 24:9–24

Puetz A (2017) Brussels Ia and international conventions on land transport. In: Carbone (ed) Brussels Ia and conventions on particular matters. The case of transports. Aracne, Rome, pp 141–179

Puetz A (2018) Rules on jurisdiction and recognition or enforcement of judgments in specialised conventions on transport in the aftermath of TNT: dynamite or light in the dark? Eur Leg Forum 18:117–125

Pustorino P (2008) Bond argentini, stato di necessità e diritti individuali nella giurisprudenza costituzionale tedesca. Diritti umani e diritto internazionale 1:142–145

Queirolo I (2013) Immunità degli Stati e crisi del debito sovrano. In: Adinolfi G, Vellano M (eds) La crisi del debito sovrano degli Stati dell'area euro. Profili giuridici. Giappichelli, Torino, pp 152–180

Queirolo I, Dominelli S (2013) Statutory certificates e immunità funzionale del registro italiano navale. Il diritto marittimo 114:152–183

Ryngaert C (2015) Jurisdiction in international law. Oxford University Press, Oxford

Sacerdoti G (1972) I contratti tra Stati e stranieri nel diritto internazionale. Giuffré, Milano

Sinclair I (1980) The law of sovereign immunity: recent developments. Recueil des cours 167:117–284

Soleti PF (2017) Brussels Ia and international air transport. In: Carbone (ed) Brussels Ia and conventions on particular matters. The case of transports. Aracne, Rome, pp 181–211

Tomz M (2007) Reputation and international cooperation. Sovereign debt across three centuries. Princeton University Press, New Jersey

Tuo CE (2017) Brussels Ia and international transports conventions: the regulation's 'non affect' clause through the lens of the CJEU case law. In: Carbone (ed) Brussels Ia and conventions on particular matters. The case of transports. Aracne, Rome, pp 33–62

Unzicker F (2003) Zur 'Argentinien–Rechtsprechung' des LG Frankfurt am Main. Recht Aktuell, III, pp 5–6

van Calster G (2016) Fahnenbrock: 'Civil and commercial' viz bearers of Greek bonds. ECJ puts forward 'direct and immediate effect'

Verheul JP (1983) The Forum Actoris and international law. In: Essays on international and comparative law in honour of Judge Erades. Martinus Nijhoff Publishers, The Hague, pp 196–209

Villata FC (2013a) Remarks on the 2012 Greek sovereign debt restructuring: between choice-of-law agreements and new EU rules on derivative instrument. Rivista di diritto internazionale privato e processuale 49:325–356

Villata FC (2013b) La ristrutturazione del debito pubblico greco del 2012: nuove prospettive per l'*optio iuris*. In: Adinolfi G, Vellano M (eds) La crisi del debito sovrano degli Stati dell'area euro. Profili giuridici. Giappichelli, Torino, pp 107–133

Vischer F (1992) General course on private international law. Recueil des cours 232:13–255

Vitta E (1972) Diritto internazionale privato, Vol. I, Parte generale. UTET, Torino

Vlas P (2016) Article 4. In: Magnus U, Mankowski P (eds) Brussels Ibis Regulation. Otto Schmidt, Köln, p 106

Wagner R (2015) Anwendbarkeit der EuZVO auf Klagen gegen den griechischen Staat wegen des Zwangsumtauschs von Staatsanleihen. Europäische Zeitschrift für Wirtschaftsrecht 17:636–637

Wagner J (2019) In another Argentinian state bankruptcy case the German Federal Constitutional Court once again rejects the existence of a state of necessity as a general principle of international law. In: GPIL – German Practice in International Law

Walter S (2019) The aftermath of the CJEU's Kuhn Judgment – Hellas triumphans in Vienna. Really. Conflictoflaws.net

Wittich S (2013) Article 2(1)(c) and (2) and (3). In: O'Keefe R, Tams C (eds) The United Nations Convention on jurisdictional immunities of states and their property. A commentary. OUP, Oxford, pp 54–72

Stefano Dominelli is a researcher in international law at the University of Genoa, where he currently teaches international law, conflict of laws, and IHL. His main research interests are private international law in contractual and insolvency matters, cross-border service of document, and State and diplomatic immunities from civil jurisdiction.

Sovereign Debt and Immunity: The Controversy of Subsequent Liability Limitation for State Bonds

Johannes Ungerer

Abstract This chapter engages with the limitations of jurisdictional immunity of states in cases of commercial transactions (*acta jure gestionis*) by looking at state bonds and immunity against claims for their repayment. There is no international consensus as to whether immunity can subsequently be restored by the issuing state through a public act of state (*actus jure imperii*) that unilaterally modifies or lifts the obligation of repayment. The chapter analyses the two opposing views that have been taken by highest courts of different countries and international courts. The reasoning behind the judicial views is elucidated in order to establish why, or why not, foreign states might subsequently assert their jurisdictional immunity when sued by private investors. Placing this controversy in the wider legal context, the chapter suggests that differing perceptions of the underlying public-private law divide can be seen as an explanation of the divergent views. The respective consequences of jurisdictional immunity against claims for repayment of state bonds are addressed subsequently.

1 Introduction

Where sovereign debt is created by states borrowing money from private investors, as it has become very common since the nineteenth century,[1] the state submits itself to private law, which governs the liability for repayment of issued bonds. However, especially in times of severe national economic crisis, which some states have encountered in the decades before and after the Millennium,[2] these states seek to avert sovereign default and to limit their liability particularly on the basis of sovereign immunity against repayment claims brought in foreign courts.

[1] Oosterlinck (2013), p. 699; Roos (2019), pp. 95ff.

[2] Roos (2019), pp. 173ff (on Argentina) and pp. 225ff (on Greece).

J. Ungerer (✉)
University of Oxford, Oxford, UK
e-mail: johannes.ungerer@law.ox.ac.uk

R. Bismuth et al. (eds.), *Sovereign Immunity Under Pressure*,
https://doi.org/10.1007/978-3-030-87706-4_15

Within the wide topic of sovereign debt and immunity,[3] this chapter focuses on the specific question whether liability for state bonds is subsequently limitable, in other words whether state immunity is subsequently restorable. Courts of various jurisdictions have had to answer this question in cases that concerned unpaid sovereign debt, first in connection with Argentina's debt moratorium in 1982 and again twenty years later in 2002, and then in the more recent Greek sovereign debt crisis when bonds were curtailed by half in 2012.[4]

Two opposing views taken by the courts can be identified and will be analysed in some detail in Sect. 2, including how they have been perceived by judges in other decisions and by legal scholars. Afterwards, Sect. 3 will take a more comprehensive perspective, addressing two resulting issues: first, practical implications for private investors will be pointed out, and secondly a jurisprudential explanation of the divergent views will be proposed. The findings of this chapter will be summarised and evaluated in the final section, which will also address the future prospects of sovereign insolvency.

2 Restricting and (Not) Restoring State Immunity for Bonds

2.1 *Issuance of State Bonds as Acta Jure Gestionis*

In contrast to the traditionally widespread understanding of absolute immunity deriving from sovereign equality,[5] states are not anymore exempted from foreign civil jurisdiction without significant exceptions.[6] Within the last decade, a restrictive understanding of state immunity has been recognised as customary international law by the International Court of Justice in its *Germany v Italy* judgment.[7] According to the restrictive perception, states may still claim to be immune concerning their exercise of sovereign power (*acta jure imperii*), but they can be held liable for

[3] See, for instance, Bröhmer (2015); Delaume (1989); Kupelyants (2018); Mola (2012); Waibel (2011); Weidemaier (2014).

[4] For a comprehensive analysis of sovereign defaults see Reinhart and Rogoff (2009); Schumacher et al. (2018).

[5] Sovereign equality is commonly based on the principle par in parem non habet imperium or par in parem non habet iudicium, see for instance Bankas (2005), pp. 37ff; Damrosch (2019), p. 42; Fox and Webb (2015), pp. 26ff; Kokott (2011), para. 35; Tomuschat (1999), p. 176. However, as noted by Finke (2010), p. 866, the League of Nations referred merely to the independence of states as the basis for their immunity, without relying on their equality, see 'Competence of the Courts in regard to Foreign States' (1927) 9 Publications of the League of Nations V, Legal, No 11, reprinted in (1928) 22 American Journal of International Law Supplement 117, 118.

[6] For an overview see Bankas (2005), pp. 329ff. For a historical overview see Fox (2019).

[7] International Court of Justice, Jurisdictional Immunities of the State judgment (Germany v Italy, Greece intervening) [2012] ICJ 99, paras. 60–61.

their non-sovereign actions (*acta jure gestionis*).[8] Not all but most states follow this restrictive understanding.[9] It has also been adopted in Part III of the UN Convention on Jurisdictional Immunities of States and Their Property, which addresses proceedings in which State immunity cannot be invoked;[10] however, this Convention has not yet entered into force.[11]

Non-sovereign and therefore non-immune activities most importantly comprise commercial transactions,[12] in addition to other areas that concern more specific situations like employment.[13] Commercial transactions are usually understood to include 'any contract for a loan or other transaction of a financial nature', such as in the UN Convention on Jurisdictional Immunities.[14] The commercial restriction on immunity is widely recognised,[15] and probably the most important in international legal practice.[16] In Article 10 of the UN Convention on Jurisdictional Immunities, the commercial exception is worded as follows:

> If a State engages in a commercial transaction with a foreign natural or juridical person and, by virtue of the applicable rules of private international law, differences relating to the commercial transaction fall within the jurisdiction of a court of another State, the State cannot invoke immunity from that jurisdiction in a proceeding arising out of that commercial transaction.[17]

Where states issue bonds to private investors and create sovereign debt to finance their spending, this is typically seen as a commercial transaction that is clearly an *actus jure gestionis*.[18] The state acts like a private corporation that voluntarily enters into a loan contract. Sometimes such exclusion of immunity is expressly agreed on,

---

[8] Orakhelashvili (2019); Stoll (2012), para. 25.

[9] Sucharitkul (1982), pp. 207ff.

[10] Articles 10ff UN Convention on Jurisdictional Immunities.

[11] Art 30(1) of the of the United Nations Convention on Jurisdictional Immunities of States and Their Property (New York, 2 December 2004) requires 30 ratifications for the entry into force of the Convention. So far, there are 28 signatories, of which 22 have ratified and become parties. For instance, France has ratified; the UK and Russia have signed but not ratified; Germany has not even signed.

[12] Banifatemi (2019); Fox and Webb (2015), pp. 399ff; Okeke (2018), pp. 107ff; Shan and Wang (2019), pp. 70–73; Shaw (2017), pp. 540ff; van Alebeek and Pavoni (2018), pp. 112ff; Yang (2012), pp. 75ff.

[13] Fox and Webb (2015), pp. 439ff; Okeke (2018), pp. 130ff; Shaw (2017), pp. 546ff; van Alebeek and Pavoni (2018), pp. 116ff; Yang (2012), pp. 132ff.

[14] Art 2(2)(c)(ii) UN Convention on Jurisdictional Immunities.

[15] Fox and Webb (2015), pp. 417ff; Yang (2012), pp. 75ff.

[16] Wittich (2013), p. 168.

[17] Art 10(1) UN Convention on Jurisdictional Immunities.

[18] Aust (2010), p. 153; Shaw (2017), pp. 542–543; Yang (2012), p. 77 with further references in footnote 23. Also see German Federal Constitutional Court (Bundesverfassungsgericht), Case 2 BvM 9/03, ECLI:DE:BVerfG:2006:ms20061206.2bvm000903, para. 35.

otherwise it is considered an implied term.[19] Therefore, in principle, the state is contractually obliged to repay at least the nominal value of the bond on maturity date and is prevented from refusing repayment due to sovereign immunity.

2.2 *Restoring Immunity Through Acta Jure Imperii*

Far more controversial and interesting are the views on the critical question whether the liability for commercial transactions like state bonds can be subsequently modified and thus limited by acts of state (*acta jure imperii*), which intend to restore sovereign immunity. All of those subsequent alterations to repayment obligations of states are problematic as they are unilaterally proclaimed by the public debtor and are intended to take retroactive effect. This might be feasible due to the allegedly restorable sovereign power of the state for public purposes, which would however be different from the powers of any private debtor. In turn, this could therefore be seen to contradict the commercial nature of the obligation that should be free from such sovereign interventions, regardless of their purpose.

Whether or not sovereign measures, which seek to limit the state's commercially agreed obligation of repayment aiming to establish subsequent sovereign immunity against debt, are given effect in foreign courts is not decided by any rule of public international law. This issue is neither addressed by the UN Convention on Jurisdictional Immunities nor by any rule of customary international law.[20] Although the European Court of Human Rights held that Article 11 of the UN Convention, which deals with contracts of employment, has to be characterised as customary international law in the decided case against France,[21] this does not analogously apply to Article 10 for commercial activities and/or to other states. The Court's decision is specific both to the distinct immunity exception in the labour context and to the French situation, because France had not only signed the UN Convention, but also initiated the ratification of it.[22] Similar to this was only the previous case against Lithuania, which also concerned Article 11.[23] Nor can a relevant rule of customary international law be based on the European Convention on State Immunity, though it has entered into force in 1976,[24] because it does not provide for a general

[19] Amirfar (2019); Okeke (2018), pp. 155ff; Shan and Wang (2019), pp. 76–77; Yang (2012), pp. 316ff.

[20] Francioni (2009), pp. 745–746 also finds that there is no basis in international law for claiming that a commercial transaction may subsequently qualify as actus jure imperii, although he evaluates this finding differently.

[21] European Court of Human Rights, Sabeh el Leil v France, Case 34869/05 (2012) 54 EHRR 14.

[22] European Court of Human Rights, Sabeh el Leil v France, Case 34869/05 (2012) 54 EHRR 14, paras. 57–58.

[23] European Court of Human Rights, Cudak v Lithuania, Case 15869/02 (2010) 51 EHRR 15, paras. 66–67.

[24] European Convention on State Immunity (Basel, 16 May 1972) ETS No 74.

commercial exception to immunity. Specific to business conducted in a foreign establishment, it only provides that:

> A contracting state cannot claim immunity from the jurisdiction of a court of another Contracting State if it has on the territory of the state of the forum an office, agency or other establishment through which it engages, in the same manner as a private person, in an industrial, commercial or financial activity, and the proceedings relate to that activity of the office, agency or establishment.[25]

Yet, highest courts of different countries and international courts have, in quite controversial ways, ruled on the issue whether or not sovereign measures seeking to restore sovereign immunity against the state's commercial obligations are given effect in foreign courts. In fact, two opposing views can be singled out, which will be discussed in the following and will be, in short, referred to as the 'Anglo-American view' and the 'Continental European view'.

2.2.1 Anglo-American Rejection Under the Principle 'Once a Trader, Always a Trader'

Starting with the view of Anglo-American courts, which can be condensed in the simplifying slogan 'once a trader, always a trader',[26] attempts to subsequently restore sovereign immunity for commercial transactions have been rejected by the highest courts both in the US and the UK.

In this respect, the leading case on sovereign debt and immunity is the US Supreme Court's ruling in *Republic of Argentina v. Weltover, Inc.*[27] Bondholders had sued Argentina because of its unilateral extension of the bond maturity date by a presidential decree as part of a currency stabilisation plan back in 1982.[28] Justice Scalia delivered the ruling of the US Supreme Court, which held that the initial issuance of the state bonds was a 'commercial activity' under the Foreign Sovereign Immunities Act 1976 (FSIA).[29] However, the US Supreme Court further found that the unilateral rescheduling of the bond repayment dates had not changed this commercial nature, and therefore Argentina could not claim immunity.[30] The Argentinian state had participated in the market like a private player; it did not act as a regulator of the market by sovereign measures.[31]

---

[25] Art 7(1) European Convention on State Immunity.

[26] It seems as if this exact expression was first used in UK House of Lords, I Congreso del Partido [1983] AC 244, 263, 269, 276. It is also used, for instance by Damian (1985), p. 105; Geimer (2017). See also Arnold and Garber (2019), p. 390; Mankowski (2019), p. 199.

[27] US Supreme Court, Republic of Argentina v Weltover, Inc (1992) 504 US 607. For a comprehensive comment, see Lew (1994).

[28] US Supreme Court, Republic of Argentina v Weltover, Inc (1992) 504 US 607, 609ff.

[29] Ibid., 610ff and 615ff.

[30] Ibid., 617ff.

[31] Ibid., 614.

The US Supreme Court backed its view in *Weltover* by referring to its earlier judgment in *Alfred Dunhill of London, Inc. v. Republic of Cuba,*[32] which was handed down before FISA entered into force. This case concerned an action that was brought by former owners of expropriated Cuban cigar companies against US importers to recover payments for cigar shipments.[33] Cuba was not granted immunity in US courts because the 1960 Cuban nationalisation of the business and assets of the cigar manufacturers did not qualify as an act of state that would subsequently have turned the commercial business liabilities into sovereign and therefore immune actions.[34]

In *Weltover,* FSIA was applied, and importantly without exception. The Act denies immunity of a foreign state in cases:

> in which the action is based upon a commercial activity carried on in the United States by the foreign state; or upon an act performed in the United States in connection with a commercial activity of the foreign state elsewhere; or upon an act outside the territory of the United States in connection with a commercial activity of the foreign state elsewhere and that act causes a direct effect in the United States.[35]

The meaning of 'commercial activity' is defined by FISA as:

> either a regular course of commercial conduct or a particular commercial transaction or act. The commercial character of an activity shall be determined by reference to the nature of the course of conduct or particular transaction or act, rather than by reference to its purpose.[36]

The Supreme Court found that Argentina could not claim immunity for issuing bonds as a particular commercial transaction by nature. With regard to the subsequent measures by Argentina, this view did not change and no exception was made, as FSIA does not provide for any counter-exceptions. This assessment is shared by many public international law scholars because it also reflects their understanding of sovereign participation in the private market.[37]

In Britain, very similarly, the only two years older UK State Immunity Act 1978 provides for the state immunity exception for commercial transactions such as state bonds. It stipulates that:

> [a] state is not immune as respects proceedings relating to a commercial transaction entered into by the state'.[38]

Insofar vital is the definition of 'commercial transaction', which rather broadly means:

[32] US Supreme Court, Republic of Argentina v Weltover, Inc (1992) 504 US 607, 613–614.

[33] US Supreme Court, Alfred Dunhill of London, Inc v Republic of Cuba (1976) 425 US 682.

[34] Ibid., 696.

[35] 28 US Code § 1605(a)(2). For a commentary, see Dickinson et al. (2004), paras. 3.034ff.

[36] 28 US Code § 1603(d).

[37] Bröhmer (2015), pp. 188–190; Herdegen (2018), § 37 para. 7; Kupelyants (2018), para. 8.33; Okeke (2018), pp. 113–114; Panizza et al. (2009), pp. 653–654; Shaw (2017), p. 544; Webb (2018), p. 330; Waibel (2011), p. 122.

[38] State Immunity Act 1978, sec 3(1)(a).

> any contract for the supply of goods or services; any loan or other transaction for the provision of finance and any guarantee or indemnity in respect of any such transaction or of any other financial obligation; and any other transaction or activity (whether of a commercial, industrial, financial, professional or other similar character) into which a State enters or in which it engages otherwise than in the exercise of sovereign authority.[39]

With regard to the question whether immunity can subsequently be restored, which is not specially addressed in the British Act either, the leading case in the UK is *I Congreso del Partido*,[40] which the House of Lords had to decide in 1981 without applying the newly introduced State Immunity Act because the facts of the case dated back into the period before its entry into force.[41] Although the case itself did not concern state bonds, but a contract for the supply of sugar, which equally comes under the Act's immunity exception for commercial transactions, it can be considered as precedent. The underlying facts of the case can be very briefly summarised like this: after a Cuban state-trading company had negotiated a sale of sugar to a company in Chile, the flag and ownership of one of the ships carrying the sugar was transferred to the Republic of Cuba itself, which then however delivered the sugar to North Vietnam. The majority of the Law Lords ruled that the whole transaction did not subsequently qualify as an act done in Cuba's sovereign capacity, so that immunity was not granted by the Court. Lord Bridge argued that:

> a sovereign state cannot justify a breach of [a purely private law] obligation on the ground that the reason for the breach was of a sovereign or governmental character.[42]

In *I Congreso del Partido,* Lord Bridge's scenario of another commercial transaction, which he illustrated to support this finding, has been particularly instructive:

> State A, having ordered uniforms for its army from a supplier in State B, repudiates the contract; when sued in the courts of State B for damages, State A cannot claim immunity on the ground that, since the placing of the contract, a government of a new political complexion has made a sovereign decision, pursuant to a policy of total disarmament, to disband its army.[43]

Following from this case law, it is assumed under the UK State Immunity Act that immunity is not restored for any attempt to limit private liability, which has arisen from a commercial transaction, even where the subsequently sought modification is made by a sovereign act.[44] According to this view, nothing else would apply in a case where a government changes its mind about the repayment of issued bonds and claims immunity for it.[45]

[39] State Immunity Act 1978, sec 3(3)(b).

[40] I Congreso del Partido [1983] AC 244.

[41] On 22 November 1978, SI 1978/1572 per State Immunity Act 1978, sec 23(5).

[42] I Congreso del Partido [1983] AC 244, 278–279.

[43] Ibid., 279.

[44] Dickinson et al. (2004), para. 4.029; Lewis (1990), p. 43; Mann (1979), p. 52.

[45] Similarly Kupelyants (2018), para. 8.24.

Worth adding to the UK's view is a striking judgment from the Mixed Tribunal of Cairo, which was handed down almost a century ago in 1925, when Egypt was a British protectorate. Being concerned with sovereign debt, the Tribunal held that:

> a government which enters into an agreement with a private individual to pay a certain sum of money thereby contracts a civil obligation; with regard to disputes arising out of this purely civil obligation it is subject to the jurisdiction of the common law. From its character as public authority a government derives no right to liberate itself from its obligation by deciding on its own will that it is released for reasons that render it the only judge of civil obligations entered into by it.[46]

That no subsequent restoration of immunity based on claims of sovereign action would be permissible becomes especially clear from the Tribunal's further findings that:

> the refusal to pay by alleging extinction of the contractual obligation which gave rise to the duty to pay, has never been an act of sovereignty, or an act of public authority.[47]

In conclusion, the Anglo-American view rejects the idea of subsequently restorable immunity by sovereign acts in the commercial context. States who have engaged once as traders are always treated like traders whose liability is not subsequently limitable by special means which are not available to traders.

2.2.2 Continental European Approval Under the Principle 'Once a Trader, Still a Sovereign'

The contrary view that state immunity for commercial transactions like state bonds can be restored through subsequent a*cta jure imperii*, which could be shortened to 'once a trader, still a sovereign', has been upheld by continental European courts, particularly by the highest civil courts of Italy, Germany, and Austria. In addition, both the Court of Justice of the European Union and the European Court of Human Rights share the underlying understanding.

In 2002, Argentina had again declared a moratorium, which had effectively frozen its issued bonds and postponed the date for their repayment, in the context of emergency measures addressing another national economic crisis. This time in Italy, Argentina was sued by a private investor for punctual repayment of bonds. Contrary to the US Supreme Court's decision in *Weltover*, the Italian Supreme Court of Cassation (Corte Suprema di Cassazione) granted state immunity to Argentina.[48] It held that:

---

[46] English translation by Borchard (1951), p. 11 of Mixed Tribunal of Cairo, NM Rothschild & Sons v Gouvernement Egyptien (1925) 350 Journal des Tribunaux Mixtes 4.

[47] Ibid.

[48] Italian Court of Cassation, Borri v Argentina, Case 11225 (2005) 88 Rivista Diritto Internazionale 856.

> while the issuing and placing in the international market of the bonds concerned are undeniably of a private law nature, the subsequent moratorium adopted by the Argentinian government [... is] not of an analogous character. [... The Argentinian] laws are clear manifestations of the sovereign power of the state [...]. This is [...] because of their purposes [...] which are manifestly public and pursued to regulate finances for the protection of the primary needs of the economic survival of the population in the context of a serious national emergency.[49]

The Court established that a foreign state may displace the *jure gestionis* nature of the commercial activity, and may successfully claim immunity through the subsequent enactment of laws which repudiate its contractual obligations. To support this finding, reference was made to an earlier judgment by the Italian Constitutional Court in a case involving Nigeria, in which it was held that subsequent measures to delay the repayment obligations of the foreign state were within its sovereign powers.[50] Restoring immunity through subsequent *acta jure imperii* was again confirmed in a later case before the Court of Cassation, in which it distinguished such acts and their effects from a mere unilateral decision not to fulfil existing commercial obligations, which could not qualify as an act *jure imperii*.[51]

Criticism against allowing subsequent limitation of liability has arisen due to the fact that the Italian judges had neither given any consideration to foreign jurisprudence, such as the *Weltover* decision, nor did they engage in any transnational judicial dialogue.[52] Although this is true, it does not reproach the Italian Court for having misjudged the issue, simply because they differed from the Anglo-American view without expressly arguing and distinguishing their opposite evaluation. Despite further criticism for self-contradiction by the Court of Cassation in allowing subsequent restoration of sovereign immunity for a commercial transaction, it has also been noted in the literature that, in terms of international level, immunity has to be granted to foreign states only on a minimum level of protection. Individual jurisdictions are neither obliged to go beyond, nor prevented from extending immunity as long as this does not result in violation of the claimants' fundamental rights of access to justice.[53] In the context here, suspicion of such violation would be far-fetched.[54] Consequently, it is understandable and acceptable that the Italian Court relied on the

[49] Quoted according to the translation by van Alebeek and Pavoni (2018), p. 116.

[50] Italian Constitutional Court, Case 329, judgment of 2 July 1992.

[51] Italian Court of Cassation, Brazil v Italplan Engineering, Environment & Transports SPA, Case 6603/2015 (IT 2015) Oxford Reports on International Law: International Law in Domestic Courts 2566, paras. 17–18.

[52] Bonafè (2006); Pavoni (2009), pp. 78–80; van Alebeek and Pavoni (2018), p. 116. Also see Francioni (2009), p. 746.

[53] Bröhmer (2015), pp. 191–192; Hess (2018b), pp. 222–223.

[54] Not even in a case of torture in and by a foreign state, the forum state is obliged to refuse immunity to this foreign state on the basis of the tortured claimant's fundamental right of access to justice under Art 6(1) European Convention of Human Rights, see European Court of Human Rights, Al-Adsani v the United Kingdom, Case 35763/97 (2002) 34 EHRR 11, paras. 52–67 (however, this decision was only made by nine votes to eight).

public purposes giving rise to the subsequent limitations of liability as *jure imperii* measures, which were able to restore Argentina's sovereign immunity.

Moving on to the Greek government debt crisis in the aftermath of the global financial crisis of 2007/08, German courts fairly recently had to deal with Greek bonds, whose repayment was subsequently curtailed in 2012. Greece adopted a series of sudden reforms and austerity measures in order to receive financial support from the Troika: the International Monetary Fund (IMF), the Eurogroup, and the European Central Bank (ECB). As part of this Greek sovereign debt restructuring, the Greek Bondholder Act was passed in February 2012 that effectively halved the nominal value of the issued bonds,[55] after a qualified majority of the private bondholders—but not all of them—had agreed. By this measure, sovereign default and potentially complete loss of investments could be averted. In particular, the Act unilaterally and retroactively inserted a Collective Action Clause (CAC) to the existing state bonds governed by Greek law, which had the effect that minority bondholders found themselves bound by the majority's decision to accept that the bond values were significantly reduced. Some of these minority bondholders sued the Hellenic Republic in German courts for full repayment of their bonds. In defence, the Greek government argued that it would be entitled to state immunity because of its public act, which reduced the bond value, and that German courts would not be permitted to judge on this issue.

In the highest instance, the German Federal Court of Justice (Bundesgerichtshof) acknowledged in a series of decisions in 2016/17 that issuing state bonds is a non-sovereign activity, which does not entail immunity, but held that Greece is immune against the repayment claims beyond the amount subsequently reduced by sovereign power.[56] The German Court emphasised that it was prevented from questioning the validity of the Greek Bondholder Act, which qualified as a public act of a foreign state that could not be subject to domestic court proceedings. The Greek state was not comparable to a private corporation refusing payment, because the reduction was enacted by statute. The subsequent limitation of state bond liability was also not comparable to a differently decided employment case where the German Federal Labour Court (Bundesarbeitsgericht) held that Greece was not immune against the claim of a teacher, who was employed at a Greek school in Germany and sought full payment of his salary, which was reduced by a newly introduced Greek salary tax.[57]

The view taken by the German Court, accepting the subsequent limitation of liability, has been criticised by scholars from a normative angle. They insist that the

[55] Greek Bondholder Act 4050/2012 (23 February 2012), Art 1.

[56] German Federal Court of Justice, Case VI ZR 516/14, ECLI:DE:BGH:2016:080316U VIZR516.14.0; Case XI ZR 217/16, ECLI:DE:BGH:2017:191217UXIZR217.16.0; Case XI ZR 247/16, ECLI:DE:BGH:2017:191217UXIZR247.16.0; Case XI ZR 796/16; ECLI:DE:BGH:2017: 191217UXIZR796.16.0.

[57] German Federal Labour Court, Case 3 AZB 5/12, Entscheidungen des Bundesarbeitsgerichts 144, 244, paras 25ff.

defendant state should not be subsequently entitled to immunity if it intervenes in its own private legal relationship by means of regulatory laws or administrative acts.[58] It is not in line with customary rules of state immunity to allow such conduct by a defendant state.[59] Otherwise, this would indicate a return to the anachronistic idea of sovereign debt as a debt of honour, not of legal obligation.[60] However, there is no superior legal reason for the critics' normative claim that continental European judges would be obliged to adhere to the view taken by their Anglo-American colleagues 'once a trader, always a trader'. Particularly, there simply is no rule of customary international law that would decide the issue either way, as it is evident from the divergent views taken by the various courts, which have given rise to the whole debate. The immunity decision 'once a trader, still a sovereign' is not unsound either considering another line of argument brought forward by the German critics, who suggest that the whole liability action should be decided on its merits and not on its admissibility.[61] As the German Court did not declare the action admissible, no decision on the merits was permissible; this logic is not refuted just because the action could have, in the eyes of the critics, been more convincingly decided its merits. Ultimately, the outcome of the action would, if it were decided on its merits, coincide with the judgment given: Liability of Greece would be denied due to the Greek statute, which—depending on the outcome of the conflict-of-laws analysis—would apply as part of the governing law or as overriding mandatory provisions;[62] this would resemble the findings in another Greek school teacher's case concerning a pay cut under the Greek austerity measures.[63]

The position of the German Federal Court of Justice in the Greek bonds cases was recently affirmed by the German Federal Constitutional Court (Bundesverfassungsgericht).[64] Although there was no expressive discussion or even disapproval of the principle 'once a trader, always a trader', it was upheld that the Greek limitation of liability was a result of the compulsory exchange imposed by Greek law. Such limitation was not available to a private market

[58] Damian (1985), pp. 106, 178; Geimer (2017); Hess (2018a), pp. 352–354; Mankowski (2018a), p. 188; Schack (2017), para. 182; Seidl-Hohenveldern (1979), p. 1091.

[59] Lorz (2017), p. 85; Weller and Fischer (2016), p. 173.

[60] Based on the idea of Politis (1984), p. 16. Also see, for instance, UK Court of Appeal, Twycross v Dreyfus (1877) 5 Ch D 605, 616.

[61] Arnold and Garber (2015), pp. 185–188; Mankowski (2018a), p. 188; Müller (2016), p. 81.

[62] Mankowski (2018a), p. 188; Müller (2018).

[63] German Federal Labour Court, Case 5 AZR 962/13, ECLI:DE:BAG:2017:260417.U.5AZR962.13.0, Entscheidungen des Bundesarbeitsgerichts 159, 69–81. Also see the preliminary ruling by the Court of Justice of the European Union, Case C-135/15 Nikiforidis, ECLI:EU:C:2016:774. For an analysis see Lehmann and Ungerer (2017/2018).

[64] German Federal Constitutional Court, Case 2 BvR 331/18, ECLI:DE:BVerfG:2020:rk20200506.2bvr033118. For an English summary see, for instance, https://gpil.jura.uni-bonn.de/2020/07/once-a-trader-always-a-state-the-federal-constitutional-court-classifies-greek-debt-restructuring-measures-as-acta-jure-imperii/.

participant, but expression of state sovereignty. As a sovereign measure by a foreign state, the limitation of the bond liability cannot be subject to German jurisdiction.

Before moving on and looking at the international case law of the European courts, it is worthwhile to consider the view of the Austrian courts, because it changed within a short time. This helps to understand the importance of the international judicial influence on the views of national courts, such as in Austria.

Initially, in 2014/15, the Austrian Court of Justice (Oberster Gerichtshof) had refused to grant immunity to Greece in a number of cases, in which private investors claimed full repayment of bonds just as in Germany.[65] As it is international consensus, the Austrian Court stated that Greece acted like any private debtor when issuing the bonds, and therefore did not enjoy immunity.[66] Yet, the Austrian Court did not find that refusing immunity was inconsistent with the Greek Bondholder Act, which it only addressed in a different part of its judgment, but not with regard to the issue of restoring immunity.[67] Very recently, however, in January 2019, the view taken in Austria changed to the opposite, and now essentially corresponds with the continental understanding that Greece is immune against claims for repayment of the amount reduced by the Greek Bondholder Act.[68]

This change in view indirectly resulted from the impression which the Austrian court gained from the *Kuhn* judgment of the Court of Justice of the European Union in 2018 in a similar (but not formally connected) case concerning the international jurisdiction of Austrian courts for the claims brought against Greece in foreign courts.[69] This is the closest that one can get to a supranational view on the Greek measures and their suitability to restore the immunity of Greece, which as such is a question solely decided on national levels.[70] Although there cannot be a binding decision by a supranational or international court on the immunity issue in this respect, such a court's view can be important guidance on issues that are relevant as general context and background for state immunity. The conceptual proximity of sovereign immunity and international jurisdiction in the Brussels Ia Regulation is

[65] Austrian Court of Justice, Case 4 Ob 227/13f, confirmed Case 8 Ob 67/15h, ECLI:AT:OGH0002:2015:RS0130470, in Case 6 Ob 122/15g, and in Case 8 Ob 125/14p.

[66] Austrian Court of Justice, Case 4 Ob 227/13f, para. 3.2.

[67] Ibid., para. 3.1.

[68] Austrian Court of Justice, Case 10 Ob 103/18x, ECLI:AT:OGH0002:2019:0100OB00103.18X.0122.000, para 1.1. For a case note, see Weller and Walter (2019), pp. 124–125.

[69] Court of Justice of the European Union, Case C-308/17 Kuhn, ECLI:EU:C:2018:911.

[70] It is undisputed that the Court of Justice cannot rule on sovereign immunity as an issue of national procedure. See particularly, Case C-292/05 Lechouritou, ECLI:EU:C:2006:700, Opinion of AG Ruiz-Jarabo Colomer, para 78; UK High Court, Grovit v De Nederlandsche Bank [2005] EWHC 2944 (QB), [47]; Mankowski (2019), p. 194; Muir Watt and Pataut (2008), pp. 68–69; Weller and Walter (2019), p. 125.

generally acknowledged.[71] Against this background, the case-law is implicitly relevant and highly interesting for the actual question of subsequent restoration of immunity, which is closely connected to the decided issue.

The Court of Justice of the European Union was asked in a preliminary ruling procedure to interpret provisions of the Brussels Ia Regulation (EU) No 1215/2012 on jurisdiction and the recognition and enforcement of judgments in civil and commercial matters.[72] The Brussels Ia Regulation only applies, as it is already apparent from the title of the Regulation and is set out in its Article 1(1):

> in civil and commercial matters [but it] shall not extend, in particular, to [...] the liability of the state for acts and omissions in the exercise of state authority (acta jure imperii).[73]

The Court of Justice found that a claim for the full repayment of the Greek bonds, whose value was reduced by statute, does not qualify as such a 'civil and commercial matter'.[74] Although not expressly stated, the Court of Justice seems to have assumed that the subsequent limitation to the repayment liability was an *actus jure imperii*. The Court considered a variety of factors before denying the civil and commercial nature of the rather sovereign action:

> having [had] regard to the exceptional character of the conditions and the circumstances surrounding the adoption of [the Greek Bondholder Act], according to which the initial borrowing terms of the sovereign bonds at issue in the main proceedings were unilaterally and retroactively amended by the introduction of a CAC.[75]

It was also highlighted, similar to the reasoning of the Italian Court of Cassation many years earlier in the Argentinian case, that the enacted statute pursued objectives in the public interest, and that the actual dispute in the Austrian court effectively centred around the Greek statute as a sovereign act, which would not be justiciable like 'civil and commercial matters' within the meaning of EU law.

German scholars have also been critical with this view as taken by the CJEU judgment, blaming it for factual or even political reasoning without a legal basis and particularly for ignoring the private-law background in this regard.[76] On the other hand, French jurists have agreed with the decision,[77] which they think differs from

---

[71] See, for instance, Arnold and Garber (2015), pp. 192–193; Hauser (2019), pp. 337–338; Hess (2018b), p. 72; Mankowski (2015), para. 9; Mankowski (2019), pp. 195–196; Stürner (2008), p. 203; Wagner (2014), p. 264; Weller and Walter (2019), p. 125.

[72] OJ L351/1.

[73] Art 1(1) Brussels Ia Regulation.

[74] Court of Justice of the European Union, Case C-308/17 Kuhn, ECLI:EU:C:2018, paras. 29ff.

[75] Ibid., para. 42.

[76] Arnold and Garber (2015), pp. 389–390; Kehrberger (2019), pp. 90–91; Hauser (2019), pp. 336ff; Kerber (2019), p. 1334; Mankowski (2018b), p. 478; Mankowski (2019), p. 195; Weller and Walter (2019), p. 124. Similarly critical from the Swiss perspective Vogl (2019).

[77] Idot (2019); Kleiner (2019); Nourissat (2019), p. 14.

the distinguishable *Fahnenbrock* case on the service of documents,[78] and they consider it to be in line with earlier relevant case-law on *acta jure imperii*.[79]

In respect of the question whether state immunity can subsequently be restored for state bonds, which the Court of Justice of the European Union did not have to address because it is not an issue regulated by EU law, the Court's findings implicitly suggest that Greece exercised its sovereign power by passing the Greek Bondholder Act, which therefore would allow Greece to successfully claim immunity against repayment obligations. At least, the Court's ruling has been considered to serve as a point of reference in this area of national adjudication.[80] Of course, this does not follow conclusively in all possible scenarios, as others have noted, because *acta jure imperii* are imaginable which are excluded from the scope of the Brussels Ia Regulation on international jurisdiction, but which do not constitute a sufficient basis for sovereign immunity.[81] Nevertheless, the *Kuhn* judgment by the Court of Justice of the European Union gave rise to the change of the Austrian Court's view in this instance, which outshines any different hypothetical scenarios.[82]

In this *Kuhn* judgment, a reference was made to a similar Greek case that was decided by the European Court of Human Rights, who dealt with the axiomatic question whether human rights had been violated by the Greek Bondholder Act.[83] Private investors claimed infringement of their right to property, as set out in the First Added Protocol to the European Convention on Human Rights,[84] and/or infringement of prohibition of discrimination,[85] by the alleged expropriation due to the reduction of the bond values. Again, similar to *Kuhn*, the actual issue was not about state immunity, but the Court of Human Rights as an international court was presented with the opportunity to characterise the nature of the Greek action. Insofar the Court of Human Rights indirectly ruled on the incidental question, which is decisive for the question of state immunity restoration, whether the Greek measures

---

[78] Court of Justice of the European Union, Case C-226/13 Fahnenbrock, ECLI:EU:C:2015:383:

[79] Court of Justice of the European Union, Case C-292/05 Lechouritou, ECLI:EU:C:2007:102.

[80] Kleiner (2019), paras. 18–21.

[81] Lorz (2017), p. 156; Mankowski (2019), p. 200; Thole (2012), p. 1794.

[82] Arguing the contrary, Weller and Walter (2019), p. 125, point towards a decision by the Austrian Court of Justice (Case 6 OB 164/18p, para 3.3) which was handed down just a few days after the Kuhn judgment and which still followed the initial view of rejecting the subsequent restoration of immunity. Most likely however, due to the short time in-between, the Austrian Court was not able anymore to adapt its view, which it did however in its later decision: Austrian Court of Justice, Case 10 Ob 103/18x, ECLI:AT:OGH0002:2019:0100OB00103.18X.0122.000. In conclusion, Weller and Walter (2019), p. 126, agree that the Austrian Court will adhere to its changed view of accepting subsequently restorable immunity.

[83] European Court of Human Rights, Mamatas v Grèce, Cases 63066/14, 64297/14 and 66106/14 [2016] ECHR 256, paras 99 and 105. For a very critical review, see Kerber (2019), pp. 1334–1336.

[84] [First] Protocol to the Convention for the Protection of Human Rights and Fundamental Freedoms (Paris, 20 March 1952), Art 1.

[85] [European] Convention for the Protection of Human Rights and Fundamental Freedoms (Rome, 4 November 1950), Art 14.

were of a sovereign nature. It is only to this extent that the decision is relevant here and to be included in the analysis.

In this respect, 'the Court had no doubt that the interference in question was 'provided for by law',[86] and that states like Greece would 'enjoy a fairly wide margin of appreciation' with regard to combating an economic crisis and that their policy choices are to be respected unless manifestly lacking a reasonable basis.[87] It held that Greece could legitimately take measures to achieve the goals of economic stability and debt restructuring in the public interest.[88] Affirming the public law character of the Greek measures contributes to supporting the view that Greece exercised its sovereign power, which might thus be understood to underpin the assessment that Greece was allowed to claim immunity against repayment obligations.

In conclusion of the continental European analysis, it can be stated that courts at national level have approved the principle of subsequently restored immunity by sovereign acts, which responded to instability and distress in times of sovereign debt crises. This principle has been indirectly supported by European courts on the supranational and international level.

3 Implications and Explanations of the Divergent Views

Given the divergent views on subsequently restorable state immunity that have been laid out above, two observations can be made on a more general level. Finally, the findings will be summarised and resulting needs for future action will be pointed out.

3.1 Practical Implications for Private Investors

First, there is an important implication from a practical point of view. Private investors have to beware of the following: they need to choose the court wisely in which they sue the foreign state whose bonds they have bought and which has then reduced or delayed repayment. It would be pointless to sue a foreign state in continental Europe, knowing that courts have no choice but to reject any claim

[86] Mamatas v Grèce, Cases 63066/14, 64297/14 and 66106/14 [2016] ECHR 256, para. 99.

[87] Ibid., paras. 88–89 and 103, with reference to earlier case law of the European Court of Human Rights, Valkov v Bulgaria, Case 2033/04 (2016) 62 EHRR 24; Frimu v Romania, Cases 45312/11, 45581/11, 45583/11, 45587/11 and 45588/11 [2012] ECHR 431; Panfile v Romania, Case 13902/11 [2012] ECHR 320; Koufaki and Adedy v Greece, Cases 57665/12 and 57657/12 [2013] ECHR 507; NKM v Hungary, Case 66529/11 (2016) 62 EHRR 33; da Conceição Mateus and Santos Januário v Portugal, Cases 62235/12 and 57725/12 [2013] ECHR 1008; Savickas v Lithuania, Case 66365/09 [2013] ECHR 328; da Silva Carvalho Rico v Portugal, Case 13341/14 [2015] ECHR 287.

[88] Mamatas v Grèce, Cases 63066/14, 64297/14 and 66106/14 [2016] ECHR 256, para. 103.

where the foreign state exercised its sovereign power in order to modify its repayment obligations, even if done so unilaterally and retroactively. Only suits filed in British or US courts seem to have a viable chance to pass the immunity objection by the defendant state, relying on the case law and most importantly the provisions and exemptions of the respective foreign state immunity acts.

This leaves private investors with the question of how to determine the competent court. As this is an issue of international jurisdiction, it is governed by the local procedural law of the court to be addressed, the *lex forum*.[89] Within the EU, international jurisdiction of civil courts is usually determined by the Brussels Ia Regulation.[90] However, in the case of state bond obligations that have potentially been modified by an *actus jure imperii*, the Court of Justice of the European Union has decided in *Kuhn* that the Brussels Ia Regulation does not apply due to its exclusion of sovereign issues.[91] Therefore, the courts of EU Member States, like courts of any other state outside the EU, apply their autonomous law of private international law in order to determine their international jurisdiction.[92] This is all but easy to determine due to the fact that the claimants do not want to sue the defendant state in its own courts. The claimants will prefer courts at their own venue, which however contradicts the internationally recognised jurisdictional principle of *actor sequitur forum rei*.[93] Hence, establishing international jurisdiction can be troublesome, even before the immunity bottleneck is approached.

3.2 *Jurisprudential Explanation of Conceptional Differences*

Secondly, from a jurisprudential perspective, there is a need for an explanation of the divergent views. The differing perceptions of whether or not a state may modify its private-law obligations by a public act can be seen to originate in differing conceptions of the public-private law divide in the respective legal systems.[94] Similar to how it has been described by *Dicey* for the nineteenth century nation states,[95] and still applies in principle today,[96] states in continental Europe envisage the government to represent the nation and general public, having special rights and duties, determined by rules and principles of public law. The continental state is thus above

[89] Briggs (2019), pp. 173ff; Torremans (2017), p. 73; Lord Collins of Mapesbury (2018), paras. 7R–001ff.

[90] Art 4ff Brussels Ia Regulation.

[91] Court of Justice of the European Union, Case C-308/17 Kuhn, ECLI:EU:C:2018, paras. 42–43.

[92] Briggs (2019), p. 39; Torremans (2017), p. 189.

[93] Mehren (2006), pp. 153ff.

[94] Similarly, Fox and Webb (2015), p. 402; Hess (2018b), pp. 89–95.

[95] Dicey (2013), pp. 237–238.

[96] Collini (1979), pp. 13ff; Horwitz (1982); van den Berge (2018), pp. 124ff. See also Allison (2000); Allison (2007); Cane (1986), p. 4; Cane (2003); Finke (2010), pp. 859–860.

the private law, which only sets the legal relations between citizens. Whether or not this perception is based on a sound analysis,[97] its impact has certainly been significant on legal academics and judges alike.[98]

Following this understanding, a state is usually not accountable under private law because there are special rules in place which govern its privileges and obligations for the greater good. By way of analogy, the situation that a state issues bonds and creates an obligation to repay them like a private corporation seems to be exceptional given the sovereignty of the state; one could say that the state descends from its superior position down to the ordinary. In turn, it is more plausible that a state does not have to stick to its private law obligation, but may rather return to its original sovereignty, and refuse to be held accountable if required and set by public law. Therefore, it is not surprising that courts in continental Europe allow a foreign state to subsequently restore its immunity because this would just restore a basic understanding: namely that the state is above the private law and may modify such obligations as required by public law in order to stabilise national economy and avert government default.

In Common Law jurisdictions, however, the state shall principally adhere to the supremacy of the law that is binding for the government like the ordinary citizens in the *Diceyan* ideal.[99] Notwithstanding specific laws for public governance, all legal subjects including the state are subjected to the law in the same way.[100] In other words, the Common Law stipulates that government and citizens alike are bound in the same legal realm.[101] In the Victorian England of *Dicey*, the legal framework for the commonwealth state could be perceived as not significantly differing from the law applicable to a private corporation.[102]

As this perception is analogously evidenced in the decisions of US and UK courts, it is understandable why they make no difference between sovereign debt and corporate debt. It seems rather consistent to treat private law obligations of states against private investors in the same way as those of private parties among themselves. In consequence, state debtors are banned from unilaterally and retroactively modifying their repayment obligation by allegedly sovereign acts, which no private debtor would ever be allowed to assert. Therefore, courts in the US and UK refuse to recognise that a foreign state could subsequently restore immunity, which it never had and will never have again with regard to a commercial obligation that is exclusively and permanently governed by private law. Particularly in Common Law jurisdictions, whose law is predominantly established and developed by judge-made case law, it must be noticed as a measure of remarkable importance

[97] Questioned, for instance, by Freedland (2006), p. 96 with reference to Loughlin (1992), pp. 153–162.

[98] Lord Bingham of Cornhill (2002).

[99] Dicey (2013), ch. 12. Also van den Berge (2018), pp. 129ff.

[100] Dicey (2013), pp. 100ff.

[101] Craig (1990), pp. 27–29.

[102] Dyson (1980), p. 52.

that legislators have enacted statutes like the US-American FSIA and the UK States Immunity Act, which provide for exceptions to state immunity in commercial transactions with a clarity that is unknown to continental European jurisdictions, the actual home of statutory codification.

4 Conclusion and Future Prospects

In conclusion, the divergence of views on the question, whether liability for state bonds is subsequently limitable, can of course not be resolved, but perhaps the divergent views 'once a trader, always a trader' versus 'once a trader, still a sovereign' can be better understood. The reasons for either side are valid, and against the background of the respective legal traditions and fundamental perceptions they are consistent. Criticism against either view can only argue for the opposite on a normative basis, but cannot call into question the foundations underlying them. Hence, as a change of minds cannot be expected nor demanded from the judges in either jurisdiction, private investors will have to live with the consequences and choose their forum accordingly.

The result of this unsatisfactory situation and the challenge to resolve sovereign default more systematically and effectively raise many complex economic and legal questions that could only be addressed and solved on an international political level, which makes it all but easy and straightforward, given the divergent national views and policies.[103] A variety of possible legal solutions have been suggested for sovereign insolvency mechanisms and the challenges, which an individual insolvent state faces within the international community of nations.[104] However, these future prospects of a state insolvency regime are not overly promising in so far as they would require international consensus regarding the national economic considerations, but also with respect to all associated social and societal implications.[105] Therefore, answering the question whether liability for state bonds is subsequently limitable, in other words whether state immunity is subsequently restorable, remains highly important, certainly in the context and aftermath of a next sovereign debt crisis.

[103] See, for instance, Roos (2019).

[104] Bolton and Skeel (2004); Buckley (2009); Hagan (2005); Ryan (2014); Schwarcz (2015). For a critical view see Gelpern (2013). Forthcoming: Sander et al. (2021).

[105] Bröhmer (2015), p. 183; Krueger (2012), pp. 165ff.

References

Allison JWF (2000) A continental distinction in the common law: a historical and comparative perspective in English public law. OUP, Oxford

Allison JWF (2007) Variations of view on English legal distinctions between public and private. Camb Law J 66:698

Amirfar C (2019) Waivers of jurisdictional immunity. In: Ruys T, Angelet N (eds) The Cambridge handbook of immunities and international law. CUP, Cambridge, pp 167–184

Arnold S, Garber T (2015) Zur Trennung privater und hoheitlicher Tätigkeit im Internationalen Zivilverfahrensrecht – Gerichtsbarkeit, internationale Zuständigkeit und die Umstrukturierung griechischer Staatsanleihen 2012. Zeitschrift für Zivilprozess International 20:171

Arnold S, Garber T (2019) Ein vermeintlicher Pyrrhussieg für Griechenland: Die Grenzen staatlicher Souveränität im Internationalen Zivilverfahrensrecht. Praxis des Internationalen Privat und Verfahrensrechts 385

Aust A (2010) Handbook of international law, 2nd edn. CUP, Cambridge

Banifatemi Y (2019) Jurisdictional immunity of states – commercial transactions. In: Ruys T, Angelet N (eds) The Cambridge handbook of immunities and international law. CUP, Cambridge, pp 125–141

Bankas EK (2005) The state immunity controversy in international law: private suits against sovereign states in domestic courts. Springer, Berlin

Bolton P, Skeel DA Jr (2004) Inside the Black Box: how should a sovereign bankruptcy framework be structured? Emory Law J 53:763

Bonafè BI (2006) State immunity and the protection of private investors: the Argentine bonds case before Italian courts. Ital Yearb Int Law 16:165

Borchard E (1951) State insolvency and foreign bondholders. Yale University Press, Yale

Briggs A (2019) The conflict of laws, 4th edn. OUP, Oxford

Bröhmer J (2015) State immunity and sovereign bonds. In: Peters A et al (eds) Immunities in the age of global constitutionalism. Brill, Leiden, pp 182–208

Buckley RP (2009) The bankruptcy of nations: an idea whose time has come. Int Lawyer 43:1189

Cane P (1986) An introduction to administrative law. Clarendon Press, Oxford

Cane P (2003) Accountability and the public/private distinction. In: Bamforth N, Leyland P (eds) Public law in a multi-layered constitution. Hart, Oxford, pp 247–276

Collini S (1979) Liberalism and sociology. CUP, Cambridge

Craig P (1990) Public law and democracy. OUP, Oxford

Damian H (1985) Staatenimmunität und Gerichtszwang. Springer, Berlin

Damrosch LF (2019) The sources of immunity law - between international and domestic law. In: Ruys T, Angelet N (eds) The Cambridge handbook of immunities and international law. CUP, Cambridge, pp 40–60

Delaume GR (1989) Sovereign immunity and public debt. Int Lawyer 23:811

Dicey AV (2013) In: Allison J (ed) Introductory to the study of the law of the constitution. OUP, Oxford

Dickinson A, Lindsay R, Loonam JP (2004) State immunity. OUP, Oxford

Dyson KHF (1980) The state tradition in Western Europe. OUP, Oxford

Finke J (2010) Sovereign immunity: rule, comity or something else? Eur J Int Law 21:853

Fox H (2019) The restrictive rule of state immunity – the 1970s enactment and its contemporary status. In: Ruys T, Angelet N (eds) The Cambridge handbook of immunities and international law. CUP, Cambridge, pp 21–39

Fox H, Webb P (2015) The law of state immunity, 3rd edn. OUP, Oxford

Francioni F (2009) Access to justice, denial of justice and international investment law. Eur J Int Law 20:742

Freedland M (2006) The evolving approach to the public/private distinction in English law. In: Freedland M, Auby JB (eds) The public law/private law divide: Une entente assez cordiale? Hart, Oxford, pp 93–112

Geimer R (2017) Vertragsbruch durch Hoheitsakt: 'Once a trader, not always a trader?' – Immunitätsrechtlicher Manövrierspielraum für Schuldnerstaaten? Praxis des Internationalen Privat– und Verfahrensrechts 344
Gelpern A (2013) A skeptic's case for sovereign bankruptcy. Houst Law Rev 50:1095
Hagan S (2005) Designing a legal framework to restructure sovereign debt. Georgetown J Int Law 36:299
Hauser P (2019) Es kann nicht sein, was nicht sein darf? Anlegerklagen gegen Griechenland keine Zivil– und Handelssache? Zeitschrift für Bank– und Kapitalmarktrecht 333
Herdegen M (2018) Völkerrecht, 17th edn. Beck, Munich
Hess B (2018a) Abgrenzung der acta jure gestionis und acta jure imperii: Der BGH verfehlt die völkerrechtliche Dimension der Staatenimmunität. Praxis des Internationalen Privat– und Verfahrensrechts 351
Hess B (2018b) The private–public divide in international dispute resolution. Recueil des cours 388:49
Horwitz MJ (1982) History of the public/private distinction. Univ Pa Law Rev 130:1423
Idot L (2019) Matière civile et commerciale. Europe 50
Kehrberger RF (2019) Zivilprozessrecht: Anwendungsbereich der EuGVVO bei staatlich angeordnetem Schuldenschnitt – Anmerkung. Europäische Zeitschrift für Wirtschaftsrecht 88
Kerber MC (2019) Sargnägel auf dem Anlegerschutz? – Anmerkungen zur Legalisierung der Zwangsumschuldung der Gläubiger griechischer Staatsanleihen durch die Urteile des EGMR vom 21.7.2016 und des EuGH vom 15.11.2018. Wertpapier–Mitteilungen 1333
Kleiner C (2019) Compétence judiciaire. Journal du droit international 854
Kokott J (2011) States, sovereign equality. In: Wolfrum R (ed) Max Planck encyclopedia of public international law. OUP, Oxford
Krueger AO (2012) Struggling with success: challenges facing the international economy. World Scientific, Singapore
Kupelyants H (2018) Sovereign defaults before domestic courts. OUP, Oxford
Lehmann M, Ungerer J (2017/2018) Applying or taking account of foreign overriding mandatory provisions – Sophism under the Rome I Regulation. Yearb Priv Int Law 19:53
Lew A (1994) Republic of Argentina v. Weltover, Inc.: interpreting the Foreign Sovereign Immunity Act's commercial activity exception to jurisdictional immunity. Fordham Int Law J 17:726
Lewis CJ (1990) State and diplomatic immunity, 3rd edn. Lloyd's, London
Lord Bingham of Cornhill (2002) Dicey revisited. Public Law 39
Lord Collins of Mapesbury et al (2018) Dicey, Morris & Collins on the conflict of laws, 15th edn. Sweet & Maxwell, London
Lorz S (2017) Ausländische Staaten vor deutschen Zivilgerichten. Mohr Siebeck, Tuebingen
Loughlin M (1992) Public law and political theory. Clarendon Press, Oxford
Mankowski P (2015) Art 1 Brüssel Ia–VO. In: Rauscher T (ed) Europäisches Zivilprozess– und Kollisionsrecht, 4th edn. Otto Schmidt, Cologne
Mankowski P (2018a) Grundsatz der Staatenimmunität, wenn die Klage auf Rückzahlungsansprüche aus Staatsanleihen gestützt ist – Anmerkung. Wertpapier–Mitteilungen – Entscheidungsanmerkungen zum Wirtschafts– und Bankrecht 185
Mankowski P (2018b) Zur internationalen Zuständigkeit für Klage einer natürlichen Person gegen Griechenland auf Erfüllung griechischer Staatsanleihen bzw. Schadensersatz ('Kuhn'). Entscheidung zum Wirschaftsrecht 477
Mankowski P (2019) Griechische Staatsanleihen und der griechische Schuldenschnitt vor dem EuGH (Folge Zwei). Zeitschrift für Wirtschaftsrecht 193
Mann FA (1979) The State Immunity Act 1978. Br Yearb Int Law 50:43
Mehren AT (2006) Adjudicatory authority in private international law. Brill, Leiden
Mola L (2012) Sovereign immunity, insolvent states and private bondholders: recent national and international case law. Law Pract Int Courts Tribunals 11:525

Muir Watt H, Pataut E (2008) Les actes jure imperii et le Règlement Bruxelles 1 – A propos de l'affaire Lechouritou. Revue critique de droit international privé 97:61
Müller MJ (2016) Internationales Wirtschaftsrecht – RIW–Kommentar. Recht der internationalen Wirtschaft 80
Müller MJ (2018) Unvereinbarkeit einer Klage wegen Vertragsansprüchen mit Staatenimmunität – Anmerkung. Neue Juristische Wochenschrift 857
Nourissat C (2019) Inapplicabilité du règlement 'Bruxelles I bis' à un recours exercé par un particulier contre un État ayant émis des obligations. Procédures 13
Okeke EC (2018) Jurisdictional immunities of states and international organizations. OUP, Oxford
Oosterlinck K (2013) Sovereign debt defaults: insights from history. Oxf Rev Econ Policy 29:697
Orakhelashvili A (2019) Jurisdictional immunity of states and general international law – explaining the Jus Gestionis v. Jus Imperii Divide. In: Ruys T, Angelet N (eds) The Cambridge handbook of immunities and international law. CUP, Cambridge, pp 105–124
Panizza U, Sturzenegger F, Zettelmeyer J (2009) Sovereign debt and default. J Econ Lit 47:651
Pavoni R (2009) A decade of Italian case law on the immunity of foreign states: lights and shadows. Ital Yearb Int Law 19:73
Politis NE (1984) Les Emprunts d'Etat en Droit International. Durand and Pedone–Lauriel, Paris
Reinhart CM, Rogoff KS (2009) This times is different: eight centuries of financial Folly. Princeton University Press, Princeton
Roos JE (2019) Why not default? The political economy of sovereign debt. Princeton University Press, Princeton
Ryan M (2014) Sovereign bankruptcy: why now and why not in the IMF. Fordham Law Rev 82:2473
Sander GG, Garašić J, Bodiroga-Vukobrat N (eds) (2021) Sovereign insolvency – possible legal solutions. Springer (forthcoming)
Schack H (2017) Internationales Zivilverfahrensrecht, 7th edn. Beck, Munich
Schumacher J, Trebesch C, Enderlein H (2018) Sovereign defaults in court. ECB Working Paper No 2135
Schwarcz SL (2015) Sovereign debt restructuring: a model–law approach. J Glob Dev 6:343
Seidl-Hohenveldern I (1979) Neue Entwicklungen im Recht der Staatenimmunität. In: Sandrock O (ed) Festschrift für Günther Beitzke. De Gruyter, Berlin, p 1081
Shan W, Wang P (2019) Divergent views on state immunity in the international community. In: Ruys T, Angelet N (eds) The Cambridge handbook of immunities and international law. CUP, Cambridge, p 61
Shaw MN (2017) International law, 8th edn. CUP, Cambridge
Stoll PT (2012) State immunity. In: Wolfrum R (ed) Max Planck encyclopedia of public international law. OUP, Oxford
Stürner M (2008) Staatenimmunität und Brüssel I–Verordnung. Praxis des Internationalen Privat– und Verfahrensrechts 197
Sucharitkul S (1982) Fourth report on jurisdictional immunities of states and their property. Yearb Int Law Commission (2):199
Thole C (2012) Klagen geschädigter Privatanleger gegen Griechenland vor deutschen Gerichten?. Wertpapier–Mitteilungen 1793
Tomuschat C (1999) International law: ensuring the survival of mankind on the eve of a new century, general course on public international law. Recueil des cours 281:9
Torremans P et al (2017) Cheshire, North & Fawcett: private international law, 15th edn. OUP, Oxford
Van Alebeek R, Pavoni R (2018) Immunities of states and their officials. In: Nollkaemper A et al (eds) International law in domestic courts: a casebook. OUP, Oxford, pp 100–169
Van den Berge L (2018) Rethinking the public-private law divide in the age of governmentality and network governance. Eur J Comp Law Gov 5:119

Vogl T (2019) Zur internationalen Zuständigkeit für Klage einer natürlichen Person gegen Griechenland auf Erfüllung griechischer Staatsanleihen bzw. Schadensersatz ('Kuhn'). Entscheidung zum Wirschaftsrecht 95

Wagner R (2014) Staatenimmunität und internationale Zuständigkeit nach der EuGVVO. Recht der internationalen Wirtschaft 260

Waibel M (2011) Sovereign defaults before International Courts and Tribunals. CUP, Cambridge

Webb P (2018) International law and restraints on the exercise of jurisdiction by national courts of states. In: Evans M (ed) International law, 5th edn. OUP, Oxford, pp 316–348

Weidemaier WMC (2014) Sovereign immunity and sovereign debt. Univ Ill Law Rev 67

Weller M, Fischer A (2016) Staatenimmunität bei Umschuldung griechischer Staatsanleihen – Anmerkung. Zeitschrift für Internationales Wirtschaftsrecht 172

Weller M, Walter S (2019) Kurzer Prozess – Neues zur Zulässigkeit von Anlegerklagen gegen den griechischen Schuldenschnitt. Zeitschrift für Bank- und Kapitalmarktrecht 123

Wittich S (2013) Proceedings in which state immunity cannot be invoked, Article 10. In: O'Keefe R, Tams CJ (eds) The United Nations Convention on jurisdictional immunities of states and their property: a commentary. OUP, Oxford, pp 167–182

Yang X (2012) State immunity in international law. CUP, Cambridge

Johannes Ungerer is the Erich Brost Lecturer in German law and European Union law at the Faculty of Law and St Hilda's College, University of Oxford. His research focuses on private international and comparative law.

Foreign Central Banks and Immunity from Execution: Too Sovereign to Be Attached?

Pierluigi Salvati

Abstract Foreign central banks traditionally enjoy a broad immunity from enforcement measures within the wider framework of immunity from execution granted to foreign States. Nevertheless, divergent approaches to sovereign immunity by some national legislation and courts have somehow limited the scope of this rule, in particular with reference to claims promoted by victims of serious international crimes (e.g. terrorism, gross violations of human rights, etc.). Said developments may raise implications also in the matter of execution against foreign central banks, influencing the emergence of new international rules. Emblematic is the case of the Central Bank of Iran which has been the subject of a number of enforcement proceedings promoted against its parent State for its role in supporting international terrorism.

1 Introduction

The question of immunity from execution of Foreign Central Banks (FCBs) is a burning issue as these institutions are increasingly subject to enforcement measures by judgment creditors although international law grants them a general immunity within the broader context of immunity from execution granted to foreign States.

On this last aspect, if the customary rule on jurisdictional immunity, as a widespread practice shows, shifted from absolute to restricted—States enjoying immunity from adjudication limited to acts performed in the exercise of public functions (*acta jure imperii*) but not extended to acts carried out under private law (*acta jure gestionis*)—the extent of immunity from execution remained for a long time broader and almost absolute. Only gradually the principle of the restricted immunity of States and their assets has established itself also in the field of enforcement, and measures of constraint have been considered admissible insofar

P. Salvati (✉)
Link Campus University, Rome, Italy
e-mail: p.salvati@unilink.it

R. Bismuth et al. (eds.), *Sovereign Immunity Under Pressure*,
https://doi.org/10.1007/978-3-030-87706-4_16

as carried out on State property not intended or destined for sovereign and public functions.

Nevertheless, if the very scope of sovereign immunity from execution remains a widely debated topic,[1] its reference to the assets of FCBs poses even further problems given their particular and diversified characteristics: *e.g.* they may enjoy a greater or lesser degree of independence from the States which have set them up (so-called 'parent State') or, although statutorily carrying out sovereign activities (supervisory policies, money supply, price stability control, etc.) they may also perform activities of private law; furthermore, they may manage assets destined for governmental purposes but also for commercial activities, or even 'mixed' accounts.

All these circumstances as well as the fact that domestic laws protecting FCBs' property from execution are very diversified among national legislation makes it difficult to identify the extent of the rules governing their immunities under customary international law, although the United Nations Convention on Jurisdictional Immunities of States and Their Property ('UNCSI')[2]—aimed at codifying general international law on the matter and not yet in force[3]—expressly grants foreign central banks an *ad hoc* general and almost absolute immunity from measures of constraint (Art. 21(1)(c)).

Some scholars, including most recently Wuerth,[4] have analyzed the different domestic provisions on the immunity of FCBs from execution, also to identify a common trait: starting from these very premises, the present contribution will first examine the most recent national legislation following the adoption of the UNCSI to verify whether a common practice (or at least a trend) among States on the matter exists. Moreover, it will try to assess if and to what extent such legislation has been influenced by the rules on immunity from execution provided for in the UNCSI and whether the latter do reflect general international law.

Then, some divergent approaches to sovereign immunity of domestic laws and courts, in particular in the US and Italy, will be considered insofar as they have somehow limited the scope of the rule with reference to claims for compensation promoted by victims of serious international crimes (*e.g.* gross violations of human

[1] See e.g. Montero and Castro (2019), Wiesinger (2016), Sportes and Simon (2016), Giuffrida (2015), Fox and Webb (2013), Stoll (2012), and Yang (2012).

[2] The UNCSI has been adopted during the 65th plenary meeting of the UN General Assembly by resolution A/59/38 of 2 December 2004 and open for signature from 17 January 2005.

[3] In accordance with Article 30 of the UNCSI, the Convention 'shall enter into force on the thirtieth day following the date of deposit of the thirtieth instrument of ratification, acceptance, approval or accession with the Secretary-General of the United Nations....'. To date, 28 States have signed the Convention and 22 States have ratified it (Austria, Czech Republic, Finland, France, Japan, Equatorial Guinea, Kazakhstan, Iran, Iraq, Italy, Latvia, Lebanon, Liechtenstein, Mexico, Norway, Portugal, Romania, Saudi Arabia, Slovakia, Spain, Switzerland and Sweden).

[4] See Wuerth (2019): the first part of this paper will methodologically follow a reconstructive path and an examination of the State practice similar to the one followed by the Author though focusing on national legislation enacted following the adoption of the UNCSI in order to highlight its possible reflections on them.

rights, terrorism, etc.) and may result in the development of new international rules also in the field of enforcement—and therefore also of immunity of the assets of foreign central banks. Emblematic is the case of the Central Bank of Iran (Bank Markazi) which has been the subject of *ad hoc* rules in the US which have unhinged its protection from execution as well as different decisions by some domestic courts, which might contribute to undermining the principle of immunity granted to FCBs.

2 Immunity from Execution of Foreign Central Banks in the Framework of General International Law on State Immunity

Domestic legislation on immunities of FCBs' assets from enforcement proceedings varies significantly from one State to another.[5]

Apart from those countries which do not have legislation on sovereign immunity at all (thus relying on the principles of general international law on the matter),[6] some States do not provide for a special legislation protecting FCBs insofar as they are considered as a part of the foreign State which has set them up and therefore subjected to the ordinary rules regulating State immunity,[7] whereas other States provide for an additional and *ad hoc* protection for FCBs' assets, such protection ranging from 'reinforced' to near absolute.[8]

[5] See Gaukrodger (2010), p. 24. Although for a long time, foreign central banks have not enjoyed a special immunity as they were not considered linked to their parent State, but separate and independent entities thus not entitled to claim sovereign immunity (see e.g. Trendtex Trading Corporation v. Central Bank of Nigeria, United Kingdom, Court of Appeal, Civil Division, 13 January 1977, 64 ILR 111, 134-1), over time State legislations have granted them a certain degree of immunity from measures of constraint, providing them with a privileged status, although in a very diversified manner.

[6] E.g. Italy does not have a specific legislation on sovereign immunity. Only by Art. 1 of the decree-law 28 April 2010, no. 6, Italy suspended the effectiveness of the enforceable titles on assets of foreign States or international organizations, if their immunity from Italian jurisdiction was controversial and the issue gave rise to a claim before the ICJ in the Jurisdictional Immunities case on the compensation due to individuals who were victims of war crimes by German occupation troops during World War II.

[7] See e.g. Art. 35(1), Australia Foreign States Immunities Act.

[8] See e.g. Section 14(4) of the UK Sovereign Immunity Act (SIA). In AIC v. Central Bank of Nigeria, [2003] EWHC 1357 (2003), the British High Court ruled that 'moneys in a bank account of a central bank with another bank are immune from execution irrespective of the source of the funds in the account or the use of the account or the purpose for which the account is maintained'. However, before the entry into force of the SIA, the UK courts did not treat foreign central bank accounts differently from ordinary bank accounts; see e.g. Trendtex Trading Corporation v. Central Bank of Nigeria, United Kingdom, Court of Appeal, Civil Division, 13 January 1977, 64 ILR 111; see also Hispano Americana Mercantil S.A. v. Central Bank of Nigeria, United Kingdom, Court of Appeal, Civil Division, 25 April 1979, 64 ILR 221. On absolute immunity of FCBs, see also Singapore Act no. 19 of 1979 (State Immunity Act), Chapter 313, Article 16(4).

The verification of the minimum extent of the protection recognized by general international law to FCBs' assets should be first reconnected to the broader principle on immunity from measures of constraint accorded to the property of foreign States.

Immunity from enforcement has to be regarded as an autonomous rule compared to the one on immunity from adjudication: as pointed out by the International Court of Justice (ICJ) in the case of *Jurisdictional Immunities of the State (Germany v. Italy, Greece intervening)* of 2012,[9] 'the immunity from enforcement enjoyed by States in regard to their property situated in foreign territory goes further than the jurisdictional immunity enjoyed by those same States before foreign courts'.[10] Although connected, the two immunities do not have a coinciding scope and can work separately[11] since to immunity from enforcement measures must be recognized a different (and even wider) sphere of application and has been long considered absolute as the 'last bastion of immunity'.[12]

The process to affirm a restricted scope of immunity also in the field of enforcement has been slower: the practice of States has gradually (and not universally) led to identify a distinction between assets destined for acts performed in the exercise of sovereign powers and assets destined for acts of a commercial nature. Many States have, in fact, guaranteed immunity to the property of foreign States destined to grant governmental activities, while ensuring execution against those intended for activities of an exclusively private legal nature.

This general approach has been clearly defined by the ICJ in the mentioned case of *Jurisdictional Immunities* where the Court stated that under a well-established practice,[13] 'at least one condition ... has to be satisfied before any measure of constraint may be taken against property belonging to a foreign State: that the property in question must be in use for an activity not pursuing government non-commercial purposes, or that the State which owns the property has expressly

---

[9] ICJ, Jurisdictional Immunities of the State (Germany v. Italy: Greece intervening), judgment, ICJ Reports 2012.

[10] ICJ, Jurisdictional Immunities of the State (Germany v. Italy: Greece intervening), judgment, ICJ Reports 2012, para. 113.

[11] According to the ICJ, 'Even if a judgment has been lawfully rendered against a foreign State, in circumstances such that the latter could not claim immunity from jurisdiction, it does not follow ipso facto that the State against which judgment has been given can be the subject of measures of constraint on the territory of the forum State or on that of a third State, with a view to enforcing the judgment in question'; ICJ, Jurisdictional Immunities of the State (Germany v. Italy: Greece intervening), judgment, ICJ Reports 2012, para. 113.

[12] Ostrander (2004), p. 541; see also Wood (2013), p. 15.

[13] The ICJ cites at para. 118 the decision of the German Constitutional Court (Bundesverfassungsgericht) of 14 December 1977 (BVerfGE, Vol. 46, p. 342; ILR, Vol. 65, p. 146), the judgment of the Swiss Federal Tribunal of 30 April 1986 in Kingdom of Spain v. Société X (Annuaire suisse de droit international, Vol. 43, 1987, p. 158; ILR, Vol. 82, p. 44), as well as the judgment of the House of Lords of 12 April 1984 in Alcom Ltd. v. Republic of Colombia ([1984] 1 AC 580; ILR, Vol. 74, p. 170) and the judgment of the Spanish Constitutional Court of 1 July 1992 in Abbott v. Republic of South Africa (Revista española de derecho internacional, Vol. 44, 1992, p. 565; ILR, Vol. 113, p. 414).

consented to the taking of a measure of constraint, or that that State has allocated the property in question for the satisfaction of a judicial claim'.[14]

This principle has been crystallized by the UNCSI as well: in particular, such Convention—largely enshrining the restrictive doctrine of immunity[15]—in confirming the different regulation between immunity from adjudication (regulated in Part II and III) and immunity from execution (regulated in Part IV), distinguishes therein the hypothesis of State immunity from pre-judgment measures of constraint (regulated under Article 18) and State immunity from post-judgment measures of constraint (regulated under Article 19).

Under Article 18, pre-judgment measures of constraint against the property of a foreign State are allowed only if 'the State has expressly consented to the taking of such measures … or the State has allocated or earmarked property for the satisfaction of the claim which is the object of that proceeding', while only post-judgment measures are also allowed, under Article 19, if ' … it has been established that the property is specifically in use or intended for use by the State for other than government non-commercial purposes and is in the territory of the State of the forum, provided that post-judgment measures of constraint may only be taken against property that has a connection with the entity against which the proceeding was directed'.

Therefore, if pre-judgment measures of constraint are always banned except with express consent by the State concerned, post-judgment measures are allowed based on the destination of the assets to be attached, Article 19 considering immune from execution the property intended for the exercise of sovereign functions but not also the one which is specifically in use or intended for use for other than government non-commercial purposes, *i.e.* destined for commercial and private activities.[16]

However, apart from the general regulation of the measures of constraint, the UNCSI also contains an *ad hoc* provision relating to the 'property of the central bank or other monetary authority of the State': under Article 21(1)(c) such property has been included among the special categories of assets that are not considered as property specifically in use or intended for use by the State for other than government non-commercial purposes under Article 19, and thus are immune from executive jurisdiction.

The Convention, therefore, provides for an absolute (and non-rebuttable) presumption that such property is, by its very nature, used or intended for use for

---

[14] ICJ, Jurisdictional Immunities of the State (Germany v. Italy: Greece intervening), judgment, ICJ Reports 2012, para. 118.

[15] UNCSI, Preamble and Article 5; under the New York Convention, a State is required to refrain from exercising jurisdiction against another State by ensuring that its courts automatically ascertain the immunity granted to a foreign State except in cases expressly provided for by the Convention; see Article 6.

[16] Moreover, said property must be located in the territory of the State of the forum and must have a 'connection' with the entity against which the proceeding was directed; see UNCSI, Article 19(c).

sovereign purposes[17] and thus should be immune from pre- and post-judgment measures of constraint, except the cases of express consent by the same FCB (or its parent State) or if the allocation is for the satisfaction of a claim which is the object of a proceeding.[18] Moreover, it should be noted that, given the extent of such provision, even in the case of property with multiple destinations (e.g. mixed accounts), such imperative presumption should be extended to the entire asset, without it being possible to attach the part of the assets allegedly destined for commercial purposes.[19]

3 Strengthening FCBs' Protection

3.1 Between a 'Reinforced' . . .

Following the adoption of the UNCSI, many States—some of which had sovereign immunity traditionally governed by case law—started to enact statutes on the matter[20] which reflect most of the general principles on immunity from execution codified therein.

On the one hand, some States have generally extended to FCBs' assets the general principles enshrined by Articles 18 and 19 of the UNCSI in relation to the immunity of assets of foreign sovereigns which are excluded, except with their express consent, from pre-judgment measures of constraint and subjected to the regime of restricted immunity in relation to post-judgment measures of constraint insofar as they are exclusively used for non-governmental purposes: therefore, under these statutes, the property of an FCB is treated like other State-owned property, *i.e.* not entitled to special protection if not used or not intended for sovereign purposes.[21]

---

[17] Wautelet, Immunity of Foreign Central Banks Assets in Belgium. 2 September 2008. conflictoflaws.net. Accessed 15 April 2021.

[18] See Articles 18 and 19, subparagraphs (a) and (b) of the UNCSI recalled by Article 21(2). It is interesting to note that the ILC's Special Rapporteur on Jurisdictional Immunities of States and Their Property (1991) suggested the addition of the words 'and use for monetary purpose' at the end of paragraph dedicated to the immunity of the assets of FCBs but said clarification was not included for lack of general support; see Yearbook of the International Law Commission, 1990, vol. II, para. 227; see also Draft Articles on Jurisdictional Immunities of States and Their Property, with commentaries, text adopted by the International Law Commission at its forty-third session, in 1991, and submitted to the General Assembly as a part of the Commission's report covering the work of that session (A/46/10, at para. 28), 59.

[19] See Giuffrida (2015), p. 284, n 57.

[20] As already noted, a broad overview is provided by Wuerth (2019).

[21] E.g. under the Israeli Foreign Sovereign Immunity Law 5769-2008, FCBs are substantially considered equivalent to foreign States and their assets are immune to the extent they are not commercial assets, or property situated in Israel to which the foreign State is entitled by the way of succession or as bona vacantia, or immovables situated in Israel; see Foreign Sovereign Immunity Law 5769-2008, Articles 1, 16 and 18.

On the other hand, most States have instead modified their domestic legislation and have provided for an *ad hoc* regulation for FCBs' assets, although with different nuances. In particular, some of them have granted foreign central banks a 'reinforced' immunity through a presumption *iuris tantum* (*i.e.* a rebuttable presumption) of destination of their assets for governmental purpose, or by listing their assets among those not eligible for execution insofar as intended for use or used by the foreign State in activities related to the exercise of sovereign authority; in both the cases, the provisions allow for actions against those assets if held and used exclusively for commercial purposes, whose burden of proof lies with the creditor.

Even before signing the UNCSI,[22] in 2005 France had inserted in its Monetary and Financial Code (MFC)[23] an *ad hoc* provision (Article L. 153-1) providing that assets of whatever kind which foreign central banks hold or manage for their own account or on behalf of the State or foreign State(s) that govern them cannot be attached. As an exception, the French statute[24] allows a creditor holding a writ of execution establishing a certain and payable debt to request the judge to authorise enforcement if he/she can establish that the assets held or managed by an FCB form part of resources allocated to a primary activity governed by private law.[25]

By this rule, France has granted FCBs immunity of their property through a presumption *iuris tantum* of sovereign destination, making it rebuttable by allowing creditors to prove that the assets subject of execution are destined for commercial purposes.[26]

This protection, although not absolute, is clearly inspired by the principles enshrined in the UNCSI, as pointed out by the French Cour de Cassation observing that the rules under Art. 153-1 MFC 's'inscrivent dans les principes posés en matière d'immunité d'exécution par le droit international coutumier, tel que reflété par la Convention des Nations Unies du 2 décembre 2004'.[27] The same Court stated that the exception referred to in Article L. 153-1 para. 2 MFC actually establishes a more favorable regime than customary international law so that if the judge—in accordance with the principle of the hierarchy of norms—were to make international law

[22] France signed the UNCSI on 17 January 2007 and ratified it on 12 August 2011.

[23] See Act no. 2005-842 of 26 July 2005.

[24] Act no. 2005-842 of 26 July 2005, Article L. 153-1 para. 2.

[25] French legislation on the matter has been also carefully analyzed by Wuerth (2019), p. 12ff.

[26] The French legislator enshrined and developed the principles already expressed by the Cour de Cassation in the case Sonatrach, where the Court found that the assets of public entities, distinct from the foreign State, whether or not enjoying legal personality, which are part of a group of assets ('patrimoine') which been dedicated to activities in the private law sector, may be seized by all creditors of the public entity: see French Court of Cassation, Société Sonatrach v. Migeon, 1 October 1985, 77 ILR 525: 'Les biens des organismes publics, personnalises ou non, distincts de l'Etat étranger, lorsqu'ils font partie d'un patrimoine que celui-ci a affecte a une activité principale relevant du droit prive, peuvent être saisis par tous les créanciers, quels qu'ils soient, de cet organisme'; see also Cour de Cassation, Creighton Ltd v. Minister of Finance of Qatar and Others, 6 July 2000, 127 ILR 154, 155.

[27] Cour de Cassation, judgment of 11 January 2018 no.16-10.661.

prevail over French law should therefore exclude any seizure of the property of foreign central banks, without even questioning their destination and/or obtaining prior authorization from the executive judge.[28]

After all, even before its entry into force, the echoes of the UNCSI have long influenced the judgments of the Cour de Cassation which made regular references to the Convention.[29] On the ground of the principles enshrined therein, France has specifically regulated the matter of immunity from execution in the context of the fight against corruption ('Loi Sapin II')[30] where it provided for a judicial prior authorization in case of provisional or enforcement measures on property owned by a foreign State[31]—although this specific requirement is not provided by the UNCSI. The statute specifies that said measures can be only authorized if the State concerned has expressly consented or it has reserved or assigned this property to the satisfaction of the request object of the procedure, or where a judgment or arbitration has been issued against the State concerned and the property in question is specifically used or intended to be used by the State other than for non-commercial public service purposes and has a connection with the entity against which the proceedings were initiated.[32]

These provisions are an almost exact reproduction of Article 19 of the UNCSI. But it is interesting to note that, even providing a list of assets '*notamment considérés comme spécifiquement utilisés ou destinés à être utilisés par l'Etat à des fins de service public non commerciales*'[33]—and thus presumptively excluded from the enforcement measures *in modum* of Article 21 of the UNCSI—French law does not list therein the property of FCBs, which remains regulated by the presumption *iuris tantum* referred to in the MFC. France has, therefore, enshrined the principles and the legislative technique as well used by UNCSI in Articles 19 and 21, with the relevant exception of the assets of the FCBs whose regulation has been referred to an *ad hoc* rule providing for a rebuttable presumption of immunity of their assets.

Belgium has also adopted specific legislation aimed at granting immunity from enforcement to the assets of foreign central banks[34] providing that assets of any kind, including foreign exchange reserves, which FCBs hold in Belgium for their own account or on behalf of third parties cannot be seized, unless the creditor with an enforceable title demonstrates that they are used exclusively for private economic or commercial activities.[35] Also in this case, although FCBs do not enjoy immunity

---

[28] Ibid.

[29] E.g. see Cour de Cassation, judgment of 13 May 2015; see amplius Sportes and Simon (2016).

[30] Law no. 1691 of 10 December 2016.

[31] French Code of civil enforcement procedures, Article 111-1-1.

[32] French Code of civil enforcement procedures, Article 111-1-2.

[33] French Code of civil enforcement procedures, Article 111-1-2 (3), para. 2.

[34] Loi 2008-07-24/42 modifiant le Code judiciaire en vue d'instituer une immunité d'exécution à l'égard des avoirs de banques centrales étrangères et d'autorités monétaires internationales.

[35] See Article 1412 quater of the Judicial Code.

from jurisdiction, the Belgian statute provides for a broad and general immunity from execution. It is interesting to note that under the Commentary to the statute, the law had neither the purpose nor the consequence of modifying or reinforcing the rules on immunity but simply to crystallize the existing juridical situation,[36] endorsing the rebuttable presumption that assets held by a foreign central bank must, in general, be considered as instrumental with respect to governmental activities. Nevertheless, the statute provides as the only exception the demonstration by judgment creditors that said assets are exclusively used for economic and commercial purposes.[37] This condition, together with the necessary authorization by the judge of the seizures, entail that property which '*présentant indéniablement une affectation de droit public*'[38] cannot be subjected to seizures.

Other States like Spain and Russia have differently strengthened the immunity granted to FCBs: even using in national law the 'list technique' of assets to be presumed as immune under the scheme of Article 21 of the UNCSI, they have affirmed their immunity 'to the extent that' they are intended for use or used by it in its own account in activities related to the exercise of sovereign authority. Thus, the effect is similar to a presumption *iuris tantum* of immunity as the burden of proof of their commercial nature lies with the judgment creditors to rebut their sovereign destination.

In particular, Article 9 of the Spanish Law no. 6/2015 of 27 October 2015 on privileges and immunities of foreign States provides for a general exception to immunity from the jurisdiction of the foreign State in case of proceedings relating to business transactions. Article 17 reaffirms the principles enshrined in the UNCSI under which the Spanish courts refrain from measures of execution or other coercive measures against foreign State property, both before and after the Court ruling, unless that State has consented. Only when a judgment is issued, Spanish courts may adopt coercive measures if it has been determined that said foreign assets are used or are intended to be used by the foreign State for purposes other than non-commercial, provided that they are in Spanish territory and have a link to the State against which the proceedings have been initiated, as well as are intended for an activity other than that which gave rise to the litigation. Under Article 20.1(c) among the assets 'in any case' used or intended to be used for non-commercial purposes are included the ones of the FCB or other monetary authority of the State 'which are intended for the purposes of these institutions'[39] which cannot be subject to measures of execution, unless the foreign State has given its consent.

---

[36] Commentaire des Articles of the Proposition de Loi modifiant le Code judiciaire en vue d'instituer une immunité d'exécutionà l'égard des avoirs de banques centrales étrangères et d'autorités monétaires internationals, déposée par Mmes Annemie Roppe et Anne-Marie Baeke et M. Luk Van Biesen, Commentary to Art. 2, 8 February 2007, p. 3.

[37] See Wautelet (2008).

[38] Commentaire des Articles of the Proposition de Loi modifiant le Code judiciaire, p. 5.

[39] Ley Orgánica 16/2015 of 27 October 2015, Article 20.1(c). Spanish case law tends to reject immunity from execution in cases where the foreign central banks exclusively act jure gestionis: e.g. in a judgment rendered before the enactment of Law no. 6/2015, the Audiencia Provincial of

Russia enacted the Federal Law 'on Jurisdictional Immunities of a Foreign State and the Property of a Foreign State in the Russian Federation' in 2015,[40] largely based on the UNCSI.[41] By said statute, Moscow modified its approach to the question of immunity, traditionally oriented towards the absolute immunity doctrine.[42] If the new statute embraces the principle of restrictive immunity, the exercise of jurisdiction does not affect immunity from pre- or post-judgment measures of constraint. In particular, the Russian law lists under Article 16 several types of property which are deemed to be used for the exercise of sovereign powers and therefore enjoy immunity from enforcement, among which, under Article 16(1)(5), property of FCBs or another supervisory body of a foreign State that is responsible for bank supervision. Furthermore, the Russian statute provides for a 'condition of reciprocity', *i.e.* Russian courts are allowed to consider limits of jurisdictional immunity of a foreign State to be determined in relation to the degree of immunity the Russian Federation enjoys in that foreign State.

3.2 ... and an Almost Absolute Immunity from Execution

Other States have instead embraced the principle of almost absolute immunity of FCBs' assets as enshrined under Article 21(1)(c) of the UNCSI, subtracting their assets from any enforcement proceeding without their parent State's (explicit or implicit) consent, although sometimes providing exceptions.

After signing the Convention,[43] Japan passed Act no. 24 of April 24, 2009 'on the civil jurisdiction of Japan with respect to a foreign State' where, after enshrining the general principle of immunity of a foreign State from jurisdiction,[44] it regulated the cases of non-immunity from proceedings of execution of temporary restraining orders and civil execution procedures against the property of foreign States. In the

---

Madrid rejected the request for recognition of immunity from execution filed by the National Bank of Cuba in a proceeding promoted by a German company with respect to a recognition of debt granted from the bank to the plaintiff considering that the FCB had acted as a private and therefore could not claim any kind of immunity; see Hachemie, Hamburger Chemikalien Gesellschaft mit Beschränker Haftung v. Banco Nacional de Cuba, Aranzadi Insignis (AP Madrid, April 10, 2000) [AC\2000\2362], cited in Montero and Castro (2019), p. 385.

[40] Federal Law no. 297-FZ of 3 November 2015 on the Jurisdictional Immunity of a Foreign State and the Property of a Foreign State in the Russian Federation.

[41] Explanatory Note to Bill on Jurisdictional Immunity of a Foreign State and a Foreign State's Property in the Russian Federation.

[42] Ibid.

[43] Japan signed the UNCSI on 11 January 2007 and accepted it on 11 May 2010.

[44] Act no. 24 of April 24, 2009 on the Civil Jurisdiction of Japan with respect to a Foreign State, Article 4. In Japan, the Supreme Court since Tokyo Sanyo Trading Co Ltd v Islamic Republic of Pakistan (60-6 Minshu 2542, 1231/2003; Supreme Court, July 21, 2006) adopted restrictive immunity, affirming that a foreign State is not immune from the jurisdiction of the Japanese courts in respect of activities involving private law or business management, except that in particular cases.

new statute, Japan limited them to the express consent of the State concerned[45] and excluded immunity only with respect to property used by the foreign State only for other non-commercial purposes. Even providing for a list of assets allegedly excluded from the execution measures,[46] the statute does not include in said list the assets of the FCBs which are regulated by an *ad hoc* provision[47] where said banks are deemed to be a foreign State for the purposes of an execution of a temporary restraining order or a civil execution procedure.

Moreover, Japanese law specifies that the general principle whereby a foreign State is not immune from execution against the property exclusively held for other than government non-commercial purposes expressly does not apply concerning the assets of a foreign central bank,[48] which confirms the imperative presumption that the assets held by an FCB are deemed as exclusively destined for sovereign purposes and excluding the possibility of acting *in executivis* against them.

The People's Republic of China (PRC) has enacted an *ad hoc* legislation as well protecting foreign central banks' assets. If Beijing has traditionally adhered to the principle of absolute State immunity,[49] in 2005 it adopted the Law 'on Judicial Immunity from Compulsory Measures Concerning the Property of Foreign Central Banks' granting foreign central banks' property judicial immunity from the compulsory measures of property preservation and execution, except where the FCB (or its parent State) waives such immunity or said property is designated to be used for property preservation and execution:[50] also, in this case, the exceptions substantially reflect those provided under Articles 18 and 19 lett. (a) and (b) of the UNCSI as recalled by Article 21(2).[51] The statute is based on an imperative presumption that the assets, unless otherwise expressly indicated by the institution, are used for governmental purposes, thus subtracting them from execution. As noted by Zhu, 'Chinese Courts, including the courts in Hong Kong Special Administrative Region (SAR) and Macao SAR, should not take any judicial measures of constraint in the whole civil proceedings, in whatsoever expressions used, such as attachment, injunction, arrest, order or execution, and in whatsoever stages, whether the pre-judgment stage or the post-judgment stage'.[52] An important exception reads that where a foreign country does not grant immunity to the property of the PRC central bank or the immunity granted is more restricted than the one provided for in

---

[45] Act no. 24 of April 24, 2009 on the Civil Jurisdiction of Japan, Article 17.

[46] Ibid., Article 18.

[47] Ibid., Article 19.

[48] Ibid., Article 19 para. 2.

[49] See Wang (2015), p. 556: 'from China's perspective, the doctrine of restricted sovereign immunity has not yet become a rule of international law'.

[50] Law of the People's Republic of China on Judicial Immunity from Compulsory Measures Concerning the Property of Foreign Central Banks, adopted at the 18th Meeting of the Standing Committee of the Tenth National People's Congress of the People's Republic of China on October 25, 2005, Article 1.

[51] In 2005, China has signed but not ratified the UNCSI.

[52] Zhu (2007), p. 76.

the Chinese law, the PRC shall apply the principle of reciprocity.[53] Therefore, the almost absolute immunity granted to FCBs applies if the same immunity is recognized by the foreign State; if absolute immunity is not recognized by the foreign country, an equivalent 'degree' of immunity will be applied by the Chinese courts in turn.

Argentina has accepted the principle of almost absolute immunity as well by enacting legislation which appears to be patterned after the Chinese example.[54] Law no. 26.961 of 7 August 2014 establishes a general rule of immunity of FCBs or other foreign monetary authorities which are immune from the jurisdiction of Argentine courts[55] except (a) in case of express consent expressed in writing; (b) counterclaim based on the same legal relationship or on the same facts as the main claim; and (c) when the claim is about an activity outside *its own functions*[56] and the jurisdiction of the Argentine courts arises from the contract invoked or international law.

Immunity from execution is regulated under Article 2[57] which provides that a foreign central bank enjoys immunity in the Argentine Courts with respect to any coercive measure ('*respecto a cualquier medida coercitiva*' in the Spanish text) that could affect its assets, either as a preemptive or as a post-judgment measure. Therefore, as observed by Laborias, 'a wider and almost absolute immunity from execution is recognized for these foreign agencies',[58] except the express waiver by the same bank. A significant limit is provided by the reciprocity clause under Article 3: accordingly, Argentina grants FCBs the same 'degree' of immunity enjoyed by its central bank in the foreign State concerned, with the consequence that its national courts are allowed to adopt the same measures of execution against an FCB as those a foreign country can adopt against the Argentina central bank.

---

[53] Law of the People's Republic of China on Judicial Immunity, Article 3.

[54] On the desire by the Argentinian government to enact a statute similar to the Chinese law, see amplius Laborias (2016); Wuerth stresses as well that the Argentinian law was 'modeled' on the Chinese one; see Wuerth (2019), p. 7.

[55] Ley 26961 of 7 August 2014, Art. 1.

[56] Emphasis added; this exception therefore provides for a reference to activities carried out by the FCB outside the broader criterion of 'its own functions' and not to the nature of the activity (commercial or otherwise) carried out or the purpose of the assets held.

[57] Ley 26961, Article 2, para. 2.

[58] Laborias (2016).

4 Divergent Approaches on Sovereign Immunity and Possible Reflections on FCBs: The Case of *Bank Markazi*

Although State practice following the signing of the UNCSI shows a general—though diversified—the trend towards a strengthening of the immunity of FCBs' assets from execution, a divergent line may come from the conflicting approaches developed by some domestic laws and judicial decisions which have limited the extent of sovereign immunity with reference to claims for compensation promoted by the victims of serious international crimes.

In particular, if the United States has provided for an explicit derogation (so-called 'terrorism exception') to immunity for foreign countries that have aided and abetted acts of terrorism, Italian Courts have similarly challenged the traditional approach to foreign State immunity: the Court of Cassation held that immunity from adjudication should be lifted in case of acts amounting to international crimes,[59] while the Constitutional Court ruled under the so-called 'counter-limits' doctrine[60] that the international customary rules on State immunity can be applied in the Italian system only insofar as they conform with the fundamental rights protected by the Italian Constitution.

Although the ICJ has clearly confirmed the extent of the principle of sovereign immunity regardless of the seriousness of the violation contested, excluding in *Jurisdictional Immunities*[61] that immunity may encounter a limit with respect to behaviors that constitute a violation of peremptory rules (*ius cogens*) as the latter is a substantive law with respect to immunity which is procedural in character and thus operating on different levels—moreover stressing the different scope of immunity from execution compared to that from adjudication[62]—the divergent trends emerged may be reflected as well in the matter of enforcement against the assets of FCBs.

Emblematic is the case of the Central Bank of the Islamic Republic of Iran (also known as 'Bank Markazi Jomhouri Islami Iran' or 'Bank Markazi') as it has been at the center of a number of enforcement proceedings promoted by judgment creditors

[59] Corte di Cassazione, judgment no. 5044/2004 ('Ferrini' judgment): according to the Italian Supreme Court functional immunity cannot be applied when the acts performed, even jure imperii, are an international crime: in that case there is no valid reason to hold the immunity of the State.

[60] For this doctrine, inaugurated by Italian Constitutional Court, judgment no. 238/2014 (reported inter alia in Rivista di diritto internazionale, 2015, 237, with commentary by E. Cannizzaro, 126) see para. 4.2.

[61] ICJ, Jurisdictional Immunities of the State (Germany v. Italy: Greece intervening), judgment, ICJ Reports 2012, paras. 58, 93. In Arrest Warrant of 11 April 2000 (Democratic Republic of the Congo v. Belgium), judgment, ICJ Reports 2002, para. 60 the Court also held that 'While jurisdictional immunity is procedural in nature, criminal responsibility is a question of substantive law. Jurisdictional immunity may well bar prosecution for a certain period or for certain offences; it cannot exonerate the person to whom it applies from all criminal responsibility'.

[62] Arrest Warrant of 11 April 2000 (Democratic Republic of the Congo v. Belgium), judgment, ICJ Reports 2002, para. 113.

against Iran for its role in supporting state-sponsored terrorism: the US has enacted an *ad hoc* regulation in order to limit its immunity while some domestic decisions might undermine the consolidated trend towards a strengthening of the immunity granted to the property of FCBs.

4.1 The US Approach to Sovereign Immunity

4.1.1 In General

The US Foreign Sovereign Immunity Act (FSIA) largely codifies the restrictive immunity doctrine[63] establishing a comprehensive legal framework on jurisdiction against foreign States and recognizing the general rule of immunity of foreign sovereigns from adjudicative and executive jurisdiction of US courts at the conditions provided by law.[64]

In 1996, the Congress modified the FSIA to create a new exception to immunity to allow legal actions by victims of terrorism (so-called 'terrorism exception'). Under 28 U.S.C. §1605(a)(7), replaced in 2008 with an expanded exception codified at 28 U.S.C. §1605A, a foreign State is not immune from the jurisdiction of courts of the United States if money damages are sought for personal injury or death that was caused by an act of torture, extrajudicial killing, aircraft sabotage, hostage taking, or the provision of material support or resources for such an act if such act or provision of material support or resources is engaged in by an official, employee, or agent of such foreign State while acting within the scope of his or her office, employment, or agency. However, a court could hear a claim under such section only if the Executive Branch has designated the sovereign as a 'State sponsor of terrorism' prior to, or as a result of, the act at issue.[65] On 13 September 2016, the US approved the Justice Against Sponsor of the Terrorism Act ('JASTA') which intervened directly on the law on jurisdictional immunity of foreign States and extended the scope of the terrorism exception[66] by eliminating the 'State Sponsor of Terrorism' requirement under the FSIA.

---

[63] Verlinden B. N. v. Cent. Bank of Nigeria, 461 U.S. 480, 488, 103 S. Ct. 1962, 76 L. Ed. 2d 81 (1983).

[64] E.g. if the foreign State waives immunity, or the action is based upon a commercial activity carried on in the United States by the foreign State. Other exceptions also cover most non-commercial torts occurring in the US and arbitration; see amplius FSIA §1605.

[65] The list of designated State sponsors of terrorism is published on April 30 of each year. Currently, Iran, Syria and Sudan are designated by the US as State sponsors of terrorism.

[66] In particular, the statute introduced the new §1605B of the US Code establishing that a foreign State shall not be immune from suits seeking money damages for personal injury or death, or for injury to property, occurring in the United States that is caused by (1) 'an act of international terrorism in the United States' and (2) a tortious act of a foreign State or its officials 'regardless where the tortious act or acts of the foreign State occurred'. The tortious act of a foreign State may not, however, be an omission or 'constitute mere negligence'.

This progressive approach narrowing the extent of foreign sovereign immunity has also been reflected in the matter of immunity from execution. The general rule under Title 28 U.S.C. §1609 provides that the ownership in the US of a foreign State or its agencies and instrumentalities is immune and can only be subject to attachment and execution as specifically provided in §§1610 and 1611. If §1610(a) establishes that the property in the United States of a foreign State used for a commercial activity in the United States 'shall not be immune from attachment in aid of execution, or from execution, upon a judgment entered by a court of the United States ... if ... (1) the foreign State has waived its immunity from attachment ... [or] (2) the property is or was used for the commercial activity upon which the claim is based', other relevant exceptions to immunity from execution have been introduced in cases where the foreign State or its instrumentality are not immune under the terrorism exception.[67]

Nevertheless, §1611(b)(1) expressly provides the so-called 'central-bank exemption' under which, notwithstanding the provisions of §1610, 'the property of a foreign State shall be immune from attachment and execution ... if the property is that of a foreign central bank or monetary authority held *for its own account*'[68] unless such bank or its parent State have explicitly waived its immunity. The expression 'for its own account' has turned out to be complicated from an interpretative point of view.[69] Some courts have in fact understood it as referring to all those assets that pertain to the performance of the traditional activities of an FCB, and thus not to its commercial functions[70] given that the Congress had noted that the funds held for the central bank's own accounts would be those 'used or held in connection with central banking activities, as distinguished from funds used solely [for]

[67] E.g. §1610(a)(7) provides that property in the United States of a foreign State that is used for a commercial activity shall not be immune from attachment and execution where the plaintiff holds a §1605A judgment against the foreign State, while §1610(b)(3) provides that any property of the agency or instrumentality of a foreign State engaged in commercial activity in the United States shall not be immune from attachment and execution in satisfaction of a judgment on a claim for which the agency or instrumentality is not immune under §1605A. Moreover, §1610(g) provides that both the property of a foreign State against which a judgment is entered under §1605A and the property of an agency or instrumentality of such a State (including 'property that is a separate juridical entity or is an interest held directly or indirectly in a separate juridical entity') are subject to attachment and execution. In Rubin v. Islamic Republic of Iran, 583 U.S. (2018), the US Supreme Court held that §1610(g) does not provide a freestanding basis for parties holding a judgment under §1605A to attach and execute against the property of a foreign State; rather, for §1610(g) to apply, the immunity of the property at issue must be rescinded under a separate provision within §1610.

[68] Emphasis added.

[69] See, e.g., Ministry of Def. & Support for the Armed Forces of the Islamic Republic of Iran v. Cubic Def. Sys., Inc., 385 F.3d 1206, 1223–24 (9th Cir. 2004).

[70] E.g. in Weston Compagnie de Finance et d'Investissement, S.A. v. Republica del Ecuador, 823 F. Supp. 1106, 1111 (S.D.N.Y. 1993) the US Court hold that the funds in a central bank account used to finance commercial transactions of private parties were not immune because the funds were not 'held for its own account'.

commercial transactions'.[71] Some other courts have instead recently interpreted the requirement by adopting a 'modified central bank functions test' according to which property of an FCB is 'presumed to be immune'[72] from attachment if the central bank uses such property for central banking functions as such functions are normally understood, and thus 'irrespective of their commercial nature',[73] the plaintiffs bearing the burden of producing evidence to rebut that presumption because they are the party against whom the presumption is directed.

In 2002 the United States also adopted the Terrorism Risk Insurance Act ('TRIA') which allowed for enforcement measures for judgments entered following the terrorism exception. In particular, §201 allows for attachment and execution in every case of judgments obtained for compensatory damages against the assets of a 'terrorist party' (defined to include *inter alia* designated State sponsors of terrorism as well as their agencies or instrumentalities)[74] previously blocked by the US Government. Thus, the TRIA, overcoming the 'central-bank exemption', allows for execution also against FCBs' assets insofar as they are blocked by the President pursuant to his authority.[75]

4.1.2 The Ad Hoc Measures Against Bank Markazi . . .

In order to facilitate the execution of claims for compensation obtained by some plaintiffs under a judgment (*Deborah D. Peterson et al. v. Islamic Republic of Iran et al.*)[76] against Iran as sponsor of international terrorism[77]—mostly arising out of

---

[71] H.R. Rep. no. 94-1487, at 31 (1976), reprinted in 1976 U.S.C.C.A.N. 6604, 6630, cited in Note, Too Sovereign to be Sued: Immunity of Central Banks in Times of Crisis, Harvard Law Review 124, no. 2 (2010), 553.

[72] In NML Capital, Ltd. v. Banco Central de la Republica Argentina, the Second Circuit stated that '[w]here funds are held in an account in the name of a central bank or monetary authority, the funds are presumed to be immune from attachment [emphasis added] under §1611(b)(1)'. Therefore, any funds that are used for central banking functions in the sense outlined by the Court—i.e. interpreting the expression in ordinary meaning—should be presumed as immune, even if they are characterized as commercial. See NML Capital, Ltd. v. Banco Central de la República Argentina, no. 10-1487- cv (L), — F.3d —, 2011 WL 2611269, pp. *19–20 (2d Cir. July 5, 2011); see also Dickinson et al. (2004), p. 14. See most recently Continental Transfer Technique, Limited v. Federal Government of Nigeria, no. 08-2026 (PLF), United States District Court, District of Columbia, 6 August 2019.

[73] NML Capital, Ltd. v. Banco Central de la República Argentina, no. 10-1487- cv(L), — F.3d —, 2011 WL 2611269, p. 194 (citing Patrikis 1982, pp. 275–277).

[74] Under the TRIA. the separate agency or instrumentality do not have to be a named party to the litigation resulting in the judgment.

[75] It must be finally noted that the recently enacted JASTA does not contain any provision limiting or modifying immunity from executive jurisdiction, thus not relating to FCBs either.

[76] Peterson v. Islamic Republic of Iran, 515 F.Supp.2d 25, 60 (United States District Court for the District of Columbia 2007.

[77] In 1984, the United States designated Iran as a 'State sponsor of terrorism', a designation still in force.

the 1983 bombing of the U.S. Marine barracks in Beirut, Lebanon—the Congress enacted an *ad hoc* law concerning certain assets held by Bank Markazi, the Iranian central bank.

In particular, in 2010, the *Peterson* plaintiffs had registered the judgment in the U.S. District Court for the Southern District of New York[78] and had moved for execution for post-judgment collection[79] to obtain an order compelling the turnover of bond proceeds allegedly owned by Bank Markazi and held in New York City through European intermediaries.[80]

While this action was pending, on 5 February 2012, President Obama issued the Executive Order (E.O.) 13599 which blocked '[a]ll property and interests in property of any Iranian financial institution, including the Central Bank of Iran, that are in the United States'.[81]

However, given that Bank Markazi claimed that the block was not covered by TRIA because the account object of the *Peterson* enforcement proceeding was not an asset 'of' Bank Markazi but of its intermediary, on 1 August 2012 the Congress passed the 'Iran Threat Reduction and Syria Human Rights Act 2012'.[82] Under this statute, assets 'held in the United States for a foreign securities intermediary doing business in the United States [. . .] equal in value to a financial asset of Iran, *including an asset of the central bank or monetary authority of the Government of Iran*[83] or any agency or instrumentality of that Government, that such foreign securities intermediary or a related intermediary holds abroad shall be subject to execution or attachment in aid of execution in order to satisfy any judgment to the extent of any compensatory damages awarded against Iran for damages for personal injury or

[78] Deborah Peterson, et al. v. Islamic Republic of Iran, et al., case no. 10-cv-4518 (S.D.N.Y.).

[79] In 2008, the plaintiffs first learned of the interests of Bank Markazi in a Citibank bank account in New York belonging to Clearstream Banking, S.A. (a Luxembourg-based bank) which held the account on behalf of Bank Markazi. In 2008, another account was opened in the interest of the Iranian central bank with Italian bank Banca UBAE S.p.A to place the interest payments from the Clearstream account.

[80] The plaintiffs allege that those bond proceeds were processed by and through a global chain of banks: as part of its foreign currency reserves, Bank Markazi held $1.75 billion in security entitlements in foreign government and supranational bonds at Banca UBAE S.p.A. (an Italian bank) which, in turn, held corresponding security entitlements in an account with another intermediary in Luxembourg, Clearstream.

Clearstream then held corresponding security entitlements in an omnibus account at Citibank, N. A., in New York.

[81] According to the US District Court for the Southern District of New York: 'E.O. 13599 had the effect of turning any restrained assets owned by the Iranian Government (or any agency or instrumentality thereof) into 'Blocked Assets'. As Bank Markazi is the Central Bank of Iran, any of its assets located in the United States as of 5 February 2012, became 'Blocked Assets' pursuant to E.O. 13599; see Deborah D. Peterson et al. v. Bank Markazi a.k.a. Central Bank of Iran et al., US District Court for the Southern District of New York, opinion and order dated 28 February 2013, p. 12.

[82] President Obama signed the 2012 Act into law on 10 August 2012. It was then codified after enactment as 22 U.S.C. §8772.

[83] Emphasis added.

death caused by an act of torture, extrajudicial killing, aircraft sabotage, or hostage-taking, or the provision of material support or resources for such an act'.[84]

Moreover, the statute specified that 'the financial assets that are identified in and the subject to proceedings in the United States District Court for the Southern District of New York in *Peterson et al. v. Islamic Republic of Iran et al.,* Case No. 10 Civ. 4518'[85] were to be subject to execution in order to satisfy any judgment to the extent of any compensatory damages awarded against Iran for damages for personal injury or death caused by an act of terrorism.

Therefore, the District Court granted summary judgment to the plaintiffs, ordering turnover of the assets:[86] in particular, the Court held that even if the blocked assets had been held for the central bank's own account under §1611(b) central-bank exemption, however the TRIA's 'notwithstanding' clause and the further legislation implemented expressly preempted any immunity.

Moreover, according to the Court of Appeals, E.O. 13599 suggested that the activities of Bank Markazi were not central banking activities that would grant §1611(b) immunity and, even if they were, 'Congress ha[d] changed the law governing this case'[87] hence, the Central Bank of Iran was not entitled to immunity.

However, although Bank Markazi claimed that the new US rules were unconstitutional because enacted as *ad hoc* legislation with reference to a single pending case, therefore violating the principle of separation of powers, the Supreme Court confirmed the decision in 2016.[88]

Although this last judgment has a relevant value mostly under a US constitutional law perspective, it is worth to note that it has in fact validated *ad hoc* measures against assets owned by an FCB despite the general immunity rule under §1611(b) of the FSIA, as well as it has led to the following lawsuit promoted by Iran against the United States before the International Court of Justice raising a case on the issue of immunity from execution for FCB assets under international law.

[84] 22 USC §8772, lett. a).

[85] 22 USC §8772, lett. b).

[86] Peterson, et al. v. Islamic Republic of Iran, Bank Markazi a.k.a. Central Bank of Iran, Banca UBAE, Citibank, and Clearstream Banking, No. 10 Civ. 4518 (S.D.N.Y., July 9, 2013); In July 2013, the district court issued an order directing turnover of the blocked assets and enjoining the parties from initiating a claim to the assets in another jurisdiction; see Peterson v. Islamic Republic of Iran, No. 10 Civ. 4518 (S.D.N.Y. July 9, 2013).

[87] Peterson v. Islamic Republic of Iran, 758 F.3d 185, 193 (2d Cir. 2014).

[88] US Supreme Court, Bank Markazi, a.k.a. the Central Bank of Iran, Petitioner v. Deborah Peterson, et al, 578 U.S. (2016); Docket no. 14-770. The ruling resulted in an order for the turnover of nearly $2 billion; in fact, the US District Court authorized the payment of the blocked assets to the judgment creditors and closed the proceedings: see Deborah D. Peterson et al. v. Bank Markazi a.k.a. Central Bank of Iran et al., US District Court for the Southern District of New York, order authorizing distribution of funds dated 6 June 2016.

4.1.3 ... and Their Challange Before the International Court of Justice: The Certain Iranian Assets Case

On 15 June 2016, the Islamic Republic of Iran filed a claim before the International Court of Justice challenging *ad hoc* US measures against Bank Markazi. Iran accused the United States of violating certain provisions of the 1955 Treaty of Amity, Economic Relations and Consular Rights between the United States and Iran ('the Treaty of Amity').[89]

If the object of the dispute has been limited to the specific violation of some provisions of the Treaty of Amity,[90] the question of immunity is indirectly involved as well.[91]

A jurisdictional question addressed by the Court was whether the Treaty of Amity obliged the US to respect the sovereign immunity to which the Iran central bank would allegedly be entitled under customary international law: Article IV.2 of the Treaty of Amity in fact guarantees a minimum of protection, stating that 'property of nationals and companies of either High Contracting Party ... shall receive the most constant protection and security within the territories of the other High Contracting Party, *in no case less than that required by international law*'.[92]

In its complaint, Iran had expressly stated that Article IV.2 incorporated customary international law, including the rules pertaining to the immunity of FCBs[93] and therefore, the US *ad hoc* measures against Bank Markazi were in violation of the jurisdictional immunities and immunities from enforcement to which Iran and Iranian State-owned companies were entitled 'under both customary international law and the Treaty of Amity'.[94] Tehran asked the Court to order and declare *inter*

---

[89] The Treaty of Amity, Economic Relations and Consular Rights between the United States and Iran was signed in Tehran on 15 August 1955 and entered into force on 16 June 1957.

[90] Article XXI (2) of the Treaty of Amity provides: 'Any dispute between the High Contracting Parties as to the interpretation or application of the present Treaty, not satisfactorily adjusted by diplomacy, shall be submitted to the International Court of Justice, unless the High Contracting Parties agree to settlement by some other pacific means'. In particular, Iran contested the alleged violation of: Articles III. 1 (recognition of the legal status of Iranian companies and enterprises), III.2 (fair and impartial access to jurisdiction), IV.1 (fair and impartial treatment of its own citizens and businesses), IV.2 (protection and security guaranteed to its own citizens and businesses), V.1 (right to acquire and dispose of goods and property), VII.1 (prohibition of restrictions on payments or transfer of funds) and Art. X.1 (freedom of trade and navigation).

[91] At the outset, the United States raised three jurisdictional objections, namely (i) the Iran claims fell outside the scope of the Treaty of Amity and the jurisdiction of the Court as the Executive Order 13599 was covered by the 'national security exception' of the Treaty of Amity; (ii) the Treaty of Amity did not give immunity to the States Parties or to any of their State entities; and (iii) the Treaty of Amity did not apply to Bank Markazi, insofar as it was not a 'company' under Articles III, IV and V thereof since, as the Central Bank of Iran, it carried out exclusively sovereign functions and was not engaged in activities of a commercial nature.

[92] Emphasis added.

[93] ICJ, Application instituting proceedings, filed in the Registry of the Court on 14 June 2016, Certain Iranian Assets (Islamic Republic of Iran v. United States of America), p. 30.

[94] Ibid., p. 26.

alia the US failure to grant immunities 'to which Iran and Iranian State-owned companies, including Bank Markazi, and their property, are entitled *under customary international law*[95] and as required by the Treaty of Amity'.[96]

On the contrary, the US assumed that the Treaty of Amity could not be understood as including sovereign immunity protections for Iran or Bank Markazi, and Iran could not rely on the Treaty of Amity as a basis for jurisdiction over sovereign immunity-related claims in the extent granted by general international law.

On 13 February 2019 the ICJ issued its decision on preliminary objections: even declaring its jurisdiction over the case, the Court denied it in the part in which Tehran's claim was based on the alleged violation of rules of international law on sovereign immunities, by restrictively interpreting the scope of the Treaty of Amity.[97]

The Court ruled that 'international law' as referred to in Article IV.2 did not govern the protections enjoyed by State entities by virtue of the principle of sovereign equality of States but only defined the minimum standard of protection for property belonging to the 'nationals' and 'companies' of one Party engaged in economic activities within the territory of the other;[98] accordingly, the examined provision did not incorporate customary rules on sovereign immunities nor did the other provisions of the Treaty of Amity on which Tehran relied to assert that sovereign immunities did fall within the scope of the Treaty.[99]

Therefore, the Court upheld the preliminary objection raised by the United States and affirmed that jurisdiction was lacking to assert claims based on the international law of State immunity.

Said ruling has restricted the scope of the case and its implications for international law since, as noted by Chachko, the ICJ has considered the *Certain Iranian*

---

[95] Emphasis added.

[96] ICJ, Application instituting proceedings, filed in the Registry of the Court on 14 June 2016, Certain Iranian Assets (Islamic Republic of Iran v. United States of America), p. 33. Iran also affirmed that the jurisdiction conferred on the Court by the Treaty included jurisdiction to determine and apply the immunities at issue to the full extent necessary (i.e. under customary international law as well) in order to decide whether the provisions invoked by the plaintiff had been breached by the United States. According to Iran, since the Court had jurisdiction to rule on the alleged breach of any of the Treaty's provisions, it therefore also had jurisdiction to apply the law of immunities in the context of Article IV.2.

[97] ICJ, Certain Iranian Assets (Islamic Republic of Iran v. United States of America), judgment on Preliminary Objections, 13 February 2019, para. 57. In particular, with reference to Article IV.2, the Court held that that 'Iran's proposed interpretation of the phrase referring to the 'require[ments of] international law' ... is not consistent with the object and purpose of the Treaty of Amity', insofar as the Parties, as stated in the preamble thereof, intended to encourage mutually beneficial trade and investments and closer economic intercourse generally between their peoples; nor the same title of the Treaty of Amity did suggest that sovereign immunities fell within the object and purpose of the instrument concerned.

[98] ICJ, Certain Iranian Assets (Islamic Republic of Iran v. United States of America), judgment on Preliminary Objections, 13 February 2019, para. 57.

[99] The Court examined as well Article XI(4), Article III(2), Article IV(1) and Article X(1).

Assets case a 'simple case about treaty interpretation'[100] thus significantly reducing the scope of what could have been a significant case on the international law of State immunity. Such case could have resulted in a pronouncement on the US practice with respect to both the *ad hoc* measures against an FCB and more generally the terrorism exception under the FSIA, considering that, already in *Jurisdictional Immunities*, the Court had noted that only the US recognized a similar exception on State immunity.[101]

In particular, the ICJ might have focused on the special immunity granted to FCBs and—also considering that it has broadly relied on the relevant and more restrictive provisions of the UNCSI (although not yet in force)—it might have clarified its extent under customary law. In fact, although the Court has shown a general resistance in recognizing new exceptions to immunity even for cases involving serious violations of *ius cogens*,[102] the correspondence between the principle of 'almost' absolute immunity as enshrined in Article 21(1)(c)[103] and general international law is anything but certain.

4.2 *The Italian Approach to Sovereign Immunity and the 'Counter-Limits' Doctrine*

Unlike other States, Italy does not have specific domestic legislation on jurisdictional immunities: consequently, the rules on sovereign immunity find their foundation in the principles of international law as implemented in the Italian law through Article 10, para. 1 of the Italian Constitution (hereinafter 'Art. 10') which provides that 'the Italian legal system conforms to the generally recognized principles of international law', thus working as a 'permanent transformer'[104] of customary international law into domestic law.

[100] Chachko (2019).

[101] ICJ, Jurisdictional Immunities of the State (Germany v. Italy: Greece intervening), judgment, ICJ Reports 2012, para. 88.

[102] The US unilateral waive of the immunity of Iran and its central bank as well as the Supreme Court decision in Peterson had been also strongly criticized as inconsistent with international law by third States and International Organizations: e.g. the Coordinating Bureau of the Non-Aligned Movement objected 'to US defiance to international law through the unilateral waiving of the sovereign immunity of States and their institutions in total contravention of the international and treaty obligations of the United States and under a spurious legal ground that the international community does not recognize'. See Communique by the Coordinating Bureau of the Non-Aligned Movement in Rejection of Unilateral Actions by the United States in Contravention of International Law, in Particular the Principle of State Immunity (5 May 2016).

[103] Subject, of course, to the possibility of waiver under Articles 18 and 19, subparagraphs (a) and (b).

[104] This definition was first used by Perassi (1957), p. 29.

The lack of an *ad hoc* internal legislation on the matter—and the related need to refer to customary international law—have involved a necessary and constant work of interpretation by the Italian courts about the application of the general rules on sovereign immunity of foreign State regarding their exact extent and limits.

Since its judgment in *Ferrini*,[105] the Italian Court of Cassation inaugurated an approach denying foreign States the benefit of jurisdictional immunity in cases of serious violations of human rights. In that decision the Italian Supreme Court recognized that the right of victims of Nazi crimes to obtain compensation for the damage suffered during second world war was prevalent over the principle of sovereign immunity, thus denying Germany immunity in the light of the violation of *jus cogens* norms 'which must have priority over the rule granting immunity from jurisdiction'.[106] To counter such an approach, Germany filed a claim before the ICJ complaining about the violation of the customary rule on the jurisdictional immunity and, with the decision issued in the *Jurisdictional Immunities* case, the Court in the Hague condemned Italy to provide to deprive Italian judgments on the matter of any effect.[107]

However, called to judge on a linked question of constitutional legitimacy,[108] the Italian Constitutional Court has nevertheless developed a particular approach to the issue of sovereign immunity: by judgment no. 238/2014,[109]it found that, although customary rules of international law have the same rank as the constitutional ones by virtue of Art. 10, in the event of a conflict between general international law (in that case, the principle of immunity from jurisdiction) and fundamental constitutional rights (in that case, the right to judicial protection granted under Article 24 and the right to dignity protected under Article 2 of the Constitution), the automatic adaptation mechanism provided by Art. 10 does not apply and then the Italian legal system does not conform to such international rules.[110]

[105] Corte di Cassazione, Joined Sections, judgment no. 5044/2004.

[106] See Iovane (2005), p. 165.

[107] Italy implemented the decision by establishing, in Article 3 of the Law no. 5 of 2013, the obligation for the Italian judge to detect in any state and degree of the process the lack of jurisdiction and to allow the revocation of the civil judgments already final.

[108] Trib. Firenze, order of 21 January 2014, case no. 1300/2012, commented inter alia by Palombino (2014), p. 501.

[109] The decision was subject to numerous comments including: De Sena (2014), Pustorino (2015), Sciso (2015) and Cataldi (2015).

[110] The Court's decision is very articulated and it is not possible here to dwell in detail on all the issues addressed; in any case the approach therein has traditionally been followed by the Constitutional Court and, before the judgment in comment, reiterated by the Court, albeit in an obiter dictum, in the judgment no. 73 of 22 March 2001 where it affirmed that 'the openness orientation of the Italian legal system towards both the generally recognized international law rules and the conventional international norms meets the necessary limits to guarantee their identity and, therefore, above all the limits deriving by the Constitution': therefore, the fundamental principles of the constitutional order and the inalienable rights of the person constitute a limit to the entry of the generally recognized international norms to which the Italian legal system conforms by virtue of the Art. 10 of the Constitution.

Under the 'counter-limits doctrine', the fundamental principles enshrined in the constitutional rules of the Italian system constitute in fact a limit to the entry of generally recognized international rules. The Constitutional Court has judged as 'completely disproportionate' the sacrifice that the victims' right to judicial protection would have suffered to respect the concurrent right of the foreign State to immunity in a case involving international crimes: according to the Court, the customary international rule on immunity from jurisdiction, within the extent defined by the ICJ in *Jurisdictional Immunities*, 'entail[ed] the *absolute sacrifice*[111] of the right to judicial protection, insofar as it denie[d] the jurisdiction of [domestic] courts to adjudicate the action for damages put forward by victims of crimes against humanity and gross violations of fundamental human rights',[112] and thus it did not enter the Italian legal system under Art. 10.

Given such an approach developed in the matter of immunity from jurisdiction, it is not clear what the consequences may be in the phase of execution and, as for the topic under discussion, in particular with reference to the assets of FCBs.

In 2018, the Italian courts have been asked to rule on the enforcement against the assets of Bank Markazi following a judgment issued by a US court.[113]

The US judgment creditors decided to enforce the judgment in Italy and, pending the exequatur proceedings, had asked for a 'sequestro conservativo' *ante causam* (*i.e.* a preventive seizure) to freeze all the assets held by Bank Markazi in Italy, including its account at UBAE bank as well as possible assets held in Bank of Italy.

In June 2018, the Court of Appeals of Rome issued an order freezing all the assets belonging to Bank Markazi, by preliminarily establishing the admissibility of preventive measures in order to neutralize the risk of loss of credit guarantee pending the exequatur proceedings.[114] The Court of Appeals deemed thus applicable the ordinary domestic preventive instruments on the condition of the existence of the criteria provided for by the Italian civil procedural code of *fumus boni iuris* (*i.e.* a *prima facie* likelihood of success on the merit of the case) and *periculum in mora* (*i.e.* a danger in the delay), both considered to exist.[115]

---

[111] Emphasis added.

[112] ICJ, Jurisdictional Immunities of the State (Germany v. Italy: Greece intervening), judgment, ICJ Reports 2012, para. 104.

[113] On 12 October 2012, the United States District Court for the Southern District of New York entered judgment no. 2624/2012 (Havlish, et al. v. bin Laden, et al.) on behalf of the victims of the 9/11 terrorist attacks and against the Islamic Republic of Iran, Bank Markazi and other Iran's agencies and instrumentalities, awarding damages to the victims and their families.

[114] Court of Appeals of Rome, order dated 14 June 2018. The Court issued this decision despite the lack of a specific provision such as those provided for intra-EU judgments by Article 47 of the Council Regulation (EC) no. 44/2001 of 22 December 2000 (no longer in force) and by Art. 40 of Regulation (EU) no. 1215/2012; see Court of Appeals of Rome, judgment of 15.7.2003; Court of Appeals of Milan, judgment of 13.03.1998; Court of Appeals of Trieste, judgment of 20.06.93, cited in the order.

[115] On 28 June 2018, Bank Markazi filed a petition in the Court of Appeals seeking rehearing of the decision and on 8 October 2018, a rehearing panel of the same Court entered an order that vacated the asset freeze: actually, the Court did not rule on the question of immunity of Bank Markazi but

However, such seizure order issued by the Court of Appeal seems to be in contrast with the general principles on immunity from execution as expressed by the ICJ in *Jurisdictional Immunities* where the Court had already condemned the Italian government not only for allowing the recognition and the declaration of enforceability of some Greek judgments in violation of the principle of jurisdictional immunity, but also for violating Germany's immunity from enforcement.[116]

In particular, the seizure ordered of the Court of Appeal was based on the judgment obtained by the plaintiffs in the United States which was considered as an element to corroborate the *fumus boni iuris* in support of the request for preventive seizure. Nevertheless, the US judgment had not yet been declared enforceable in Italy[117] and therefore, pending the exequatur proceedings, the seizure order granted by the Italian court should be qualified as a coercive pre-judgment measure aimed at guaranteeing the satisfaction of the creditor claim by preventing the dispersion of the assets by the debtor before the recognition of the foreign judgment. But if the UNCSI enshrines the principle of restrictive immunity in relation to post-judgment measures of constraint, it excludes pre-judgment measures without the express consent by the foreign State concerned.

The Court of Appeal should have verified the correspondence of the extent of Article 18 of the UNCSI with general international law and, once ascertained,[118] applied it pursuant to Art. 10. Therefore a pre-judgment measure of constraint against property of a foreign State (or its instrumentalities as an FCB) should have

---

found, from an exclusive point of view of domestic law, the defect of the requirement of periculum in mora, thus revoking the seizure order. On January 3, 2019, the Havlish plaintiffs filed a second request for an asset freeze before the Court of Appeals of Rome claiming that Bank Markazi had already made several attempts to shield its funds at UBAE bank, among which moving the funds out of its account at UBAE to unknown destinations outside the jurisdiction of Italian courts. Bank Markazi and Iran solicited the aid of the Italian government by asking it to intervene on its behalf in the proceedings: with a note dated March 28, 2019, the US judgment creditors formally requested that the Italian government reject the Iranian government's request to intervene in its support in the Italian court proceedings, explicitly recalling the decision of the Italian Constitutional Court no. 238 of 2014 which has affirmed that acts resulting in crimes against humanity cannot benefit from immunity in Italian courts, at the same time requesting assistance in the ongoing judicial proceedings in Italy.

[116]Italy had allowed the mortgage registration on 'Villa Vigoni', site of an Italian-German cultural center destined for favor cultural exchanges between the two countries. The Court found that 'the registration of a legal charge on Villa Vigoni constituted a violation by Italy of its obligation to respect the immunity owed to Germany'; see ICJ, Jurisdictional Immunities of the State (Germany v. Italy: Greece intervening), judgment, ICJ Reports 2012, para. 120.

[117]The ICJ stated that a court decision declaring a foreign enforceable ruling constitutes a violation of immunity from jurisdiction and not from enforcement; see ICJ, Jurisdictional Immunities of the State (Germany v. Italy: Greece intervening), judgment, ICJ Reports 2012, paras. 121–133, in particular para. 128.

[118]Broad international practice on sovereign immunity tend to allow pre-judgment attachments with a requirement that the express consent by a foreign State has been provided: see e.g. Sec. 1610(d) of the US FSIA, Sec. 13(2)(a) and 13(3) of the UK SIA, Sec. 10(1) of the Canadian SIA, Art. 23 of the European Convention on State Immunity.

been declared inapplicable and it would have been even irrelevant to determine whether the property was specifically used or intended for use by the State for other than government non-commercial purposes—a circumstance however not even considered by the Court.

Indeed, the freezing order by the Court of Appeals is actually grounded on the often-referred principles enshrined in the ruling no. 238 of 2014 of the Italian Constitutional Court and on the 'counter-limits' doctrine developed therein. Yet this latest decision focused on the issue of immunity from jurisdiction while it is not clear whether and to what extent the principles established therein also concern immunity from execution.[119]

Immunity from execution has a wider scope than the one from jurisdiction as pointed out not only by the ICJ[120] but also by the same Italian Constitutional Court which ruled that 'the immunity of foreign States from the preventive and executive jurisdiction of the State of the forum is not a simple extension of immunity from the jurisdiction of cognition'.[121]

A *sic et simpliciter* application of the principles developed by the Constitutional Court to immunity from execution does not seem to be so automatic. In the case ruled in judgment no. 238 of 2014, the customary international rule on jurisdictional immunity entailed the 'absolute' sacrifice of the constitutional right to judicial protection insofar as it denied the jurisdiction of domestic courts to adjudicate the claim for damages put forward by victims of crimes against humanity and gross violations of fundamental human rights. In that case, the impossibility of effective judicial protection of the victims under the international law of State immunity (acknowledged by the same ICJ in *Sovereign Immunities*)[122] made evident the contrast between said principle and the fundamental rights protected by the Italian Constitution which led the Court to declare the prevalence of the latter because of the particular gravity of the humanitarian crimes perpetrated.[123]

The same conclusion is not necessarily reached in the event of immunity from execution on assets of FCBs, also considering that the Constitutional Court outlined a non-absolutist conception of counter-limits.[124] In case of execution of a foreign

[119] In the sense of the exclusion of the latter, see Pustorino (2015), p. 52.

[120] ICJ, Jurisdictional Immunities of the State (Germany v. Italy: Greece intervening), judgment, ICJ Reports 2012, para. 113.

[121] Constitutional Court, judgment no. 329 of 1992, para. 3.

[122] The same Court expressly acknowledged that the lack of jurisdiction of the Italian judges involved a sacrifice of the fundamental rights of the subjects who have suffered the consequences of the crimes committed by the foreign State and has identified in the opening of a new negotiation the only tool under international law to define the issue; see ICJ, Jurisdictional Immunities of the State (Germany v. Italy: Greece intervening), judgment, ICJ Reports 2012, para. 102.

[123] Constitutional Court, judgment no. 329 of 1992, para. 3.

[124] With regard to cases of immunity from jurisdiction of States provided by general international law, the Constitutional Court has recognized that, in cases involving foreign States, 'the fundamental right to judicial protection can be further limited, beyond the limitations provided by Art. 10. However, this limit has to be justified by reasons of public interest potentially prevailing over the

judgment against an FCB's assets, no 'absolute' sacrifice of constitutional principles is evident as there is not a complete infringement of the right to judicial protection or other fundamental right as in the case of total immunity from adjudication. Immunity from execution entails a lower sacrifice since the judgment creditors could have been however satisfied 'by equivalent'[125] by attaching other assets of the foreign State, unless otherwise proved.[126] Finally, it has been also already observed that the seizure order of the Court of Appeals does not contain any reference to the destination of Bank Markazi assets.[127]

It should be noted that the Italian case-law has long claimed to be unable to apply the principle of jurisdictional immunity where compensation for damages has been requested following a terrorist act which represents an international crime committed in violation of human rights.[128] However, even after the ruling by the Constitutional Court, some courts have stated that customary international law does not allow executive or preventive actions concerning the assets of foreign States that are destined for the exercise of sovereign functions or public purposes.[129] The Court of Cassation has also repeatedly stated that a foreign State can be condemned before Italian courts, but not all its assets are subject to execution.[130]

---

principle of Article 24 Constitution, one of the 'supreme principles' of the constitutional order (judgment no. 18/1982). Moreover, the provision that establishes the limit has to guarantee a rigorous assessment of the [public] interest in light of the concrete case (judgment no. 329/1992)'; see Constitutional Court, judgment no. 329 of 1992.

[125]The principle of protection by equivalent is recognized also by the European Court of Human Rights (ECtHR): the Strasbourg Court, even considering the principle of State immunity a legitimate limit to the individual's right of access to court protected under Article 6(1) of the European Convention on Human Rights recognized as well the necessity of balancing the granting of immunity with the right of access to courts and the right to an effective remedy. See ECtHR, Al-Adsani v. United Kingdom, Grand Chamber judgment of 21 November 2001, Application no. 35763/97, § 54; see also Cudak v. Lituania, Grand Chamber judgment of 20 March 2010, Application no. 15869/02, § 60; and Sabeh El Leil, v. France, Grand Chamber judgment of 29 June 2011, Application no. 34869/05, § 52.

[126]The same reasoning developed by the Constitutional Court in judgment no. 238/2014 has been criticized because it did not adopt of an 'effective' and 'comprehensive' balancing model insofar as grounded on the sole gravity of the crimes object of the proceedings, which was considered per se as a circumstance not allowing exceptions to the right to judicial protection: no emphasis was given to the possibility that that protection could take place by equivalent through alternative means of satisfaction to judicial action; see De Sena (2014).

[127]If this approach may be perhaps formally corrected as the fumus boni iuris required by the Italian law to issue a seizure order should be found in the probability of recognition of the foreign judgment (probability in fact existing in the light of the principles expressed by the Constitutional Court), however it would lead to the substantial paradox for which the preventive seizure could be granted but, after the recognition of the foreign judgment, there could be no execution.

[128]Corte di Cassazione, Joint Sections, judgment no. 21946 of 28 October 2015.

[129]See e.g. Court of Appeals of Milan, judgment no. 1278 of 27 January 2015.

[130]'due to the principles of jurisdictional immunity of foreign States, established by customary international law (to which Article 10 of the Constitution refers), there is no jurisdiction of the Italian judge with regard to the enforcement or preventive action on assets belonging to said [foreign] States or to their public bodies, in the case of goods intended for the exercise of their

Nevertheless, the broad interpretation of the scope of the Constitutional Court's ruling on enforcement has recently been affirmed by the same Supreme Court which held that:

> immunity from the civil jurisdiction of foreign States ... is a prerogative (and not a right) recognised by international customary rules, whose operation or applicability in Italy is in any case precluded in our legal system, following the Court's judgment cost. n. 238 of 2014, for the *delicta imperii, i.e.* for those crimes committed in violation of international norms of *ius cogens*, since they are detrimental to universal values that transcend the interests of the individual state communities ... It follows that Italian judges, both those who have been charged with the cognitive judgment and *those charged with the enforcement of judicial titles*[131] ... have the institutional duty, in inescapable compliance with the regulatory framework determined by judgment no. 238 of 2014 of the Constitutional Court, to deny any exemption from that jurisdiction on the liability recognised elsewhere that may be invoked before them, both in the place where the judgment of cognizance or deliberation of the foreign judgment is made, and in the place ... of enforcement based on it.[132]

The approach of the Supreme Court of Cassation is therefore still contradictory as to the complete applicability of the principles of the 'counter-limits' doctrine and the extent thereof also to the enforcement process although the principles indicated by the Constitutional Court seem to direct national jurisprudence towards limiting the extent of State immunity also in the field of enforcement, including with specific reference to FCBs.

5 Conclusion

As observed by Wuerth,[133] the analysis of the most recent national legislation shows a general trend—although with different nuances—towards a greater immunity granted by most States to the assets of FCBs from measures of constraint.

This trend is linked on the one hand to the willingness of States to strengthen their economic competitiveness[134] and thus attract the assets of FCBs while guaranteeing

sovereign functions or, in any case, of their public purposes' see Corte di Cassazione, III Section, judgment no. 14885 of 25 March 2018; see also Corte di Cassazione, Joint Sections, judgment no. 173 of 12 January 1996; according to the Constitutional Court, judgment no. 329/1992 and Corte di Cassazione, Joint Sections, judgment no. 5888/1997 it is not the foreign State that is subjectively immune from the executive jurisdiction but its assets cannot be subject to execution if they are destined for the fulfillment of its public functions.

[131] Emphasis added.

[132] Corte di Cassazione, III Section, judgment no. 21995 of 25 June 2019.

[133] See amplius Wuerth (2019).

[134] E.g. in the Commentaire des Articles of the Proposition de Loi modifiant le Code judiciaire, the Proposers expressly provided that 'La présente proposition vise à renforcer la compétitivité de la Belgique', p. 3. Also the US Federal Reserve Bank of New York noted that 'an inadequate or uncertain immunity law might prompt central banks to move their reserves to more hospitable jurisdictions', in Brief of Amicus Curiae the Federal Reserve Bank of New York, NML Capital, 2010 WL. See also Laborias (2016); see amplius Waibel (2011), pp. 19–20.

greater protection and, on the other hand, to the incisive influence of the principles of international law on immunity from execution provided by the UNCSI, also with particular reference to the strong protection granted to FCBs under Article 21 which provides States with an authority they can rely on to strengthen the national protection afforded to such institutions' assets.

As noted, if some States have enshrined also with reference to FCBs the principles relating to immunity from executive jurisdiction by applying the principles provided for in Articles 18 and 19 of the UNCSI, other States have instead based their legislation on the rules provided in Article 21 on certain categories of assets which must be deemed immune from executive jurisdiction on the basis of an absolute presumption that they cannot be considered as property specifically in use or intended for use by the State for other than government non-commercial purposes.

However, if Articles 18 and 19 UNCSI seem to be generally considered as a codification of general international law[135]—although the ICJ in *Jurisdictional Immunities* did not rule on whether all aspects of Article 19 reflect current customary international law[136]—as instead for the extent of Article 21(1)(c) granting an almost absolute immunity to foreign central banks, it seems to have a purely conventional extent. Lacking a general *opinio juris* as well as an affirmed *diuturnitas* among States, given the differences in national legislation on the matter, the regulation provided by the UNCSI on the immunity granted to FCBs seems rather to indicate a progressive development of the matter, not corresponding at present to a generally recognized rule of international law.

In fact, many States having recently adopted said principle came, in large part, from absolute immunity regimes and therefore, their approach in regulating the assets of FCBs has remained substantially unmodified although in a context of a more general re-orientation towards restricted immunity. In addition, many of them provided in their statutes a condition of reciprocity, thus limiting the effective scope of the (almost) absolute immunity principle to those States which apply it in their turn.

Therefore, at present, the minimum level of protection recognized by general international law to the assets of FCBs from post-judgment measures of constraint seems to be the one granted to the property owned by foreign States under the rule

[135] E.g. see the judgments given by the European Court of Human Rights on 17 July 2012 in the case Wallishauser v. Austria (application no. 156 / 04) and in the case of Oleynikov v. Russia, 14 March 2013 (application no. 36703/04). See also Luzzato and Queirolo (2006), p. 219. On the contrary, according to Brown and O'Keefe (2013), p. 306, it is premature to affirm that Article 18 reflects customary international law.

[136] ICJ, Jurisdictional Immunities of the State (Germany v. Italy: Greece intervening), judgment, ICJ Reports 2012, para. 117; in support of its claim before the Court, Germany provided for by Article 19 of the UNCSI considering it as a codification, in relation to the issue of immunity from enforcement, of the existing rules under general international law, and therefore binding regardless of the entry into force of the UNCSI; see Case concerning jurisdictional immunities of the States, Memorial of the Federal Republic of Germany, 12 June 2009, para. 104 reading that 'The UN Convention on Jurisdictional Immunities of States and Their Property has recently codified the rules existing under general international law'.

and exceptions provided by under Article 19 of the UNCSI depending on whether their assets are used or intended for use for sovereign functions (sometimes the reference being to the 'typical functions' of central banks) or for commercial purposes.

Nevertheless, the immunities guaranteed to foreign monetary institutions are increasingly reinforced by many States in their domestic legislation (without regard to whether the bank is independent from its parent State). Such 'reinforcement' is carried out through either a presumption *iuris tantum* of destination of the same property for sovereign purposes or listing their assets among those not eligible for execution 'insofar as' they are intended for use or used by the foreign State in activities related to the exercise of sovereign authority, whose burden of proof to the contrary lies in both the cases with the creditors.

This entails a strengthened protection of FCBs from execution, the destination of their assets for exclusive commercial purposes appearing to be the decisive element in order to allow enforcement measures. Therefore, if FCBs' funds destined for governmental functions should be considered immune, mixed assets keep presenting relevant problems, even though some national courts hold that in order to be liable to attachment, the State property has to be shown to serve 'solely' commercial purposes, and thus mixed assets cannot be attached.[137]

The divergent approaches followed by the US and Italy do not seem to contradict these conclusions.

The US terrorist exception to State immunity is from many quarters considered contrary to customary international law[138] and it remains a somewhat isolated practice among States.[139] Moreover, it has not affected the general rule of immunity from enforcement with respect to FCBs, the US maintaining a substantial protection of these assets when used for typical central banking functions (and irrespective of their 'commercial' nature). Nor do the *ad hoc* measures against Bank Markazi,

---

[137] See e.g. Leasing West v. Democratic Republic of Algeria, Austria, Supreme Court, 30 April 1986, Case No. 3 Ob 38/86, 116 ILR 526, 529; I GmbH v. A, Austria, Supreme Court, 25 August 1998, Case No. 1 Ob 100/98g; in Alcom v. Republic of Colombia (United Kingdom, House of Lords, 12 April 1984, [1984] 2 All ER 6, 74 ILR 170, 187), the House of Lords held that a general mixed bank account of an embassy was immune from enforcement measures and the funds could not be dissected into commercial and sovereign purposes.

[138] A clear concern about a possible lack of compatibility between the provisions of the JASTA and the international norms was expressed in his veto message (which was overcome by the vote of the Congress) by the same US President who noted that 'JASTA would upset longstanding international principles regarding sovereign immunity, putting in place rules that, if applied globally, could have serious implications for U.S. national interests'; see Veto Message from the President S.2040, available at https://www.whitehouse.gov/. Accessed 15 April 2021. On the contrary, see Dodge (2016).

[139] Cîrlig and Pawlak (2016). On May 5, 2016, 120 nations of the Non-Aligned Movement addressed a letter to the UN Secretary General rejecting the unilateral actions of the US as violations of the principle of State immunity. Many international actors have censored the JASTA as well: e.g. the EU has expressly claimed that it 'conflict[s] with fundamental principles of international law and in particular the principle of State sovereign immunity'; see Statement of the EU Delegation to the United States of 9 October 2016.

although they are a significant precedent, represent a consolidated deviation from this trend.

On the other side, the Italian case-law on immunity from adjudication inaugurated since *Ferrini* has been censored by the ICJ and considered as not conforming to customary law by some foreign domestic courts.[140] Moreover, although such an approach limiting the scope of sovereign immunity has been recently confirmed by the Italian Court of Cassation which held that the effects of the 'counter-measures' doctrine developed by the Constitutional Court not only affect the adjudication process but also the enforcement process, also with specific reference to the assets of FCBs, its effective extent in this last field remains debatable.

However, if it is significant that many global financial destinations (UK, Singapore, China, Japan) have already enshrined near-absolute protection, in the future, the entry into force of the UNCSI is likely to entail a further general strengthening of the immunity of the assets of the FCBs under Article 21(1)(c) almost absolute immunity rule, with possible consequences also from the point of view of the practice of the States, thus potentially influencing the development of a new customary rule on the matter. Nor the relatively low number of parties that have signed and ratified the New York Convention is enough to limit its influence:[141] as observed by Webb, 'the Convention's influence is not necessarily dependent on its entry into force ... the belief that the Convention would have a harmonizing effect on law and practice ... is ... more realistic than the slow rate of ratifications suggests'.[142]

References

Brown C, O'Keefe R (2013) Article 18. In: O'Keefe R, Tams C (eds) The United Nations Convention on jurisdictional immunities of states and their property. A commentary. OUP, New York, pp 293–307

Cataldi G (2015) La Corte costituzionale e il ricorso ai 'contro-limiti' nel rapporto tra consuetudini internazionali e diritti fondamentali: 'oportet ut scandala eveniant', Diritti Umani e Diritto Internazionale, pp 41–50

Chachko E (2019) Certain Iranian assets: the International Court of Justice splits the difference between the United States and Iran. In: Lawfare.com

Cîrlig CC, Pawlak P (2016) Justice against sponsors of terrorism JASTA and its international impact, EPRS | European Parliamentary Research Service

[140] See e.g. House of Lords, 14.6.2006, Jones v. Ministry of Interior of the Kingdom of Saudi Arabia and others, in ILM, 2006, 992.

[141] E.g. the Dutch Hoge Raad (Supreme Court) has applied the principles enshrined in Article 19 even though the Netherlands has not signed the UNCSI; see Supreme Court of the Netherlands, Netherlands v. Servaas, 14 October 2016, cited in Webb, United Nations Convention on Jurisdictional Immunities of States and Their Property, Introductory note, in United Nations Audiovisual Library of International Law (2019).

[142] Webb, United Nations Convention on Jurisdictional Immunities of States and Their Property, Introductory note, in United Nations Audiovisual Library of International Law (2019).

De Sena P (2014) Spunti di riflessioni sulla sentenza 238/2014 della Corte costituzionale. In: SIDI Blog
Dickinson A et al (2004) State immunity: selected materials and commentary. OUP, New York
Dodge WS (2016) Does JASTA violate international law?. Just Security
Fox H, Webb P (2013) The law of state immunity, 3rd edn. OUP, New York
Gaukrodger D (2010) Foreign state immunity and foreign government controlled investors, OECD Working Papers on International Investment 2010/02
Giuffrida R (2015) L'immunità dei beni degli Stati dalla giurisdizione esecutava e cautelare nel diritto internazionale ed italiano. In: Ordine Internazionale e Diritti Umani, pp 273–287
Iovane M (2005) The Ferrini judgment of the Italian Supreme Court: opening up domestic courts to claims of reparation for victims of serious violations of fundamental human rights. Ital Yearb Int Law:165–193
Laborias AR (2016) Immunity of foreign central banks: a comparison between the legislations in Argentina and China. Ambito Juridico
Luzzato R, Queirolo I (2006) Sovranità territoriale, 'Jurisdiction' e regole di immunità. In: Carbone SM, Luzzatto R, Santa Maria A (eds) Istituzioni di Diritto Internazionale. Giappichelli, Milano, pp 203–242
Montero FJ, Castro P (2019) Waivers of sovereign immunities in enforcement proceedings and the 1958 NY Convention. In: Gómez KF, López Rodríguez AM (eds) 60 years of the New York Convention key issues and future challenges. Alphen aan den Rijn, pp 369–397
Ostrander J (2004) The last bastion of sovereign immunity: a comparative look at immunity from execution of judgments. Berkeley J Int Law 22:541–582
Palombino F (2014) Quali limiti alla regola sull'immunità degli Stati? La parola alla Consulta, in Rivista di diritto internazionale, pp 501–561
Patrikis ET (1982) Foreign central bank property: immunity from attachment in the United States. Univ Ill Law Rev:265–288
Perassi T (1957) Lezioni di diritto internazionale, Padova
Pustorino P (2015) La sentenza n. 238 del 2014 della Corte costituzionale: limiti e prospettive nell'ottica della giurisprudenza italiana, Diritti Umani e Diritto Internazionale, pp 51–60
Sciso E (2015) La regola sulla immunità giurisdizionale dello Stato davanti alla Corte costituzionale, Diritti Umani e Diritto Internazionale, pp 61–84
Sportes C, Simon S (2016) Immunity from enforcement: when national law supplements customary international law. La Revue, Squire Patton Boggs
Stoll PT (2012) State immunity. In: Wolfrum R (ed) Max Planck encyclopedia of public international law. OUP, Oxford
Waibel M (2011) Sovereign defaults before international courts and tribunals. CUP, Cambridge
Wang G (2015) International investment law: a Chinese perspective. Routledge, London
Wautelet P (2008) Immunity of Foreign Central Banks Assets in Belgium. In: Conflictoflaws.net
Wiesinger E (2016) State immunity from enforcement measures. University of Vienna
Wood M (2013) Immunity from jurisdiction and immunity from measures of constraint. In: O'Keefe R, Tams CJ (eds) The United Nations Convention on jurisdictional immunities of states and their property. A commentary. OUP, New York, pp 13–18
Wuerth IB (2019) Immunity from execution of central bank assets. In: Ruys T, Angelet N, Ferro L (eds) The Cambridge handbook of immunities and international law. CUP, Cambridge, pp 266–284
Yang X (2012) State immunity in international law. CUP, Cambridge
Zhu L (2007) State immunity from measures of constraints for the property of foreign central banks: the Chinese perspective. Chin J Int Law 6:67–81

Pierluigi Salvati is an Adjunct Professor of international and EU law at Link Campus University of Rome. He holds a PhD in International Order and Protection of Rights from the University of Naples 'Federico II'. Pierluigi is also a lawyer admitted in Italy mainly focusing on international trade, large infrastructure projects, international commercial contracts and related litigation, including arbitration.

Expanding Immunity from Execution Through the Backdoor: The French Example

Régis Bismuth

Abstract In December 2016, France enacted a new Statute—the 'Sapin 2 Law'—containing certain provisions governing State immunity from execution. This initiative, which gave rise to a vigorous debate in which diplomatic concerns as well as economic interests were prevalent, has resulted in a new legal framework significantly reinforcing the protection enjoyed by State property. Measures of constraint targeting State property are now subject to a new procedure of prior judicial authorization which, in practice, may complicate the enforcement of creditors' rights. The new statute also clarifies the rules governing the seizability of assets, which depends on their use or intended use by the State as well as on whether the State has waived its immunity from execution. Within this framework, the statute grants a specific protection to diplomatic property. While the original declared intent was to devise a new framework based on customary international law, as reflected by the 2004 United Nations Convention on Jurisdictional Immunities of State and their Property (UNCSI), it turns out that it significantly and purposefully deviates from it in many ways. In this light, doubts might be raised as to whether the new statute is in line with the requirements of the European Convention on Human Rights.

1 Introduction

In light of its title, the French Statute No. 2016-1691 of 9 December 2016 on 'Transparency, the Fight against Corruption and the Modernization of Economic Life'[1] has *prima facie* nothing to do with the issue of immunity from execution. It is clearly not in its Title IV 'On the Strengthening of Financial Regulation' that we would have imagined finding provisions on that matter, just after new rules relating to market abuse and the powers of the French financial regulatory authorities. It is

[1] JORF (10 December 2016), No. 287.

R. Bismuth (✉)
Sciences Po Law School, Sciences Po, Paris, France
e-mail: regis.bismuth@sciencespo.fr

R. Bismuth et al. (eds.), *Sovereign Immunity Under Pressure*,
https://doi.org/10.1007/978-3-030-87706-4_17

also surprising that such a sensitive subject has been addressed in a text discussed before the Parliament in the framework of an accelerated legislative procedure,[2] without dealing with issues that could have been included in a broader statute on sovereign immunities, for instance a statute that would have dealt with immunity from jurisdiction of States and/or immunity from execution of international organisations.

A close examination of the legislative *travaux préparatoires* holds a few surprises and denotes that the issue of immunity from execution is placed at the intersection of multiple interests, public and private, often intertwined and sometimes contradictory. The record of the Senate debates of 7 July 2016 is particularly instructive in this regard.[3] Between 10:25 pm and 00:30 am,[4] when more than twenty million viewers were vibrating in front of France-Germany for the semi-final of the UEFA European Championship and fans were pouring into the streets of the capital noisily celebrating the qualification, a few blocks away, a handful of senators and members of the government were discussing several amendments concerning the provisions relating to immunity from execution. Three topics were at the centre of discussions.

The first issue concerned what is now Article 59 of the Sapin 2 Law, which has amended the *Code des procedures civiles d'exécution* (CPCE—Code of Civil Enforcement Procedures) with regard to interim and enforcement measures targeting foreign State property. Minister Michel Sapin, the initiator of the bill, said that the proposed rules (need for prior judicial authorization, conditions relating to waiver of immunity from execution, categories of seizable State property and reinforced protection of diplomatic property) intend to protect the property of foreign States 'within the framework of the UNCSI'[5] (the United Nations Convention on Jurisdictional Immunities of States and Their Property—UNCSI), and added that certain initiatives undertaken by creditors were 'very damaging, notably for our diplomatic relations,' mentioning, in passing, the cases of 'Russia today' and 'Argentina yesterday.'[6]

The second issue concerned what is now Article 60 of the Sapin 2 Law, which has established a more restrictive immunity regime with regard to interim and enforcement measures targeting foreign State property when the underlying claim is related to a sovereign default. According to Michel Sapin, this measure aims at 'fighting against what is sometimes called "vulture funds"' and 'against the abnormal behaviour of a certain number of speculative funds.'[7]

---

[2]However, it should be noted that 'no constitutional provision requires the Government to justify the use of the accelerated procedure' and that, consequently, recourse to this procedure does not require the characterization of an emergency situation (Conseil constitutionnel, Decision No. 2012-649 DC (15 Marchs 2012), Loi relative à la simplification du droit et à l'allègement des démarches administratives, para. 4).

[3]JO Sénat (2016), No. 76 S. (C.R.), p. 12422.

[4]JO Sénat (2016), No. 76 S. (C.R.), p. 12523 and p. 12566.

[5]JO Sénat (2016), No. 76 S. (C.R.), p. 12540.

[6]JO Sénat (2016), No. 76 S. (C.R.), p. 12540.

[7]JO Sénat (2016), No. 76 S. (C.R.), p. 12544.

The third issue was related to a Senator's amendment proposal (eventually not included in the final text) that would have prohibited a garnishment when the payment of the claim in the hands of the garnishee was unenforceable against the debtor in a foreign court.[8] This seemed a rather surprising proposal in that context since it does not concern the issue of immunity from execution. Actually, it was much less surprising when one considers that several French companies owing social charges, taxes or royalties to a foreign State have been targeted by its creditors as third-party debtors. This was the case, for example, of Total or Air France in the context of garnishments filed in France against Argentina.[9] If such measures do not fully discharge these companies from their monetary obligations, they are put at risk of paying twice. As the senator noted, 'the current situation is very costly to our companies based abroad, especially those that export and thus contribute to our balance of trade.'[10]

The issues discussed during these few hours of parliamentary work raise several questions. Why do States legislate on immunity from execution? Is it to preserve their diplomatic relations and/or to avoid offending certain powerful States? Is it to find a palliative remedy to sovereign debt problems?[11] Is it to preserve the competitiveness of domestic companies and their activities abroad? And this also leads to other questions. Could we consider that a more restrictive framework on immunity from execution also affects the possibility of domestic companies to secure the payment of their claims against foreign States? Does it also affect the attractiveness of Paris as an arbitration centre since the enforcement of awards will become more complex? Could it also affect in turn the 'small creditors' of States, such as employees of diplomatic missions, who find themselves unable to enforce a judgment in their favour, and who are likely to be the first victims of this new system, much more than investment funds and other types of sophisticated creditors having other means of exerting pressure on their debtors? And, more generally, although the law of sovereign immunities is obviously affected by political as well as economic considerations and constraints, to what extent is it possible to modify and even manipulate these rules at the national level—rules which are supposed to be at the heart of delicate balances resulting from a long process of formation of customary international law?

It should be borne in mind that these provisions of the Sapin 2 Law have been enacted with the specific purpose of making more restrictive in France measures of

[8] JO Sénat (2016), No. 76 S. (C.R.), p. 12546 (the text of the proposal provided: '*Lorsque, sans faute du tiers saisi, le paiement de la créance saisie entre les mains du même tiers est, devant un tribunal étranger, inopposable au débiteur saisi, et sauf renonciation expresse et irrévocable du débiteur à poursuivre le tiers, la saisie-attribution est privée d'effet*') (Author's translation).

[9] Bismuth (2015), p. 633

[10] JO Sénat (2016), No. 76 S. (C.R.), p. 12547 ('*la situation actuelle coûte très cher à nos sociétés installées à l'étranger, en particulier celles qui exportent et contribuent ainsi à notre balance commerciale*') (Author's translation).

[11] On the link between sovereign insolvency and immunity from execution, see Fox and Webb (2013), p. 480.

constraint against foreign State property, in particular diplomatic property. The provisions on immunity from execution, also labelled in the general press as 'the Putin Amendment,'[12] have been included in response to enforcement proceedings targeting Russian assets located in France in the wake of the Yukos arbitration,[13] while also having in mind enforcement measures stemming from Argentina's sovereign default. The impact assessment of the bill noted that 'these measures will have a positive impact on France's diplomatic relations.'[14]

It is also important to note that, from a legal perspective, French authorities intended to place these new rules in the orbit of the UNCSI. This treaty, ratified by France in 2011[15] but not yet in force, reflects, to a large extent, customary international law, as pointed out by the International Court of Justice (ICJ).[16] The underlying objective was to ensure the legitimacy of the Sapin 2 Law initiative by 'docking' the statute with the UNCSI. It should also be remembered that the case law on immunity from execution was characterized by high degree of instability.[17] Notably, in three decisions of 2013 (*NML v. Argentina*)[18] and of 2015 (*Commisimpex v. The Republic of Congo*),[19] the French *Cour de cassation* adopted two divergent solutions on the issue of the waiver or immunity from execution but,

---

[12]For instance, see in 'L'amendement Poutine adopté dans la loi Sapin 2' (10 juin 2016) Le Figaro.

[13]Tranchant (2017), p. 838 et s.

[14]Étude d'impact – Projet de loi relatif à la transparence, à la lutte contre la corruption et à la modernisation de la vie économique, NOR: FCPM1605542L/Bleue-1 (30 March 2016), p. 95 ('*ces mesures auront un impact positif sur les relations diplomatiques de la France*') (Author's translation).

[15]Loi No. 2011-734 autorisant la ratification de la convention des Nations unies sur les immunités juridictionnelles des États et de leurs biens, JORF (29 June 2011), p. 10953.

[16]The ICJ mentioned that the UNCSI sheds 'light on the content of customary international law' on the basis of a 'State practice of particular significance [which] is to be found in the judgments of national courts faced with the question whether a foreign State is immune, the legislation of those States which have enacted statutes dealing with immunity, the claims to immunity advanced by States before foreign courts and the statements made by States, first in the course of the extensive study of the subject by the International Law Commission and then in the context of the adoption of the United Nations Convention' (Jurisdictional Immunities of the State (Germany v. Italy: Greece intervening), Judgment of 3 February 2012, [2012] ICJ Rep. 99, p. 123, para. 55; p. 128, para. 66). On the specific issue of immunity from execution, the Court stated that 'it is unnecessary for purposes of the present case for it to decide whether all aspects of Article 19 [of the UNCSI] reflect current customary international law' but that it suffices 'to find that there is at least one condition that has to be satisfied before any measure of constraint may be taken against property belonging to a foreign State : that the property in question must be in use for an activity not pursuing government non-commercial purposes, or that the State which owns the property has expressly consented to the taking of a measure of constraint, or that that State has allocated the property in question for the satisfaction of a judicial claim' (at p. 148, paras. 117–118).

[17]Étude d'impact – Projet de loi relatif à la transparence, à la lutte contre la corruption et à la modernisation de la vie économique, NOR: FCPM1605542L/Bleue-1 (30 March 2016), p. 91.

[18]Cass. Civ. 1ère (28 March 2013), Nos. 10-25.938, 11-10.450 and 11-13.323, NML v Argentine, Total Austral et Air France. See, Muir Watt (2013) and Bismuth (2015).

[19]Cass. 1ère civ. (13 May 2015), No. 13-17.751, Commissimpex v Republique du Congo. See Muir Watt (2015) and Glucksmann (2017).

nonetheless, considered that both decisions were based on rules of 'customary international law.'

Surprisingly, the government and the parliamentarians both claimed that their proposals were in line with the convention, even though they were diverging one from another.[20] The *travaux préparatoires* show above all that the UNCSI was an element of legitimation of the various proposals and that, although the final text relies on some portions of the UNCSI, the Sapin 2 Law is not in conformity with the convention. In fact, it differs from it in many respects. The same is true for the 1961 Vienna Convention on Diplomatic Relations, which has been mentioned during the *travaux préparatoires*,[21] but has proven not to be relevant in all respects, for example, with regard to the immunity of the bank accounts of diplomatic missions.

An analysis of the provisions of the Sapin 2 Law relating to immunity from execution therefore requires particular attention not only to identify the various obstacles that creditors will encounter in practice even though they do not appear explicitly in the statute, but also to question their conformity with customary international law, as well as with certain constitutional requirements and with the European Convention on Human Rights (ECHR). Our analysis will focus on article 59 of the Sapin 2 Law, which inserts the new articles L.111-1-1 to L.111-1-3 into the CPCE.

Two issues deserve to be discussed in this context. First, the Sapin 2 Law modifies the procedure applicable to coercive measures concerning the property of foreign States by making them subject to a new procedure of prior judicial authorization (Sect. 2). Second, the new Statute clarifies the applicable rules determining the seizability of State property, which depends essentially on its actual or potential use and on whether the State has waived its immunity from execution (Sect. 3).

2 The Questionable Addition of a Procedural Hurdle: The Prior Judicial Authorization

The new CPCE article L.111-1-1 provides that 'interim or enforcement measures may only be implemented on foreign State property with the prior authorization of the judge by an order on motion.'[22] This new procedure of prior judicial

[20] For instance, in the same senatorial session, Minister Sapin underlined that the government's amendment proposal was 'within the framework of the UNCSI' (JO Sénat (2016) No. 76 S. (C.R.), p. 12540) whereas the commission's amendment proposal had, according to the rapporteur, 'accurately transposed the UNCSI) (at p. 12541).

[21] See for instance the advisory opinion of the French Council of State (No. 391.262 (24 March 2016), para. 27) pointing out that the provisions of the bill 'also respect the rules of international custom ... which is consistent with the Vienna Convention on Diplomatic Relations.'

[22] '*Des mesures conservatoires ou des mesures d'exécution forcée ne peuvent être mises en œuvre sur un bien appartenant à un État étranger que sur autorisation préalable du juge par ordonnance rendue sur requête*' (Author's translation).

authorization is mainly intended to filter out abusive requests from creditors, but it has the effect of creating obstacles that are difficult to overcome for certain creditors acting in good faith (Sect. 2.1). Moreover, an analysis of the mechanism shows that its legality is questionable, in particular with regard to the case law of the European Court of Human Rights (Sect. 2.2).

2.1 A Procedural Hurdle Aimed at Filtering Abusive Requests but with Excessively Restrictive Effects

By introducing a new requirement of prior judicial authorization, CPCE article L.111-1-1 constitutes an exception to the ordinary law in matters of enforcement measures according to which 'a creditor in possession of an enforceable title establishing a due monetary debt may pursue its forced execution on the debtor's property'[23]—given that it is the judge's responsibility to intervene *ex post* to control whether such measures had been carried out in an irregular manner if a dispute arises.[24] The same principles apply as regards interim measures since the CPCE provides that 'a prior authorization of the judge is not necessary when the creditor avails himself of an enforceable title or a court decision which is not yet enforceable.'[25] But in the context of the Sapin 2 Law applicable to coercive measures targeting State property, the ordinary chronological sequence (measure of constraint)/(judicial control) is reversed.

2.1.1 A New Procedure Paved with Good Intentions

The new CPCE article 111-1-1 has experienced many vicissitudes since both parliamentary assemblies opposed its inclusion in the final text[26] and it was systematically reinstated at the initiative of the Government until its final adoption. At first sight, the objective of this new procedural requirement is commendable: allowing the judge to review the coercive measure requested to ensure compliance with the substantive provisions of the Sapin 2 Law, supposedly based on the UNCSI, and thus preventing the State on whose territory the property is located from violating its international obligations.[27]

According to the French Government, this *ex ante* control is necessary to neutralize abusive procedures carried out by certain creditors initiating enforcement

---

[23] CPCE, article L.111-2 ('*le créancier muni d'un titre exécutoire constatant une créance liquide et exigible peut en poursuivre l'exécution forcée sur les biens de son débiteur*') (Author's translation).

[24] Mouralis (2017), para. 15.

[25] CPCE, article L.511-2.

[26] Heymann (2017), p. 176.

[27] See more generally about preventive measures of that nature, Audit et al. (2019), p. 380.

measures of dubious legality within the framework of a strategy of procedural harassment. As Minister Sapin noted:

> certain creditors knowing that their request is not necessarily completely legitimate or sound nevertheless process it by means of bailiffs who are not necessarily familiar with all the subtleties of international law. At the end of the day, several months later, they are rejected. But, between the [measure] and the moment when justice puts things in order, the creditor is in a position of strength to discuss with the State concerned. This does not seem to us to be a good thing.[28]

Similarly, the impact study emphasized that this procedure is justified 'due to the complexity of the verifications to be carried out to ensure the seizability of State property.'[29]
The bailiffs are regarded as insufficiently reliable, but actually the same distrust applies to all French courts given that, under the new framework, only the 'enforcement judge' (*juge de l'exécution*) of the Paris *Tribunal de Grande Instance* has authority to decide on measures of constraint targeting State property.[30] This rule of special competence, which exists for matters relating to national security such as terrorism,[31] is surprising and barely justifiable in light of the low technicality of the legal issues at stake. The possibility that French authorities had in mind favouring the emergence of a more controlled judicial policy with regard to immunity from execution through the centralization of the decision-making process cannot be excluded.

The procedure of prior judicial authorization is not a complete novelty in French law. Indeed, this procedure has already been implemented since 2005 for measures of constraints specifically targeting the assets of foreign central banks.[32] Under article L.153-1 of the *Code monétaire et financier* such measures are in principle prohibited, but can be authorized by a court only to the extent it is proven that these assets 'are part of resources allocated to an activity governed by private law.'[33]

---

[28] JO Sénat (2016) No. 76 S. (C.R.), p. 12540 ('*certains créanciers qui savent que leur demande n'est pas forcement tout à fait légitime ou solide la mettent néanmoins en œuvre par le biais d'huissiers ne connaissant pas forcément l'ensemble des subtilités du droit international. Au bout du compte, plusieurs mois après, ils sont déboutés. Mais, entre le moment où ils font fermer tel ou tel consulat ou saisir tel ou tel bien et celui où la justice remet les choses en ordre, le créancier s'est trouvé en situation de force pour discuter avec l'État concerné. Cela ne nous paraît pas être une bonne chose*') (Author's translation).

[29] Étude d'impact – Projet de loi relatif à la transparence, à la lutte contre la corruption et à la modernisation de la vie économique, NOR: FCPM1605542L/Bleue-1 (30 March 2016), p. 94.

[30] CPCE, article R. 111-1.

[31] Code de procédure pénale, articles 706-17 and 706-25-2; Code de la sécurité intérieure, articles L.229-1, L.229-4 and L.229-5.

[32] Enacted through Law N° 2005-842 of 26 July 2005 (Loi pour la confiance et la modernisation de l'économie).

[33] Article 153-1§2 of the *Code monétaire et financier* provides that '*par exception aux dispositions du premier alinéa, le créancier muni d'un titre exécutoire constatant une créance liquide et exigible peut solliciter du juge de l'exécution l'autorisation de poursuivre l'exécution forcée dans les conditions prévues par la partie législative du code des procédures civiles d'exécution s'il établit*

Parliamentary debates show that this specific provision was devised—in the words of a senator—to improve the 'competitiveness of the Paris financial centre . . . for the asset management of foreign central banks,'[34] which implies to 'provide sufficient security.'[35] How much clearer can it be?

The requirements of article L.153-1 of the *Code monétaire et financier* have made more difficult attachment of foreign central banks' assets, given that the creditor has the obligation of proving that the assets at stake 'are part of resources allocated to an activity governed by private law.'—which is all the more difficult to reach, given bank secrecy. This led creditors to challenge the constitutionality of article L.153-1 but, surprisingly, the French *Cour de Cassation* considered that the issue was not 'of a serious nature'[36] and decided not to refer the matter to the *Conseil Constitutionnel*. This is also why doubts have been raised as to whether that provision is in conformity with the European Convention on Human Rights (ECHR).[37] The government was perfectly aware of the obstacles stemming from article L.153-1 and, through the Sapin 2 Law, it knowingly decided to extend its application to all foreign States' property.

The procedure of prior judicial authorization has also been implemented in Belgium. The Belgian statute of 23 August 2015 amended the *Code judiciaire* and inserted a new article 1412*quinquies* 'governing the seizure of assets belonging to a foreign power or to a supranational or international organization of public law' and requiring a prior judicial authorization as well. It is worth noting that, instead of 'States' this new statute uses the expression 'foreign power' which is quite unusual in the twenty-first century and was more common in the nineteenth century when the doctrine of absolute immunity prevailed. The *travaux préparatoires* of the Belgian Statute have been a valuable source of inspiration for the French legislator to the extent that similar arguments have been raised in the Belgium context. Indeed, the Belgian minister supporting the bill pointed out, just like Michel Sapin a year later, that measures of constraint can 'be made in such a short period of time and sometimes without the intervention of a judge that one cannot presume a perfect knowledge of international law on the part of those involved.'[38] The Belgian constitutional court, which upheld the constitutionality of the procedure of prior judicial authorization,[39] also confirmed that the legislator relied on a similar procedure recognizing 'the principle of unseizability of assets held or managed by foreign

---

que les biens détenus ou gérés pour son propre compte par la banque centrale ou l'autorité monétaire étrangère font partie d'un patrimoine qu'elle affecte à une activité principale relevant du droit privé.'

[34] JO Sénat (2005), pp. 5133–5134.

[35] JO Sénat (2005), pp. 5133–5134.

[36] Cass. 2ème civ. (11 July 2013), No. 13-40.036, QPC, Novoparc Healthcare International v Central Bank of Iraq.

[37] Bismuth (2015), p. 639 et s.

[38] Doc. parl., Chambre (2014–2015), DOC 54-1241/005, p. 9.

[39] Cour constitutionnelle (27 April 2017), No. 48/2017.

central banks and international monetary authorities in Belgium as well as the exception to this principle when the creditor can demonstrate that the assets he intends to seize are exclusively allocated to an economic or commercial activity governed by private law.'[40]

2.1.2 A New Procedure Neutralizing Creditors' Requests in Practice

According to the French government, the procedure of prior judicial authorization by order on motion has a protective dimension for creditors to the extent that the decision is made *ex parte* without an adversarial procedure, thus neutralizing the risk that the debtor State would be informed of this initiative and would have an opportunity to relocate its assets abroad. This is, moreover, the position of the *Conseil constitutionnel* when the issue of the potential infringement of creditors' rights was raised. In this respect, the Constitutional Council limited itself to indicating that the absence of an adversarial debate 'protects the creditor from the relocation of the assets covered by the protective or enforcement measure.'[41]

However, the reality of enforcement proceedings against foreign States is quite different and the litigation relating to the implementation of article L.153-1 of the *Code monétaire et financier* has already given a glimpse of the almost insurmountable obstacles that creditors will face. In the context of a seizure or attachment of bank accounts, how can creditors prove, in the context of an *ex parte* procedure, the commercial or non-commercial, diplomatic or other destination of the funds targeted when the court considers that banking secrecy is applicable?[42] The question was raised before the Belgian Constitutional Court, which simply indicated that the burden of proof weighing on the creditor as regards the use of the assets 'does not appear to be impossible to provide in all cases.'[43] This is a far cry from discovery procedures ordered by US courts in the context of the dispute between the Argentine Republic and its creditors![44] The Belgian court's expeditious argument is unconvincing and it is very difficult to assess the viability of the procedure of prior judicial authorization without taking into account rules on bank secrecy and those concerning the different types of seizable assets (diplomatic assets, assets allocated to an economic activity governed by private law, etc.). Moreover, the Belgian

[40] Cour constitutionnelle (27 April 2017), No. 48/2017, para. B.23.3 ('*Le législateur s'est par ailleurs inspiré de la procédure similaire prévue par l'article 1412quater du Code judiciaire, qui établit l'insaisissabilité de principe des avoirs détenus ou gérés par les banques centrales étrangères et les autorités monétaires internationales en Belgique ainsi que l'exception à ce principe lorsque le créancier peut démontrer que les avoirs qu'il entend saisir sont exclusivement affectés à une activité économique ou commerciale de droit privé.*') (Author's translation).

[41] Conseil constitutionnel, Decision No. 2016-741 DC (8 December 2016), Loi relative à la transparence, à la lutte contre la corruption et à la modernisation de la vie économique, para. 72.

[42] Audit et al. (2019), p. 383.

[43] Cour constitutionnelle (27 April 2017), No. 48/2017, para. B.25.2.

[44] Kleiner (2015), p. 771; Glucksmann (2018), p. 311; Audit et al. (2019), p. 386.

Constitutional Court noted in the same decision that, given the inviolability of 'bank account statements and records [which] constitute archives and documents protected by Article 24 of the Vienna Convention on Diplomatic Relations of 18 April 1961,' the foreign State 'cannot be compelled to produce them in court, so that the judge could not compel the debtor, a foreign power, to prove that these funds have been used for government non-commercial purposes.'[45]

Due consideration shall also be given to what is likely to happen in practice. Given that States could be informed of seizure initiatives at a preliminary stage, it is not excluded, as pointed out by the Senate's Commission on Legislation, which disapproved the principle of prior authorization, that this procedure 'would allow the foreign State to relocate the most mobile assets like a bank account'[46] and that finally 'the proposed reform would be likely to deprive the creditors of any capacity to obtain the enforcement of a final court decision.'[47]

The procedure of prior judicial authorization was based on the government's desire to limit the risk of violation of the rules on immunity from execution. It would be no exaggeration to say that the underlying ambition of the current framework is to eliminate every risk of enforcement. It is in this light that the legality of the prior authorization procedure ought to be examined.

2.2 *Assessing the Legality of the Procedure of Prior Judicial Authorization*

The rapporteur of the bill in the Senate considered the procedure of prior judicial authorization to be 'a manifestly excessive infringement of the right of creditors and the right to obtain the enforcement of court decisions, both guaranteed by the Constitution.'[48] But the *Conseil constitutionnel* did not carry out an in-depth review

---

[45] Cour constitutionnelle (27 April 2017), No. 48/2017, para. B.26.2. ('*Il découle de cette inviolabilité que l'Etat étranger ne saurait être contraint de les produire en justice, de sorte que le juge ne pourrait contraindre le débiteur, puissance étrangère, à prouver l'utilisation de ces fonds à des fins de service public non commerciales*') (Author's translation).

[46] Sénat, Rapport fait au nom de la Commission des lois sur le projet de loi relatif à la transparence, à la lutte contre la corruption et à la modernisation de la vie économique, No. 712 (vol. 1) (22 June 2016), p. 144.

[47] Sénat, Rapport fait au nom de la Commission des lois sur le projet de loi relatif à la transparence, à la lutte contre la corruption et à la modernisation de la vie économique, No. 712 (vol. 1) (22 June 2016), p. 144.

[48] Sénat, Rapport fait au nom de la Commission des lois sur le projet de loi relatif à la transparence, à la lutte contre la corruption et à la modernisation de la vie économique (Nouvelle lecture), No. 79 (vol. 1) (26 October 2016), p. 74. The rapporteur mentions the two following decisions of the French Constitutional Council: Conseil constitutionnel, Decision No. 2010-607 DC (10 June 2010), Loi relative à l'entrepreneur individuel à responsabilité limitée (concerning creditors' rights); Conseil constitutionnel, Décision No. 2014-455 QPC (6 March 2015), M. Jean de M. (concerning the right to obtain the enforcement of court decisions).

of the Sapin 2 Law, and just noted 'laconically'[49] the protection of foreign states' property[50] and the protection against the risk of dissipation of assets were general interest objectives.[51] The reluctance to scrutinize the constitutionality of the statute echoes what the *Cour de cassation* did when it refused to refer a case to the *Conseil constitutionnel* concerning the constitutionality of the same procedure for central bank assets.[52] Moreover, the same can be said for the analysis made by the *Conseil d'Etat* in its advisory opinion on the bill, which considered that all the provisions, and in particular the procedure of prior judicial authorization, 'were strictly in conformity with international law,'[53] 'did not raise any constitutional difficulty, nor did they run counter to the provisions of the European Convention on Human Rights and Fundamental Freedoms.'[54] However, a more detailed and nuanced analysis indicates that doubts could be raised as to the conformity of the procedure of prior judicial authorization with the ECHR to the extent that this additional protective procedure is not required by the UNCSI.

2.2.1 A Procedure Not Required by the UNCSI

First, it is necessary to examine the conformity of the procedure of prior judicial authorization with the UNCSI. The UNCSI does not require such an authorization in the context of pre- and post-judgment measures of constraint under its articles 18 and 19. This was not denied either by the impact study (this authorization is 'not required by the international treaties to which France is a signatory')[55] or by the Minister during the parliamentary debates, Michel Sapin noting: 'I will say straight away that this provision is not necessary in order to comply with the United Nations Convention', but then adding that 'It is not contrary to it either.'[56]

The question then arises as to whether an additional condition for the implementation of a measure of constraint targeting the property of foreign States, not provided for by the UNCSI but not explicitly prohibited by it, constitutes a violation of international law. This question leads us to examine the status of the international law of sovereign immunity and, in particular, the issue of whether it consists only of interstate obligations or whether some of its rules are likely to generate symmetrical

---

[49] Tranchant (2017), p. 843.

[50] Conseil constitutionnel, Decision No. 2016-741 DC (8 December 2016), Loi relative à la transparence, à la lutte contre la corruption et à la modernisation de la vie économique, para. 69.

[51] Conseil constitutionnel, Decision No. 2016-741 DC (8 December 2016), Loi relative à la transparence, à la lutte contre la corruption et à la modernisation de la vie économique, para. 72.

[52] Cass. 2ème civ. (11 July 2013), No. 13-40.036, QPC, Novoparc Healthcare International v Central Bank of Iraq.

[53] Conseil d'Etat, avis No. 391.262 (24 March 2016), para. 27.

[54] Conseil d'Etat, avis No. 391.262 (24 March 2016), para. 27.

[55] Étude d'impact – Projet de loi relatif à la transparence, à la lutte contre la corruption et à la modernisation de la vie économique, NOR: FCPM1605542L/Bleue-1 (30 March 2016), p. 94.

[56] JO Sénat (2016), No. 76 S. (C.R.), p. 12541.

rights for the benefit of private persons. As we previously noted, the choice made by a State to offer other States a more extensive protection with regard to sovereign immunity than the one prescribed by custom does not in itself constitute a violation of the international law of sovereign immunity *stricto sensu* because sovereign immunity is conceived as a floor and not as a ceiling of protection.[57] This idea is supported by the ICJ's position in *Jurisdictional Immunities of the State*. While the Court considered that 'it is unnecessary for purposes of the present case for it to decide whether all aspects of Article 19 [*of the UNCSI*] reflect current customary international law,'[58] it nonetheless pointed out that:

> it suffices . . . to find *that there is at least one condition that has to be satisfied* before any measure of constraint may be taken against property belonging to a foreign State : that the property in question must be in use for an activity not pursuing government non-commercial purposes, or that the State which owns the property has expressly consented to the taking of a measure of constraint, or that that State has allocated the property in question for the satisfaction of a judicial claim[59]

The State therefore complies with the international law of sovereign immunity if at least one of these conditions is met when exercising a coercive measure against the property of a foreign State. It may therefore grant additional protections to the benefit of States, such as the procedure of prior judicial authorization not provided for by the UN Convention. But any additional protection not required by international customary law is a relevant element to take into account when it comes to assessing its compatibility with the ECHR.

2.2.2 The Doubtful Legality of the Procedure with the ECHR

The Strasbourg Court has long held that ECHR Article 6 on the right to a fair trial does not only imply the right to be heard or the right to obtain a court decision, but also includes the enforcement of decisions, because the right to a court 'would be illusory if a Contracting State's domestic legal system allowed a final, binding judicial decision to remain inoperative to the detriment of one party.'[60] The creditor's property rights may also be affected under Article 1 of Protocol No. 1 to the Convention.[61] This right to the enforcement of judicial decisions is not absolute, however, and may be subject to limitations if such limitations 'pursue a legitimate

[57] Bismuth (2015), p. 646.

[58] Jurisdictional Immunities of the State (Germany v. Italy: Greece intervening), Judgment of 3 February 2012, [2012] ICJ Rep. 99, p. 148, para. 117.

[59] Jurisdictional Immunities of the State (Germany v. Italy: Greece intervening), Judgment of 3 February 2012, [2012] ICJ Rep. 99, p. 148, para. 118 (Emphasis added).

[60] ECtHR, No. 18357/91, Hornsby v Greece, Judgment of 19 March 1997, para. 40.

[61] ECtHR, No. 43892/04, Pennino v Italy, Judgment of 24 September 2013, para. 53; ECtHR, No. 43870/04, De Luca v Italy, Judgment of 24 September 2013, para. 39.

aim and if there is not a reasonable relationship of proportionality between the means employed and the aim sought to be achieved.'[62]

State compliance with the international law of sovereign immunity is one of the legitimate aims that the Court takes into account. As it pointed out, 'the Convention should so far as possible be interpreted in harmony with other rules of international law of which it forms part, including those relating to the grant of State immunity."[63] Consequently, 'measures taken by a High Contracting Party *which reflect generally recognised rules of public international law on State immunity* cannot in principle be regarded as imposing a disproportionate restriction on the right of access to a court as embodied in Article 6§1.'[64]

The margin of appreciation of States is therefore limited, and the question that must guide the national court to ensure compliance with the requirements of ECHR Article 6 is the following: in allowing the exception based on sovereign immunity, do the limitations imposed on the applicant go beyond what is prescribed by international law when they confer additional protection on the foreign State? In other words, does the protection go beyond what is required by the UNCSI? This was the approach of the Strasbourg Court in *Cudak v. Lithuania* in which it recognized that 'the application of absolute State immunity has, for many years, clearly been eroded'[65] and that it was necessary to consider the exceptions to immunity existing in customary international law as reflected in the UNCSI, in this case the exception of Article 11 relating to contracts of employment. By granting the foreign State additional protection beyond the floor of international law, the High Contracting Party has failed 'to preserve a reasonable relationship of proportionality',[66] overstepped its margin of appreciation and consequently violated ECHR Article 6.

It is in this light that the conformity with the ECHR of the new CPCE article L.111-1-1 needs to be examined. As pointed out above, the procedure of prior judicial authorization implies in certain situations (in particular with regard to bank accounts) a *de facto* quasi-impossibility of taking a measure of constraint if one also takes into account the allocation of the burden of proof, bank secrecy and the risk of dissipation of funds.[67]

A similar question has already been put to the French courts when the legality of article L.153-1 of the *Code monétaire et financier* was assessed in a case involving an attachment of funds belonging to the Central Bank of Iraq. In 2015, the *Cour d'appel de Versailles* dismissed the argument of non-compliance with the ECHR by simply recalling the 'legitimate aim' pursued by 'the respect of generally recognized

[62] ECtHR, No. 26083/94, Waite and Kennedy v Germany, Judgment of 18 February 1999, para. 59.

[63] ECtHR, No. 35763/97, Al-Adsani v United Kingdom, Judgment of 21 November 2001, para. 55.

[64] ECtHR, No. 35763/97, Al-Adsani v United Kingdom, Judgment of 21 November 2001, para 56 (Emphasis added).

[65] ECtHR, No. 15869/02, Cudak v. Lithuania, Judgment of 23 March 2010, para. 64.

[66] ECtHR, No. 15869/02, Cudak v. Lithuania, Judgment of 23 March 2010, para. 74.

[67] See also, Audit et al. (2019), p. 385.

international rules on State immunity' and that if 'article L.153-1 places a difficult burden of proof on the creditor as to the nature of the funds and their allocation, it does not establish an impossible proof,' thus concluding that there is no 'disproportionate restriction' to ECHR Article 6.[68] The case was brought before the *Cour de cassation*, which, identically concluded that this provision 'does not place a disproportionate restriction on the right to enforcement in relation to the legitimate aim pursued and does not disregard the requirements of a fair trial,' and added that the burden of proof arising from these provisions 'does not have the effect of violating the principle of equality of arms resulting from the right to a fair trial.'[69]

The position of the *Cour d'appel de Versailles* and of the *Cour de cassation*—which, it may be recalled, considered that the question of the constitutionality of Article L.153-1 was 'not of a serious nature'[70]—was insufficiently argued in comparison with the meticulous examination carried out by the European Court of Human Rights in *Cudak v. Lithuania*. It would therefore be premature to say that the debate on the conformity of CPCE Article L.111-1-1 with the ECHR is closed in the absence of a clear position of the Strasbourg Court on that matter.[71] Given that the procedure of prior judicial authorization is not required under international customary law, this additional protection is likely to be considered by the Court as a disproportionate restriction.

These questions are also difficult to dissociate from the issues relating to the applicable legal standards to determine the seizability of State property, for which the Sapin 2 Law has also deviated from international customary law.

3 The Questionable Standards Governing the Seizability of State Property

Once an application has been made to the *juge de l'exécution* (the 'enforcement judge'), he or she has to determine whether a measure of constraint may be taken against the targeted State property. On that matter, the Sapin 2 Law clarifies the regime of immunity from execution which had been defined by an unstable case law in the wake of the Argentine sovereign debt litigation. Two main situations need to be considered to determine the seizability of assets, depending on the absence (Sect. 3.1) or presence (Sect. 3.2) of a waiver of immunity from execution. The new mechanism is *prima facie* inspired by the UNCSI, in particular its articles 18, 19

[68] CA Versailles, 16ème ch. (1 October 2015), No. 14/05200. See Bismuth (2016).

[69] Cass. 2ème civ. (11 January 2018), No. 16-10.661. See, Haftel (2018); Bazille and Bismuth (2018).

[70] Cass. 2ème civ. (11 July 2013), No. 13-40.036, QPC, Novoparc Healthcare International v Central Bank of Iraq.

[71] See also Grandaubert (2021), pp. 541–544.

and 21, but some questionable deviations from the convention have also been incorporated in the final text.

It is useful to briefly mention beforehand Article 60 of the Sapin 2 Law, which is not codified in the CPCE, and which establishes a specific discipline intended to counter the usual procedural strategy of so-called 'vulture funds.'[72] Under article 60, a measure of constraint against a foreign State and requested on the basis of a sovereign debt instrument cannot be authorized when the following three conditions are met: (1) the State was on the list of recipients of official development assistance established by the OECD Development Assistance Committee when it issued the debt instrument in question, (2) the debt instrument was acquired by the creditor when the State was in default or had proposed a modification of the issuance agreement, (3) the situation of default must have existed for less than 48 months at the time when the creditor seeks the prior judicial authorization. In substance, article 60 of Sapin 2 Law does not concern the general regime of immunity from execution, but pursues an objective similar to that of certain 'anti-holdout' legislations which have been adopted in the United Kingdom or in Belgium.[73] The underlying objective is to incentivize recalcitrant creditors to participate in collective action mechanisms instead of pursuing the enforcement of their claim.

However, it may be noted that Article 60(V) provides that 'for the purposes of this article, the central State, the federated States and their public institutions shall be treated as foreign States.' This definition of a 'State' has not been extended to the provisions of Article 59, which does not incorporate the definition of a 'State' contained in the UNCSI. In any case, Article 60(V) restricts the eligibility of the anti-holdouts mechanisms to the financial instruments of the central state, federated states and their public institutions. Other types of territorial subdivisions (municipalities, regions, etc.) are not mentioned and cannot benefit from this protective regime.

3.1 *The Scope of Seizable Property in the Absence of Waiver of Immunity from Execution*

Before the Sapin 2 Law, the position of French courts was guided by the 1984 *Cour de cassation*'s ruling in *Eurodif* which held that the immunity from execution enjoyed by foreign States 'may nevertheless be waived in exceptional cases; this is the case when the seized property has been allocated to the economic or commercial activity governed by private law which gives rise to the action.'[74] The conditions for lifting the immunity were restrictive since it was necessary to establish a link

[72] JO Sénat (2016), No. 76 S. (C.R.), pp. 12542–12546.

[73] Bismuth (2012), pp. 499–503.

[74] Cass. Civ. 1ère (14 March 1984), No. 82-12462, SA Eurodif et Sofidif v République islamique d'Iran.

between the seized property and the activity at the origin of the action, which had to be governed by private law, something difficult to prove in practice. The *Eurodif* ruling has given rise to difficulties of interpretation and has also generated an overlapping between issues of immunity from jurisdiction and from execution by linking the question of enforcement to the nature of the activity giving rise to the action.[75]

The Sapin 2 Law breaks with the *Eurodif* approach and implements a framework that, at least apparently, is closer to that of the UNCSI. To better understand the evolutions the new statute introduces, the relevant provisions of the English translation of the law[76] and of the English version of the UNCSI are mirrored in the following table:

Sapin 2 Law (Article 59)	UNCSI
CPCE Article L.111-1-2 Provisional or enforcement measures in respect of property belonging to a foreign State may be authorized by the judge only if one of the following conditions is met: . . . 3° Where a judgment or award has been rendered against the State concerned and the property in question is specifically used or intended to be used by that State other than for non-commercial public service purposes and has a connection with the entity against which the proceedings was directed.	**Article 19 – State immunity from post-judgment measures of constraint** No post-judgment measures of constraint, such as attachment, arrest or execution, against property of a State may be taken in connection with a proceeding before a court of another State unless and except to the extent that: . . . . . . c) it has been established that the property is specifically in use or intended for use by the State for other than government non-commercial purposes and is in the territory of the State of the forum, provided that post-judgment measures of constraint may only be taken against property that has a connection with the entity against which the proceeding was directed.
For the purposes of 3°, the following assets, in particular, are considered to be specifically used or intended to be used by the State for non-commercial public service purposes: (a) Property, including bank accounts, used or intended for use in the performance of the functions of the State's diplomatic mission or its consular posts, special missions, missions to international organizations, or delegations to organs of international organizations or to international conferences; (b) Property of a military character or property used or intended use in the performance of military functions;	**Article 21 – Specific categories of property** 1. The following categories, in particular, of property of a State shall not be considered as property specifically in use or intended for use by the State for other than government non-commercial purposes under article 19, subparagraph (c): (a) property, including any bank account, which is used or intended for use in the performance of the functions of the diplomatic mission of the State or its consular posts, special missions, missions to international organizations or delegations to organs of international organizations or to international conferences;

(continued)

[75] Giansetto (2017), p. 377 et s.

[76] Author's translation.

Sapin 2 Law (Article 59)	UNCSI
(c) Property forming part of the cultural heritage of the State or part of its archives and not placed or intended to be placed on sale; (d) Property forming part of an exhibition of objects of scientific, cultural or historical interest and not placed or intended to be placed on sale; (e) Tax or social security receivables.	(b) property of a military character or used or intended for use in the performance of military functions; (c) property of the central bank or other monetary authority of the State; (d) property forming part of the cultural heritage of the State or part of its archives and not placed or intended to be placed on sale; (e) property forming part of an exhibition of objects of scientific, cultural or historical interest and not placed or intended to be placed on sale.

It may be noted that, in the absence of a waiver of immunity from execution, measures of constraint may be requested only on the basis of an existing judgment or an arbitral award. On that matter, there is a convergence between the rules of the Sapin 2 Law and of the UNCSI. But two other issues need to be addressed: the question of the identification of the seizable entity and the identification of the seizable assets belonging to that the entity.

3.1.1 Identification of the Seizable Entity

It is possible to note a break with the *Eurodif* precedent on an important aspect that opens new perspectives for creditors.[77] Whereas *Eurodif* was based on an approach that could be described as 'substantive' (the existence of a substantive link between the seized property and the activity at the origin of the claim), the Sapin 2 Law as well as the UNCSI adopt a 'personalist' approach (the property 'has a connection with the entity against which the proceedings was directed').[78] This means that, *prima facie,* the scope of the debtor's assets likely to be targeted is much wider since the whole of his patrimony is potentially concerned—with some limits that will be detailed below. Relying on international customary law, the *juge de l'exécution* had the occasion to abandon the *Eurodif* precedent for seizures carried out prior to the entry into force of the Sapin 2 Law but challenged afterwards, by holding, for example, that 'according to customary international law, the allocation of the seized assets to an operation falling under private law constitutes a sufficient condition, without it being necessary for the seized assets to be linked to the claim that was the subject of the procedure.'[79]

[77] Tranchant (2017), p. 850; Glucksmann (2018), p. 294.

[78] The ILC Draft Articles adopted in 1991 retained both substantive and personalist approaches. Its article 18(c) referred to the property having 'a connection with the claim which is the object of the proceeding or with the agency or instrumentality against which the proceeding was directed' (ILC, Draft Articles on Jurisdictional Immunities of States and their Property (1991) YILC vol. II (Part 2), p. 56.

[79] TGI Paris (9 mai 2017), No. 18/83221, États-Unis v Bellelis.

One can also wonder about the meaning of the expression 'property that has a connection with the entity against which the proceeding was directed' that appears in both the Sapin 2 Law and the UNCSI. In this regard, it is necessary to turn to the Annex of the UNSCI which provides that 'the words "property that has a connection with the entity" . . . are to be understood as broader than ownership or possession.' It is therefore conceivable to target assets that have been fraudulently transferred by this entity to third parties in order to avoid measures of constraint.

The personalist approach also implies that the distinctions between legal persons under the domestic law of the foreign State must in principle be respected. In the absence of a waiver of immunity from execution, it is only possible to target the property of one of the components of the State (the State as a legal person under domestic law, or an organic or territorial dismemberment of the State) if the judicial decision on which the measure is based has been obtained against that component of the State—of course leaving aside the possibility of seizing the assets of its emanations.[80] In other words, it would not be possible to target in France the assets of the province of Quebec if the debtor is the Province of Ontario or Canada.

This solution resulting from the personalist approach could be different if the debtor is the foreign State (e.g. Canada) and accepts a waiver to its immunity from execution which would constitute an international commitment from a public international law standpoint (e.g. the waiver is included in a treaty or was made by an *ex officio* representative of the State). In that case, the international obligation would arguably be binding on the foreign State as an international legal subject and, given that a State cannot rely on its own domestic law to limit the scope of its international obligations,[81] such waiver would therefore cover all its organs, including its organic or territorial subdivisions.

3.1.2 Identification of the Seizable Property

Once the entity (or its emanations) on which seizures can be made have been identified, the scope of the seizable property must be delimited more precisely, since certain types of assets are subject to specific protection and can be seized only when there is a waiver of immunity from execution. In the absence of such a

---

[80] This is indeed permitted under the Annex to the UNCSI which states that 'article 19 does not prejudge the question of "piercing the corporate veil", questions relating to a situation where a State entity has deliberately misrepresented its financial position or subsequently reduced its assets to avoid satisfying a claim, or other related issues.' The same solution has been followed by the *Cour d'appel de Paris* which considered that 'it is accepted that the creditor's right to sue is extended in the event of confusion of assets, in particular to public bodies which are so dependent on a foreign State that they are merely an emanation of it. The qualification as an emanation of the State, a question of fact, must be assessed according to the functional independence and the autonomy of the assets of the entity concerned, which are the attributes of legal personality' (CA Paris (27 June 2017), No. 16/08522, Veteran Petroleum v Arianespace et Roscosmos).

[81] Free Zones of Upper Savoy and the District of Gex (Second Phase) (France v Switzerland) (Order) [1930] PCIJ Rep Series A No. 24, p. 12.

waiver, only property 'specifically used or intended to be used by that State other than for non-commercial public service purposes' is seizable.

On this point, there is no significant difference between the Sapin 2 Law and the UNCSI, both using a double negative which does not serve the clarity of the text. However, differences are to be noted in the lists of types of assets that the statute and the convention consider to be 'specifically used or intended to be used by that State other than for non-commercial public service purposes.' Both texts mention diplomatic and military property, property forming part of the cultural heritage, archives and property forming part of an exhibition of objects of scientific, cultural or historical interest—types of assets that cannot be seized in the absence of renunciation. The Sapin 2 Law does not mention the property of central banks, contrary to the convention, but a reference to them is already made in article L.153-1 of the *Code monétaire et financier*.[82]

The main difference lies in paragraph (e) of the text of the Sapin 2 Law, which includes in this list 'tax or social security receivables' whereas there is no reference to those in the UNCSI. The words 'in particular' suggests that the list article 21 draws is not exhaustive, but this addition in the French statute raises several questions. First, it is inspired more by the litigation before French courts on immunity from execution than by a general practice. Indeed, the Argentine sovereign debt litigation in France that gave rise to the judgments of the *Cour de cassation* of 28 March 2013 mainly concerned enforcement measures relating to tax and social security receivables owed by French companies to Argentina.[83] The *travaux préparatoires* of the Sapin 2 Law shows that this provision reflects more a desire to protect the overseas activities of French companies than a careful reflection of what could be in international customary law the meaning of a property 'specifically used or intended to be used by that State other than for non-commercial public service purposes.' What constitutes a 'tax or social security receivables' is also a tricky question. For instance, in *NML v Argentina* the French *Cour de cassation* considered that oil royalties fall into that category even though royalties could be contractually negotiated between the State and the foreign company. Also, should we consider as a 'tax or social security receivables' what is considered as such under the law of the foreign State or under the law of the State where enforcement measures are sought? Just another question that has remained unanswered in the statute and that may be a harbinger of future difficulties for the *juge de l'exécution*.

Lastly, the Sapin 2 Law leaves open the question of what constitutes property 'specifically used or intended to be used by that State other than for non-commercial public service purposes.' The notion of 'allocation' ('*affectation*') of the property in the *Eurodif* ruling has raised certain questions of interpretation,[84] but the picture is less clear when it comes to determining the possible or potential use of the property.

[82] On the relationship between the Sapin 2 Law and article L.153-1 of the *Code monétaire et financier*, see Wuerth (2019), p. 275.

[83] Bismuth (2015), p. 637; Glucksmann (2018), p. 295.

[84] El Sawah (2012), p. 268.

Some assets are indeed objectively assigned to a sovereign function (the premises of an embassy, a military ship, etc.) unless proven otherwise. This is less obvious for claims, bank accounts and financial assets. For instance, tax and social security receivables can be linked to the exercise of sovereign prerogatives, but how can one determine their use? How can one prove the possible non-diplomatic use of an embassy bank account if bank secrecy is an obstacle?

Thus, despite a legal framework that seems *prima facie* more predictable and favourable to creditors than the one resulting from the *Eurodif* ruling, enforcement measures in the absence of a waiver of immunity from execution should be limited in practice.

3.2 The Scope of Seizable Assets in Presence of a Waiver of Immunity from Execution

Before exploring the legal regime of waivers, it may be noted that CPCE article 111-1-2(2) provides that enforcement measures against foreign State property may be authorized if the State 'has allocated or earmarked property for the satisfaction of the claim which is the object of that proceeding.' This provision is directly inspired by article 18(b) and 19(b) of the UNCSI and concerns cases where, for example, the foreign State has granted security interests.[85] This hypothesis can also be understood as a case where the foreign State has expressly waived its immunity from execution for an identified asset in the context of a specific dispute.

The situation is not so clear with respect to the provisions of the Sapin 2 Law applicable to the waiver of immunity from execution, which allow—at least in theory—broadening the scope of seizable assets for creditors by including those that are not deemed to be used or intended to be used by the State 'other than for non-commercial public service purposes.' The CPCE deviates from the UNCSI on some important aspects. Just like the specific provision on 'tax and social security receivables' mentioned above, the statute is more the result of national considerations than of an intent to follow the path of the UNCSI.

3.2.1 In General

The first point of divergence between the law and the Convention concerns the modalities of waiver. Leaving aside the question of the special waiver for diplomatic property, which will be discussed below, both the law and the Convention indicate that the State must have 'expressly consented' to the application of measures of constraint, which may include both post- and pre-judgment measures. It can be noted that the statute uses the singular ('the State has expressly consented to … such a

[85] Herman and Hanotin (2017).

measure') and the convention the plural ('the State has expressly consented to ... measures'). The latter expression leaves more latitude to the court in the sense that the waiver clause formulated in a general way (for example, an undertaking to enforce an award) refers to all possible enforcement measures subsequent to the judgment.

The text of the statute, which uses the singular, could require a specific mention of the enforcement measure envisaged, thus giving the court the possibility of controlling waiver clauses in a more restrictive manner. Moreover, the UNCSI refers in particular to a waiver made 'by international agreement' or 'by an arbitration agreement or a written contract.' There is no such reference in the new CPCE article L.111-1-2. This has led some authors[86] to consider that the *Creighton* precedent, which recognized that the commitment made by the State to enforce the award pursuant to the ICC Arbitration Rules 'implies a waiver by that State of its immunity from enforcement,'[87] could be called into question.

3.2.2 For Diplomatic Property

While the UNCSI envisages only a single waiver regime regardless of the nature of State property,[88] the new CPCE article L.111-1-3 imposes specific waiver procedures when the targeted property relates to the exercise of diplomatic functions. More specifically, this article provides that 'interim and enforcement measures may not be implemented on property, including bank accounts, used or intended to be used in the performance of the functions of the States' diplomatic mission or its consular posts, special missions, missions to international organizations, only in presence of an express and special waiver [accepted by] the States concerned.'

Such a deviation from the UNCSI cannot be understood without a quick look at the fluctuating case law of the *Cour de cassation* on the matter. In 2011, the court, basing its decision on 'customary international law,' held that diplomatic missions enjoy 'autonomous immunity from execution which can only be waived in an express and special manner.'[89] In three rulings in 2013, the same court, this time basing its decision on 'customary international law, as reflected in the United Nations Convention,' stated that 'while States may waive ... their immunity from execution in respect of property or categories of property used or intended to be used for public purposes, this may only be waived in an express and special manner, by mentioning the property or category of property in respect of which the waiver is granted.'[90] The condition of special waiver is thus extended to all property used or

[86] Mouralis (2017), para. 86.

[87] Cass. 1ère civ. (6 July 2000), No. 98-19.068, Creighton v Qatar.

[88] Brown and O'Keefe (2013), p. 346; Dopagne (2019), p. 400.

[89] Cass. Civ. 1ère (28 September 2011), No. 09-72.057, NML v Argentine.

[90] Cass. Civ. 1ère (28 March 2013), Nos. 10-25.938, 11-10.450 and 11-13.323, NML v Argentine, Total Austral et Air France.

intended to be used for public purposes, whereas in 2011 the Court justified the requirement of special waiver for diplomatic property in view of the autonomous character of diplomatic immunities. This is one of the reasons why these decisions, which seem to be part of a movement to extend immunity, are in disharmony one with another as to their legal justification.[91] Perhaps aware of the fragility of its case law, the same court held in 2015 that even for the property of diplomatic missions, 'customary international law does not require anything other than an express waiver of immunity from execution.'[92] Ironically, it is in this decision, which does not mention the UNCSI, that the Court of Cassation adopts the position that best complies with it.

To the extent that the Sapin 2 Law deviates on this matter from the UNCSI, the issue of the conformity of the requirement for a special waiver in the case of diplomatic property with the ECHR deserves to be raised. The Belgian Constitutional Court is of the opinion that this requirement finds its source in the 1961 Vienna Convention on Diplomatic Relations, which makes it in line with the case law of the ECHR.[93] It thus decided to censor the condition of special waiver included in the Belgian law, but only to the extent that it applies 'to property which is not assigned to the exercise of the functions of the diplomatic mission of the foreign power or of its consular posts, its special missions, its missions to international organizations or its delegations to the organs of international organizations or to international conferences.'[94] Would the position of the European Court of Human Rights be the same? If so, CPCE article L.111-1-3 would be preserved. The argument based on the specific nature of diplomatic immunity is, however, questionable since the 1961 Vienna Convention does not include any specific provision relating to the modalities of waiver of immunity from execution concerning the diplomatic mission's property.[95] It is more likely in an evolution of State practice and an emerging customary norm than in a debatable interpretation of the 1961 Vienna Convention that a requirement

---

[91] For a critical assessment, see Bismuth (2015), p. 638 et s.

[92] Cass. 1ère civ. (13 May 2015), No. 13-17.751, Commissimpex v Republique du Congo.

[93] Cour constitutionnelle (27 April 2017), No. 48/2017, para. B20.1.

[94] Cour constitutionnelle (27 April 2017), No. 48/2017, para. B21.

[95] On this aspect, see Bismuth (2015), p. 640. See also Dopagne (2019), p. 402; Fox and Webb (2013), p. 518.

for a special waiver is to be found.[96] So far, this requirement exists not only in France and Belgium, but also in Germany[97] and Australia.[98]

However, the key concern for creditors is not the possibility of seizing property actually used strictly in the context of a diplomatic mission such as an embassy, but the availability of adequate procedures to obtain evidence as to the actual or potential use of property formally designated as 'diplomatic.' Without such evidentiary safeguards, the special waiver clause—which could not have been fully contemplated by creditors before these recent developments in France or Belgium—could eventually encourage States to designate as 'diplomatic' certain assets (such as bank accounts) that are not used for their alleged purposes.

4 Conclusion

The provisions of the French Sapin 2 Law on immunity from execution offer an interesting illustration of how international customary law can be used and manipulated at the domestic level for purely political motives. While the stated intention was to ensure compliance with international customary law as reflected by the UNCSI, it turns out that the French statute significantly and purposefully deviates from it in many ways for some different reasons: preserve peaceful diplomatic relations, avoid offending certain powerful States, avoid interference with sovereign debt restructurings, but also preserve the competitiveness of domestic companies and their activities abroad.

But when rules on immunity from execution are modified for whatever reason, they are applicable to all types of enforcement measures and not only for those for which they have been designed. They may affect enforcement measures sought by so-called vulture funds, but also those requested in the context of the payment of arbitral awards, damages for torts or compensation to be paid to embassy employees.

States' creditors in the weakest position to obtain enforcement measures are those who cannot usually rely on a waiver by the State of its immunity from enforcement.

Some precedents have shown that claimants such as former embassy employees who cannot generally rely on such a waiver are in the most precarious situation. Faced with the obstacle of immunity from execution, they will have no choice but to

[96] On the evolution of State practice, see Grandaubert (2021), pp. 506–511. See also Dopagne (2019), p. 402.

[97] BVerfG (6 December 2006), No. 2 BvM 9/03, S v. Ministro de Economía Hipolito Yrigoyen, para. 59 (according to which it cannot be inferred from the VCDR, the work of the International Law Commission and the international law literature 'that a general rule of international law exists according to which a blanket waiver of immunity would be suitable for waiving the diplomatic immunity of embassy accounts'). (Translation from the author).

[98] Australia Foreign States Immunities Act 1985, sec. 31(4) ('a waiver does not apply in relation to property that is diplomatic property or military property unless a provision in the agreement expressly designates the property as property to which the waiver applies').

bring in France a 'strict liability claim' before administrative courts to engage the State's responsibility on the basis of a personal damage caused by the implementation of a treaty or a rule of customary international law.[99] It will therefore be up to the French taxpayer to bear the financial consequences of the successful invocation by the foreign State of its immunity from execution—and leaving it freed from its monetary obligations.

More sophisticated creditors, such as corporations, whether or not they benefit from a waiver of immunity from execution, could be tempted, faced with difficulties in executing their claims, to sell them at a lower price to financial funds specialized in the recovery of sovereign debts. Some precedents show that this secondary market can be particularly unscrupulous. For example, Vivendi had been waiting since 1997 for the settlement of a claim on Argentina and, given the difficulties with regard to enforcement, decided to sell its claim to the financial fund Gramercy for 25% of its value and by being paid in Argentine bonds—while the fund was already secretly negotiating with Argentina to whom it sold the claim for more than 60% of its value. The obstacles that creditors face as a result of the more restrictive rules on immunity from execution could therefore encourage the development of a secondary market for sovereign debt dominated by opaque actors, likely to encourage embezzlement and dishonorable collection practices. This would be another unfortunate side effect of a law on 'Transparency, the Fight against Corruption and the Modernization of Economic Life.'

References

Audit M, Angelet N, Van den Bossche MC (2019) Immunity from execution and domestic procedural rules – preventive control, burden of proof and discovery. In: Ruys T, Angelet N, Ferro L (eds) The Cambridge handbook of immunities and international law. CUP, Cambridge, pp 379–388

Bazille JS, Bismuth R (2018) Immunité d'exécution – Renonciation par un Etat à son immunité. JDI 2018:570–583

Bismuth R (2012) L'émergence d'un 'ordre public de la dette souveraine' pour et par le contrat d'emprunt souverain ? Quelques réflexions inspirées par une actualité très mouvementée. AFDI 58:489–513

Bismuth R (2015) NML c. Argentine. In: Pellet A, Miron A (eds) Les grandes décisions de la jurisprudence française de droit international public. Dalloz, Paris, pp 633–651

Bismuth R (2016) Débat autour de la conventionnalité de l'immunité spéciale des biens des banques centrales étrangères en France. La Semaine Juridique (Edition Générale) 2016:739–742

Brown C, O'Keefe R (2013) Article 21. In: O'Keefe R, Tams C (eds) The United Nations Convention on jurisdictional immunities of states and their property. A commentary. OUP, New York, pp 334–347

Dopagne F (2019) Waivers of immunity from execution. In: Ruys T, Angelet N, Ferro L (eds) The Cambridge handbook of immunities and international law. CUP, Cambridge, pp 389–408

[99] CE (14 October 2011), No. 329788, Om Hashem Saleh et autres.

El Sawah S (2012) Les immunités des États et des organisations internationales – Immunités et procès equitable. Bruylant, Bruxelles

Fox H, Webb P (2013) The law of state immunity, 3rd edn. OUP, New York

Giansetto F (2017) Le traitement juridictionnel de l'insolvabilité de l'Etat. Institut Universitaire Varenne, Paris

Glucksmann E (2017) Commisimpex v. Republic of Congo. AJIL 111:453–460

Glucksmann E (2018) L'affirmation de la protection des biens des États étrangers destinés aux missions diplomatiques, l'apport de la loi Sapin 2. Revue de Droit International d'Assas 1:287–323

Grandaubert V (2021) L'immunité d'exécution de l'Etat étranger et des organisations internationales en droit international. Dissertation, Université Paris Nanterre (forthcoming Pedone, Paris)

Haftel B (2018) La Cour de cassation, la cohérence et la sécurité juridique – À propos du nouveau revirement dans l'affaire Commisimpex. Recueil Dalloz 2018:541–546

Herman H, Hanotin G (2017) Le nouveau régime applicable aux mesures conservatoires et mesures d'exécution prises contre des États étrangers issu de la loi Sapin 2. Gazette du Palais 2017 (18):14–17

Heymann J (2017) La loi Sapin 2 et les immunités d'exécution – A propos de la loi n° 2016-1691 du 9 décembre 2016. La Semaine Juridique (Edition Générale) 2017:176–180

Kleiner C (2015) Les affaires relatives à la dette souveraine argentine – Un contentieux collectif et transnational en quête de règles et de tribunal. AFDI 61:751–783

Mouralis D (2017) Le contentieux des sentences arbitrales internationales devant le juge de l'exécution. Les Cahiers de l'Arbitrage/Paris J Int Arbitr 2017:189–252

Muir Watt H (2013) De la renonciation à l'immunité de juridiction des Etats. RCDIP 2013:671–677

Muir Watt H (2015) Immunité d'exécution des États (renonciation) : Portée du droit international coutumier. RCDIP 2015:652–655

Tranchant B (2017) L'immunité étatique et l'exécution en France des sentences arbitrales internationales. RGDIP 2017:837–861

Wuerth I (2019) Immunity from execution of central bank assets. In: Ruys T, Angelet N, Ferro L (eds) The Cambridge handbook of immunities and international law. CUP, Cambridge, pp 266–284

Régis Bismuth is a Professor of Law at Sciences Po Law School (Paris), specializing in public international law, international economic law, and international adjudication. He is the author of several publications in these fields and more particularly on the law of international organizations, sovereign immunity, extraterritoriality, anti-corruption law, economic sanctions, WTO law, international investment law and arbitration, State capitalism, sovereign debt, international standards, financial regulation, internet regulation, and the responsibility of multinational corporations. He is Co-Editor-in-Chief of *The Law and Practice of International Courts and Tribunals* (LPICT) and Director of Studies of the French Branch of the International Law Association (ILA). Régis is also a member of the International Monetary Law Committee of the ILA (MOCOMILA) and a Fellow at the International Academy of Financial Crime Litigators. He has advised public institutions and private entities on matters of international law.

Part IV
Conclusion

Conclusions: State Immunity Under Pressure

Vera Rusinova

Abstract The main tenet of this volume is that State immunity not only finds itself in the state of flux, but is 'under pressure' in many of its dimensions. From a pluralistic understanding of the legal reality, which is based on the application of different global meta-principles of legal authority, the concept of State immunity (in its material and procedural dimensions) is at the forefront of the coexisting and sometimes contesting systems with their norms, values and actors: a rules-based legal order and a realist anarchy, the US hegemony, globalisation, regionalism and nationalism, liberalism and paternalism. The cornerstone in this variety and complexity is the notion of authority. This explanation of the genesis of states' approaches to State immunities, as well as of their current transformations (or, vice versa, their lack) does not, however, preclude the value-based, axiological 'reading' of the pressing forces shaping this legal doctrine. Both sovereignty and humanity—as values—can be used as a tool in the struggle and (re)distribution of authority. However, the current legal order continues to be based on the sovereignty of states and reflects more a neo- than a post-Westphalian model and we are able to predict only a cautious and slow evolution of the international customary law on State immunity balancing between costs and benefits of possible changes.

While considered as one of the most ancient institutions of international law and one of the cornerstones of the international legal order, State immunity is still qualified as 'disputable,' 'vague,' or 'unclear.'[1] If State immunity can be regarded as an illustration of the 'relative indeterminacy' doctrine,[2] it surely takes a hypertrophic form,

[1] On the seminal writing on State immunities concludes by diagnosing a 'loss of a single unifying concept of immunity' and posing the question of whether it should by 'deplored or welcomed'. See Fox and Webb (2015), p. 614.

[2] Koskenniemi (2005), pp. 36–41.

V. Rusinova (✉)
Faculty of Law of the National Research University Higher School of Economics, Moscow, Russia

R. Bismuth et al. (eds.), *Sovereign Immunity Under Pressure*,
https://doi.org/10.1007/978-3-030-87706-4_18

embracing its legal nature and normative content, including the general rule itself and exceptions therefrom.

From a formalistic perspective, however, this problem does not appear to be unsurmountable. State immunity stems from the principle of sovereign equality taken together with the principle of sovereignty of states,[3] and its concrete implementation is a matter in the hands of states, which neither requires, nor denies the existence of precise customary rules. To some extent, State immunity can be conceived 'as a floor and not as a ceiling of protection'[4] and this perspective offers an explanation of the contemporary heterogeneity of national approaches, as shown by the contributions to this volume, including the choice of states between restrictive and absolute conceptions of State immunity, the application of distinctive criteria for the differentiation between jure imperii and jure gestionis acts, the introduction of new exceptions and for the possibility to take into account considerations of comity and reciprocity.[5]

Another way to provide a—potentially complementary—explanation is to consider that we are witnessing the final stage of the crystallization of the restrictive conception of State immunity with only a few 'last bastions' left such as the specific position of a limited number of States[6] as well as specific areas of regulation.[7] Under this perspective, territorial torts, labour disputes and to a larger extent the fight against terrorism and grave violations of human rights endure an uneasy and prolonged way for the formalization as customary exceptions to the general rule of immunity for acta jure imperii.

However, these possible normative explanations do not go beyond the frames of the descriptive legal discourse. The main tenet of this volume is, nonetheless, that State immunity not only finds itself in the state of flux, but is 'under pressure' in many of its dimensions. Evolution of the State immunity regime as well as its stability may be well indicative of the appearance of new forces and persistence of the old ones. What are these forces? The roots of the shift from the absolute to restrictive State immunity can be found in the economic realm (increasing commercial activity of states) and in the idea that 'private persons must be given greater legal

[3]Jurisdictional Immunities of the State (Germany v. Italy: Greece intervening), Judgment of 3 February 2012, [2012] ICJ Rep. 99, para. 57 (*Jurisdictional Immunities case*). See also about the different roots of State immunity, Johannes Ungerer's contribution to this volume (chapter "Sovereign Debt and Immunity: The Controversy of Subsequent Liability Limitation for State Bonds").

[4]See Régis Bismuth's contribution to this volume (chapter "Expanding Immunity from Execution Through the Backdoor: The French Example").

[5]Finke (2010), pp. 871–879.

[6]See Peng Wang's contribution to this volume (chapter "From Diplomacy to Law: Half-way in Institutional Transition of Chinese Regime on State Immunity").

[7]Including the 'greater immunity' granted to the assets of foreign central banks (see Pierluigi Salvati's contribution—chapter "Foreign Central Banks and Immunity from Execution: Too Sovereign to Be Attached?") and the European approach regarding disputes relating to sovereign bonds ('once a trader, still a sovereign') (see Johannes Ungerer's contribution—chapter "Sovereign Debt and Immunity: The Controversy of Subsequent Liability Limitation for State Bonds").

protection through the courts than in the past, not only against their own State but also against foreign States.'[8] The changes in the position of an individual in international law[9] articulated 'at least a quest' for further exceptions from the State immunity in the name of a more effective protection of the most fundamental rights of individuals.[10] In addition, the significant increase of the number of states supporting the restrictive doctrine proportionally reduces the utility of adherence to absolute State immunity.[11] However, the current stance of State immunity in international law reveals a far richer and more complicated picture.

The permanence of State immunity, despite its transformations and being subject to resistance and contestation, should be apprehended from a pluralistic understanding of the legal reality. According to this complex view, 'there are various contending global meta-principles of legal authority, or 'orders of order" that make a residual state-sovereigntist position 'to compete for ascendancy with hierarchical, unipolar, regional, integrity-based, legal-field'[12] approaches. The concept of State immunity (in its material and procedural dimensions) is at the forefront of the coexisting and sometimes contesting systems with their norms, values and actors: a rules-based legal order and a realist anarchy, the US hegemony, globalisation, regionalism and nationalism, liberalism and paternalism.

The cornerstone in this variety and complexity is the notion of authority. The interest- or identity-based approaches (post-colonial, socialist, developing/developed states) are able to provide some explanations of the approaches taken by states with respect of State immunity, but these explanations finally serve to shed more or less light on the genesis of stances taken by different states with respect to the exercise and distribution of authority in international community.

In the words of Chimène Keitner, who provides an analysis of the US legislation on foreign sovereign immunity, the structural function of State immunity transcends its substantive meaning since it 'allocates authority among states to adjudicate the conduct of certain actors in the international system.'[13] US legislative reforms consisting of the introduction of a terrorism exception as a new waiver from State immunity does not sustain a check for the ability to create a new customary international law norm. While inclined to waive the immunity of foreign states, the US has reacted vigorously to any attempt of others to rely on a similar approach with respect of them. A possibility of the reciprocal application of the same exception may also have a very limited 'unintentional effect of changing the rules of State

[8] Claim against the Empire of Iran Case (Federal Republic of Germany, Federal Constitutional Court) (1963), 16 BVerfGE 27 (1964)), 45 ILR 57.

[9] See about these changes Orakhelashvili (2001), pp. 241–276 and Peters (2016), pp. 408–435, albeit expressing divergent views with respect to the international legal personality of the individual.

[10] Peters (2014), p. 2.

[11] See Verdier and Voeten (2015), pp. 211, 217.

[12] Walker (2008), p. 386.

[13] See Chimène Keitner's contribution to this volume (chapter "Sovereignty, Humanity, and Justice – Reflections on the U.S. Law of Foreign Sovereign Immunity").

immunity for international crimes.'[14] Thus, both the adoption and application of the terrorism exception and its possible reciprocal mirroring does not exceed the frame of US hegemony. As Rana Essawy stresses in her contribution, although 'negative reciprocity' can factually erode the rule of state immunity, it 'does not lead to a change in customary rules of international law.'[15]

The new French law on 'Transparency, the Fight against Corruption and the Modernization of Economic Life' (known as the 'Sapin 2 Law') provides for a legal framework that 'significantly and purposefully deviates from' international customary rules on State immunity from execution for some different reasons, including the necessity to 'preserve peaceful diplomatic relations, avoid offending certain powerful States, avoid interference with sovereign debt restructurings, but also preserve the competitiveness of domestic companies and their activities abroad.'[16]

Latin-American states, although having divergent approaches, still have in common one central feature: almost all of them, except Argentina that generally adheres to the restrictive immunity doctrine, have not enacted domestic legislation on State immunity.[17] This readiness to apply—allegedly evolving—international customary rules is a clear signal of the reliance on the rule-based international legal order. At the same time, however, this stance can be also read from the lenses of authority as a submission to the structure of force crystallizing in the international community. This structure only idealistically can be perceived as being neutral and universal.

A colonial past and the hard-won independence of African states along with the continuum between State immunity and the immunities of State officials (and, thus, a 'link between sovereign and leadership immunities'—as Appollin Koagne Zouapet points out) is a 'part of the African perspective.'[18] This acceptance of the functional approach to State immunity remains constrained by their 'strong attachment to the immunity from execution.'[19] The fear of possible foreign domination through the transformation of the immunity regime as well as the fight for participation (the fact that 'their voice counts on the international scene'[20]) fuel the African approach to the State immunity regime.

---

[14] See Rana Essawy's contribution to this volume (chapter "The United States Hegemony and Reshaping the Norms of State Immunity for International Crimes").

[15] Rana Essawy's contribution to this volume (chapter "The United States Hegemony and Reshaping the Norms of State Immunity for International Crimes").

[16] See Régis Bismuth's contribution to this volume (chapter "Expanding Immunity from Execution Through the Backdoor: The French Example").

[17] See Facundo Pérez-Aznar's contribution to this volume (chapter "State Immunity Regimes in Latin America: A First Approximation to a Global Analysis").

[18] See Apollin Koagne Zouapet's contribution to this volume (chapter "Too Hard-Won to be Wasted ... Sovereignty, Immunities and Values: a (Sub-Saharan) African Perspective").

[19] See Apollin Koagne Zouapet's contribution to this volume (chapter "Too Hard-Won to be Wasted ... Sovereignty, Immunities and Values: a (Sub-Saharan) African Perspective").

[20] See Apollin Koagne Zouapet's contribution to this volume (chapter "Too Hard-Won to be Wasted ... Sovereignty, Immunities and Values: a (Sub-Saharan) African Perspective").

Showing that China is 'in an early stage of institutionalizing its State immunity regime,' Peng Wang finds the roots of the ongoing (albeit still rather fragmented or embryonic) transformations of the old diplomatic-centric approach in its rupture with 'the new normal of a rising China' as a major global player.[21]

Although through its new law adopted in 2015 Russia has switched to the restrictive immunity doctrine, the new framework does not reflect a free choice and acceptance of the liberal regime of State immunity. Indeed, the official position is unequivocal on the grounds: Russia was 'forced' to this shift and the pressing force was to be found in a disregard of Russia's consent by foreign states,[22] which has been perceived as an 'assault on Russian sovereignty.'[23] It required 'counterbalancing relations with foreign states that disregard Russian state immunity.'[24] A sovereignty-centered approach still influences Russian legal policy with respect to State immunity, as the application of the restrictive immunity doctrine by its national courts is based on a restrictive pro-sovereignty interpretation of new rules—which, according to Vladislav Starzhenetskiy, only confirms a defensive and deterrent meaning of the Russia's historic deviation from the doctrine of absolute immunity.

This explanation of the genesis of states' approaches to State immunities, as well as of their current transformations (or, vice versa, their lack) does not, however, preclude the value-based, axiological 'reading' of the pressing forces shaping this legal doctrine. Both sovereignty (equality of States, independence, non-interference in domestic affairs) and humanity (human dignity, human rights, fight against impunity for international crimes) are both able to be translated into the language of power/authority or the language of values. Sovereignty and humanity—as values—can be used as a tool in the struggle and (re)distribution of authority.

In such a situation as when the ICJ in the Jurisdictional Immunities case refused to interpret international law relying on the hierarchical application of the competing legal norm,[25] there is a place for the policy-based legal approaches, which, albeit not un-controversially, extend these limitations. Together with a well-known Italian

[21] See Peng Wang's contribution to this volume (chapter "From Diplomacy to Law: Half-way in Institutional Transition of Chinese Regime on State Immunity").

[22] Explanatory Note to the Draft of the Federal Law 'On Jurisdictional Immunities of Foreign State and its Property in the Russian Federation' (2015), Committee of the State Duma on the Property Issues (available at https://sozd.duma.gov.ru/bill/855485-6?sortEventsByNum=num_down&sortEventsByDate=date_up).

[23] See Vladislav Starzhenetskiy's contribution to this volume (chapter "Russian Approach to State Immunity: If You Want Peace, Prepare for War?").

[24] See Vladislav Starzhenetskiy's contribution to this volume (chapter "Russian Approach to State Immunity: If You Want Peace, Prepare for War?").

[25] Jurisdictional Immunities of the State (Germany v. Italy: Greece intervening), Judgment of 3 February 2012, [2012] ICJ Rep. 99, para. 93. See also Giulia Bernabei's contribution to this volume (chapter "The Law of State Immunity and the Role of the International Court of Justice: Looking for the Guiding Star").

saga,[26] some less reported examples have been explored in this volume. In 2013, the Constitutional Court of Colombia decided that conflicts of norms involving State immunity 'should be resolved with due regard to the principle pro homine, giving the greatest possible scope to solutions that favour human rights.'[27]

Although State immunity and the immunity of State officials share similar purposes, it 'does not mean that the two types of immunity are identical' and subject to the same legal rules.[28] However, the development of the immunity of State officials[29]—at least, at the axiological level—influences the changes with respect to the immunity of states. But Appolin Zouapet's warning deserves to be pointed out: 'while committed to these values, African states and the African Union stress the difficulty of implementing them in an inherently unequal society.'[30]

The current legal order continues to be based on the sovereignty of states and reflects more a neo- than a post-Westphalian model.[31] This neo-Westphalian model is still far from a possibility to be qualified as a product of a trend described by Anne Peters as the 'constitutionalisation of the international legal system—a process which notably implies that human rights protection (not state sovereignty) should function as the Letztbegründung of the international order.'[32] State immunity as an international legal concept, a principle, and a rule is under pressure, but still delineates the balance between different forces. The fact that some states started to accept the restrictive immunity doctrine about 150 years ago[33] and that many states have since then still pursued the doctrine of absolute immunity signals the diverging values that states attach to their adjudicative and enforcement jurisdiction. Given the

[26]Ferrini v Federal Republic of Germany, No 5044 (Italy 2004), ILR 2006, vol 128, p. 659; Jurisdictional Immunities of the State (Germany v. Italy: Greece intervening), Judgment of 3 February 2012, [2012] ICJ Rep. 99; Judgment of the Constitutional Court of 22 October 2014, No 238/2014. See Anna Wyrozumska's and Giulia Bernabei's contributions to this volume (Chapters "Can Human Rights Overcome State immunity? National Courts at the Crossroads" and "The Law of State Immunity and the Role of the International Court of Justice: Looking for the Guiding Star").

[27]See Facundo Pérez-Aznar's contribution to this volume (chapter "State Immunity Regimes in Latin America – A First Approximation to a Global Analysis").

[28]International Law Commission, Fourth Report on the Immunity of State Officials from Foreign Criminal Jurisdiction, by Concepción Escobar Hernández, Special Rapporteur, 29 May 2015, para. 96–117.

[29]International Law Commission, Fifth Report on Immunity of State Officials from Foreign Criminal Jurisdiction, by Concepción Escobar Hernández, Special Rapporteur, 14 June 2016; See also Apollin Koagne Zouapet's and Stefan Oeter's contributions to this volume (chapters "Too Hard-Won to be Wasted ... Sovereignty, Immunities and Values: a (Sub-Saharan) African Perspective" and "Sovereign Immunity from a Comparative Perspective: The Case of Germany").

[30]See Apollin Koagne Zouapet's contribution to this volume (chapter "Too Hard-Won to be Wasted ... Sovereignty, Immunities and Values: a (Sub-Saharan) African Perspective").

[31]Kress (2014), pp. 25–40.

[32]Peters (2014), p. 2. See also See Elisa Ruozzi's contribution to this volume (chapter "Shrinking of Jurisdictional Immunities and Victims' Rights: from Separation to Synergy").

[33]If we consider the 1857 judgment of the Belgian court as the starting point. See van Alebeek (2008), p. 14.

unwillingness of international courts to solve the conflict between jus cogens norms and State immunity, the place has been left for national actors. As Giulia Bernabei put it, 'the international adjudicators' are urged 'to pursue the goal of consistency, rather than that of uniformity.'[34]

Even at the national level the main actors—governments, legislators, and the courts—in different states play different roles in the refinement of the rules applicable to State immunities and their interpretation. Moreover, these actors may not necessarily be in concordance with each other with respect to the scope of state immunities. It is rather complicated to give a uniform answer to the question as to who has 'the 'ball' in a game between State immunity and human rights, responsibility for jus cogens violations and justice.'[35] In the US and Canada, the developments of the national regime of State immunities took a legislative form, albeit Italy has revealed a strong case of the enhanced role of the national courts, and in particular—of the Constitutional Court. The non-implementation of the ICJ Judgment on the Jurisdictional Immunities case,[36] though being subject to considerable criticism,[37] highlighted at the same time the role of the national courts in shaping a 'trend towards a stronger respect of human rights,' which may be sought by domestic courts even 'against the international legal order.'[38]

As it was rightly pointed by Stefan Oeter '[t]he law of jurisdictional immunities thus functions like a mirror that allows us to espouse a different perspective on our beliefs of what international law is and should be, where it comes from and where it is going in its further development.'[39] Taking into account that even the 'club of liberal democracies'[40] is not ready to give precedence to the fundamental norms (and values), and that the terrorism exceptions introduced by the US do not exceed the one-way hegemonic application of law,[41] and, finally, even the labour rights protection is qualified as an exception from the State immunity on a restrictive basis,[42] we predict a cautious and slow evolution of the international customary law balancing between costs and benefits of possible changes.

---

[34] See Giulia Bernabei's contribution to this volume (chapter "The Law of State Immunity and the Role of the International Court of Justice: Looking for the Guiding Star").

[35] See Anna Wyrozumska's contribution to this volume (chapter "Can Human Rights Overcome State immunity? National Courts at the Crossroads").

[36] On whether this falls under the 'principled resistance' see Breuer (2019), pp. 324–326.

[37] Kolb (2014), pp. 6, 11–16.

[38] Lando (2015), p. 1038.

[39] Oeter (2014), p. 355.

[40] See von Bogdandy and Hering (2020), pp. 275–279.

[41] See Rana Essawy's contribution to this volume (chapter "The United States Hegemony and Reshaping the Norms of State Immunity for International Crimes").

[42] As pointed out in Giovanni Ardito's contribution to this volume (chapter "Assessing State Jurisdictional Immunities through the Lenses of the European Court of Human Rights: Embassy Employment Disputes as Test Bench for Restrictive Immunity"), a number of European states follow the restrictive approach of the ECtHR.

References

Breuer M (2019) 'Principled resistance' to ECtHR judgments: an appraisal. In: Breuer M (ed) Principled resistance to ECtHR judgments – a new paradigm? Springer, Berlin, pp 323–350
Finke J (2010) Sovereign immunity: rule, comity or something else? Eur J Int Law 21:853–881
Fox H, Webb P (2015) The law of state immunity, 3rd edn. OUP, Oxford
Kolb R (2014) The relationship between the international and the municipal legal order: reflections on the Decision no 238/2014 of the Italian constitutional court. Questions Int Law 1:5–16
Koskenniemi M (2005) From ppology to Utopia. CUP, Cambridge
Kress C (2014) Major Post-Westphalian shifts and some important Neo-Westphalian hesitations in the state practice on the international law on the use of force. J Use Force Int Law 1:11–54
Lando M (2015) Intimations of unconstitutionality: the supremacy of international law and Judgment 238/2014 of the Italian constitutional court. Mod Law Rev 78:1028–1056
Oeter S (2014) The law of immunities as a focal point of the evolution of international law. In: Peters A, Lagrange E, Oeter S, Tomuschat C (eds) Immunities in the age of global constitutionalism. Brill, Leiden/Boston, pp 353–366
Orakhelashvili A (2001) The position of the individual in international law. Calif West Int Law J 31:241–276
Peters A (2014) Immune against constitutionalisation? In: Peters A, Lagrange E, Oeter S, Tomuschat C (eds) Immunities in the age of global constitutionalism. Brill, Leiden/Boston, pp 1–19
Peters A (2016) Beyond human rights. The legal status of the individual in international law. CUP, Cambridge
van Alebeek R (2008) The immunity of states and their officials in international criminal law and international human rights law. OUP, Oxford
Verdier P-H, Voeten E (2015) How does customary international law change? The case of state immunity. Int Stud Q 59:209–222
von Bogdandy A, Hering L (2020) In the name of the European club of liberal democracies. On the identity, mandate and national buffering of the ECtHR's case law. In: Ruiz Fabri H, Nunes Chaib A, Venzke I, von Bogdandy A (eds) International judicial legitimacy – new voices and approaches. Nomos, Baden-Baden
Walker T (2008) Beyond boundary disputes and basic grids: mapping the global disorder of normative orders. I•CON 6:373–396

Vera Rusinova is a Professor at the Faculty of Law of the National Research University Higher School of Economics, where she heads the School of International Law. The main fields of her research activities comprise international human rights law, international humanitarian law, use of force, the theory of international law, and the application of international law to cyber operations. She is a Co-Chair of the International Law Association's Committee on Use of Force: Military Assistance on Request. Vera is also a member of the Editorial Groups/Boards of 'International Justice', 'Journal of International Humanitarian Legal Studies', and 'International Cybersecurity Law Review'. Her lecture on 'Human Rights in Armed Conflicts' was placed in the UN Audiovisual Library of International Law.

Correction to: The Law of State Immunity and the Role of the International Court of Justice: Looking for the Guiding Star

Giulia Bernabei

Correction to:
Chapter 8 in: R. Bismuth et al. (eds.), *Sovereign Immunity Under Pressure*, https://doi.org/10.1007/978-3-030-87706-4_8

The book was inadvertently published with a mistake in footnotes 37 and 232 of Chapter 8. The correction has been updated now.

The updated online version of this chapter can be found at
https://doi.org/10.1007/978-3-030-87706-4_8

R. Bismuth et al. (eds.), *Sovereign Immunity Under Pressure*,
https://doi.org/10.1007/978-3-030-87706-4_19

The manufacturer's authorised representative in the EU is Springer Nature Customer Service Centre GmbH, Europaplatz 3, 69115 Heidelberg, Germany. If you have any concerns regarding our products, please contact ProductSafety@springernature.com

Printed and bound by CPI Group (UK) Ltd, Croydon, CR0 4YY
30/09/2026
02225690-0016